Handbook of Research on Learning in Language Classrooms Through ICT–Based Digital Technology

Rajest S. Suman
Bharath Institute of Higher Education and Research, India

Salvatore Moccia
EIT Digital Master School, Spain

Karthikeyan Chinnusamy
Veritas, USA

Bhopendra Singh
Amity University, Dubai, UAE

R. Regin
SRM Institute of Science and Technology, India

A volume in the Advances in Educational
Technologies and Instructional Design (AETID)
Book Series

Published in the United States of America by
IGI Global
Information Science Reference (an imprint of IGI Global)
701 E. Chocolate Avenue
Hershey PA, USA 17033
Tel: 717-533-8845
Fax: 717-533-8661
E-mail: cust@igi-global.com
Web site: http://www.igi-global.com

Library of Congress Cataloging-in-Publication Data

Names: Suman, Rajest S., 1988- editor. | Moccia, Salvatore, 1968- editor. |
  Chinnusamy, Karthikeyan, 1973- editor. | Singh, Bhopendra, 1974- editor.
  | Regin, R., 1985- editor.
Title: Handbook of research on learning in language classrooms through
  ICT-based digital technology / Rajest S. Suman, Salvatore Moccia,
  Karthikeyan Chinnusamy, Bhopendra Singh, and R. Regin, Editors.
Description: Hershey, PA : Information Science Reference, [2023] | Includes
  bibliographical references and index. | Summary: "This book is a
  collection of chapters concerning technology from the fields of ICT
  Based Digital Technology, that facilitate learning, teaching
  development, language, and linguistics and assesses the effectiveness of
  technology uses in ICT Based Digital Technology and language
  classrooms"-- Provided by publisher.
Identifiers: LCCN 2022039727 (print) | LCCN 2022039728 (ebook) | ISBN
  9781668466827 (hardcover) | ISBN 9781668466865 (paperback) | ISBN
  9781668466834 (ebook)
Subjects: LCSH: Language and languages--Study and teaching--Technological
  innovations. | Language and languages--Study and
  teaching--Computer-assisted instruction. | Web-based instruction. |
  LCGFT: Essays.
Classification: LCC P53.855 .H374 2023 (print) | LCC P53.855 (ebook) |
  DDC 418.0078/5--dc23/eng/20221115
LC record available at https://lccn.loc.gov/2022039727
LC ebook record available at https://lccn.loc.gov/2022039728

British Cataloguing in Publication Data
A Cataloguing in Publication record for this book is available from the British Library.

All work contributed to this book is new, previously-unpublished material. The views expressed in this book are those of the authors, but not necessarily of the publisher.

For electronic access to this publication, please contact: eresources@igi-global.com.

Advances in Educational Technologies and Instructional Design (AETID) Book Series

Lawrence A. Tomei
Robert Morris University, USA

ISSN:2326-8905
EISSN:2326-8913

MISSION

Education has undergone, and continues to undergo, immense changes in the way it is enacted and distributed to both child and adult learners. In modern education, the traditional classroom learning experience has evolved to include technological resources and to provide online classroom opportunities to students of all ages regardless of their geographical locations. From distance education, Massive-Open-Online-Courses (MOOCs), and electronic tablets in the classroom, technology is now an integral part of learning and is also affecting the way educators communicate information to students.

The **Advances in Educational Technologies & Instructional Design (AETID) Book Series** explores new research and theories for facilitating learning and improving educational performance utilizing technological processes and resources. The series examines technologies that can be integrated into K-12 classrooms to improve skills and learning abilities in all subjects including STEM education and language learning. Additionally, it studies the emergence of fully online classrooms for young and adult learners alike, and the communication and accountability challenges that can arise. Trending topics that are covered include adaptive learning, game-based learning, virtual school environments, and social media effects. School administrators, educators, academicians, researchers, and students will find this series to be an excellent resource for the effective design and implementation of learning technologies in their classes.

COVERAGE

- Educational Telecommunications
- Virtual School Environments
- Hybrid Learning
- Classroom Response Systems
- Instructional Design Models
- Digital Divide in Education
- Instructional Design
- Bring-Your-Own-Device
- Adaptive Learning
- Higher Education Technologies

IGI Global is currently accepting manuscripts for publication within this series. To submit a proposal for a volume in this series, please contact our Acquisition Editors at Acquisitions@igi-global.com or visit: http://www.igi-global.com/publish/.

The Advances in Educational Technologies and Instructional Design (AETID) Book Series (ISSN 2326-8905) is published by IGI Global, 701 E. Chocolate Avenue, Hershey, PA 17033-1240, USA, www.igi-global.com. This series is composed of titles available for purchase individually; each title is edited to be contextually exclusive from any other title within the series. For pricing and ordering information please visit http://www.igi-global.com/book-series/advances-educational-technologies-instructional-design/73678. Postmaster: Send all address changes to above address. Copyright © 2023 IGI Global. All rights, including translation in other languages reserved by the publisher. No part of this series may be reproduced or used in any form or by any means – graphics, electronic, or mechanical, including photocopying, recording, taping, or information and retrieval systems – without written permission from the publisher, except for non commercial, educational use, including classroom teaching purposes. The views expressed in this series are those of the authors, but not necessarily of IGI Global.

Titles in this Series

For a list of additional titles in this series, please visit: www.igi-global.com/book-series/advances-educational-technologies-instructional-design/73678

Handbook of Research on Perspectives in Foreign Language Assessment
Dinçay Köksal (Çanakkale 18 Mart University, Turkey) Nurdan Kavaklı (Izmir Demokrasi University, Turkey) and Sezen Arslan (Van Yuzuncu Yil University, Turkey)
Information Science Reference • © 2023 • 400pp • H/C (ISBN: 9781668456606) • US $270.00

Practices That Promote Innovation for Talented Students
Julia Nyberg (Purdue University Global, USA) and Jessica Manzone (University of Southern California, USA)
Information Science Reference • © 2023 • 300pp • H/C (ISBN: 9781668458068) • US $215.00

Strategies for Promoting Independence and Literacy for Deaf Learners With Disabilities
Nena Raschelle Neild (Ball State University, USA) and Patrick Joseph Graham (Rochester Institute of Technology, USA)
Information Science Reference • © 2023 • 320pp • H/C (ISBN: 9781668458396) • US $215.00

New Approaches to the Investigation of Language Teaching and Literature
Aitor Garcés-Manzanera (University of Murcia, Spain) and María Encarnacion Carrillo García (University of Murcia, Spain)
Information Science Reference • © 2023 • 325pp • H/C (ISBN: 9781668460207) • US $215.00

Handbook of Research on Facilitating Collaborative Learning Through Digital Content and Learning Technologies
Jared Keengwe (University of North Dakota, USA)
Information Science Reference • © 2023 • 495pp • H/C (ISBN: 9781668457092) • US $270.00

Handbook of Research on Advancing Teaching and Teacher Education in the Context of a Virtual Age
Aaron Samuel Zimmerman (Texas Tech University, USA)
Information Science Reference • © 2023 • 412pp • H/C (ISBN: 9781668484074) • US $270.00

Handbook of Research on Interdisciplinary Preparation for Equitable Special Education
Dena D. Slanda (University of Central Florida, USA) and Lindsey Pike (University of Central Florida, USA)
Information Science Reference • © 2023 • 657pp • H/C (ISBN: 9781668464380) • US $270.00

Shaping the Future of Online Learning Education in the Metaverse
Gürhan Durak (Balıkesir University, Turkey) and Serkan Cankaya (Izmir Democracy University, Turkey)
Information Science Reference • © 2023 • 350pp • H/C (ISBN: 9781668465134) • US $215.00

701 East Chocolate Avenue, Hershey, PA 17033, USA
Tel: 717-533-8845 x100 • Fax: 717-533-8661
E-Mail: cust@igi-global.com • www.igi-global.com

List of Contributors

B. R., Aravind / *Kalasalingam Academy of Research and Education, India* 1

Barot, Himanshu / *Karnavati University, India* 298

Bharti, Anupama / *Himachal Pradesh University, India* 175

Bhojia, Sudeshna Jayant / *Visamo Kids Foundation, India* 256

Bhuvaneswari, G. / *Vellore Institute of Technology, India* 127

Borah, Rashmi Rekha / *Vellore Institute of Technology, Chennai, India* 127

Costin, Alina / *Aurel Vlaicu University of Arad, Romania* 213

Demeter, Edgar / *Aurel Vlaicu University of Arad, Romania* 213

Dhiman, Viney / *Panjab University, Chandigarh, India* 175, 187

G. G., Lakshmi Priya / *Department of Multimedia, Vellore Institute of Technology, Vellore, India* 102

G., Bhuvaneswari / *Vellore Institute of Technology, India* 1

Gaur, Gaurav / *Panjab University, Chandigarh, India* 187

Hussain, Moon Moon / *B.S. Abdur Rahman Crescent Institute of Science and Technology, India* .. 127

Kem, Deepak / *Jamia Millia Islamia, India* 117

Kulkarni, Shalaka Mahesh / *Karnavati University, India* 162

Kumar, Sandeep / *Karnavati University, India* 200, 274

Kumar, Tribhuwan / *Prince Sattam Bin Abdulaziz University, Saudi Arabia* 54

Lile, Raul / *Academy of Romanian Scientists, Romania* 213

Lu, Shiqi / *Nanjing Normal University, China* 139

M., Raja / *Department of Multimedia, Vellore Institute of Technology, Vellore, India* 102

Nobre, Ana / *Universidade Aberta, Portugal* 85

Nuryana, Zalik / *Universitas Ahmad Dahlan, Indonesia* 139

P. M., Sreejith / *Cochin University of Science and Technology, India* 241

Padmanabhan, Jayakumar / *Sathyabama Institute of Science and Technology, India* 41

Patel, Sunil H. / *Karnavati University, India* 298

Pradhan, Sambit K. / *Karnavati University, India* 162

Rad, Dana / *Aurel Vlaicu University of Arad, Romania* 213

Rad, Gavril / *Aurel Vlaicu University of Arad, Romania* 213

Rai, Gayatri / *Karnavati University, India* 200

Rajest, S. Suman / *Bharath Institute of Higher Education and Research, India* 1, 41

S., Sreejith / *Cochin University of Science And Technology, India* 241

Tiwari, Shweta Vivek / *Karnavati University, India* 230

Torkos, Henriette / *Aurel Vlaicu University of Arad, Romania* 213

Vancu, Gabriela / *Aurel Vlaicu University of Arad, Romania* 213

Venkateswaran, P. S. / *PSNA College of Engineering and Technology, Dindigul, India* 12

Verma, Anurag / *Karnavati University, India*.. 149
Veronica, J. Josephin / *Sathyabama Institute of Science and Technology, India* 41
Xu, Wenbin / *Nanjing Normal University, China*... 139
Yastibaş, Ahmet Erdost / *Gazi University, Turkey* 23, 68

Table of Contents

Preface xviii

Chapter 1
ICT-Based Digital Technology for Testing and Evaluation of English Language Teaching 1
    Aravind B. R., Kalasalingam Academy of Research and Education, India
    Bhuvaneswari G., Vellore Institute of Technology, India
    S. Suman Rajest, Bharath Institute of Higher Education and Research, India

Chapter 2
Evaluation of the Efficiency of Online Learning Programs in Higher Education 12
    P. S. Venkateswaran, PSNA College of Engineering and Technology, Dindigul, India

Chapter 3
Giving Feedback Online on EFL/ESL Student Writing Through Talk and Comment: A Review 23
    Ahmet Erdost Yastibaş, Gazi University, Turkey

Chapter 4
A Study on the Orthography and Grammatical Errors of Tertiary-Level Students 41
    Jayakumar Padmanabhan, Sathyabama Institute of Science and Technology, India
    S. Suman Rajest, Bharath Institute of Higher Education and Research, India
    J. Josephin Veronica, Sathyabama Institute of Science and Technology, India

Chapter 5
Incorporating Technology as a Tool Into English Language Teaching and Learning 54
    Tribhuwan Kumar, Prince Sattam Bin Abdulaziz University, Saudi Arabia

Chapter 6
The Use of Zoom in Giving Writing Conferences in Foreign Language Writing Classes 68
    Ahmet Erdost Yastibaş, Gazi University, Turkey

Chapter 7
Walking Side by Side: Digital Humanities and Teaching-Learning of Foreign Languages 85
    Ana Nobre, Universidade Aberta, Portugal

Chapter 8

The Revolution in Integrating Virtual Reality in E-Learning... 102
> Raja M., *Department of Multimedia, Vellore Institute of Technology, Vellore, India*
> Lakshmi Priya G. G., *Department of Multimedia, Vellore Institute of Technology, Vellore, India*

Chapter 9

Implementing E-Learning Applications and Their Global Advantages in Education........................ 117
> Deepak Kem, *Jamia Millia Islamia, India*

Chapter 10

Reading Habits Among University Students Studying Engineering in the Digital Age.................... 127
> Rashmi Rekha Borah, *Vellore Institute of Technology, Chennai, India*
> G. Bhuvaneswari, *Vellore Institute of Technology, India*
> Moon Moon Hussain, *B.S. Abdur Rahman Crescent Institute of Science and Technology, India*

Chapter 11

Curriculum Innovation Based on Learning Styles to Help Teachers Become Professionals:
Towards a Successful Educational System 139
> Zalik Nuryana, *Universitas Ahmad Dahlan, Indonesia*
> Wenbin Xu, *Nanjing Normal University, China*
> Shiqi Lu, *Nanjing Normal University, China*

Chapter 12

Study on Learning of Communication Channels at the Grassroots Level With Reference to Social
Issues.. 149
> Anurag Verma, *Karnavati University, India*

Chapter 13

Learning Technology of Communication in the Rise of Exhibition Design in Museums.................. 162
> Shalaka Mahesh Kulkarni, *Karnavati University, India*
> Sambit K. Pradhan, *Karnavati University, India*

Chapter 14

An Empirical Study of Managing Education During the Pandemic Situation 175
> Viney Dhiman, *Panjab University, Chandigarh, India*
> Anupama Bharti, *Himachal Pradesh University, India*

Chapter 15

An Overview of Field Work Education in the Social Work Profession in India and Abroad............. 187
> Viney Dhiman, *Panjab University, Chandigarh, India*
> Gaurav Gaur, *Panjab University, Chandigarh, India*

Chapter 16
Effectiveness of Visuals in Learning Social Media Awareness During the Pandemic 200
    Gayatri Rai, Karnavati University, India
    Sandeep Kumar, Karnavati University, India

Chapter 17
Romanian Preschool Teachers' Perceptions About Early Childhood Online Education: A
Qualitative Study on the Inclusiveness of Zoom Kindergartens 213
    Dana Rad, Aurel Vlaicu University of Arad, Romania
    Raul Lile, Academy of Romanian Scientists, Romania
    Alina Costin, Aurel Vlaicu University of Arad, Romania
    Gabriela Vancu, Aurel Vlaicu University of Arad, Romania
    Henriette Torkos, Aurel Vlaicu University of Arad, Romania
    Edgar Demeter, Aurel Vlaicu University of Arad, Romania
    Gavril Rad, Aurel Vlaicu University of Arad, Romania

Chapter 18
Review of the Research on Design Education and Practices 230
    Shweta Vivek Tiwari, Karnavati University, India

Chapter 19
Systematic Literature Review on the Relationship Between Entrepreneurship and Cultural Capital
in the Role of Transnationality, Education, and Gender 241
    Sreejith P. M., Cochin University of Science and Technology, India
    Sreejith S., Cochin University of Science And Technology, India

Chapter 20
Underprivileged Children and COVID-19: Visamo Kids Case Studies in Ahmedabad Shelter 256
    Sudeshna Jayant Bhojia, Visamo Kids Foundation, India

Chapter 21
Mobile Journalism and Dissemination: Use of Smart Phones in Traditional News Reporting 274
    Sandeep Kumar, Karnavati University, India

Chapter 22
An Empirical Study of Distraction in Work-Life Balance of Teachers During COVID-19 Turmoil
Circumstances 298
    Himanshu Barot, Karnavati University, India
    Sunil H. Patel, Karnavati University, India

Compilation of References 313

About the Contributors 352

Index 357

Detailed Table of Contents

Preface xviii

Chapter 1

ICT-Based Digital Technology for Testing and Evaluation of English Language Teaching 1

    Aravind B. R., Kalasalingam Academy of Research and Education, India
    Bhuvaneswari G., Vellore Institute of Technology, India
    S. Suman Rajest, Bharath Institute of Higher Education and Research, India

The present research was carried out to check computer-based English language testing through the easy test maker application. Also, to collect English language teachers' perceptions on using the easy test maker application for language testing. Eighty English language teachers participated in the study. The practitioner research methodology was employed in the study. A perception scale questionnaire was circulated to rate the instructional testing method. The research findings revealed that the teachers' computer-based testing yielded a positive outcome after exploring the easy test maker application in the sessions. The perception scale results also confirmed that 75 participants out of 80 responded that they were satisfied with the easy test maker application on an overall level. Detailed descriptions of the usefulness of testing and evaluation of the English language are given in the investigation.

Chapter 2

Evaluation of the Efficiency of Online Learning Programs in Higher Education 12

    P. S. Venkateswaran, PSNA College of Engineering and Technology, Dindigul, India

Online education helps students from different economic and social backgrounds, places, and times by avoiding distance and cost. An essential scientific and practical question that will be studied for a long time is how well students learn. All the communication channels make it easier for students to talk to their teachers and other people. The playing field is more level, making it easier for people to talk to each other, and for everyone in the class can participate. When students think about how many online courses are available, distance education's value also increases. Budgets being reduced for the government and private sector and decreased college enrollment are favourable trends. The efficiency of online learning courses in higher education is investigated using the SEM method. According to the e learning survey for the higher education students' e-learning classes, cloud meetings are better for learning than live conversations. Students are showing more interest towards the online courses with cloud meetings if they think e-learning with cloud meetings is better.

Chapter 3
Giving Feedback Online on EFL/ESL Student Writing Through Talk and Comment: A Review 23
Ahmet Erdost Yastibaş, Gazi University, Turkey

Teaching writing requires English as a foreign language (EFL)/English as a second language (ESL) students to use their knowledge of English to produce a piece of language through which they can communicate their ideas, feelings, and beliefs. Giving feedback on EFL/ESL students' writing plays a critical role in teaching writing because feedback enables students to see their strengths and weaknesses and improve their writing by working on their weaknesses. Such feedback can be given face-to-face or online. Different programs such as Word and Google Docs can be used in giving online feedback. One of these methods is Talk and Comment. This study aimed to review this technology and indicate how it can be used to provide feedback on EFL/ESL students' writing. Therefore, this technology was reviewed in two stages: First, its features were described. Second, it was evaluated critically. Thus, its use to give feedback on EFL/ESL students' writing was explained step by step in this study.

Chapter 4
A Study on the Orthography and Grammatical Errors of Tertiary-Level Students 41
Jayakumar Padmanabhan, Sathyabama Institute of Science and Technology, India
S. Suman Rajest, Bharath Institute of Higher Education and Research, India
J. Josephin Veronica, Sathyabama Institute of Science and Technology, India

Writing is one of the most important skills in language abilities. It is a primary basis for judging one's learning and intellect. Writing skills equip us with communication and thinking skills. Writing is very important in communication. More importantly, in writing, the learners of English should have error-free sentences in their orthographic and grammatical areas. Because if there is incorrect grammar, the sentences will be unclear and meaningless. The proper syntactic structure of the paper shows a huge difference in one's speaking and writing, and it also indicates sound knowledge of the speaker. A combination of diverse features of English is required for effective communication. The study aims to explore the writing skills of tertiary-level students and to find out the difficulties in writing, especially the orthographic and grammatical errors.

Chapter 5
Incorporating Technology as a Tool Into English Language Teaching and Learning 54
Tribhuwan Kumar, Prince Sattam Bin Abdulaziz University, Saudi Arabia

Educators and teachers generally use a traditional approach in English language teaching. They use books, flashcards, and whiteboards to organize a lecture. However, at present times, teaching through traditional methods is not considered effective. We live in the advanced technology age, where teaching through a blended method is more practical and effective. For this reason, a teacher should be acquainted with the various technology tools to be used effectively in the classroom. The use of technology plays playing a significant role in English language teaching and learning (ELTL). In this paper, the authors will explore the uses of technology such as the internet, websites, electronic dictionaries, softwares and social networking technologies in English language teaching and learning.

Chapter 6
The Use of Zoom in Giving Writing Conferences in Foreign Language Writing Classes 68
Ahmet Erdost Yastibaş, Gazi University, Turkey

To give feedback during Covid-19, language instructors used digital programs such as Zoom. Accordingly, the present study aimed to find out and describe the experiences of a language instructor who held online writing conferences through Zoom. It was designed as a single case study conducted with a participant language instructor. The data were collected through a semi-structured interview and content analyzed. The findings indicated that online writing conferences had advantages such as saving time, and disadvantages, including technical issues. They also showed that online writing conferences could be affected positively and negatively by several factors such as time-saving and technical issues. According to the findings, though the content of feedback in them was the same as the one in face-to-face writing conferences, there were differences including student prejudice between them. The findings were discussed, pedagogical implications of the study were mentioned, and suggestions for further research were made.

Chapter 7

Walking Side by Side: Digital Humanities and Teaching-Learning of Foreign Languages..............85
Ana Nobre, Universidade Aberta, Portugal

The digital humanities have become a new avatar of scientific and educational progress and are part of the ideology of progress, of a linear and cumulative science. Therefore, our work questions the marketing pretension of the new digital learning environments for languages that herald an educational revolution registering itself in the idea of technological progress and addresses digital technologies in the teaching of a foreign language. We will insist in particular on the need not to ignore the term innovation, and we will see that a pedagogy that aims to be truly innovative requires a fundamental reflection, both at the educational level and at the technological levels to meet the needs of the current mobility of international students.

Chapter 8

The Revolution in Integrating Virtual Reality in E-Learning..............102
Raja M., Department of Multimedia, Vellore Institute of Technology, Vellore, India
Lakshmi Priya G. G., Department of Multimedia, Vellore Institute of Technology, Vellore, India

The virtual reality (VR) concept has been in existence for more than half-a-century. This technology's growth has been predominant recently because of the availability of plenty of technological solutions that support VR content. Coronavirus (COVID-19), a virus outbreak, has taken the whole world to an unexpected critical phase where social distancing is an inevitable part of life. Notably, the education sector faces a huge challenge, and VR technology has become the need of the hour during this pandemic as most learning takes place in virtual mode. VR equipment and software applications were highly priced at one point. Still, the present scenario is entirely different, with plenty of hardware and software resources available at affordable pricing. This study aims to identify the benefits, needs, and opportunities open for virtual reality-enabled e-learning and offer a generic methodological framework for efficiently implementing VR in e-learning. Analysis of this study indicates that VR technologies have rebooted their presence in the education.

Chapter 9

Implementing E-Learning Applications and Their Global Advantages in Education..............117
Deepak Kem, Jamia Millia Islamia, India

This paper aims to understand e-learning, and to classify its advantages as well impacts on individuals and also their global development. While understanding e-learning and its importance, the primary objectives of this paper will also be to measure the market growth of the e-learning industry, analyze the essence of e-learning courses, and identify the global advantage gained by e-learning. The present paper is a review paper dependent on data, literature, and information provided by various sources such as online journals and articles. It is a proven fact that e-learning has facilitated the development of educational practices in the global world by developing and providing learning opportunities to all. Keeping this in mind, the present attempt presents an analysis and discussion with a strong focus on e-learning and its global advantages, especially during the forced situations of the COVID-19 pandemic. Addressing the advantage of e-learning, this article evaluates the manner in which learners can interact with their peers worldwide through group discussions and private chats.

Chapter 10

Reading Habits Among University Students Studying Engineering in the Digital Age....................127
    Rashmi Rekha Borah, Vellore Institute of Technology, Chennai, India
    G. Bhuvaneswari, Vellore Institute of Technology, India
    Moon Moon Hussain, B.S. Abdur Rahman Crescent Institute of Science and Technology,
        India

In this study, engineering students from universities all around India will have their reading interests and habits examined. Reading habits have changed as a result of technology; the most popular change is the rise of text reading from computer screens. Teachers and students face a variety of difficulties and opportunities as a result of the widespread use of screen reading. The usage of annotations and other forms of text interaction by engineering students when reading academic publications is examined in this work along with their general reading preferences, habits, and attitudes. The opinions of 109 students who participated in an online survey were examined. The report highlights a number of issues with engineering students' preferences and habits, and how those issues affect their capacity for critical thought. The researcher presented recommendations to encourage reading habits among engineering students in the continually technologically driven environment of today after conducting research to acquire a thorough overview of millennials' reading preferences.

Chapter 11

Curriculum Innovation Based on Learning Styles to Help Teachers Become Professionals:
Towards a Successful Educational System 139
    Zalik Nuryana, Universitas Ahmad Dahlan, Indonesia
    Wenbin Xu, Nanjing Normal University, China
    Shiqi Lu, Nanjing Normal University, China

Learning style is the perfection and operationalization of the cognitive approach used in education due to the overall pattern providing direction to training and teaching. This emphasizes the cognitive, affective, and psychological characteristics based on how students perceive, interact, and respond to their learning environment. Therefore, this study aims to explain the integration of curriculum innovations regarding learning styles, to help teachers become professionals towards a successful educational system. The results showed that curriculum integration provided convenience for teachers and students, leading to educators' accommodation of learning styles. This curriculum began with teachers' teaching style, which included pre (introduction lessons), core (learning process), and post (evaluation) activities. The results also revealed that this integration increased students' interests and helped teachers become professionals in the educational system.

Chapter 12

Study on Learning of Communication Channels at the Grassroots Level With Reference to Social Issues...149

Anurag Verma, Karnavati University, India

Communication helps an individual to survive, grow, progress, and develop within a structure. Communication also creates a common pool of ideas and beliefs through a systematic process. When it comes to rural areas, the role of communication and communicators becomes more important because of the educational background of people. The Indian rural population faces a lot of social issues like girl's education, dowery, domestic violence, etc. The government always initiates number of programs in rural areas to make people aware regarding the social issues. Also, the change agents like educators and NGO workers work along with the government agencies, but most of the time, the campaign fails to impress the people at grassroot level. The communication at grass root level allows rural people to be at the centre of any initiatives. There are so many formal channels of communication in rural areas and there are some informal channels of communication at grass root level which helps people to understand information as they are.

Chapter 13

Learning Technology of Communication in the Rise of Exhibition Design in Museums.................. 162

Shalaka Mahesh Kulkarni, Karnavati University, India
Sambit K. Pradhan, Karnavati University, India

In today's world, museums are seen in a very different and peculiar way because they are created by putting the audience in charge of the making. Museums now are more human-centered than earlier, with only one objective, which was a display of artifacts. Also, how exhibition design evolved with time and was incorporated within museums to enhance the visitor's experience. What better way could it be to explain the evolution of museums, shifting focus from the narrative style to making the museum-going experience interactive, and how these two areas overlap each other? Over the last two hundred years, there has been a massive change in the relationship between the museum and its visitors. By offering background on the artwork and artifacts on show, museum directors have empowered visitors to create their interpretations.

Chapter 14

An Empirical Study of Managing Education During the Pandemic Situation 175

Viney Dhiman, Panjab University, Chandigarh, India
Anupama Bharti, Himachal Pradesh University, India

Education is an important part of society, and Coronavirus radically influenced the educational system. Foundations have started the use of electronic modes in the educational system; also, comparative abilities can be gotten to through different stages. ToThis paper presents a concentration on acknowledgment of online education toas an answer to the Coronavirus pandemic, especially at Panjab College, Chandigarh (India). The present chapter overviewed several secondary and primary sources. For this purpose, total of 50 respondents interacted with mobile phones: 20 undergraduate students, 20 post-graduate students, also ten each PhD scholars from different streams of Punjab University, Chandigarhto. They were asked their view as university convened online classes from the last week of March 2020 tountil the 15th May 2020. In addition to the ten faculty members of Panjab University, there were also others interviewed online toin order to find their perception of the current system's efficacy in responding toto the pandemic.

Chapter 15
An Overview of Field Work Education in the Social Work Profession in India and Abroad............. 187
    Viney Dhiman, Panjab University, Chandigarh, India
    Gaurav Gaur, Panjab University, Chandigarh, India

In the social work education field, learning plays a significant role as it allows the field instructors and the social work educators to know the knowledge gained by the student during the field education experience. Field learning helps the instructors to get aware of the way through which the students learn and develop in social work agencies. The article helps examine the field of learning in social work education and compares India and abroad. The articles will focus on the multifaceted nature of field learning that shows the sociocultural approaches associated with the nature of learning settings for understanding the student's learning process in social field education. The article will focus on the cross-comparison of the role of field training in social work education practices across India and other countries, including Australia, Uganda, Canada, Vietnam, Norway, and Sweden. The article helps develop social work education with its practices in various countries.

Chapter 16
Effectiveness of Visuals in Learning Social Media Awareness During the Pandemic....................... 200
    Gayatri Rai, Karnavati University, India
    Sandeep Kumar, Karnavati University, India

The study aimed to identify whether social media visual advertisements can engage and influence individuals during the pandemic period. Further, it also aims to identify the important factor influencing an individual in social media visual advertisements in the awareness campaign. From the results obtained through analysis, it can be interpreted that most of them agree and strongly agree that visual advertisements in social media influence them to engage some of their time perceiving the content. Further from the mean score, it can be well interpreted that most agree and strongly agree that visual advertisements in social media influence their decision. Also, it was found that quotes, timing of advertisements, picture presentations, and celebrities are the most influencing factor in visual advertisements in the awareness campaign.

Chapter 17
Romanian Preschool Teachers' Perceptions About Early Childhood Online Education: A
Qualitative Study on the Inclusiveness of Zoom Kindergartens.. 213
    Dana Rad, Aurel Vlaicu University of Arad, Romania
    Raul Lile, Academy of Romanian Scientists, Romania
    Alina Costin, Aurel Vlaicu University of Arad, Romania
    Gabriela Vancu, Aurel Vlaicu University of Arad, Romania
    Henriette Torkos, Aurel Vlaicu University of Arad, Romania
    Edgar Demeter, Aurel Vlaicu University of Arad, Romania
    Gavril Rad, Aurel Vlaicu University of Arad, Romania

COVID-19 replaced face-to-face instruction with online learning. This study examines preschool teachers' online ECE attitudes. 375 preschool teachers took an online course on quality and inclusive early childhood education. 195 out of 375 preschoolers completed this study's online questionnaire about internet learning. The authors coded responses to find pros, cons, and mixed viewpoints. Romanian preschool instructors see the challenge of online learning in Zoom kindergarten, the requirement of online teaching instead of not retaining contact with kids and families, and tightening the connection with parents as advantages of early childhood online education. Romanian preschool teachers have mixed opinions about Zoom kindergarten's pros and cons, including that online classes can be used as integrated online educational sequences but never replace traditional kindergarten.

Chapter 18
Review of the Research on Design Education and Practices..230
Shweta Vivek Tiwari, Karnavati University, India

Since time immemorial, the space where teachers and students assembled for traditional learning was the classroom. But the internet has changed how people think about place, time, and space. The physical dimension no longer confines space; it also includes the virtual domain. Futuristic methods of teaching and learning have emerged based on improved cognitive understanding. As a result, the concept of a classroom has expanded and evolved. Spaces are no longer defined by their physical notions but identified by their intangible usefulness. Today, though technology and the internet have drastically reduced the importance of distance, space is still a crucial determinant for collaborative creative work. Building on the premise that the physical environment influences learning, this research intends to identify spatial characteristics that play a role in facilitating creativity and innovation, especially in the context of design education.

Chapter 19
Systematic Literature Review on the Relationship Between Entrepreneurship and Cultural Capital in the Role of Transnationality, Education, and Gender..241
Sreejith P. M., Cochin University of Science and Technology, India
Sreejith S., Cochin University of Science And Technology, India

Along with the upcoming opportunities it presents in the market, entrepreneurship is a topic that receives a great deal of attention in academic study. The nature of running a business has been shifting for some time now, which has resulted in many changes to the dynamics of entrepreneurship in more recent times. The revolution that has taken place in the cultural and social components of society has also contributed to the occurrence of this transition. The approach that Bourdieu takes to entrepreneurship deals with the cultural components of the subject matter and delivers a great lot of insightful new information. For the purpose of this study, a comprehensive review was carried out in order to determine the primary topics that correspond to the connection between the two. Transnational entrepreneurship, the role of gender, and the impact of education and skills on the concept of entrepreneurship are the three subjects that have been identified for the study.

Chapter 20
Underprivileged Children and COVID-19: Visamo Kids Case Studies in Ahmedabad Shelter........256
Sudeshna Jayant Bhojia, Visamo Kids Foundation, India

The pandemic has disrupted lives and is continuing to affect the right to education across the world; a shelter home housing underprivileged kids in the state of Gujarat is no exception. The crisis that hit the world unannounced, and led to hurried closing down of the educational institutions for indefinite periods. After a hiatus, a new mode of imparting education was sought to be adapted –the online mode. And the inequalities in access to education were striking. With online education becoming an only way to maintain continuity, the fragility of the public education system and institutions that were under funded became vivid. The pressure on the parents, educators, and administrators increased manifold. A tiny section of students at a shelter home in Ahmedabad—the Visamo Kids Foundation—endeavoring to access quality education in the finest English medium schools under RTE, were marginalized and deprived of their right to access to quality education.

Chapter 21
Mobile Journalism and Dissemination: Use of Smart Phones in Traditional News Reporting 274
    Sandeep Kumar, Karnavati University, India

Communication and dissemination of information forever changed after 1990, and media is changing to adapt or survive the emerging trends in use with new media. Smartphones with touch screens and online connectivity are more prevalent than computers in the digital age. Emerging new technologies have changed the journalism and styles of news presentation and dissemination as smartphones changed their audience. Mobile journalism is a journalistic practice in which a reporter uses a smartphone for reporting, recording, editing, and even uploading content on media port or air. The researcher is studying how journalists adapt the culture of mobile journalism in their journalistic tasks and the effects of mobile journalism on their work. It also tries to analyze news organizations' responses toward using mobile phones in journalism instead of traditional equipment and studio setups.

Chapter 22
An Empirical Study of Distraction in Work-Life Balance of Teachers During COVID-19 Turmoil Circumstances 298
    Himanshu Barot, Karnavati University, India
    Sunil H. Patel, Karnavati University, India

COVID-19 was a crucial time to survive and created unprecedented challenges for every industry globally. This unexpected event distracted the work-life balance to where many are physically and mentally tired. Being pushed to quickly adapt to the new work environment and online teaching pedagogy was a challenge for the entire education system. Many studies have been conducted on the impact of COVID-19 in work-life balance of teachers, but the authors observed not a single study has revealed the strength of association between gender, employability, post lecture energy, and domestic responsibilities. This study aimed to measure the strength of this association using chi-square and Cramer's v analysis as well as impact of the pandemic on teaching faculty and subsequent implications of policy. The major outcomes of the study are that personal and professional life was imbalanced with affected mental health, which leads to less productivity.

Compilation of References 313

About the Contributors 352

Index 357

Preface

The globe has seen a spectacular increase in communication, computer, and digital innovation during the last few years. The creation of new internet connectivity services and the integration of machines and telecommunications have opened up many opportunities for using new technological tools in instruction and learning systems. With its capacity to integrate, enhance, and meaningfully interact with each other over a vast physical distance to meet educational objectives, the combination of computers and telecommunication gives educational systems previously unimaginable opportunities. Instructors and learners now have access to a world outside the curriculum thanks to the development of these telecommunications and digital systems and their simplicity of use, power, and variety of information conveyance. It can alter the structure and method of the educational setting and imagine a new learning culture. In the ICT-assisted environment, ease, flexibility, and interactivity have taken over. ICT expands learning possibilities by allowing users to access, extend, alter, and share knowledge in various multimodal communication formats. It supports learner-centered and collaborative learning principles, fosters the sharing of learning materials and spaces, and improves learners' problem-solving, analytical thinking, and imaginative thought abilities. The integration of technology and information is known as ICT. The use of computers allows for creative work. However, they are constrained by their access options. Adding a networking channel, such as the web or other informational services, greatly increases the system's capacity. Additionally, it can be used to overcome geographical limitations, get educational knowledge, and collaborate constructively with others. ICT refers to a field of computing that processes and exchanges data to serve human needs. ICT will undoubtedly take over the leadership role in the destiny of education.

ICT in education refers to the knowledge processing, transmission capabilities, and characteristics that enable teaching, learning, and various educational activities. It is essential to address the use of ICT in education by focusing mostly on computer-based technology because, in the age of digital technology, the word ICT primarily refers to the infrastructure, tools, and resources of information technology. ICTs can enrich instruction and study processes while accelerating, enhancing, and deepening student learning, motivating and engaging students, and bridging the gap between the classroom and the workplace. Information and technology integration may energize both educators and pupils. Offering instructional support in challenging topic areas can aid in improving and improving the quality of education. ICT concept and nature: Computer and connection technology (ICT) describes the processes and tools that make it possible to create, collect, process, store, present, and determine information. Data appears whenever and everywhere we identify or make patterns. Data should be accurate, current, meaningful, startling, and action-oriented. It should also conform with prior learning and related to it. Both contemporary culture and education are growing overly complex, with students receiving an ever-increasing amount of knowledge. ICT contributes to developing this new teaching-learning environment that improves interaction and knowledge reception. Every aspect of life now makes use of ICT. By offering and supporting resource-based, student-centered environments and by allowing education to be tied to environment and practice, teaching methodologies using contemporary ICTs offer many potentials for reconstructive learning. Especially in elementary education, computer training is required. For instructors to fulfill their responsibility as those who design training environments, they must understand ICT skills and use technology to enhance teaching and learning. Although some research supports the use of ICT in technical contexts, there is limited information regarding the best instructional frameworks and teaching methodologies for usage in learning and training. How can these digital learning and instructional environments be created so that they are founded on particular epistemologies or cognitive bases? What will the new pedagogy digital fusion vision and driving ideas be for instructor development? Training and study will differ from prior as we rely more and more on ICT. To achieve our new objective and vision, we must use the numerous fascinating options provided by modern educational technologies. We must comprehend the significant fundamental shifts in academia that have occurred recently to comprehend the integration of ICT in instruction and learning fully. Under that aegis of an ICT-enabled learning environment, academia worldwide is going through significant paradigm transformations in educational methods of instructing and learning. Training through initiatives and problems, investigation and design, exploration and invention, originality and diversity, movement and contemplation is likely more appropriate for the modern era than learning through facts, exercise, practices, regulations, and procedures, which was more responsive in earlier times. The worldview shift from learner concentration to teacher emphasis is the primary indicator of this learning transfer. In actuality, the training and study processes have been revolutionized by all of these technologies.

Knowledge and contact methods include television and recent digital technology like computers and the internet. They have been pictured as potent enablers of educational reform. Various ICTs can improve education quality, strengthen the educational process, and increase access to education. ICT is useful in many academic fields. Thanks to ICT, which offers several options, students can select the educational elements that best suit them. ICT can help students of all ages strengthen their critical thinking and reasoning skills. This is crucial in the current environment because most educational institutions do not emphasize students' ability to reason and think critically. The enhancement of the teaching-learning interaction is the primary goal of ICT-based education. Knowledge and technology integration may energize both educators and pupils. Offering interdisciplinary support in challenging topic areas can aid in improving and developing the integrity of education. Teachers must be active in group projects and the creation of innovation change initiatives, which might include using ICT in classroom partnerships.

ORGANIZATION OF THE BOOK

The book is organized into 22 chapters. A brief description of each of the chapters follows:

Chapter 1 examined easy test maker's computer-based English language testing. Also, gather English teachers' opinions on Easy Test Maker for language testing. Eighty English teachers participated. This study used practitioner research. An instructional testing method perception scale questionnaire was distributed. According to the research, the Easy Test Maker tool helped teachers with computer-based testing. 75 out of 80 participants were happy with Easy Test Maker, according to the perception scale. The analysis illustrates the value of English testing and evaluation.

Chapter 2: Online education avoids distance and costs for students from different backgrounds, regions, and times. How well students learn is an important scientific and practical question. All the communication channels help students talk to teachers and others. Everyone in the class can participate since the playing field is level. Distance education's value improves when students consider the number of online courses. Government and business budget cuts and declining college enrollment are positive trends. SEM is used to evaluate online courses in higher education. Cloud meetings are better for learning than live conversations, says an e-learning poll for college students. If they think e-learning with cloud meetings is superior, students are more interested in them.

Chapter 3 reviews EFL/ESL students must use their English skills to communicate their ideas, feelings, and opinions through writing. Feedback on EFL/ESL students' writing is important for teaching writing since it helps students understand their strengths and limitations and improve their writing by addressing their inadequacies. Face-to-face or online feedback is available. Online feedback uses Word and Google Docs. Talk and Comment is one. This study examined how this technology can deliver writing feedback to EFL/ESL students. This technology was reviewed twice: First, it was described. It was critically evaluated. This study explains how to utilize it step-by-step to give comments on EFL/ESL students' writing.

Chapter 4 introduces language skills, including writing. It's used to measure intelligence and learning. Writing improves communication and thinking. Communication is better written. English learners should write orthography- and grammar-free sentences. Incorrect grammar causes confused and meaningless sentences. The proper syntactic structure illustrates the distinction between speaking and writing and the speaker's knowledge. Effective communication requires multiple English elements. Sentences with a proper grammatical sequence are significant. The study intends to explore tertiary-level students' writing skills and find their writing issues, specifically Orthography and Grammatical faults. BA. English literature students will be tested to detect problems. Test results show the student's faults and problems. This study qualitatively and quantitatively assessed data.

Chapter 5: English teachers adopt a traditional approach. Lectures are organized with books, flashcards, and whiteboards. Traditional teaching isn't effective today. In this age of advanced technology, blended learning is more successful. A teacher should be familiar with successful classroom digital tools. Technology is important for teaching and studying English (ELTL). This article explores the usage of technology like the internet, websites, electronic dictionaries, software, and social networking in English language teaching and learning. Modern technology has contributed additional ELTL tools and applications. Students learn faster with technology and are interested in educational developments. We can use technology to teach and learn English based on these assumptions.

Chapter 6 used Zoom to give feedback during Covid-19. The present study aims to describe a language instructor's Zoom writing conferences. It was a single-case study with a language teacher. The interview data were analyzed. According to the research, online writing conferences have time-saving benefits and technological challenges. Time-saving and technical difficulties might affect online writing conferences positively and negatively. Even though the criticism was the same as in face-to-face writing sessions, student prejudice was different. The findings, pedagogical implications, and future research were discussed.

Chapter 7 is about digital humanities, a new avatar of scientific and educational progress and part of a linear, cumulative science. Digital Humanities, digital literacies, and multimodality are part of this "educational pedagogy." Our work investigates the marketing pretensions of new digital learning environments for languages that herald an educational revolution based on technological advancement and confronts digital technologies in foreign language instruction. We'll explore if the new language learning environments are part of a didactic heritage or a real evolution by merging cyberculture and social semiotics. We will emphasize the necessity to not dismiss the term innovation, and we will show that a creative pedagogy demands fundamental reflection at both the educational and technology levels to satisfy the needs of international students.

Chapter 8 develops that virtual reality (VR) has been around for more than 50 years. Plenty of technological solutions support VR content, which has fueled its expansion. The coronavirus (COVID-19) has brought the globe to a crucial phase where social alienation is unavoidable. The education sector has a big challenge, and VR technology is needed because most learning is virtual. VR hardware and software were once expensive. Presently, there are plenty of economical hardware and software resources. This paper identifies the benefits, needs, and prospects for virtual reality-enabled e-learning and offers a methodological framework for using VR in e-learning. This report shows VR's resurgence in education. Appropriate technology improves learning outcomes, student accomplishment, motivation, and concept-learner connections.

Chapter 9 seeks to understand e-learning and classify its benefits and worldwide influence. This study will quantify the e-learning industry's market growth, analyze the substance of e-learning courses, and define e-global learning's advantage. This paper is a literature review based on internet publications and articles. E-learning has helped establish global educational practices by providing learning possibilities to everybody. This analysis and discussion focus on e-learning and its global benefits, notably during the COVID-19 epidemic. This article examines how e-learning allows students to communicate with classmates globally through group discussions and private chats. The reasons offered are mostly drawn from academic journals, essays, and other works that answer issues about e-learning, its market growth, achievements, and ambitions, focusing on e-global learning's advantages.

Chapter 10 examines engineering students' reading interests and habits in India. Because of technology, more people are reading from computer displays. Screen reading presents teachers and students with challenges and opportunities. This work examines engineering students' use of annotations and other text interactions when reading academic articles, as well as their reading preferences, habits, and attitudes. 109 students were surveyed online. The report examines how engineering students' preferences and habits affect their critical thinking. After researching millennials' reading preferences, the researcher recommended encouraging engineering students to read in today's digitally driven workplace. Less reading could lead to a knowledge gap, making it tougher to connect outside digital materials.

Chapter 11: Learning style perfects and operationalizes the cognitive approach utilized in education because of its overall pattern. This stresses how students perceive, interact, and respond to their learning environment. This study explains curriculum changes in learning styles to help teachers build a successful educational system. According to the results, curriculum integration facilitated teachers' and students' learning styles. This curriculum contained pre (introduction lessons), core (learning process), and post (assessment) exercises. This integration raised students' interests and helped teachers become educators.

Chapter 12 helps a person live, grow, advance, and develop. Systematically, communication develops a pool of ideas and beliefs. In rural locations, education levels make communication and communicators more vital. Rural Indians suffer social difficulties, including girl education, dowery, and domestic abuse. Government activities in rural areas raise social awareness. Change agents like educators and NGO workers collaborate with government organizations, but the campaign rarely impresses grassroots people. Grassroots communication puts rural people at the center of efforts. In rural areas, formal and informal communication channels assist people in interpreting information. This paper examines grass-roots communication. From 250 samples, 184 were eligible for data analysis.

Chapter 13: Today's museums are unique because they put the public in control of making them. Before, museums just displayed items and had no human focus on how Museums incorporate exhibition design over time to improve the visitor experience. What better method to show how museums have evolved from narrative to interactive, and how do the two overlap? Over 200 years, the museum's inter-action with its visitors has changed drastically. Museum directors encourage visitors to generate their interpretations by providing background on artwork and artifacts. Because the objects lacked context labels, visitors had trouble making connections. This article addresses how museums and exhibition design have changed to embrace technological innovations, making art more accessible to the public.

Chapter 14 discusses coronavirus drastically changed the school system. Foundations have started using electronic modes for overseeing instruction, and comparing abilities can be attained through sev-eral stages. Focus on online education to combat the Coronavirus pandemic, notably at Panjab College, Chandigarh (India). The chapter reviewed secondary and primary sources. For this reason, 50 respondents interacted with mobile phones, 20 undergraduate students, 20 postgraduate students, and ten Ph.D. re-searchers from different streams of Punjab University, Chandigarh, to know their views as the university convened online classes from March 2020 to May 2020. Ten Panjab University faculty members were also interviewed online about the system's pandemic response capability. Mean Value analyses data. They're restless since they don't know about online training platforms and are apprehensive about how their presentation will be rated.

Chapter 15 addresses social work education; learning is important because it lets field instructors and social work educators know what students learned in the field. Fieldwork teaches educators how students learn and grow in social work agencies. The article contrasts Indian and international social work education. The essays will focus on the multidimensional nature of field learning, showing socio-cultural perspectives connected with learning locations for understanding student learning in social field education. The essay compares field training in India to Australia, Uganda, Canada, Vietnam, Norway, and Sweden. The essay promotes social work education in several countries.

Chapter 16 examined if Social Media Visual Ads can impact people during a pandemic. Identify the key influencers of Social Media Visual Ads in the awareness campaign. Analysis shows that most agree or strongly agree that Visual Ads in Social Media impact their spending time seeing the content. Further from the mean score, most agree and strongly agree that visual social media ads influence their decision. Quotes, ad timing, picture presentations, and celebrity are the most influential factors in aware-ness campaign visual ads.

Chapter 17 classifies COVID-19 replaced face-to-face training with online learning. This study evalu-ates online ECE views of preschool teachers. 375 preschool teachers took an online inclusion course. 195 of 375 preschoolers completed our online survey. Coding pros, disadvantages, and mixed views. Romanian preschool teachers regard online learning in Zoom kindergarten, the need for online teaching to maintain touch with kids and families, and tightening the link with parents as benefits of early childhood online education. Romanian preschool teachers have mixed opinions about Zoom kindergarten's pros and cons, including online classes can be used as integrated online educational sequences but never replace traditional kindergarten, parents' reliance on online educational activities, Zoom kindergarten's age ap-propriateness, the inability to replicate an authentic socio-emotional connection, and children's shorter attention spans. Concerns include online learning, lack of physical interaction, lack of socio-emotional support, Zoom kindergarten's impersonation and emotionlessness, total parental dependence, lack of feedback in consolidating skills, preschoolers' lack of self-regulation, and rural-urban parental technology knowledge and resource disparities. Lifelong learning helps preschool teachers adapt. Advanced ECE ICT Online preschool is studied. Online early childhood education in Romania may require teacher input.

Chapter 18: Since forever, teachers and students have gathered in classrooms to study. The internet has transformed how people view place, time, and space. The physical dimension now encompasses the virtual domain. Improved cognitive comprehension has led to futuristic learning approaches. The classroom has altered as a result. Spaces are now defined by their intangible usefulness. Despite technology and the internet, space is still important for collaborative creative work. Based on the concept that the physical environment affects learning, this research aims to uncover spatial qualities that foster creativity and innovation in design education. The physical environment affects student involvement, creativity, and well-being in design education. This study tries to determine the spatial features of a design studio that positively influence creativity in design schools.

Chapter 19 adapts along with market opportunities, and entrepreneurship is a popular academic topic. The changing nature of business has altered the dynamics of entrepreneurship in recent years. The cultural and social revolution contributed to this change. Bourdieu's approach to entrepreneurship focuses on the subject's cultural aspects and offers new insights. This study used a comprehensive review to identify the main subjects relating to the two. The study will focus on transnational entrepreneurship, gender, and the impact of education and skills on entrepreneurship. As the number of multinational organizations rises, it's crucial to understand foreign cultures. Along with education or skills, one of today's most sought things is to motivate more women to seek entrepreneurial jobs.

Chapter 20 has disrupted lives and education globally. Gujarat's orphanage is no exception. Unannounced catastrophe forced schools/colleges/universities to close indefinitely. No early warning signals or time to prepare were given. Online schooling followed a gap. Education disparity was notable. Online education became the only way to maintain continuity, showing public education's fragility. Parents, teachers, and administrators experienced pressure. A few children at Ahmedabad's Visamo Kids Foundation were denied a proper education in the best English-medium institutions under RTE. This study examines 12 kids who fought to attend school during the lockdown. Each storey shows virus-caused vulnerability. The study investigates the shelter's impact, adjustments, coping mechanisms, best practises, civil support groups, and problem-solving collaborations.

Chapter 21: After 1990, media changed to adapt to or withstand new patterns in media use. Smartphones with touch screens and internet access are more popular than desktops. New technology revolutionized journalism, and news presentation approaches as cell phones transformed their audience. Mobile journalism is when a reporter utilizes a smartphone to report, record, edit, and upload content. The researcher studies how journalists adapt mobile journalism culture to their profession. It also analyses news companies' use of mobile phones instead of traditional equipment and studios.

Chapter 22 discusses COVID-19 poses significant challenges for every industry internationally. This unforeseen occurrence disrupted the work-life balance, leaving many exhausted. The school system struggled with online teaching pedagogy. COVID-19's impact on teachers' work-life balance is well-studied. No study has linked gender, employment, post-lecture energy, and home obligations. This study used chi-square and Cramer's v to determine the pandemic's influence on teaching faculty and policy implications. Personal and professional lives unbalanced mental health and productivity. The study indicated that gender and online hours, post-lecture vitality, and work-life balance are independent; nonetheless, female teachers find household chores difficult. Not all teachers have been affected. Educational institutions must acknowledge policy inequities to avoid these results.

Rajest S. Suman
Bharath Institute of Higher Education and Research, India

Salvatore Moccia
EIT Digital Master School, Spain

Karthikeyan Chinnusamy
Veritas, USA

Bhopendra Singh
Amity University, Dubai, UAE

R. Regin
SRM Institute of Science and Technology, India

Chapter 1
ICT–Based Digital Technology for Testing and Evaluation of English Language Teaching

Aravind B. R.
https://orcid.org/0000-0001-7872-8171
Kalasalingam Academy of Research and Education, India

Bhuvaneswari G.
https://orcid.org/0000-0002-2897-7265
Vellore Institute of Technology, India

S. Suman Rajest
https://orcid.org/0000-0001-8315-3747
Bharath Institute of Higher Education and Research, India

ABSTRACT

The present research was carried out to check computer-based English language testing through the easy test maker application. Also, to collect English language teachers' perceptions on using the easy test maker application for language testing. Eighty English language teachers participated in the study. The practitioner research methodology was employed in the study. A perception scale questionnaire was circulated to rate the instructional testing method. The research findings revealed that the teachers' computer-based testing yielded a positive outcome after exploring the easy test maker application in the sessions. The perception scale results also confirmed that 75 participants out of 80 responded that they were satisfied with the easy test maker application on an overall level. Detailed descriptions of the usefulness of testing and evaluation of the English language are given in the investigation.

1. INTRODUCTION

Tests can serve pedagogical purposes (Bachman & Palmer, 1996) and can be classified differently in

DOI: 10.4018/978-1-6684-6682-7.ch001

terms of various criteria. According to Buck (2001), "the basic purpose of language testing is to provide opportunities for learning," and this applies to both the students taking the exams and the teachers and professors who create and grade them. The exams should be fair, reliable, and valid, but the ability to learn something is the most important factor. When someone takes a good test, we are able to draw accurate conclusions about the communicative language abilities of the person taking the test. Tomlinson (2005) also contributed to the discussion and supported the idea that "tests are not generally perceived as events in which new learning takes place. However, it is feasible for students to acquire new information, as well as develop new awareness and abilities, while they are in the process of completing an examination.

1.1. Testing

Tests may be considered instruments or tools used to measure abilities or performance to make evaluative judgements or statements. Tests are activities designed for learners to display their performance, usually within a given period and with limited focus. Carroll (1968) describes it thus, "a psychological or educational test is a procedure designed to elicit certain behavior from which one can make inferences about certain characteristics of an individual".

1.2. Measurement and Assessment

Measurement is the activity by which the results of tests are quantified, and judgments about characteristics and relative performances are made available. Here specific rules and procedures are employed to objectively rate the learners' abilities. Numerical indices are assigned to data in a meaningful and consistent manner. Assessment is the process of estimating ability using scores, marks or grades. At best, it may involve presenting data about relative performance, but it does not necessarily make value judgments. Chan (2007) defined assessment as multiple, comprising vocabulary, sentence patterns, songs and rhymes, and the skills of listening, speaking, reading, and writing. Assessment can also be multiple in terms of tools. It can involve the traditional paper-and-pencil test or multiple media such as a computer, tape recorder, or video recorder.

1.3. Evaluation

As the word "evaluation" suggests, this process involves placing a value judgement on the outcomes that were reached. The term "evaluation" refers to the comprehensive process of accumulating relevant information and drawing relevant conclusions from that data. The testing, measuring, and evaluating are all included in the evaluation.

1.4. Principles of Evaluation

- Determining whether learners' objectives have been achieved or not by the teaching what is to be evaluated.
- Selecting suitable techniques to achieve the purposes identified.
- Combining a range of strategies for a more comprehensive or holistic evaluation of the learning activity.
- Determining and estimating the strengths and limitations of the techniques selected.

- Using evaluation as a means to an end, not an end.

1.5. Importance of Evaluation in Education

Evaluation is used majorly in three types of situations (figure 1).

- To evaluate student performance
- To evaluate teacher activities
- To evaluate the programme or curriculum.

Figure 1. Interrelation of Teaching and Evaluation

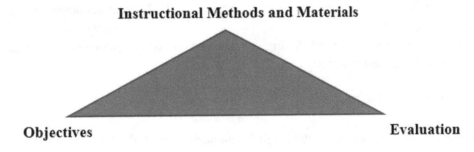

2. REVIEW OF LITERATURE

Mobile applications and owning a mobile phone have been trending in recent times, Li (2022) conducts a study on spoken English assessments in China Universities with the effective use of the mobile-assisted language learning application (MALL) "IELTS Liulishuo" (speaking English fluently in the IELTS test). The positive impact of using the MALL is that it improves automatic speech recognition in factors like the accuracy and fluency of English learners in China colleges.

Muzaza and Tembo (2020) argue in their study that tests are used to enhance learning and motivate students, or it simply prevails as the mean for accessibility of students' performance in the language. Several groups of examinations were conducted with the motive of separating testing from teaching.

Few researchers, like Khan (2019), believe that trainees or teachers lack the professional method of improving their language exams and assessment literacy in the Saudi EFL context. The author reveals that language tests and their benefits vary in several contexts similarly, and there are practical constraints as well. Comparatively, Wieman (2019) claims that universities face a big threat in teaching students more complex thinking and problem-solving skills, which is the need of the hour. The author highly believes that established expertise in teaching these skills which have to be a constant practice to bring about in nature of teaching and creates a huge impact on higher education.

Huang (2016) shows a linear result in the study where the learning motivation and performance of 80 EFL students using the FSVL strategy and mobile learning tool were much more beneficial than the traditional learning tools in a situational English vocabulary learning environment. Similarly, Liu and Kunnan (2016) conducted an analytical study on applying "WriteToLearn" tests. They evaluated the performance in terms of scoring ability and the accuracy of its error in English majors' essays. Second-year

Chinese undergraduates collected one hundred sixty-three samples. The results showed that undergraduates had difficulty identifying the errors in using articles, prepositions, word choice, and expression.

Foreign language teacher training programs need to revamp and innovative in English language testing, and evaluation (ELTE) courses in Turkey declared in the article by Hatipoglu (2015), since future teachers will have good scope for challenges of language assessment. One hundred twenty-four pre-service English language teachers' data was collected using need analysis from questionnaires and interviews. The aftermath of the analysis brought out the perceptions of teachers' needs in language assessment literacy.

3. RESEARCH OBJECTIVES

- To check Computer-based testing on various aspects of the English language through the Easy Test Maker application.
- To collect the perception of English language teachers on using computer-based testing through the Easy Test Maker application

4. RESEARCH QUESTIONS

- Is the computer-based testing of the English language through the Easy Test Maker application sufficient to check learners' performance?
- What is English language teachers' perception of using computer-based testing through the Easy Test Maker application?

5. SIGNIFICANCE OF THE STUDY

The current study places an emphasis on combining computer-based testing with the process of learning a language. Particularly the responsibility that comes along with the testing environment has been taken over by digital platforms. Therefore, the activities that engaged the students were significantly expanded and more thorough than those that took place in a conventional classroom. Therefore, by investigating the usability of computer-based testing for language educators, there is an unquestionable improvement in the accessibility of novel technologies, which in turn raises the quality of the testing and evaluation process. Computer-based testing, on the other hand, has an advantage in that it is both ageless and completely objective, which is beneficial to both teachers and students.

6. RESEARCH METHODOLOGY

The Practitioner Research Methodology was adopted to explore the usability of computer-based testing to 80 English language educators. Kemmis (2006) designates quality practitioner research as "not just a matter of technical excellence but a matter of addressing important problems in thought and actions, in theory, and practice…in and for our communities, in and for our shared world" (p.471). Groundwater-Smith and Mockler (2005) argue that practitioner research should be "collaboration in its nature and transformative in its intent and action" (p.7). Campbell and McNamara (2009) said, "practitioner research is characterized with a view to evaluation and improvement". All 80 educators were given Easy Test Maker and instructed to respond to the data collected at the end.

6.1. Rationale for Easy Test Maker

Easy Test Maker is an online application that allows us to generate online tests. This application permits us to create and manage tests that are customized by our preference. It further admits its users to create, print, and publish the online tests that we customize. The application name discloses it and makes it meaningful just has the name "Easy Test Maker"; it makes it easy and feasible for the teachers' to frame the format of the question types can be multiple or alternate. Follows, an exclusive feature to print alternate versions and publish the online tests on the website. Some of the exceptional features provided by the application are as follows:

- Online test graded automatically- this feature allows you to view and print your student's result and even grade it. Online tests published are graded automatically.
- Formatted tests allow us to create all question patterns like multiple choice, fill-ups, short answers, and true or false questions. It further permits giving instructions and dividing the sections into multiple ones.
- Question bank – this feature enables the teachers to form a test with an entire question bank. It automatically gives a random set of questions to each test taker.
- Analysis report – accessible to quick reports to check the participation of the test takers.
- Shuffling version to reduce malpractice – alternative sections are available with no additional work, and the questions and answer choices are automatically shuffled accordingly in a different order.
- Messy to Easy – creates hassle-free work of creating tests in just a few clicks. Added to it, we can copy any question from one to another; also, any test can be downloaded in both Word document or PDF to save and print for future reference.

6.2. Sample and Sample size

To study the objectives, the current research was conducted with the help of 80 English language educators teaching both in colleges. The language educators were randomly selected from the English discipline.

6.3. Procedure of the Study

The research study was explored with English language educators by inviting them to a Practitioner Research approach. The language educators briefly explained the nature and aim of the study during the registration process. Eighty English language educators were registered to take part in exploring computer-based testing. The scheduled meeting was planned systematically with four sessions. In the session, I, the instructor (researcher), introduced the Easy Test Maker application and its uses with a few demonstrations to the participants (educators). In session II, the instructor (researcher) would play the role of a teacher with the Easy Test Maker application, and the participants (educators) would act as a student while using the computer-based testing. During session III, the participants (educators) were

Table 1. Items in perception scale questionnaire

S.No	Items in the questionnaire
1	The Easy Test Maker application was easy to use
2	Easy Test Maker was easy to test and evaluate
3	Comfortable customizing the test items
4	I would use the Easy Test Maker application again
5	The app made it convenient to measure learners' performance
6	I felt comfortable communicating with students using the Easy Test Maker
7	Easy Test Maker helped me manage my students' learning effectively
8	The app improved my access to students' assessment service
9	Easy Test Maker has the necessary tools to test. I expected it to have
10	Overall, I am satisfied with this Easy Test Maker app

given the role of a teacher to conduct, assign, and assess the class with the Easy Test Maker application. The final session of the meeting was the perception of the participants (educators) after experiencing the Easy Test Maker application. Additionally, language educators were given a perception scale to reassure and rate educators' comprehension of computer-based testing of the Easy Test Maker application.

7. RESULTS AND DISCUSSION

The study's findings were used to check and collect English language teachers' perceptions of using computer-based testing on various aspects through the Easy Test Maker application. The items in the perception scale questionnaire are presented in Table 1. The statistical data of the perception of English language teachers was graphically represented in Fig. 2.

The current research aimed to check the computer-based testing using the Easy Test Maker application related to English language testing and assessment by English language teachers. The findings indicated to the teachers that the Easy Test Maker application could design reliable and valid assessment instruments. The application was ready to customize and pick appropriate assessment methods for instructional testing based on learners' performance levels. Also, the application was ready to administer, score and interpret the results by the provisions in-built into the application (fig.3)

As the unique features were discussed previously, the study findings overlaid for the teachers to create a hassle-free task to create a test in this application (figure 4). The ripples set off for the teachers with additional features like adding images for a conspicuous view in understanding the questions. Despite several applications trending this, Easy Test Makers prevails as the game-winning one since it's user convenient and is exclusively built for teachers or instructors. Given the problem of teachers, setting different question papers for each batch was a tedious process. Still, this application just permits you to create a question bank, and it alternates or shuffles the questions accordingly to test takers of different batches. It is also protected with a passcode from the teacher; until then, the students cannot access the questions of their choice, similar to traditional access to the question paper individually.

Figure 2. Graphical Representation of Teachers' Perception of Easy Test Maker

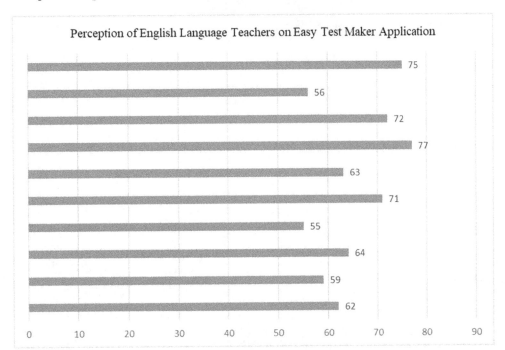

The Easy Test Maker application makes it suitable for teachers or instructors because after the tests are scheduled, they can be stress-free as it automatically evaluates and publishes the grades on the website without any further command (figure 5). The teachers need not take the burden of the evaluating part, which is, again, a tiring task. This application does the entire process once the question banks are created in the particular account. As mentioned in the perception questionnaire, the teachers or instructors are satisfied with the necessary tools or features available in the application. The reason behind that is as per the data recorded by the students or the test-takers, the application evaluates it accordingly by grading.

Figure 3. Adding questions in Easy Test Maker Application

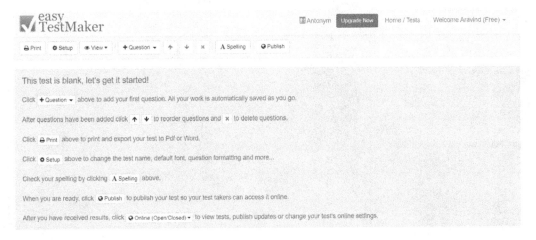

Figure 4. Sheet to fill the questions in Easy Test Maker Application

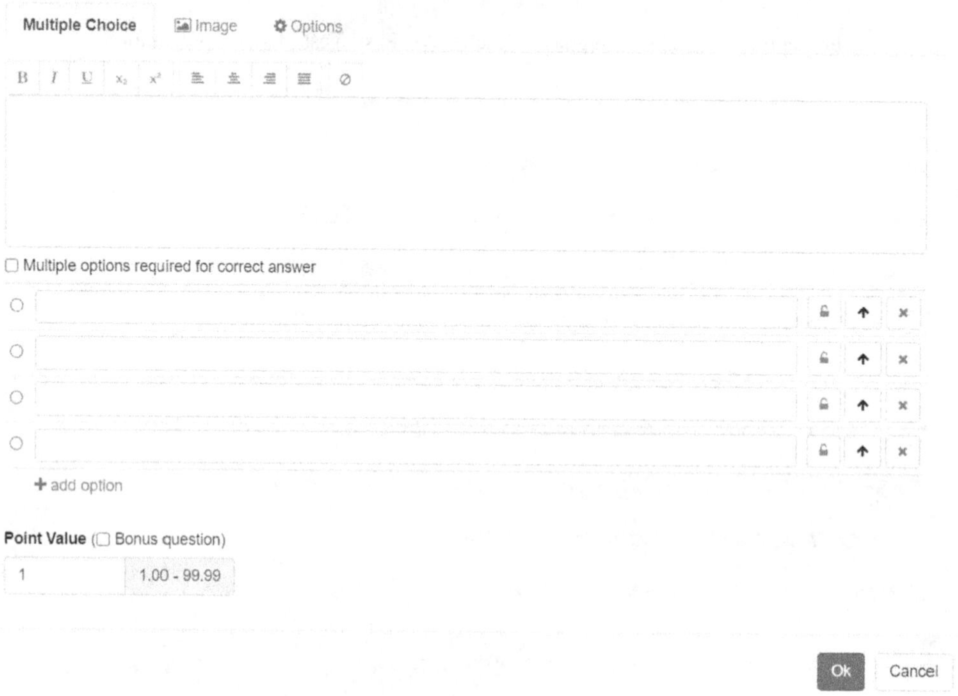

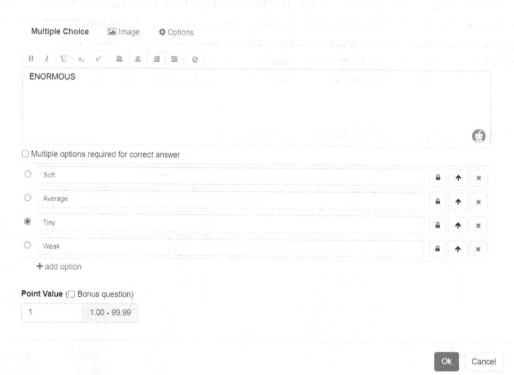

Figure 5. Finalizing and locking the questions in Easy Test Maker Application

Figure 6. Final output of the questions

Additionally, the analysis report instantly given by the application for quick verification of participants or students taken and not taken the test marks it as a satisfactory output, making it an acceptable change for the teachers to utilize the computer-based testing applications shortly. The teachers were gratified by the Easy Test Maker application for the alternatives or shuffling of the question format for each test taker, which is considered to be a time-consuming task, and it was a cakewalk for them. The option of changing the questions to another question paper is the best part, I believed the teachers, and it was such a thought-provoking one. The significant feature is that the teachers can download the results both in Word or PDF format; if any corrections are to be made, they can edit in the Word document.

Easy Test Maker application employed the test results for individual students' performance, planning, and designing the curriculum for better outcomes of the instructional learning and testing of items (fig.6). The application has the feature of developing a valid grading system according to the pupils' scores. Additionally, the teachers' evaluations in this Easy Test Maker application revealed that they found testing skills, knowledge, reliability, and validity were useful and more relevant to their evaluation method. It was revealed that computer-based testing was considered a continuous practice of digital evaluation of testing and evaluation process, which will produce more active and effective tools for assessing students' progress. Hence the teachers felt it was appropriate to assess students' performances and outcomes through computer-based testing (figure 7).

7.1. Major Findings of the Study

- 62 participants out of 80 responded that the Easy Test Maker application was easy to use
- 59 participants out of 80 responded that Easy Test Maker was easy to test and evaluate
- 64 participants out of 80 responded that the app was Comfortable customizing the test items
- 55 participants out of 80 responded that they would use the Easy Test Maker application again
- 71 participants out of 80 responded that the app made it convenient to measure learners' performance
- 63 participants out of 80 responded that they felt comfortable communicating with students using the Easy Test Maker
- 77 participants out of 80 responded that Easy Test Maker helped them manage their students' learning effectively
- 72 participants out of 80 responded that the app improved their accessing process to students' assessment service

- 56 participants out of 80 responded that Easy Test Maker has the necessary tools to test they expected it to have
- 75 participants out of 80 responded that, Overall, they are satisfied with this Easy Test Maker app

Figure 7. Stages in Easy Test Maker Application

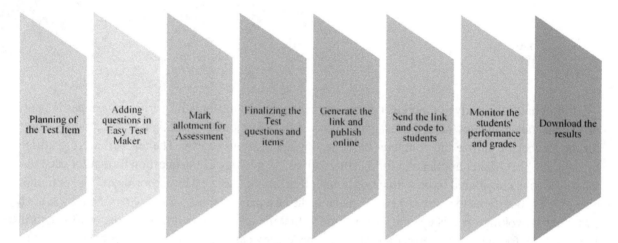

Planning of the Test Item | Adding questions in Easy Test Maker | Mark allotment for Assessment | Finalizing the Test questions and items | Generate the link and publish online | Send the link and code to students | Monitor the students' performance and grades | Download the results

8. CONCLUSION

From the discussion of the study, computer-based testing through Easy Test Maker provides an effective formulation for English language testing and evaluation. Because testing and evaluation play take a pivotal role in language learning and teaching. Easy Test Maker allows the teacher to customize the test items for a standardized evaluation process. Hence testing and evaluation process would have a systematic channel to test the students' performance. Easy Test Maker application acts as a computer-based testing tool that collects, analyses and interprets pupils' attainment as part of a recognized pattern of scoring its effectiveness. Nevertheless, the application is useful for teachers in selecting, grading, scoring, predicting, diagnosing, and self-correction test items. The findings of the participants gave serious thought to the teaching, learning and evaluation process within the domain of testing and evaluation, keeping in mind providing quality and digitally engaged language education. The result reflects the usability of testing and evaluation through Easy Test Maker, where testing is now offered at computer-based testing. Therefore, English language teachers must be trained first on using digital tools for testing. Also, results suggest that computer-based testing is widely applicable to English language training, determined by Easy Test Maker experiments in digital testing in multimedia e-learning academic environments on the usability of computer-based testing.

REFERENCES

Bachman, L. F., & Palmer, A. S. (1996). *Language Testing in Practice*. Oxford University Press.

Buck, G. (2001). *Assessing listening*. Cambridge University Press. doi:10.1017/CBO9780511732959

Campbell, A., & McNamara, O. (2009). Mapping the field of practitioner research, inquiry and professional learning in educational contexts: a review. In A. Campbell & S. Groundwater-Smith (Eds.), *Connecting inquiry and professional learning in education: international perspectives and practical solutions* (pp. 10–26). Routledge.

Carroll, J. D. (1968). Generalization of Canonical Correlation Analysis to Three of More Sets of Variables. APA.

Chan, Y. C. (2007). Elementary school of EFL teachers' beliefs and practices of multiple assessments. *Reflections on English Language Teaching, 7*(1), 53.

Groundwater-Smith, S., & Mockler, N. (2005, July 4-6). *Practitioner research in education: Beyond celebration.* Paper presented to the Australian Association for Research in Education Focus Conference, James Cook University, Cairns, Australia.

Hatipoğlu, Ç. (2015). English language testing and evaluation (ELTE) training in Turkey: Expectations and needs of pre-service English language teachers. *ELT Research Journal, 4*(2), 111–128.

Huang, C. S., Yang, S. J., Chiang, T. H., & Su, A. Y. (2016). Effects of situated mobile learning approach on learning motivation and performance of EFL students. *Journal of Educational Technology & Society, 19*(1), 263–276.

Kemmis, S. (2006). Participatory action research and the public sphere. *Educational Action Research, 14*(4), 459–476. doi:10.1080/09650790600975593

. Khan, A. (2019). Testing in English Language Teaching and its Significance in EFL Contexts: A Theoretical Perspective. *Global Regional Review (GRR), 4.*

Li, X. (2022, January). The Effectiveness of Mobile-assisted Language Learning (MALL) Applications on the Spoken English Assessments in China's Universities. In *2021 International Conference on Social Development and Media Communication (SDMC 2021)* (pp. 751-756). Atlantis Press. 10.2991/assehr.k.220105.137

Liu, S., & Kunnan, A. J. (2016). Investigating the Application of Automated Writing Evaluation to Chinese Undergraduate English Majors: A Case Study of "WriteToLearn". *calico journal, 33*(1), 71-91.

Muzaza, S., & Tembo, G. (2020). Testing and Evaluation Towards Teaching and Testing. *Journal Educational Verkenning, 1*(1), 21–24. doi:10.48173/jev.v1i1.26

Tomlinson, B. (2005). Testing to learn: A personal view of language testing. *ELT Journal, Oxford University Press, 59*(1), 44. doi:10.1093/elt/cci005

Wieman, C. E. (2019). Expertise in university teaching & the implications for teaching effectiveness, evaluation & training. *Daedalus, 148*(4), 47–78. doi:10.1162/daed_a_01760

Chapter 2
Evaluation of the Efficiency of Online Learning Programs in Higher Education

P. S. Venkateswaran
ⓘ https://orcid.org/0000-0001-8958-103X
PSNA College of Engineering and Technology, Dindigul, India

ABSTRACT

Online education helps students from different economic and social backgrounds, places, and times by avoiding distance and cost. An essential scientific and practical question that will be studied for a long time is how well students learn. All the communication channels make it easier for students to talk to their teachers and other people. The playing field is more level, making it easier for people to talk to each other, and for everyone in the class can participate. When students think about how many online courses are available, distance education's value also increases. Budgets being reduced for the government and private sector and decreased college enrollment are favourable trends. The efficiency of online learning courses in higher education is investigated using the SEM method. According to the e learning survey for the higher education students' e-learning classes, cloud meetings are better for learning than live conversations. Students are showing more interest towards the online courses with cloud meetings if they think e-learning with cloud meetings is better.

1. INTRODUCTION

Aulkemeier et al. (2019) talked about "digital collaboration platforms" that could help the social innovation process by letting people share information, work together, and connect. The Delloite research (2019) indicates that online education tools in the IT field increase productivity, the quality of interaction, class morale, and output, all of which are important in business and education today.

Heggart & Yoo (2018) discussed how to use Google Classroom for primary school educators teach kids and improve their teaching methods for future use and improvement. The research showed that

DOI: 10.4018/978-1-6684-6682-7.ch002

Google Classroom got students more interested in learning and helped them learn more. It made the classroom environment better.

Under the auspices of the Digital India initiative, Nedungadi et al. (2018) stated that rural people benefitted due to the inclusion of a digital literacy framework, financial literacy, and e-safety. The cell phone helps a lot for online curriculum and flexible learning method and guide the students in practical classes, motivation, attitude building and creating subject interest through online video lectures, videos.

Online instruction provides a better learning environment for students, teachers, and others in a better way (Dogbey et al., 2017). Kaliisa and Picard (2017) examine how much cellphone devices can help students in higher education. They found that students and teachers work together more when using mobile devices.

Annamdevula and Bellamkonda (2016) say that online services help university administrators to set aside the right amount of money to improve educational services, such as support services and facilities.

Brahimi & Sarirete (2015) criticize online technology that higher education today is moving towards commercialization instead of pedagogical enhancement via MOOCs. Chatterjee and Nath (2015) stated that the lack of digital literacy in India had been a problem for MOOCs over the past 20 years. However, membership is still relatively high, demonstrating distant regions' need and thirst for information, particularly in HEI.

Sooryanarayan and Gupta (2015) investigated the influence of several motivating variables on Indian students' motivation to use MOOCs. Cremona et al. (2015) analyze the contributing aspects while focusing on the framework of the digital platform.

Fletcher and Bullock (2015) examine how existing digital behaviours may impact the future development of teaching methodologies for education systems. Multiple factors influence flipped learning at institutions of higher education where collaborative and communicative education are required.

In digital learning for HEI, social presence is a critical construct that, along with other characteristics that support discourse-based learning, should be given substantial weight. The framework enables students, increases their potential, boosts their well-being, and decreases the danger of exploitation and further focused on a teaching technique in which internet-based social interaction among students facilitates learning.

El Massah and Fadly (2017) found participants' leading causes of learning efficacy were personal and social qualities.

Scheerens (2016) says that a school's learning effectiveness is determined by how well it meets its goals. Its significance is acknowledged globally as a crucial factor in growth. Researchers used the symbolic cognition perspective to find that personal and social factors affect how well people learn.

Using the representational cognition theory, researchers found that personal and social factors affect how well people learn. Researchers developed three aspects: absorptive ability, knowledge acquisition initiative, and learning orientation. Network links, how well groups did, and pro-sharing norms were identified as social factors.

Research shows that individual motivations are essential for improving learning efficacy because they help make goals relevant. Higher education institutions (HEIs) worldwide have used e-learning as a major one after the COVID 19.

In India (Swayam, NPTEL) and worldwide (Edraak, Coursera, Udacity, Open 2 Study, Future Study, FUN, and Iversity) for commercial purposes, students have benefited from learning at their speed and from remote locations. Students who wished to update their resumes by enrolling in a few courses or increasing their skill set embraced MOOCs in India in recent years. The popularity of e-learning may also be owing to its cost-effective adaptability. According to Broadbent (2017), the online learning market rises at a rate of 7.07 per cent and reach $65.41 billion by 2023.

Online teaching brings more innovative ideas in teaching methods and more benefits to the teaching and learning community. Due to the flipped classroom's (FC) introduction, student's leadership talent has increased. The teamwork and work completion among them improved well. Along with the advantages, the combination of online teaching in the FC has increased efficiency and improved student-learning outcomes. However, more research still needs to be done to improve the effectiveness of online teaching, especially in high schools.

ONLINE EDUCATION

Several studies have found that online instruction is better for students learning than traditional face-to-face instruction. On line learning measured through the test marks, student's positive attitude, motivation and interest towards the curriculum and development and fewer students dropping out or failing (Nguyen, 2015). Numerous students are attracted to online education due to its adaptability, availability, and ease.

Convenience: Students prefer the online learning than the traditional classrooms because they can learn from their location itself. It highlights ease as the primary benefit of online education. Online education facilitates a strong connection among professors and students in cyber classes (Fedynich, 2013).

Participation: In the online mode student's participation is high. Students can easily attend the online classes from the location. The major adaptable thing in cyber learning is the ability of pupil to attend in their home atmosphere. There are several formats for online education, like power point presentation, white board flipped classroom etc.

Morrison et al. (2019) say students participate online classes through their mobile in live or interact through chat rooms or discussion boards. Higher education institutes are offering online education, students' admission, enrollment in school, colleges and University grows, hence revenue increases.

2.1 Distribution of Classrooms

Numerous students are drawn to online learning because of its adaptability, accessibility, and ease. Moreover, online education will remain a vital part of higher education. Some students choose online education because it is more convenient than attending a regular classroom. It highlights ease as the primary benefit of online education.

Schools need less space than the national average, so they need fewer classrooms. This cuts down on their power and maintenance costs (Briggs, 2015). Engagement is evaluated by a student's level of interest, the frequency with which they interact with other students, and their willingness to acquire course content.

In their 2016 research, Jaggars and Xu discovered a correlation between online course participation and performance on quizzes and examinations. This connection is crucial. According to Barteit et al. (2020), online learning is highly accepted by HEIs, due to its availability, low cost and high-quality resources for learners and easy approach to the student's community. The acceptability of e-learning by educators and students globally is crucial to the growth of e-learning.

The growth of online learning depends on the acceptance level of teachers and students-learning is in high demand because of learning innovations in engineering and sustainability (Rodrigues et al., 2019), analytics, and AI-based assessment (Sedrakyan et al., 2020).

E-learning has been used successfully in business and education, improving teaching and learning and making students happier (Chang, 2016). Waheed et al. (2016) looked into how learners felt about the quality of the information they learned, the types of content that could be found on online tools, and how this affected the success of e-learning environments. Engagement is vital for producing the intended effects.

Students' engagement is one of the essential factors in learning results. The most important thing is how effective e-learning can provide a better result to the learning problems. Early models of e-learning efficacy were made to help people understand how they used technology to learn online (Chu & Chen, 2016).

User-to-user learning cooperation is used more and more on the Internet (Rahimi et al., 2015), which contributes to the globalization of education and gives much room for growth and change in the digital age. Existing difficulties in the online learning must be removed for the betterment of online learning.

2.2. Academic Proficiency

The change from teacher-centred to learner-centred learning strategies is mainly responsible for emphasizing learning outcomes to measure student progress. So, analyzing learning outcomes helps many people, like students, teachers, academic advisors, and accrediting bodies, reach learning goals that have already been set (Mahajan & Singh, 2017). According to the findings, behavioural intentions result in actual conduct. Students should be proficient with technology and the contents of the online learning programmes to be utilised should be designed with the teacher's assistance in a way that puts the student at the centre. Instead than forbidding the use of technology in the classroom, educators should make sure that students have access to sufficient technological infrastructures and technical support for their learning activities. Moreover, online education should be integrated into standard classroom curriculum, and its usage as a supplement to traditional schooling should be encouraged and expanded.

3. REVIEW OF LITERATURE

3.1. Technology Acceptance Model

3.1.1. Perceived Ease of Use (PEOU)

F. D. Davis (1989) mentioned that PEOU method is not a tough technology to use in the classroom or higher education environment. The previous study has indicated that the PEOU has a strong and significant relationship with behavioural intention to use (BI) (Jaber., 2016). In e-learning, perceived ease of use (PEOU) is how much a student thinks using an e-learning system will not take much work and will be easy. The PEOU was measured using the following variables: E-learning is easier to use, E-learning makes learning easier, and E-learning gives more practical learning support.

3.1.2. Perceived Usefulness (PU)

Perceived utility (PU) is how individuals feel a new technology will enhance their work performance. Considerable empirical research reveals that P.U. is a crucial factor in technology adoption (Tarhini et al., 2017). Students will only adopt a learning method if they perceive it to improve their academic achievement. The earlier study on e-learning has shown a substantial positive relationship between perceived utility (PU) and behavioural intention to use the e-learning system (Mahmodi, 2017). These variables were utilized to calculate the PU: E-learning allows learning more rapidly, effectively, and with remarkable ability.

3.1.3. Attitude Towards Use (ATU)

Attitude is "the extent to which a person has a favorable or unfavorable view of e-learning technologies" (Hussein., 2017). Research has demonstrated that attitude directly affects behavioral intent. The ATU was measured based on the following variables: I am hopeful about e-future learning, I like using the online learning system, and the online learning system helps a lot for better learning and provide a congenial environment to the learning community.

3.1.4. Behavioral Intention to Use (BI)

Regarding e-learning, behavioural intention (BI) refers to the learners' current and future purpose in using e-learning systems. It entails consistent use. Multiple studies have proven that behavioural intent influences actual use directly and significantly of an e-learning system (Mou, Shin, & Cohen, 2017). I like to participate in online learning in the future, I strive to participate in online learning in the future, and I wish to engage in BI-calculating online learning in the forthcoming.

4. RESEARCH METHOD

4.1 Data Collection

Online surveys are administered to undergraduate engineering students from specific colleges in the Madurai District. Due to the difficulties of taking a random sample of all college students utilizing e-learning systems, this study collects sample data by convenience sampling. 250 Engineering (UG) graduates in e-learning programs have been requested to submit a survey online. There is no missing information in the poll, which was filled out by 218 students. Of those who answered, 42% are men and 58% are women.

5. RESULTS

The software packages SPSS and Amos are used to examine the data. The results are disclosed in the sections that follow.

5.1. Measurement Model

Table 1 gives proof of the reliability of the three tested components. All constructs have statistically significant favorable factor loading and, with composite reliability (CR) greater than 0.70, extracted average variance (EAV) more than 0.50, and Cronbach's alpha exceeding 0.70. The measures employ a Likert scale with five points. Each instrument's mean is more than 3, suggesting a favorable perception of e-learning. From the respondent's opinion, perceived usefulness and attitude towards use have the higher advantage in the online learning compared with other two variables since their mean vale are 3.904 and 3.849.

Table 1. Reliability analysis

	Mean	Standard Deviation	CR	AVE	Cronbach alpha
Perceived Ease of Use	3.738	0.917	0.794	0.671	0.849
Perceived Usefulness	3.904	0.966	0.826	0.718	0.904
Attitude Towards Use	3.849	0.706	0.871	0.744	0.871
Behavioral Intention to Use	3.771	1.063	0.942	0.829	0.926

Source: Primary data

Table 2. Discriminant validity

	Perceived Ease of Use	Perceived Usefulness	Attitude Towards Use	Behavioral Intention to Use
Perceived Ease of Use	0.509			
Perceived Usefulness	0.671	0.628		
Attitude Towards Use	0.722	0.551	0.703	
Behavioral Intention to Use	0.683	0.729	0.795	0.812

Source: Primary data

From the table 2, all the constructs have a strong correlation between them. The constructs have discriminant validity if the square root of the average variance derived from indicators within a construct is greater than any two constructs, creating a strong correlation between them. The constructions exhibit indicators of adequate measurement quality.

5.2. Structural Model

The structural equation model in the figure 1 explains the various path coefficients connected with each variable. The path coefficients value indicates their standardized value and how their relationships are correlated with other variables in linear function or not. Figure 1 shows the SEM analysis output. At p.01, the positive associations between PEOU and PU, as well as PU and Intention (IN), are statistically significant. Both path coefficients were standardized (0.48 and 0.43) exceed the specified optimal sig-

Figure 1. SEM model

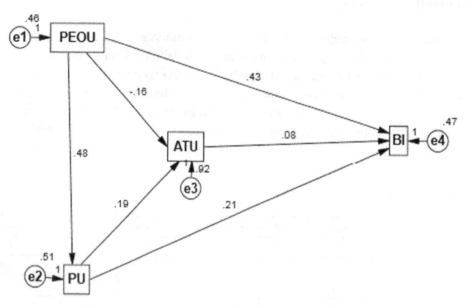

nificance requirement of 0.30. The below figure shows the regression weights, intercepts, Covariance, variances of the variables in the model.

Null hypothesis - H01: There is no influence of PEOU on PU, ATU, BI at 5 percent significant level. *Influence of Perceived Ease of Use:*

From the above model, it is clear that, Perceived Ease of Use of the online learning tools in the HEIs has a strong influence on Perceived Usefulness and Behavioral Intention to Use and which is significant at 5 percent level (H0 Rejected). Hence, all these variables are having a strong effect on QWL. i.e. QWL of the nurses are good. There is a negative and poor influence of Perceived Ease of Use on Attitude Towards Use, hence the null hypothesis is accepted at 5 percent level.

Null hypothesis - H02: There is no influence of PU on ATU and BI at 5 percent significant level.

From the above model, it is clear that, Perceived Usefulness of the online learning tools in the HEIs has a moderate influence on Attitude Towards Use and Behavioral Intention to Use and which is significant at 5 percent level (H0 Rejected).

Null hypothesis - H02: There is no influence of ATU on BI at 5 percent significant level.

From the above model, it is clear that, Attitude Towards Use of the online learning tools in the HEIs has a weak influence on Behavioral Intention to Use and which is significant at 5 percent level (H0 Rejected).

Figures 1 and Table 3 summarize the behaviors of the chosen fit indices during fitting the sample. In this case, we display the distributions of the average sample estimates for each fit index across all

Table 3. SEM output

Path analysis			Estimate	S.E.	C.R.	P
PU	←	PEOU	.480	.071	6.738	0.001
ATU	←	PEOU	-.156	.106	-1.474	0.141
BI	←	PEOU	.432	.075	5.724	0.001
ATU	←	PU	.187	.092	2.042	0.041
BI	←	PU	.214	.066	3.249	0.001
BI	←	ATU	.079	.048	1.646	0.100

simulations. RMSEA .06, CFI >.95, and SRMR .08 are often used benchmarks for judging how well a model fits the data (Hu & Bentler, 1999). Results demonstrated that the most crucial parameters, such as the p-value for x2, are more significant than 0.05 when using the average sample RMSEA as the outcome. The values of RMR, RMSEA, GFI, and CFI all represent the perceived goodness-of-fit of the structural model.

6. CONCLUSION

According to the research, E-learning will increase the accessibility and quality of higher education. However, existing online education systems must be enhanced because of the high dropout rate. The absence of real-time dialogue between students and teachers may contribute. Real-time cloud meetings with real-time talks might be included in the e-learning environment to make studying more straight-forward and more inspiring for many students. Learners' impressions of a course's usefulness and ease of use are strongly affected by the quality of the course, how it is graded, and how the technology is designed. Pedagogically driven e-learning solutions may significantly affect how satisfied students are with these aspects. The students survey shows that e-learning courses suggests that cloud meetings facilitate learning more effectively than live conversations. Online learning classes attended students felt more advantageous are more inclined to enroll in online courses. Cloud meetings have made it possible for students and teachers to talk and openly exchange ideas. It has made learning more accessible and more effective. By lowering transactional distance, open interactions improve learner engagement and retention. In addition, the results support the concept of online distance education in that cloud-based communications and learner-to-learner interactions may increase student motivation, learning pleasure, and effectiveness.

6. REFERENCES

Al-Gahtani, S. S. (2016). Empirical investigation of e-learning acceptance and assimilation: A structural equation model. *Appl. Comput. Inform.*, *12*(1), 27–50. doi:10.1016/j.aci.2014.09.001

Annamdevula, S., & Bellamkonda, R. S. (2016). Effect of student perceived service quality on student satisfaction, loyalty, and motivation in Indian universities: The development of HiEduQual. *Journal of Modelling in Management, 11*(2), 488–517. doi:10.1108/JM2-01-2014-0010

Aulkemeier, F., Iacob, M. E., & van Hillegersberg, J. (2019). Platform-based collaboration in digital ecosystems. *Electronic Markets, 29*(4), 597–608. doi:10.100712525-019-00341-2

Barteit, S., Guzek, D., Jahn, A., Barnighausen, T., Jorge, M. M., & Neuhann, F. (2020). Evaluation of e-learning for medical education in low- and middle-income countries: A systematic review. *Computers & Education, 145*, 103726. doi:10.1016/j.compedu.2019.103726 PMID:32565611

Brahimi, T., & Sarirete, A. (2015). Learning outside the classroom through MOOCs. *Computers in Human Behavior, 51*(1), 604–609. doi:10.1016/j.chb.2015.03.013

Briggs, A. (2015), Ten ways to overcome barriers to student engagement online. *Online Learning Consortium.* https://onlinelearningconsortium.org/news_item/tenways-overcomebarriers-student-engagement-online/

Broadbent, J. (2017). Comparing online and blended learners' self-regulated learning strategies and academic performance. *The Internet and Higher Education, 33*, 24–32. doi:10.1016/j.iheduc.2017.01.004

Chang, V. (2016). Review and discussion: E-learning for academia and industry. *International Journal of Information Management, 36*(3), 476–485. doi:10.1016/j.ijinfomgt.2015.12.007

Chatterjee, P., & Nath, A. (2015). Massive open online courses (MOOCs) in education – a case study in Indian context and vision to ubiquitous Learning. *Proceedings of the 2014 IEEE International Conference on MOOCs, Innovation and Technology in Education,* (pp. 36–41). IEEE.

Chu, T. H., & Chen, Y. Y. (2016). With Good, We Become Good: Understanding e-learning adoption by the theory of planned behaviour and group influences. *Computers & Education, 92*, 37–52. doi:10.1016/j.compedu.2015.09.013

Cremona, L., Ravarini, A., & Viscusi, G. (2015). *Fitness of business models for digital collaborative platforms in clusters: a case study. Lecture Notes in Business Information Processing.* Springer Verlag.

Cruz-Benito, J., Sanchez-Prieto, J. C., Theron, R., & Garcia-Penalvo, F. J. (2019). Measuring students' acceptance to AI-driven assessment in eLearning: proposing a first TAM-based research model. *International Conference on Human-Computer Interaction,* (pp. 15–25). Springer, Cham, 10.1007/978-3-030-21814-0_2

Davis, F. D. (1989). Perceived usefulness, perceived ease of use, and user acceptance of information technology. *Management Information Systems Quarterly, 13*(3), 319–340. doi:10.2307/249008

Dogbey, J., Kumi-Yeboah, A., & Dogbey, J. (2017). Dialogue pedagogical strategies perceived to enhance online interaction: The instructor's perspective. *International Journal of Online Pedagogy and Course Design, 7*(3), 70–85. doi:10.4018/IJOPCD.2017070105

El Massah, S. S., & Fadly, D. (2017). Predictors of academic performance for finance students: Women at higher education in the UAE. *International Journal of Educational Management, 31*(7), 854–864. doi:10.1108/IJEM-12-2015-0171

. Fedynich, L. V. (2013). Teaching beyond the classroom walls: The pros and cons of cyber learning. *Journal of Instructional Pedagogies, 13.*

Fletcher, T., & Bullock, S. M. (2015). Reframing pedagogy while teaching about teaching online: A collaborative self-study. *Professional Development in Education, 41*(4), 690–706. doi:10.1080/19415257.2014.938357

Heggart, K. R., & Yoo, J. (2018). Getting the most from Google Classroom: A Pedagogical Framework for Tertiary Educators. *The Australian Journal of Teacher Education, 43*(3), 140–153. doi:10.14221/ajte.2018v43n3.9

Hu, L. T., & Bentler, P. M. (1999). Cutoff criteria for fit indexes in covariance structure analysis: Conventional criteria versus new alternatives. *Structural Equation Modeling, 6*(1), 1–55. doi:10.1080/10705519909540118

Hussein, Z. (2017). Leading to Intention: The Role of Attitude in relation to an Acceptance Model in E-Learning. *Procedia Computer Science, 105*, 159–164. doi:10.1016/j.procs.2017.01.196

Jaber, O. A. (2016). An examination of variables influencing the acceptance and usage of e-learning systems in Jordanian higher education institutions. [PhD dissertation, London School Commerce, Cardiff Metropolitan Univ., Cardiff, U.K].

Jaggars, S. S., & Xu, D. (2016). How do online course design features influence student performance? *Computers & Education, 95*, 270–284. doi:10.1016/j.compedu.2016.01.014

Kaliisa, R., & Picard, M. (2017). A systematic review on mobile learning in higher education: The African perspective. *The Turkish Online Journal of Educational Technology, 16*(1), 1–18.

Linjawi, A. I., & Alfadda, L. S. (2018). Students' perception, attitudes, and readiness toward online learning in dental education in Saudi Arabia: A cohort study. *Advances in Medical Education and Practice, 9*(1), 855–863. doi:10.2147/AMEP.S175395 PMID:30538597

. Mahajan, M., and Singh, M.K.S. (2017). Importance and benefits of learning outcomes. *OSR Journal of Humanities and Social Science (IOSR-JHSS), 22*(3), 65–67.

. Mahmodi, M. (2017). The Analysis of the Factors Affecting the Acceptance of E-Learning in Higher Education. *Interdisciplinary Journal Virtual Learn. Med. Sci., 8*(1), e11158.

Morrison, G. R., Ross, S. J., Morrison, J. R., & Kalman, H. K. (2019). *Designing Effective Instruction.* John Wiley & Sons.

Mou, J., Shin, D. H., & Cohen, J. (2017). Understanding trust and perceived usefulness in the consumer acceptance of an e-service: A longitudinal investigation. *Behaviour & Information Technology, 36*(2), 125–139. doi:10.1080/0144929X.2016.1203024

Nedungadi, P. P., Menon, R., & Raman, R. (2018). Towards an inclusive digital literacy framework for digital India. *Education + Training, 60*(6), 516–528. doi:10.1108/ET-03-2018-0061

Nguyen, T. (2015). The effectiveness of online learning: Beyond no significant difference and future horizons. *Journal of Online Learning and Teaching, 11*(2), 309–319.

Rahimi, E., van den Berg, J., & Veen, W. (2015). Facilitating student-driven constructing of learning environments using Web 2.0 personal learning environments. *Computers & Education*, *81*, 235–246. doi:10.1016/j.compedu.2014.10.012

Rodrigues, H., Almeida, F., Figueiredo, V., & Lopes, S. L. (2019). Tracking e-learning through published papers: A systematic review. *Computers & Education*, *136*, 87–98. doi:10.1016/j.compedu.2019.03.007

Scheerens, J. (2016). Educational effectiveness and ineffectiveness. A Critical Review of the Knowledge Base, 389. Springer.

Sedrakyan, G., Malmberg, J., Verbert, K., Jarvela, S., & Kirschner, P. A. (2020). Linking learning behaviour analytics and learning science concepts: Designing a learning analytics dashboard for feedback to support learning regulation. *Computers in Human Behavior*, *107*, 105512. doi:10.1016/j.chb.2018.05.004

Sooryanarayan, D. G., & Gupta, D. (2015). Impact of learner motivation on MOOC preferences: transfer vs made MOOCs. *International Conference on Advances in Computing, Communications, and Informatics,* (pp. 929–934). IEEE. 10.1109/ICACCI.2015.7275730

Tarhini, K., Hone, K., Liu, X., & Tarhini, T. (2017). Examining the moderating effect of individual-level cultural values on users' acceptance of E-learning in developing countries: A structural equation modelling of an extended technology acceptance model. *Interactive Learning Environments*, *25*(3), 306–328. doi:10.1080/10494820.2015.1122635

Vidanagama, D. U. (2016). Acceptance of E-learning among undergraduates of computing degrees in Sri Lanka. *Int. J. Mod. Educ. Comput. Sci.*, *8*(4), 25–32. doi:10.5815/ijmecs.2016.04.04

Waheed, M., Kaur, K., & Qazi, A. (2016). Students' perspective on knowledge quality in eLearning knowledge quality in eLearning. *Internet Research*, *26*(1), 120–145. doi:10.1108/IntR-08-2014-0199

Chapter 3
Giving Feedback Online on EFL/ESL Student Writing Through Talk and Comment:
A Review

Ahmet Erdost Yastibaş
(iD) https://orcid.org/0000-0002-1886-7951
Gazi University, Turkey

ABSTRACT

Teaching writing requires English as a foreign language (EFL)/English as a second language (ESL) students to use their knowledge of English to produce a piece of language through which they can communicate their ideas, feelings, and beliefs. Giving feedback on EFL/ESL students' writing plays a critical role in teaching writing because feedback enables students to see their strengths and weaknesses and improve their writing by working on their weaknesses. Such feedback can be given face-to-face or online. Different programs such as Word and Google Docs can be used in giving online feedback. One of these methods is Talk and Comment. This study aimed to review this technology and indicate how it can be used to provide feedback on EFL/ESL students' writing. Therefore, this technology was reviewed in two stages: First, its features were described. Second, it was evaluated critically. Thus, its use to give feedback on EFL/ESL students' writing was explained step by step in this study.

INTRODUCTION

Writing is one of the productive skills which require English as a foreign language (EFL)/English as a second language (ESL) students to use their knowledge of English, including grammar, vocabulary, spelling, and pronunciation to produce a piece of language through which they can express themselves, communicate their feelings, ideas, and beliefs, and convey their messages. As a result, teaching writing plays an essential role in English language teaching.

DOI: 10.4018/978-1-6684-6682-7.ch003

Considering its significance in English language teaching, teaching writing successfully necessitates careful planning in which writing is presented to EFL/ESL students in different stages, including brainstorming, outlining, first draft, proofreading, editing, final draft, and publication. In each stage, EFL students are supposed to do several interrelated writing activities to produce a piece of writing. For example, after writing their first draft, they try to improve their writing in the proofreading and editing stages by concentrating on different aspects of writing, including their use of language (e.g., grammar, spelling, punctuation), their choice of vocabulary, and the organisation of their ideas. In the proofreading and editing stages, they may not be proficient enough to find out their strengths and weaknesses, so they may not be able to enhance their writing by working on their weaknesses. Therefore, they need other people who are more proficient such as teachers and peers, to give them feedback on their writing, which makes feedback significant to know.

Feedback

Feedback can affect what students learn and achieve academically due to the information that focuses on students' performance and understanding (Hattie & Timperley, 2007). The effectiveness of feedback depends on how well it is done (Brookhart, 2017). If it shows students their current level of learning, what they should do to improve their learning, and why they should do so, and if it is understandable for them, it can be considered good feedback (Brookhart, 2017), which makes it effective in students' learning. Depending on this information, it can be defined as the information given to students about their academic work, shows their strengths and weaknesses, enables them to work on their weaknesses, and helps them enhance their learning.

The general information about feedback above is also valid for the feedback given on EFL/ESL students' writing because if it shows EFL/ESL students their strengths and weaknesses in their writing and provides them with the information necessary to work on and overcome their weaknesses, and if EFL/ESL students can comprehend it, it can enhance their writing. Such feedback can be given face-to-face or online.

Giving Online Feedback on EFL/ESL Students' Writing

Online feedback is a type of feedback students receive on their academic work through different technologies such as email and Moodle. It can be given on EFL/ESL students' writing, and this (i.e., online feedback on EFL/ESL students' writing) has been researched in the literature in terms of three aspects separately or together: online teacher feedback (Saiful, Sulistyo, Mukminatien, 2019; Vadia & Ciptaningrum, 2020; Widyaningsih, 2018; Wihastyanang, Kusumaningrum, Latief, & Cahyono, 2020), online peer feedback (Abri, 2021; Chuaphalakit, Inpin, & Coffin, 2019; Ebadi & Alizadeh, 2021; Daweli, 2018; Gao, Samuel, & Asmawi, 2016; Ma, 2019; Saiful et al., 2019; Shang, 2017, 2019; Vadia & Ciptaningrum, 2020; Wihastyanang et al., 2020; Yang & Meng, 2013; Yuk, 2021), and automated corrective feedback (Shang, 2017, 2019).

Although two of these studies (Saiful et al., 2019; Wihastyanang et al., 2020) found out that online teacher and peer feedback did not increase students' academic performance in writing, the other studies indicate that online feedback can contribute to students' writing positively (Lv, Ren, & Xie, 2021; Vadia & Ciptaningrum, 2020; Yang & Meng, 2013; Yoke et al., 2013). Online peer feedback can improve students' writing (Chuaphalakit et al., 2019; Daweli, 2018; Ma, 2019; Yang & Meng, 2013) and writing ability/skills (Ebadi & Alizadeh, 2021; Yuk, 2021) and can enable them to enhance their sentence writing and increase different types of lexical items (Shang, 2017, 2019) as well as reduce their grammatical errors (Abri, 2021; Shang, 2019). Online teacher feedback can also improve students' writing skills (Widyaningsih, 2018). In addition, automated corrective feedback can help students to enhance their writing by improving their vocabulary (Shang, 2019). Besides these, online feedback can help improve students' self-confidence and interest them in writing (Vadia & Ciptaningrum, 2020).

Some Technologies Used to Give Feedback on EFL/ESL Students' Writings Online

Several different technologies have been used in the studies on online feedback given on EFL/ESL students' writing. These technologies include Wiki (Ma, 2019), a system designed for the study (Yang & Meng, 2013), email (Widyaningsih, 2018; Yoke et al., 2013), Moodle (Shang, 2017, 2019), automated corrective feedback systems such as Cool Sentence Corrective Network (Shang, 2017, 2019), Edmodo (Vadia & Ciptaningrum, 2020; Wihastyanang et al., 2020; Yuk, 2021), weblog such as Qzone (Gao et al., 2016), Google Docs (Alharbi, 2019; Chuaphalakit et al., 2019; Daweli, 2018; Ebadi & Alizadeh, 2021), and Schoology (Saiful et al., 2019). In addition to these programs, Kaizena (Pearson, 2021), Microsoft Word and Adobe (to give feedback on PDF files) can be used to provide feedback online on EFL/ESL students' writing.

Research That Has Reviewed Technologies Used to Teach, Learn, and/or Practice Different Aspects of a Language

There is a growing literature on the studies which have reviewed technologies, including websites and applications that can be used to teach, learn, and/or practice a language. In these review studies, the features of such technologies are generally described, and those technologies are evaluated in terms of how they can be used in language teaching and learning. Table 1 below presents some of these studies, the technologies reviewed in these studies, and how they can be used to teach, learn, and/or practice different aspects of a language.

As understood from Table 1, different kinds of technologies can be used to teach, learn, and/or practice the macro skills (i.e., reading, listening, speaking, and writing) and micro-skills (i.e., pronunciation, grammar, and vocabulary) of a language, and such technologies are among common research topics.

Aim of the Research and Research Questions

The present study aimed to review Talk and Comment and indicate the use of it to give feedback on EFL/ESL students' writing online so that it can contribute to the existing literature on the reviews of technologies used to teach, learn, and/or practice a language by trying to answer the following research questions:

1. What are the features of Talk and Comment?
2. How can Talk and Comment be used to give feedback on EFL/ESL students' writing?

Table 1. Some technology review studies, the technologies reviewed in these studies, and how the reviewed technologies can be used to teach, learn, and/or practice different aspects of a language

Study	Technology reviewed	Their use in teaching, learning, and/or practicing a language
Bakoko & Waluyo (2021)	newsela.com	It can help students to practice reading in a foreign language (Bakoko & Waluyo, 2021).
Barrot (2020)	Grammarly	It can be used as an automated corrective feedback tool by students in their writing in English (Barrot, 2020).
Beck & Flinn (2021)	Say It: English Pronunciation	EFL/ESL students can improve their pronunciation, listening, and speaking in English (Beck & Flinn, 2021).
Cheng (2018)	WordSift	It can be used by students to learn vocabulary in a language (Cheng, 2018).
Ezeh (2020)	storyjumper.com	Language teachers can use it to support and improve their storytelling activities in their language classes (Ezeh, 2020).
Garib (2021)	lyricstraining.com	It can enable language teachers to teach a language with music and students to learn and practice a language with music (Garib, 2021).
Hess (2019)	www.bookcreator.com	Language teachers can use it to enable students to create a book in a language, and it can enhance students' receptive and productive skills if the book created is integrated with the necessary items such as audio (Hess, 2019).
Hetesi (2021)	Kahoot and Socrative	They are games and can be used to practice a language by students and to make language teaching more enjoyable by language teachers (Hetesi, 2021).
Hu, Deng, & Liu (2022)	WordSift	It can be used by students to enhance their vocabulary knowledge and so their reading in a foreign language (Hu et al., 2022).
Kochem (2019)	Mondly for Kids	It can be used to teach English to young learners (Kochem, 2019).
Kohnke & Moorhouse (2020)	Zoom	It can provide synchronous online language learning in online language classes with the features it has such as breakout rooms (Kohnke & Moorhouse, 2020).
Kohnke & Moorhouse (2021)	Kahoot	It can be used by language teachers to enhance students' engagement in language lessons and their academic achievement by enabling students to play games (Kohnke & Moorhouse, 2021).
Koltovskaia (2019)	www.storybird.com	Students can create their own stories in a language with it, and language teachers can use it to support their storytelling activities (Koltovskaia, 2019).
Kurt (2022)	Speakometer	Students can use it to practice and improve their pronunciation skills (Kurt, 2022).
Mehdizadeh (2020)	National Public Radio	It can be used to enhance their listening comprehension in English (Mehdizadeh, 2020).
Mei, Huang, & Zhao (2021)	Clips	It can be used for pronunciation instruction and provide feedback on students' pronunciation (Mei et al., 2021).
Mei, Qi, Huang, & Huang (2022)	Speeko	It can be used to improve students' public speaking skills (Mei et al., 2022).
Miller (2019)	Youglish	It can be used for pronunciation instruction (Miller, 2019).
Moorhouse & Kohnke (2022)	Wordwall	Language teachers can use it for vocabulary instruction (Moorhouse & Kohnke, 2022).
Nicklas (2017)	Memrise	Students can enhance their vocabulary knowledge with this program (Nicklas, 2017).
Nushi & Momeni (2021)	English Listening and Speaking – speakingenglishdaily.com	It can be used by students to enhance their listening and speaking skills in English (Nushi & Momeni, 2021).
Pearson (2021)	Kaizena	It can be used to give feedback on students writing (Pearson, 2021).
Tan (2021)	Study Intonation – studyintonation.org	It can be used for pronunciation instruction (Tan, 2021).
Todey (2019)	MReader	Language teachers can assess students' extensive readings with it (Todey, 2019).
Winans (2021)	Grammarly	It can be used by students to improve their writing (Winans, 2021).
Wright (2020)	Voyant tools	It is "a text mining software used for reading and analyzing texts" (Wright, 2020, p. 1).
Yeh (2018)	Voxy	It is an eLearning platform designed for language students to study the target language and its culture through synchronous and asynchronous language courses (Yeh, 2018).
Zhang (2022)	Mentimeter	Language teachers can use it to prepare their presentations (Zhang, 2022).
Zhao (2022)	Wordtune	It can be used by students to improve their writing (Zhao, 2022).

The Significance of the Present Study

As the literature presented above indicates, different technologies can be used by English language teachers to teach different aspects of English, such as four skills, and to enable their students to practice different aspects of English. Considering the improvements in the educational technology that can be used in language education, including English language teaching, technology review studies, such as the ones mentioned in the literature review of the present study, can be considered significant because English language teachers may not be digitally and technologically literate to use such technologies in their English language classes. They may need a guide to understand how such technologies work and how they can use them in their English classes. In accordance with this, the present study reviewed Talk and Comment in terms of its features and how it can be used to give feedback on EFL/ESL students' writing step by step, which can be considered important for English language teachers who teach English online or in a blended way as the present study can serve as a guide for them to follow in their use of Talk and Comment in their classes. Also, English language teachers can use Talk and Comment as a tool for their students to give peer feedback on each other's writing, as it will be shown in the findings of the present study. Considering these possible contributions of the present study to English language teaching and learning, the present study has instructional implications that can affect just English language teachers and EFL/ESL students. In addition, the scope of the present study was Talk and Comment like the scopes of the studies reviewed in the present study because such studies are not empirical, but they are review studies.

Methodology

Teaching English as a Second Language Electronic Journal (TESL-EJ) includes review articles in which different technologies are generally reviewed in terms of description and evaluation. In the first part, the technology to be reviewed is introduced in terms of its features, such as its sections, how users register, how they prepare their assignments, and so on. These features can change from technology to technology. The second part evaluates the technology to be reviewed in terms of how it can be used to teach, learn, and/or practice different aspects of a language. In some studies, technologies have been evaluated depending on some frameworks. Yet, in some other studies, technologies have been evaluated according to their potential uses in teaching, learning, and/or practising different aspects of a language. This study was designed according to this structure followed in TESL-EJ because most of the studies in Table have been published in this journal. As a result, this study first introduced Talk and Comment by focusing on its features and then evaluated how it can be used to give feedback on EFL/ESL students' writing.

Findings

The findings were presented according to the structure mentioned in the methodology part. First, Talk and Comment was introduced depending on its features. Second, it was evaluated in terms of how it can be used to give online feedback on EFL/ESL students' writing.

Description

Talk and Comment, developed and operated by Zaigood Inc., was described depending on its educational use with Google Docs on Google Chrome to give feedback on EFL/ESL students' writings. It can be downloaded from Chrome Web Store and used without registration and payment (yet, in this study, Talk and Comment was evaluated in terms of giving online feedback on EFL/ESL students' writing by us-

Figure 1. The image of a microphone icon with a sticky note on it on the screen

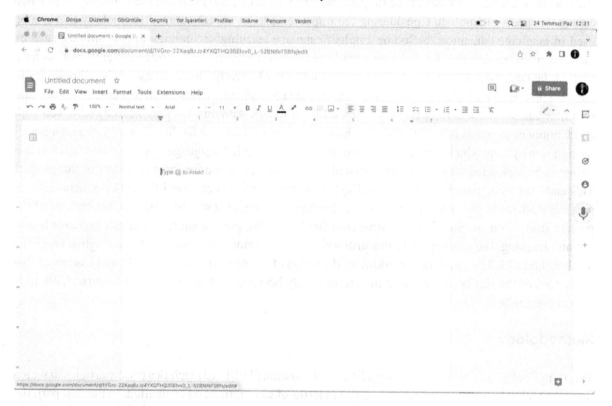

ing it with Google Docs, so to use it with Google Docs, users may need to have a Gmail account to use Google Docs.) It works as an extension on Google Chrome, so it should be used with Google Chrome. After it is downloaded and installed, a microphone icon with a sticky note image appears on the screen, as seen in Figure 1 below.

After the microphone icon appears on the screen, it first should be clicked on, and then it starts recording the voice automatically, as Figure 2 below shows.

To finish recording, the green tick should be clicked on. Then, Talk and Comment automatically creates a link, as Figure 3 below indicates.

In the last step, first, the part of a student's writing (e.g., a word, a phrase, or a sentence) is chosen. Secondly, three images appear on the screen, and the one "add comment" is selected. Then, the copied link of the recording is pasted there. These stages are presented in Figures 4, 5, and 6.

Evaluation

Talk and Comment was evaluated in terms of how it can be used to give feedback on EFL/ESL students' writings in four ways: (a) audio teacher feedback, (b) written teacher feedback supported with audio teacher feedback, (c) audio peer feedback, and (d) written peer feedback supported with audio peer feedback. The feedback giving activities in all the figures in this part were made by the researcher himself to exemplify the explanations provided about four types of feedback created through Talk and Comment; therefore, they are just examples created for this chapter.

Figure 2. How to record voice on Talk and Comment

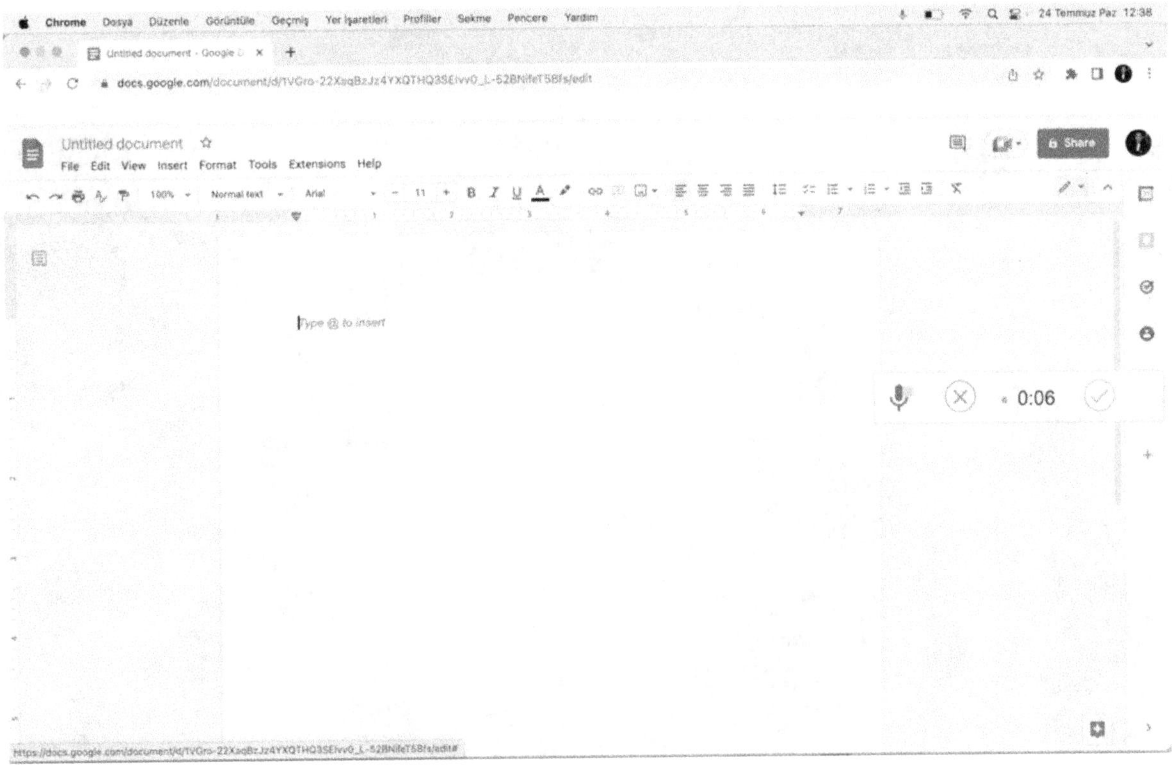

Audio Teacher Feedback

An English language teacher can choose the mistake that their EFL/ESL student has made in their writing, record their comment about the mistake by using Talk and Comment and add it by clicking on "add comment" and pasting the link of the recording created by Talk and Comment into the comment box on Google Docs. Figure 7 demonstrates a sample activity in which audio feedback was given on the sample paragraph written by the researcher with five mistakes that EFL/ESL students may make in their paragraph.

Written Teacher Feedback Supported with Audio Teacher Feedback

Google Docs enables an English language teacher to give feedback by choosing the mistake and writing a comment about that mistake. EFL/ESL students can understand some kinds of mistakes, such as spelling mistakes. Still, they may have difficulty in understanding mistakes such as subject-verb agreement, so it can be better for them to understand their mistake if the written feedback is supported with the audio feedback. The English language teacher can select the mistake that their EFL/ESL student has made in their writing, write their comment about the mistake, and record their comment by using Talk and Comment, depending on the type of the mistake. Then, they can integrate their written and audio feedback by clicking on "add comment," writing their comment about the mistake, and pasting the link of the recording created by Talk and Comment into the comment box on Google Docs. Figure 8 indicates

Figure 3. How Talk and Comment creates a link of the recording automatically to copy and paste

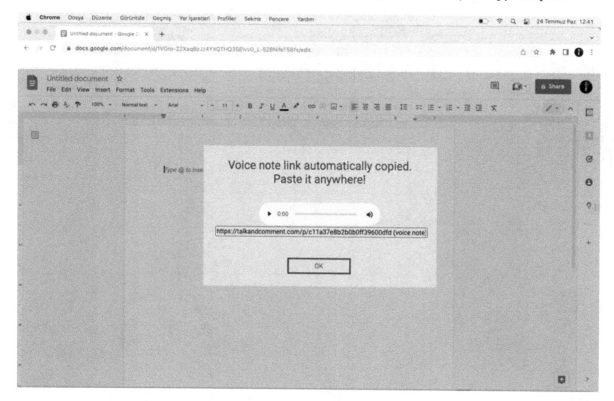

a sample activity in which written feedback was integrated with audio feedback. The paragraph that the researcher wrote is the same paragraph used in Figure 7 and includes four mistakes.

Audio Peer Feedback

Before an English language teacher gives feedback on their students' writing in an EFL/ESL writing class, they can pair students to check and provide feedback on each other's writing by using a peer feedback checklist because such checklists can help students to understand what they are supposed to do in peer feedback. A peer can choose the mistake in their peer's writing, record their comment about the mistake via Talk and Comment, and add their comment by pasting the link of the recording created by Talk and Comment into the comment box on Google Docs. Figure 9 is an example of a peer feedback activity in which a peer provided audio feedback on a sample paragraph containing four errors written by the researcher.

Written Peer Feedback Supported with Audio Peer Feedback

When students are paired and asked to give feedback on each other's writing on Google Docs, they can write comments about the mistake in their peers' writing by selecting it and clicking "add comment." If they think their peers need further explanation about the mistake that the written feedback is given, they can record their explanations through Talk and Comment. After they record, they can integrate their audio feedback with their written feedback by pasting the link of the recording into the comment box on Google Docs. If they think further explanation is not necessary for a mistake, they can just give written feedback. Figure 10 depicts written and audio peer feedback provided on the researcher's paragraph, which has four errors.

Figure 4. "Add Comment" section on Google Docs

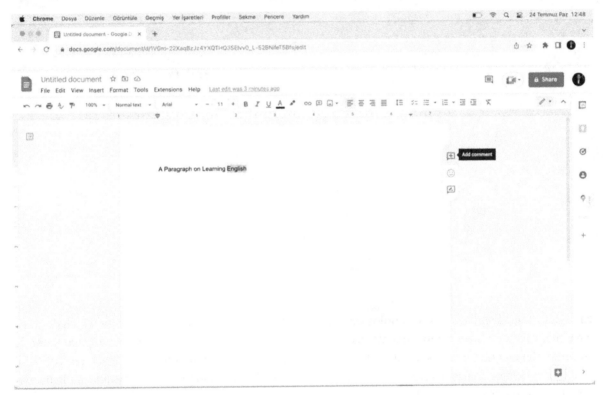

DISCUSSION

In this technology review, Talk and Comment was reviewed depending on its educational use with Google Docs on Google Chrome to give online feedback on EFL/ESL students' writing. The findings of the present study were discussed regarding this.

Talk and Comment can be downloaded and installed by English language teachers easily. As figures 1, 2, 3, 4, 5, and 6 indicate, it can also be used easily by them because all they need to do is choose the mistake they want to give feedback on, record their voice, and copy the link, and paste it. Being downloaded, installed, and used easily can be considered significant for English language teachers to pay attention to when they want to use a new technology in their English classes because they may not have enough technical skills and be technological and digital literate, so a technology which cannot be downloaded, installed, and used easily may demotivate them and prevent them from using it in their English classes. This is also important when English language teachers want their students to give online peer feedback on each other's writing by using technology since, like teachers, students may not have

Figure 5. Pasting the link created by Talk and Comment

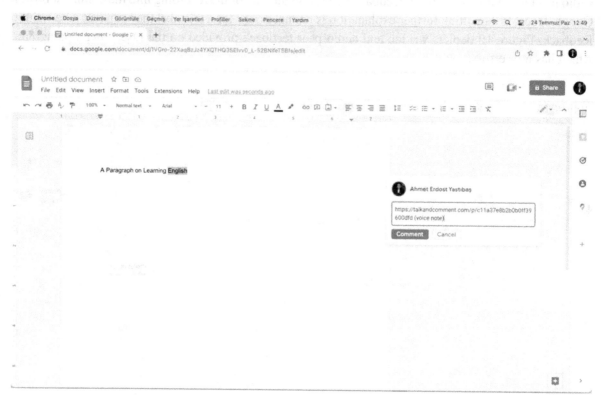

enough technical skills and be technological and digital literate; therefore, a technology which does not have these features may avoid students' using it, may demotivate them, and may not engage them. In addition, the fact that it can be used for free can make it useful for giving online feedback on EFL/ESL students' writing because if a technology is expensive, both English language teachers and students may not afford to purchase a technology.

Online feedback can be given on EFL/ESL students' writing in three ways: (a) online teacher feedback (Saiful et al., 2019; Vadia & Ciptaningrum, 2020; Widyaningsih, 2018; Wihastyanang et al., 2020), (b) online peer feedback (Abri, 2021; Chuaphalakit et al., 2019; Ebadi & Alizadeh, 2021; Daweli, 2018; Gao et al., 2016; Ma, 2019; Saiful et al., 2019; Shang, 2017, 2019; Vadia & Ciptaningrum, 2020; Wihastyanang et al., 2020; Yang & Meng, 2013; Yuk, 2021), and (c) automated corrective feedback (Shang, 2017, 2019). In line with this literature, as the evaluation of Talk and Comment shows, an English language teacher can use Talk and Comment to give online feedback to EFL/ESL students' writing in four ways: (1) audio teacher feedback, (2) written teacher feedback supported with audio teacher feedback, (3) audio peer feedback, and (4) written peer feedback supported with audio peer feedback. In the first way of giving online feedback, EFL/ESL students may not have a chance to receive face-to-face feedback in online English classes, so they may not ask English language teachers questions about the mistake(s) that they may make in their writing, but listening to the comments which are recorded by English language teachers and which include detailed information about each mistake can help them to understand their mistakes and how they can overcome them in their writing. In the second way of giving online feedback, English language teachers can choose which parts of their written feedback students might have trouble

Figure 6. The message formed with the link created by Talk and Comment

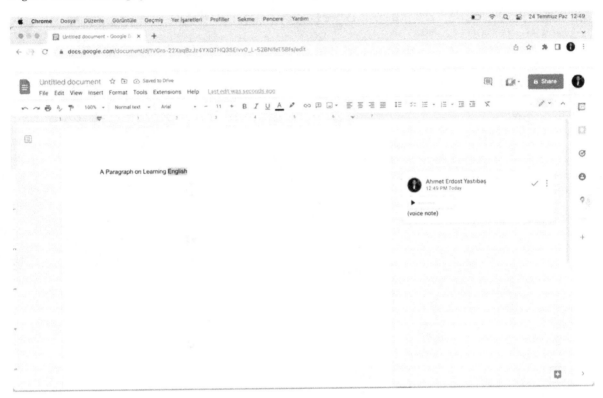

understanding and add audio feedback only to those parts. This helps students understand the written feedback and work on their mistakes to improve their writing more effectively. In the third way of giving online feedback, on the condition that students are provided with a checklist to give audio peer feedback, they can understand their peers' feedback better in online English classes because they may not be able to ask their peers questions about their feedback face-to-face or online. In the fourth way to give online feedback, students can be selective and integrate written feedback that they think their peers might have trouble understanding with their audio feedback. This way, students who get written feedback that is supported by audio feedback can understand it better and work on their mistakes to make their writing better. As all these feedback-giving activities are done on Google Docs, EFL/ESL students can also have a chance to receive online feedback on their writing through Google Docs because it can also be used as a tool to give feedback Google Docs (Alharbi, 2019; Chuaphalakit et al., 2019; Daweli, 2018; Ebadi & Alizadeh, 2021) due to its spellcheck feature which can give automated corrective feedback on grammar and spelling mistakes.

FUTURE RESEARCH DIRECTIONS

The present study has reviewed Talk and Comment in terms of its features and how it can be used to give online feedback on EFL/ESL students' writing depending on its use with Google Docs. Further research can try to find out what EFL/ESL students' attitudes toward audio teacher feedback given through Talk

Figure 7. Audio teacher feedback given via Talk and Comment

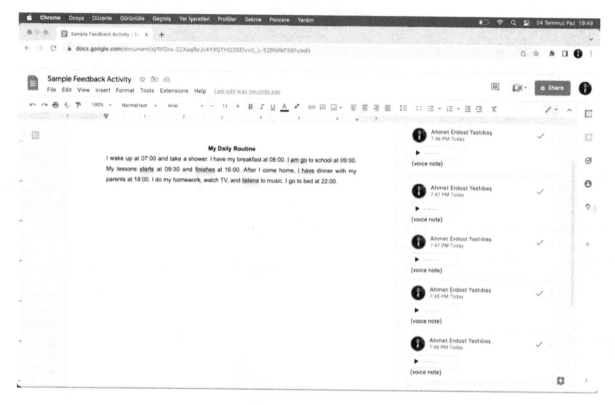

and Comment and how it may affect their writing performance and improvement. In further experimental or quasi-experimental research, online written teacher feedback supported with audio teacher feedback given via Talk and Comment can be investigated to find out the attitudes of EFL/ESL students toward it and its effect(s) on their writing. In addition, further studies can focus on audio peer feedback and try to reveal the attitudes of EFL/ESL students toward it and its impact(s) on their writing. Also, further studies can concentrate on online written peer feedback supported with audio peer feedback given through Talk and Comment and try to find out what EFL/ESL students' attitudes toward it and how it may influence their writing.

CONCLUSION

This study has reviewed Talk and Comment to give online feedback on EFL/ESL students' writing when it is used with Google Docs on Google Chrome by first describing its features and then evaluating its educational use as a tool to give feedback. The findings of this technology review study have tried to show how English language teachers can use Talk and Comment step by step in different modes of feedback. Its voice recording can enable an English language teacher to record his/her feedback or add explanations to his/her written feedback in case their students may not understand his/her written feedback. In addition to teacher feedback, if EFL/ESL students are trained about how to use it in peer feedback, they can give feedback on each other's writing by recording their voices or adding explana-

Figure 8. Written teacher feedback supported with audio teacher feedback given via Talk and Comment

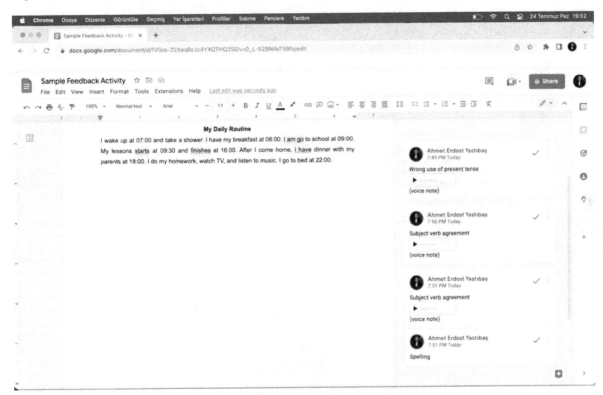

tions to their written peer feedback. As understood, Talk and Comment can be integrated with EFL/ESL classes by English language teachers to provide audio teacher feedback, written teacher feedback supported with audio teacher feedback, audio peer feedback, and written peer feedback supported with audio peer feedback on their students' writing.

Figure 9. Audio peer feedback given via Talk and Comment

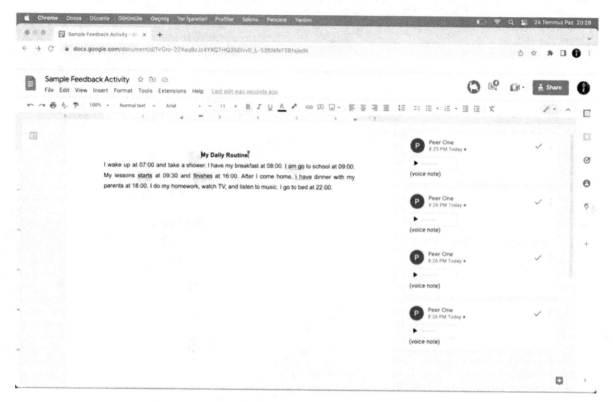

Figure 10. Written peer feedback supported with audio peer feedback given via Talk and Comment

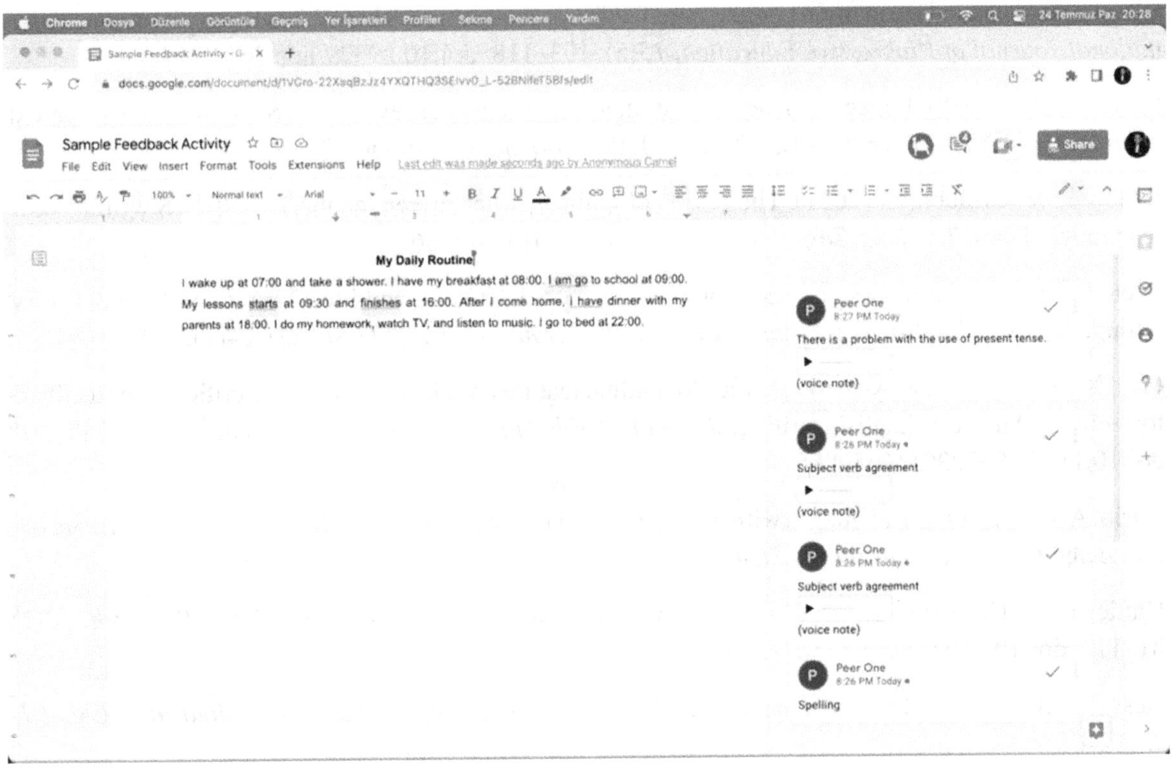

REFERENCES

Abri, A. A. (2021). Exploring EFL learners' comments on web-based peer feedback: Local and global revisions. *English Language Teaching*, *14*(6), 114–124. doi:10.5539/elt.v14n6p114

Alharbi, M. A. (2020). Exploring the potential of Google Docs in facilitating innovative teaching and learning practices in an EFL writing course. *Innovation in Language Learning and Teaching*, *14*(3), 227–242. doi:10.1080/17501229.2019.1572157

Bakoko, R., & Waluyo, B. (2021). Learning reading through current news events: Newsela.com. *Teaching English as a Second Language Electronic Journal (TESL-EJ)*, *25*(3), 1-6.

Barrot, J. S. (2020). Integrating technology into ESL/EFL writing through Grammarly. *RELC Journal*, 0033688220966632.

Beck, J., & Flinn, A. (2021). Say it: English pronunciation. *Teaching English as a Second Language Electronic Journal (TESL-EJ)*, *25*(2), 1-7.

Brookhart, S. M. (2017). *How to give effective feedback to your students*. ASCD.

Cheng, D. (2018). WordSift: Having fun with learning words. *Teaching English as a Second Language Electronic Journal (TESL-EJ)*, *22*(2), 1-9.

Chuaphalakit, K., Inpin, B., & Coffin, P. (2019). A study of the quality of feedback via the Google Classroom-mediated-anonymous online peer feedback activity in a Thai EFL writing classroom. *International Journal of Progressive Education*, *15*(5), 103–118. doi:10.29329/ijpe.2019.212.8

Daweli, T. W. (2018). Engaging Saudi EFL students in online peer review in a Saudi university context. *Arab World English Journal*, *9*(4), 270–280. doi:10.24093/awej/vol9no4.20

Ebadi, S., & Alizadeh, A. (2021). The effects of online learner-driven feedback on IELTS writing skills via Google Docs. *Teaching English with Technology*, *21*(3), 42–66.

Ezeh, C. (2020). A comparison of Storyjumper with Book Creator, and Storybird for multimodal storytelling. *Teaching English as a Second Language Electronic Journal (TESL-EJ)*, *24*(1), 1-9.

Gao, X., Samuel, M., & Asmawi, A. (2016). Online features of Qzone weblog for critical peer feedback to facilitate business English writing. *Journal of Educational Technology Systems*, *45*(2), 285–301. doi:10.1177/0047239516659865

Garib, A. (2021). Learn languages with music: Lyrics Training app review. *Teaching English as a Second Language Electronic Journal (TESL-EJ)*, *24*(4), 1-11.

Hattie, J., & Timperley, H. (2007). The power of feedback. *Review of Educational Research*, *77*(1), 81–112. doi:10.3102/003465430298487

Hess, E. (2019). Book Creator. *Teaching English as a Second Language Electronic Journal (TESL-EJ)*, *23*(1), 1-9.

Hetesi, S. (2021). A comparative review of Kahoot and Socrative. *Teaching English as a Second Language Electronic Journal (TESL-EJ)*, *24*(4), 1-11.

Hu, K., Deng, Y., & Liu, X. (2022). WordSift: Reading easier by understanding key words. *RELC Journal*, 00336882221087464. doi:10.1177/00336882221087464

Kochem, T. (2019). Mondly for kids. *Teaching English as a Second Language Electronic Journal (TESL-EJ)*, *23*(1), 1-7.

Kohnke, L., & Moorhouse, B. L. (2021). Using Kahoot! to gamify learning in the language classroom. *RELC Journal*, 1–7.

Kohnke, L., & Moorhouse, B. L. (2022). Facilitating synchronous online language learning through Zoom. *RELC Journal*, *53*(1), 296–301. doi:10.1177/0033688220937235

Koltovskaia, S. (2019). Storybird. *Teaching English as a Second Language Electronic Journal (TESL-EJ)*, *23*(1), 1-9.

Kurt, S. (2022). Speakometer: English pronunciation coach. *Teaching English as a Second Language Electronic Journal (TESL-EJ)*, *26*(1), 1-6.

Lv, X., Ren, W., & Xie, Y. (2021). The effects of online feedback on ESL/EFL writing: A meta-analysis. *The Asia-Pacific Education Researcher*, *30*(6), 643–653. doi:10.100740299-021-00594-6

Ma, Q. (2020). Examining the role of inter-group peer online feedback on wiki writing in an EAP context. *Computer Assisted Language Learning, 33*(3), 197–216. doi:10.1080/09588221.2018.1556703

Mehdizadeh, M. (2020). National Public Radio. *RELC Journal, 51*(3), 461-465.

Mei, B., Huang, S., & Zhao, Q. (2021). Using clips in the language classroom. *RELC Journal*, 1–4.

Mei, B., Qi, W., Huang, X., & Huang, S. (2022). Speeko: An artificial intelligence-assisted personal public speaking coach. *RELC Journal*, 1–5. doi:10.1177/00336882221107955

Miller, M. (2019). Youglish. *Teaching English as a Second Language Electronic Journal (TESL-EJ), 23*(2), 1-10.

Moorhouse, B. L., & Kohnke, L. (2022). Creating the conditions for vocabulary learning with Wordwall. *RELC Journal*, 1–6. doi:10.1177/00336882221092796

Nicklas, R. (2017). Memrise. *Teaching English as a Second Language Electronic Journal (TESL-EJ), 21*(1), 1-12.

Nushi, M., & Momeni, A. (2021). English listening and speaking: A review. *Teaching English as a Second Language Electronic Journal (TESL-EJ), 25*(3), 1-8.

Pearson, W. S. (2021). A review of the Kaizena app for feedback on second language writing. *RELC Journal*, 1–5. doi:10.1177/00336882211045776

Saiful, W., Sulistyo, G. H., & Mukminatien, N. (2019). Confronting effect of online teacher and peer feedback on the students' writing performance. *Problems of Education in the 21st Century, 77*(5), 650-666.

Shang, H. F. (2017). An exploration of asynchronous and synchronous feedback modes in EFL writing. *Journal of Computing in Higher Education, 29*(3), 496–513. doi:10.100712528-017-9154-0

Shang, H. F. (2022). Exploring online peer feedback and automated corrective feedback on EFL writing performance. *Interactive Learning Environments, 30*(1), 4–16. doi:10.1080/10494820.2019.1629601

Tan, A. (2012). Study intonation: A mobile-assisted pronunciation training application. *Teaching English as a Second Language Electronic Journal (TESL-EJ), 25*(3), 1-8.

Todey, E. (2019). MReader. *Teaching English as a Second Language Electronic Journal (TESL-EJ), 22*(4), 1-9.

Vadia, M. N., & Ciptaningrum, D. S. (2020, August). Improving students' writing skill using online feedback. In *1st International Conference on Language, Literature, and Arts Education (ICLLAE 2019)* (pp. 178-182). Atlantis Press. 10.2991/assehr.k.200804.034

Widyaningsih, T. L. (2018). An analysis of online corrective feedback implementation in writing class. *BRIGHT: A Journal of English Language Teaching. Linguistics and Literature, 2*(1), 63–78.

Wihastyanang, W. D., Kusumaningrum, S. R., Latief, M. A., & Cahyono, B. Y. (2020). Impacts of providing online teacher and peer feedback on students' writing performance. *Turkish Online Journal of Distance Education, 21*(2), 178–189. doi:10.17718/tojde.728157

Winans, M. D. (2021). Grammarly's tone detector: Helping students write pragmatically appropriate texts. *RELC Journal, 52*(2), 348–352. doi:10.1177/00336882211010506

Wright, J. (2020). Researchers, teachers, and learners seeing new possibilities with Voyant tools. *Teaching English as a Second Language Electronic Journal (TESL-EJ), 24*(2), 1-10.

Yang, Y. F., & Meng, W. T. (2013). The effects of online feedback training on students' text revision. *Language Learning & Technology, 17*(2), 220–238.

Yeh, E. (2018). Voxy. *Teaching English as a Second Language Electronic Journal (TESL-EJ), 22*(3), 1-10.

Yoke, S. K., Rajendran, C. B., Sain, N., Kamaludin, P. N. H., Nawi, S. M., & Yusof, S. (2013). the use of online corrective feedback in academic writing by L1 Malay learners. *English Language Teaching, 6*(12), 175–180.

Yuk, A. C. K., & Yunus, M. M. (2021). Using peer-modo feedback at the pre-writing stage to improve year 4 pupils' writing performance. *Journal of Education and e-Learning Research, 8*(1), 116-124.

Zhang, D. (2022). Engaging, impressing and captivating language learners by interactive presentations – a review of Mentimeter. *Teaching English as a Second Language Electronic Journal (TESL-EJ), 26*(1), 1-8.

Zhao, X. (2022). Leveraging artificial intelligence (AI) technology for English writing: Introducing Wordtune as a digital writing assistant for EFL writers. *RELC Journal,* 1–5. doi:10.1177/00336882221094089

KEY TERMS AND DEFINITIONS

Feedback: Feedback is the information given to students about their academic work, shows their strengths and weaknesses, enables them to work on their weaknesses, and helps them enhance their learning.

Online feedback: Online feedback is the one that students are provided with on their academic work through different technologies such as email and Moodle.

Chapter 4
A Study on the Orthography and Grammatical Errors of Tertiary–Level Students

Jayakumar Padmanabhan
Sathyabama Institute of Science and Technology, India

S. Suman Rajest
https://orcid.org/0000-0001-8315-3747
Bharath Institute of Higher Education and Research, India

J. Josephin Veronica
Sathyabama Institute of Science and Technology, India

ABSTRACT

Writing is one of the most important skills in language abilities. It is a primary basis for judging one's learning and intellect. Writing skills equip us with communication and thinking skills. Writing is very important in communication. More importantly, in writing, the learners of English should have error-free sentences in their orthographic and grammatical areas. Because if there is incorrect grammar, the sentences will be unclear and meaningless. The proper syntactic structure of the paper shows a huge difference in one's speaking and writing, and it also indicates sound knowledge of the speaker. A combination of diverse features of English is required for effective communication. The study aims to explore the writing skills of tertiary-level students and to find out the difficulties in writing, especially the orthographic and grammatical errors.

INTRODUCTION

Learning the English language is a very important process in this generation. It plays a vital role in communicating between people from different cities, states, countries, and continents. Because we all know that English is also known as the universal language. Several factors make English essential to

DOI: 10.4018/978-1-6684-6682-7.ch004

communication in the present time. It is the most widely spoken foreign language in the world. Whenever possible, when two people from different countries need to communicate with one another, they will use English. So that you can be more globally aware, it is essential that you learn English. You can communicate more easily with people from all over the world if you can speak to them in their native tongue rather than just English (Kudto et al., 2022).

Children in a lot of different countries are exposed to English as a second language and given the opportunity to study it (Guiamalon, 2021). Even in nations like the Netherlands and Sweden, where English is not an official language, the majority of syllabi and curricula in the fields of science and engineering are written only in English (Lumapenet, 2017). This is due to the fact that English is the language that is used for the majority of research and studies in the scientific community. Students in many nations are required to study the majority of their subjects in English during their time at the university level. This is done either to make the material more accessible to international students or to use the material themselves (Lumapenet & Usop, 2022). One more reason why knowing English is important is that it opens up more doors for professional advancement and employment. In light of the current economic climate, we are all aware that companies are actively seeking to increase their workforce, and one of the qualities they value is employees with English language skills. Because of this, if we are all fluent in English and can use it effectively, we will have a greater number of opportunities to find work (Kudto, et al., 2022). In addition, if you have sufficient data in English, the likelihood of promotion to any position is significantly increased (Guiamalon & Hariraya, 2021).

In brief, language helps us have precise thinking and feelings to talk, exchange views, and connect with people and people wherever we live. Furthermore, within the world, English is taken into account because it is the main language of better communication. English is now taking a crucial part in the chance required employment. Hence, we predict that the English language will still develop and convey more advantages shortly, and maybe someday, English will be the world's sole language. When it comes to Teaching the English language, we must consider from which part of the world the student is.

Teaching English requires not only fluency in the language itself, but also an intimate familiarity with the student's native dialect, culture, and traditions. Working with international clients requires fluency in English. In Chinese universities, students learn nothing practical about the language. They are unable to provide their students with an environment where English is spoken. As a result, many college grads lack fundamental competence in the English language. Only humans have the extraordinary ability to communicate with one another through the medium of written language. For centuries, the written word has helped people share information, work together, and issue urgent warnings; in turn, entire civilizations have benefited from the preservation of their past and present through writing. It is up to you to decide how best to put your writing skills to use in the modern world.

Our child's ability to express himself or herself through words is greatly enhanced by a rich vocabulary. There will be no ambiguity in their communication, as they will have a variety of terms at their disposal for describing a given situation or feeling. Our kid benefits from this because she/he can better comprehend what she/he reads and what other people are saying. Words and phrases are the building blocks of comprehension. When our child encounters an unfamiliar word while reading, that word creates a gap in his or her comprehension. It helps them comprehend concepts and think in a more rational way. The greater our child's vocabulary, the more ideas he or she will be able to understand and appreciate from others. Our kid's persuasive skills will benefit greatly from this. Our kid's ability to communicate will be greatly enhanced by his or her exposure to a more sophisticated vocabulary. Using the same word or phrase to explain a complex idea over and over again will make your explanation sound repetitive and weak. It aids our kids in making sincere first impressions. Our child's level of articulacy will greatly contribute to the impression that he or she makes on others.

An in-depth familiarity with the student's native language, culture, and traditions is also necessary for effective English language instruction. Speaking English fluently is crucial for interacting with international visitors and getting their jobs done. Most of what passes for "English class" in China's universities is merely theoretical instruction. It's unable to offer a language-learning environment in English. As a result, many graduates from higher education institutions lack proficiency in basic forms of English communication. Only humans have evolved the capacity for written language. For centuries, the written word has helped people share information and ideas, coordinate efforts, and issue urgent warnings; in turn, societies have benefited from the preservation of their past and the accumulation of their collective knowledge. It is up to you to decide how best to put your writing skills to use in today's world.

The ability to express oneself through words is a crucial skill for our child to learn. They have a wide range of expressions at their disposal, so they can be specific when describing events or feelings. Our kid benefits from this because she/he is better able to comprehend what she/he reads and what others are saying. Having a solid vocabulary is essential for gaining insight. Unfamiliar words create gaps in the text that prevent our child from gaining a full understanding of what was read. This helps them comprehend concepts and think in a more rational manner. Our child's capacity to grasp the meaning of what others say grows in tandem with his or her vocabulary. Our kid's persuasive abilities will benefit from this. If our child has a sophisticated vocabulary, she or he will be able to express themselves more interestingly. If you only have one or two words to describe an idea, you'll sound repetitive and unconvincing. But if you have a vocabulary of ten or fifteen words, you'll have plenty of options. It aids our children in making genuine connections with others. The extent to which our kid can communicate effectively will have a major impact on how people view him or her.

LITERATURE REVIEW

Both "review" and "literature" are part of the literature review. Here, literature means something other than what it usually means. When we say "knowing," we mean that we have a firm grasp on whatever subject we're studying, whether that's theory, practice, or the latest scientific research on a particular technique. The purpose of a review is to demonstrate the study's value to its field by systematically organizing relevant information in that field into a unified knowledge base. The literature review process is both inventive and laborious because it requires the researcher to synthesize the existing knowledge on the topic in a way that provides justification for his study. It contains two separate clauses. Part of the first sentence entails locating all relevant literature on the topic. Create the foundation for the research's thoughts and conclusions (second sentence).

Thus, a literature review is a piece of writing that aims to summarize the most crucial aspects of the current state of knowledge and the most prominent methodological approaches to a specific issue. It is most closely associated with scholarly works like these, and it typically precedes a research proposal and yields a chapter. It lays the groundwork for other endeavors, such as further study in the field, but its primary function is to keep the reader abreast of the most recent literature on a given subject.

According to Charter V. Good (2004), "a survey of related literature is necessary for proper planning, execution and developing right concepts of the problem and solutions. It provides hypothesis, suggestive of investigation and comparative data for the interpretative purpose."

Best (1986) believes that

a summary of the writings of recognized authorities and previous research provides evidence that the researcher is familiar with what is already known and what is still unknown and untested.

As a result, the literature evaluation provides a conceptual framework of reference for the proposed study. It proposes methodologies, processes, data sources, and statistical techniques that are acceptable for solving the challenges. The researcher will be able to justify the research.

Writing is a great tool for thinking because it allows students to control their thoughts. It has an impact on how they see themselves and the world. It contributes to their development and influences environmental change. On the other hand, writing is a difficult task for many ESL students. Writing, as everyone knows, is the hardest of all skills. Students have a difficult time writing something on their own. Writing is mostly a social activity (Hyland, 2002).

Many types of research have been performed on various themes related to developing English writing abilities at various stages. Below is a collection of them in an organized and logical manner:

1. In a study titled "The Analysis of the Writing Skills in English of the U.G. Students of Technology in Mumbai", Uma Padmanabhan (1998) uses communicative language learning methodologies in the classroom. The pupils (twelve high achievers and five poor achievers) have been advised to write with the aims and the audience in mind. They were all inspired to pick the words and phrases they wanted to repeat and practice. The study found that both high and poor performers improved their writing skills to various degrees.

2. Uma Chitra (2000) conducted a study to improve writing abilities using a silent film. The goal of this novel practice is to make English language learning easier. Writing was a talent that needed to be improved. The precise goals were to ensure that the students fully comprehended the five and could interpret and articulate themselves in grammatically acceptable English. Questions and worksheets incorporated the unique practice necessary to build writing abilities in the courses. A group of fifteen secondary school pupils was exposed to the innovation. The pupils were divided into four groups and given activities. For the first three days, speaking skills activities were provided. Each group's leader read the paragraph they had written, which was then evaluated through the implementation of a follow-up program. The class demonstrated that films might boost motivation levels to new heights and ended up with delightful learning experiences.

3. Kamala (2003) created communicative tactics to help college students improve their written communication skills in English. The researcher chose the challenge of producing a tale based on a specific framework. The tactics proposed have been proven to be successful. The study's goals are to:
    ◦   Establish a task-based, genre-oriented approach to writing instruction and assess its impact on written communication.
    ◦   to determine the impact of the kind and type of tasks on the learners' performance,

      ○   to determine the relationship between improved input and the quality of input in the process of improving writing and communication abilities

      ○   to investigate the impact of educating the writing process on the development of written communication skills

      ○   to establish a connection between training and the strategic application of skill development

      ○   to determine the progress in content and forms toward the process of improving written communication skills, and

      ○   to identify the relationship between students' knowledge of main subjects and their competence in written communication skills.

4.   The research titled "An Analysis of Creative Writing Skills in English among College Students and Development of Creative Mobilization Technology" was undertaken by Rao (2006). The study's goals are:

      ○   to ensure and analyze college students' creative writing abilities in English, and

      ○   to identify innovative mobilization technology for creative writing skills in English.

In this study, the descriptive summary approach was used. It used both qualitative and quantitative methodologies. The probability sampling approach was used to select a sample of 1440 students. Jayakumar and Ajit (2017) studied the sentence structure concerning the verb *eat*. In that study, the proper sentence structure of verb phrases was made with the use of the word *eat* in 500 different sentences. Jayakumar and Ajit (2017) also studied the importance of grammar in speaking and writing. The study was about basic English verb forms' brief roots and routes. In 2020 they studied the importance of online education and the outcomes of learners' LSRW skills in 2022.

Findings: Urban students had stronger creative writing skills, whereas assisted students had lower creative writing abilities, implying that students under the situations emphasized in the cross-case study made better progress.

ROLE OF LANGUAGE SKILLS

Therefore, a literature review is a piece of writing that aims to summarize the most critical aspects of current knowledge and methodological approaches to a specific issue. In academic papers like these, it typically precedes a research proposal and yields a chapter. Its ultimate goal is to keep the reader abreast of the most recent literature on a subject, and it lays the groundwork for other objectives, such as further study in the area.

- One of the most challenging aspects of learning a new language is honing one's receptive skills, specifically listening. This occurs frequently because they feel pressured to grasp every meaning. The receiver needs to focus solely on the listening process. Listeners have a responsibility to pay close attention as well. Everyday context, the identity of the communicator, and any available visual cues aid in understanding what is being said. One needs to be able to tune out distractions so they can focus on taking in the information. The act of listening to the sound of a language is thought to improve listening skills. Having this information would aid them in pronouncing words correctly.

- Communicating Orally: Language Is a Tool For Talking. Communication allows us to share our thoughts and learn about those of others. To a greater extent than the output (speaking and writing) level, the input (listening and reading) level will be greater. Playing games and engaging in pair work activities where the target language is used are effective methods of introducing the target language to the sources. Acquiring an awareness of para-linguistic features like voice quality, volume, tone, modulation, articulation, pronunciation, etc., would aid in developing this ability. Conversations and arguments could help this along too.

- Reading is an essential skill for education. It's useful for honing every facet of one's linguistic abilities, from vocabulary to spelling to grammar to composition skills. It's useful for training one's language intuition to use the proper form. The mind then "copies" these sentences in order to convey the intended meaning. It is essential to highlight the keyword as you read. Students who are able to read the material and draw their own conclusions benefit greatly. Reading regularly from newspapers, articles, books, and magazines is another great way for students to expand their vocabularies.

- Writing allows students to see concrete results of their efforts and progress over time. The other language skills are complemented by this one, and the learner's grasp of vocabulary and structure is solidified. It's useful for getting a handle on the texts and for composing essays. The ability to synthesize and freely employ the target language can be bolstered in this way. It takes mastery of many techniques to write fluently and correctly. Compositions and imaginative writing should be prioritized. Additionally, they need to ensure that their written language is consistent and logical.

FOCUSING ON THE FOURTH LEVEL – WRITING

Writing is the hardest of the four language skills to master, but it is a crucial ability for ESL students to master. Though writing is regarded as the hardest talent to master, it is not impossible to master. Reading, practicing, thinking, and producing are all ways in which someone with a passion for writing might improve their writing talents. Writing aids in evaluating one's ability to utilize language in a clear, concise, effective, and organized manner. Writing is a stimulating, creative, and intellectual activity that aids in developing language abilities. Writing competence is the ability to make readers think, reconsider, and even generate. Low writing abilities are caused by a lack of understanding of English sentence structures, a lack of reading, a lack of exposure to writing, poor vocabulary, a fear of making grammatical errors, a lack of practice, and a lack of awareness of writing culture.

Writing is a talent that not everyone finds easy; some people have a natural flow when they write, while others struggle. There are a variety of genres that might help you improve your writing talents. Some people master writing abilities, while others, while having a large vocabulary, fail to effectively construct even a few phrases. On the other hand, writing talents may be well-developed with the correct mindset, a passion for writing, and consistent practice. Writing involves the activities of reading and thinking. Thoughts are free to be spoken, but they must be purified before being written down. You can't just write what you're thinking. The most crucial tools for writing are reading and thinking. Writing necessitates the ability to think.

When a writer is aware of complicated accents while composing a text, his or her writing knowledge is comprehensive. The following are crucial considerations while writing texts:

Figure 2. Capitalization

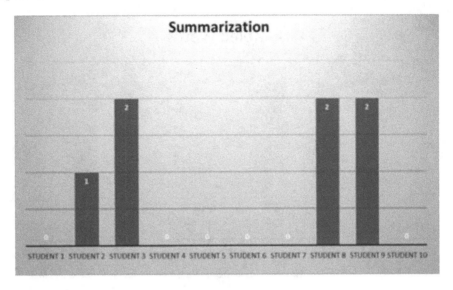

Figure 3. Misspelt Words

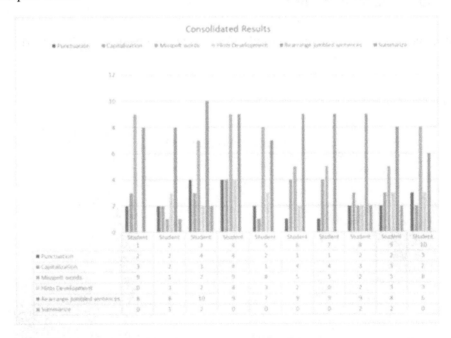

Results of Misspelt Words Test

The marks obtained by the students in Misspelt word test are given below (figure 3).

Results of Hints Development Test

The marks obtained by the students in the Hints development test are given below (figure 4).

Figure 4. Hints Development

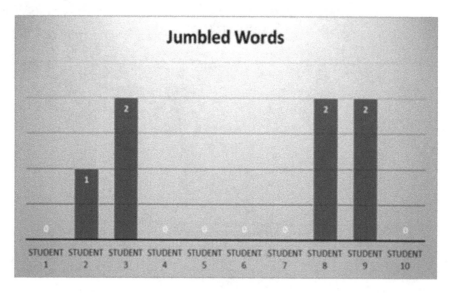

Results of Jumbled Words Test

The marks obtained by the students in the Jumbled words test is given below (figure 5).

Figure 5. Jumbled Words

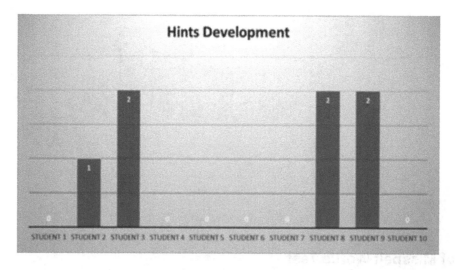

Results of Summarization Test

The marks obtained by the students in the Summarization test are given below (figure 6). Based on the above result can be consolidated below (figure 7).

Figure 6. Summarization

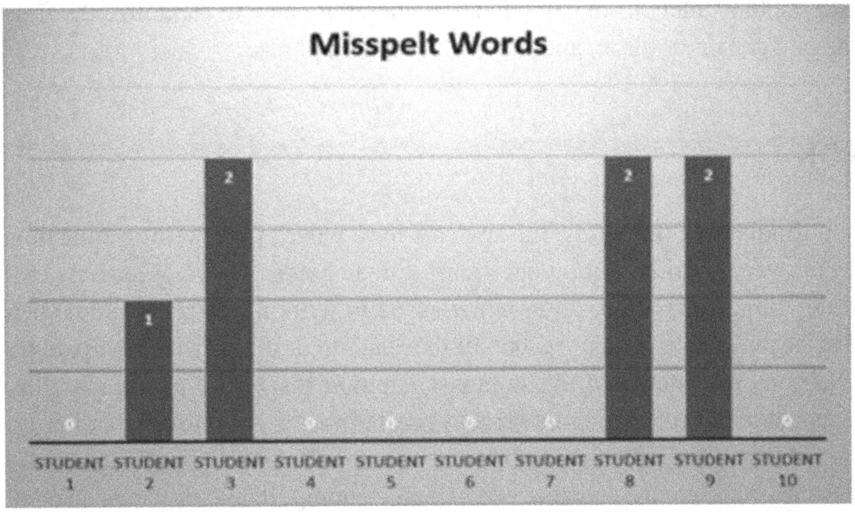

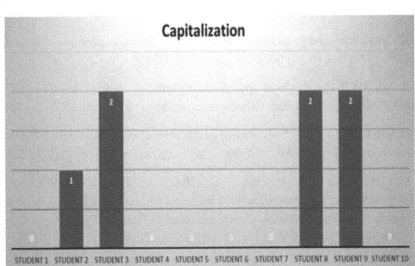

RESULTS AND DISCUSSION

According to the findings, the category of Jumbled Words was the one in which the greatest number of students achieved high marks, followed by Misspelled Words. Hints Development and Summarization were the areas in which all of the students received the lowest possible grades. Students are able to make the fundamental changes in capitalization, but when it comes to punctuation, they struggle to recognize the correctly punctuated word.

The difficulties that arise for students majoring in English Literature at the Bachelor of Arts level are dissected in this chapter. It has been observed that students have trouble writing sentences that are completely original to them. In particular, the portion of the event that was supposed to summarize the

Figure 7. Consolidated Results

story almost nobody showed up for. It is possible to rewrite the words even if they are jumbled. Students are familiar with the fundamentals of capitalization, including how to capitalize the first letter of a sentence, the name of a person or place, and the beginning of a phrase.

CONCLUSION

According to the findings of this study, the students have a hard time writing something on their own initiative. They are very good at writing questions with a choice of several answers, but they show no interest in writing paragraphs at all. After being asked to write a paragraph, some people decided to abandon the discussion. Some people try, but all they end up doing is filling the paragraphs with more prepositions. No one even attempted to use phrases in their respective paragraphs. The vast majority of people are incapable of recognizing incorrectly spelled words. Grammar is an important subject for students to study if they want to become proficient users of a language because it teaches them how to organize words and sentences in a way that gives them meaning. If students have a better understanding of grammar, they will be able to construct better sentences in their writing and speaking performances. If you use correct spelling, grammar, and punctuation in your writing, the people who read it will have more faith in the person (or company) with whom they communicate. Your employees will have an easier time comprehending your instructions and will experience less confusion as a result of your attention to detail regarding the correct spelling and use of punctuation.

REFERENCES

Guiamalon, T. (2021). Teachers Issues and Concerns on The Use of Modular Learning Modality. *IJASOS-International E-journal of Advances in Social Sciences*, *7*(20), 457–469. doi:10.18769/ijasos.970927

Guiamalon, T. S., & Hariraya, P. G. (2021). The K-12 Senior High School Programl: The Case Of Laboratory High School, Cotabato City State Polytechnic College, South Central Mindanao, Philippines. *IJASOS-International E-journal of Advances in Social Sciences*, *7*(19), 391–399. doi:10.18769/ijasos.820171

Hyland, K. (2002). Authority and invisibility: Authorial identity in academic writing. *Journal of Pragmatics*, *34*(8), 1091–1112. doi:10.1016/S0378-2166(02)00035-8

Jayakumar, P., & Ajit, I. (2016). Android app: An instrument in clearing Lacuna of English grammar through teaching 500 sentence structures with reference to the verb eat. *Man in India*, *96*(4), 1187–1195.

Jayakumar, P., & Ajit, I. (2017). The Pedagogical Implications on the Root and Route of English Basic Verbs: An Extensive Study through Android Application. *Social Sciences*, *12*(12), 2244–2248.

Jayakumar, P., Suman Rajest, S., & Aravind, B. R. (2022). An Empirical Study on the Effectiveness of Online Teaching and Learning Outcomes with Regard to LSRW Skills in COVID-19 Pandemic. In *Technologies, Artificial Intelligence and the Future of Learning Post-COVID-19* (pp. 483–499). Springer. doi:10.1007/978-3-030-93921-2_27

Kudto, N. M., Lumapenet, H. T., & Guiamalon, T. S. (2022). Students' Learning Experiences in The New Normal Education. *Central Asian Journal of Theoretical & Applied Sciences*, *3*(5), 221–233.

Lumapenet, H. (2017). Determinants of Bangsamoro Teacher's Identity. In Lumapenet, HT, & Sagadan, SA Determinants of Bangsamoro Teacher's Identity. 7th CEBU International Conference on Civil, Agricultural, Biological and Environmental Sciences (CABES-17) Sept (pp. 21-22).

Lumapenet, H., Usop, M. (2022). School Readiness towards the Delivery of Learning in the New Normal. International Journal of Early Childhood Special Education (INT-JECSE), Vol 14, Issue 03 2022, 2629-2637.

Rao, C. (2006). An analysis of creative writing skills in English among college students and development of creative mobilization technology. Indian Educational Abstracts, 6(2). Best, J. W. (1986). *Research in Education*, 1986.

ADDITIONAL READING

Bhuvaneswari, G., Swami, M., & Jayakumar, P. (2020). Online classroom pedagogy: Perspectives of undergraduate students towards digital learning. *International Journal of Advanced Science and Technology*, *29*(04), 6680–6687.

Doff, A. (1988). *Teach English trainer's handbook: A training course for teachers* (Vol. 2). Cambridge university press.

Pathan, A. (2021). The Most Frequent Capitalization Errors Made by the EFL Learners at Undergraduate Level: An Investigation. *Sch Int J Linguist Lit*, *4*(3), 65–72. doi:10.36348ijll.2021.v04i03.001

Rivers, J. (2022). *5.5: Proofreading for Mechanics*. Communication at Work.

Somasundaram. G (2017) The effect of mixed approach in developing the writing skills in English Language. *Teaching and Learning at Tertiary*.

Walters, L. (1983) "A theoretical model for teaching students to write." English Teaching Forum: 17-22

Wimmer, H., & Landerl, K. (1997). In C. A. Perfetti, L. Rieben, & M. Fayol (Eds.), *"How learning to spell German differs from learning to spell English,"* in *Research, Theory and Practice Across Languages* (pp. 81–96). Erlbaum.

Chapter 5
Incorporating Technology as a Tool Into English Language Teaching and Learning

Tribhuwan Kumar
Prince Sattam Bin Abdulaziz University, Saudi Arabia

ABSTRACT

Educators and teachers generally use a traditional approach in English language teaching. They use books, flashcards, and whiteboards to organize a lecture. However, at present times, teaching through traditional methods is not considered effective. We live in the advanced technology age, where teaching through a blended method is more practical and effective. For this reason, a teacher should be acquainted with the various technology tools to be used effectively in the classroom. The use of technology plays playing a significant role in English language teaching and learning (ELTL). In this paper, the authors will explore the uses of technology such as the internet, websites, electronic dictionaries, softwares and social networking technologies in English language teaching and learning.

1. INTRODUCTION

Different scholars have defined technology. Technology is a practical method used in different ways to handle specific tasks. The convention of technology does not only use tools and apparatus like computers, and it may be comprised of prearranged groups of students or humans, equipment, and the atmosphere (İşman, 2012; Alotaibi & Kumar, 2019; Benyo et al., 2022). We can use the term technology assimilation for the use of technology, and technology assimilation is defined as the use of technology to improve the educational system. Technology assimilation helps students and teachers teach and learn using computers instead of paper (Dockstader, 2008; Ali, 2022). Technology assimilation is also defined as a phase of using technology to develop human activities for different purposes (Çakmak et al., 2021).

The use of technology has considerably changed the ELTL process and makes the teaching and learning process easy and interesting for both teachers and students by providing opportunities (Patel, 2013; Khan et al., 2022). Modern technologies have played a fundamental role in the education department

DOI: 10.4018/978-1-6684-6682-7.ch005

and proved obliging for teachers and students, particularly in English language teaching and learning. The learning process is flattering and effortless day by day with the development of modern technologies. The communication process is not easy in the earlier period as presently available. The use of new technologies (such as the internet web, social media, digital media, Online dictionaries and softwares) has made the teaching and learning process so simple and successful. The globalization hurdle has been minimized for students and teachers, who can communicate using IPAD, the internet web and other social media sites and learn a lot without any complications (Sarica & Cavus, 2009; Pan et al., 2021).

Technology innovation has changed the social and educational framework of life. Several technologies are beneficial for ELTL: Web base technology, information & communication technology and educational technology (Taylor, 2001; Ahmed et al., 2022). Web-based internet technologies offer modern potential in every field of life. Still, it has a powerful impact on English language teaching and learning because English is the only language involved in globalization. Besides this, English is considered an international language for worldwide trade, and it is very important to learn English to express thoughts and use technology. The teaching and learning process can be simple, faster and successful by using technology in educational institutions to fulfil the time requirement (Edelson, 1998; Kumar, 2020; Bacha et al., 2021). It is found that computer technology builds up an effective method of learning, plays a significant role in language-fixing efforts, and generates a passion among learners to do work at their own pace, which has been proven supportive for both students and teachers (Hoven, 1999). Technology makes the ELTL process attractive and creative for students and generates interest among students to learn the English language precisely (Min, 2013; Ajmal & Kumar, 2020). Thus, it is essential to study how technology can be used to develop the ELTL process and make ELTL simple and successful.

2. RESEARCH QUESTIONS AND OBJECTIVES

Here are some research questions and objectives:

- How can we improve ELTL process?
- Which technologies are beneficial for students in the English learning process?
- Which learning skills can be improved by using technology?
- Can teachers use technology for the teaching process?
- How can we use technology to make English teaching and learning easy?

3. DISCUSSION

3.1. Technology in English Teaching

Several technologies can be used in the ELTL process and in creative learning, such as computerized learning, web-based learning, online dictionaries, software and digital media; Facebook, Skype, What's an app, E-mail, IMO and other social media sites. These technologies play fundamental roles in 4 learning skills: listening, reading, writing, and speaking. All of these skills are interrelated with each other. The use of technology is very important for the development of these English learning skills (Benyo & Kumar, 2020).

These four learning skills are divided into two categories by Harmer receptive skills and productive skills. Receptive skills comprise reading and listening skills, which are proposed to absorb the meaning of a text, and productive skills can be defined as the skills in which something can be created or produced as speaking and writing skills (Harmer, 2007; Mahmood et al., 2020). On the other hand, another scholar Brown, recommended his thought as oral and written are both productive performances of human beings while auditory and reading are receptive performances. Both productive and receptive skills can be improved by using technology which can be helpful in the ELTL process.

3.2. Computerized Technologies such as Tablet, PC, Cell Phones and iPods

The research was done extensively on using tablets, PCs, cell phones and iPods to develop the English language. It was found that using a Cell phone and tablets can enhance students' English reading capabilities. At the same time, during the discussion with the class group, texting can improve their writing skills and vocabulary. During the classroom, it helps students to understand English paragraphs easily. Both types of devices, handhelds and desktop devices assist students and teachers in the ELTL process (Schcolnik et al., 2007; Kumar, 2021a). Most students preferred to use handheld devices like cell phones and tablets for academic reading purposes. Literature on English learning using mobile technology was well organized in a journal (Yamada et al., 2013). The information collected from this paper concluded that there are several varieties of mobiles which can improve the ELTL process, and learning through tablets, PC, cell phones, and iPods have a great impact on listening comprehension and inspiration to students' academic knowledge (Table 1).

Table 1. Literature on using Tablet, PC, cell phones, and iPods

Publication	Conclusion
Yamada et al. (2013)	• Study the use of tablets, PCs, cell phones and iPods for English language development. • There are numerous varieties of cell phones which can improve the ELTL process and learning through Tablet, PC, cell phones and iPods have a great impact on listening comprehension and inspiration to students' academic knowledge

4. MULTIMEDIA

Multimedia technology has made the ELTL process easy for students and teachers. Several scholars write about the importance of multimedia as it is used for displaying images with text during lectures or presentations Stemler (1997). Another scholar, Parveen and Rajesh (2011), demonstrated that multimedia technology could explain any content with text, graphics, animations or real video with English text, which explains the whole lesson in the easy form, and students take an interest to see images and learn English stories easily by using multimedia.

Multimedia combines text, videos, images, graphics, sounds and animation, which can be handled using computer technology during presentations. It is a simple way of communicating English content by using daily life examples with images. It looks like a real-life story happening in our real life (Chunjian, 2009). ELTL process can be made understanding and creative by arranging lectures in multimedia. Teachers understand their students' mental capabilities and interests and put images and animations according to their interests, so students listen and watch lectures on multimedia. It saves time and also makes the teaching process easy.

In some schools, teachers use multimedia technology using slide and film-strip projectors. Teachers used higher scholarly language to improve their students' pronunciation and vocabulary with video cassette recorders and DVD players. Many English books and stories available in recorded form are used in multimedia projectors to improve students' pronunciation and listening skills. This is the way how can we use multimedia technology to improve the improvements of English language.

5. E-LEARNING TECHNOLOGY

In the past, E-learning technology was used by the name of web-based technology; afterwards, it changed into distance learning; with the innovation of internet technology, it is now known as E-learning technology. E-Learning technology greatly impacts the ELTL system and makes it an easy learning process. Several e-learning tools, such as e-mail, blogs, Electronic dictionaries, and chatting, etc., can be used to develop English language learning skills and make the ELTL process easy and sympathetic Storey et al., (2002). E-Learning makes life easy for students and teachers and develops the ELTL system. Schools have made their websites and put information regarding school activities and syllabus contents on websites. Teachers deliver their English lectures in video form and upload them on websites for students. It facilitates students in English language learning, and students don't miss their lectures if they cannot attend class due to any issue; they can collect lectures from school websites. Different types of software are available on the internet, which helps students to improve English spelling and grammar. Quiz and grammar tests are available on internet sites, and teachers can use them to check their student's progress.

On a large scale, websites made the ELTL process simple and time-saving for teachers and students. Teachers made their personal websites, shared data for the whole class, and shared the link with students who downloaded data for learning purposes. Students read data effectively in an easy environment, which develops their English reading and listening skills, saves time for both students and teachers, and makes the ELTL process easy. There are several websites (e.g. www.teachingenglish.org.uk) where website holders upload English content data. Teachers can search data related to their contents, lectures, exercises and other evaluation materials and make notes for students, which saves time and make easy teaching process. There are several types of data which can be downloaded from websites for the ELTL process as:

- Pictures
- Notes
- English worksheets
- English lesson plans
- Tenses
- crossword puzzles
- The manuscript for reading and gap filling
- Vocabulary and grammar workout
- Group of students' management and instructions.

6. E-MAIL

E-mail is a frequently used technology from ancient times and is a very useful technology for ELTL purposes. For learners of English, e-mail is an outstanding way to communicate with their teachers because of its value and charity. It is the best communication technology used to improve the English language. Both teachers and students can get assistance through a single e-mail account LeLoup, (1997).

E-mail accounts can be made on several websites such as Yahoo, Hotmail, and Gmail on specific names. English teachers can share their motto and present the main ideas or topic to students and, after some time, get their reviews. Teachers may give a topic and data to students and ask them to write in their wording; it will enhance students' understanding, writing skills and vocabulary.

E-mail technology can make the ELTL process easy when many students are present in classrooms. Teachers can get attention individually by using the e-mail address of students. E-mail helps students brainstorm as teachers give headings or topics to students, and at home, students write paragraphs and mail to their teachers through e-mail; it facilitates students to develop creative writing, enhance their passion for learning and improve communication way in the classroom. The teacher may prepare their students for debates by giving them a topic and preparing for discussion. It helps them improve their vocabulary and understanding level (Ramazani, 1994). When teachers convey their lecture, they said to prepare a summary of understandings and write in your own words through e-mail. It enhances students' mental capability towards creative writing and saves teachers time in the classroom.

7. USE OF ELECTRONIC (ACADEMIC, GENERAL) DICTIONARIES AND ELECTRONIC GLOSSES

With the development of modern technologies, English language teaching and learning are becoming easy and timesaving for students and teachers. Several electronic (academic, general) dictionaries assist students during English language learning. A qualitative investigation was done on the use of dictionaries by literature review at a small scale, but no quantitative literature was found on the use of dictionaries.

Students can use two types of dictionaries:

- ◦ Online dictionary
- ◦ Offline dictionary

Both types of dictionaries help students in the English learning process. Students can download different types of dictionaries on their mobiles and laptops. Dictionaries help students with reading, writing, listening, and speaking skills. Students can write words and listen to their pronunciation by using audio dictionaries. It helps to improve vocabulary and pronunciation.

By using online dictionaries, students can find the meaning of tough words in English and Urdu, which makes the ELTL process easy.

Academic dictionaries can be used during English content learning and understanding. In contrast, general dictionaries can be used to speak and learn general knowledge words, facilitating students throughout daily routine and communications (table 2).

Table 2. A literature review on the use of electronic (academic, general) dictionaries and electronic glosses for the ELTL process

Publication	Summary
Sakar & Ercetin (2004)	Electronic dictionaries assist in the meaning of words.
Lenders, O. (2008)	Electronic glosses explain sentences which can't understand easily.
Poole, R. (2011)	Electronic dictionaries help in the ELT process.
(Golonka et al., 2014)	ESP process can be made simple by using electronic (academic, general) dictionaries and electronic glosses

8. SOCIAL MEDIA TECHNOLOGIES

Research work was done on the use of social media technologies for the development of the English language teaching and learning process. Social media is a commonly used technology, and it greatly impacts the learning process in modern times. Social media technology assists students in learning vocabulary, reading, writing, and speaking skills. Social media applications like Twitter, Line, Facebook, WhatsApp, and Skype are used to improve the ELTL process (table 3). Figure 1 shows the statistics of global social networking technology.

Table 3. High-ranked social networking technology usage worldwide

	Created By	Released Year	website	Users
Twitter	Jack Dorsey Evan Williams Biz Stone	March 21 2006	twitter.com	126 million in 2020
Line	Naver	Spring 2011	line.me/en/	194 million in 2019
Whatsapp	Jan Koum Brian Acton	February 24, 2009	WhatsApp.com	2 billion users in 2020
Facebook	Mark Elliot Zuckerberg	February 4, 2004	www.facebook.com	2.50 billion active users on December 31 2019
Skype	Niklas Zennstrom	August 29 2003	www.skype.com	300 million users in march 2020
You Tube	Chad Hurley, Steve Chen and Jawed Karim	February 14 2005	www.youtube.come	2 billion users

8.1. Twitter

The Twitter app was first time installed in 2006. Previous studies were not perceived on the importance of Twitter. Twitter is a modern-age social networking and micro-blogging technology which can be used on mobiles or computers in the presence of the internet and used as a source of communication among students and teachers. Twitter has made great contributions to ELTL process development and progress. Teachers can share creative activities on Twitter with students, and students learnt from those activities. It developed the ELTL process, saved time, and overcame complications in the classroom.

Figure 1. The statistics of global social networking technology

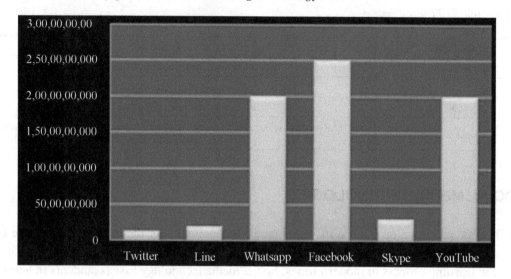

Twitter creates interest in communication among student groups or teachers and students, which develops English learning skills and improves vocabulary in an authentic framework. Twitter technology induces a sense of learning and participation among students.

Few publications, such as Sabater and Fleta (2015), reveal the importance of Twitter in developing the English language. He concluded that Twitter helps improve students' vocabulary and communication methods and encouraging students understanding levels.

Twitter enables students to take part in debates competition. Teachers conduct debates among students and assign any topic to organize speech in English. Teachers conduct debates at specific times in class groups and permit students to send their English speeches in video form after listening to the video announce students' positions. It enhances students' passion towards debates and improves English vocabulary.

8.2. Line

Naver installed the line app in 2011. It is a social media application that can be used as a source of joint learning, such as group video or group chatting, which improves the English communication skills of students and teachers. The teacher can convey their lecture to the whole class on video group calls without a problem. This way, students' English vocabulary improved, and the ELTL process was easy and comfortable. Scholars Van De Bogart and Wichadee, (2015) discussed in their publication that line application has been playing a constructive role in English for students with specific purposes (ESP).

The line helps students and teachers in the development of the ELTL process. Students can make groups and discuss their class issues in line groups, improving their communication and English writing skills. Students put their DP's in English quotations which develops understanding and passion for English language learning.

8.3. WhatsApp

WhatsApp is fast social networking technology and plays an important role in developing the ELTL process. WhatsApp was first launched by Jan Koum and Brian Acton in 2009, and over 2 billion people use it worldwide. The following features which can be used are the progress English language audio, voice text, video, text messages, images and GIFs. All of these features assist in developing the English language of students. While using WhatsApp, most people use an English keyboard, which automatically improves their English language. Students can learn English easily by using WhatsApp by making WhatsApp groups. There are many WhatsApp groups which are working on the development of the English language. WhatsApp makes online learning systems easy and comfortable for students. There are many methods which are used on WhatsApp for learning purposes:

- Teachers send notes in pdf or MS word office documents and ask students to read those notes and ask questions verbally.
- In COVID-19, WhatsApp has played a significant role in students' English learning. Due to the lockdown, online learning systems developed fastly, and teachers made it an alternative source of study. In this situation, students attend online classes through WhatsApp groups. Teachers make special groups for class and deliver their lectures through video calls using screen recording, PPT or audio messages. Students read out notes and listen to audio and video and ask questions regarding any issue in lectures. After that, teachers take assessments or viva from delivered content and give grades in the form of results.

Following are some objectives regarding the ELTL process which can be achieved by using WhatsApp technology:

- Students can easily download WhatsApp on any android phone and PC.
- Students' English listening skills can be improved by using WhatsApp, which positively impacts the ELTL process.
- Speaking English with teachers and students on WhatsApp can progress students speaking skills.
- WhatsApp improved students are reading and writing skills.
- Using WhatsApp improved students' vocabulary, which led to an enhanced ELTL process.
- WhatsApp makes the learning process easy for students.
- WhatsApp enhances students' confidence to talk with instructors easily and saves time in reaching out to the teachers and instructors.
- Students from backward areas who can't attend spoken English classes can join online learning groups and learn English easily.
- Discussion with WhatsApp group members improves speaking skills and vocabulary.
- Audio or video messaging on WhatsApp improves students speaking and listening skills.
- During class, students can learn from others students' mistakes and easily conquer their own.
- Confidence in English speaking is very important, and WhatsApp can develop confidence among students and make the ELTL process easy.
- Students can ask questions from their instructors easily by using WhatsApp.
- WhatsApp makes the ELTL process easy and beneficial.

8.4. Facebook

Mark Elliot Zuckerberg created Facebook in 2004. Facebook is a universally used social networking technology that can be used on cell phones or computers. Facebook plays a significant role in making the ELTL process easy and interesting. There are several groups on Facebook named English language learning which are working on the development of the English language. Names of some major English learning groups are:

- Learning English
- English chat and learning groups
- Learn spoken English
- Let's learn English together
- English global
- Grammar (English) learning on Facebook
- English conversation group
- Learn English daily
- Learn English
- English learning and fun

Teachers can develop the ELTL process by making Facebook groups for their class students and delivering knowledge and activities on Facebook groups. When teachers put any information in a group, students receive notification and can also discuss any issue regarding notification. These ways of communication improve students' English learning capabilities and develop confidence among students to discuss their issues. Also, it makes teaching easy for teachers and saves them time (Kabilan et al., 2010; Kumar, 20021b). Students also form groups and proceed with their English grammar and communication skills. Learning skills like reading, writing, listening and speaking can be developed using Facebook technology and improved ELTL process.

- Reading skills can be improved when a teacher posts information regarding English content, and students read and understand it and discuss it in commenting section.
- When teachers give a topic to students and ask them to write something on that specific topic and ask questions from that paragraph, it develops their English writing skills.
- Teachers record video lectures and upload them in the group; students listen to lectures and understand and discuss dilemma regarding that lectures, which develop students' listening skills.
- When the teacher asks a question from students and asks them to present in video or audio form, in this method, students speaking skills and vocabulary improve.

8.5. YouTube

YouTube videos can be used to develop the ELTL process and facilitate teachers and students in various aspects. It helps students learn vocabulary, improve receptive and productive skills, pronunciation, voice intonation and several other problems. The teacher can easily prepare their lectures from YouTube channels and understand daily life examples. Many scholars deliver lectures in authentic ways and upload them on their channels. Students can also download information regarding their issues and content from YouTube, which makes the ELTL process easy and simple. Teachers can teach by using YouTube videos and improves students' English language, just as Teachers can give English movie title to their students and ask them to watch the movie and write it in their own words. It enhances students writing and listening skills in the English language, makes them creative, and saves teacher time in teaching English language students.

Teachers can also make their YouTube Channel and upload their daily lectures and send links to students to listen to lectures carefully, and after one week, teachers can conduct tests on the base of those lectures.

Tenses are a big issue in English language learning. Teachers can record video clips on tenses with daily life examples and upload them on their YouTube channels. Students can get benefit from those videos. Teachers can upload exercise questions related to English content, share the link with their class, and ask them to solve the exercise and check in the classroom. In this way, we can articulate that YouTube channels make the ELTL process simple and time-saving for teachers and students (figure 2).

Figure 2. Social Networking Technology used for ELTL Process

8.6. Skype

Skype is a social networking technology which has made the ELTL process easy and comfortable for students and teachers. Nowadays, almost every student has an android phone with front cameras and a laptop with desktop cameras. They can discuss their problems with their teachers and even attend online classes on Skype (Wu, 2005; Ghahderijani et al., 2021). Face-to-face discussions on Skype video calling improved students' pronunciation and vocabulary. Research work can be done with the assistance of an instructor on Skype. Students can also write literature with the help of their instructor assistance on Skype.

Students can attend online English classes on the internet and get knowledge worldwide. Teachers arrange classes and collect a fee from students and issue roll numbers. After that teacher can take a class on group chat or group call. Students can ask questions individually from an instructor. And students can communicate with native speakers of verbal communication and contrast their verbalization, for example, with a native lecturer. Along with civilizing their fictional information by discussing planned fictional works with the native lecturer of English, particularly at a higher level, teaching staff can improve their speaking skills. Skype assist in improving the ELTL process worldwide and provide the potential for students and teachers to work together.

9. CONCLUSION

This study was conducted to determine the importance of technology in English language teaching and learning. It is found that the uses of technology such as the internet, E-learning, Electronic dictionaries, E-Mails and other social networking sites like Twitter, Line, Facebook, Whatsapp, YouTube and Skype are playing a significant role in the development of the English language and improving ELTL process. The use of technology has made the ELTL process easy and beneficial for both students and teachers. Now students can learn a lot in any corner of the world without going anywhere by using technology. And teachers can easily find out teaching material from websites and share data with their students by making specific websites. In this paper, we discussed the use of technology for the ELTL process theoretically. Further study is necessary to explore the use of each technology statistically and provide feedback.

Abbreviations used: ELTL (English Language Teaching and Learning), ESP (English for a specific purpose), EFL (English as a foreign language)

REFERENCES

Ahmed, A. A., Kumar, T., Iksan, M., Subrahmanyam, S., Kokhichko, A. N., Ali, M. H., Tuama, H. M., & Mousavi, M. S. (2022). Comparing the effectiveness of massive open online course (MOOC) and flipped instruction on EFL learners' reading comprehension. Education Research International. doi:10.1155/2022/6543920

Aicha, B. A. (2014). The impact of Whatsapp mobile social learning of the achievement and attitudes of females students and compared with face to face learning in the classroom. *European Scientific Journal, 10*(22), 116–136.

Ajmal, M., & Kumar, T. (2020). Using DIALANG in assessing foreign language proficiency: The interface between learning and assessment. Asian ESP Journal, *16*(2.2), 335 - 362.

Aktas, B. Ç., & Can, Y. (2019). The effect of Whatsapp usage on the attitudes of students toward English self-efficacy and English courses in foreign language education outside the school. *International Electronic Journal of Elementary Education, 11*(3), 247–256. doi:10.26822/iejee.2019349249

Ali, A., Ishtiaq Khan, R. M., Kumar, T., Shahbaz, M., & Alourani, A. (2022). An investigation of the educational challenges during COVID-19: A case study of Saudi students' experience. *European Journal of Educational Research, 11*(1), 353–363. doi:10.12973/eu-jer.11.1.353

Alotaibi, S. S., & Kumar, T. (2019). Promoting teaching and learning performance in mathematics classroom through e-learning. Opción, Año 35. *Especial, 2019*(19), 2363–2378.

Andújar-Vaca, A., & Cruz-Martínez, M. S. (2017). Mobile instant messaging: WhatsApp and its potential to develop oral skills. Comunicar. *Media Education Research Journal, 25*(1), 43–52. doi:10.3916/C50-2017-04

Bacha, M. S., Kumar, T., Bibi, B. S., & Yunus, M. M. (2021). Using English as a lingua franca in Pakistan: Influences and implications in English Language Teaching (ELT). *Asian ESP Journal., 17*(2), 155–175.

BasmaIssa, A. A. (2013). The effect of "Whatsapp" electronic dialogue journaling on improving writing vocabulary word choice and voice of EFL undergraduate Saudi students. *Arab World English Journal, 4*(3), 213–223.

Bensalem, E. (2018). *The impact of WhatsApp on EFL students' vocabulary learning. Arab World English Journal* (Vol. 9). AWEJ.

Benyo, A., Alkhaza'leh, B. A., & Kumar, T. (2022). Using unfair means in undergraduate E-learning programmes in English: An analytical survey. *World Journal on Educational Technology: Current Issues., 14*(1), 329–341. doi:10.18844/wjet.v14i1.6761

Benyo, A. & Kumar, T. (2020). An analysis of Indian EFL learners' listening comprehension errors. *Asian ESP Journal, 16*(5.2), 69-85.

Brown, H. D. (2016). *Teaching by Principles. An Interactive Approach to Language Pedagogy*. Prentice Hall.

Çakmak, F., Namaziandost, E., & Kumar, T. (2021). CALL-enhanced l2 vocabulary learning: Using spaced exposure through CALL to enhance l2 vocabulary retention. Education Research International. doi:10.1155/2021/5848525

Chunjian, Z. (2009). Application of multimedia in English Teaching and learning. *Journal of Technology for ELT*.

Damanik, E. S. D. (2020). Student attitude toward the use of Whatsapp in EFL class. *Vision (Basel), 15*(2).

Dockstader, J. (2008). *Teachers of the 21st century know the what, why, and how of technology integration*. MIT. http://the-tech.mit.edu/Chemicool

Edelson, P. J. (1998). *The organization of courses via the internet, academic aspects, interaction, evaluation, and accreditation. ERIC*. National Autonomous University of Mexico.

Ghada, A. (2016). Effect of WhatsApp on critique writing proficiency and perceptions toward learning. *Cogent Education*, 1-26.

Ghahderijani, B. H., Namaziandost, E., Tavakoli, M., Kumar, T., & Magizov, R. (2021). The comparative effect of group dynamic assessment (GDA) and computerized dynamic assessment (CDA) on Iranian upper-intermediate EFL learners' speaking complexity, accuracy, and fluency (CAF). *Language Testing in Asia, 11*(1), 25. doi:10.118640468-021-00144-3

Golonka, E. M., Bowles, A. R., Frank, V. M., Richardson, D. L., & Freynik, S. (2014). Technologies for foreign language learning: A review of technology types and their effectiveness. *Computer Assisted Language Learning, 27*(1), 70–105. doi:10.1080/09588221.2012.700315

Harmer, J. (2007). *The Practice of English Language Teaching*. Pearson Education Limited.

Hoven, D. (1999). A Model for reading and viewing comprehension in multimedia environments. *Language Learning & Technology, 3*(1), 88–103.

İşman, A. (2012). Technology and technique: An educational perspective. *The Turkish Online Journal of Educational Technology, 11*(2), 207–213.

Kabilan, M. K., Ahmad, N., & Abidin, M. J. Z. (2010). Facebook: An online environment for learning of English in institutions of higher education? *The Internet and Higher Education, 13*(4), 179–187. doi:10.1016/j.iheduc.2010.07.003

Khan, R. M. I., Kumar, T., Benyo, A., Jahara, S. F., & Haidar, M. M. F. (2022). The reliability analysis of speaking test in computer-assisted language learning (CALL) environment. Education Research International. doi:10.1155/2022/8984330

Kumar, T. (2020). Assessing language need and proficiency of English graduates of Prince Sattam Bin Abdulaziz University for designing pre-placement training and workshops. *Asian ESP Journal., 16*(4), 153–168.

Kumar, T. (2021a). 'Desire to learn, learn to shine': Idolizing motivation in enhancing speaking skill among L2 learners. *Cypriot Journal of Educational Science., 16*(1), 411–422. doi:10.18844/cjes.v16i1.5542

Kumar, T. (2021b). Social Networking Sites and Grammar Learning: The Views of Learners and Practitioners. *International Journal of Early Childhood Special Education (INT-JECSE), 13*(2), 215-223. doi:10.9756/INT-JECSE/V13I2.211057

LeLoup, J. W. (1997). But I only have e-mail—What can I do? *Learning Languages, 2*, 10–15.

Lenders, O. (2008). Electronic glossing–is it worth the effort? *Computer Assisted Language Learning, 21*(5), 457–481. doi:10.1080/09588220802447933

Mahmood, R., Shah, A. H., & Kumar, T. (2020). English language learning and its socio-cultural effects: A comparative study of private and government schools of Islamabad. *Asian EFL Journal, 27*(3.3), 150-164.

Min, P. (2013). The use of multimedia technology in English language teaching: A global perspective. Crossing the border. *International Journal of Interdisciplinary Studies, 1*(1), 29–38.

Pan, H., Xia, F., Kumar, T., Li, X., & Shamsy, A. (2022). Massive open online course versus flipped instruction: Impacts on foreign language speaking anxiety, foreign language learning motivation, and learning attitude. *Frontiers in Psychology, 13*, 833616. doi:10.3389/fpsyg.2022.833616 PMID:35197908

Parveen, J. J., & Rajesh, V. (2011). Multimedia in English Language Teaching: An empirical analysis. *Journal of Technology for ELT, 1*(4), 112–116.

Patel, C. (2013). Use of multimedia technology in teaching and learning communication skill: An analysis. *International Journal of Advancements in Research & Technology, 2*(7), 116–123.

Pérez-Sabater, C., & Montero-Fleta, B. (2015). ESP vocabulary and social networking: The case of Twitter. Ibérica. *Revista de la Asociación Europea de Lenguas para Fines Específicos*, (29), 129–154.

Poole, R. E. (2011). Concordance-based glosses for facilitating semantization and enhancing productive knowledge of academic vocabulary [Doctoral dissertation, University of Alabama Libraries, USA].

Ramazani, J. (1994). *Student writing by e-mail: Connecting classmates, texts, instructors*. University of Virginia. https://www.virginia.edu/~trc/tcemail.htm

Sakar, A., & Ercetin, G. (2004). Effectiveness of hypermedia annotations for foreign language reading. *Journal of Computer Assisted Learning*, *21*(1), 28–38. doi:10.1111/j.1365-2729.2005.00108.x

Sarica, G. N., & Cavus, N. (2009). New trends in 21st century English learning. *Procedia: Social and Behavioral Sciences*, *1*(1), 439–445. doi:10.1016/j.sbspro.2009.01.079

Schcolnik, M., Kol, S., & Oren, A. (2007, June). Are handhelds suitable for reading academic texts? In EdMedia+ Innovate Learning (pp. 888-895). Association for the Advancement of Computing in Education (AACE).

Stemler, L. K. (1997). Educational characteristics of multimedia: A literature review. *Journal of Educational Multimedia and Hypermedia*, *6*, 339–360.

Storey, M. A., Phillips, B., Maczewski, M., & Wang, M. (2002). Evaluating the usability of Web-based learning tools. *Journal of Educational Technology & Society*, *5*(3), 91–100.

Taylor, M. C. (2001). *The Moment of Complexity: Emerging Network Culture*. University of Chicago Press.

Van De Bogart, W., & Wichadee, S. (2015). Exploring students' intention to use LINE for academic purposes based on technology acceptance model. *International Review of Research in Open and Distributed Learning*, *16*(3), 65–85. doi:10.19173/irrodl.v16i3.1894

Vyver, A. G., Williams, B., & Marais, M. A. (2015). Using social media as a managerial platform for an educational development project: Cofimvaba. *International Journal of Information and Education Technology (IJIET)*, *5*(12), 910–913. doi:10.7763/IJIET.2015.V5.636

Wu, W. S. (2005). Web-based English learning and teaching in Taiwan: Possibilities and challenges. *Paper presented at The First Hsiang-shan Area Intercollegiate International Conference on English teaching*. Crane Publishing.

Yamada, M., Kitamura, S., Shimada, N., Utashiro, T., Shigeta, K., Yamaguchi, E., & Nakahara, J. (2011). Development and evaluation of English listening study materials for business people who use mobile devices: A case study. *CALICO Journal*, *29*(1), 44–67. doi:10.11139/cj.29.1.44-66

Chapter 6
The Use of Zoom in Giving Writing Conferences in Foreign Language Writing Classes

Ahmet Erdost Yastibaş
https://orcid.org/0000-0002-1886-7951
Gazi University, Turkey

ABSTRACT

To give feedback during Covid-19, language instructors used digital programs such as Zoom. Accordingly, the present study aimed to find out and describe the experiences of a language instructor who held online writing conferences through Zoom. It was designed as a single case study conducted with a participant language instructor. The data were collected through a semi-structured interview and content analyzed. The findings indicated that online writing conferences had advantages such as saving time, and disadvantages, including technical issues. They also showed that online writing conferences could be affected positively and negatively by several factors such as time-saving and technical issues. According to the findings, though the content of feedback in them was the same as the one in face-to-face writing conferences, there were differences including student prejudice between them. The findings were discussed, pedagogical implications of the study were mentioned, and suggestions for further research were made.

INTRODUCTION

Writing in a foreign language requires foreign language learners to produce a piece of language by using their knowledge of the language(s) so that they can communicate their ideas, feelings, and beliefs to other people in the foreign language(s) they learn. Therefore, the communicative purpose of writing has rendered teaching writing an essential part of foreign language teaching, which has also made approaches, methods, and/or techniques used to teach writing significant for foreign language teachers to be familiar with and use in their writing classes. One of these methods is writing conferences.

DOI: 10.4018/978-1-6684-6682-7.ch006

BACKGROUND

The background of the study was presented by first explaining what writing conferences are, their nature, the roles of teachers and learners in writing conferences, and giving feedback online during Covid-19.

Writing Conferences

Writing conferences can be defined as the conversations/talks that a teacher and a learner make with each other one-on-one and that concentrate on the learner's writing (Bayraktar, 2012). As the definition indicates, a language teacher and a language learner come together, the teacher talks with the learner about their writing (e.g., a paragraph, an essay, a report, or a research paper), and they work on the writing together to improve it in a writing conference in foreign language teaching. Also, a writing conference can be made between a teacher and an individual learner, as the definition mentions, between a teacher and a pair of learners (Yeh, 2017), or between a teacher and a group of learners (Mochizuki, 2017).

The Significance of Writing Conferences

A writing conference is an effective teaching method for language teachers to know because it can enable language learners to become better writers in the languages they learn (Bayraktar, 2012; Brown, 2018; Ji, 2017; Maliborska & You, 2016; Phusawisot, 2018; Yang, 2022; Yeh, 2017). There are several reasons for this. According to Bayraktar (2012), it can make language learners more independent in writing in a foreign language, promote their sense of authority or ownership in their writing, and improve their self-efficacy in writing. It can also enhance their confidence in their writing (Brown, 2018; Phusawisot, 2018). Language learners can receive personalized instruction about their writings in writing conferences (Yeh, 2017) since the focus of a writing conference between a language teacher and a language learner is on the learner's writing, the teacher only deals with the learners, and he spends time talking about the strengths and weaknesses about the writing with the learner individually. As a result, they can be provided with individualized/personalized and tailored support (Yang, 2022) and feedback (Brown, 2018; Sowell, 2020) for their writing. Oral (Alfalagg, 2020) or written can be given. Personalized feedback provided in a writing conference causes them to value it (Brown, 2018). With personalized instruction, feedback, and support, they can discuss their progress in their writing with their teachers (Maliborska & You, 2016).

The Nature of Writing Conferences

The nature of writing conferences can be characterized as interactive (Gilliland, 2014; Yang, 2022) and negotiating (Chang, 2021; Ewert, 2009; Mirzaee & Yaqubi, 2016; Taylor, 2021). That a writing conference is made between a teacher and a learner makes it interactive as the teacher and learner dialogue with each other in a writing conference, so dialogue is valued in writing conferences (Aldohon, 2021). The nature of this interaction is essential for effective writing conferences now that Gilliland (2014) emphasized that language learners can be engaged in a writing conference through constructive interactions. Constructive interactions can enable them to be socialized academically by learning about the academic use of the language, yet unhelpful interactions may create obstacles that may avoid learners' language (i.e., writing) development (Gilliland, 2014). Constructive interactions between language teachers and learners can promote negotiations which are required pedagogically in writing conferences (Taylor,

2021). Teachers and learners negotiate how the weaknesses in learners' writings can be improved with each other in writing conferences because writing conferences provide them with plentiful opportunities for this purpose (Mirzaee & Yaqubi, 2016). Negotiations can contribute to the talks on the content of learners' writings (Chang, 2021). When such negotiations focus on learners' use of language, teachers use scaffolding which is also necessary for writing conferences (Chang, 2021; Ewert, 2009). When teachers give feedback on the use of language to learners, scaffolding can enable them to present the feedback in a clear and understandable way to learners so that they can use feedback effectively to work on their weaknesses. According to Ewert (2009), the use of negotiation and scaffolding together can help teachers increase the number of ways that they can provide learners with assistance according to their level of proficiency and the rate of learners' participation in writing conferences.

The Roles of Teachers and Learners in Writing Conferences

The interactive and negotiating nature of writing conferences makes the roles of language teachers and learners significant to the effective implementation of writing conferences. Bayraktar (2012) stated that a teacher should be patient, friendly, and approachable to learners and place learners in the center of writing conferences by enabling them to self-evaluate their writings and consider their comments or responses to their questions. Similarly, the participants in Aldohon's study (2021) listed the features of a good tutor in writing conferences as engaging learners in writing conferences, being supportive, caring, and patient, taking into consideration and meeting their needs, and having a good relationship with them, and facilitating their learning in writing though achieving to have these features may be time-consuming for language teachers (Yeh, 2017) and require a lot of preparation time (Maliborska & You, 2016). With language teachers who have these features and do these things, learners can be provided with an opportunity to find and suggest solutions to the problem(s) in their writings (Bayraktar, 2012; Strauss & Xiang, 2006). Also, learners are the ones who revise their writings in writing conferences with the guidance of their teachers (Ji, 2017; Mirzaee & Yaqubi, 2016; Phusawisot, 2018). These explanations point out the fact that language learners should be active in writing conferences, as supported by Aldohon's study (2021), in which the participant teachers expect learners to take responsibility for their learning writing and enhance their writing. To achieve this, learners are expected to be independent and confident writers (Aldohon, 2021). Yet, learners may influence this expectation for them negatively because they may be reluctant to attend writing conferences. Consalvo and Maloch (2015) reported that learners may perform five resisting actions during writing conferences. They may ignore the comment(s) given to them by their teacher(s), seem to be engaged in writing conferences, but in fact, they may be disengaged, try to change the subject during writing conferences, refuse that writing conferences are beneficial, or may lie and approach their teacher(s) hostilely (Consalvo & Maloch, 2015). In addition, their writing self-efficacy may affect their active participation in writing conferences negatively (Bayraktar, 2013). In such cases, writing conferences may become ineffective for them. To overcome this situation, writing conferences can be made predictable (Bayraktar, 2012), which means both language teachers and learners can know what will be expected from them at the beginning, during, and at the end of a writing conference. Their focus can be mostly on learners' responses to teachers' comments (Bayraktar, 2012). Collaborative and non-directive writing conference strategies such as listening to learners actively and building a good rapport with learners can be adopted and used by teachers (Aldohon, 2021). Writing conferences can be built on a philosophy which promotes a holistic, relevant-to-learners-English-proficiency, and non-directive approach to writing conferences as well as flexible for teachers to adjust according to the emerging needs of learners (Eckstein, 2013). In addition, different techniques such as Rogerian reflections (Phusawisot, 2018) can be used to create a non-threatening atmosphere in writing conferences. These measurements can help make writing conferences effective so that language teachers can facilitate their learners' learning in writing classes (Yang, 2022). Also, with such measurements, language learners can become more self-confident, have an increased sense of ownership of their writings, respond to their teachers' comment(s), and revise their writings accordingly (Phusawisot, 2018).

Giving Feedback Online During Covid-19

The outbreak of Covid-19 led to the closure of schools and universities and the transition from face-to-face to online/distance education. As an aspect of education, giving feedback to learners was affected by these cases. Technology was used more to give feedback (AbuSa'aleek & Shariq, 2021; Jiang & Yu, 2021; Mahapatra, 2021; Phoophuangpairoj & Pipattarasakul, 2022), which added new components to the delivery of teacher feedback (Xu, Chen, Wang, & Suhadolc, 2021), yet this made giving feedback to learners challenging for teachers (Jiang & Yu, 2021) and pre-service language teachers (Yang, Mak, & Yuan, 2021). These challenges include learners' preference, areal, financial, and technical issues (AbuSa'aleek & Shariq, 2021) as well as trouble in keeping learners' responses secure, increased feedback workload, and reduction in formative feedback (Jiang & Yu, 2021). In addition, language teachers might not use the data they could obtain from their learners' online assessment, though they could engage them in several ways (Mahapatra, 2021). Despite this, language teachers were reported that their attitudes toward giving feedback online were positive (AbuSa'aleek & Shariq, 2021) and think that the online implementation of assessment and feedback practices was successful (Mäkipää, Hahl, & Luodonpää, 2021). Online feedback practices could also create learning opportunities (Yang et al., 2021) and positive changes in language teachers' motivation to give feedback and the design of their feedback (Jiang & Yu, 2021). Similarly, Xu et al. (2021) found that online teacher feedback could improve language learners' language learning (oral presentation in this case). Learners were found to have positive attitudes toward (Xu, 2021; Xu et al., 2021) and perceptions (Ma, Wang, & Teng, 2021) about online teacher feedback. Ma et al. (2021) revealed that learning-oriented assessment could foster learners' feedback literacy in different aspects of feedback literacy such as appreciating the feedback given. Besides, Xu (2021) mentioned that language learners could review the feedback given to them by their teachers online indefinitely, so they could have a comfortable learning environment. In addition, the online interaction between language teachers and learners could make learners more engaged in teacher feedback (Xu, 2021). Also, teaching practices could help pre-service language teachers to improve their online feedback-giving practices (Koşar, 2021). As this part indicates, the studies concentrated on different aspects of giving online feedback, but they did not focus on the use of technology (in this case, Zoom) in giving online writing conferences used to give foreign language learners' writing a lot.

The Aim of the Research and Research Questions

The literature review above has indicated that language teachers could give feedback to language learners online by using technology despite some challenges they encountered. In one of the universities where the researcher worked, Zoom was used for this purpose in online writing conferences and to teach a foreign language (i.e., English) to language learners. This case study aimed to find out and demonstrate how writing conferences were held through Zoom to give feedback to language learners during Covid-19 by answering the research questions below.

1. What does the language instructor think about online writing conferences?
2. What is/are the advantage(s) of online writing conferences, according to the language instructor?
3. What is/are the disadvantage(s) of online writing conferences, according to the language instructor?
4. What may affect online writing conferences positively, according to the language instructor?
5. What may affect online writing conferences negatively, according to the language instructor?
6. What is/are the similarity/similarities between face-to-face and online writing conferences, according to the language instructor?
7. What is/are the difference(s) between face-to-face and online writing conferences, according to the language instructor?
8. What is the preference of the language instructor to give feedback to her learners: face-to-face writing conferences or online writing conferences?

In the present study, online writing conferences refer to the writing conferences held between the participant and her learners through Zoom.

Significance of the Present Study

As the literature review indicates, technology has become the dominant tool for giving feedback to foreign language learners, and the studies reviewed in the present study focused on different aspects of giving online feedback. The aim of the present study was to contribute to this existing and growing literature by investigating the use of Zoom, whose use increased because of the pandemic, in giving writing conferences to give feedback to foreign language learners' writing. The findings of the present study can be used by foreign language institutions which organize online foreign language courses, including the ones in foreign language writing, to make feedback giving process more effective by using a program such as Zoom because the findings can demonstrate what may be experienced by a foreign language teacher while using technology to give feedback in an online writing conference, so by using the findings of the present study, solutions can be developed to deal with possible problems that can be encountered in this process. Also, a foreign language teacher who wants to vary how he/she can give feedback through a writing conference can benefit from the present study's findings if he/she wants to use technology in this process. By doing so, the present study can be used in local and global contexts.

METHODOLOGY

Research Design

The present study was designed as a single case study investigating one contemporary phenomenon (i.e., holding writing conferences through Zoom) in its natural context, as Yin (2009) mentioned.

Participant

A Turkish English language instructor who worked in a Turkish university participated in the research. She was 31 years old and had nine years of teaching experience. She was chosen through criterion sampling in which the criterion was to hold online writing conferences with language learners (English language learners in this case) during Covid-19.

Data Collection Tool

The data were collected through a semi-structured interview which was made in Turkish. Eight questions were prepared according to the research questions in the interview (see Appendix 1). The questions focus on the thoughts of the instructor about online writing conferences, the advantage(s) and disadvantage(s) of online writing conferences, the factor(s) that may affect online writing conferences positively and negatively, the similarity/similarities and difference(s) between face-to-face and online writing conferences, and the instructor's preference to give feedback to her learners.

Data Analysis

The data collected from the semi-structured interview were analyzed through content analysis. The codes were derived from the transcriptions of the semi-structured interview after several readings and categorized according to the themes developed depending on the similarities between the codes. The themes were used to organize and present the findings without adding any researcher comments. Then, the findings were interpreted in harmony with the description of the data. To make the content analysis of the data trustworthy, two strategies were used: (a) thick descriptions in which the findings were supported by the quotations from the semi-structured interview and (b) member-check or participant-check in which the content analysis of the data was shared with the participant, and her thoughts and comments about the analysis were learned and taken into consideration when the content analysis of the data was finalized.

FINDINGS

The findings of the present study were presented according to the themes shown in Table 1 below in order.

Thoughts of the Instructor Bbout Online Writing Conferences

The participant language instructor thought that *face-to-face feedback was more effective* for her learners. To illustrate:

Teacher: *"When I gave [online feedback], I thought there was no difference in face-to-face and online feedback, but for me, it seemed to make no difference. Yet then I later realized that when we [language instructors] shifted face-to-face [education], it is more effective for the children, the students, to do this [giving feedback] face-to-face."*

Table 1. The themes developed and codes derived from the semi-structured interview

Themes	Codes
Thoughts of the instructor about online writing conferences	Face-to-face feedback's being more effective
	Not being interested
Advantages of online writing conferences	Time-saving
	Effective feedback-giving
Disadvantages of online writing conferences	Learners' difficulty in paying attention to online writing conferences
	Not producing original writings
	Technical issues
Factors that may affect online writing conferences positively	Reading comments before the lessons
	Time-saving
Factors that may affect online writing conferences negatively	Technical issues
	Learners' preference for face-to-face feedback
Similarities between face-to-face and online writing conferences	The content of feedback
Differences between face-to-face and online writing conferences	Learners' prejudice/viewpoint
	Instructor's concerns
	Providing effective feedback
	Improving technological skills
	Learners' willingness to receive feedback
Preferring online writing conferences	Time-saving
	Giving better feedback

She also thought that her learners *were not interested* in online writing conferences, as understood from the quotation below.

Teacher: *"The students did not seem to be like something in this online [writing] conference like they were not asking a lot of questions. It was only what I told [them]. They were as if they did not pay attention [to online feedback]. I mean, I realized this when we [language instructors] shifted face-to-face feedback."*

Advantages of Online Writing Conferences

According to the participant instructor, online writing conferences were advantageous because they were timesaving for both her and her learners. The quotation below shows this clearly.

Teacher: *"The most [positive] side of it [online writing conference] for me is its being timesaving. Students can access [online writing conferences] whenever they want and wherever they want. For them it is. I think it is the same for us [language instructors]. Being timesaving is its [online writing conference] most important thing."*

She also mentioned that online writing conferences make *feedback-giving effective*. The quotation below indicates this.

Teacher: *"They [students] actually see the thing [the comments and the writing]. For example… We [language instructors] did this on Zoom. There, I sent things like error codes before sending comments. For the children [students], who are really looking [at the things sent], reading [them], [and] interested, seeing both things [the comments and the writing] at the same time both visually by sharing the screen and orally through the conference would be tidier, more something, [and] more effective. It was also easier for me to see both things [the comments and the writing] at the same time when they [students] came by reading the comments beforehand because they did not do this a lot in face-to-face [writing conferences]."*

Disadvantages of Online Writing Conferences

The participant language instructor mentioned three disadvantages of online writing conferences. The first disadvantage of online writing conferences for the participant instructor was *learners' difficulty in paying attention to online writing conferences*. To illustrate:

Teacher: *"The disadvantage of online writing conferences, I think, is… At that time, it could also be because we [language instructors and students] moved on to these online things since the pandemic had just started. I do not know whether this is its disadvantage or the conference's, but the children [students] sometimes had difficulty in paying attention. Because this [giving feedback] is online, because they did not see it [feedback] in their hands concretely, it might be a little distracting for them [students]."*

According to her, the second disadvantage of online writing conferences was *learners' not producing original writings*. The quotation below reveals this.

Teacher: *"I will say a thing, that is, as students used Google translate or copied and pasted from a source on the internet, as this [student writings] was not their work, receiving feedback to something that they did not write did not motive them a lot. In fact, this is the disadvantage of both online writing and online assessment, and I think the conference."*

The third disadvantage of online writing conferences was *technical issues* for her. The quotation below highlights this finding.

Teacher: *"Anything else? Issues… If technical issues often occur, it can also be distracting for students if Zoom often cuts off."*

Factors That May Affect Online Writing Conferences Positively

According to the participant language instructor, *learners read her comments before the lessons* and *that online writing conferences are timesaving* were the factors that affected online writing conferences positively, as understood from the following quotation.

Teacher: "As I said, the students who benefitted from the process the most were the students who came to the [online writing] conference after they read the error code comments beforehand, and they were very motivated. This made me... I gave them [students] extra writing [assignments], [and] we [the participant and her learners] held more writing conferences. Seeing that they benefited from this, seeing that they were motivated also motivated me, but the thing that made me motivated personally the most was its [online writing conferences] being timesaving. When we [language instructors] were doing hybrid education after the pandemic ended, we continued the feedback for a while and the writing [practices] in the same way [online]. The thing that motivated me the most is its [online writing conference's] timesaving; it can be done anywhere, anytime."

Factors That May Affect Online Writing Conferences Negatively

The participant language instructor explained that *technical issues* and *learners' preference for face-to-face feedback* were the things that affected online writing practices negatively. The following quotation indicates this clearly.

Teacher: "I think it is mostly technical things such as internet glitch, internet-related issues, computer-related issues [affect online writing conferences]... At first, students could not solve these technical issues. Then they started to solve technical issues more easily, but they experienced such problems in the beginning. Then there were also those [students] who said "OK, teacher. Do not do it" and gave up as they could not cope with technical problems. In my opinion, the most negative is basically technical glitches for me and the students. Any other negatives? I mean it is a general concept to say, "Teacher, I wish the lessons were face-to-face, I wish feedback were face-to-face for some children [students]. So as a viewpoint... The child [student] feels themself more comfortable. It [online writing conference] may also be negative for some students."

Similarities Between Face-To-Face and Online Writing Conferences

The participant language instructor said that *the content of the feedback given* was the similarity between face-to-face and online writing conferences, as understood from the following quotation.

Teacher: "Their [face-to-face and online writing conferences] similarities are... In both of them, in terms of content, you focus on the same content in feedback, that is, both content and organization. You give feedback with the same method and in the same way... You give everything that you need to give to students, I can say the content is the similarity. That, the content of feedback, can be their [face-to-face and online writing conferences] similarities."

Differences Between Face-To-Face and Online Writing Conferences

The participant language instructor listed five differences between face-to-face and online writing conferences. The first difference between them was *learners' prejudice/viewpoint*. The following quotation clearly supports this.

Teacher: *"In my opinion, their [face-to-face and online writing conferences] are completely the prejudice of students, their viewpoint. "Teacher, I understand better in face-to-face [education]" may be a prejudice, a truth, or their viewpoint. I think this is the difference, the students' viewpoint."*

The second difference between face-to-face and online writing conferences was *the instructor's concerns,* as indicated by the quotation below.

Teacher: *"Similarly, the teacher, I had concerns about whether both [face-to-face and online writing conferences] would be the same."*

The third difference between face-to-face and online writing conferences was *providing effective feedback.* The following quotation supports this.

Teacher: *"Also, I think we [language instructors] do the thing, this error code thing, namely both the comment and writing one, better online. Naturally, I think it works in the [online writing] conference, especially for the children [students] who are visual. I think we [language teachers] cannot do it in face-to-face [writing conferences] by hand that effectively."*

According to the participant, the fourth difference was *improving technological skills,* as the quotation below shows this.

Teacher: *"Besides, I think the student get used to things, getting used to doing something on the computer, doing it online, doing it more practically. It [online writing conference] has such an advantage over face-to-face [writing conferences] differently."*

The participant stated that the last difference was *learners' willingness to receive feedback.* The quotation below reveals this.

Teacher: *"It is as if it [online writing conference] engages the student more. I mean, they take the trouble to wake up, [and] log in Zoom. If they really come there, it does not apply to all of them, but to receive feedback... In the class, for example, you [language instructor] can give [feedback to the student] by force by saying "Come here, son. You did not write this," but in online [writing conferences], there is something, willing [to join online writing conferences] - I do not know its name in the literature -, there is an effort. Maybe that can be more motivating for kids [students] in online [writing conferences]."*

Preferring Online Writing Conferences

The participant language teacher preferred online writing conferences because she thought that online writing conferences were *time-saving.* The following quotation supports this.

Teacher: *"So I prefer online [writing conferences], but this is all about personal reasons. I prefer online lessons because it [online lesson] is time-saving. For example, writing lessons can be online; in fact, it can be more productive. Regarding its being time-saving, I prefer [online writing] conferences."*

The second reason why she preferred online writing conferences was that she believed she could *give better feedback* in online writing conferences, as understood from this quotation "In addition, I think I give online writing feedback better."

DISCUSSIONS

According to the findings of the present study, the participant language instructor considered that face-to-face feedback was more effective than online feedback for her language learners and thought that her learners were not interested in online writing conferences through Zoom. The second finding is in line with the literature because language learners may perform resisting behaviors in writing conferences (Consalvo & Maloch, 2015). These two findings are related and may result from the fact that both the participant and her learners may not have had any training on or experience with online/distance language education and online/distance giving/receiving feedback. Lack of training and experience for her language learners may have resulted in their disinterest and disengagement in online writing conferences. Similarly, the participant may not have known how to make online writing conferences more engaging and interesting for her learners in the beginning due to the lack of training or experience, so she might have considered face-to-face feedback more effective. Also, this situation may have created concerns for her, which she mentioned was a difference between face-to-face and online writing conferences.

The findings indicated that online writing conferences created two advantages for the participant: being timesaving and being an effective feedback-giving practice. Unlike the literature which claims that writing conferences are time-consuming (Yeh, 2017) and require a lot of preparation time (Maliborska & You, 2016), the participant claimed that they are timesaving. The reason she gave for this finding was that language learners could receive feedback whenever and wherever they were. Another reason for this finding may be the positive attitude of the participant toward online/distance education because she mentioned in the interview that she would like writing lessons to be online. The technical skills of the participant may have also helped her turn her online writing conferences into a time-saving practice because she may not have spent a lot of time trying to learn how to use Zoom and how to use an office program to give feedback to her learners' writing. Instead, she could have used most of her time providing feedback to her learners in online writing conferences. As a result, she may have considered being timesaving as a factor that could positively affect online writing classes, and they may help her understand why she preferred online writing conferences. The way Zoom enables a language teacher to give feedback caused her to think that online writing conferences were an effective feedback-giving practice since the learner could see their writing with the participant's feedback on the screen and be informed orally about the feedback. This reason could help to understand why she preferred online writing conferences and why she considered it a difference between face-to-face and online writing conferences.

The findings of the present study revealed that the participant thought her language learners had difficulty paying attention to online conferences due to not seeing the feedback in their hands. The reason that she gave for this finding may be related to the learners' lack of training on and experience with online writing conferences. That is, before the breakout of Covid-19, they may have been used to receiving feedback on their writing face-to-face, so this accustomedness may have caused them to believe online feedback would not be as effective as face-to-face feedback. When online/distance language education, they may have continued this belief and reflected it through their behaviors and attitudes in online writing conferences. Therefore, they may have preferred face-to-face writing conferences, which she considered was another factor that could affect online writing conferences through Zoom negatively. This was also mentioned as a difference between face-to-face and online writing conferences by her. The second disadvantage of online writing conferences for the participant was learners' not producing original writings, which she thought demotivated them to receive feedback on something that they did not write. In face-to-face language classes, the presence of a language teacher may have prevented language learners from plagiarism, but their physical presence could not exist in online language classes, which may have been misused by some learners when it comes to writing in a foreign language. The last disadvantage of online writing classes was technical issues, which was also corroborated by the literature on giving feedback during Covid-19 (Jiang & Yu, 2021). As everything depends on technology in online/distance language education, any technical problem in this process can affect any instructional activity negatively, like they affected online writing conferences held by the participant language instructor through Zoom. Consequently, the participant may have considered technical issues as one of the factors that could negatively affect online writing conferences through Zoom.

According to the literate, language learners are supposed to be active in writing conferences (Aldohon, 2021; Bayraktar, 2012; Ji, 2017; Mirzaee & Yaqubi, 2016; Phusawisot, 2018; Strauss & Xiang, 2006). Similarly, when the language learners of the participant became active in online writing conferences by reading the comments of the participants sent before the conferences, they could benefit from online writing conferences, which the participant thought could positively affect online writing conferences through Zoom. According to the present study's findings, such students were willing to receive feedback, so their willingness may have caused them to read the participant's comments before online writing conferences were held, which the participant stated as another difference between face-to-face and online writing. Finally, she mentioned that online writing conferences were different from face-to-face writing conferences in terms of improving her learners' technological skills since her learners were supposed to use technology actively in online writing conferences, so this may have improved their technological skills. Despite several differences between online and face-to-face writing conferences, according to her, there is one similarity between them: the content of the feedback. This may have stemmed from the fact that the participant may have given face-to-face and online feedback on learners' writings in terms of language, content, and organization.

Despite her thoughts about online writing conferences in the first paragraph, the findings revealed that the participant also thought online writing conferences through Zoom were effective, as found out in the literature (Bayraktar, 2012; Brown, 2018; Ji, 2017; Maliborska & You, 2016; Phusawisot, 2018; Yang, 2022; Yeh, 2017). The possible reasons for this may be that online writing conferences can be time-saving, help to give feedback effectively, and be beneficial for willing learners.

FUTURE RESEARCH DIRECTIONS

The present study was limited due to its research design and the number of participants. Future research can be conducted with more participants and collect both quantitative and qualitative data. In addition, future research can be conducted with the students who joined online writing conferences through Zoom to receive feedback on their writing. Besides them, researchers can design an experimental study in which face-to-face and online writing conferences can be used and their effects on language learners' writings compared with each other. They can also design a quasi-experimental study in which online writing conferences through Zoom can be used, and its effects on language learners' writings can be found out.

CONCLUSION

The present study investigated and described how the participant language instructor held writing conferences through Zoom with her language learners. According to the study's findings, the participant thought that face-to-face feedback was more effective for language learners, and they were not interested in online writing conferences. The findings of the study also showed that, according to the participant, being timesaving and an effective feedback-giving practice were the advantages of online writing conferences through Zoom. In contrast, technical issues, learners' difficulty in paying attention to online writing conferences, and their not producing original writings were the disadvantages of online writing conferences through Zoom. In addition, the study's findings revealed that learners' reading comments before the lesson and being timesaving were the factors that might affect online writing practices positively, whereas technical issues and learners' preferences for face-to-face feedback were the factors that might affect online writing conferences negatively. According to the findings of the study, the content of the feedback given in face-to-face and online writing conferences was the same. Yet, there were several differences (i.e., learners' prejudice/viewpoint, the instructor's concerns, providing effective feedback, improving technological skills, and learners' willingness to receive feedback) between them. The findings of the study finally indicated that the participant preferred online writing conferences through Zoom because they were timesaving, and she believed she could give better feedback to her learners.

The information presented above has led to two pedagogical implications of the study. They are as follows:

1. Language learners should be trained to use the feedback given in online writing conferences to improve their writing.
2. Any technical issues related to online writing conferences should be dealt with appropriately by schools, universities, and governments.

REFERENCES

AbuSa'aleek, A. O., & Shariq, M. (2021). Innovative practices in instructor e-feedback: A case study of e-feedback given in three linguistic courses during the COVID 19 Pandemic. *Arab World English Journal (AWEJ) Special Issue on Covid 19 Challenges* (1), 183 -198. doi:10.24093/awej/covid.14

Aldohon, H. (2021). Writing centre conferences: Tutors' perceptions and practices. *Educational Studies*, *47*(5), 554–573. doi:10.1080/03055698.2020.1717931

Alfalagg, A. R. (2020). Impact of teacher-student writing conferences on frequency and accuracy of using cohesive devices in EFL students' writing. *Asian-Pacific Journal of Second and Foreign Language Education*, *5*(1), 1–19. doi:10.118640862-020-00104-z

Bayraktar, A. (2012). Teaching writing through teacher-student writing conferences. *Procedia: Social and Behavioral Sciences*, *51*, 709–713. doi:10.1016/j.sbspro.2012.08.229

Bayraktar, A. (2013). Nature of interactions during teacher-student writing conferences, revisiting the potential effects of self-efficacy beliefs. *Eğitim Araştırmaları-Eurasian Journal of Educational Research*, *50*, 63–86.

Brown, D. A. (2018). *Instructor-student conferencing as pedagogy: Measuring ISC pedagogy's impact on student writing and self-Efficacy* [Doctoral dissertation, Indiana University of Pennsylvania].

Chang, Y. (2021). Investigating L2 teacher-student writing conferences in a college ESL composition classroom. *English Teaching*, *76*(2), 25–55. doi:10.15858/engtea.76.2.202106.25

Consalvo, A., & Maloch, B. (2015). Keeping the teacher at arm's length: Student resistance in writing conferences in two high school classrooms. *Journal of Classroom Interaction*, 120–132.

Eckstein, G. (2013). The interaction of theory, philosophy, and practice in ESL writing conferences. *The CATESOL Journal*, *24*(1), 174–186.

Ewert, D. E. (2009). L2 writing conferences: Investigating teacher talk. *Journal of Second Language Writing*, *18*(4), 251–269. doi:10.1016/j.jslw.2009.06.002

Gilliland, B. (2014). Academic language socialization in high school writing conferences. *Canadian Modern Language Review*, *70*(3), 303–330. doi:10.3138/cmlr.1753

Ji, S. (2017). *Exploring L2 writing conferences: Discourse and effects* [Doctoral dissertation, Purdue University].

Jiang, L., & Yu, S. (2021). Understanding changes in EFL teachers' feedback practice during COVID-19: Implications for teacher feedback literacy at a time of crisis. *The Asia-Pacific Education Researcher*, *30*(6), 509–518. doi:10.100740299-021-00583-9

Koşar, G. (2021). The progress a pre-service English language teacher made in her feedback giving practices in distance teaching practicum. *Journal of English Teaching*, *7*(3), 366–381. doi:10.33541/jet.v7i3.3145

Ma, M., Wang, C., & Teng, M. F. (2021). Using learning-oriented online assessment to foster students' feedback literacy in L2 writing during COVID-19 pandemic: A case of misalignment between micro-and macro-contexts. *The Asia-Pacific Education Researcher*, *30*(6), 597–609. doi:10.100740299-021-00600-x

Mahapatra, S. K. (2021). Online formative assessment and feedback practices of ESL teachers in India, Bangladesh and Nepal: A multiple case study. *The Asia-Pacific Education Researcher*, *30*(6), 519–530. doi:10.100740299-021-00603-8

Mäkipää, T., Hahl, K., & Luodonpää-Manni, M. (2021). teachers' perceptions of assessment and feedback practices in Finland's foreign language classes during the covid-19 pandemic. *CEPS Journal*, *11*(Special Issue), 219–240.

Maliborska, V., & You, Y. (2016). Writing conferences in a second language writing classroom: Instructor and student perspectives. *TESOL Journal*, *7*(4), 874–897. doi:10.1002/tesj.249

Mirzaee, M., & Yaqubi, B. (2016). A conversation analysis of the function of silence in writing conferences. *Iranian Journal of Language Teaching Research*, *4*(2), 69–86.

Mochizuki, N. (2017). Contingent needs analysis for task implementation: An activity systems analysis of group writing conferences. *TESOL Quarterly*, *51*(3), 607–631. doi:10.1002/tesq.391

Phoophuangpairoj, R., & Pipattarasakul, P. (2022). Preliminary indicators of EFL essay writing for teachers' feedback using automatic text analysis. *International Journal of Educational Methodology*, *8*(1), 55–68. doi:10.12973/ijem.8.1.55

Phusawisot, P. (2018). The use of Rogerian reflections in responding to doctoral student's research paper in one-on-one writing conferences. *LEARN Journal: Language Education and Acquisition Research Network*, *11*(1), 110–124.

Sowell, J. (2020). Let's be direct: Making the student-teacher writing conference work for multilingual writers. *MEXTESOL Journal*, *44*(4), 1–8.

Strauss, S., & Xiang, X. (2006). The writing conference as a locus of emergent agency. *Written Communication*, *23*(4), 355–396. doi:10.1177/0741088306292286

Taylor, L. (2021). Discursive stance as a pedagogical tool: Negotiating literate identities in writing conferences. *Journal of Early Childhood Literacy*, *21*(2), 208–229. doi:10.1177/1468798419838596

Xu, J. (2021). Chinese university students' L2 writing feedback orientation and self-regulated learning writing strategies in online teaching during COVID-19. *The Asia-Pacific Education Researcher*, *30*(6), 563–574. doi:10.100740299-021-00586-6

Xu, Q., Chen, S., Wang, J., & Suhadolc, S. (2021). Characteristics and effectiveness of teacher feedback on online business English oral presentations. *The Asia-Pacific Education Researcher*, *30*(6), 631–641. doi:10.100740299-021-00595-5

Yang, L. (2022). Focus and interaction in writing conferences for EFL writers. *SAGE Open*, *12*(1), 1–13. doi:10.1177/21582440211058200

Yang, M., Mak, P., & Yuan, R. (2021). Feedback experience of online learning during the COVID-19 pandemic: Voices from pre-service English language teachers. *The Asia-Pacific Education Researcher*, *30*(6), 611–620. doi:10.100740299-021-00618-1

Yeh, C. C. (2017). Shared time, shared problems? Exploring the dynamics of paired writing conferences. *Pedagogies*, *12*(3), 256–274. doi:10.1080/1554480X.2017.1356232

Yin, R. K. (2009). *Case study research: Design and methods* (4th ed.). SAGE Publications, Inc.

KEY TERMS AND DEFINITIONS

Writing conference: Writing conferences can be defined as the conversations/talks that a teacher and a learner make with each other one-on-one and that concentrate on the learner's writing (Bayraktar, 2012).

Online writing conference: An online writing conference is a writing conference held online between a teacher and a learner.

Face-to-face conference: A face-to-face writing conference is a writing conference that is held between a teacher and a learner face-to-face.

APPENDIX

The semi-structured interview questions are presented below.

1. What do you think about online writing conferences with your students?
2. What do you think is/are the advantage(s) of online writing conferences? Why do you think so?
3. What do you think is/are the disadvantage(s) of online writing conferences? Why do you think so?
4. What do you think affected your online writing conferences with your students positively? Why do you think so?
5. What do you think affected your online writing conferences with your students negatively? Why do you think so?
6. What do you think is/are the similarity/similarities between online and face-to-face writing conferences?
7. What do you think is/are the difference(s) between online and face-to-face writing conferences?
8. Which one do you prefer to hold a writing conference: face-to-face or online writing conferences? Why do you think so?

Chapter 7
Walking Side by Side:
Digital Humanities and Teaching–Learning of Foreign Languages

Ana Nobre

 https://orcid.org/0000-0002-9902-1850

Universidade Aberta, Portugal

ABSTRACT

The digital humanities have become a new avatar of scientific and educational progress and are part of the ideology of progress, of a linear and cumulative science. Therefore, our work questions the marketing pretension of the new digital learning environments for languages that herald an educational revolution registering itself in the idea of technological progress and addresses digital technologies in the teaching of a foreign language. We will insist in particular on the need not to ignore the term innovation, and we will see that a pedagogy that aims to be truly innovative requires a fundamental reflection, both at the educational level and at the technological levels to meet the needs of the current mobility of international students.

INTRODUCTION

The marketing strategy for digital environments and inverted classrooms hammers the idea that digital brings an "educational revolution". Who could refuse progress, this pedagogical revolution? Who could disagree with improving the quality of education and providing everyone with quality education? Are digital humanities in the field of education able to instill a new spirit of innovation? Digital humanities have become a new avatar of scientific and educational progress. We will try to define the components of this Revolution/New Pedagogy. This first point constitutes our theoretical construct. Then we focus on the Language Didactics and some characteristics. We propose to maintain in perspective the permanent articulation between didactic reflection and pedagogical reflection. In this part we will talk more specifically about language teaching and in particular how digital technology would have made it pos-

DOI: 10.4018/978-1-6684-6682-7.ch007

sible to revolutionize its methodology. Under what conditions can we say that digital evolution leads to an educational revolution?

Let us remember, without detaining us in the four major learning currents that support pedagogical approaches: behaviourism, cognitivism, constructivism, and socio-constructivism. These four currents are always present. However, to continue the path of our multidisciplinary exploration, it is necessary to open this definition to reflections that focus on digital literacy and multimodality.

Finally, we present two digital language learning environments. The objective of our analysis is to exemplify that these digital devices can herald a pedagogical renewal.

LEARNING IN THE DIGITAL AGE

New learning environments are one of the benefits of the digital age for education. Three elements characterize them: the massive aspect, the hybridity of the devices and, finally, the exploration of digital artifacts. Let us recall the four major learning currents that support pedagogical approaches: behaviourism, cognitivism, constructivism, and socio-constructivism. Let's start with the words of Lévy (1997) about cyberspace and "cyberculture". We can retain three main features. The first, interconnection, emphasizes a situation where everything is connected and available, everyone can send, receive and respond to messages. Cyberspace is made up of continuous flows that can no longer be frozen into formalizable and definitive knowledge. We are thus facing a general chaos of fluid information that moving constantly. This essential feature is the basis of the massive aspect of networks. The second aspect concerns ubiquity: we can participate in a face-to-face and virtual event at the same time. We interact both in cyberspace and in "real" society. The hybridity of training systems recalls this quality of ubiquity. Lévy adds a final element that refers to digital artifacts that allow not only to communicate, but also to automatically transform, according to computer algorithms, a reality that we want to share. Intellectual digital technologies thus enhance human culture. Collective intelligence is the synergy of social, symbolic and digital systems. The new pedagogy can only be thought of in an approach that considers "cyberculture", through learning communities, and not simply a way of transmitting content to isolated and disconnected individuals. For Lévy, the teacher is more a facilitator of collective intelligence than a transmitter of knowledge.

Siemens (2004) and Downes (2012) have a similar perspective that emphasizes interconnectedness and community learning. The first MOOC, of which they are the authors (2008), made it possible to put this pedagogical approach to connectivism into practice. The objective is to promote the collective intelligence of the participants, based on the principle that it is the interconnections they will create that matter. For this, it is essential to promote the emergence of communities of practice and learning (Wenger 2005) through specific events that involve real participation and permanent dialogue. A process of cooperation and dialogue is essential, we are witnessing a true "communicational action" (Habermas 1987) in cyberspace. Each participant creates and exchanges an artifact according to their own cultural vision. These cultural objects will be discussed, shared and recreated. Knowledge is the result of a dialogic co-creation (Longuet 2016) from a chaotic, complex space, in constant movement. Therefore, there cannot be a specific place that we call a classroom or learning platform. Siemens (2004) and Downes (2012) highlight collective intelligence located in social relationships. This pedagogical approach is an approach to social action that is part of both social constructivism and connectivism. We found the keywords interconnectivity, community and collective intelligence. Lévy's cyberculture and

Siemens and Downes' connectivism thus provide essential complementary elements to our definition of the new pedagogical approach.

For these reasons, we limit ourselves to three approaches: the traditional, behaviourist approach, the cognitivist/constructivist approach, and a social action approach that is both socioconstructivist and connectivism.

For language learning, this unfolds as follows: the communicative approach of the 1980s was part of the cognitivist/constructivist current, but actually maintained a strong behaviourist colour; With the Common European Framework of Reference for Languages (Council of Europe 2001), the task-based approach of the first decade of the 2000s failed to evolve into a real, so-called action-oriented approach to social action and is part of the cognitivist/constructivist current (Huver & Springer 2011). Is a pedagogical approach "revolutionary" with the following components: cyberculture, social action, collective intelligence, creativity and competences?

Digital Literacies and Multimodality

It is necessary to reflect on digital literacies and multimodality. There are several definitions: information literacy (Prague Declaration, 2003) was concerned with processing information on the web and with the competence necessary for gathering information. Information literacy has become as essential for any citizen of the digital age as traditional functional literacy (knowing how to read and write). This definition was revised and expanded in 2008 with the notion of information and media literacy (media and information literacy, media and information education). In order to search and process the many information present on the web, it is essential to know how to search, organize information and understand how old and new media work. Some people prefer to talk about transliteration (Thomas et al., 2007), which would consist of synergizing three skills to be a competent citizen in the digital age (computer, information and media literacy). In this way, transliteration provides an essential toolbox for functional digital action. All these proposals developed within the scope of UNESCO resulted in competence frameworks for teachers. However, these definitions focus on the technical aspects and do not consider the social, human and semiological aspects.

Kress (2009) emphasizes that education neglects the principles of the new communication that is no longer based on a pre-defined code and a grammar fixed by the writing tradition. In fact, the screens are presented in the form of "texts" whose multimodal composition is complex. The sought-after semiotic effects can no longer be reduced to the single mode of writing. Furthermore, cyberculture is no longer reserved only for traditional media authorized to produce information. It is dynamically and permanently enriched by a multitude of informal communities that produce multimodal "texts" integrating all available artifacts to create meaning (Kress & Leeuwen, 2001). The notion of multimodality (Kress 2009) thus allows us to go beyond a technological approach to digital literacies that is mainly interested in human-computer interaction and information processing. The question of meaning that emerges from multimodal messages becomes essential for learning. Lebrun and his team (Lebrun et al., 2012) talk about "multimodal media literacy", a formula that focuses more on the meaning of messages than on the technological aspects of media education. We are then placed in a perspective of social semiotics which brings us back to Halliday ("learning is learning to signify and expanding one's own potential for signifying," 1993, p. 113). Any "text" is part of social and, therefore, cultural practices.

It is now possible to maintain three criteria for analyzing digital language learning environments: the transliterated aspect, the connectivism/cyberculture aspect and the multimodality/social semiology aspect.

Language Didactics: A Digitally Compatible Discipline?

We are at the heart of mother tongue and foreign language teaching. A priori, it can be thought that Language Didactics is a sensitive discipline that is compatible with the three aspects of digital technology: the transliterated aspect, the connectivism/cyberculture aspect and the multimodality/social semiology aspect. In the past, it was strongly marked by audio-visual technology that allowed to process (in parallel) text, image, and sound. However, Tardy (1966) already criticized the essentially technicist approach of the audio-visual revolution, insofar as he ignored the semiotic dimension of audio-visual languages. The digital age must be a godsend as we have original multimodal documents to delight language educators. Two streams characterize Language Didactics: the first focuses on issues related to functional literacy, the second studies the impact of computers and the web on language learning. The main concern of language learning (both native and foreign) is to ensure that all students have access to functional literacy (Larruy 2012). The paradox of Language Didactics is to assert the primacy of orality when in reality it is written and cultivated language that are targeted. Each monolingual didactic, therefore, focuses learning on written code (lexicosyntax). In Europe as in Canada, to better to integrate multilingualism in globalized societies, the idea of plurilingual or pluriliterate competence has become essential (Moore & Coste 2006). We moved away from the standard of writing to ponder the sociolinguistic aspects and the repertoires of families and students. Sociolinguistic researchers are interested in everyday plurilingual social practices and are at the heart of the didactics of plurilingualism. The boundaries between linguistic systems, which seemed immutable and definitive, are deconstructed in favour of a mixed and variable vision. In Canada, the plurilingual perspective offers a more open view of literacy: "the approach to literacy as a socially situated practice is based on the multimodality of the spoken, written and visual, perceived as systems of representations that build our perception of reality and the world around us" (Sabatier, Moore, & Dagenais, 2013). In this case, and in theory, we go beyond the (multi)linguistic concerns of literacy, to consider a certain multimodality. We observe that concerns about cyberculture and transliteration remain the second stream, that of computer-assisted instruction and computer-mediated language learning, which questions the impact of digital technology (Warschauer & Kern, 2000), should account for and explore aspects of cyberculture and multimodality. Much research in this field focus on the study of human-machine interactions and pedagogical communication with online tutors (Chanier & Vetter, 2006). in the choice of modes (audio, chat, etc.) to carry out the proposed school tasks, as well as the tutor's interactions (verbal and non-verbal). Thus, we remain in an essentially technological approach (the choice of artifacts offered by socio-technical platforms) and centred on teaching (the role of tutors in the pedagogical relationship). We are not in a multimodal approach that is interested in synergising modes and means to make sense and make sense. If we go back to our criteria, we can say that this current, which should be more open to digital specificities, does not contemplate the full dimension of the new elements of cyberculture, connectivism and social semiotics. In summary, Language Didactics offers a varied landscape, on the one hand, through monolingual functional literacy and, on the other, through transliteration.

DIGITAL HUMANITIES: DIGITAL TRANSFORMATION FOR BETTER OR FOR WORSE?

Digital is the new avatar of progressive ideology. Education, considered too conservative, must adapt to modernity, and play its role in the digital revolution. We will approach today's society as a learning society, a digital society and highlight its characteristics, namely the openness and freedom offered by the Web. Scientific resources must be "free" and, consequently, knowledge must constitute common goods, a network of open access to all, without borders, with unlimited and free resources. The knowledge produced by the educational community is considered the common property of humanity. We think of the open access movement for scientific publication.

The Digital Educational Revolution

Education is at the heart of technological evolution. Revolutionary enthusiasm is displayed everywhere! We experience the "MOOC revolution", the "Learning revolution", the "flipped classroom revolution", the "mobile learning revolution", the "educational revolution" and since 2020, with pandemic crises COVID-19, the "digital education". Education is thus a privileged field for digital transformation. What would its characteristics be? Three adjectives constitute the main markers of the discourse on the digital revolution in education: the massive aspect, the free/open aspect and, finally, the distance/online aspect. Training courses of the MOOC type (massive open online courses) are in fact the model of the desired change and constitute an evolution of distance education within the framework of the technological possibilities offered by the Web. In the early 2000s, two events allowed the development of the "open/free" aspect. This is MIT's decision to offer its courses in open access with the Open course ware platform available (open and free). At the same time, Lessig (2001) developed the Creative Commons (CC) system to combat copyright legislation that blocked the development of digital creation. It is from there that we witness the movement of free education with the universal availability of educational resources. The first UNESCO forum on open educational resources was created in 2002 and the need for universal access to quality education and open educational resources was asserted. The Paris Declaration (UNESCO 2012) reaffirms the importance of free software for education and goes hand in hand with the idea that the Web is the place for creativity, sharing and collaboration. Lessig (2001) shows that the global architecture of the Web was initially thought to avoid any central control and to connect each machine in an open and unlimited way.

Siemens (2004) proposes a new approach to learning that he calls connectivism (see also Downes (2012): learning is chaotic, it is continuous, it is complex, it consists of making connections between information, one does not seek certainties, in short, learning is a co-creation from a collective intelligence. Creativity can only develop if the code and the learning environment remains open and free. This approach is opposed to the traditional training that gives the teacher a dominant position in the transmission of knowledge. We understand that this learning can only be participatory and horizontal, not centralized, Lessig (2001). Resources are unlimited and available. Everyone can be creators of new resources, the result of sharing and collaboration, knowing that it is always a matter of co-creation. Creativity in this context consists of reusing, transforming, modifying, combining, redistributing intellectual and artistic productions. The consequence for everyone, to use Lessig (2001), is being able to move from a consumer's life to a creator's life. We have somehow rediscovered the new pedagogies of the early 20th century.

Digital Environments and Language Learning

This last part concerns more specifically the didactics of languages and in particular how digital technology would have made it possible to revolutionize its methodology. Under what conditions can we say that digital evolution leads to an educational revolution? The aforementioned characteristics that define the Web: the multiple and massive relationship that transforms any individual into an actor connected to an infinity of other connected actors. This first aspect constitutes a new reality for learning, that of the always connected learning actor (Nobre, 2021). The second element refers to the idea of creativity Lessig (2001), which is at the heart of the Web. The connected learning actor learned to create collaboratively, that is, to reuse, modify, transform a resource and publish the new creation. Many applications work this way and are used massively and continuously by connected learning actors. It is important to add a third feature that concerns the content shared on the Web. The digitization of contents has, in fact, made it possible to transform the classical written form into a multimodal form whose meaning is the result of the different methods used (writing, video, music, drawing, etc.). We are moving from the classic (multi)literacy of language teaching (the written text) to a multimodal digital text. This multimodal social semiotics takes us on the one hand to Halliday (1978), who described the symbolic capacity to signify in social relations, and on the other to Kress and Leeuwen (2001) for whom canvases offer multimodal universes. The question of meaning that emerges from multimodal messages becomes, therefore, essential for learning. In this way, we become both writer and reader of multimodal texts that we constantly exchange and recompose. The choices made are not left to chance. They contribute to the power of significance of the proposed message. Siemens (2004) and Downes (2012) thus propose a new learning approach.

As we have already mentioned, three approaches currently coexist in language teaching: the traditional approach based on linguistic content and the mastery of classical literacy, the task-based approach, based on Common European Framework of Reference for Languages (2001), that is, situations of everyday life and pluriliteracy and the third approach in tune with the digital, both socioconstructivist and connectivism, taking into account the multimodal specificity of digital content. These three approaches do not succeed each other but are present in face-to-face and digital contexts.

The teaching and learning of foreign languages in digital environments must therefore implement the third approach. In addition to linguistic boundaries, the issue of multilingualism must also be addressed as proposed by the second approach to didactics. In short, the connected learning actor, plurilingualism and multimodal digital literacy (Lebrun & al., 2012) must constitute the new approach.

Digital and Educational Innovations?

Following what was mentioned above, we can ask ourselves what innovation is in digital and pedagogical terms. To do this, we must therefore think about inventing new digital tools and certainly also new practices. With that in mind, we would like to launch a reflection on what is now commonly called the digital transition.

The speed with which information has reached each individual in society makes it experience changes very quickly and tenaciously. Education, in particular, is led to absorb, almost in real time, the different demands and desires that emerge from different areas of knowledge.

Educational environments are responsible for forming critical and autonomous citizens, characteristics that are present in the daily life of today's society and are permeated by the use of Digital Information and Communication Technologies (TDIC) as an interaction and learning tool (Almeida et al., 2013). Thus, it is important that the school environment, in addition to providing conditions for teaching and learning, offers the student conditions to interact with colleagues and teachers, not only in person, but also in a virtual way, since learning does not only occur in the classroom, but also ubiquitous.

Foreign language classrooms, for example, are favourable environments for students to interact, not only with the people present there, but also with others from different locations. Social networks have contributed to the interaction and sharing of information and can also be used to assist in the teaching and learning of students.

At the pedagogical level, namely in the teaching and learning of a foreign language in a digital environment, the creation of a hybrid training involving situations of teaching and learning at a distance leads us to rethink the content and organization of this training (Charlier et al., 2006). It is impossible to escape the creation of new educational tools, namely to avoid falling into a simplistic transposition of a face-to-face course. It is, therefore, a matter of counting on the possibilities of the digital platform used and of imagining didactic paths. Thus, in French Foreign Language teaching, reflecting on the development of educational sequences and promoting autonomous learning, our path goes through a conceptualization of tools, activities and exercises that do not yet exist because that is what their transposition to the digital space requires. New tools, new devices and new teaching and learning practices thus become priorities and research objects in their own right.

Virtual social networks are considerable in everyone's everyday life, especially among students who are often easier to reach via Snapchat, WhatsApp or Facebook than through academic online channels (Setién, Nobre, & Chenoll, 2017). The study of social uses thanks to these new means of inter-individual communication constitutes in itself an important field in the field of digital humanities (Deouël & Granjon, 2011) and Didactics of Languages (Grassin, 2016) A student today benefits from permanent connectivity and there is no doubt that these new practices contribute to the construction of the social people and citizens of tomorrow (Martin, 2012).

The democratization of digital uses is linked to the development of commercial engineering of portals and/or applications for learning a foreign language (Nissen, 2011). Creating scripts for a foreign language teaching-learning course means entering the digital age of learning. Learning a foreign language means following a path, experiencing a series of sequences. In today's society, marked by the daily uses of digital mediation, mainly thanks to smartphones that make it possible to go beyond the ancestral and obsolete (albeit etymological) work/suffering association to walk towards learning/pleasure. It then becomes possible for the student to cross levels, score points, get bonuses as they progress along their learning path. The student born around the year 2000 having always known digital interfaces, it seems essential to take this parameter into account when thinking about the educational organizations of tomorrow. Self-training took a big turn in the 2000s (Barbot and Pugibet, 2002), in our opinion because it offers this adaptation device to the student, for example in terms of managing the pace of learning and its progression (Nobre 2018a). Therefore, the reflection is guided by certain specificities between the possibilities of this increasingly present digital mediation and the issues present in the learning of a foreign language (ibid).

SOME DIGITAL LANGUAGE LEARNING ENVIRONMENTS

We are at the center of technological evolution. Let's look more specifically at some digital technologies for language teaching/learning, which should bring learners together and facilitate the modes of interaction characteristic of cyberculture. These new devices must offer a true pedagogical evolution and consider hybrid, interconnected and community aspects. Many types of digital environments are present on the web today: the flipped classroom, specialized platforms for language learning (like LiveMocha, Duolingo, BBC Learning English, etc.) and social networks.

Whatsapp

According to Nobre (2018b), social networks are Internet sites that promote interaction and communication between people from different social groups. It is noticeable that, through the use of technological tools and social networks, the teacher develops the role of mediator of teaching, since he will provide the necessary materials so that the desired activity can be developed. According to Souza (2015), it is up to the teacher to act as a verbal exchange partner in the virtual environment, so that students feel comfortable, without thinking they are being monitored.

In addition to the benefits already described, the use of social networks contributes to student autonomy. In this regard, Leandro and Weissheimer (2016) describe that collaborative autonomous learning can happen when French Language students interact through a Facebook group in a mixed learning environment, in which they can "debate issues, share information and materials and, thus, collaboratively build knowledge about the target language, while substantially increasing the degree of exposure to that language" (p. 127).

In this way, it is clear that stimulating students' autonomy and motivating them so that they want to have contact with the foreign language not only during face-to-face classes, but also at other times, using existing digital resources present in the lives of these students, it is an essential part of the teaching and learning process. For example, in the activity proposed in this work, which aims to work on students' orality and writing using the WhatsApp tool.

WhatsApp allows "[...] to share with people, individually or through groups, multimedia and textual resources instantly, as well as recording audio and, [...] making voice calls" (Costa and Lopes, 2015, p. 47-48). Such a tool can be used through the use of cell phones, tablets and also personal computers (using its own application or browsers present on the computer).

It is important to note that the pedagogical use of WhatsApp is not new. In a quick search in the Google database, it is possible to identify some successful experiences pointed out by Kaieski, Grings and Fetter (2015), such as the one by Rambe and Bere (2013) in South Africa; Plana, Hopkins, Gimeno and Appel (2013) in Spain and Mudliar and Rangaswamy (2015) in India that establish a dialogue between education and the use of this tool.

WhatsApp groups provide a digital environment for fostering dialogue and interaction, so that students can clarify their doubts and queries outside the classroom - a situation that richly favours the learning condition of the actors involved, not just limited to to the student. Nevertheless, it is possible to verify that, initially, WhatsApp was not created with the purpose of meeting the demands of education or teaching, but this tool proved to be very useful in various educational contexts. The examples range from the simple sharing of content, to the inverted classroom with the protagonism of the students.

Based on this scenario, using the WhatsApp communication tool, we worked on "les verbes auxiliaries". So, every day, the teacher asked questions like *"Qu'est-ce que vous ne voulez pas faire aujourd'hui? Est-ce que vous savez cuisiner? Est-ce que vous aimez apprendre le français?* and students had to respond both orally and in writing. For this, the objectives are: to analyze the orality and written production of students from an activity of "Verbes Auxiliaires" on WhatsApp; as well as evaluating the pronunciation in French of these students.

By pointing to the analysis of orality as one of the objectives of this work, it is important to emphasize that orality is the transmission of information through speech, which can be transmitted spontaneously, through everyday conversations, or in the form of reproduction of a written text.

According to Kaieski, Grings and Feer (2015, p. 04) "one of the great financial advantages of WhatsApp is its cost, as sending messages is free, requiring only an internet connection to enable sending messages and making connections." In other words, the presence of a WIFI network and the use of mobile data from the cell phones themselves collaborates in the use of the tool, as it is with these forms of data distribution that it is possible to make use of WhatsApp for free.

In 2020 and 2021, during the two confinements due to the COVID-19 pandemic, schools closed, and WhatsApp was used in an emergency way to send classes, activities and communication with parents and guardians, representing, in many cases, the only tool for Communication.

Now, with the gradual return to classes in the face-to-face format, the idea is to enjoy and extract the best of each moment: if in person there is much easier interaction between teaching staff, employees and students than online, WhatsApp can to be used as a supplement to school.

Now and in the coming years, we will have to work on reducing the lag with personalization of teaching, which can be done with homework and school reinforcement with complementary content sent by WhatsApp. We have to use this tool not as a solution to a big problem, but as part of the teaching-learning process that can indeed help students to monitor their studies in this new stage of learning.

Mobile learning

For our work, we chose the definition authored by Agnes Kukulska-Hulme and Lesley Shield (2008) where mobile learning refers to learning mediated by portable devices and potentially available anytime and anywhere. This learning is formal or informal. These devices emphasize the continuity or spontaneity of access and the more immediate interaction that occurs in different contexts of use (ibid.). Likewise, Kukulska-Hulme (2009) finds that there is no fixed definition for mobile learning, on the one hand due to the rapid evolution of the field, on the other hand due to the ambiguity of the term mobile: it is the term related to technology or learner mobility? In recent years, the focus has been on the student and the intersection of formal and informal learning. In particular, informal aspects of learning are emphasized. Basically, there is always the same idea of the learner's active role and of how he can better personalize and adapt his learning (see chap. 2.2). According to Kukulska-Hulme (2009: 160), the effects of mobility can include new ways of sharing time and crossing borders. With the right technology, mobile learners can participate in activities that directly relate to their ever-changing locations and learning can take place, for example, during their daily travels (ibid.). Students can direct their own teaching (Haelewyck 2014: 18). Often, mobile apps allow you to repeat the same exercise an unlimited number of times. Thus, the student can train on his weaker skills that require more practice (ibid.)

However, when mobile technology advances, the performance of mobile devices is considered sufficient for language learning purposes and compared to more traditional methods, mobile technology offers different ways of learning. For those who prefer speech, voice recognition can be a better way to learn than writing or typing. Because all foreign language teachers have already evidenced students who are inhibited from speaking in the classroom, are ashamed to practice production orally before other people (Nobre and Martin-Fernandes 2018).

In this work, we focus on smartphones, which are mobile phones equipped with a touchscreen that allows access to the Internet. The first smartphones already existed in the late 90s, but they were extremely expensive, and had very few features compared to current phones. The launch of the iPhone in June 2007 on the commercial market made the smartphone concept familiar to everyone (Reed 2010). A decade later, they are increasingly a part of our daily lives. Despite their cost and thanks to the new communication and connectivity options they offer, in many communities' smartphones have become essential items (Godwin-Jones 2017). That's why we wanted to develop an experiment to study the use of smartphones in language learning and their functioning as learning tools.

Duolingo

The idea was to test the usability and functioning of the Duolingo application. We asked to 16 adult students on a vocational training course to test the app for at least 15 minutes a day during the months of October and November 2021. There were no time limits and therefore participants could exceed this time if they wanted to use the app longer. The apps are partially paid, but participants were asked to use only the free versions. The experience was unsupervised due to its mobile nature, participants were allowed to use the apps at their convenience.

Duolingo seems to be the most studied and probably the best known app on the market. Thus, it is not surprising that the application was already familiar by name to some participants and others had already used it. Overall, participants found Duolingo easy to use and its structure and categories clear. According to the responses, it was also easy to track your own progress and the app gave a lot of feedback. One of Duolingo's main merits was the look and feel that participants commented positively on:

R1. Nice with lots of colours, so motivating.
R2. I like the look of Duolingo, the sound effects and the various exercises are fun.
R3. The set is reasonably constructed, functional categories, visually stimulating.
R4. I liked the look, it was motivating.
R5. The appearance was very motivating and clear! The graphics are of good quality. R6. App appearance is very colourful and there were many animated effects.

Duolingo works on the experience point system and there are classes with a series of exercises (translation, writing, listening, pronunciation). The learner must choose a daily objective as soon as the application is opened (4 options) and the level to study the basic level and the more advanced level, accompanied by a diagnostic assessment at will. To motivate the user, Duolingo sends email notifications to remind the user to practice. One of the students replied that he returned to using the app because of this.

Furthermore, Duolingo frames learning with constant progress monitoring, which is quite effective according to one of the students: After completing an exercise, the app reports my level in the game at that moment, which made me play longer. (R9)

However, some participants feel that parts of Duolingo are missing, such as correct word definitions or verb conjugations. Duolingo does not have a section for grammar and according to R10 it can be demanding if there is no linguistic knowledge. R8 and R11 wish there was a section to check verb conjugations. Also, according to R7, the opportunity to practice pronunciation is both an advantage and a disadvantage: If you train at home, it's a nice option, but if you're from somewhere else, you won't want to use it. Practicing pronunciation aloud with application when surrounded by others can feel awkward, as Kukulska-Hulme (2012) has noted.

In addition, Duolingo offers shortcuts with which the student can progress more quickly in the most demanding topics and exercises. It is also possible to retake the course when desired. Admittedly, this autonomy-friendly feature isn't unique to Duolingo, but in this app shortcuts are more consistently integrated. While these shortcuts exist, progress in the application was not optimal according to some participants. R13 thinks that the language learned is repeated too much and thinks that the same words and themes are addressed too often. She found it sad that she couldn't pick the points she wanted to review herself. R14 also found that the exercises were repetitive, and it would be better to advance more with vocabulary. These examples show that Duolingo doesn't work perfectly in the autonomy category, as it doesn't offer enough freedom in the choice of exercises to improve the learning itself.

We believe that the coverage of digital media, the scripting of training, as well as the technological organization of a platform can make it possible to respond in a precise and relevant way to this need for flexibility. It should be noted in passing that the implementation of a digital device could constitute an equally relevant complement to face-to-face education, justifying the necessary hybridization of training and offering a possible way of considering the existing heterogeneity in the classroom (especially in an educational institution that receives several hundred students per semester from dozens of different countries).

As we see here, this constant need to invent, to innovate, both in digital practices and at a pedagogical level, invites us to think about didactic innovation. The lines of thought are conditioned by the organization and fluidity of the constitution of an individual program adapted to a specific learner, which includes a number of exercises and activities sufficient to respond to different possible scenarios: it will no longer be necessary to spend time training to work on perception, the other will be able to spend more on repetition exercises with an integrated self-learning option. In addition, the reinvestment of these essential mechanical training will also have to find its place in authentic online conversation activities, which implies, for the teacher, thinking of a synchronous conversation methodology to put what has been learned into practice, oral comprehension and production.

CONCLUSION

The framework of competences for teachers, produced by UNESCO (2012), allows us to understand the path to be followed for a real consideration of cyberculture and social semiotics. We can say that some "digital activists" are still at level 1 of digital literacy that consists of integrating digital into teaching and whose skills are mainly related to transliteration. The UNESCO reference system offers a level 2 that proposes to advance towards a teaching centered on the collaborative resolution of complex tasks. In this case, it is about knowing how to manage information and understand the media, using open digital artifacts to carry out projects. Finally, the final target, level 3 (knowledge creation), highlights skills such as "the ability to solve problems, communicate, work collaboratively, experiment, exercise critical thinking and show creativity". The school becomes a learning and inclusive organization. We saw, during the two confinements in 2020 and 2021 due to the COVID-19 pandemic, with the example of "collaborative" Whatsapp, that it is possible, in an institutional environment, to glimpse the citizen utopia of an inclusive learning society.

In the Whatsapp digital environment, based on the collected data, in a first analysis we saw that most students participated in the activities, totaling 99% of the participants. Even though the students did not perform all the commands requested by the teacher, they were able to progress in learning a foreign language.

The objectives of the study, which consisted of analyzing the orality and written production of students from an activity on WhatsApp, were achieved, since it was possible to analyze both the oral and written production of these students, when participating in the proposal carried out in the WhatsApp application in the extracurricular period.

It was noticed that when the contents are worked on in a practical way, using current and easily accessible tools, to which students are exposed daily, they are able to acquire knowledge in order to use it properly in the long term. Thus, in this activity, the student was able to present his interpretation of the pronunciation of words in the foreign language, and, in addition, understand the speech of the colleague. As a result of this, the student was able to make the appropriate comment according to the audios posted in the application, thus practicing their oral production skills (by recording their own audio), oral comprehension (by listening to the audios of their colleagues), written production (when writing comments about colleagues' audio) and written comprehension (when reading comments written by colleagues).

We observed that digital activities tend to have positive effects, since they involve technologies present in the students' lives, which works as a motivating factor for them during the activities.

However, it would be naive to believe that educational organizations and the teaching community are willing to move in such a revolutionary and demanding direction.

Digital transformation deserves more than a simple enchantment to make us believe in the benefits of all digital. The arts industry, that of new digital technologies, is causing significant changes in our view of culture. We could see, taking as an example the digital language learning environment Duolingo, that technological change leads to social and educational improvements, however, these digital devices do not change the didactic approach much, the traditional cognitive-behavioural approach remains mostly. Already in 2016, Grégoire said more generally that pedagogy has not changed. Economic and technological imperatives point to the strengthening of the traditional approach to education. Collaborative and connectivism learning implies the possibility of using and transforming the resources available on the Web. However, these become the property of private companies, consortia that claim rights over resources and data. Many free apps, which allow for creativity, are turned into paid private apps in the form of a premium offer. Collaborative learning is therefore kept to a minimum. We went from a school, university as closed spaces, to an unlimited virtual space.

Digital technology is quickly emerging as a means of revolutionizing human communication and cognition, which affects the way people interact, access and share information. In the past, the invention of printing had to await the completion of the Industrial Revolution. In contrast, today, digital technology is developing simultaneously with the communicational process and globalization, thus ensuring a much faster impact on communication practices, literacy, literacy. Thus, new knowledge production models need to be re-signified, along with the distribution of materials, multimodal resources, construction of interactive environments and a better understanding of the concept of technology and literacy within the teaching and learning process.

Integrating digital tools into pedagogy requires devising alternatives from a wide variety of options regarding theory and practice to produce meaningful learning environments. Digital technologies are a reality and language teachers need to face them head on in the 21st century.

Education is interactional in the sense that teachers and students interact dynamically, with teachers mediating students who are at different levels of learning. Furthermore, it should be noted that while some technologies simply replace an existing task or activity with an automated version, others require teachers to change the way they interact with students, how they select and use teaching resources, and occasionally reconceptualize their roles and obligations as teachers.

Transforming and developing Education does not mean being fully digital.

The question of "what to convey?" arises, because knowledge is everywhere on the web. This is a fact. But we certainly defined the knowledge contained in books and libraries during the Renaissance without sufficiently think in the human factor. It is necessary to get out of this knowledge to avoid continually writing books about books. This is a path that the digital humanities can explore, just as they can question human digital interactions. This work of ours is only a partial exploration of digital learning environments for teaching and learning foreign languages. The analysis has been reduced to two examples which constitute a particularly significant input. Our journey through digital environments was based on contextualizing (conducting concrete experiences and analysing experiences), decontextualizing (generalization and conceptualization) and then recontextualizing (experimentation and application through exercises). Of course, it would be interesting to take another path analysing digital exchanges and interactions.

In this article, we seek to highlight a certain number of elements to propose an approach to pedagogical adaptation via digital technology in language teaching, questioning concepts that seem fundamental to us. Digital technologies have potential (collaboration, cooperation, communication, inventiveness, etc.), but pedagogy must change first. The issue of the digital transition seems to us above all unavoidable and deserves in itself to re-examine the teaching and learning of foreign languages in general, French as a foreign language in particular, at the didactic and pedagogical level.

Innovating in this area involves innovative proposals, both in substance and in form, to finally achieve the objectives established by the various curricula. Considering the digital uses of current and future students, it is essential to reflect the evolution of these social, linguistic and technological practices to design innovative activities in digital environments. Today, mobile learners may not move geographically, but thanks to digital mediation, they benefit from virtual mobility (Nobre, 2020). The teaching and learning of a foreign language require a particular reflection regarding its transposition in the context of a digital interface, in a remote and independent way.

Digital Humanities in Education constitute a space for interdisciplinary dialogue on changes linked to digital, in the construction and dissemination of knowledge, for an active educational community, with a collaborative, critical, reflective approach, production of tools, methods or resources.

Therefore, we think that in the future, in this post-pandemic world, we must:

- Make better use of spaces and times to teach and learn;
- Rethink the models of transmission of knowledge and skills;
- Involve students;
- Reverse roles and ensure that students are teachers too.

REFERENCES

Almeida, R., Bueno, T., & Gimenez, T. (2013). O uso das tecnologias de informação e comunicação para aprendizagem colaborativa: percepções de alunos e professores do ensino médio de uma escola pública de Londrina. In *Denise Ismênia Bossa Grassano Ortenzi, Kleber, Aparecido da Silva, Luciana Cabrini Simões Calvo et al. (Orgs.). Re exões sobre ensino de línguas e formação de professores no Brasil: uma homenagem à professora Thelma Gimenez* [The use of information and communication technologies for collaborative learning: perceptions of high school students and teachers at a public school in Londrina. In Denise Ismênia Bossa Grassano Ortenzi, Kleber, Aparecido da Silva, Luciana Cabrini Simões Calvo et al. (Org.). *Reactions on language teaching and teacher education in Brazil: a tribute to Professor Thelma Gimenez]*, (pp. 389–410). Pontes.

Barbot, M. J., Pugibet, V. (2002). *Apprentissages des langues et technologies: usages en émergence.* Paris: Clé International. Berdal-Masuy, F., Briet, G. & Pairon, J. (2004). Apprendre seul, à son rythme et encadré. *Études de linguistique appliquée* [Learning languages and technologies: emerging uses. Paris: Key International. Berdal-Masuy, F., Briet, G. & Pairon, J. (2004). Learn alone, at your own pace and supervised. Studies in Applied Linguistics], *134*(2), 173-190.

Chanier, T., & Vetter, A. (2006). *Multimodalité et expression en langue étrangère dans une plate-forme audio-synchrone* [Multimodality and foreign language expression in an audio-synchronous platform]. (Vol. 9). Alsic.

Charliet, B., Deschryver, N., Peraya, D. (2006). Apprendre en présence et à distance: une définition des dispositifs hybrides. *Distances et savoirs* [Learning in the presence and at a distance: a definition of hybrid devices. Distances and knowledge], *4*(4), 469-496.

Costa, D., Lopes, J. (2015). *A perspectiva docente quanto ao uso do WhatsApp como ferramenta adicional ao ensino de inglês: um experimento em um curso livre de idiomas* [The teaching perspective regarding the use of WhatsApp as an additional tool for teaching English: an experiment in a free language course].

de l'Europe, C. (2001). *Cadre européen commun de référence en langues* [Common European Framework of Reference for Languages]]. Didier.

Deouël, J., & Granjon, F. (Eds.). (2011). *Communiquer à l'ère numérique. Regards croisés sur la sociologie des usages.* Presses des Mines. [Communicate in the digital age. Perspectives on the sociology of uses. Paris: Presses des Mines] doi:10.4000/books.pressesmines.387

Depover, C., De Lièvre, B., Peraya, D., Quintin, J., & Jaillet, A. (2011). *Le tutorat en formation à distance* [Distance education tutoring. Louvain-la-Neuve, Belgium] De Boeck Supérieurdoi:10.3917/dbu.depov.2011.01

Downes, S. (2012). Connectivism and Connective Knowledge: essays on meaning and learning networks. *Stephen Downes Web.* https://www.downes.ca/post/58207

Godwin-Jones, R. (2017). Smartphones and language learning. *Language Learning & Technology, 21*(2), 3–17. 10125/44607

Grassin, J.-F. (2016). Échanges en ligne sur un réseau social dans le cadre d'une formation en Français Langue Étrangère: pratiques discursives et modes de participation [Online exchanges on a social network as part of a French as a Foreign Language course: discursive practices and modes of participation]. In Liénard, F. & Zlitni, S. (éd.), Médias numériques et communication électronique, Actes de colloque, Bruges, 295-303.

Grégoire, R. (2016). *Cours en ligne ouverts et massifs: état des lieux et adoption au Canada français. Guide et bilan de l'impact des cours en ligne ouverts et massifs (CLOM) au Canada francophone* [Open and massive online courses: inventory and adoption in French Canada. Guide and assessment of the impact of open and massive online courses (OLOC) in French-speaking Canada]. REFAD.

Habermas, J. (1987). *Théorie de l'agir communicationnel* [[Communication action theory]]. Fayard.

Haelewyck, S. (2014). *L'acquisition du français à l'usage d'applications mobiles: un état de question.* (Mémoire de Master). Université de Gent. [*The acquisition of French for the use of mobile applications: a state of question.* [Master memory, University of Gent]

Halliday, M. (1993). Towards a language-based theory of learning. *Linguistics and Education, 5*(2), 93–116. doi:10.1016/0898-5898(93)90026-7

Huver, E., & Springer, C. (2011). *L'évaluation en langues* [Language assessment]. Didier.

Kaieski, N., Grings, J. A., & Fetter, S. A. (2015). Um Estudo Sobre as Possibilidades Pedagógicas de Utilização do WhatsApp. *Renote - Novas Tecnologias na Educação* [A Study on the Pedagogical Possibilities of Using WhatsApp. Renote - New Technologies in Education], *13*(2), 1–10.

Kress, G. (2009). *Multimodality: A Social Semiotic Approach to Contemporary Communication.* Routledge. doi:10.4324/9780203970034

Kress, G., & Van Leeuwen, T. (2001). *Multimodal discourse: The modes and media of contemporary communication.* Edward Arnold.

Kukulska-Hulme, A. (2009). Will mobile learning change language learning? *ReCALL, 21*(2), 157–165. doi:10.1017/S0958344009000202

Kukulska-Hulme, A. (2012). Mobile-Assisted Language Learning. In *C. A. Chapelle (dir.), The Encyclopedia of Applied Linguistics.* Blackwell Publishing. doi:10.1002/9781405198431.wbeal0768

Kukulska-Hulme, A., & Shield, L. (2008). An overview of mobile assisted language learning: From content delivery to supported collaboration and interaction. *ReCALL, 20*(3), 271–289. doi:10.1017/S0958344008000335

Leandro, D., & Weissheimer, J. (2016). Facebook e aprendizagem híbrida de inglês na universidade. In *Júlio Araújo & Vilson Le a (Orgs.). Redes sociais e ensino de línguas: O que temos de aprender?* [Facebook and hybrid English learning at university. In Júlio Araújo & Vilson Le a (Orgs.). *Social networks and language teaching: What do we have to learn?*]. Parábola Editorial.

Lebrun, M., Lacelle, N., Boutin, J.F. (2012). *La littératie médiatique multimodale De nouvelles approches en lecture-écriture à l'école et hors de l'école.* Presses de l'université du Québec. [Multimodal Media Literacy New approaches to reading-writing in and out of school. Press of the University of Quebec.]

Lessig, L. (2001). *The Future of Ideas–The fate of the commons in a connected world*. Random H House.

Lévy, P. (1997). *L'intelligence collective: pour une anthropologie du cyberspace* [[Collective intelligence: for an anthropology of cyberspace.]]. Ed. La Découverte.

Longuet, F. (2016). Former des enseignants par le biais d'environnements d'apprentissage numérique multimodaux [Train teachers through multimodal digital learning environments]. In Revue de Recherches en LMM (r2lmm.ca), vol. 3.

Mangenot, F., & Soubrié, T. (2014). *Le web social au service de tâches d'écriture* [The social web at the service of writing tasks]. Recherches.

Marquillo Larruy, M. (2012). «Littératie et multimodalité ici & là-bas... [Literacy and multimodality here & there]». *Recherches en didactique des langues et des cultures: Les Cahiers de l'Acedle*, n° 9 (2): 47- 84.

Martin, G. (2012). Les amis de vos amis sont-ils vos amis ? *Idées économiques et sociales* [Are your friends' friends your friends? Economic and social ideas], 169(3), 1-1. Doi:10.3917/idee.169.0001

Moore, D., & Coste, D. (2006). *Plurilinguismes et école* [[Plurilingualism and school]]. Didier.

Mudliar, P., & Rangaswamy, N. (2015). Offline Strangers, Online Friends: Bridging Classroom Gender Segregation With Whatsapp. In *Conference on Human Factors in Computing Systems - Proceedings* (Vol. 2015-April, p. 3799– 3808). 10.1145/2702123.2702533

Nissen, E. (2011). Variations autour de la tâche dans l'enseignement / apprentissage des langues aujourd'hui [Variations around the task in language teaching/learning today]. *Alsic*, *14*(Vol. 14). Advance online publication. doi:10.4000/alsic.2344

Nobre, A. (2018a). Multimedia Technologies and Online Task-Based Foreign Language Teaching-Learning. *Tuning Journal for Higher Education*, *5*(2), 75–97. doi:10.18543/tjhe-5(2)-2018pp75-97

Nobre, A. (2020). *The Pedagogy That Makes the Students Act Collaboratively and Open Educational Practices* in Personalization and Collaboration in Adaptive E-Learning. IGI_Global. Doi:10.4018/978-1-7998-1492-4.ch002

Nobre, A. (2021). Educational Practices Resulting From Digital Intelligence in Handbook of Research on Teaching With Virtual Environments and AI. IGI_Global. Doi:10.4018/978-1-7998-7638-0.ch003

Nobre, A., & Martin-Fernandes, I. (2018b). «Pratiques pédagogiques de mobile-learninget FLE: une étude de cas [Pedagogical practices of mobile-learning and FLE: a case study]». Thélème. Revista Complutense de Estudios Franceses, Vol. 33. *Núm.*, *2*, 195–211.

Peraya, D., Bonfils, P. (2014). Détournements d'usages et nouvelles pratiques numériques: l'expérience des étudiants d'Ingémédia à l'Université de Toulon [Diversion of uses and new digital practices: the experience of Ingémédia students at the University of Toulon]. *Revue des sciences et techniques de l'information et de la communication pour l'éducation et la formation*, 21. Doi:10.3406/stice.2014.1098

Plana, M. G., Hopkins, J. E., Gimeno, A., & Appel, C. (2013). Improving Learners Reading Skills Through Instant Short Messages: A Sample Study Using WhatsApp. In *IV World CALL Conference* (p. 10–13).

Rambe, P., & Bere, A. (2013). Using Mobile Instant Messaging to Leverage Learner Participation and Transform, Pedagogy at a South African University of Technology. *British Journal of Educational Technology*, *44*(4), 544–561. doi:10.1111/bjet.12057

Reed, B. (2010, 23.09). *A brief history of smartphones*. Blog Post.

Sabatier, C., Moore, D., & Dagenais, D. (2013). Espaces urbains, compétences littératiées multimodales, identités citoyennes en immersion française au Canada [Urban spaces, multimodal literacy skills, civic identities in French immersion in Canada]. *Glottopol*, *21*, 138–161.

Setién, A., Nobre, A., Chenoll, A. (2017). El proceso de enseñanza-aprendizaje en contextos ubicuos y universitarios.Tres estudios de casos Virtualidad, Educación y Ciencia [The teaching-learning process in ubiquitous and university contexts. Three case studies Virtuality, Education and Science], *14* (8), pp. 123-135.

Siemens, G. (2004). Connectivism: A learning theory for the digital age. http://www.ingedewaard.net/papers/connectivism/2005_siemens_ALearningTheoryForThe DigitalAge.pd

Souza, C. (2015). Aprendizagem sem distância: tecnologia digital móvel no ensino de língua inglesa. In *Texto Livre*. Linguagem e Tecnologia. [Learning without distance: mobile digital technology in English language teaching. In Free Text: Language and Technology] doi:10.17851/1983-3652.8.1.39-50

Tardy, M. (1966). *Le professeur et les images* [The teacher and the pictures]. PUF.

Thomas, S. (2007). "Transliteracy: Crossing divides". Web. October 2015.

UNESCO. 2012. *TIC UNESCO: Un référentiel de compétences pour les enseignants* [UNESCO ICT: A competency framework for teachers]. Paris. https://unesdoc.unesco.org/images/0021/002169/216910f.pdf

Warschauer, M., & Kern, R. (2000). *Network-based language teaching: Concepts and practice*. Cambridge University Press. doi:10.1017/CBO9781139524735

Wenger, E. (2005). *La théorie des communautés de pratique. Apprentissage, sens et identité* [The theory of communities of practice. Learning, meaning and identity]. Les Presses de l'université Laval.

Chapter 8
The Revolution in Integrating Virtual Reality in E–Learning

Raja M.

Department of Multimedia, Vellore Institute of Technology, Vellore, India

Lakshmi Priya G. G.

Department of Multimedia, Vellore Institute of Technology, Vellore, India

ABSTRACT

The virtual reality (VR) concept has been in existence for more than half-a-century. This technology's growth has been predominant recently because of the availability of plenty of technological solutions that support VR content. Coronavirus (COVID-19), a virus outbreak, has taken the whole world to an unexpected critical phase where social distancing is an inevitable part of life. Notably, the education sector faces a huge challenge, and VR technology has become the need of the hour during this pandemic as most learning takes place in virtual mode. VR equipment and software applications were highly priced at one point. Still, the present scenario is entirely different, with plenty of hardware and software resources available at affordable pricing. This study aims to identify the benefits, needs, and opportunities open for virtual reality-enabled e-learning and offer a generic methodological framework for efficiently implementing VR in e-learning. Analysis of this study indicates that VR technologies have rebooted their presence in the education.

1. INTRODUCTION

Virtual reality is a scenario where the simulation is very close enough to the real-world situation, which suspends the users' beliefs by immersing them in the simulated environment. This technology's vast applications include games, education, construction/architectural visualizations, military training, medical training, etc. This COVID-19 pandemic has pushed the world to adopt computer-based communication tools to help learners continue their studies wherever they are. Despite engaging the students with multimedia tools like PowerPoint presentations, videos, graphics content, games for learning, etc., students still get less time or almost no time to interact with the teachers remotely through the learning manage-

DOI: 10.4018/978-1-6684-6682-7.ch008

ment systems. Recent studies show that the use of VR in education has shown increased effectiveness in the teaching-learning process.

Virtual reality concepts and applications can help support online education, like how it supports brick-and-mortar education. The concepts of VR discussed in this paper will effectively help overcome the online teaching-learning process. For this purpose, the researchers have worked together to identify and propose a new architecture for e-learning with VR by modifying the existing generic architecture for e-learning. Figure 1 shows the most straightforward architecture widely followed for remote teaching-learning. Not all e-learning courses are the same; they differ based on the syllabus and learner cohort. Corresponding to the course's weightage, content depth, and delivery styles, e-learning architecture is categorized as receptive, directive, and guided discovery (Clark, 2005).

Figure 1. E-learning Architecture

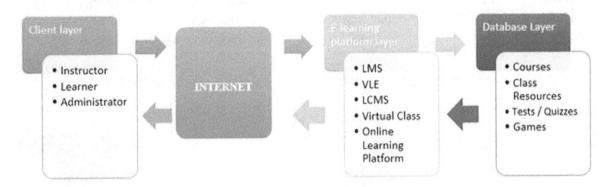

There is a significant increase in learning digitally through online mode, which is different from the usual learning methods that mostly use text alone (Parong & Mayer, 2018). Especially during the pandemic times, online education is the only alternative to regular studies. As juxtaposed in Table 1, a total of 1,091,439,976 learners were affected by COVID-19 school closure, which is 62.3% of the total enrolled users from 123 countries.

The projected data clearly shows a definite need for online education with a more robust capacity that would not be lower than regular instruction standards. Figure 2 highlights this alarming issue's importance, as the global pandemic has been widespread for about four months.

It is vital to understand that preparing ourselves for a virtual learning space opens international doors for teaching and learning. This new normal of education is a big challenge for all educational institutions across the globe as it forces them to shift from offline to online mode (Dhawan, 2020). VR offers a wide range of benefits when used offline or online; understanding VR's benefits is the first step in using this technology in a virtual classroom.

Table 1. Schools Closure – Global Data

Date	Affected Learners	% of Enrolled Learners	No. of Countries
As on 16/02/2020	999,014	0.1%	1
As on 16/03/2020	770,882,424	44%	110
As on 16/04/2020	1,576,873,546	90.1%	190
As on 16/05/2020	1,218,486,850	69.6%	159
As on 16/06/2020	1,091,439,976	62.3%	123

2. VIRTUAL REALITY NI EDUCATION

Education is one of the most affected domains in any pandemic situation, directly impacting every country's future generation. Providing online learning is considered the highest priority for any educational institute, whether preschool, primary school, secondary/senior secondary school, college, or university.

Figure 2. Global monitoring of schools closure (a) as of 16/02/2020; (b) as on 16/06/2020

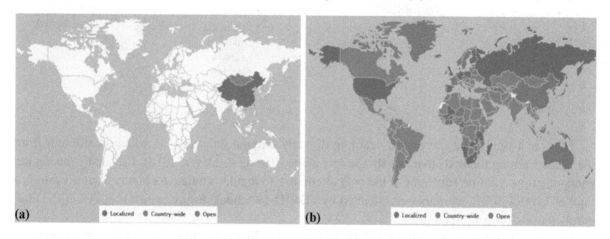

The biggest challenge in online education is student engagement. It is challenging to retain the student's attention span and concentration levels during an online session. Research shows that engaging content should be delivered in the first eight seconds to grab the students' attention in an online class. VR enhances the students' attention span (Cho et al., 2002) and offers several other benefits, as illustrated in Figure 3.

2.1 Creates Interests

The students' interest levels are high when they learn through VR than the traditional methods (Zhao et al., 2020). In a remote learning setup, the learner is the driver of the learning process and will decide on the pace at which the learning should take place. The interest in watching and learning is comparatively higher in a virtual environment than in a video or multimedia output. Understanding this novel reason should eradicate negative learning rates. An experiment conducted with the CAVE environment by (Bakr et al., 2018) shows that the participants were very interested, and their interest levels varied according to age.

2.2. Increases Students' Engagement and Curiosity

The younger generation seeks a comfortable learning environment that utilizes modern techniques to disseminate knowledge, making them curious to explore and increase engagement (Kamińska et al., 2019). This technology paves the way for the "learning by doing" concept that sharply increases users' participation because they can explore a new world that anybody would be curious to see.

2.3. Eliminates Language Barriers

Various content is available on the internet in different languages; people from other locations use their computers to access the courses. Google translate helps us translate text, signs, menus, etc., in more than thirty languages. Still, understanding the language is a barrier for some learners as they cannot cope with the translations because it doesn't precisely match their mother tongue or dialect. Learning through VR eliminates this barrier as it provides opportunities for learning to explore, experience, and learn rather than listening or reading (Solomon et al., 2019).

2.4. Promotes Experiential Learning

Experiential learning is considered one of the vital aspects of all learning paradigms. It emphasizes that the learner should experience and learn the content instead of the teacher forcing them to do it (Kolb & Kolb, 2012). To keep it simple, students get a chance to discover and obtain knowledge in a minimally guided learning atmosphere.

2.5. Facilitates Safer Experiments

Studies reveal that lab experiments are carried out to help achieve learning outcomes and be safe. Students often make mistakes when they practice lab experiments because they have limited chances to practice. Such incidents can be avoided by giving them a safer practice environment using VR because it enables them to practice safely and remember until they do some live experiments in physical labs. Specific lab experiments require teachers' strict supervision; failing may lead to mild or severe injuries. Classics like chemistry and medical training demand a safer lab environment to avoid trauma. Tailor-made applications for this purpose have reported higher satisfaction with no barriers to using the technology (Dunnagan et al., 2020).

2.6. Eliminates Distractions

VR comprises three basic ideas: immersion, interactivity, and imagination restricting the user from refining external distractions. In an online course, the learners are put before the computer screens, and minimal tasks keep them engaged. A student could be easily carried away by mobile phones, social networking applications, television, or the conversation around the surrounding. When the student is

Figure 3. Benefits of using VR in Education

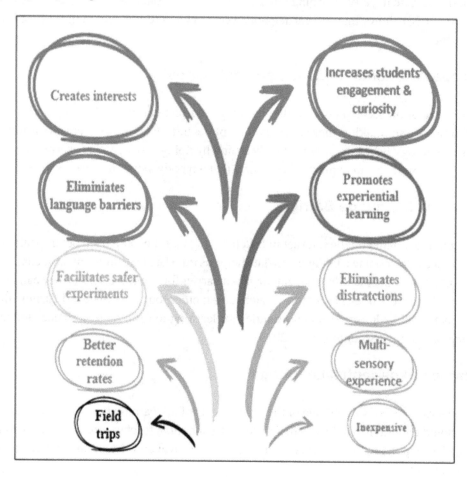

wearing a Head Mounted Display (HMD), it completely disconnects the user from the external world, thus providing a way to concentrate on the task entirely (Schrader & Bastiaens, 2012).

2.7. Better Retention Rates

Teachers adopt different delivery styles to cater to students' needs with varying learning abilities, where the retention rates differ from person to person. VR aims to make users feel their presence inside the virtual environment and feel "being there" (Cummings & Bailenson, 2016). The connection between presence in VR and retention or recall of a concept is secure, proved by the results of several pieces of research (Parong et al., 2020).

2.8. Multi-Sensory Experience

Even the first VR device, 'Sensorama', aimed to give a multi-sensory experience to the users, including sight, sound, smell, motion, and the force of the wind (Kim et al., 2013). The level of immersion increases if multiple senses are activated. Advanced VR applications combined with specific hardware offer a fully immersive experience by provoking the maximum human senses. A complete accident scene was brought in front of the user's eyes where they could hear the patients screaming and moaning; the facility to check their pulse rates with the help of haptic feedback was also given to increase the multi-sensory experience (Servotte et al., 2020). Simultaneously, these sensory elements should be handled swiftly by the users because over-immersion may lead to decreased quality of learning.

2.9. Fieldtrips

Field trips are essential and mandatory for specific courses. Even at the primary, secondary or tertiary levels of education, field trips play an important role in helping the students to conceptualize the learned theories and relate them to practical scenarios. In one of the experiments, the authors compared VR-based field trips with traditional ones, and the results demonstrated that the students using VR showcased high results with improved motivation (Bowen, 2018). Notably, taking the students on a field trip is impossible during pandemic times. Teachers can use VR's opportunity and choose the right application that syncs with their syllabus.

2.10. Inexpensive

Several Virtual Reality hardware is available at an affordable cost for the end-users. The development of applications for a particular task involving extensive travel or huge expenses can be tried by users across the Globe with VR applications that cut down the time spent and the costs incurred. One such application was developed and tested during a research study where the users could mobilize virtually to several places of their choice, which is inexpensive and practical.

3. NEED OF THE HOUR

The pandemic has pushed the entire world to a different scenario where virtualization plays a vital role. Amongst the safety measures to avoid this contagious virus, social distancing is one of the crucial suggestions given to the public (Anderson et al., 2020). The time frame for the students to return to their campuses is a million-dollar question. In such situations, educators will have to face many formidable challenges and issues, including offering lectures and conducting lab experiments, assessments, and evaluations. The education system is forced to embrace an e-learning methodology for which educators must prepare themselves to adapt to technological tools that act as a platform for distant learning. Unlike the traditional classroom setting, e-learning is the only platform through which students can learn and interact with teachers and/or students in different locations across boundaries (Dhawan, 2020). Compared to the generic e-learning methods, the VR component's addition has the highest potential to elevate the teaching-learning process. In any traditional teaching-learning setting, as highlighted by Hermann Ebbinghaus's forgetting curve, if a student's absorption rate is 100% on the first day, there will be loss of learning and retention as the days move on (Murre & Dros, 2015). Virtual Reality acts as a medium to challenge the learning curve by offering experiential learning with peculiar features like immersion and interaction (figure 4).

Figure 4. Visualization of Forgetting Curve with VR

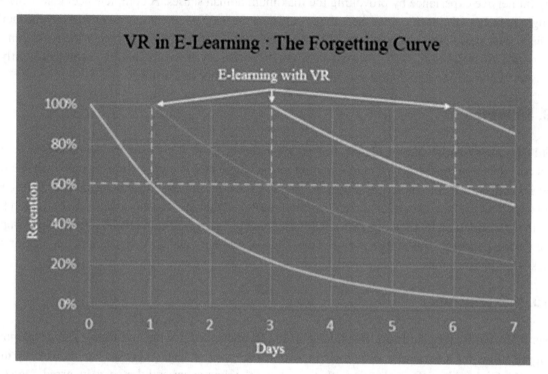

Research has already proven that immersion provides a real experience that enhances the learners' retention power (Parong et al., 2020), which in turn actively helps to break the forgetting curve. Compared to a traditional e-learning setting, when the integration of VR takes place as an additive component, teaching-learning goals can be achieved better.

4. OPPORTUNITIES

In contrast with the face-to-face teaching, in an e-learning environment, it is difficult to monitor the students and keep them engaged throughout the session. But, with the integration of VR into e-learning, it is possible to overcome the drawbacks to a greater extent and achieve our goals. A few essential educational goals and VR's support to achieve them are discussed in Table 2.

A comprehensive study from the Scopus database showed Virtual Reality technology's present state and integration into e-learning. As shown in Figure 5, The search shows that there are 2443 documents related to this topic within the 5+ years ranging from 2015 – 2019. Data shows that the research opportunities are widening year by year.

One important factor contributing to integrating VR into e-learning is creating the necessary materials for the teaching-learning process. According to the analysis, 27% of the research projects were funded, the remaining 73% are non-funded research, and country-wise segmentation shows that the United States of America tops the funding list.

The results highlight the importance of encouraging educators and researchers. The analysis also reveals that India's United States has the most research on Virtual Reality and E-learning. In contrast,

Table 2. Educational Goals and the Role of VR to achieve them

Goal	Description	Role of VR
Spaced Repetition	Reviewing information at a more significant time interval	Virtual worlds can be experienced as often as needed, thus resulting in a less steep forgetting curve.
Experiential Learning	Practicing or applying the learned skills through laboratory equipment, software, field trips, etc.,	Enables the users to interact naturally with materials in a realistic setting, thus providing useful and realistic experiences that can be achieved even with low-cost VR devices.
Enhance Retention	Information that is disseminated with an association with the student increases retention rates.	Virtual games and simulations foster an excellent learning platform that enables users to master the subject and remember what they experience.
Comprehensive Understanding	It is a more precise method of understanding the concepts, associated theories, and underlying insights.	VR labs are more robust to suit the e-learning architecture, enabling students to understand comprehensively.

India holds the 14th position in the chart (Figure 7). More funding support from the institution and other agencies would encourage researchers to develop feasible VR solutions for education.

The amount of research and development in VR denotes the need for this technology hour. Regarding research related to VR linked with education, countries like the USA and China are way ahead of all the other countries. Educational institutions must embrace this technology at the earliest to shift their standard to a global positioning by offering value-added education (figure 6).

Figure 5. Documents Published between 2015-2019

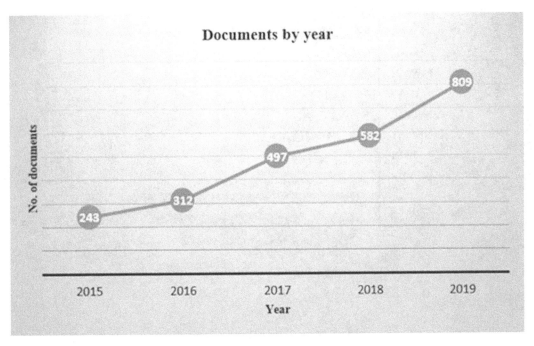

Figure 6. Funded Vs. Non-Funded Research

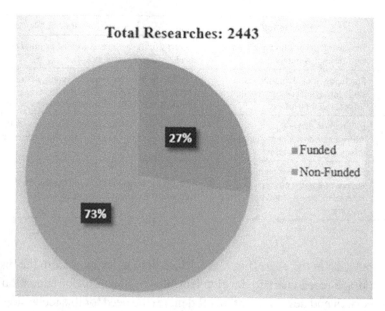

Figure 7. Country-wise Segmentation of Publications

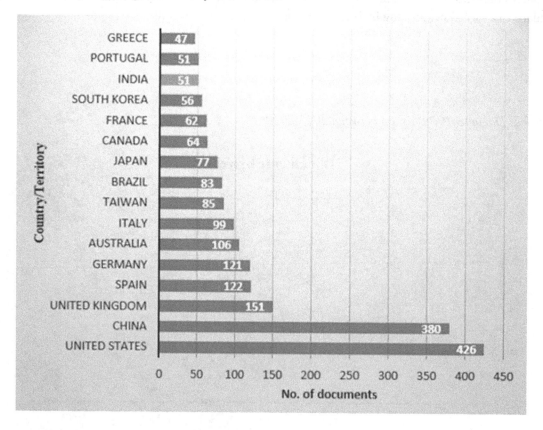

5. METHODOLOGICAL FRAMEWORK FOR IMPLEMENTING VR IN E-LEARNING

Technological readiness, content readiness, parental support, and institutional initiative are crucial in integrating VR into e-learning architecture. These four criteria are integrated into the client layer of existing e-learning architecture, as shown in Figure 8. It is also essential to define the methods of integrating the VR component into the e-learning architecture. This section proposes a methodological framework for implementing VR in e-learning.

5.1. Technological Readiness

Technology has always supported education when used wisely, and it helps promote students' critical thinking, thus contributing to the teaching-learning process (Saidin et al., 2015). Teachers must spend a predominant amount of time coping with technological advancements. Even if the technology is available easily, teachers' willingness to come forward and use it decides the implementation rate.

5.2. Content Readiness

Creating a 3-dimensional virtual application is not a cup of coffee for all educators. Essential training on using technology will help educators prepare themselves for the new normal. But, the availability of content is a challenge regarding VR applications because of the development costs involved in the projects. Most of it is not available for free. Even if the content is available, matching them to the curriculum and using them correctly is challenging. Virtual Reality can be infused into the curriculum design, and appropriate content can be made available for the required topics to overcome the material's lack of availability.

5.3. Parental Support

Technology supports a student in learning autonomously. VR applications designed for a specific purpose serve the uses by offering a safer learning environment, fostering an interactive space that responds in the form of feedback, and enhancing retention power (Phipps et al., 2002). Parental influence must be present to promote technological use at home as it is a vital parameter that encourages the kid to use technological devices for educational purposes. Motion sickness caused due to the prolonged use of VR HMDs (Olmos et al., 2018) is one of the parents' concerns that directly affect their kid's health. Secondly, the strain caused in the eyes or blurred vision due to close contact with the screen is also a concern. Parental education is a must to get support from them. A crucial step toward the plan is to give a good overview of the pros and cons of using a VR application and suggest using the technology without affecting their kid's health.

5.4. Institutional Initiative

In the early stages of introducing VR technologies, institutions were reluctant to adopt them because of the high costs involved. Now that the technology is available to everyone at an affordable price, embedding it in the curriculum is not a problem. Despite the few challenges, it is high time that institutions realize the importance of implementing VR into their curriculum (Abulrub et al., 2011). Fifteen million

Table 3. Instructional Design Approaches and the Role of VR to achieve them

Approach	Benefits	Role of VR
Receptive	o It helps to make an analogy of previous learnings o Enables faster problem-solving ability by enriching the focus on encoding information.	VR helps present the content more excitingly and responsively. A deeper understanding of the subject/topic happens using appropriate virtual platforms to support teaching-learning.
Directive	o This method supports the practical training of a concept that promotes long-term learning. o Supports higher learning outcomes by providing a platform to master the content.	VR tools make practical exercises more comfortable, safe, and affordable. Especially in e-learning, hands-on experience is the most critical challenge educators face.
Guided Discovery	o This method comes in place after infusing the necessary foundation using the other two techniques; it concentrates on real-world problems. o Domain-specific knowledge roots up in this phase.	Usually, this stage is executed in a regular classroom with field trips or industrial visits to expose students to real-world problems. With VR, it is possible to integrate a real functioning of any industry as an assignment or practical exercise.

educational users of VR technology are projected for 2025. The institute's initiative gives more autonomy and authority to educators to implement VR in their classes.

It is noticeable that online learning follows one or more of the following instructional design approaches (Clark, 2005):

- Receptive
- Directive
- Guided Discovery

Virtual Reality supports all three instructional designs on a satisfactory scale. Table 3 showcases the use of the different approaches, their benefits, and VR's role in helping them.

The proposed methodological framework highlights how VR is incorporated during the regular e-learning platform. Integration of VR can happen in one of the following ways:

- Flipped Classroom
- Regular E-learning
- Blended mode

5.5. Flipped Classroom

Several researchers have concluded that the flipped classroom methodology has a positive impact on the student's achievement levels. Integrating the flipped classroom methodology into e-learning yields fruitfulness in creating a better learning platform (Dhawan, 2020). Virtual reality content distributed to students before they attend the online classes helps foster a better understanding of the subject and advancement in learning (Xiao-Dong & Hong-Hui, 2020). The flipped classroom also paves the way for the receptive instructional design that fosters students to make an analogy of their previous learning.

Figure 8. A methodological framework for implementing VR in E-Learning

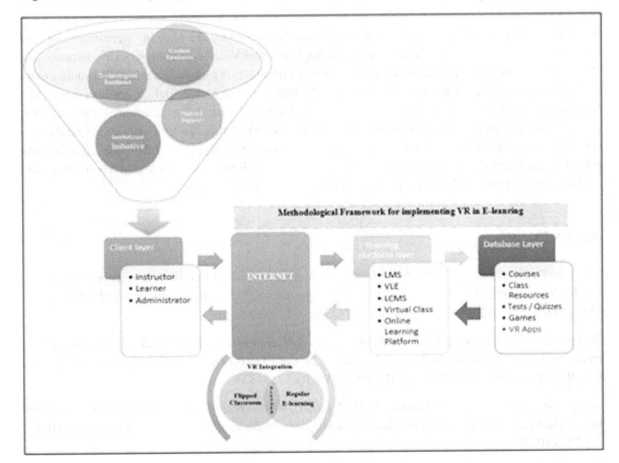

5.6. Regular E-Learning

Wherever possible, and there is a need, it is good to use VR for content that requires social interaction, which supports the directive instructional design. Learning occurs in a better setting when learners receive timely feedback on their work progress (Hattie & Timperley, 2007). Notably, in an e-learning setting, it is difficult for the instructor to control the class and direct them on step-by-step procedures. VR helps the learners by allowing them to rehearse even when the instructor is unavailable but still receive feedback on their progress.

5.7. Blended Mode

Sometimes it is an excellent choice to choose both the flipped classroom approach and regular e-learning. This choice is essential if the taught course or the topic is complicated or involves a guided discovery instructional approach that insists on real-world problems.

6. CONCLUSION

The benefits, needs, and opportunities open for Virtual Reality enabled e-learning were examined, and a feasible generic methodological framework for implementing VR in e-learning at ease was proposed. Pieces of literature reveal a definite need to implement Virtual Reality into e-learning. VR fosters a more in-depth understanding of the subject, eliminates the barrier of the non-availability of labs in a virtual learning space, aligns more precisely with the key instructional designs, and eliminates the forgetting curve. While insisting on the benefits of using VR in e-learning, this research also identified the factors that contribute to the successful implementation of this technology by embedding them into the e-learning architecture. In the future, a comprehensive study will be conducted to evaluate the proposed methodological framework for integrating VR into e-learning architecture.

REFERENCES

Abulrub, A. G., Attridge, A. N., & Williams, M. A. (2011). Virtual reality in engineering education: The future of creative learning. *2011 IEEE Global Engineering Education Conference (EDUCON)*, (pp. 751–757). IEEE. 10.1109/EDUCON.2011.5773223

Anderson, R. M., Heesterbeek, H., Klinkenberg, D., & Hollingsworth, T. D. (2020). How will country-based mitigation measures influence the course of the COVID-19 epidemic? *Lancet*, *395*(10228), 931–934. doi:10.1016/S0140-6736(20)30567-5 PMID:32164834

Bakr, A. F., El Sayad, Z. T., & Thomas, S. M. S. (2018). Virtual reality as a tool for children's participation in kindergarten design process. *Alexandria Engineering Journal*, *57*(4), 3851–3861. doi:10.1016/j.aej.2018.10.003

Bowen, M. M. (2018). Effect of virtual reality on motivation and achievement of middle-school students. *ProQuest Dissertations and Theses,* 125. https://search.proquest.com/docview/2050000008?accountid=156 37%0Ahttp://sfx.car.chula.ac.th:3410/sfxlcl41?url_ver=Z39.88 -2004&rft_val_fmt=info:ofi/fmt:kev:mtx:dissertation&genre=di ssertations+%26+theses&sid=ProQ:ProQuest+Dissertations+%26+T heses+Global&at

Butt, A. L., Kardong-Edgren, S., & Ellertson, A. (2018). Using Game-Based Virtual Reality with Haptics for Skill Acquisition. *Clinical Simulation in Nursing*, *16*, 25–32. doi:10.1016/j.ecns.2017.09.010

Cho, B.-H., Ku, J., Jang, D. P., Kim, S., Lee, Y. H., Kim, I. Y., Lee, J. H., & Kim, S. I. (2002). The effect of virtual reality cognitive training for attention enhancement. *Cyberpsychology & Behavior*, *5*(2), 129–137. doi:10.1089/109493102753770516 PMID:12025879

Clark, R. C. (2005). Multimedia Learning in e-Courses. In R. Mayer (Ed.), *The Cambridge Handbook of Multimedia Learning* (pp. 589–616). Cambridge University Press. doi:10.1017/CBO9780511816819.036

Cummings, J. J., & Bailenson, J. N. (2016). How Immersive Is Enough? A Meta-Analysis of the Effect of Immersive Technology on User Presence. *Media Psychology*, *19*(2), 272–309. doi:10.1080/152132 69.2015.1015740

Dhawan, S. (2020). Online Learning: A Panacea in the Time of COVID-19 Crisis. *Journal of Educational Technology Systems*, *004723952093401*(1), 5–22. doi:10.1177/0047239520934018

Dunnagan, C. L., Dannenberg, D. A., Cuales, M. P., Earnest, A. D., Gurnsey, R. M., & Gallardo-Williams, M. T. (2020). Production and Evaluation of a Realistic Immersive Virtual Reality Organic Chemistry Laboratory Experience: Infrared Spectroscopy. *Journal of Chemical Education*, *97*(1), 258–262. doi:10.1021/acs.jchemed.9b00705

Hattie, J., & Timperley, H. (2007). The Power of Feedback. *Review of Educational Research*, *77*(1), 81–112. doi:10.3102/003465430298487

Kamińska, D., Sapiński, T., Wiak, S., Tikk, T., Haamer, R. E., Avots, E., Helmi, A., Ozcinar, C., & Anbarjafari, G. (2019). Virtual reality and its applications in education: Survey. *Information (Switzerland)*, *10*(10), 1–20. doi:10.3390/info10100318

Kim, J.-H. K., Thang, N. D. T., Kim, T.-S. K., Voinea, A., Shin, J., Park, S. B., Jang, S. H., Mazuryk, T., Gervautz, M., & Smith, K. (2013). Virtual Reality History, Applications, Technology and Future. *Digital Outcasts, 63*(ISlE), 92–98.

Kolb, A. Y., & Kolb, D. A. (2012). In N. M. Seel (Ed.), *Experiential Learning Theory BT - Encyclopedia of the Sciences of Learning* (pp. 1215–1219). Springer US. doi:10.1007/978-1-4419-1428-6_227

Murre, J. M. J., & Dros, J. (2015). Replication and analysis of Ebbinghaus' forgetting curve. *PLoS One*, *10*(7), 1–23. doi:10.1371/journal.pone.0120644 PMID:26148023

Olmos, E., Cavalcanti, J. F., Soler, J.-L., Contero, M., & Alcañiz, M. (2018). In S. Yu, M. Ally, & A. Tsinakos (Eds.), *Mobile Virtual Reality: A Promising Technology to Change the Way We Learn and Teach BT - Mobile and Ubiquitous Learning: An International Handbook* (pp. 95–106). Springer Singapore. doi:10.1007/978-981-10-6144-8_6

Parong, J., & Mayer, R. E. (2018). Learning science in immersive virtual reality. *Journal of Educational Psychology*, *110*(6), 785–797. doi:10.1037/edu0000241

Parong, J., Pollard, K. A., Files, B. T., Oiknine, A. H., Sinatra, A. M., Moss, J. D., Passaro, A., & Khooshabeh, P. (2020). The mediating role of presence differs across types of spatial learning in immersive technologies. *Computers in Human Behavior*, *107*, 106290. doi:10.1016/j.chb.2020.106290

Phipps, L., Sutherland, A., Seale, J., Ball, S., Dilloway, M., Evans, S., Lakey, M., Peacock, S., Skelton, J., & Wiles, K. (2002). Access All Areas: disability, technology and learning. In *Access All Areas: disability*. https://eprints.soton.ac.uk/6181

Saidin, N. F., Halim, N. D. A., & Yahaya, N. (2015). A review of research on augmented reality in education: Advantages and applications. *International Education Studies*, *8*(13), 1–8. doi:10.5539/ies.v8n13p1

Schrader, C., & Bastiaens, T. J. (2012). The influence of virtual presence: Effects on experienced cognitive load and learning outcomes in educational computer games. *Computers in Human Behavior*, *28*(2), 648–658. doi:10.1016/j.chb.2011.11.011

Servotte, J. C., Goosse, M., Campbell, S. H., Dardenne, N., Pilote, B., Simoneau, I. L., Guillaume, M., Bragard, I., & Ghuysen, A. (2020). Virtual Reality Experience: Immersion, Sense of Presence, and Cybersickness. *Clinical Simulation in Nursing*, *38*, 35–43. doi:10.1016/j.ecns.2019.09.006

Solomon, Z., Ajayi, N., Raghavjee, R., & Ndayizigamiye, P. (2019). In S. Kabanda, H. Suleman, & S. Gruner (Eds.), *Lecturers' Perceptions of Virtual Reality as a Teaching and Learning Platform BT - ICT Education* (pp. 299–312). Springer International Publishing.

Xiao-Dong, L., & Hong-Hui, C. (2020). Research on VR-supported flipped classroom based on blended learning— A case study in "learning english through news.". *International Journal of Information and Education Technology (IJIET)*, *10*(2), 104–109. doi:10.18178/ijiet.2020.10.2.1347

Zhao, J., Xu, X., Jiang, H., & Ding, Y. (2020). The effectiveness of virtual reality-based technology on anatomy teaching: A meta-analysis of randomized controlled studies. *BMC Medical Education*, *20*(1), 127. Advance online publication. doi:10.118612909-020-1994-z PMID:32334594

Chapter 9
Implementing E-Learning Applications and Their Global Advantages in Education

Deepak Kem
Jamia Millia Islamia, India

ABSTRACT

This paper aims to understand e-learning, and to classify its advantages as well impacts on individuals and also their global development. While understanding e-learning and its importance, the primary objectives of this paper will also be to measure the market growth of the e-learning industry, analyze the essence of e-learning courses, and identify the global advantage gained by e-learning. The present paper is a review paper dependent on data, literature, and information provided by various sources such as online journals and articles. It is a proven fact that e-learning has facilitated the development of educational practices in the global world by developing and providing learning opportunities to all. Keeping this in mind, the present attempt presents an analysis and discussion with a strong focus on e-learning and its global advantages, especially during the forced situations of the COVID-19 pandemic. Addressing the advantage of e-learning, this article evaluates the manner in which learners can interact with their peers worldwide through group discussions and private chats.

1. INTRODUCTION

E-learning or electronic learning is sharing knowledge through various advanced technologies such as mobile phones, webinars, and tablets. Basically, e-learning implies the process of teaching and learning using digital tools or resources. This has resulted in many students changing their learning platform from offline to e-learning. This is due to the reason e-learning helps in making instruction easier and more productive. Various benefits of e-learning will be discussed further in the study. Thus, to define the term, e-learning is system-based learning which depends on electronic technologies and the Internet. Students receive classes through various online modes and through technologies considered to be interesting, like watching television or video on a mobile phone. However, with technological advancements in learning

DOI: 10.4018/978-1-6684-6682-7.ch009

technology, e-learning has attracted many customers. E-Learning can be understood as a type of learning that is mediated, facilitated and supported by the use of Digital technologies popularly known as Information Communication technologies (ICT). Such ICT enabled learning empowers learners to learn anywhere and anytime keeping their convenience in mind. To put it more simply technology assisted learning is harnessing the power of technology to connect educators and the learners who are separated physically. This mode of learning entails heavy usage of multimedia to boost learning. In the corporate world too e-learning is used for training, timely deliverance of information and expert counsel. There is no denial that teaching and learning can take place anywhere, be it inside or outside the four walls of classrooms, but today computer and the internet comprise as a major component of learning. Technology mediated learning may also be designated as a delivery of network based transfer of education, knowledge and/or skills to mass learners at the same time instantly. In today's world technology is evolving at an alarming pace and all sectors of our society have taken support of technological advancements. Education too has taken the support of technology and equipped itself to offer more innovative, convenient and flexible means to enhance the reach of education as digital platform of teaching and learning provides that flexibility of place, time and access for upgradation of skills, knowledge and qualification.

E-learning is the most preferred mode of learning in the corporate sector and amongst the working class as it helps conduct multiple training programs and orientations for employees across the Globe. Different sectors in the world are introducing e-learning courses, and it is believed that it will help in the progress of nations and countries. It has been reported that e-learning is not only concerned with educating school and college students; it also helps to provide various programs and events in sectors such as medicine, transportation, entertainment, finance and many more. The rise of e-learning has led to a revolution across the Globe. According to Waller *et al.* (2019), it was observed that in the United Kingdom, the market growth (2022-2026) of E-learning would be US $11.57 billion. The main components of e-learning are Market drivers and Market Challenges, which allow e-learning to grow in the market. Besides the telecom revolution which has made Information Communication Technologies penetration possible and affordable, "Rising in-house content development" is one of the factors which contribute to e-learning's market growth. Enhancing the academic sector is an important market driver for e-Learning towards their market growth. The online learning system provides various assessments and training to multiple institutions, which has gained adaptation and recognition in the market. This has resulted in gaining acceleration for personnel development and adaptive learning. It is now a globally accepted fact that e-learning has many advantages over traditional face to face classroom learning. To give a few examples some such advantages would include the opportunity for learners to use self-paced learning and select a learning environment that suits their needs. Moreover, the model of e-learning is not only cost-efficient and cost-effective, it also eliminates the geographical barriers that are often seen to be related with the traditional system of education. On the basis of the advantages it provides and the benefits it has to offer, it will safe to state that the present tendencies of the e-learning market show extraordinary progress for the industry. E-learning initially was not accepted due to lack of human element in the system but with the meteoric advancements in technology the mode has been now positively accepted by the masses. It was the introduction of computers in the education sector in particular, that formed the backbone of this revolution and with the continuous usage and introduction of smartphones and hand held devices etc. technology now finds a significant place in the learning process. E-learning is a an education platform where the learner is provided with a an opportunity to choose a self-guided process where in the absence of educator/instructor the learners have the flexibility to choose their convenient time and place of learning. This flexibility for the learner allows them to adjust learning

Figure 1. E-Learning market in the UK
(Source: PR Newswire, June 2022)

according to their busy day to day scheduled. It is a fact that it becomes difficult for e-learning to be engaging and impactful in the absence (physical) of an educator, but by introducing interactive, engaging and other multimedia content it is possible to achieve and maintain the desired level of learner engagement and retention as using such techniques to gain learner interest, leaves a lasting impact on learners and helps them to retain more and apply more. In 2015 the worldwide revenue of the e-learning market was slated to be $107 Billion, according to Market research firm Global Industry Analysts, but now it is expected to grow to $325 Billion by 2025, which is remarkable considering the fact that the number was three times smaller.

One of the most daunting tasks for any government is to ensure quality learning opportunities for all learners irrespective of their backgrounds. We must realize that education is an ongoing process as it starts right from the birth and continues lifelong. One of the key aspects of learning is education. Both education and learning are vital facets for an individual as they lead to attainment of knowledge, increasing their awareness enhance personality. In other words, the process of education provides for overall development, implying greater access to their intellectual as well as skills enabling every learner to operate on their maximum potential. It must also be accepted that just like other systems of education the e-learning system of education too is not perfect and could mean to sacrifice of some sort. Besides the risk of malpractices during assessments, there is always a fear of lack of communication skill and social isolation. These are some of the challenges or disadvantages that need to be addressed. Having said so, e-learning offers numerous uses across all sections of society and the fact that e-learning has been used effectively is plentiful can be seen in its meteoric growth. Furthermore, this has provided various opportunities for students to learn multiple courses and subjects. In addition, e-learning offers learners different course materials according to their needs and requirements. This factor has accelerated the growth of e-learning in the market all over the Globe (fig.1).

There is a plethora of work that suggests the importance, standing and significance of e-learning and the advantages it has to offer on a global basis. In order to accelerate the growth and progress of a nation, important sectors such as services, medicine education, agriculture are now making changes to incorporate the concept of e-learning especially those who operate from offices spread across the country and need a solution that allows employees, experts and stakeholders connect easily from all official locations, any time. Such arrangement offers an opportunity to employees in acquiring new proficiencies and better their skill sets. It stands equally true for sectors where learning by training is a constitutive part, the e-learning system has been enormously fruitful in creating a positive impression. To bring together employees from different parts of the country for the purpose of training is not only outlandish but also an unnecessary wastage of time, money and effort. E-learning in such a scenario has provided the solution and the answer as it is the most effective means for professionals across the globe who are desirous to acquire requisite skills while in the comfort of their office or home. What technology-mediated learning has done is that it has empowered the learners to learn without disturbing their daily schedules and as per their availability, allowing them to manage their day better. As an example, one such study conducted by International Business Machines (IBM) in 2019, has reported that the price of training provided to the employees necessitates an investment of between $1 and $30 in productivity. The cost was low as the employee only gained relevant knowledge regarding the company's focus and put the learning into practice as soon as possible. It was also reported in the same report that IBM Company was able to successfully save $200 million after the implementation of the e-learning program and also the training result revealed five times more value within the given time (IBM, 2019).

Similarly, according to another study by Brandon Hall (2017) it was observed that e-learning saves time (fig.2). It said that e-learning needs 40 to 60% lesser time than the traditional teaching-learning model. The same report also makes a striking observation that the e-learning market has risen from 200 to 900% in a very short time (Hall, 2017). Furthermore, according to a report by Global Market Insights Inc. in 2019, it has been observed and reported that the e-learning business/market will reach $300 billion by 2025. But due to the COVID-19 pandemic-induced online teaching and learning the estimations of this have been proven to be incorrect as due to the pandemic as the e-learning industry is estimated to cross $315 billion mark by 2021 (GM Insights, 2022). What the pandemic has done is that it has positively impacted the e-learning industry and accelerated the process of adopting digital modes of teaching and learning by various educational institutions, globally. E-learning has also garnered the support of governments towards improving the infrastructure and strengthening the digital platform, especially in developing countries. Thus, it becomes imperative to assess and observe how e-learning is bringing revolution to the education industry by replacing the dull and boring traditional classroom learning by interactive and fun-filled learning. Recently, e-learning has been seen to be a new age of learning where the life of the students and teachers has been made easy. Students can learn anytime and anywhere with a stable internet connection (Gunawan *et al.* 2018) making learning and teaching easy, fast, independent and flexible. In some countries, particularly third world countries, geographical boundaries were a major factor for teachers and students, but by eliminating such barriers e-learning has revolutionized the education sector. The transformation results in a new self-learning trend that has evolved and is increasing rapidly. E-learning systems use various methods such as online courses, webinars and virtual conferences for the do-it-yourself approach instead of using the traditional learning model. According to a survey by Global learner, it was shown that approximately 76% of students agree to go for online courses rather than attending traditional schools and colleges (Baisel *et al.*, 2020). This was the main reason for various companies in India like BYJU'S, Vedantu, LinkedIn Learning and Un Academy, to provide online courses and multiple opportunities for different classes and subjects side by side keeping their needs and interest. These interests and needs of the learners are gratified by the digital

Figure 2. Covid-19's Impact on the increase in E-Learning
(Source: World Economic Forum, 2020)

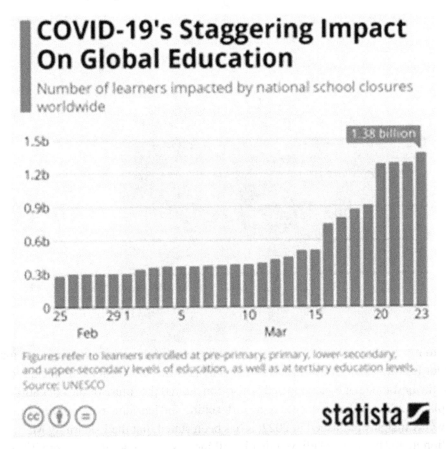

mode of learning by providing quality education anytime and anywhere as per their interest, convenience and within their affordability bracket, making it cost-efficient (fig.3).

2. ANALYSIS AND DISCUSSION

The **need to analyse** is required as a discussion will provide the difference between the current state of e-learning and its benefits and the desired future. Thus, one of the biggest advantages that e-learning yields in the current situation are learners' access to selected classes and courses at their time of suitability. This has provided individuals to attend classes flexibly according to their convenience just by using their digital device (computer, laptop, mobile phone, i pad or desktop) simply because all the teaching and learning are conducted online, i.e., in a virtual mode. Because all the content is saved online and is accessible to all learners, any content saved in a video format can be replayed as many number of times as the learner desires till he/she comprehends the teaching materials clearly. This has made learning easy and as per the suitability of the learners as they can learn/train/comprehend/clarify the content personally without the help of teachers and employers. According to (Soni 2020), it has been observed that e-learning is quite sufficient in comparison to the traditional teaching-learning model as there are

Figure 3. Global E-Learning Market size
(Source: Global Newswire, 2022)

various ways to resolve issues for a learner in digital learning. A learner can always opt for a video call with the mentor for further clarification and solving any issues. The recent pandemic has confirmed that e-Learning is the best mode of education and is also considered the future of the educational sector. This mode will replace traditional face to face classroom teaching and learning in the coming future. According to a report by GM Insights published in 2022, it has been stated that the E-learning Market will surpass US$ 315 billion in 2021, and it is believed that it will increase at a rate of 20% from 2022 to 2028 (GM Insights, 2022). As technology progresses it is ultimately filling the gaps in various sectors. The same is also applicable to the education sector which is now marked by the presence of technology-aided and mediated learning. E-learning has facilitated the paradigm shift from traditional learning to continuous learning, which gives the learners an opportunity to acquire new/expand their existing skill set to match the requirements of the developing modern environment.

A good learning environment is one of the most essential factors in learning, especially in the e-learning process. Because both the learner and the educator are separated physically, the educator may be of the opinion that he/she may not be able to do much to improve the learning environment for the students, but there are quite a few things that can be done to impact this. Any learning process is impacted by a variety of factors such as attentiveness or mental capability to concentrate. As well as other factors, having a calm environment to focus without any disturbance benefits learners do better and therefore learn better. But it is equally true that an educator or instructor cannot possess control over the learning environment of the learner. The environment analysis depicts the best environment for e-Learning so that the individual will learn and be provided support.

It is quite essential to appreciate the components involved in the making of a good e-Learning environment. First of all, every educator is required to adopt a creative approach towards teaching and learning their discipline. In order for the learners to experience the best learning environment coupled with effective retention of the content imparted via the e-learning process, it is significant to provide these learners with all resources and tools. For designing any effective e-learning environment, the instructor must keep the engagement of the learner and secondly the engagement of the learner's interest in mind. Adding strategies of self-assessment like quizzes and simple components of interactive activities to the curriculum will not only augment learner engagement but also elevate learners' retention of the content. This will help the learner to gain knowledge and enhance their performance. The setting for e-Learning varies from person to person, as few are habituated to listening to podcasts. In contrast, some are habituated to learning in a room, and some engage in independent learning. A few factors benefit the environment due to e-Learning, which are as follows. First, the energy consumption for powering up the devices for e-Learning is very high compared to the energy supply in schools and offices; this is considered minimal energy consumed. Thus, it can help in energy saving. This also helps reduce transportation, which can finally reduce Carbon dioxide emissions by approximately 148 pounds yearly (Nielsen 2021). The other reason is that it reduces paper use, as millions of textbooks are thrown out yearly. Thus, changing the mode to e-learning will help reduce paper waste. The online learning environment provides innovative access to teaching and learning; therefore, it may be biased to limit e-learning merely to some documents and/or PPT's only. In the e-learning environment the learners experience more than just reading documents over the internet and watching slides, they learn through live interactive sessions, recorded videos, assignments, animated videos and other fantastic educational resources. It is very clear that videos make learning easier and more interesting. It is equally true that not all audio-visual content is interesting but video content made well-made positively impacts not only the teaching and learning experiences but also the education environment.

Conversely, another e-learning environment that may sound complicated is gamified learning. It is more popular and used at the primary level of education. One of the most popular examples of gamified learning are quizzes and drag-and-drop games, making the e-learning interesting as well as interactive. A lot of LMS stepped up their games by providing easy interactions for educators. We all would agree that simple games become a habit which in turn leads to encouraging learners to actively participate. Now one of the biggest tasks for any educator is to keep the learners motivated. It obviously becomes easy once the learner grasps how interesting and enjoyable it is to learn about a subject (science, maths, history), but till that moment or time, making and keeping the learners involved in a new subject can be very unnerving for an educator. Here the concept of gamification or gamified learning is employed in order to encourage learning. The beauty of this approach is that it this approach creates an environment that helps learners become motivated and they actively participate in the activities and tasks.

More and more innovative pedagogies like simulations and gaming are being introduced to kindle learner interest. Such methodologies provide opportunities to learners to learn by doing through the application-based knowledge. Such opportunities to perfect skills by practising infuses in the learner a sense of confidence while ensuring better quality and greater productivity of work. With growing interest of the industries to implementing technology-based learning as their preferred method of learning and training, makes it seem that e-learning is here to stay change the way we learn, radically. The task analysis of e-Learning helps break tasks into smaller ones for specific job roles. This includes various factors such as task description, the importance of the study, subordinate mission, length and frequency of the survey provided, and tools required for task completion. This is conducted to determine how the job is completed and whether it is a step-by-step method. This analysis helps ensure an individual's learning and performance capabilities with the job the individual needs to perform (Al Rawashdeh et al. 2021). The second point is that it can help analyze the total scope and the complexity of the task and manuals that need to be taught. This analysis is also helpful in confirming the fact that external learning is required to learn the goals and topics. There are three steps to performing Task Analysis: identifying the primary procedure, which helps determine the preceding procedures that the individuals are expected to perform. The second step is to list the main tasks with the help of the main task and sub-task. And the last is to list the sub-tasks, which is to break the main functions into sub-tasks which helps in the completion of task analysis. The audience analysis of e-Learning is mainly done to classify the audiences into various groups for those who will participate in training and the characteristics of the groups made (Farrah and Al-Bakri, 2020). There are multiple ways to identify the audiences based on "Demographics", which are the age and gender of the audience. The second way is the "cognitive characteristics", which are based on education level, linguistics, knowledge regarding the subject and learning preferences. Other various ways for audience analysis are roles and responsibilities in jobs, interests and attitudes.

3. CONCLUSION

The above presented topic discusses the e-learning system of education, the evolution and its impact on the education sector in particular along with the benefits it brings and offers for various other sectors and its explicit contribution in the raise of these sectors, industries and/or organizations. At the core, the topic discusses diverse students at schools and colleges that benefit from e-learning. E-Learning provides *University students* with updated content and lots of interaction with various teachers, providing all educational/academic services for the learners online. Due to the implementation of e-learning the students are able to enrol in more than one course of their choice and interest. Also, the e-learning platform delivers the relevant online courses and learning modules. For the learner's interest and retention e-learning provides various tasks, assessments and quizzes to test their knowledge, making learning fun and entertaining.

E-Learning has empowered the students with the authority to express what they want to learn and when they want to learn. Thus, with the emergence of e-learning, the kind of education a learner desires is in the hands of the learners themselves, right from setting their mindsets to engaging in learning from the devices. This has proved to be a spectacular facility as many students proceeded to courses selected by pressure from their families and society (Vainshtein *et al.* 2019). This will help them to do an adjacent course that interests them. Career is one of the most important factors that college students think of. Due to various online courses, they are provided with certification increasing their chances of getting their dream job.

E-Learning has also provided benefits to the teachers, such as flexibility, reduced workload and building a better student-teacher relationship. This has helped the teachers work from their homes during summer and winter breaks. It is also a good option for extra income by giving lectures on different sources provided by E-Learning technology. E-Learning has also reduced the teachers' workload as making other teaching materials such as presentations, videos and quizzes using different technologies are easy. Thus, teachers are dependent on the benefits of E-Learning. Moreover, during an e-learning class, the teacher is the main element of concentration of the course. Thus, students' minds are set that the teacher is the only person who can rectify and test their skills and knowledge. Therefore, e-learning helps build a good student-teacher relationship (Hoque *et al.* 2019). Therefore E-Learning is a revolution in this digital world and can develop various personal factors that are lacking during a career, so adopting E-Learning teaching as fast as possible is advisable.

REFERENCES

Al Rawashdeh, A.Z., Mohammed, E.Y., Al Arab, A.R., Alara, M. and Al-Rawashdeh, B., (2021) "Advantages and disadvantages of using e-learning in university education: Analyzing students' perspectives." *Electronic Journal of e-Learning, 19*(3), pp.107-117.

Alharahsheh, H. H., & Pius, A. (2020). A review of key paradigms: Positivism vs interpretivism. *Global Academic Journal of Humanities and Social Sciences, 2*(3), 39–43.

Atmowardoyo, H. (2018). Research methods in TEFL studies: Descriptive research, case study, error analysis, and R & D. *Journal of Language Teaching and Research, 9*(1), 197–204. doi:10.17507/jltr.0901.25

Baisel, A., Vijayakumar, M., & Sujatha, P. (2020). An Experiential Study on the Learners' Perception of E-Learning and Traditional Learning. In *Innovations and Technologies for Soft Skill Development and Learning* (pp. 46–52). IGI Global. doi:10.4018/978-1-7998-3464-9.ch006

Farrah, M., & Al-Bakry, G. H. (2020). Online learning for EFL students in Palestinian universities during corona pandemic: Advantages, challenges and solutions. *Indonesian Journal of Learning and Instruction, 3*(2), 65–78.

Global Newswire. (2022). Global Online Education Market (2022 to 2027). https://www.globenewswire.com/fr/news-release/2022/02/03/2378224/28124/en/Global-Online-Education-Market-2022-to-2027-by-User-type-Provider-Technology-and-Region.html

Gunawan, W., Kalensun, E. P., Fajar, A. N., & Sfenrianto. (2018). E-Learning through social media in the virtual learning environment []. IOP Publishing.]. *IOP Conference Series. Materials Science and Engineering, 420*(1), 012110. doi:10.1088/1757-899X/420/1/012110

Hall, B. (2017). *Following the Latest Trends to Shape Customized E-Learning Experiences*. Brandon Hall [online]. https://www.brandonhall.com/blogs/tag/e-learning/

Hoque, M., Yusoff, A. M., Toure, A. K., & Mohamed, Y. (2019). Teaching Hadith Subjects through E-Learning Methods: Prospects and Challenges. *International Journal of Academic Research in Progressive Education and Development, 8*(2), 507–514. doi:10.6007/IJARPED/v8-i2/6164

IBM. (2019). *IBM e-learning content*. IBM. https://www.ibm.com/training/W961341C20522X82,

Insights, G. M. (2022). E-Learning Market Size. Competitive Market Share & Forecast, 2022 – 2028. *GM Insights*. https://www.gminsights.com/industry-analysis/elearning-market-size#:~:text=E%2DLearning%20Market%20size%20surpassed,to%20economical%20internet%20connectivity%20plans

Newswire, P. R. (2022). E-Learning Market Size in the UK to grow by USD 11.57 billion by 2026. *Technavio*. https://www.prnewswire.com/news-releases/e-learning-market-size-in-the-uk-to-grow-by-usd-11-57-billion-by-2026--packaged-content-segment-to-be-significant-for-revenue-generation--technavio-301563094.html

Nielsen, J. (2021 November 7). 6 Environmental Benefits of Online Learning That Will Blow Your Mind. *Sustainable Business Toolkit.* https://www.sustainablebusinesstoolkit.com/social-and-eco-be nefits-of-online-learning/

SoniV. D. (2020)" Global Impact of E-learning during COVID 19. https://ssrn.com/abstract=3630073 doi:10.2139/ssrn.3630073

Vainshtein, I. V., Shershneva, V. A., Esin, R. V., & Noskov, M. V. (2019). Individualization of Education in Terms of E-learning: Experience and Prospects. *Journal of Siberian Federal University. Humanities & Social Sciences, 12*(9), 1753–1770. doi:10.17516/1997-1370-0481

Waller, R. E., Lemoine, P. A., Mense, E. G., & Richardson, M. D. (2019). Higher education in search of competitive advantage: Globalization, technology and e-learning. *International Journal of Advanced Research and Publications, 3*(8), 184–190.

Woiceshyn, J., & Daellenbach, U. (2018). Evaluating inductive vs deductive research in management studies: Implications for authors, editors, and reviewers. Qualitative Research in Organizations and Management: An International Journal, 13(2), pp.183-195. doi:10.1108/QROM-06-2017-1538

World Economic Forum. (2020). The COVID-19 pandemic has changed educa-tion forever. *We Forum.* https://www.weforum.org/agenda/2020/04/coronavirus-education -global-covid19-online-digital-learning/

Chapter 10
Reading Habits Among University Students Studying Engineering in the Digital Age

Rashmi Rekha Borah
Vellore Institute of Technology, Chennai, India

G. Bhuvaneswari
 https://orcid.org/0000-0002-2897-7265
Vellore Institute of Technology, India

Moon Moon Hussain
B.S. Abdur Rahman Crescent Institute of Science and Technology, India

ABSTRACT

In this study, engineering students from universities all around India will have their reading interests and habits examined. Reading habits have changed as a result of technology; the most popular change is the rise of text reading from computer screens. Teachers and students face a variety of difficulties and opportunities as a result of the widespread use of screen reading. The usage of annotations and other forms of text interaction by engineering students when reading academic publications is examined in this work along with their general reading preferences, habits, and attitudes. The opinions of 109 students who participated in an online survey were examined. The report highlights a number of issues with engineering students' preferences and habits, and how those issues affect their capacity for critical thought. The researcher presented recommendations to encourage reading habits among engineering students in the continually technologically driven environment of today after conducting research to acquire a thorough overview of millennials' reading preferences.

INTRODUCTION

In a digital age, reading interests and habits change quickly. As digital natives, millennials have unlim-

DOI: 10.4018/978-1-6684-6682-7.ch010

ited access to materials, including research papers and lecture notes on the internet. Our lives have a significant amount of technological integration. Information overload is technology's most significant negative effect. Information transfer is only a click away. Most traditional information transfer through printed documents has been supplanted by online data. This modification has impacted both what and how individuals read. The outcomes of a survey carried out by the researchers found that the students' reading habits have shifted away from reading on paper and more toward reading on electronic devices, specifically the internet. Reading provides the foundation for the growth of other key language talents like as speaking, listening, and writing, and its importance cannot be overstated.

Teachers shouldn't disregard this change in students' reading preferences. Younger people are rapidly embracing digital formats for information and pleasure, according to Karim, Hasan, and Shahriza (2006). Liu (2005) adds that there is an increase in the amount of time people spend using electronic reading media and that the new reading preferences are influenced by the quick expansion of digital information available. These findings provide evidence that the advent of the digital age has already had an effect on people's reading habits. The purpose of this study is to evaluate how current reading habits, behaviours, and attitudes of engineering students in the digital age affect their capacity for critical thought.

OBJECTIVES

1. To find out the reading preferences
2. To find out the library attendance frequency
3. To find out the role of technology in reading habits

RESEARCH QUESTIONS

- In the digital age, what books do engineering students prefer to read?
- In a typical week, do college students prefer reading online content over offline content?
- What sort of content do engineering students typically read online?
- How closely related are the habits of engineering students to their demographic characteristics, including age, gender, location, economic situation, educational attainment, JEE scores, work status, and personal online time?

METHODOLOGY

Participants

The data for the study were gathered using a survey methodology. 99 replies to the survey were obtained based on the 109 samples that were selected. University students from Chennai, India's Engineering Vellore Institute of Technology made up the questionnaire's participants. On campus, the sample was chosen at random. This university is well known for preparing professionals in engineering, science, and technology through its 4-year, 5-year integrated, and graduate programmes. They consisted of 109 responders, of which 34 were men and 75 were women. They were primarily second-year students, ranging in age from 18 to 20. They pursued engineering studies in a variety of programmes and fields. The majority of students are from various Indian cities, towns, and villages.

Instrument and Procedure

For this investigation, a 20-item questionnaire is created (see Appendix A). Six categories make up the questionnaire: a demographic category, a category for how frequently respondents read, a category for what they read online, a category for what they do online, a category for what they read online, and a category for topics of interest they find online. The following steps were used to create, test, and revise the instrument. First, the researcher came up with the research questions while keeping in mind the goals of the study, basing them on the intended uses and potential research topics. The questionnaire was then peer reviewed by two colleagues of the researcher. The questionnaire's shortcomings were discussed by the researcher and the teachers, who then amended the original version.

Third, a pilot study using a questionnaire was conducted with a class of ten students. Fourth, the researcher changed the questionnaire and created the present questionnaire after examining the findings of the pilot study. The researcher then distributed surveys via Google Forms. A total of 109 legitimate surveys were gathered. Following the collection of the questionnaire, the frequency and percentages of replies for each of the 20 items were added together to analyse the data. The data were analysed using Chi-square tests and standard deviation. Analyses of the mean, standard deviation, and frequency were done to determine the association between reading habits and the demographic characteristics of the pupils.

Data Collection Procedures

A questionnaire was used to learn more about university students' reading preferences. For them to feel comfortable answering the questions honestly, the students were not asked for their true names. The researcher gathered questionnaires from participants, examined them, and discovered the frequency of reading levels.

LITERATURE REVIEW

Everyone, regardless of age or gender, can benefit from developing the habit of reading. It makes it easier for someone to obtain a decent education, a job, pass a test, be an excellent communicator, an exceptional orator, or acquire status for studying (Kurtus, 2002). Reading is the finest habit to instil in children, according to Fisher (1996). Early on in elementary school, the majority of pupils like reading their favourite novels. Books like Panchatantra and Aesop's fables, which are predominantly read to or heard about by children, have the power to permanently alter the reading habits of its potential readers.

For some of these readers, their family may try to get them more reading material at a later basic level. Boys choose adventure, mysteries, and biographies, while ladies prefer magazines and teen novels in junior high school, according to many students who keep reading logs Fisher (2007). Fisher has extensively discussed these gender disparities in reading interests and behaviours (2007). Students become more serious readers in high school and lose interest in classics and individual writers. They are capable of comprehending the writing craft of an author at the college and university levels.

Gender, race, and education were found to be predictors of participants' reading habits, while race and education were found to be predictors of reading patterns (Scales and Rhee, 2001). According to Scales and Rhee (2001), students' reading patterns and habits are influenced by their gender, race, and educational background. There is only one option for students to improve their learning—reading—if they want to advance their social standing and academic performance at the university level. However, it has been noted that students' propensity for digitising reading has sufficiently harmed the entire educational process. My weak grasp of the subject and passing exams have been replaced by gaining a thorough understanding of it.

The researchers' survey indicates that library visits have drastically decreased. Nothing good comes from making someone read something they are not interested in. In order to help young people develop their reading habits for later learning, it is crucial to pay attention to their reading preferences. Engineering students' reading habits are declining in India. Teachers fall short in encouraging students to read and fail to emphasise the value of reading books outside of those required for university courses. In India, engineering students' reading habits are declining due to a variety of social factors. Shah and Saleem (2010) claim that the low literacy rate, lack of reading orientation, limited purchasing power, inadequate educational system, inappropriate library structure, unfavourable reading environment, and low motivational library staff are all contributing factors to Pakistanis' poor reading habits. In India, the issue is similar in that changing engineering students' reading habits involves a change in both attitude and practise.

A lot of changes in the reading habits of college students have been observed by researchers. This change is apparently due to the digital media impact made available through the Internet (Liu, 2005). India's plummeting data prices have hit a new low. According to a BBC report, the country has the lowest mobile broadband prices in the world. Many Indian users said they were paying less than $0.10 a GB. Reading habits have changed as a result of technology, and the most popular new reading method is reading from computer displays (Vandenhoek, 2013). Teachers and students face a variety of difficulties and opportunities as a result of the widespread use of screen reading. Reading books could soon become obsolete due to the rise of electronic media, much like how stamp collecting as a hobby is no longer practised.

The participants favour electronic reading while doing so for fun, but they favour printed reading when studying for tests. Although the so-called "digital natives" have access to smartphones and other digital platforms as well as a wide variety of reading materials, many of them opt not to read (Abidin, Zainol, Majid, Lean & Choon 2011).

Recreational reading has altered for millennials in an age of eBooks, laptops, and hours spent online. Different mediums are widely accessible to students. With the development of the Internet, information can be transmitted swiftly. By skimming and exploring the less structured and non-linear hypertexts, reading time for digital media is reduced. Millennials prefer reading screen-based content, according to Liu's 2005 research. To read more slowly, students often print out the material they need for exams. According to research, reading conventional novels is no longer popular. Students may read on their mobile devices, play computer and web games, and have access to the solutions thanks to Google.

It is undoubtedly available to the majority of students, but colleges around the world have seen that the ability to raise challenging questions has often lessened.

Students must keep up with technological advancements if they want to make reading enjoyable and maintain the habit. If online reading and gaming are taken into account, reading has likely increased in the digital age. For those who prefer to read in Chinese, there are now search engines available in that

Figure 1. Materials Read by Students

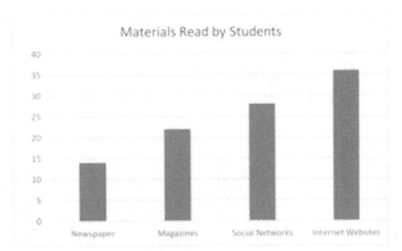

language. More tech-savvy pupils would be encouraged to read for leisure as a result of this. In many EFL circumstances, English is studied more for exam purposes than as a tool for daily life.

Yang claims that most students don't utilise English outside of the classroom and only read English-language literature because they have to, not for fun (2007). In contrast to Yang, a study done by the researcher Priajana (2013) highlighted the students' reading habits, attitudes, and preferences, all of which were highly favourable because they valued reading in their free time and thought it was essential to their life.

Academic programmes, different kinds of reading materials, and reading resources, especially websites, all differ significantly from one another. Participants who were male and female showed different reading interests and attitudes. Using gadgets like Android phones, PCs, e-books, and PDAs and without the use of any printed documents, technology has made reading more immediate and slightly non-linear. Karim, Hasan and Shahriza (2007).

ANALYSIS

The questionnaire's results were revealed when participants were asked to list the resources they had read: newspapers (14%), magazines (22%) and social networks (28%), internet websites (36%). When asked to draw their ideal reading area, participants always included books and computers (desktop computers, laptops or tablets) (figure 1).

According to the report, readers view the website as a reading resource that is becoming more significant. Academic programmes, reading materials, and reading resources, particularly websites, all differ significantly from one another. Participants from both genders saw disparities in reading attitudes and behaviours.

75 (68.8%) of the 109 responders were females, and 34 (31.19%) were males. The demographic breakdown of the respondents is shown in Table 1.

Table 2 indicates that while 22.02% of the students enjoy reading, 4.58% never read. The frequency ranges between a minimum of 4.58% to a maximum of 46.78% (figure 2).

Table 1. Demography of Respondents

Demographic Variable	Item	Frequency	Percentage (%)
Gender	Male	34	31.19
	Female	75	68.81
	Total	109	100

Mean = 18 Min = 16 Max = 22 SD= 3.17

Table 2. Frequency of Leisure Reading

	Frequency	Percentage
Always	24	22.01
Frequently	29	26.60
Seldom	5	4.58
Sometimes	51	46.78
	109	100

Mean = 27.27 Min = 5 Max = 51 SD = 13.64

Figure 2. Materials Read by Students

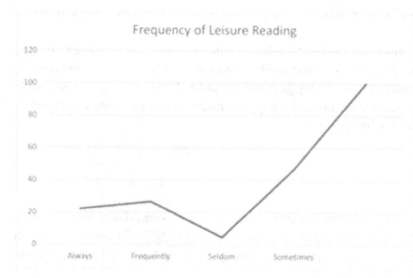

Table 3. Preference of Books over technology

	Frequency	Percentage
Books	72	66.05
Technology	37	33.94
	109	100

Mean = 54.5 Min = 37 Max = 72 SD = 27.25

Figure 3. Books over Technology

The result of table 3 is highly promising that the respondents preferred books over technology (figure 3). Factors Contributing to Leisure Reading has measured in table 4 and shown in figure 4 also.

Table 4. Factors Contributing to Leisure Reading

Reasons	Frequency	Percentage
Enhances my knowledge	60	55.04
Helps in my research	4	3.66
Makes me smart and stand out in the crowd	27	24.77
My hobby	18	16.53
Total	109	100

Mean = 27.25 Min =4 Max = 60 SD = 37.18

Preference over reading materials Digital Vs. Library reading has measured in table 5 and shown in figure 5.

DISCUSSION

The teachers and the textbooks are said to be the two main elements influencing a student's performance in college. Reading is frequently seen as a means of acquiring ideas that cannot be communicated verbally. When children read effectively, they expand their horizons intellectually and increase their opportunities. (Satija, 2002). Therefore, the development of computer technology and the Internet has

Figure 4. Factors contribute to Leisure Reading

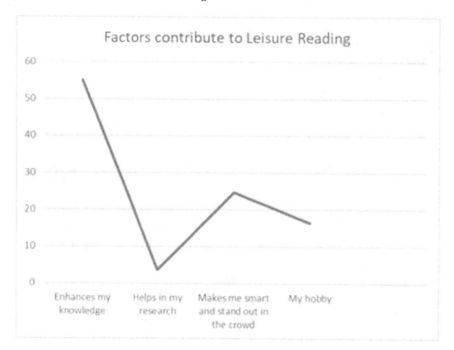

created a new digital environment, which has an impact on all occupations and people in general. Now that everything has shifted from traditional to digital, it has been observed that college students' reading habits are deteriorating daily.

The findings indicate that the majority of students love reading for pleasure. It is also noted that, despite the fact that reading has several benefits, knowledge improvement is the main one. Academic reading naturally includes reading for research reasons, and it should be noted that the majority of students prefer reading because they wish to stand out from the crowd. The fact that students still favour books over computers, despite technology's growth and pervasiveness, is quite encouraging. This essay makes the case for the academic community to provide additional possibilities for extracurricular reading that can be included into the curriculum. To promote reading habits among the students, a library that contains exclusively books for leisure reading should be made available to the students.

Reading fosters critical thinking in kids and enhances reading comprehension, which is advantageous in all of the subject areas examined in this study. The advantages of leisure reading, however, extend beyond the classroom. Students carry their reading-based talents into adulthood and, into the labour

Table 5. Preference over reading materials Digital Vs. Library reading

	Frequency	Percentage
I would borrow a book from the library rather than surf online:	65	59.63
Never, I will rather surf online	44	40.36
Total	109	100

Mean = 54.5 Min = 44 Max = 65 SD = 27.25

Figure 5. Percentage

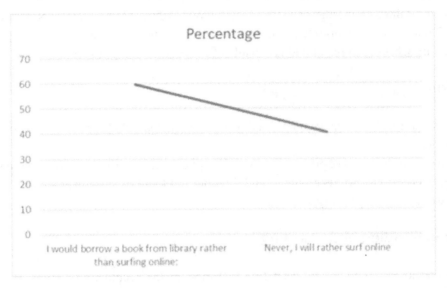

force and society after that. Unfortunately, state-mandated testing, state curricula, and an ongoing push to introduce more technology into the classroom reduce the amount of time students have available to spend reading while in school, despite evidence to the contrary that leisure reading is overwhelmingly beneficial to student progress.

Need of the hour

Knowing what would help them in their career progress would enable students to understand the need for the reading - to upskill their knowledge level, grow professionally, become competent in any career path that they are planning to undertake. There are in numerous books and reference materials available, and students can easily get lost in their reading. To get the most out of their reading habits students should be able to identify where their interest lies on and what is really needed to focus on. We do not have the luxury of time to invest in reading all the material available in this world. It warrants one to be vigilant on spending one's time in reading only materials that really matters.

Though many students spend their time on reading it does not bear them the benefit that they wanted to reap. The reality is many of the students are clueless, helpless and they end up wasting their quality time on elsewhere. Learning these skills early in their student life, will help them stand out all through their career.

The skilled people know how to read and what to read. They also know to attain mastery what kind of tools that they should have. Reading any or reading however you want will dilute the efforts you are trying to put towards attaining the skill.

Retention

While reading enhances one's skill, retaining what we learnt is a different skill altogether for any student. There are several study techniques and study methodologies that would help students to retain what they learn over the period of time. These techniques can be learnt by anyone and if one applies this technique wisely, then the retained knowledge can help them to move to the next level such as Speed reading, Deep reading and Rapid skill acquisition etc., Willingness to explore and having the curiosity to go to the depths of understanding what our human mind is capable of – would help any students to excel in their deeds.

Application

Research says that most of what we read in a day is lost in the next 24 hours unless we re-read it or we put it to practical use.

Obviously, the 10000 rules of practicing any skill applies here as well. Deliberate reading, systematic learning, focussed effort towards retaining and then putting them to systematically practice what one has learnt - would help to gain mastery in any skill.

Continuous Reading and Learning

We can say confidently without any hesitation that most of the successful people that we see in our professional life are regular readers. In simple terms – Successful people are readers. Once the reading habit is cultivated, one should make it as a regular practice that it is continued all through one's life. For one who practices all through this life will see to that he remains successful in achieving all the goals one tries to accomplish. Yes, the magic lies in practicing it regularly and consistently all through one's life. The person who does this regularly builds psychological and mental stamina that no other person can compete with. The changes that happen during this skill acquisition is neurophysiological. Every time something is rehearsed or reread, it strengthens the ability to retain the knowledge that we acquire.

CONCLUSION

The majority of kids, according to the report, simply read for test purposes and don't enjoy it. Most students like to read books and publications. However, students prefer using electronic reading materials. Furthermore, studies show that social networking sites are bad for children's reading habits. If students are encouraged to read from a young age, reading habits can be formed. It's important for parents, teachers, and peers to support students' reading habits and foster positive attitudes about reading. Additionally, reading improves pupils' academic and professional performance. Students must so appreciate the importance of reading, make time for it, and develop a passion for it.

Guthrie (2000) asserts that readers appreciate the process of learning through literature. They exhibit self-efficacy and are certain of their reading skills. Additionally, they are mastery-oriented, genuinely motivated, and they strive to comprehend what they read.

The study found that younger generations are more at ease using all types of technology and have been embracing all technological advancements with a positive attitude. Engineering students have been seen using laptops, smartphones, and other sophisticated electronic gadgets for their studies. The survey found that the digital transition has had an effect on engineering students' reading habits as well. However, the development of the Internet has given students access to instant information, which is why they are gravitating toward digital reading rather than traditional reading.

Recommendations

In their spare time, university students may have access to a variety of reading materials. University students can be encouraged to develop reading habits, and activities to promote frequent reading among university students may be arranged. The engineering students who read the most might present to the other students and inspire them by sharing their positive book-reading experiences. Through events like these, engineering students can meet with visitors like authors, journalists, and publishers. Events could also be planned to promote books that students think you should read.

Reading fosters critical thinking in kids and enhances reading comprehension, which is advantageous in all of the subject areas examined in this study. The advantages of leisure reading, however, extend beyond the classroom. Students carry their reading-based talents into adulthood and, into the labour force and society after that. Unfortunately, state-mandated testing, state curricula, and an ongoing push to introduce more technology into the classroom reduce the amount of time students have available to spend reading while in school, despite evidence to the contrary that leisure reading is overwhelmingly beneficial to student progress.

Limitations of the Study

Due to the fact that this study was conducted at a single university, its generalizability is limited. The scope of this study was restricted to one engineering school with participants from comparable socio-economic backgrounds. As a result, the study may not be generalizable to students in other disciplines or other nations. The study might have been able to produce the outcomes as intended by the study's aims. The outcomes, however, can be different in a different situation.

REFERENCES

Abidin, M. J. Z., Mohammadi, M. P., & Lean, O. C. (2011). *The Reading Habits of Malaysian Chinese University Students*. In *Journal of Studies in Education, 1*(1), E9.

Fisher, P. J. L. (1996). Who reads when and why. In E. H., Cramer, M. Castle (Ed.). Fostering the love of reading: The effective domain in reading education. Newark: International Reading Association.

Guthrie, J. T. (2000). Contexts for engagement and motivation in reading. Handbook of reading Research, (vol 3), 1-15.

Karim, A., Hasan, A., & Shahriza, N. (2007). Reading Habits and Attitude in the Digital Age: Analysis of Gender and Academic Program Differences in Malaysia. *The Electronic Library*. http://umpir.ump.edu.my/5/1/Reading_habits_and_attitude _at_digital_age_-_amelia_2.pdf

. Kurtus, R. (2002, January 27). Gaining knowledge by reading. *The Courier Mail*, p. 22.

Liu, Z. (2005). Reading behavior in the digital environment: Changes in reading behavior over the past ten years. *The Journal of Documentation*, *61*(6), 700–712. doi:10.1108/00220410510632040

Priajana, N. (2013). *Student teachers' reading habits and preferences.*In [JEFL]. *Journal on English as a Foreign Language*, *3*(2), 71. doi:10.23971/jefl.v3i2.65

Scales, A. M., & Rhee, O. (2001). Adult reading habits and patterns. *Reading Psychology, 22*(3), 175–203. doi:10.1080/027027101753170610

Vandenhoek, T. (2013). Screen reading habits among university students. *International Journal of Education and Development using ICT, 9*(2). https://www.learntechlib.org/p/130282/

Yang, A. (2007). Cultivating a reading habit: Silent reading at school. *Asian EFL Journal, 9*(2), 115–129.

Chapter 11
Curriculum Innovation Based on Learning Styles to Help Teachers Become Professionals:
Towards a Successful Educational System

Zalik Nuryana
Universitas Ahmad Dahlan, Indonesia

Wenbin Xu
Nanjing Normal University, China

Shiqi Lu
Nanjing Normal University, China

ABSTRACT

Learning style is the perfection and operationalization of the cognitive approach used in education due to the overall pattern providing direction to training and teaching. This emphasizes the cognitive, affective, and psychological characteristics based on how students perceive, interact, and respond to their learning environment. Therefore, this study aims to explain the integration of curriculum innovations regarding learning styles, to help teachers become professionals towards a successful educational system. The results showed that curriculum integration provided convenience for teachers and students, leading to educators' accommodation of learning styles. This curriculum began with teachers' teaching style, which included pre (introduction lessons), core (learning process), and post (evaluation) activities. The results also revealed that this integration increased students' interests and helped teachers become professionals in the educational system.

INTRODUCTION

Learning is a compulsory process for humans willing to change from illiterate to knowledgeable dimen-

DOI: 10.4018/978-1-6684-6682-7.ch011

sions through a formal (school) and non-formal (experiential) method impacting cognitive, affective, and psychomotor factors. Based on this process, each country reportedly has its policy to regulate education to produce a golden generation with the continuous learning ability to compete at the international level. This explains that no suitable learning method is observed for all students, which tendencies are based on the application of their techniques. Since students do not realize this educational tendency, the potential is not subsequently maximized. Learning style is also a refinement and operationalization of the cognitive style used in education due to being the overall pattern providing direction to training and teaching. This emphasizes the cognitive, affective, and psychological characteristics based on the methods by which students understand, interact, and respond to their learning environment (Rourke, 2000). According to Simon, learning styles were used to design student academic achievements, clinical/medical training, career development, and educational policies (Cassidy, 2004). This proved that each individual had their habits and tendencies, as some preferred quiet atmospheres with easier learning abilities by listening to music and vice versa. In Learning, students' attitudes are often influenced by the conditions of activities and educational processes, with each training style found to be very important.

Based on Kolb, learning styles were divided into four types: The Converger, Diverger, Assimilator, and Accommodator. This proved that the educational approach was a two-way combination to process the conditions containing Abstract Conceptualization, Concrete Experience, Active Experiment, and Reflective Observation. Furthermore, learning style affects student achievement (Bhatti & Bart, 2013), with the new assumption that teaching should consider the learners' training approaches due to their patterns of reacting and using the stimulus obtained in the educational process. It is also a combination of methods where a person absorbs, organizes, and manages the information obtained. From the study of Bobbi de porter and Mike Hernacki in Quantum Teaching, learning styles were the characteristics and preferences regarding how humans concentrate, absorb, obtain, manage, respond, and assume information, respectively (Prasnig, 2007; Singer-Nourie, 2001). These styles are the strong individual characteristics leading to consequences in knowledge absorption due to being a key variable towards developing the concept and design of a more leveraged learning process (Hayes & Allinson, 1996). In this condition, students also have various learning motives based on characters, such as age, gender, school background, and training attitude. By preparing good learning designs through a structured curriculum, teachers and schools are found to subsequently influence students' motivation and academic achievement (Bruinsma, 2004). This leads to new ideas for preparing a learning style-based curriculum, as no study has been observed to evaluate these procedural tendencies to improve student achievement. Therefore, the role of this curriculum is found to be very important with the foundation of learning preparation, to effectively and efficiently perform training operations towards the maximization of student achievement.

According to the predictive process of text learning, the topic interest influenced training persistence and was related to affective responses. Based on the styles and integration into the curriculum innovation, learning interests provide new directions and solutions for the world of education, specifically schools, to maximize student development towards better achievement. This is used to analyze each student's interest in a subject, with learning styles being utilized in helping teachers to maximize students' selective activities. Meanwhile, the integration of curriculum is a new holistic approach, where learning style-based interest is referentially included and implemented by teachers.

Power of Learning Styles

The style emphasizes differences in individuals' most effective learning patterns. Many opinions explain that optimal education is obtained when the diagnosis of training and teaching approaches are appropriate (Pashler et al., 2008b). Over the last decade, some previous studies revealed that student achievement improved while teaching methods were appropriate to their learning styles, biological enhancements, and developmental characteristics. These results confirmed that some of these factors affected the learning patterns, with no best or worst styles being observed. Each learning style also had its characteristics, indicating that students were not solely labelled on a specific approach. Stronger tendencies were also observed for the learning styles (Klavas, 2002), which were very dangerous when used to punish students (Kolb & Kolb, 2005). Subsequently, many previous studies focused on learning styles from various perspectives. In this present study, the relationship of these styles to the human senses was evaluated, with the adopted developed concept based on the theory of Bobbi De Porter and Mike Hernacki, namely audio, visual, and kinesthetic approaches (DePorter & Hernacki, 1992), as shown in Figure 1.

Figure 1. Types of audio, visual, and kinesthetic styles were adopted from Christian Jarrett (Jarrett, 2018)

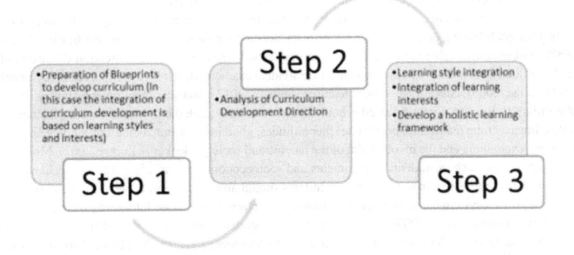

According to Figure 1, the three learning styles had their characteristics, with the visual approach emphasizing the aspect of vision. This explained that the people with the ability quickly understood the subject matter through writing or pictures. Although more prominent in some people, visual acuity is still very strong in other individuals due to the brain containing more devices for processing optical information than the remaining senses. Visual students are at their best when provided with realistic examples, diagrams, idea maps, icons, pictures, etc. In addition, students are encouraged to create many symbols and pictures in their notes, with mind maps a great tool in any subject. This is because visual students learn best when they understand the whole picture.

Figure 1 also explained that the audio style emphasized the auditory aspect, as people with this approach learn quicker when the learning materials are delivered through hearing aids. This revealed that the human hearing mind was more powerful than expected, with the ears constantly capturing and storing audio information without actual realization. These types of students prefer to learn from sound, dialogue, reading aloud, silent hearing repetition, and telling others about their experiences through recorded lessons. In repetitive information, listening to lectures, examples, and stories are the most important learning method for auditory learners due to the preference to repeatedly record information rather than write notes. They may repeat what they said. There are also students who habitually listen to music while studying, with others observing it as a distraction. According to Figure 1, the kinesthetic style was also observed as a learning pattern emphasizing motion and touch. This revealed that students with the ability preferred applied projects and learned quicker by performing what was being taught. Subsequently, these learners prefer to learn through movement and are best at memorizing information by associating motion with each fact. Students are also unable to be constantly static, as the body's movement is needed to keep the mind alive.

FACTORS AFFECTING LEARNING ACHIEVEMENT

Several factors affect student learning outcomes, including teachers and learning media. These media are specifically designed for a teacher, through the presentation of faces, voices, and motions (not cartoons) having an impact on student achievement (Yılmaz & Kılıç-Çakmak, 2012). In mathematics, e.g., class size, teaching characteristics often have a role in improving achievement, indicating that the main focus of teacher goals has a greater influence on students' accomplishment (Meece et al., 2006; Rivkin et al., 2005). Other considerable factors affecting learning achievement are parental attention (Castro et al., 2015; Wilder, 2014), students' involvement and individual character (Carini et al., 2006; Klem & Connell, 2004; Taras, 2005), educational system features (Spinath, 2012), and school autonomy (Finlay, 1969). According to Brophy, a goal-oriented school should meet several elemental requirements, including a safe climate, strong leadership, positive teacher attitudes, good instruction/curriculum, student and staff progress evaluation, and the involvement of the parents and society (Becker & Luthar, 2002). Moreover, external factors, such as students' assignments and socioeconomic status, affect learning achievement (Winne & Nesbit, 2010). In the classroom, students should always be calm for learning conditions not be tense, with a system being subsequently provided to teachers to ensure interesting educational processes (Laukenmann et al., 2003). Based on this concept, student achievement was influenced by internal and external factors. This showed that the internal factors were intrinsically obtained from students' individual development or external awareness stimuli, such as health, talents, interests and motivations, methods, and learning styles. Meanwhile, external factors were extrinsically obtained from the individual students, such as the family, school, and community environmental conditions. As stated by Cardoso, the factors rarely observed for producing good academic achievements were the relationships between teacher-students, students-students, and vice versa (Cardoso et al., 2011).

NEED FOR INNOVATION IN LEARNING STYLE-BASED CURRICULUM DESIGN

Innovation is directed at the success and progress in one, some, or all aspects of education, such as theory and practice, curriculum, Learning, policy, technology, institutions, administration, institutional culture, and teachers. All these aspects reportedly can be applied in all educational sectors due to having a positive impact on students (Serdyukov, 2017). The curriculum is purposefully designed to establish the important principles and concepts that can provide opportunities and in-depth exploration in various educational contexts. It also aims to provide real opportunities in the preparation of quality work instructions (Bertenthal; & Curtis, 2002). Various operations have reportedly been carried out by the secondary (Junior and Senior High Schools) and tertiary (Universities) institutions towards designing a curriculum to develop students' achievements. These were conducted through the knowledge of the learners' learning styles, educational and family backgrounds, and other factors, with the schools being expected to maximize their potential (Vasquez & Duran, 1985). In this case, the factors affecting the achievements should be appropriately designed, with parents' involvement in the academic progress also found to be very influential.

Furthermore, the consideration of students by their parents is found to have a good impact on academic achievements. Family and educational backgrounds, intellectual ability, gender (Papanastasiou, 2002), and homework also affect student achievement (Fehrmann et al., 1987). This explains that the strength of the curriculum is needed to design a suitable model, based on the tendency of students' learning styles. When the learning design is not adequately designed through the curriculum, its operations are unable to be optimally performed. Therefore, this curriculum innovation aims to improve students' academic achievement.

CURRICULUM INNOVATION INTEGRATION OF LEARNING STYLES, TEACHING STYLES, LEARNING STRATEGIES, AND LEARNING EVALUATION

Blended Learning aims to play the teachers' main role in guiding, inspiring, and monitoring the teaching process due to combining the advantages of traditional and modern methods. It also aims to fully reflect students' initiative, enthusiasm, and creativity, as the main part of the learning process (Grasha & Yangarber-Hicks, 2000). The sole focus on learning styles is insufficient to improve student achievement, as schools should subsequently consider other factors, such as teaching approaches. With the utilization of technology, integrating these styles is a very suitable solution for modern developments (Schibeci, 1989). External factors also affect student achievement (Pashler et al., 2008a), as teachers are recommended to identify suitable subject matters through visual or audio aids. This should be accompanied by selecting a suitable method for the learning and teaching styles (Kirby et al., 1988). However, knowing students' learning styles ensures an easier and more optimal educational design for teachers. For instance, "when a lesson requires visual aids suitable for specific students, what about those with other learning style tendencies?" This is a problem for teachers and students, as a comprehensive understanding is highly needed (PASK, 1976). In this condition, combining Learning (Joore et al., 2016; Schroeder, 1993) and assessment (Riener & Willingham, 2010)strategies is a powerful weapon to improve student achievement. Figure 2 explains the methods by which curriculum development served as a tool for organizing supportive learning concepts.

The concept of learning styles should be understood by considering several aspects, e.g., (1) Students do have differences from one another, indicating that teachers should broadly assume many external factors towards improving learning achievement, (2) The belief in learning styles is compatible with the egalitarian educational perspectives, which stated that each student had different values, strengths, and characters. This difference does not require the knowledge of learning style theory due to being a basic ability, and (3) The theories on learning styles have become a common knowledge, as results cannot be used as student justification. For example, can students with a hearing predisposition with auditory as-

Figure 2. The concept of curriculum development as a tool to organize the concept of education to maximize learning outcomes

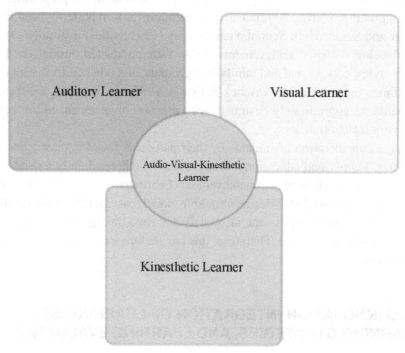

sociations possibly learn geography by hearing? And Is it possible for students with visual styles to be better at music by observing? Therefore, these conditions cannot be referentially used to justify students (Bureau, n.d.).

The problem associated with this study is that students have not explained what underlies the differences in learning style tendencies, as a series of educational processes were also commonly unclear, very uniform, and detrimental (Reynolds, 1997). Therefore, the curriculum integration to design learning style programs is very important, based on being an innovation to be futuristically used as a reference for schools, specifically universities (Figure 3). Moreover, the central or school-based curriculum for each major field/subject has set learning goals and objectives, such as knowledge, abilities, values, and attitudes. Assessment is also the practice of obtaining learning evidence in various aspects (including process and outcomes), such as data interpretation, the education system, and the performance assessment for providing feedback to students, teachers, schools, parents, and other stakeholders. This indicates that assessment is integral to the curriculum, Learning, and feedback cycles. In this case, the importance of curriculum integration should be conveyed as a reference in implementing education.

Each school has the flexibility to design a adaptive curriculum that can help students overcome learning problems and improve their achievements. The curriculum development innovation is shown in Figure 3, where three steps served as a reference for creating the innovations designed for school needs, such as integrating educational styles, strategies, and evaluation, respectively. Therefore, this integration should be designed in the curriculum as a reference in implementing education and teaching within the classroom. Despite being easy, it is often not considered by schools.

Figure 3. Steps of curriculum development innovation based on learning styles and interests

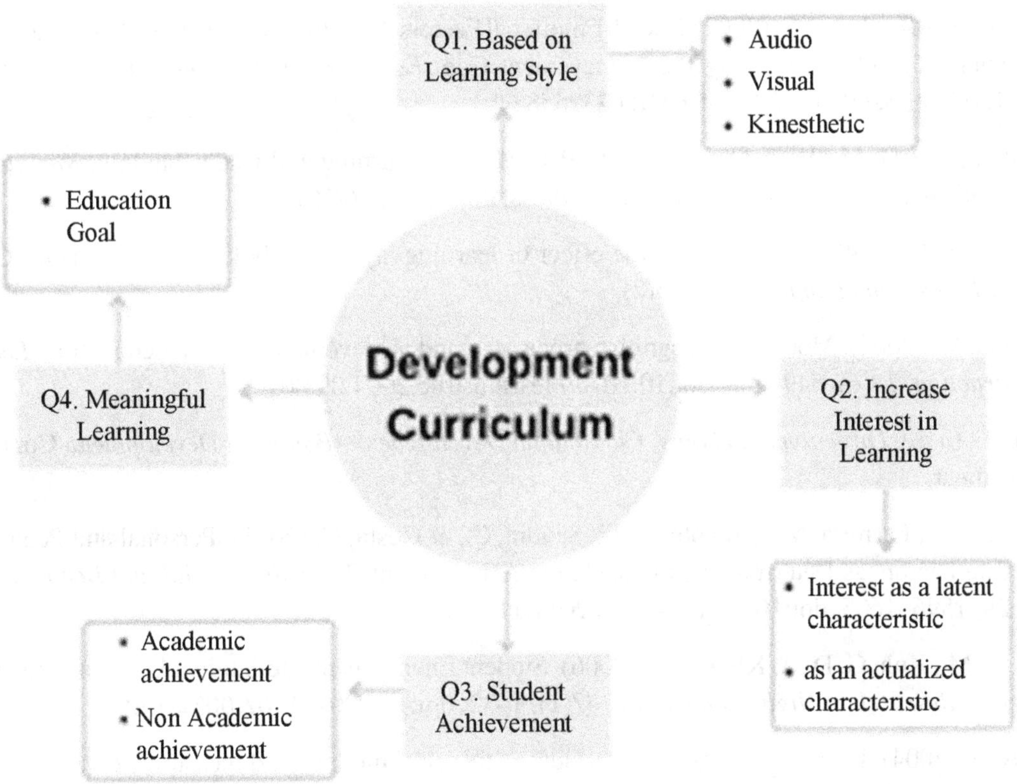

CONCLUSION

Due to the overall pattern that provides direction to training and teaching, learning style is the perfection and operational definitions of the cognitive approach used in education. This emphasizes cognitive, affective, and psychological factors based on how students perceive, interact, and respond to their learning environment. This confirmed that each student tended towards different learning styles, with teachers being required to accommodate learners' educational approaches. Teachers should also understand the character and the teaching styles accommodating all student needs. Furthermore, curriculum integration helped students, teachers, parents, and related parties provide solutions to maximizing learning achievement. The development of a learning-based curriculum also began with the following: (1) the concept of audio, visual, and kinesthetic learning style tendencies, (2) increasing students' learning interest by understanding the tendency of each style, (3) developing both academic and non-academic students' achievements, and (4) ensure meaningful learning objectives, for educational styles to improve student achievement.

REFERENCES

Becker, B. E., & Luthar, S. S. (2002). Social-Emotional Factors Affecting Achievement Outcomes Among Disadvantaged Students: Closing the Achievement Gap. *Educational Psychologist*, *37*(4), 197–214. doi:10.1207/S15326985EP3704_1 PMID:23255834

Bertenthal; J. P. G. M. W., & Curtis, J. B. L. P. C. (2002). Learning and Understanding. *Kartografija i Geoinformacije*, *12*(20). National Academies Press. doi:10.17226/10129

Bhatti, R., & Bart, W. M. (2013). On the effect of learning style on scholastic achievement. *Current Issues in Education (Tempe, Ariz.)*, *16*(2).

Bruinsma, M. (2004). Motivation, cognitive processing and achievement in higher education. *Learning and Instruction*, *14*(6), 549–568. doi:10.1016/j.learninstruc.2004.09.001

Bureau, E. (n.d.). *Direction of Schools' Curriculum Development - Balanced Development*. Continuous Enhancement.

Cardoso, A. P., Ferreira, M., Abrantes, J. L., Seabra, C., & Costa, C. (2011). Personal and Pedagogical Interaction Factors as Determinants of Academic Achievement. *Procedia: Social and Behavioral Sciences*, *29*, 1596–1605. doi:10.1016/j.sbspro.2011.11.402

Carini, R. M., Kuh, G. D., & Klein, S. P. (2006). Student Engagement and Student Learning: Testing the Linkages*. *Research in Higher Education*, *47*(1), 1–32. doi:10.100711162-005-8150-9

Cassidy, S. (2004). Learning Styles: An overview of theories, models, and measures. *Educational Psychology*, *24*(4), 419–444. doi:10.1080/0144341042000228834

Castro, M., Expósito-Casas, E., López-Martín, E., Lizasoain, L., Navarro-Asencio, E., & Gaviria, J. L. (2015). Parental involvement on student academic achievement: A meta-analysis. *Educational Research Review*, *14*, 33–46. doi:10.1016/j.edurev.2015.01.002

DePorter, B., & Hernacki, M. (1992). *Quantum learning: Unleashing the genius in you*. Dell.

Fehrmann, P. G., Keith, T. Z., & Reimers, T. M. (1987). Home Influence on School Learning: Direct and Indirect Effects of Parental Involvement on High School Grades. *The Journal of Educational Research*, *80*(6), 330–337. doi:10.1080/00220671.1987.10885778

Finlay, S. E. (1969). Student Achievement. *Lancet*, *294*(7618), 495. doi:10.1016/S0140-6736(69)90200-1 PMID:4185483

Grasha, A. F., & Yangarber-Hicks, N. (2000). Integrating Teaching Styles and Learning Styles with Instructional Technology. *College Teaching*, *48*(1), 2–10. doi:10.1080/87567550009596080

Hayes, J., & Allinson, C. W. (1996). The Implications of Learning Styles for Training and Development: A Discussion of the Matching Hypothesis. *British Journal of Management*, *7*(1), 63–73. doi:10.1111/j.1467-8551.1996.tb00106.x

Jarrett, C. (2018). *"Another nail in the coffin for learning styles" – students did not benefit from studying according to their supposed learning style.* The British Psychological Society. https://digest.bps.org.uk/2018/04/03/another-nail-in-the-coffin-for-learning-styles-students-did-not-benefit-from-studying-according-to-their-supposed-learning-style/

Joore, P., Brezet, H., & Care, S., Sykes, A. O., Giesen, D., Meertens, V., Vis-visschers, R., Beukenhorst, D., Moghimipour, I., & Seminar, E. (2016). Online library : Digital copies. *BMJ Open*. doi:10.1177/1468794107071408

Kirby, J. R., Moore, P. J., & Schofield, N. J. (1988). Verbal and visual learning styles. *Contemporary Educational Psychology, 13*(2), 169–184. doi:10.1016/0361-476X(88)90017-3

Klavas, R. D. J. S. B. A. (2002). California Journal of Science Education. *Journal of Science Education, II*(2), 75–98.

Klem, A. M., & Connell, J. P. (2004). Relationships Matter: Linking Teacher Support to Student Engagement and Achievement. *The Journal of School Health, 74*(7), 262–273. doi:10.1111/j.1746-1561.2004.tb08283.x PMID:15493703

Kolb, A. Y., & Kolb, D. A. (2005). Learning Styles and Learning Spaces: Enhancing Experiential Learning in Higher Education. *Academy of Management Learning & Education, 4*(2), 193–212. https://www.jstor.org/stable/40214287. doi:10.5465/amle.2005.17268566

Laukenmann, M., Bleicher, M., Fuß, S., Gläser-Zikuda, M., Mayring, P., & von Rhöneck, C. (2003). An investigation of the influence of emotional factors on learning in physics instruction. *International Journal of Science Education, 25*(4), 489–507. doi:10.1080/09500690210163233

Meece, J. L., Anderman, E. M., & Anderman, L. H. (2006). Classroom Goal Structure, Student Motivation, and Academic Achievement. *Annual Review of Psychology, 57*(1), 487–503. doi:10.1146/annurev.psych.56.091103.070258 PMID:16318604

Papanastasiou, C. (2002). Effects of Background and School Factors on the Mathematics Achievement. *Educational Research and Evaluation, 8*(1), 55–70. doi:10.1076/edre.8.1.55.6916

Pashler, H., McDaniel, M., Rohrer, D., & Bjork, R. (2008a). Learning Styles. *Psychological Science in the Public Interest, 9*(3), 105–119. doi:10.1111/j.1539-6053.2009.01038.x PMID:26162104

Pashler, H., McDaniel, M., Rohrer, D., & Bjork, R. (2008b). Learning Styles Concepts and Evidence. *Psychological Science in the Public Interest, 9*(3), 105–119. doi:10.1111/j.1539-6053.2009.01038.x PMID:26162104

Pask, G.PASK. (1976). Styles And Strategies Of Learning. *The British Journal of Educational Psychology, 46*(2), 128–148. doi:10.1111/j.2044-8279.1976.tb02305.x

Prasnig, B. (2007). *The Power of Learning Styles :Memacu Anak Melejitkan Prestasi dengan Gaya Belajarnya.* Kaifa.

Reynolds, M. (1997). Learning Styles: A Critique. *Management Learning, 28*(2), 115–133. doi:10.1177/1350507697282002

Riener, C., & Willingham, D. (2010). The Myth of Learning Styles. *Change: The Magazine of Higher Learning*, *42*(5), 32–35. doi:10.1080/00091383.2010.503139

Rivkin, S. G., Hanushek, E. A., & Kain, J. F. (2005). Teachers, Schools, and Academic Achievement. *Econometrica*, *73*(2), 417–458. doi:10.1111/j.1468-0262.2005.00584.x

Rourke, L. & Lysynchik, L. (2000). *The Influence of Learning Style on Achievement in Hypertext [microform]*. ERIC Clearinghouse. https://eric.ed.gov/?id=ED446102

Schibeci, R. A. (1989). Influences on Student Attitudes and Achievement in Science. *Science Education*, *73*(1), 13–24. doi:10.1002ce.3730730103

Schroeder, C. C. (1993). New Students—New Learning Styles. *Change: The Magazine of Higher Learning*, *25*(5), 21–26. doi:10.1080/00091383.1993.9939900

Serdyukov, P. (2017). Innovation in education: What works, what doesn't, and what to do about it? *Journal of Research in Innovative Teaching & Learning*, *10*(1), 4–33. doi:10.1108/JRIT-10-2016-0007

Singer-Nourie, B. D. P. M. R. and S. (2001). *Quantum Teaching*. Kaifa.

Spinath, B. (2012). Academic Achievement. In *Encyclopedia of Human Behavior* (pp. 1–8). Elsevier. doi:10.1016/B978-0-12-375000-6.00001-X

Taras, H. (2005). Physical Activity and Student Performance at School. *The Journal of School Health*, *75*(6), 214–218. doi:10.1111/j.1746-1561.2005.00026.x PMID:16014127

Vasquez, M. J. T., & Duran, R. P. (1985). Hispanics' Education and Background: Predictors of College Achievement. *The Journal of Higher Education*, *56*(2), 233. doi:10.2307/1981674

Wilder, S. (2014). Effects of parental involvement on academic achievement: A meta-synthesis. *Educational Review*, *66*(3), 377–397. doi:10.1080/00131911.2013.780009

Winne, P. H., & Nesbit, J. C. (2010). The Psychology of Academic Achievement. *Annual Review of Psychology*, *61*(1), 653–678. doi:10.1146/annurev.psych.093008.100348 PMID:19575616

Yılmaz, R., & Kılıç-Çakmak, E. (2012). Educational interface agents as social models to influence learner achievement, attitude and retention of Learning. *Computers & Education*, *59*(2), 828–838. doi:10.1016/j.compedu.2012.03.020

Chapter 12
Study on Learning of Communication Channels at the Grassroots Level With Reference to Social Issues

Anurag Verma

Karnavati University, India

ABSTRACT

Communication helps an individual to survive, grow, progress, and develop within a structure. Communication also creates a common pool of ideas and beliefs through a systematic process. When it comes to rural areas, the role of communication and communicators becomes more important because of the educational background of people. The Indian rural population faces a lot of social issues like girl's education, dowery, domestic violence, etc. The government always initiates number of programs in rural areas to make people aware regarding the social issues. Also, the change agents like educators and NGO workers work along with the government agencies, but most of the time, the campaign fails to impress the people at grassroot level. The communication at grass root level allows rural people to be at the centre of any initiatives. There are so many formal channels of communication in rural areas and there are some informal channels of communication at grass root level which helps people to understand information as they are.

INTRODUCTION

Effective communication is one of the most important factors in Rural Development. The communication channels developed amongst government agencies, rural institutions, and individuals create the chances to make a certain segment of information and experience desirable for rural development (Fowsar et al., 2020). Government agencies have been initiating and running various social issues campaigns in rural areas, which stretches in all directions. There are so many successful campaigns that make people aware of various social issues. Rural audiences must be involved in all grassroots communications because they

DOI: 10.4018/978-1-6684-6682-7.ch012

are central to any development initiative (Fowsar, 2020). The responsibility of mass media in progress can be split into three parts, i.e., information, instruction, and participation (Rameez et al., 2020). To initiate information, it is very important to keep all concerned in the loop so it can lead to instructions and then the participation of the larger group. When it comes to rural areas, the communication channel is not in the hand of one authority, but there are so many officials involved (Rameez, 2019). Whether it is a government-appointed person, a local teacher with no official designation, or any other powerful 'opinion leader' of the village. Rural areas, specifically areas far from any city or major spot and with no concrete communication infrastructure, always face a problem of getting authentic information. In such cases, the informal source of communication helps government agencies a lot (Rameez, 2018). It has been observed that the people in rural areas listen to their local influencers and try to get wisdom and knowledge about the various awareness programs from them. It is also reflected in the cinemas where the person who is literate and considered to be knowledgeable, people always take his/her advice. Communication in primitive social structures not only satisfies people's needs but also achieves society's functional and persistent needs. In any rural social structure, informal communication sources help maintain traditional knowledge. Indeed, the rural areas in India are now equipped with television networks, mobile phones, the internet, various public service advertising, etc. Still, on the other hand, it is also true that illiterate audiences are very easy to be manipulated, and they don't easily decode the core of the communication. Most of the time, the rural audiences act like laggards, i.e., the last ones to adopt effective communication about social issues. Such an audience waits for others (Early Adopters) to follow or adopt any new communication, and they see their reaction. If the communication is helping the early adopters, then the laggards follow the same (Fowsar et al., 2022).

The change agencies are running many campaigns to make people aware, and in rural areas, the role of opinion leaders is very important in spreading such information. The opinion leader is an entity that can change the attitude and beliefs of another individual (Rogers, 1962). Opinion leaders are kind of unannounced leaders whom people trust and listen to his/her wise words. Change agents within a certain social structure use the opinions of such leaders as lieutenants in awareness campaigns. The same experience can also be seen in the first chapter of The Passing of Traditional Society, The Grocer, and The Chief (Lerner, 1958). The reason for ineffective communication can be so many. It can be the background of the receiver, the attitude of the social structure, or the inability of the Communicator. In many things, communication is also considered to be ineffective when people do not want to be changed or the opinion leader is very traditional. One of the recent examples of such a situation can be seen in the web series Panchayat (Rameez and Fowsar, 2018). The change agent is trying to spread awareness about birth control through wall paintings, and one of the citizens cannot decode the message. This is truly an example of day-to-day life in rural India.

REVIEW OF LITERATURE

Various researchers, authors, thinkers, and change agencies have tried to explore communication in rural development. Wilbur Schramm (1977), in his book Mass Media, and National Development, talks about the involvement of media channels with various interpersonal channels at the local level. Development in underdeveloped and developing countries can take place quickly when big change agencies shake hands with local-level change agents who always have a grip on their people. On the other hand, Katz (1961) says:

that it is inconceivable to design new information without any back story of the social order in which potential beneficiaries are located. It is always hard to design communication messages without knowing the social structure where the communication will be diffused. In His Book Diffusion of Innovations, Everett M. Rogers (1962) talks about the role of opinion leaders in a particular social system. By their quiet compliance with the structure's customs, opinion leaders act as an appropriate example for the innovative actions of their admirers. When opinion leaders matched their supporters, it was noted that they are more visible to all types of outside communication and have slightly above average public level. The same opinion leaders can be very useful in any diffusion of information at a place where people gather to discuss causes. Parhi and Mohanty (2011), Folk and Traditional Media: A Powerful Rural Development Tool talks about the folk medium of spreading information. Their study reveals that most people use various folk mediums to gather information. Still, in this digital technology era, folk mediums are being replaced by digital awareness campaigns. Misra (2002) found that the participation of local people in the administration and other change initiatives was less, and it was not helping the social structures. He suggested that the involvement of local people is very important in any development initiatives. Pandey and Kumar (1999) indicate that rural people prefer to use local interpersonal communication channels, like friends, relatives, shopkeepers, etc. Uma Narula (2006) also claims in her book Development Communication- Theory and Practice that people participation, that the participation of the local audience is very important in any communication. Bella Mody (1991) says that development would have to include mobilization and reorganization of the marginalized majority within the community.

OBJECTIVES

The objectives of the study are

- To find out the use of media in rural areas to get information in day-to-day life
- To analyze the channels of communication at the grassroots level
- To see the involvement of informal sources of communication in rural areas
- To study the impact of formal sources of communication in rural areas

THEORETICAL FRAMEWORK

The Social Support theory is being followed in the study to study the objectives of the study. This theory is about how people in a social system support each other and establish a network of communication to spread information. People also experience physical, emotional, and monetary support from these networks. The researcher has also taken guidance from opinion leadership theory, where people take the help of opinion leaders to authenticate a piece of information (Varma and Verma, 2017).

METHODOLOGY

The study primarily uses primary data collected by survey. The researcher has used a self-made closed and open-ended questionnaire to gather information. Researchers have used a multistage sampling method

Table 1. The demography of the respondents

S. No.	Variables	Category (S)						
1	Gender	Male			Female			
		113 (61.4%)			72 (39.1%)			
2	Age (In years)	18-26	27-35	36-44	45-53	54-62		Above 63
		39 (21.2%)	35 (19%)	41 (22.3%)	32 (17.4%)	26 (14.1%)		11 (6%)
3	Education	Illiterate	Neo literate	Primary	Secondary	Senior Secondary	Graduate	Postgraduate
		22 (12%)	25 (13.6%)	32 (17.4%)	27 (14.7%)	36 (19.6%)	26 (14.1%)	18 (9.8%)
4	Profession	Housewife	Govt. Employees	Private Employees	Business	Agriculture	Labor	Student
		21 (11.4%)	17 (9.2%)	22 (12%)	30 (16.3%)	40 (21.7%)	26 (14.1%)	27 (14.7%)

for this study to collect the right sample. Based on certain parameters, two villages of Rajasthan state, Mundoti and Bandarsindiri, were selected to carry out the study. Both the villages are remote and are situated far from the city. A total of 250 samples were collected, and out of those 184 samples were found suitable for the study. Data is analyzed on SPSS, and Cronbach's Alpha is applied to check the reliability.

INTERPRETING DATA

This study's data was organized, coded, and analyzed using Statistical Packages for Social Science (SPSS). Frequency and percentage were used to present the results (table 1).

After analyzing the data in the table, it is revealed that

- 61.4% of males and 39.1% of females participated in the study.
- In the context of age, 22.3% of respondents were in the age group of 36-44, followed by 21.2% of respondents who belonged to the 18-26 age group. 19% belong to the 27-35 age group, followed by 17.4% of respondents who belong to the 45-33 age group. 14.1% were between 54 to 62 and above 63, and there were only 6% of respondents.
- 19.6% of respondents completed high school, while 17.4% completed primary school. 14.1% of respondents are graduates and 14.7% are matriculated. 13% of respondents are illiterate or neoliterate. 9.8% of respondents are postgraduates.
- 21.7% of participants do agriculture as their profession, followed by 16.3% who are in business. 14.7% are students, followed by 12% in private jobs. 14.1% of respondents work as laborers. 11.4% are housewives, and 9.2% of respondents have government jobs.

Respondents' media use is displayed.

Table 2 shows the different sources of information people use to get information. 88% prefer TV, followed by 74.5%, i.e., newspaper. 37% of respondents use the radio, and 23.4% use the internet to get information. The data in table 2 are mixed, i.e., people were given the option to choose multiple sources of information. Figure 1 shows the individual responses of participants regarding various sources of information they prefer.

Table 2. The different sources of information people

No.	Response	Frequency	%
1	Newspaper	137	74.5%
2	TV	162	88.0%
3	Radio	68	37.0%
4	Internet	43	23.4%

Figure 1. Individual responses of participants regarding various sources of information

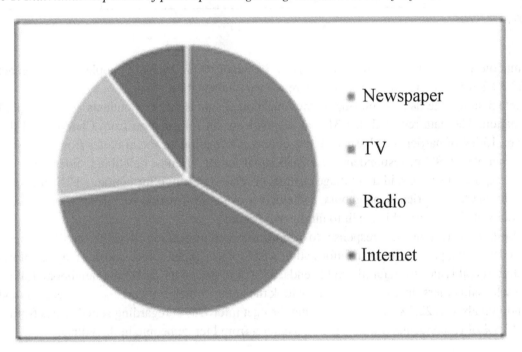

Table 3 reveals participants' responses toward formal communication channels in rural areas. 18.5% of respondents prefer to take information from the panchayat, newspaper, and social worker. 16.3% of respondents take information from social workers. 15.8% of respondents prefer newspapers to take information on social issues. 14.1% of respondents take information from village heads, newspapers, and journalists. 10.9% of participants have said they take information on various social issues from the village head. 9.2% of respondents have said about the village head, social worker, and journalists, and only 6% of participants said they get information from the panchayat. The above data shows how people use and believe formal communication channels. It is observed that social workers are the most trustworthy source in rural areas, and people usually take information from them. After social workers, people take information from newspapers and other available sources.

Table 4 and figure 2 show respondents' responses to formal social communication channels. 51.1% of respondents trust social workers' advice. 50% of participants said that newspapers give more relevant

Table 3. Displays the responses of participants toward the sources of formal communication channels

No.	Response	Frequency	%
1	Panchayat	11	*6.0%
2	Village head	20	*10.9%
3	Social worker	30	*16.3%
4	*Village head and Social worker	17	*9.2%
5	Newspaper	29	*15.8%
6	*Panchayat, Newspaper and social worker	34	*18.5%
7	*Village head, newspaper and journalist	26	*14.1%
8	*Village head, journalist and Social worker	17	*9.2%

*Multiple responses

information. The frequency of village heads is 41.3% out of 100%. 25.5% of people have said panchayat, and 22.3% have said journalists can give more relevant information.

Table 5 shows the data of informal communication channels that respondents use for social issues information. The data revealed that 31% of respondents get information from Chaupal and their co-workers. 15.8% of participants have said they collect information on social issues from a neighbor and literate people. 29.9% of respondents have said about family, friends, neighbors, elders, and chaupal. 13% of respondents have said that village chaupal provides relevant information. 10.3% of respondents have said that family, friends, neighbors, and elders provide information on various social issues. 8.2% of participants have given this credit to family and friends.

Table 6 shows respondents' responses to the informal communication channels. 66.8% of respondents have said that Chaupal gives relevant information. 41.8% of respondents have said that they get information regarding social issues from family and friends. 38% of respondents said about neighbors, followed by 29.9% who said others. In this category, they took the name of their co-workers, shopkeepers randomly met individuals, etc. 22.3% of people said that they get information regarding social issues from elders. Only 15.8% of respondents said they get information from literate people in the village.

Table 4. Individuals toward the formal information channel for social issues

S. No.	Response	Frequency	%
1	Panchayat	47	*25.5%
2	Village head	76	*41.3%
3	Newspaper	92	*50.0%
4	Journalist	41	*22.3%
5	Social worker	94	*51.1%

*Multiple responses

Figure 2. Individual responses of respondents regarding the formal channels of communication for social issues

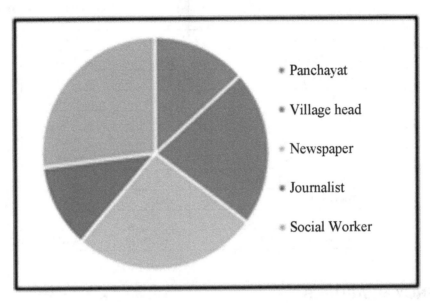

Table 5. Reveals responses toward the in-formal information channel for social issues

SN	Response	Frequency	%
1	Friend	15	8.2%
2	Chaupal	24	13.0%
3	*Family, friends and Chaupal	15	8.2%
4	*Neighbor and Literate people	30	16.3%
5	*Chaupal and others	55	29.9%
6	*Family friend, Neighbor and elder	19	10.3%
7	*Family, friends, neighbors, Elder and chaupal	26	14.1%

*Multiple responses

Table 6. Respondents' views on informal social information channels issues

SN	Response	Frequency	%
1	Family friend	77	41.8%
2	Neighbor	70	38.0%
3	Literate people	31	16.8%
4	Elder	41	22.3%
5	Chaupal	123	66.8%
6	Others	55	29.9%

Table 7. The internal consistency of communication channels

No.	Channels for health information	Mean	Correlation Item-Total	Deleted Cronbach's Alpha
1	Trust on Panchayat	3.51	0.965	0.983
2	Trust in Village head	3.27	0.964	0.983
3	Trust on Newspaper	3.09	0.957	0.984
4	Trust in Social worker	4.1	0.916	0.986
5	Trust on Journalist	3.92	0.911	0.985
6	Trust in family and friends	3.2	0.939	0.984
7	Trust on Neighbors	3.87	0.947	0.984
8	Trust in the Literate people of the village	4.12	0.919	0.986
9	Trust on Elders	3.75	0.907	0.985
10	Trust on Chaupal	3.67	0.909	0.985
11	Trust on Internet	2.45	0.892	0.985

CONSISTENCY MEASURES

After conducting the reliability test on SPSS, the Cronbach alpha had been obtained .986, which is more than the cut-off value (.7). In table 7, corrected items to total correlation values are acceptable, and if item Deleted value is greater than the calculated reliability value (.986), that item should be dropped from the questionnaire and not considered for further study.

Table 8. The beliefs on various communication channels for social issues

No.	Response Category	Very less	Less	Can't say	High	Very high
1	Panchayat	14 (7.6%)	30 (16.3%)	29 (15.8%)	66 (35.9%)	45 (24.5%)
2	Village head	26 (14.1%)	28 (15.2%)	33 (17.9%)	61 (33.2%)	36 (19.6%)
3	Newspaper	27 (14.7%)	41 (22.3%)	31 (16.8%)	50 (27.2%)	35 (19%)
4	Social worker	0	10 (5.4%)	26 (14.1%)	92 (50%)	56 (30.4%)
5	Journalist	0	24 (13%)	28 (15.2%)	64 (34.8%)	68 (37%)
6	Family friends	25 (13.6%)	27 (14.7%)	37 (20.1%)	64 (34.8%)	31 (16.8%)
7	Neighbors	14 (7.6%)	38 (20.7%)	36 (19.6%)	51 (27.7%)	45 (24.5%)
8	Literate people	0	0	41 (22.3%)	71 (38.6%)	72 (39.1)
9	Elders	9 (4.9%)	11 (6%)	27 (14.7%)	84 (45.7%)	53 (28.8%)
10	Chaupal	13 (7.1%)	11 (6%)	31 (16.8%)	82 (44.6%)	47 (25.5%)
11	Internet	46 (25%)	60 (32.6%)	35 (19%)	25 (13.6%)	18 (9.8%)

Table 8 shows responses to social content communication channels. As shown in Table 8, 35.9% of respondents trust high on the information provided by the panchayat, and only 7.6% of respondents don't trust on panchayat. Table 8 shows 33.2% trust in the village head. Table 8 shows 27.2% of respondents trust high newspapers. It is also observed that almost 50% of people trust high on the information provided by change agents, which is shown in table 8. Table 8 shows that 37% of people trust journalists very highly, and 34.8% trust their family and friends. 27.7% of people trust the information provided by neighbors, shown in table 8.

Regarding information provided by literate people, 39.1% trust them very highly, followed by 45.7% of people who trust their elders for their wisdom words on social issues. Chaupal also plays an important role in spreading information; as shown in table 9, 44.6% of people get information during an informal get- together. 32.6% trust level is very less on the information they get on the internet.

Table 9. Showing responses towards attention on wall paintings

No.	Response	Frequency	%
1	Very less	7	3.7%
2	Less	24	12.1%
3	Can't say	38	18%
4	High	45	26.7%
5	Very high	71	37.1%

In rural areas, messages are drawn on the wall almost everywhere. The above data shows (table 9) the same only. Almost 37.1% of respondents said that whenever they see any message related to social issues, they see messages painted on the wall, 26.7 percent of respondents said they notice wall messages. 18% of people are unsure about it, and 12.1% and 3.7% don't pay attention to the message.

Table 10. Showing (individual) responses toward the information channels for government schemes

No.	Category	Frequency	%
1	Chaupal	97	*52.7%
2	Elders	65	*35.3%
3	Government employee	56	*30.4%
4	Newspaper	29	*15.8%
5	Social worker	81	*44.0%
6	Friend	27	*14.7%

*Out of 100%

Table 10 shows the individual responses of respondents regarding the information channels for government schemes. The data revealed that 52.7% of respondents take information regarding various government schemes from chaupal. 44% of respondents take information from social workers. 35.3% of respondents take information from elders. Out of all, 30.4% of respondents receive information from

Table 11. Expression of Views on Social Issues

No.	Response Category	Frequency	Percentage
1	Open Events	57	31.0%
2	Debating	49	26.6%
3	Discussions with Government Officers	23	12.5%
4	*Open Events and Debates	25	13.6%
5	*Discussions with various authorities	28	15.2%
6	All above	13	7.1%

*Multiple responses

government employees, followed by 15.8% who take information from newspapers. Only 14.7% of respondents receive information regarding government schemes from friends.

The above data reveals how people in rural areas express their views on social issues. 31% of people take participation in open events (table 11). They express their views on various social issues in public meetings. 26.6% of people debate various social issues. It is also observed during the survey that people think debating on social issues can be very helpful in rural development. 12.5% of people talk directly to government officers. People also said they use multiple platforms to express their views on social issues.

DISCUSSION

It is never an easy task to find out what's in the mind of rural audiences. The present study has tried to get an idea about the sources of communication channels that people prefer in rural India. After analyzing the data, the researchers observed that the informal communication channel in rural areas, like educated persons, the village head, and shopkeepers, can play an important role in disseminating any new message related to social issues. However, people also get information through television channels, but when it comes to local-level information, newspapers and change agents play an important role. It can also be seen in the study that people feel the internet does not give authentic information. Every social structure has its own needs and cannot be compared with other rural areas. As mentioned by Everett M. Rogers, every social structure is based on its own set of ideologies, and when it comes to adopting the modern culture, it takes the traditional mindset lot of time. Most of the time, people fight back as they don't want to change themselves, and then the role of opinion leaders becomes more important. Rural people are also very vocal about their rights and leave no opportunity to raise their voices against social issues. But social issues are always created by the people in the system, and it will always take time to solve all the problems at the grassroots level. Campaigns like Beti Bachaao, Beti Padhaao, Pulse Polio, and Sarv Siksha Abhiyan have positively impacted people. Still, the contribution of local change agents also cannot be ignored. Government agencies can find such change agents in rural areas with a hold on the people. It can be a good medium for spreading awareness and making people more sensitive toward social issues.

During the discussions, people accepted that sometimes they could not decode the message and the reason behind this is mixed. It can be the message's language, difficult words, more technicality, or any other thing. The mind behind such messages must understand the background of its audience. When researchers asked about the easiest way to understand a message, people said talking directly about social issues in their village would be a good idea. There is no point in discussing and designing awareness campaigns about any issues irrelevant to a certain village or social structure. To support their statement, one of the respondents tried to explain his thoughts through an example,

"There might be a gambling problem in any village, the campaigns related to gambling can be good for that village, but it might not be effective for our village as we don't have such issues."

CONCLUSION

The suggestions of the opinion leaders and other local villagers can be taken before designing any social campaigns. It is very important to understand the need for social structure. Designing local-language messages can also be a good step toward effective communication. Since the study is carried out on a small sample size and universe, there is a scope for doing the study on a larger scale. But, in a country like India, where government and other change agencies always initiate messages for social development and where the country's maximum population belongs to rural areas and 3rd tier cities, identifying opinion leaders, informal sources of communicators, and effective methods of awareness dissemination will help the rural masses in a more systematic and real way. Government agencies can work with informal opinion leaders to design communications for development and make people more aware of social issues and their solutions. Most of the time, people don't even know about their rights, the scheme started by the government or any other important factor related to any issues. In such cases, the help of opinion leaders and other informal communication channels in rural areas can bring a change.

REFERENCES

Fowsar, M. A. M. (2020). Local Democratic Crises in Sri Lanka: A Study based on Kalmunai Municipal Council. *Journal of Educational and Social Research*, *10*(5), 34–43. doi:10.36941/jesr-2020-0085

Fowsar, M. A. M., Raja, N. K. K., & Rameez, M. A. M. (2022). COVID-19 Pandemic Crisis Management in Sri Lanka. Slipping away from Success. In D. Brisen, T.T.T. Nguyen, & Q.M. Pham (Eds.). Times of Uncertainty: National Policies and International Relations under Covid 19 in Southeast –Asia and Beyond (401-422). Kanishka Publishers.

Fowsar, M. A. M., Rameez, M. A. M., & Rameez, A. (2020). Muslim Minority in Post-war Sri Lanka: A Case Study of Aluthgama and Digana Violence. *Academic Journal of Interdisciplinary Studies*, *9*(6), 56–68. doi:10.36941/ajis-2020-0111

Katz, E. (1961). The social itinerary of technical change: Two studies on the diffusion of innovation. *Human Organization*, *20*(2), 70–82.

Lerner, D. (1958). *The passing of traditional society: Modernizing the Middle East*. APA.

Misra, Y. (2002). *Empowering People - Grassroots Organizations and Rural Development*. UOC.

Mody, B. (1991). *Designing messages for development communication: An audience participation based approach*. Sage Publications.

Mohanty, M., & Parhi, P. (2011). Folk and traditional media: A powerful tool for rural development. *Journal of Communication*, 2(1), 41–47. doi:10.1080/0976691X.2011.11884781

Mohanty, M., & Pritishti, P. (2011). Folk and Traditional Media: A Powerful tool for Rural Development. *Journal of Communication*, 2(2), 2011. doi:10.1080/0976691X.2011.11884781

Narula, U. (2006). Dynamics Of Mass Communication. Theory And Practice. *Atlantic Publishers & Dist*.

Pandey G. P. (1999). Traditional media and development. *Communicator, July-Sept. 1999*.

Rameez, A. (2018). Political Participation of Women in Local Governance: Case Study of Selected Local Government Bodies in Eastern Sri Lanka. *Journal of Asian and African Studies*, 53(7), 1043–1061. doi:10.1177/0021909618762559

Rameez, A. (2019). English Language Proficiency and Employability of University Students: A Sociological Study at Faculty of Arts and Culture, South Eastern University of Sri Lanka. *International Journal of English Linguistics*, 09(4), 199–209. doi:10.5539/ijel.v9n2p199

Rameez, A., & Fowsar, M. A. M. (2018). An Empirical Survey on Factors Affecting Citizens' Trust in Public Institutions in the Eastern Province of Sri Lanka. *Journal of Politics and Law*, 11(2), 88–100. doi:10.5539/jpl.v11n2p88

Rameez, A., Fowsar, M. A. M., & Lumna, N. (2020). Impact of Covid-19 on Higher Education Sectors in Sri Lanka: A Study based on South Eastern University of Sri Lanka. *Journal of Educational and Social Research*, 10(6), 341–349. doi:10.36941/jesr-2020-0132

Rogers, E. M. (1962). *Diffusion of innovations*. Free Press.

Schramm, W. (1964). *Mass Media and National Development: The role of information in the developing countries*. Stanford University press.

Srinivas, M. N. (Ed.). (1993). *India's Villages*. Media Promoters & Publishers.

Varma, M., & Verma, A. (2017). Rural development and channels of grass root communication with reference to health information. *Journal of Content, Community & Communication*, 6(12), 101–110.

Yadav, J. S. (1979). Communication strategy and the challenge of rural development. *Communicator*, 14(2), 6.

ADDITIONAL READING

Paul, H., Patil, B. R., & Dighe, A. (1989). *The mass media and village life: An Indian study*. Sage Publications.

Rogers, E. M., Singhal, A., & Quinlan, M. M. (2014). Diffusion of innovations. In *An integrated approach to communication theory and research* (pp. 432–448). Routledge.

Sambhaji, D. P. (2014). Impact of the Media in Rural Development. *International Journal of Management and Commerce Innovations*, 2(2), 339–340.

Chapter 13
Learning Technology of Communication in the Rise of Exhibition Design in Museums

Shalaka Mahesh Kulkarni
Karnavati University, India

Sambit K. Pradhan
Karnavati University, India

ABSTRACT

In today's world, museums are seen in a very different and peculiar way because they are created by putting the audience in charge of the making. Museums now are more human-centered than earlier, with only one objective, which was a display of artifacts. Also, how exhibition design evolved with time and was incorporated within museums to enhance the visitor's experience. What better way could it be to explain the evolution of museums, shifting focus from the narrative style to making the museum-going experience interactive, and how these two areas overlap each other? Over the last two hundred years, there has been a massive change in the relationship between the museum and its visitors. By offering background on the artwork and artifacts on show, museum directors have empowered visitors to create their interpretations.

INTRODUCTION

Learning technology of communication exhibition design has played a pivotal role in the evolution of museums, starting from the Universal survey museums to the technology-oriented and virtual museums in today's life (Roman et al., 2020). It has always been the responsibility of exhibition designers to create graphics and communication tools and build buildings, display furniture, and showcases within exhibition spaces to provide context for the things on display. This technique, in recent years, has embraced technology and has embedded a relationship between the viewer and the object (Rad et al., 2020).

DOI: 10.4018/978-1-6684-6682-7.ch013

To better understand what caused the evolution of exhibition design, we must understand the need for it and how the public took it as an area of concern (Rad et al., 2019). The impact of modern art movements like De Stijl, the Bauhaus, Constructivism, and Futurism in Europe in the early twentieth century and how it impacted museum heads' understanding of their institution's mission and how to serve visitors effectively (Demeter et al., 2021).

Museums were originally built and supported by the higher class so that they could utilize art as a reflection of art and culture to make themselves seem more educated and global (Balas-Timar & Lile, 2015). The modern movements challenged these class distinctions (Gao & Liu, 2021). Artists and designers found new ways to broaden their perspective of art. Parallel with these movements was the development of stagecraft design; many designers were into stage and exhibition design (Shaffer, 2017).

Understanding the Role of Museums

The museum is a place where the first traces of human and environmental history can be studied and preserved for future generations. The nine muses of Roman mythology are the patrons of art and science, and their name, mice, originated the Latin word museum. There are numerous goals for building museums for recreational facilities, educational resources, intellectual venues, to attract tourism, to contribute to the quality of life of communities where they are situated, to inspire civic pride, or even to impart ideological beliefs. Despite their varied appearances and purposes, all of these cultural artefacts share the goal of preserving and explaining the intangible aspects of a society's history and heritage (Richman-Abdou, 2018).

HISTORY AND EVOLUTION OF MUSEUMS

Humans have a natural inclination to collect and learn more about the world around them, which is why museums exist. The cave mobiliary art provides evidence of communication through the finds, and there have been collections of artefacts from Palaeolithic burials.

Ancient inscriptions were copied around 2000 BCE in Larsa, Mesopotamia, for use in classrooms.

During the reign of Florence's Emperor Lorenzo de' Medici in the 15th century, the term "museum" was resurrected in Europe to describe his extensive collection. That wasn't the name of a structure, though; it was a metaphor for completeness.

By the 17th century in Europe, the word "museum" had come to denote a place where oddities were kept. When the Act that established the British Museum in 1753 was being created, there were significant concerns raised about the role of museums. Nonetheless, in the 18th century, a public institution was founded to store and exhibit a collection for the benefit of visitors.

In the 19th and much of the 20th century, the term "museum" referred to a public institution housing cultural artefacts.

Gradually, when museums responded to the societies that created them, the emphasis on the building started shifting. There were open-air museums where there were a series of museums comprised of objects and eco-museums that portrayed all aspects of the outdoor environment. And lastly, virtual museums exist in electronic form on the internet.

Table 1. Name of the Museum

Name of the Museum	Year	Artifacts
The Musei Capitoli, Rome, Italy	1471	Pope Sixtus IV gifted the city with bronze statues. This institution first welcomed visitors in 1734 and is considered a forerunner of today's universal survey museums.
The Statuario Pubblico, Venice, Italy	1593	Two hundred-item antique statue collection
Ashmolean Museum, England, United Kingdom	1683	Archaeological-focused repository
The British Museum, London, United Kingdom	1759	Primarily a library, it was also the repository for Sir Hans Sloane's assortment of scientific oddities.
The Uffizi Gallery, Italy	1765	Collection holdings of the Medici family in Florence

Universal Survey Museums

Museums dedicated to displaying works of art by the general public first opened their doors in Europe in the early nineteenth century. They are the "most prestigious and authoritative places for seeing original works of art," as described by Carol Duncan and Alan Wallach, who call these museums "universal survey museums" and outline a specific method for displaying artwork and artefacts based on their time period, location, and type. According to Shaffer (2017):

Before the nineteenth century, Europe was home to museums and galleries where the general public could view works of art and other things (table 1).

Although the early Universal survey museums were open to the public, their initial visitors were the same scholars, educated clients interested in collecting and examining art for years.

The Louvre Museum (1793)

The Louvre museum is the world's largest art museum and a historic monument in Paris, France. In 1747, under the rule of Louis XV, an art critic published a pamphlet recommending an art gallery at the Louvre Palace open to the public. Although the building was not in a proper state, it had a huge amount of royal art collection and was a National symbol for the people of France. Even though it was open to the masses, the aristocratic and educated people used it to showcase their wealth and status. They desired a visitor's experience as being seen in that environment rather than viewing the art (figure 1).

A new style for exhibition or display was adopted, the Style de salon (painting frames abutting stacked on top of the other from floor to ceiling) in the 19th century.

The museum was more of quantity than quality because although the quality maintained an accepted taste of artworks, people were more overwhelmed by the quantity, and there was no credit given to the individual work. One of the most crucial drawbacks was no record of signage for museum labels at the Louvre, so the viewer did not know what he was looking at, and every artwork was presented without description. So, the ability to enhance one's understanding, a narrator was a must; without him, the viewer would be lost (Goefrey D.Lewis, 2018) (figure 2).

Figure 1. The Louvre museum (Wikipedia, Louvre Museum, 1793)

Figure 2. The Public Viewing David's Coronation (Metropolitan Museum of Art, 1810)

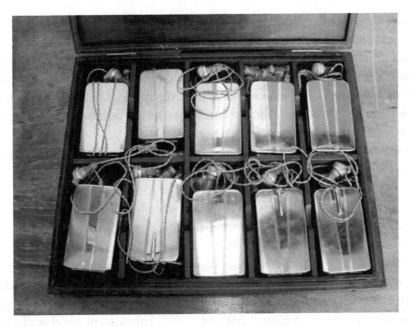

Purpose of the Museums

Following this trend, art museums sprung up fast in different parts of the United States, with the dual goals of increasing the general public's exposure to refined aesthetics and showcasing the cultural wealth of a given area. Public art museums were already well-established by the late 19th century in Europe and the United States, depicting civic/state pride and offering a stage for the wealthy to display their power (the museums were over-flooding with artworks and objects).

At meetings held during this time, museum directors discussed the concerns about whether a common man could understand the collection in the museums like the upper class. Many questions were raised, and a thorough evaluation was made of the museum's displays in terms of what was on exhibit, how it was displayed, whether or not any explanation was necessary, and the museum's composition as a whole, with each piece considered separately. Also, among all these questions, one of the most important questions was how the museums acted as a mediator to showcase the artists' artworks and provide a platform for the public to view and understand their artworks.

Another challenge which they came across was how to attract working-class people to come to their museums. Firstly, the working-class people were more susceptible, and future artists would emerge from them. Then it was decided to publish guides as factual textbooks to educate and inspire the viewers.

Also, in the meeting, many practical concerns were raised about architecture, corridor-like arrangement, waste of space, and money over a huge stair hall.

The 19th century's attempt to educate the people by filling museums with artworks and items backfired because there was simply too much knowledge created for a 'working man' to grasp.

IMPACT OF MODERNISM GIVING RISE TO EXHIBITION DESIGN

As many questions were raised regarding the museum's mission, artists joined many social movements during the same years in the 20th century in Bauhaus.

Europe, which rapidly spread to the United States as well. These movements questioned a lot of topics, for instance, the role of women, the socioeconomic condition of the poor, industrial society, and the authority of such museums. These modernists were the members of De Stijl, Constructivists, The Bauhaus, and the Futurists. On one side, modern philosophers and writers expressed their issues in their books, and artists, on the other side, targeted museums.

The artists were upset that the museum administrators were given exclusive access to the works of painters who had long since passed away.

It shouldn't be up to museum administrators, as Russian constructivist Alexandr Rodchenko argued in his Declaration of Museum Management. Nonetheless, the artist should be allowed the final say. Rodchenko and his contemporaries held that the artist/maker was in a special position to connect the dots between historical and contemporary efforts.

Upon taking stock of the situation, he realised that there was a chasm between the creative culture's past and present that needed to be bridged in order to provide visitors with a more enriching experience. As a means of resolving the issue of legitimacy, he rejected all the presumptions of art-school disciples by include the fields of design and architecture. Following this, a plethora of novel artefacts and structures, including sculptures, paintings, interior design, furniture design, buildings for both living and working, typography, illustration, and textiles, arose. As a new century dawned, a new breed of creatives set out to reimagine the 20th.

Aspirations of the new, contemporary authors were taken into account by costume and set designers in theatrical works, which also embraced the reinvention method. Exhibition design as we know it now is a product of the work of theatre set designers, building architects, and product designers.

The New Stagecraft is a Pioneer of Modern Exhibition Design

The importance of set design is shown in this investigation. Nonetheless, it is significant because it bridges the gap between the evolution of stage design and the advent of contemporary Exhibition design. This implies that many of the first prominent exhibition designers, like Frederick Kiesler, Joseph Urban, Norman Bel Geddes, and many more, got their start in the industry working as stage designers.

When looking at the wide range of theatre historians, the Swiss-born Adolphe Appia (1862-1928) and the Englishman Edward Gordon Craig (1872-1966) stand out as two designers who fully recognised the possibilities to transform the stagecraft. When it came to carrying out a specific scene, each had their own unique methods.

In the 20th century, innovations in stagecraft occurred on the one hand, but other forms of design and ornamental art also advanced. Walter Gropius, the director of the Kunstschule and the Kunstgewerbeschule in Saxony, amalgamated the two schools in 1919 to create the Staatliche Bauhaus in Weimar, Germany, with a new department of architecture. The initial version of his programme said, "Bauhaus aims to bring all creative endeavour into a whole." A theatre workshop was not a part of the original curriculum until 1921, when it was expanded to incorporate stagecraft design. To find a solution to the issue of visual display, Gropius sought out new research into the nature of exhibitions. After being incorporated in the printing workshop's experimental efforts about 1925, Exhibition design went on to become a recognised academic discipline in its own right.

It has been noted that the job of a stage designer foreshadows that of an exhibition designer because both are concerned with the effective utilization of space by whoever occupies it, from its creators (the artists) to the audience (viewers).

A New Perspective in Exhibition Design- Frederick Kiesler

Frederick Kiesler was an architect, theoretician, theatre designer, artist, and sculptor. He was a part of the De Stijl group, and taking from the experience of stage design, and he applied the principles of the use of abstract form to create three-dimensional surfaces; he gave a different paradigm to Exhibition Design. In 1924, he was allowed to design.

The International Exhibition of New Theatre Technique in Vienna Over 600 works by artists, designers, and filmmakers were on display, including sketches, posters, pictures, designs, and models for avant-garde stage plays.

To prevent damage to the artworks and items and the subsequent requirement for patching and painting, Kiesler constructed a L & T system for display. This meant that there were two basic layouts for Exhibition fixtures: the horizontal 'L' type (Leger-type), which provided a variety of viewing angles from a range of different heights, and the vertical 'T' type. Cantilevered viewing platforms were secured in place by vertical Trager-type ('T') fittings that were oriented to the visitor (figure 3).

After applying the L & T fixtures with the exact measurement of the room, Kiesler estimated he had created three times more space than the traditional approach of displaying objects. He understood that the amount of material provided to the viewer should be absorbed by him/her to create a good experience. In his new works, Kiesler integrated the essence of the primary colors - red, blue, and yellow - In two years, Frederick Kiesler, with his clear vision and determination, positioned himself at the forefront of Exhibition design.

Figure 3. International Exhibition of New Theater Technique (Kiesler, 1924)

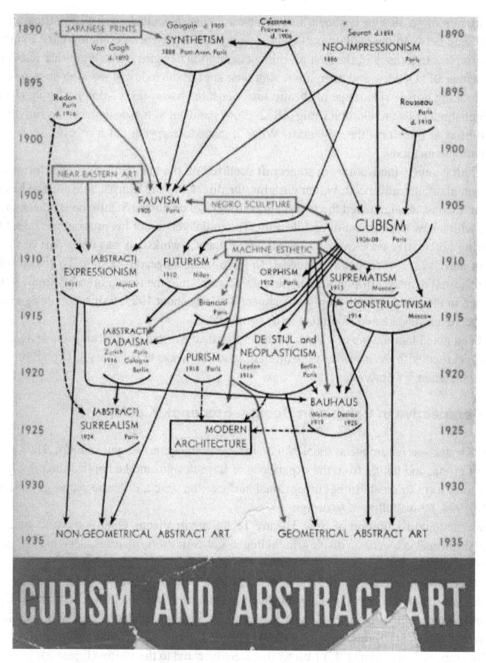

Figure 4. The Constitution of the Soviets and The Newspaper Transmissions (El Lissitzky,1928)

Adapting Communication Techniques to Improve the Viewer Experience

So, during this evolution stage of museums, the designers merged both to create a multimedia platform to enhance the visitor's experience through conducting a two and three-dimensional environment. Also, by using graphic tools for explaining purposes, the exhibition aimed to display artworks and objects and educate the viewer (figure 4).

El Lissitzky was a Russian artist, designer, photographer, typographer, polemicist, and architect. He was also known as the "father of constructivism." In addition to being a pupil of Kazimir Malevich and a prominent figure in the Russian avant-garde who contributed to the development of suprematism, he was also responsible for the design of several exposition exhibits for the Soviet Union. (El Lissitzky, Wikipedia). As the picture to the right shows, he utilised the multimedia strategy developed by Kiesler and amplified the scale of display as well as the graphic graphics in order to provide a novel experience for the spectator.

Text and images were included into the design of the Exhibition, which violated some of the principles set out by the more conventional method. This demonstrated the beginning of a new era in the design of exhibitions. A visual language was developed in order to present structures in a way that enables the audience to obtain additional information and go away from the exhibition with a deeper comprehension of the topic at hand.

Figure 5. Cubism and Abstract Art exhibition catalogue cover (Barr, Alfred H, 1936)

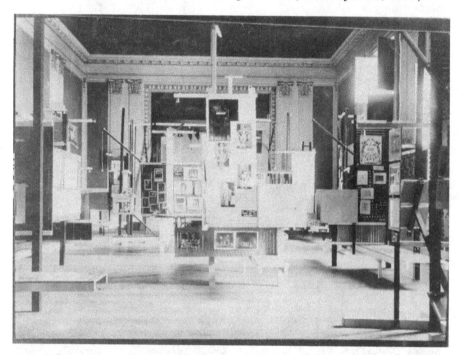

The Museum of Modern Art (MoMA), 1929

New York City's Museum of Modern Art hosted a gathering of exhibition designers from fields other than museums who shared an interest in giving alternative perspectives on museum-based displays. Early on, it was able to accommodate all of the art and design-focused departments of the museum, which contributed to its rapid rise to prominence in the institution's early years. More than seventy exhibitions had been held at the Museum of Modern Art by the time that the year 1936 rolled around. These exhibitions included displays of works by American and European painters, sculptures, architects, photographers, designers of industrial products, and winners of contests for poster and typography design.

Alfred Barr, the founding director of the Museum of Modern Art, made the decision to broaden the museum's scope in 1936 by displaying works of cubism and abstract art. This was done with the intention of better explaining the paradigm shift that took place in the field of art in the early 20th century. In an effort to make things easier to understand for his group, he drew out a timeline that detailed the important occurrences that took place over the course of history and indicated with arrows how they followed one another. A few years later, this diagram that Picasso had developed was included on the cover of an exhibition at the Museum of Modern Art titled Cubism and Abstract Art (figure 5).

The exhibition's objective was to chart the development of cubism and abstract art from its inception up till the current day by showing works in a chronological order and focusing on the influence that these artistic forms have had on contemporary artists.

During the middle of the 20th century, rapid democratisation of universal survey museums led to the development of new technologies, such as computers and digital technology, as well as the integration of these technologies with architecture and communication mediums. Wexhibition designers had previously developed these technologies (Shaffer, 2017).

Figure 6. The first museum audio guides (Holland et al., 1952)

USE OF TECHNOLOGY TO ENHANCE THE VISITOR'S EXPERIENCE

The rise of digital technology has transformed museums into places of "unpredictable experience," including the universal survey museums. In contrast to the traditional method of narration, modern museum visitors can now interact with exhibits through technological equipment such as audio tours, smartphone apps, touch displays, etc (figure 6).

Beginning in 1937, Willem Sandberg held the position of curator at the Stedelijk Museum. He gave Philips, a Dutch technology firm, the task of developing a radio headset that visitors to the museum could use to take themselves on a self-guided tour of the museum's contents in order to make the institution more accessible. He developed this idea as if the museum were having a conversation with an individual and listening to that conversation in order to increase spectator involvement. The walls of the museum were filled with many new and innovative gadgets, such as the Cooper Hewitt pen, which allowed visitors to access information and blurred the divide between the manufacturer and the user. Other new and innovative technologies also joined the museum.

Digital Technology: A Tool for Exhibition Designers

As museums continued to adopt new forms of technology, exhibition designers were faced with the challenge of determining how best to include and operate the many mechanical components in order to provide visitors with a satisfying experience. The younger people who are interested in technological gadgets and who visit museums and have these devices (smartphones) to access information immediately for an engaging experience make up part of the target audience for these kinds of exhibits.

Figure 7. Timeline Multiple touch table (Image Source- Pinterest)

The ability to use technology shouldn't take precedence over other aspects of the museum experience; this is the challenge that faces exhibition designers, despite the fact that the proliferation of technological trends in museums does not negate the fact that people go to museums to view some form of art.

To provide visitors a more engaging and thought-provoking experience with the museum's collection, museums are increasingly integrating digital media into their displays. These displays aim to present visitors with a more immersive and interactive experience.

In spite of this, the function of an exhibition designer has evolved throughout the years. Nevertheless, he or she will always be the means via which information may be communicated from the creator to the user, and they will also be the ones responsible for navigating among locations that have the appropriate installations (Shaffer, 2017).

Mosti – Interactive Science and Technology Museum in Saudi Arabia

The museum was commissioned by MTE studios and made by an exhibition maker in Dubai. Formula D interactive and its partners developed 21 digital installations for this museum (figure 7).

An interactive audiovisual presentation shows a variety of mathematical, chemical, botanical, medical, astronomical, artistic, and architectural aspects of the technical and scientific advancements made in the Muslim world from 700 BC to 1700 BC. Touch tables, touch screen displays, and other interactive items displaying a timeline and supplying information by connecting directly to the viewer are included in the installations. The interactive table with various touch points covers a thousand years and provides information on three hundred significant occurrences.

Museums Should be Multiple Active Senses, and not Just the Eyeball- Ellen Lupton

Ellen Lupton, who is a curator at the Cooper Hewitt Design Museum in New York City, is one of the speakers at a TedX (MidAtlantic) lecture. She begins by stating that "museum curators adore eyes," and that "do not touch" is the most popular mantra that museum curators like to utilise. She entertained the idea of putting together a display that was not geared toward the eyes, but rather one that the audience could feel, taste, smell, and listen to. She was putting the finishing touches on this display before she gave it the title "made for the senses to move beyond the eyeball." She claims that designers are coming up with a variety of new items to stimulate the senses, so making the environment more exciting and welcoming to more people. An exhibition's design understanding is contingent upon the environment that has been produced there. The design of an exhibition can facilitate communication with the target audience and the technical transfer of information.

CONCLUSION

The position of museums as wealthy institutions has swiftly transformed into that of user-centered institutions, bringing with it a fast transformation in museums' evolution and identities. Every single legal gap resulted in a significant shift in the way museums were constructed. The design of exhibitions was a significant contributor to this development because it altered people's perceptions of the world around them, emphasised the importance of experience, and is still undergoing development in order to improve its appearance and become more compatible with modern technological advancements. The increasing prevalence of cutting-edge exhibition design in museums has, in a sense, contributed to the development of a relationship with the audience. In modern museums, visitors are asked what they would like to see and their suggestions are included into the building's architecture. This is an excellent method since it allows visitors to have a stronger connection to the organisation they are visiting.

REFERENCES

Balas-Timar, D., & Lile, R. (2015). The story of Goldilocks told by organizational psychologists. *Procedia: Social and Behavioral Sciences*, *203*, 239–243. doi:10.1016/j.sbspro.2015.08.288

Barr, A. H. (1936). *Cubism and Abstract Art exhibition catalogue cover. Museum of Modern Art (1902-1981), Jr. Cubism and Abstract Art*. The Museum of Modern Art.

Demeter, E., Rad, D., & Balas, E. (2021). Schadenfreude and General Anti-Social Behaviours: The Role of Violent Content Preferences and Life Satisfaction. BRAIN. *Broad Research in Artificial Intelligence and Neuroscience*, *12*(2), 98–111. doi:10.18662/brain/12.2/194

Gao, T., & Liu, J. (2021). Application of improved random forest algorithm and fuzzy mathematics in physical fitness of athletes. *Journal of Intelligent & Fuzzy Systems*, *40*(2), 2041–2053. doi:10.3233/JIFS-189206

Holland, A., & Museum, S. (1952). *The first museum audio guides*. Stedelijk Museum.

Kiesler, F. (1924), International Exhibition of New Theater Technique. Vienna, 1924, *Avant-garde on Display: Frederick Kiesler's Exhibition of New Theatre Technique*.

Lewis, G. D. (2018). Museum- Definition, history, types & operation. *Britannica*. https://www.britannica.com/topic/museum-cultural-institution

El Lissitzky (1928), The Constitution of the Soviets and The Newspaper Transmissions. Soviet Pavilion, Pressa, Cologne, 1928, Pinterest.

Metropolitan Museum of Art. (1810), The Public Viewing David's 'Coronation' at the Louvre Louis Léopold Boilly. Metropolitan Museum of Art.

Rad, D., Balas, E., Ignat, S., Rad, G., & Dixon, D. (2020). A Predictive Model of Youth Bystanders' Helping Attitudes. Revista romaneasca pentru educatie multidimensionala-*Journal for Multidimensional Education, 12*(1Sup2), 136-150.

Rad, D., Dughi, T., Demeter, E. (2019). The Dynamics of the Relationship between Humor and Benevolence as Values. Revista romaneasca pentru educatie multidimensionala-Journal for Multidimensional Education, *11*(3), 201-212.

Richman-Adbou, K. (2018). How Museums Evolved Over Time From Private Collections to Modern Institutions. *Cabinets of Curiosities.*

Roman, A., Rad, D., Egerau, A., Dixon, D., Dughi, T., Kelemen, G., Balas, E., & Rad, G. (2020). Physical Self-Schema Acceptance and Perceived Severity of Online Aggressiveness in Cyberbullying Incidents. *Journal of Interdisciplinary Studies in Education, 9*(1), 100–116. doi:10.32674/jise.v9i1.1961

Shaffer, W. R. (2017), Exhibition Design and The Evolution of Museum-goer Experience. Master's Green, Cooper Hewitt, PA]. https://repository.si.edu/bitstream/handle/10088/35449/Shaffer%20Thesis.pdf?sequence=1&isAllowed=y

Chapter 14
An Empirical Study of Managing Education During the Pandemic Situation

Viney Dhiman
Panjab University, Chandigarh, India

Anupama Bharti
Himachal Pradesh University, India

ABSTRACT

Education is an important part of society, and Coronavirus radically influenced the educational system. Foundations have started the use of electronic modes in the educational system; also, comparative abilities can be gotten to through different stages. ToThis paper presents a concentration on acknowledgment of online education toas an answer to the Coronavirus pandemic, especially at Panjab College, Chandigarh (India). The present chapter overviewed several secondary and primary sources. For this purpose, total of 50 respondents interacted with mobile phones: 20 undergraduate students, 20 post-graduate students, also ten each PhD scholars from different streams of Punjab University, Chandigarhto. They were asked their view as university convened online classes from the last week of March 2020 tountil the 15th May 2020. In addition to the ten faculty members of Panjab University, there were also others interviewed online toin order to find their perception of the current system's efficacy in responding toto the pandemic.

INTRODUCTION

Guidance is underpinning of social structure of a country; it is a pacesetter for social resurgence also monetary change (Unnikrishnan vs State of A.P., 1993) Education goes probably as a synergist expert in making and also understanding a nation's human resource. (Chadah, 2010)

DOI: 10.4018/978-1-6684-6682-7.ch014

Education and Pandemic

Emergency destructive upset schooling system also pushed to apply innovation through different stages, counting Zoom (Zoom Video Interchanges, San Jose, CA), WebEx (Cisco Webex, Milpitas, CA), also Skype (Skype Advancements, Palo Alto, CA). Likewise, this configuration permits us toto record all meetings (aside from persons through safeguarded data, like bleakness also mortality) also can undoubtedly be re-utilized. (Chick et al., 2020)

For supporting tutoring, many, including business progressed learning stage providers, have rushed toto offer their assistance also 'plans', now also again in vain. Furthermore, before Covid, there has been growing examine of how tutoring tech is renaming also decreasing instructing also learning thoughts. It is battled that 'preparing is broken, also it should also can be fixed with development. Such technology, regularly viewed as impartial, is immovably associated with educationalization, for instance compelling creating social issues for guidance toto decide. Consequently, this is a crucial point in time toto consider what instructive foundations' ongoing decisions could mean for Corona virus schooling also web based learning. In any case, inquiry emerges entrepreneur edge toto help education system will advance training according toto all-encompassing human development also prepare toto a positive eventual fate of schooling. (Roy, 2020)

While the Corona virus pandemic has been seething across the mainland's, performing expressions teachers have untaught and changed their teaching methods in course conveyance to overcome the difficulties brought about by the Corona virus pandemic. Dependent upon the Corona virus pandemic circumstance facilitating in Hong Kong and all over the planet, the entire schooling area is by all accounts returning to typical step by step. In the meantime, there are successful illustrations and bits of knowledge to be gained from the mixture teaching method during the pandemic, which could additionally help the new typical period (post-pandemic) of performing expressions training. To inspect the ongoing act of computerized learning among understudies and personnel (perspectives toto crossover, on the web, and eye to eye learning and inclinations about learning mode for proficient turn of events/preparing studios), this exact review takes a gander at 408 understudies and 17 employees at a main performing expressions foundation in Hong Kong. This study finds the central questions for performing expressions instructors in regards to on the web/cross breed educating and learning. It presents examples and bits of knowledge for quality protection and improvement. Discoveries can advise the future advancement regarding computerized educating and learning for the performing expressions as well with respect to other practice-based subjects. (Sarkar, 2020)

Performing expressions educating and learning exercises are normally led in an eye to eye setting. For a really long time, the "sage on the stage" and "gain from the expert" was the main approaches to learning. Nonetheless, the pandemic has transformed movements of every sort into different web based learning models. To empower a smooth virtual instructing and learning climate, a wide cluster of drives has been executed in performing expressions training. That remembers the utilization of innovations for educating; learning, creation, and expert turn of events. To conquer the difficulties of the Corona virus pandemic, a half and half learning teaching method was first proposed and carried out in performing expressions schooling in Hong Kong. (Li et al., 2021) A survey research was carried out at the Hong Kong Academy for Performing Arts to validate this hybrid learning style and investigate areas for future improvement (HKAPA). One of the world's top institutions for performing arts is HKAPA. According to QS Rankings 2022, The Academy is ranked No. 10 globally and No. 1 in Asia in the discipline of Performing Arts in 2022. About 1000 students can choose from the Academy's undergraduate and graduate programmes. It has approximately 120 academic staff members spread over its six schools, including the schools of Chinese Opera (CO), Dance (DA), Drama (DR), Film and Television (FTV), Music (MU), and Theatre and Entertainment Arts (TEA) (TEA). Between September and October 2021, a survey of students and academic staff was undertaken to examine the four research questions. According to their prior educational experiences, academic staff and students' attitudes toward hybrid, online, and face-to-face learning are as follows: (1) What are the current digital practises in performing arts teaching and learning?; (2) What are their preferences for professional development and training workshops?; (3) What are their attitudes toward professional development and training workshops?; (4) How would the anticipated technology infrastructure improve teaching and learning quality?; This study also provides information regarding whether or not the online learning environment is advantageous for teachers' instruction and students' learning. Additionally, it exposes their preparedness, preferences, and suggestions for additional enhancements. (Li et al., 2022)

Covid Pandemic also Push toto Online Learning: As referred toto earlier, COvid-19 pandemic fuming all around the planet has caused gigantic degree official also direct 'shock effects' in various areas of human activity, including tutoring. Impact on understudies is incredible: on 9 April 2020, there were more than 1,500,000,000 students generally from crucial for tertiary level, who couldn't go to class (UNESCO, 2020). As a result of colossal also surprising terminations, influenced countries also organizations have been constrained to search for helpful arrangements in diverse modernized learning stages (Jandric, 2020). These quick moves from homeroom to electronic training have saved more critical requests associated with public educational procedures also speculative grounds also premises. Present statuses of formal tutoring frameworks can be portrayed using serious solid areas for Philip's model of pandemic cerebrum science containing three one after other also covering plagues: fear, explanation, also action. Strong purposes 'plague' as a representation addressing total mental reactions to an epidemiological crisis. Fundamental perspective incorporates a plague of fear also opens up a request: How should tutoring frameworks also individual understudies adjust to extraordinary situation?

The ensuing perspective is a scourge of explanation also talks: 'People probably won't have option to close whether one more disorder or another eruption is unimportant or something enormously critical. They swing backward also forward beginning with one point of view then onto following. (Strong, P., 1990) All while, different performers in definitive positions give their records of how to understand situation also assurance continuation of teaching also learning. Legislators are at extreme forefront of educational methodology making, meanwhile setting restrictions also measures considering prosperity experts' assessments also fostering their power also genuine records. Online amusement grant trained professionals also youngsters to give their goal also nonsensical viewpoints to little adjust. Lockdowns impact students in more than one manner, developing variations also putting them under cordial also mental tension. Gatekeepers also managers are influenced too, also an enormous number of them get it, perhaps strangely, social justification behind tutoring framework also its capacity to structure everyday presence.

Third perspective is a pandemic of act. It shows how informative establishments also educators generally trade their work from homerooms also assembly rooms to modernized organizes essentially for now. This quick change has also uncovered openings also lacks in how electronic learning has or has not been taken on in educational foundations. Attempts to cover these openings have made various kinds of assist with preferring drop-in gatherings, free web-based classes also blog sections, emergency procedure files (Doucet et al., 2020), also even models acquired from before school lockdowns. (Czerniewicz, 2020) Perhaps more fundamentally, condition has transformed into one more market an entryway for business mechanized learning stage providers. Thusly, methodology, execution also use of private Capital are focal factors to get moving online preparation.

A couple of sorts of emergency online learning are rebuked for deteriorating to follow to comprehensive instructive norms, best practices, also earlier exploration. (Hodges et al., 2020) By means of electronic diversion, undeniable experts have investigated reasons driving a couple of individuals, affiliations, also associations so eagerly to provide guidance, taking into account whether their inspiration has been driven by marketplace reasons (Siemens, 2020). Others have seen normal unfavorable outcomes expecting that educational advancement convenient arrangements are executed without changing their results (Selwyn, 2020; St. Amour, 2020). Quickly focusing on learning stages also web learning has in like manner raised stresses over security also perception also impact on student's lives also human regard. (Harwell, 2020) Further, if confidential players expecting excited about placing assets into help of internet preparing, it is moreover vital to know whether their incentive is benefit driven or regard goes before them to take a such action.

The Corona virus pandemic has struck schooling system all over the planet. The pandemic started a prompt and complete lockdown of the relative multitude of instructive organizations, to keep social removing. As per medical services experts, lockdown and social separating could assist with levelling the disease bend and decrease complete fatalities from the Corona virus pandemic. It has impacted over 90% of the world's students, as the customary learning approaches are not fitting in that frame of mind of the standard times and web based learning appears to have turned into a basic salvation for learning, the instructive establishments endeavour to limit the local area spread of the illness. Every one individuals taking part in the school system acknowledged that educating and learning techniques should be modified in the time of Corona virus as the circumstance prompted constrained variation of e-learning strategies. This paper researches and assesses the students' discernment in an advanced education establishment of India and looks at the distinction in the view of similar understudies in Pre and Post Corona virus period, involving the Factual Bundle for Sociologies program (SPSS) rendition 23.0 and JASP 0.14.1 programming applications for illustrative and logical measurements for example medium, least, most extreme, matched t-test and relationship. The consequence of this papers affirmed that there exists a measurably huge distinction in the understudies' discernment to the Pre-Pandemic and Post-Pandemic learning techniques, which shows that understudies have a higher view of the Pre-Pandemic learning mixed learning, than that of the Post Pandemic learning web-helped learning (Dutta, S., 2020).

The lockdown because of Corona virus appears to seriously affect the learning of advanced education understudies as they were in their even semesters and this lockdown forced on them, prompted a change in their learning strategies. These understudies couldn't learn on a one-on-one premise with their teachers, as the pandemic started a prompt and complete closedown of the relative multitude of instructive foundations, the change in gaining from customary homeroom figuring out how to PC based learning became quite possibly of the best scholastic change which the understudies expected to adapt to. The ongoing review has been embraced to fathom the understudy's discernment about the forced changes in learning techniques because of Corona virus issue at advanced education organizations. Hence, it helps in growing better comprehension of required instructive changes in the pandemic and post pandemic times, as the need might arise to be changed essentially as opposed to sitting tight for predictability. This examination work affirms the impacts of Corona virus on advanced education Organizations in India. Analyzing the effects of the pandemic on the educational and learning systems in different Indian states, as well as the impact on tertiary education. The illustrative and educational organized studies and library examination are utilized to accumulate the information, dissected in this exploration. The accumulated information examined through chi sq. quantifiable instrument at five rate level of importance that was presented inside the style of recurrence and rates. The examinees for this study are 1100 teachers from various territories of India. The assessment and examination uncovered that viral flare-up altogether affects advanced education establishments in India.

In a crisis, enlightening affiliations should consider their selections concerning online education also preparing development. These selections could resonate in upcoming as new relations of control also control, new sorts of student awkwardness also difference, also other uncommon effects (Selwyn 2020). to direct possible unfavorable outcomes, educational affiliations should use past data on electronic progressing as something that can be more contrasted than just a technique for conveying information. Regardless, they are in danger of falling into catch of commendable Bourdeausian 'misrecognition' (Bourdieu, P., 1984), that is, into translating mechanized progressing as a clearly self-evident also clearing reply for huger issues of current mass preparation also directed teaching also learning.

Web learning can take many designs, together with those informatively extra noteworthy number of innovative also interfacing with than generally rummage-sale data movement also assessment processes. It will in general be taught also shaped by different tutoring philosophical also educational underpinnings. (Teras & Kartoglu, 2017) Thusly, electronic learning should not be seen as 'a specific something' or showing strategy through its own effort.

Electronic gaining is regularly seen as indistinguishable from content-driven self-study, where advantages are limited to (a relative) opportunity of presence. Regardless, a mechanized learning environment which includes solely of text-based reports also talk get accounts shared through an acquiring board structure is very surprising from a modernized education environment that utilizes an organized web learning plan like valid learning framework (Herrington, Reeves, & Oliver, 2010) which concentrates helpful data advancement also amazing, genuine learning. In addition, dazzling teachers also students in new growth, execution, also usage of preparing advancement can impact how successfully innovation can uphold significant instructing also learning (Bates & Sangra, 2011; Howland et al., 2011).

It is contended that there is a more extensive cultural exchange about motivations behind training also sort of society we need to create in Corona virus world. Innovation also its suppliers ought to take action accordingly. On off chance that we are to gain something important from Solid's (1990) model of pestilence brain research, we ought to try not to rehash three phases of social 'scourges', dread, clarification, also activity. As (Fuchs, C., 2020) has brought up, our 'existential feelings of trepidation also requirements can be instrumental zed', also thus, we could acknowledge corporate instruction tech also different types of mastery as given. This has made an exceptional push for web-based learning. Generally speaking, instructive establishments have tracked down convenient solutions with ed-tech to guarantee continuation of studies. (Teras et al., 2020)

Advanced education: Advanced education in India is developing decisively. Quantity of Colleges has expanded multiple times from 20 out of 1950 to 677 out of 2014.quantity of Focal Colleges is 48, State Colleges 399, Considered to be Colleges 126 also State Private Colleges 334.above figure uncovers that complete number of colleges in India is 907. 900 93 colleges, 39931 Universities also 10725 independent organizations are recorded on their entrance, adding to training (DNS Kumar, 2020). Regardless of these numbers, global training rating organizations have not set numerous foundations inside best-of-the-world positioning. Likewise, India has neglected to create a-list colleges. Information Commission furthermore suggests an increment of no less than 1.5% of Gross domestic product for advanced education out of a sum of no less than 6% of Gross domestic product for schooling generally speaking. There are a few lacuna in advanced education such as (Gupta, 2012) Low college rank, a gigantic staff deficiency, unfortunate foundation, political obstruction, nature of training, low certification, also low interest in innovative work. (Kumar, Anuj, & Ambrish, 2015)

Influence on Advanced education also pandemic: Covid has genuinely affected hard also fast educational system of India also globe anyway likely most impacted areas of high-level training in India. It obliged debilitated each also every informative activity (Pravat, 2020). various activities like affirmation, evaluations, entrance tests, also serious appraisals coordinated by various sheets/schools/colleges/ universities are conceded, also experts are making a plan for modernized evaluations. UGC has conveyed Rules on Appraisals also Academic timetable considering Covid pandemic also coming about lockdown on 29th April 2020 (UGC notice, 2020). All terminal evaluations have been deferred also moved to July 2020, also proposed inception of classes is from August 2020. UGC has similarly set up a complete timetable for academic gathering 2020-2021 with new dates keeping in view lockdown. A part of electronic drives of UGC also MHRD for high level training for sharing information during Covid are raised underneath:

1. E-GyanKosh by Indira Gandhi Public Open College (IGNOU).
2. Gyandarshan works with sound guiding live conversations with instructors also specialists
3. Gyandhara Swayam gives Enormous Open Web-based Courses (MOOCs) with 140 college endorsedcredit move highlights. Swayam Prabha gives excellent informative projects through 32DTH channels communicating instructive material.
4. E-PG Pathshala (Pravat, 2020).
5. E-Adhyayan (computerized books) is a phase that gives 700+ computerized books to Post-Graduate courses. All computerized books are gotten from e-PG Pathshala courses. It is like manner works with playlists of video content.
6. E-Pathya (Separated Induction)
7. The Public Modernized Library of India (NDLI) is a vault of e-content on different disciplines for many clients like students (of all levels), teachers, trained professionals, overseers, library clients, specialists, surprisingly abled clients also any leftover dependable understudies.
8. E-Yantra outfits dynamic contribution in embedded structures. It has around 380 Labs also made 2300+ colleges benefit.
9. FOSSEE is a short construction for nothing/Libre, also Open Source Programming for Preparing made to propel open source programming for guidance also master use.
10. Virtual Labs has made web-engaged instructive program based tests planned for far off action. It has more than 100 Virtual Labs including around 700 web-engaged tests expected for distant movement. It gives remote - permission to Labs in various disciplines of science also planning. These Virtual Labs deal with students at undergrad level also post-graduate levels as well as to investigate scientists (Selwyn, 2020).
11. E-Shodh Sindhu is a grouping of e-journals; e-journal records also computerized books on a somewhat long access premise. It has at least 10,000 e-journals, 31, also at least 35,000 advanced books. It gives induction to emotional electronic resources, including full-text, bibliographic also evident informational indexes, to insightful foundations at a lower participation rate.
12. Shodhganga is a phase for research students to store their PhD propositions also make them open to entire shrewd neighborhood open access. Document can get, record, store, scatter also save electronic recommendations also compositions introduced by trained professionals.
13. VIDWAN is a central informational collection also public assessment network with profiles of scientists/subject matter expert's also different representatives.

14. National Educational Alliance for Development (Great) is a drive for skilling understudies in latest advances through a Public-Private association model between Open powers (through its executing association AICTE) also Tutoring Advancement associations of India. It gets best imaginative things preparing informative strategy on a lone stage for understudies' advantage.

15. SAKSHAT is Quit Tutoring Section for watching out for all preparation also learning-related prerequisites of students, specialists, educator's also dependable understudies. Doorway gives latest news, public explanations, achievements, etc., associated with Administration of HRD. So one can visit SAKSHAT to known universe of web learning (Kapasia et al., 2020).

Working from home can help different associations in agreeing with any law during pandemic circumstances. This study explores the connection of embracing working from home in the association during the critical circumstance and how it empowers the representative to perform, fulfil, focused on working with full adequacy. Moreover, this exploration evokes different factors, for example, worker commitment and how it supports the work independence of people to control or shape proficient elements associated with liability and the climate. The specialist has utilized elucidating measurements, coefficient of connection and one example t-test strategy to break down information, and the outcome demonstrated which shows a decent connection between worker responsibility and occupation fulfilment during the reception of working from home strategy in an association. Additionally saw from the review, working from home can side by side routine work and official gatherings during the ongoing circumstances. It is additionally suggested that representatives ought to guarantee the workplace appropriately before embrace with working from home technique.

In the ongoing circumstance, there are many cloud-based advances that make remote work more successful and proficient than the conventional office. Tele working assists most bosses with arriving at an enormous number of representatives by permitting labourers access because of the Covid danger. Telecommuting is viewed as one of the significant instruments which causes work closeness to reinforce and stronger by empowering telecommuters to remain useful and use to keep up with social ties and associations. (Tracy & Lara, 2020) In the perspective on an association, working from home can give an answer for any issues utilizing lessening overheads or diminishing truancy. There are many explanations behind businesses to give representatives to telecommute, contingent upon the idea of the gig and innovation because of any pandemic conditions. Working from home gives part of the labour force, particularly for rustic inhabitants to whom it gives the chance to dwell any place they need. It gives a business way to benefit from individual abilities, which have any incapacity or disease that expects them to remain at home. Working from home has been utilized effectively by allowing representatives with the individuals who have any sickness or during any pandemic conditions to work at home and have more useful existences. (Jogan, 2019)

EMPIRICAL OBSERVATION ON EDUCATION & PANDEMIC CRISIS

Empirical Observation

For empirical study, 50 students interacted; ten faculty members also interacted. It is desirable to know about Punjab University Chandigarh.

Punjab University Chandigarh

Panjab College is situated in Chandigarh, India. Started in 1882 as College of Punjab Lahore, it was migrated to Chandigarh in 1947 as East Punjab College after parcel of India, where college was parted among India also Pakistan. College has 78 educating also research division's also ten focuses/seats for educating also research at principal grounds in Chandigarh. It has 188 subsidiary universities spread overweight locale of Punjab state also association domain of Chandigarh, with Territorial Focuses at Muktsar, Ludhiana also Hoshiarpur urban areas in, Punjab state. It is perhaps of most all around positioned college in India. After Lockdown College is dealing with showing framework in web-based mode. Specialists additionally educated educators to take assistance regarding YouTube for posting talks or introductions for understudies also could answer to inquiries through video conferencing. Holding intuitive discussions through Skype or Zoom was additionally proposed. It has additionally been recommended that Public Program on Innovation Upgraded Learning (NAPTEL) stage ought to to be utilized for designing courses. (Punjab University Guidelines, 2020)

It has finished continuous semester from last seven day stretch of spring to fifteenth May 2020, also respondents' perspectives were just broke down for this period. As of now, just long-lasting staff has been engaged with educating; neither legally binding nor visitor personnel have been engaged with showing continuous class. Be that as it may, mid-semester understudies have been elevated to following class. This situation joblessness will be reflected significantly felt in college as some employees consistently sit tight for their joining (Kumar, 2020).

RESULTS

The Factors Have Been Analyzed

Awareness of Students

Awareness of students try culled out from respondents based on taking fifteen factors, also details have been provided in upcoming table.

The above table 1 shows that only 46 percent of students were aware of online support system, also 56 per cent did not know at all.

Problems Faced by Student

Problems Faced by Students while availing of online education has tried made known based on four Indicators also responses of respondents put forward in next table 2.

Responses brought to notice that 90% of students were faced with Anxiety, 85% encountered Network Issues, 60% raised an issue they had not Smart a phone, also 75% felt bottleneck of Language Barriers.

Teachers' Responses

Teacher's responses regarding upgrading university infrastructure have been actualized based on their views also try identified in subsequent table 3.

Table 1. Responses of Students about Awareness of Online Support System

Awareness of Factors	Yes (in %)	No (in %)
e-GyanKosh	90	10
Gyandarshan	70	30
Gyandhara	65	35
Swayam	35	65
e-PG Pathshala	82	18
e-Adhyayan	87	13
e-Pathya	37	63
e-Yantra	22	78
Free/Libre also Open Source Software for Education	17	83
Virtual Labs	35	65
e-ShodhSindhu	25	75
Shodhganga	90	10
VIDWAN is a premier database	10	90
National Educational Alliance for Technology (NEAT)	10	90
SAKSHAT	15	85
Mean Value	690/15=46	810/15=54

N=50

The above discussion pointed out that some respondents advised providing teacher training to tackle online education. Further, 98% of respondents favored a change in curriculum. Lastly, cent per cent rued regarding Development of Infrastructure to cope with new demands of Digitalization of Education.

Table 2. Problems Faced by Student

Factors	Yes (In %)	No (In %)
Anxiety	90	10
Network issue	85	15
Problems of Smartphone	60	40
Language Barriers	75	25

N=50

Table 3. Teachers' Responses for Infrastructure development for online education

Factors	Yes (In %)	No (In %)
Training of Teacher	100	0
Change in Curriculum	98	2
Development of Infrastructure	100	0

N=10

CONCLUSION

This study assessed that in light of static examination of mental elements also issues understudies face not having needed innovation also language obstructions. Education provided after Covid-19 appears to is a widely approved online or virtual education programme, which may or may not be a separate educational system. Numerous effects of COVID-19 on higher education in India have been examined in this study. Current epidemic presented a chance for pedagogical techniques to shift also to adopt virtual education at all educational levels. Education provided after Covid-19 appears to is a widely approved online or virtual education programme, which may or may not be a separate educational system. However, students in India, with a low Internet penetration rate also network problems, are also anxious because they are unaware of various platforms that support online education also are concerned about how their performance will be assessed. However, there is an immediate need for curriculum revision also a demand for teacher training.

REFERENCES

Bates, T., & Sangra, A. (2011). Managing technology in higher education: strategies for trans forming teaching and learning. *Wiley/Jossey-Bass*. https://www.researchgate.net/publication/279513336_Managing_Technology_in_Higher_Education_Strategies_for_Transforming_Teaching_and_Learning

Bourdieu, P. (1984). *Distinction. A Social Critique of the Judgement of Taste* (R. Nice, Trans.). Harvard University Press.

Chadah, S. (2010). Operationalising right to Education Act: Issues and challenges. *The Indian Journal of Public Administration*, 56(3), 616–634. doi:10.1177/0019556120100318

Chick, R. C., Clifton, G. T., Peace, K. M., Propper, B. W., Hale, D. F., Alseidi, A. A., & Vreeland, T. J. (2020). Using technology to maintain the education of residents during the COVID-19 pandemic. *Journal of Surgical Education*, 77(4), 729–732. doi:10.1016/j.jsurg.2020.03.018 PMID:32253133

Czerniewicz, L. (2020). What we learnt from "going online" during university shutdowns in South Africa. *Phil on EdTech*. https://philonedtech.com/what-we-learnt-from-going-online-during-university-shutdowns-in-south-africa/

Doucet, A., Netolicky, D., Timmers, K., & Tuscano, F. J. (2020, March 2). *Thinking about pedagogy in an unfolding pandemic (Version 2.0).* Independent Report written to inform the work of Education International and UNESCO. https://issuu.com/educationinternational/docs/2020_research_covid-19_eng

Dutta, S. (2020, May 20). Telemedicine is the new call for action at the moment. *The Indian Express.*https://indianexpress.com/article/lifestyle/health/in-telemedicine-virtual-healthcare-futu re-scope-india-mindsets-doctors-6421192/

Fuchs, C. (2020b). *Communication and capitalism: A critical theory.* University of Westminster Press., doi:10.16997/book45

Harwell, D. (2020). Mass school closures in the wake of the coronavirus are driving a new wave of student surveillance. *Washington Post*. https://www.washingtonpost.com/ technology/ 2020/04/01/online-proctoring-college-exams-coronavirus/

Herrington, J., Reeves, T. C., & Oliver, R. (2010). *A guide to authentic e-learning*. Routledge. https://researchrepository.murdoch.edu.au/id/eprint/1903/1/a_guide_to_authentic_learning.pdf

Howland, J. L., Jonassen, D. H., & Marra, R. M. (2011). *Meaningful learning with techn ology* (4th ed.). Pearson Education.

Jandrić, P. (2020). Deschooling. In M. Peters (Ed.), *Encyclopedia of teacher education*. Springer. doi:10.1007/978-981-13-1179-6_115-1

Jena, P. K. (2020). Challenges and Opportunities created by Covid -19 for ODL: A case study of IGNOU. International Journal for Innovative Research in Multidisciplinary, *6*(5):217-222.7.https://10.31235/doi:osf.io/jy2td

Jogan, S. N. (2019). Higher Education in India: Avision of 2030. *International Journal of Research*, *6*(7), 365–370. https://files.eric.ed.gov/fulltext/ED596145.pdf

Kapasia, N., Paul, P., Roy, A., Saha, J., Zaveri, A., Mallick, R., Barman, B., Das, P., & Chouhan, P. (2020). Impact of lockdown on learning status of undergraduate and postgraduate students during COVID-19 pandemic in West Bengal, India. *Children and Youth Services Review*, *116*, 105194. doi:10.1016/j.childyouth.2020.105194 PMID:32834270

Kumar, D. N. S. (29 April 2020). Impact of COVID-19 on Higher Education. *Higher Education Digest*. https://www.highereducationdigest.com/impact -of-covid-19-on-highereducation/

Kumar, D. N. S. (2020, April 29). Impact of COVID-19 on higher education. *Higher Education Digest*. https://www.highereducationdigest.com/impact-of-covid-19-on-higher-education/

Kumar, A. & Ambrish. (2015). Higher Education: Growth, Challenges and Opportunities. *International Journal of Arts, Humanities and Management Studies*, *1*(2). https:// www.academia.edu/11996755/Higher_Education_Growth_Challenges_And_Opportunities

Li, Q., Li, Z., & Han, J. (2021). A hybrid learning pedagogy for surmounting the challenges of the COVID-19 pandemic in the performing arts education. *Education and Information Technologies*, *26*(6), 7635–7655. doi:10.100710639-021-10612-1 PMID:34220284

Li, Z., Li, Q., Han, J., & Zhang, Z. (2022). Perspectives of hybrid performing arts education in the post-pandemic era: An empirical study in Hong Kong. *Sustainability*, *14*(15), 9194. doi:10.3390u14159194

Loh, T. H. & Fishbane, L. (2022, March 8). COVID-19 makes the benefits of telework obvious. *Brookings*. https://www.brookings.edu/blog/the-avenue/2020/03/17/covid-19-makes-the-benefits-of-telework-obvious/

Punjab University. (2020). *Guidelines.* Punjab University. https://www.edexlive.com/news/2020/mar/25/panjab-uni ve rsity-issues-guidelines-for-online-teaching-through-google-classroom-10873.html

Roy, A. (2020). The pandemic is a portal: An online teach-in. *Arundhati Roy.*

Sarkar, S. (2020). GC goes ahead with final year exam plan, students and teachers highlight digital divide, anxieties. *The Hindu.*

Selwyn, N. (2020). After COVID-19: The longer-term impacts of the corona virus crisis on education. *Melbourne Monash University.* https://educationfutures.monash.edu/all%2D%2D-pre sent/after-covid-19

Siemens, G. (2020). A Google scholar search of prominent voices quickly reveals those who have earned the right to provide guidance [tweet]. *Twitter.*

St. Amour, M. (2020). Privacy and the online pivot. Inside Higher Ed, 25.

Strong, P. (1990). Epidemic psychology: A model. *Sociology of Health & Illness, 12*(3), 249–259. doi:10.1111/1467-9566.ep11347150

Teras, H., & Kartoglu, U. (2017). A grounded theory of professional learning in an authentic online professional development program. *The International Review of Research in Open and Distributed Learning, 18*(7). doi:10.19173/irrodl.v18i7.2923

Teras, M., Suoranta, J., Teras, H., & Curcher, M. (2020). Post-Covid-19 Education and Education Technology 'Solutionism': a Seller's Market. Postdigital Science and Education. Google Scholar.

UNESCO. (2020). *COVID-19 educational disruption and response.* UNESCO. https://en.unesco. org/ covid19/educationresponse

Unni Krishnan, J.P. & Ors. Vs State of Andhra Pradesh & Ors. *1993 AIR 217, 1993 SCR (1) 594, 1993 SCC (1) 645, JT 1993 (1) 474, 1993 SCALE (1)290.*

Chapter 15
An Overview of Field Work Education in the Social Work Profession in India and Abroad

Viney Dhiman
Panjab University, Chandigarh, India

Gaurav Gaur
Panjab University, Chandigarh, India

ABSTRACT

In the social work education field, learning plays a significant role as it allows the field instructors and the social work educators to know the knowledge gained by the student during the field education experience. Field learning helps the instructors to get aware of the way through which the students learn and develop in social work agencies. The article helps examine the field of learning in social work education and compares India and abroad. The articles will focus on the multifaceted nature of field learning that shows the sociocultural approaches associated with the nature of learning settings for understanding the student's learning process in social field education. The article will focus on the cross-comparison of the role of field training in social work education practices across India and other countries, including Australia, Uganda, Canada, Vietnam, Norway, and Sweden. The article helps develop social work education with its practices in various countries.

INTRODUCTION

A combination of theoretical; and practice learning is required in social work education based on practiced professionalism. Both types of learning play an important role in becoming professional social workers. Field learning can be provided outside the university classroom through the experience of field education. The learning process is critical for the student in both classroom and field setting as it helps them acquire, practice, and improve the values and skills needed in their profession. Learning helps students to become ethical professional social workers and helps in the development process that starts at the

DOI: 10.4018/978-1-6684-6682-7.ch015

early stages of the students. (Salsberg et al., 2017) stated that learning influences the whole education process and is considered a long-term development and critical process. Learning is considered critical for the student's future, and field education and social work education show how students develop in the classroom and field settings. The fieldwork focuses on the operational and task-oriented nature of learning compared to the learning process. The field experience underestimates the value of critical reflection in student learning; however, field education is important to understand the role of social work and its professional identities gained from the field experience. (Hossain et al., 2020) The article will discuss the field in learning social work education and compare India abroad. From the existing literature, it has been clear that learning is divided into various types, including formal and informal learning. Formal and informal learning are differentiated in the social work education literature to provide a framework that helps understand the different types of student learning as an adult learner. The formal learning process involves the knowledge obtained from the institution, including classroom-based learning and academic or laboratory learning. The behavior of formal learning is highly structured, and it is learned outside the social work practice environment. Formal learning processes are also involved in the daily work that includes the on-the-job training course, and Formal learning is directly linked to the explicit knowledge that can be learned through courses, books, and lectures. Informal and non-formal learning takes place in the workplace or field placement setting. The informal learning process involves various daily activities and is highly unstructured. The informal learning process is also involved in the formal institutional context that can be between students and students to exchange the knowledge, skills, and values that will help in the social work progression. (Khan et al., 2017)

Field learning is classified as informal learning that helps the students to acquire knowledge, skills, and values for the social work profession. Both learning processes are influenced by social, cultural, political, and historical content. The formal and informal learning processes are associated with adult education due to their field nature and learned-centred focus. The curriculum of social work schools worldwide is influenced by field learning. Social work education has revealed that field learning is used to evaluate students' learning and measure performance in various schools and countries. Field learning is considered experiential learning by the social work students involved in the social work educational process. Social work students move from class-based learning to learning by doing during the field practicum, which marks the entrance into the world and enhances learning demands through the work. Field learning helps the students to improve their personal development with professional development. The student's personal development takes place through field learning in various ways as the students interact with the different categories of people during the fieldwork experience. Field learning helps social work students to discover new idea that helps in their professional development (Jena, 2020). Field learning allows social work students to deal with democratic ideals and humanitarian values based on the people's worth, equality, and dignity. Behind social action, human rights and social justice are considered the main motivation. The social work profession can alleviate poverty, and it helps students to uplift the oppressed and vulnerable people in society. Field learning helps students to achieve social inclusion and development through social field learning.

The full potential of the people of the communities is developed by the profession that helps the people to prevent dysfunction. The human condition is improved by incorporating other social workers' that help to change the condition of society in response to chronic problems such as unemployment, poverty, malnutrition, prostitution, human trafficking, terrarium, discrimination, etc. (Ansari & Khan, 2020). Field learning helps to understand the challenges and issues faced by the people in society, and through field learning, other issues can be understood and solved at the ground level. Social work education is a national education system in all countries; however, the pedagogy, octet, and practices in all the countries differ. However, there is no universal pattern for social education. In this study, we will discuss the role of field learning in social work education in India and other countries such as Australia. India & Australia are both prominent countries in Asia and the Pacific region of the world (Lokhandwala & Gautam, 2020).

An accessible, multi day overall field experience program for distance tutoring and close by cordial work students at an Australian regional school is portrayed in this paper. Student learning, student pack connection, capable obligation and motivation, as well as an extended excitement for worldwide social work, grassroots neighbourhood work, social assortment, normal freedoms, and social liberties issues, were all on a very basic level impacted by overall survey understanding, as shown by pre-and post-program evaluation studies. During dynamic time of program, positive, rational responsibilities to circumstance associations and ceaseless relationship with social liberties projects in India were two other constructive outcomes. Accentuation of need of acceptable insightful preparation, correspondence, on-going educational assistance, and help of passing concentrate abroad ventures. This paper bases on habits by which a get-together of Australian social work students participated in a multi-day overall gather abroad program in India helped them with encouraging their master characters. Program's general effects were surveyed using a mixed methodologies approach. Students' impression of social equality, normal freedoms, direction, environment, worldwide social work, and master character were inspected through pre-and post-program appraisal outlines and smart studios. This paper takes a gander at rich portrayals of experiences and's the manner by which students could decipher their own capable characters was affected by collaboration in multi day program by focusing in on a subset of these master character data. Paper closes by causing to see a couple of repercussions for students and teachers of social work who are enthused about expected benefits of transient concentrate abroad ventures.

MATERIALS AND METHODS

Specifically, the study looked at the role of field learning in social work education in the United States, Canada, the United Kingdom, Australia, and India. The Asian and Pacific Association of Schools of Social Work has 78 member institutions. Social work is typically taught in the undergraduate curriculum in a number of Asian countries. According to the Asia Pacific Association for Social Work Education, more than one hundred schools and colleges in China offer social work programs. Yet Japan has 81 graduate schools of social work and 143 undergraduate institutions dedicated to social education, while Vietnam has only three. There are reportedly five schools of social work in Malaysia (Kinni, 2020). Many different social work programmes can be found in countries like India, Australia, and the Philippines, all of which hold graduate social work education to very high standards. It's been seven decades since India first introduced the idea of field learning, and it's since become a major influence on the country's social work curriculum. The study of social work has made its mark in both public and private institutions of higher education. The social work profession in Australia can trace its roots to the United Kingdom and the United States. Social work education in Australia got its start in 1940. In Australia, the social service industry is part of the public or non-profit sector. There have been shifts in both the professional model and the de-professionalized approach to social work in Australia.

Table 1. Institutions dedicated to social work in India's several regions

Zone	State & Cities	Social Work Institutions
North	Chandigarh, Delhi, Haryana, Himachal Pradesh, Jammu & Kashmir, Punjab, Uttarakhand, Uttar Pradesh	49
West	Rajasthan, Goa, Gujarat, Maharashtra	111
Central	Chhattisgarh, Madhya Pradesh	79
East	West Bengal, Odisha, Bihar, and Jharkhand	21
North-East	This includes the Indian states of Arunachal Pradesh, Assam, Manipur, Meghalaya, Mizoram, Nagaland, Sikkim, and Tripura.	22
South	This is in the state of Tamil Nadu, Telangana, Tamil Nadu, Puducherry (UT), Andhra Pradesh, Karnataka, and Kerala	244
	Total	526

STRUCTURE AND CONTENT OF SOCIAL WORK

This article proposes the following framework for comparing culturally competent social work education and practise in India and overseas:

India

Across India's educational institutions, the semester is the standard unit of assessment for social work courses. The Bachelor of Social Work (BSW) is the entry-level professional degree in the area of social work, and it is enhanced through field learning. Field learning provides proactive-based knowledge regarding the challenges present in society, and it also helps the students to get connected with people. The bachelor's social work degree involves families, communities, and organizations (Arrow and Grant 2021). India is a large country separated into numerous zones based on different criteria depending on the cause for the division. Based on their socio-geographic location and proximity, (Bhatt, S., 2016) categorized the development of social work education into North, West, Central, East, North-East, and South zones (table 1).

The aforementioned schools of social work offer a wide variety of study programmes, course offerings, fieldwork opportunities, training/field placement, and other specialised experiences. The 2016 research by Professor Bhatt provides data on Indian social work organisations. Although it took a while to get established, SWEI has steadily expanded into the north-eastern region since the first school of social work was founded there in the early 1990s. SWEI density is highest in the South zone, which consists of five states and one UT, and lowest in the North zone, which has seven states and one UT. The second-largest concentration of SWEIs is located in the Western Hemisphere (Rajasthan, Goa, Gujarat, and Maharashtra). While there is an older SWEI in West Bengal, and a newer one in Odisha, SWEIs have been established in Bihar, Jharkhand, and Odisha, the other states in this zone, during the last decade. The number of SWEIs is lowest in the Eastern region.

There have also been rapid advances in the establishment of SWEIs in the north-eastern region, which encompasses the land of seven sisters and Sikkim. The TISS campuses in Guwahati and Nagaland are located in this region and are run in conjunction with the Nagaland Gandhi Ashram. Given that the vast majority of social work education institutions (SWEIs) focus on graduate-level instruction, it is high time that an undergraduate generic/base/preparatory course, such as a BA (Social Work) with limited field work exposure, be considered. Earning a master's degree in social work allows students to focus on developing their interests. Professional entry-level positions often call for at least a bachelor's degree. This study expects to think about proficient social work rehearses, educational plan, examination, hands on work, and training in India and Australia. It analyzes advancement of social work training in these two countries and its best practices. This is finished with aim of grasping social government assistance and social work approaches in the two nations. preparing in friendly work started in India in 1936, though it started in Australia in 1940 at College of Sydney. Course work expert in India is College Awards Commission (UGC) and Public Certification and Appraisal Committee (NAAC), while in Australia, proficient affiliation known as Australian Relationship for Social Work (AASW) is liable for license. Objective of social work training in Australian colleges is to create graduates with a large number of abilities that can be utilized in a wide assortment of training settings. Coursework in India can be conventional or specific. Oddly, social work has not yet been enlisted with any state or government office in any of nations. Self-guideline, on other hand, is empowered, as are peer oversights and continuous expert turn of events. Australian Social Work Training and License Norms (ASWEAS), which likewise control and direct educational plan advancement for Australian social work programs, are responsible for keeping up with training principles in Australia. Understudies in friendly and local area work depend on help and assets given by chiefs of social assistance organizations for their hands on work arrangements.

The focal point of this article is orientation mistreatment and impacts that a momentary global review program had on Australian social work understudies' cognizance of civil rights and common freedoms issues. Composed assessments and subjective information from an intelligent studio are utilized to portray and explore understudies' appearance on program's opportunities for growth. Proficient information base and social work concentrate on abroad projects are thought about. Program enhanced comprehension understudies might interpret worldwide issues like orientation abuse, civil rights, and common liberties, as well as built up need for personnel drove worked with, intelligent getting the hang of, as per discoveries. Need to lay out global principles for social work schooling is developing. As a component of their plan for worldwide joint effort and diverse drenching in calling, different global colleges have started expanded open doors for worldwide trade in educating and educational experience. Understudies in friendly work who partook in worldwide trades valued need for worldwide needs and procedures to propel social work training, exploration, and practice ability advancement, which has likewise prompted future joint effort between these foundations. In any case, there are various deterrents for both assistant and establishments included, which ought to be considered at different phases of trade. Have establishment's fastidious arranging is expected for this. In view of creator's very own insight, this paper centres on need for worldwide social work, hardships of global temporary jobs, and cycle and content of field training for global understudies. Motivation behind this paper is to offer a general model for worldwide field instruction that both host foundation and home organization can settle on.

This may help to popularise the course as a prerequisite for MSW programs as a basic or introductory course. The crucial fieldwork component of social work education, which includes concurrent fieldwork training under the direct supervision of a faculty member, is also harmed. As a result, pupils cannot develop the skills required for social work. The geophysical structure and socio-economic development of India's north, east, west, and south areas differ. Field learning in the different regions of India differed from each other due to their different social-cultural areas. North states of India act as a bridge in building the teachers' training facilities and helps the state to prepare holistic planning for field training. The field training of south India is different from that of north India due to their social culture. In south India, field training regarding social work education involves providing education on psychology education, homework, literacy, and pre-primary education. The east state of India includes west Bengal, Odisha, and Jharkhand focus on providing field training to the students. The universities in the eastern state of India provide field training to the students that guides them to work for social purposes. Bachelor's and master's degrees differ from one another. The school and the colleges provide field training to improve the professional development of the students. The fieldwork component plays an important role in the training; the faculty supervise the study tour in the bachelor's. In social work, the master's course bears 80 to 90 credits of the requirement. Field training is less in India as only credit is provided for field training. Across the schools in India, there is a large variation in the specialization provided. Some of their schools in India allow a three-step process for the selection of national-level written exams, group discussions, and personal interviews. However, employment for social workers in the government sector is limited in India. Most of the social workers in India are employed in the non-government sector (Drolet & Harriman, 2020).

Australia

In Australia, four years, of course, is provided for the bachelor of social, and it is mandatory for getting employment in the field of social work. Some universities in Australia also offer a two years graduation course for the bachelor of Social work. The Australian Association of Social Workers recognizes all the courses related to social work education. For social workers, there is no requirement for registration in Australia which is needed in India. Employers in Australia need prospective employees who become eligible to be a member of AASW. Professional social work education in Australia issues core and common knowledge, values, and skills applied across the practice settings. (Dhodmise, 2021) states that Australia's professional social work program involves well-being and doing. Field training helps the students enhance their critical thinking, innovation, and ability to solve problems. Field training helps the students identify core values, including human rights, social justice, and human dignity and equality. In Australia, contemporary pedagogical knowledge is followed for building the students' professional development. It has been recognized by the AASW that there is tension present in the content requirement and the learning process. For the appropriate balance, these standards have strived. Australian social work education recognizes social work as it influences the people, cultural, special, spiritual, and physical environments. Field learning is also considered the core component in Australian entry-level provision of teaching, field learning is marginalized by Australian social workers, mental health, cross-cultural practice, child well-being, and protection and practice with aboriginal and Torres Strait Islander people and communities are the specific curriculum included in the Australian social work. (Williamson, 2020) Social work programmers' in school should be taught in a way that helps them to be social workers. An IASSW practice is followed by the Australian social work for the fieldwork practice. The field training in Australia includes mental health, child well-being, Aboriginal and Torres Strait Islander cultures, income security, aging, cultural and linguistic diversity and removing the locations, housing and homelessness, and international practices and education (Archer-Kuhn et al., 2020).

Sweden

Due to neoliberal globalisation, field learning in Sweden's social work programmes faces a number of obstacles. Because of the country's skewed development and rising inequality, social work education there has been revamped. The government of England can help more students get ready to work in the new global context by implementing field-based learning into the field of social work. Mid The Social Work Department at Mid Sweden University (MIUN) has become a centre for critical and international understanding. An integral part of any social work curriculum should include time spent in the field gaining practical experience. Social work education programmes at Mid-Sweden University combine classroom study with practicum and internship experiences. Students in Sweden have access to high-quality social-learning education through international field training. MIUN organises a wide range of field training opportunities so that students can gain exposure to a wide range of social issues and service opportunities. Global field studies give students a virtual window into the world's most pressing social issues.

Norway

The NTNU Social Work Program at the Norwegian University of Science and Technology emphasises practical experience. Fieldwork at NTNU can be difficult because it contributes to inequality in postcolonial and non-liberal settings. The social work curriculum in Norway typically lasts for three months and is taught by university professors. Seminars and classes in social work are available to students at the University of Norway.

Uganda

In 1969, Makerere University introduced its new Bachelor of Social Work and Social Administration degree programme for undergraduates. The purpose of the three-year curriculum is to train social workers who are competent in working with clients at all levels of society. To that end, social work education in Uganda is given within the framework established by the Universities and Other Tertiary Institutions Act of 2001, which regulates higher education in Uganda. All educational establishments are obligated to include the Act's content standards for social work education and training into their respective curricula. To wit: (Kgosietsile, N., 2018)

Canada

Specifically, the field component of social work education in Canada integrates theory and practise. Field education requirements established by the 12 member institutions of the Canadian Association of Schools of Social Work (CASSW, 1998) range from 900 hours for a 2-year MSW (after BA) programme to 450 hours for a 1-year MSW programme and 700 hours for a Bachelor of Social Work programme (post-BSA). Under the supervision of a trained professional, students must put their knowledge and abilities to use in the real world. Training for agency-based field instructors and participation from professional groups in accreditation evaluations are two examples of how the same accreditation criteria can serve as bridges between the professional community and the academic establishment.

Vietnam

In recent years, social work has been recognised at Vietnamese universities. The new social work curriculum in Vietnam is on line with other Bachelor of Arts degree programmes. The four-year programme consists of 210 units: 84 for foundational skills in politics, Marxism, and other languages; and 106 for specific knowledge and practise (of which only 52 credits are spent on specialised professional knowledge). Some subjects, including as politics, Marxism, Ho Chi Minh Ideology, and themes relating to professional training, are required by the Ministry of Education and Training (MOET) and are taught at all grade levels as part of a standardised programme (Durst, D., Thai, N. T., & Loan, L. H., 2010).

RESULTS AND DISCUSSION

Future Needs of Social Work

The quality of social work education can be enhanced at the postgraduate level. It is important to tackle the possibilities and challenges in social work education. In Indian society, it is important to learn and adopt both method of field training that helps in improving Indian social work practices worldwide. In social work education, there are major needs that should be followed. In rural India, it is important to establish several social work institutions. Field training should be increased to fulfil the gap between rural and urban social work institutions. The field training aims to produce high-quality social workers who can reduce poverty and society's vulnerabilities. (Petra et al., 2020) stated that professionally trained social workers also needed to produce highly qualified social workers for the development programmer of the country into reality. (Borgmeyer et al., 2021) stated that, in India and Australia, there is a lack of proper funding for the institution of social work. Therefore, they are not capable of research and development, and there is a need for a greater fund that can motivate social workers to bring innovative changes across the country by sharing ideas without compromising quality. All the schools of social work should be linked up through online knowledge based on their respective resources. Across the country, a standard curriculum for social work education should be developed that is preferred by all your local contexts of different regions of social work education. In adobe, it has been mentioned that the quality of the social work education in various institutions is substandard, and most of the institutions are privately based that should be funded for the development of the country and the people belonging to vulnerable groups (Monrad & Mølholt, 2017). Unfortunately, some schools have limited and paid seats that take a capitation charge from the students.

The fieldwork training in these institutions is weak; therefore, field training is considered the most important factor in social work education in India. It is important to control the fee structure of these institutions. It should be followed during the accreditation process. (Hitchcock et al., 2019) stated that institutions that fail to respect ideology should not be granted acceptance regarding social work education. The high fee structure of the schools and colleges leads to an increase in the growth of the distance education sector for social work courses. Many students consider distance education the most economical, and it is considered the best option to get a postgraduate degree in social work. The standards of the social work profession are affected by these standards as distance education is not providing a good quality of personal experience. It is important to delink this specialization from the social work education field training is the best way to understand the challenges present in society. The National Council for Social Work Professions should be established to license the social work practice that is effectively introduced, which helps to enhance the social work standards. (Parga & Doyle, 2020) The pre-existing framework of social work should be enhanced by social work education in the local context.

(Mathiyazhagan, 2021) argues that initiatives that are too generalised ought to be phased out and replaced with ones that are better suited to the unique social and cultural conditions of rural areas. New institutions of social work education should be created in more remote locations. Some social work education in the north of the country is housed in the university system, and therefore it is necessary to keep social work departments distinct from other departments so that they can have more autonomy and room for growth. The social work curriculum varies greatly between the various schools in Northern India. The market economy and a focus on employment heavily shape the majority of schools' social work (Meler & Mahajne, 2021). Social work and its educational infrastructure face a number of challenges, as reported by (Durst, D., Thai, N. T., & Loan, L. H., 2010). Vietnam's social work curriculum is based on the "Global Standards for Social Work Education and Training" (IASSW/IFSW, 2004) that establishes international best practise standards. While the criteria are based on a Western understanding of social work. It might be challenging to identify theoretical and practical approaches that are both culturally sensitive and suited to the context and culture of Vietnam. Even though field education accounts for up to a third of the credit hours in Canadian social work programmes, it is often seen as a lesser priority than the classroom instruction. In most Canadian universities, the field coordinator is viewed as a professional and has a lower academic standing than teaching academics. Canada also has a problem with insufficient practise, but Vietnam has it considerably worse. Field education, or practical training, is an integral part of a Canadian student's academic experience. As much as a third of a degree programs required coursework can be spent on field education. In Vietnam, just nine practise units across social work (six units) and community development (three units) are required to graduate from the MOLISA programme.

From a diploma course to a doctoral degree, professional field education in India's four scores of social workers has grown significantly. As well, curriculum has changed. Despite a few issues, such as insufficient contributions, inadequate contextualization, thematic restrictions, Sometimes, advancements are held back, making country's curriculum for literature in social work narrow. Indian context of social work education and curriculum is subject of article. It examines social work education and curriculum in India and is primarily based on a literature review of articles, chapters, and books published in India and abroad. There have been attempts to investigate social work curriculum, reasons why it needs to be revaluated, and any potential new additions that could be made to broaden scope of field.

This paper examines effects and challenges of a two-week study abroad program in India on Australian social work students' understanding of real-world environment using a critical social work lens. A brief study on environmental social work was conducted in 2011 using a mixed method approach. It included pre- and post-program surveys, as well as a facilitated reflective workshop. Program improved students' conventional socio-cultural understanding of environment and global dimensions of environmental degradation, according to results, which are discussed. Although this is encouraging and suggests some justification for international study abroad program, it also raises other concerns about program's neo-colonial and complex cultural issues. need for novel and creative teaching methods in field of social work education has been demonstrated by tidiest photo voice model of qualitative research in social work classroom has been cited as a model that meets these requirements by some. photo voice model is implemented in three different social work courses, as shown in this paper: 1) Social Work on a Global Scale; 2) Public Service; 3) Social work orientation paper gives four different examples that show how photo voice can be used creatively in learning processes of students. In light of significance of creativity in framework for social work education, these examples are discussed: facilitating internalization of social work's values, professional goals, and methods of action; and a phenomenological look at social realities in a way that lets student "freeze" certain parts of learning experience and think critically about how these realities are interpreted.

According to (Sandstrom, 2007), Swedish National Agency for Higher Education and new national goals for social work degrees are two factors that affect social work education in Sweden. National Agency for Higher Education in Sweden evaluates degree programmes and courses before approving universities to hand out academic credentials. After getting this green light, topics and programmes will be examined every six years. In Uganda, since persons trained in other professions also work as social workers, there is no regulation to support its formation at practice level. Therefore, it is still unregulated, making it unclear whether graduates will find employment after graduating. Vietnam's understanding of "fieldwork" is lacking. Amount of time allotted for practicum in current Hanoi program is quite small (only ten credits). Either social work is seen as a "good job" that everyone can perform or as a completely theoretical field. Practice-oriented nature of social work is one of its defining characteristics in Canada. A method of understanding individuals and societal institutions known as practice orientation is described as being comprehensive and systemic. Various practice environments and jurisdictions use this strategy widely. Theory and practice are linked in Canadian social work education, especially regarding field component. Social work education in Australia is also influenced by westernization, and curriculum of social work in Australia is taken from western social work. Australia follows American model, and it follows British model for social work of education. Teachers present in school in Australia belong to Britain or from America. Professors regarding students' curriculum and training provided to students. In Australia, most social work program components are same as social work school in America (Bell et al., 2013). Australia needs to develop a system that focuses on local context rather than following American model. In Australia, Public sector is considered a major sector where social worker gets employment due to high-quality social work practice norms present in public sector of Australia. Field of social work in India needs to create openings for its practitioners and allow social work schools to seize them. A look at Australia's accreditation system may be useful for India. A social work curriculum and field that is appropriate for political and socioeconomic climate of India is urgently required. Development grounded in social work education requires an influx of experts and ideas from all over world.

CONCLUSION

The importance of fieldwork in social work education in India and abroad has been illuminated by this research. The research has yielded a thorough comprehension of the prerequisites, obstacles, and openings for experiential learning in each of the four countries. For this reason, all countries' social work curricula, which are now mostly based on western models, need to be indigenized. One of the most pressing issues in the field of social work education is the lack of sufficient financing in many regions. The key issues in field training in all countries are the diversity of the regions, the proliferation of the supplied social work institutions, the great difference in the curriculum, and the diversity of the regions. Because of this diversity, it is impossible to provide a universal curriculum description. Accreditation for social work degrees in India needs development, however, because the country has a tough time keeping up with the growing number of social workers.

REFERENCES

Ansari, J. A., & Khan, N. A. (2020). Exploring the role of social media in collaborative learning the new domain of learning. *Smart Learning Environments*, *7*(1), 9. doi:10.118640561-020-00118-7

Archer-Kuhn, B., Samson, P., Damianakis, T., Barrett, B., Matin, S., & Ahern, C. (2020). Transformative learning in Field education: Students bridging the theory/Practice gap. *British Journal of Social Work*, *51*(7), 2419–2438. doi:10.1093/bjsw/bcaa082

Arrow, K. M., & Grant, Z. S. (2021). Pandemic Possibilities in Crip Time: Disrupting Social Work Field Education. *Intersectionalities: A Global Journal of Social Work Analysis. Research, Polity, and Practice*, *9*(1), 98–114.

Bell, K. & Anscombe, A.W. (2013). International field experience in social work: Outcomes of a short-term study abroad programme *Social Work Education* to India., *32*(8), pp.1032-1047. doi:10.1080/02 615479.2012.730143

Bhatt, S. (2016). Social Work Educational Institutions in India: An Analysis. *Journal of Social Work Education, Research and Action*, *2*, 46-67. https://www.researchgate.net/publication/34932 4328_Social_Work_Educational_Institutions_in_India

Borgmeyer, A. R., Garand, J. C., & Wilks, S. E. (2021). Examining academic entitlement through the lens of field education. *Social Work Education*, *41*(6), 1336–1350. doi:10.1080/02615479.2021.1950672

Dhodmise, T. (2021). Values in Field work for social work: Value ethics for sustainable and ethical future, for the field work in social work. *Mahratta*, *1*(1), 1–3.

Drolet, J., & Harriman, K. 2020. A conversation on a new Canadian social work field education and research collaboration initiative. *Field Educator*, *10*(1). https://fieldeducator.simmons.edu/article/a-conversation-on-a-new-canadian-social-work-field-education-and-research-collaboration-initiative/

Durst, D., Lanh, T. H., & Pitzel, M. (2010). A Comparative Analysis of Social Work in Vietnam and Canada: Rebirth and Renewal. *Journal of Comparative Social Work*, *5*(2), 77–88. doi:10.31265/jcsw.v5i2.63

Fox, M., McHugh, S., Thomas, D., Kiefel-Johnson, F., & Joseph, B. (2021). Bringing together podcasting, social work field education and learning about practice with Aboriginal peoples and communities. *Social Work Education*, 1–17. doi:10.1080/02615479.2021.1972963

Hitchcock, L. I., King, D. M., Johnson, K., Cohen, H., & Mcpherson, T. L. (2019). Learning outcomes for adolescent SBIRT simulation training in social work and nursing education. *Journal of Social Work Practice in the Addictions*, *19*(1-2), 47–56. doi:10.1080/1533256X.2019.1591781

Hossain, M. A., Jahid, M. I., Hossain, K. M., Walton, L. M., Uddin, Z., Haque, M. O., Kabir, M. F., Arafat, S. M., Sakel, M., Faruqui, R., & Hossain, Z. (2020). Knowledge, attitudes, and fear of COVID-19 during the rapid rise period in Bangladesh. *PLoS One*, *15*(9), e0239646. doi:10.1371/journal.pone.0239646 PMID:32970769

Jena, R. (2020). Measuring the impact of business management student's attitude towards entrepreneurship education on entrepreneurial intention: A case study. *Computers in Human Behavior*, *107*, 106275. doi:10.1016/j.chb.2020.106275

Kgosietsile, N. (2018). *Social Work Education and Human Rights A Comparative Study of Learning and Teaching of Human Rights in University of Gothenburg, Sweden and Makerere University, Uganda* [Master's thesis, University of Gothenburg]. https://gupea.ub.gu.se/bitstream/handle/ 2077/57127/gupea_2077_57127_1.pdf;jsessionid=8C59CF3D24AF9DBBC53DA6D2FBF027FA?sequence=1

Khan, M. J., Chelliah, S., & Ahmed, S. (2017). Factors influencing destination image and visit intention among young women travellers: Role of travel motivation, perceived risks, and travel constraints. *Asia Pacific Journal of Tourism Research*, *22*(11), 1139–1155. doi:10.1080/10941665.2017.1374985

Kinni, R. (2020). Integration of theory and practice in social work education. Analysis of Finnish social work students' field reports. *Social Work Education*, *40*(7), 901–914. doi:10.1080/02615479.2020.1754385

Lokhandwala, S., & Gautam, P. (2020). Indirect impact of COVID-19 on environment: A brief study in Indian context. *Environmental Research*, *188*, 109807. doi:.2020.109807 doi:10.1016/j.envres

Mahajne, I., & Meler, T. (2021). Retraining in social work for Arab academic women: Motivation and integration into the Field. *Affilia*, *37*(2), 300–319. doi:10.1177/08861099211057504

Mathiyazhagan, S. (2021). Field practice, emerging technologies, and human rights: The emergence of tech social workers. *Journal of Human Rights and Social Work*, *7*(4), 441–448. doi:10.100741134-021-00190-0 PMID:34518805

Monrad, M., & Mølholt, A. (2017). Problem-based learning in social work education: Students' experiences in Denmark. *Journal of Teaching in Social Work*, *37*(1), 71–86. doi:10.1080/08841233.2016.1271382

Parga, J., & Doyle, K. (2020). Field Instructor Training: Implications of Low Completion Rates. *Field Educator*, *10*(2). https://fieldeducator.simmons.edu/article/field-instructor-training-implications-of-low-completion-rates/

Petra, M. M., Tripepi, S., & Guardiola, L. (2020). How many hours is enough? The effects of changes in field practicum hours on student preparedness for social work. *Field Educator*, *10*(1). https://fieldeducator.simmons.edu/article/how-many-hours-is-enough-the-effects-of-changes-in-field-practicum-hours-on-student-preparedness-for-social-work/

Salsberg, E., Quigley, L., Mehfoud, N., Acquaviva, K. D., Wyche, K., & Silwa, S. (2017). *Profile of the Social Work Workforce*. Health Sciences Research Commons. https://hsrc.himmelfarb.gwu. edu/sphhs_policy_workforce_ facpubs/16

Sandström, G. (2007). Higher education for social work in Sweden. *Australian Social Work*, *60*(1), 56–67. doi:10.1080/03124070601166711

situation have caused further issues, and this pressure was felt on the global healthcare system. Lack of clarity on COVID, its symptoms, its strength, its variants, and possible treatments added to the problem. At one stage world, powers and countries had to accept and announce that it was a pandemic and the world was not ready for this; precautions were the best possible solution at the time. A large population of the world is people who aren't aware of the seriousness and severity of the problem and are unaware of any useful facts about it. Here, in this regard, the objective is to identify the potential of visuals to spread customer knowledge and how effective these adverts are.

A researcher has used an online survey to obtain data from 456 samples of people, which has been subsequently analyzed concerning collecting information on 408. Data were randomly obtained from participants on the internet using a quick, free-response online questionnaire. During the period between May 2019 and January 2020, the data was obtained. It was seen that digital media is responsible for two factors: "Information Sharing" and "Health Care in the Digital" are essential in getting Covid-19 attendees to know about the topics. Therefore, the conclusions from this study were confirmed by all the results that showed the importance of digital media and social media during the healthcare crisis and the success and efficacy of other research on that mentioned. Thus, the researchers concluded that further analyses of Covid-19's social media audiovisual communication impact on public consciousness should be done, as these results make clear the crisis of how social media was effective.

People on social media use many media, emphasizing images, text, and geographic details. For government organizations, it is a faster medium for sharing information about social development schemes. For corporations, the information could be used to shape their management practices; for politicians, it may be useful in tracking public sentiment; and for public bodies, it could be used to understand the spread of illness or respond to natural disasters. Some researchers see social networking as a window into the collective mind. Many benefits come from utilizing social networks; however, there are certain difficulties with using data from social networks. This medium has a large potential and is normally transmitted in radio waves. The data is often multidimensional, with varying quality, and highly context-dependent.

Regarding social networking, communication patterns are rapidly occurring in various forms. There are several developed disciplines, such as artificial intelligence and data analysis, for processing and understanding such large, complicated data. A machine intelligence technique for discovery method that looks for identifiable patterns in data that can be described algorithmically.

Users may work through interactive visualization to explore intriguing associations by mapping dynamic data to visual types. The sidebar on Social Media Visual Advertisements addresses the systems' core methodological properties. The use of visual advertisements on social network data exemplifies the numerous advantages of this integrated strategy. The abundance of social media info and the resources it provides to different stakeholders has ignited a lot of interest in visual advertising. There are two types of Univariate Analysis; visual advertisements in social media influence you to spend more time perceiving the material, and therefore, visual advertisements in social media influence decision-making. Multivariate analysis is another factor in visual advertising that influences an Awareness Campaign the most.

Instead of working through these challenges, the medical practitioners returned to conventional approaches. By the third month of the disease had emerged, millions of cases were recorded from across the whole regions of the planet, and it rapidly became a global catastrophe. Severe Acute Respiracirus has already surpassed its disease severity after significantly increased incidences of Severe Acute Respiratory Syndrome (SARS- CoV). To prevent the Coronavirus from spreading, as it is in Africa, the participating nations are looking into needed help and training requirements, along with assistance in the development of pharmaceutical research, to create greater healthcare capacities in those countries. The World Health

Organization has recently collaborated with several media outlets to improve public literacy and increase awareness. Understanding this need It is imperative to raise understanding of Coronavirus has increased; hence it is necessary to keep it from getting worse. As a result, the world community has produced several guidelines, such as the use of wheelchairs and transport travel accommodations. Other than that, healthcare awareness promotional programs often teach us about the circulation and consequences of this pandemic, and other efforts are being made to raise awareness about it. The number of Coronaviruses is rising, and we learn new stuff daily about it. This is why more and better knowledge for the public is now available, and less spectacular public data on sources, risk factors, and precautionary steps is vital.

Several prototype data-crunchingeware programs have been developed to extract multidimensional data from social networks and correlate it with quotations, photos, as well as appearances of celebrities, and marketing strategies. COVID-related studies proposed a visual identity "visual discovery and tracking mechanism" as an example of natural pandemics and natural disasters as a visual way to detect geographical patterns in Twitter data and locate Subject streams, as explained in the earlier paragraph. A timeline of subjects and participants; typical discussions about various news issues such as pandemics, political statements, and natural disasters (central); while the visualization of different viewpoints by images (not shown) aids online debates regarding international sporting tournaments offers both graphic and actual discovery. On the project side, we've studied fresh and innovative ways to visualize community-provided photo galleries, real-or video-streamed live news, and daily time series of geo-referenced microblog updates. Organizations may generate, distribute, and disperse their content through social networking 'Social networking represents a type of 'owned' media. Social networking encompasses several types of platforms used to meet specific brand-building goals for brands, marketers, and managers microblogging, video-sharing platforms (e.g., Instagram), social media (e.g., Facebook), image-sharing sites (e.g., Pinterest), and traditional networking (e.g., LinkedIn) all got off the ground during the last decade. Among the most common social media sites, Instagram, Pinterest, and Snapchat demonstrate that visual advertisements are a significant element of social media marketing.

Media outlets will increase general knowledge that Coronavirus is lethal for those with compromised immune systems. As well as the value of media-based healthcare programs was also brought up; likewise, media health campaigns were found to be powerful sources of intelligence. Most of the population, particularly in rural areas, remains unaware of any prior health problem. There is some empirical evidence that media-based advertisements have a greater ability to assist in persuading people regarding the benefits of implementing health-enhancing habits than other ads. Preventing people from being infected is crucial for their well-being, and to preserve it, distancing people from the infected is also important. Nevertheless, despite accepting social distancing as a key determinant, a significant population remains ignorant.

On the other hand, social networking can reach an incredibly large number of users; thus, providing important content to these people in addition to conventional media is valuable. The new measures in place to keep humanity from breeding are increasing its population size and are having unintended side effects that cause things like more people acting irrationally. Regardless of whether or not consumers may be sensitized by new contact channels such as social media, many customers are affected by being exposed to ads by various means. Due to the technological ability to move to digital media, it is now possible to stop these information-gathering methods, making it possible to take advantage of these online resources to promote knowledge. How well social media messaging works is shown when they say that they believe that it influences viewer behavior is confirmed by citing social media as an influential channel. According to the researchers, increased digital marketing use continues to affect how people see the world and their decisions. It is a straightforward task; allowing people to collect more people with appropriate information increases their options and lets them decide. Social media advertisers formulate content campaigns emphasizing consumer desires and intentions in mind. Traditionally, Digital ads entice the audience and follow a sequence of stages, which is what it is intended to do. This concept is known to be true around the board; contemporary marketing and advertisement affect behavior and can be advantageous in several ways. We should say that social media usage enables them to keep current on events globally, including Coron's virus outbreak. Using social media to extend our contact and involvement and reach our target demographic, we will include them in our campaign, help them to understand how to engage with us, and inspire them to get involved in how to follow up to the delivery and culmination of our goal with Coronavirus.

REVIEW OF LITERATURE

Immersive visualization combines automated data processing, and fresh and innovative technologies emerge. The application of this approach to massive, complicated data, such as that provided by social networking, will support several realms. Simultaneously, researchers must conquer several obstacles. Visual analytics framework designers must strive for a perfect balance between automated processing and manual immersive discovery. Today's programs often place an excessive amount of emphasis on one of these factors. However, in many situations, this is not the optimal division of labor between the robot, which excels at automated interpretation, and human observers, who excel at the imagination and visual recognition (El-Awaisi, et al., 2020).

The software and hardware workflows used to overcome real-world problems can be used to maximize the relative computational capacities of the two. The code can, for example, choose the best analysis measures to investigate and the resulting set of promising data views. Additionally, a refined taxonomy that includes graphic designers will better comprehend functional relationships across different dimensions. It is essential to approach data holistically to provide a full understanding (Venigalla et al., 2020) .

Diverse panels of researchers have started to explore the multiple data analysis applications of visual analytics, which can be seen in the "Diverse Panel of Experts" subhead of "Visual Analytics" (Hackley, 2014). The media concentrated on different forms of social communications and connections, including face-to-to-face, correspondence, and conference calls, as well as social media, such as audio and video, emphasizing teeming. If work is to be completed, social networking must be a vital component (Hawn, 2009).

When technology adapts to be more human-friendly, it incorporates different dimensions, such as operating systems focusing on social aspects, digital applications mostly centered on networking, and media of contact across social networks, which are becoming increasingly important. To date, social networking outlets have been critical for disseminating information during the coronavirus outbreak of 2019. (COVID- 19). It has published several statements and works, as well as numerous other healthcare schemes, on guidance regarding the square measure over the years. Many people have been aware of coronaviruses being discovered and spoken about because of the rise in popularity of the internet, and so, as a result, have others who use search through the internet; it's common to see their activity in turn influence and dwarf discussions about it (Radwan and Radwan, 2020).

COVID has led to more users using social media to talk to others they know, to connect with friends and family, and to connect with public leaders. This latest analysis from observations and resolve was recently made available. So simply put, certain programs have a certain degree of freedom. According to a recent survey of over 25,000 people conducted from March 14-24, the app-based messaging service WhatsApp, which aims to be a social networking tool, saw a statistically significant increase in the number of users. Because Facebook is in control, we have increased from the twenty-seventh day up to the forty-first. As suggested by Kantar's research, usage has risen by 51% in countries where the pandemic is present (Khalifa, et al., 2020).

WhatsApp has seen a growth in Europe of 76%. The one-influential study discovered that the most rapid rise in electronic communications occurred among the 18- to 34-year-old demographic. Facebook and Instagram had a 40% rise in use, and WhatsApp usage went up by that much. Twitter has done well through the recent Chinese influenza outbreak, of course, but so has WeChat and Weibo, as we have seen in the past. In total, Facebook is being used 37% more times, where social apps have been designed and produced in China, which is an improvement over the earlier reported figure of 26%. According to Kantar, social media shows growth in a social irruption; individuals are more focused on social media than disseminated content and hence seem to stay away from other citizens (Sutton et al., 2020).

The various forms of media found themselves obsessing about various social topics, focusing on information that had an expanded meaning of social interaction, such as communication across both traditional and new channels, interactive voice and video while reporting about how different people were showing their involvement in new forms of media such as text and speech, blogs, instant messaging, and also making posts over the conference, as well as it, and illustrating various positions with photos (Lee et al., 2018).

In each organization, people are vital to productivity. In other words, a social network is necessary for the members to accomplish their tasks and projects. That would be possible if different technologies were used in combination. These may include systems centered on OS that adjusts to people's interests as well as social applications which focus on communication on social networks or OS whose functions are aimed at using social software but are especially targeted at communication as well as an interface that includes media methods via a social media networks. The diverse content supplied by general attention companies, including Twitter and other media (which currently covers many platforms), is how fast to act and react to changes in conditions are vital for dealing with uncertainty (Brindha, Jayaseelan, and Kadeswaran, 2020).

Let's use the word "expand" as an example. In this context, the government has pointed out or designated several expansion alternatives to a better comprehension of the province, as well as encouraging greater social dispersal; to date, social networking sites have been critical in allowing the return of case data in response to the coronavirus re-spreading (COVID- 19). World Health Organization (WHO) is a hub for alternative health services across many channels. The realization that Facebook and Twitter as search engines were taking a huge place in the conversations around disaster-related data provided a possible expansion for groups which expanded the group's networking capabilities, causing organizations to wonder whether other major media platforms could serve the same functions. During this economic recession, COVID finds an opportunity; greater social media usage has gained popularity (Habes et al., 2020).

Therefore, families, acquaintances, and relatives turn to social media to find information. In contrast, government accounts find them must-have information, and search engines that provide it are not as reliable. This latest in-Insights and data from Kantar now show the % of application owners and the number of higher echelons [i.e., Exclusive, valuable] customers their apps have. According to a survey of over 25,000 consumers in thirty markets conducted from March 14 to 24, the mobile service WhatsApp, which functions as a social networking app, has seen the greatest boost due to COVID-19. For Facebook consumption to rise, the product must be ranked high in the "WhatsApp" menu, so today, it gained user's attention in the WhaApps' Growth era' and also accounts for a high rank on the "App Store" list in less than two weeks under the influenza pandemic. As the use of WhatsApp has increased across the nation and district, it's speculated that use is about to be more prevalent among nations in the latter phase of the latest pandemic outbreak, according to Kantar figures (Bal, 2008).

The number of WhatsApp users in Europe rose by 76 percent, for instance, in the countries that had previously seen SMS banking. Moreover, it was observed that use grows the most within the 18- to 34-year-old demographics in all of the electronic messaging channels, as opposed to the traditional demographics of those 35 to which the user growth is reported. Not only has the use of the three famous messaging apps—WhatsApp, Facebook, Instagram, and Viber—gone up, but the number of people using such services has increased by 40 percent. A notable number of social networking platforms saw success after the global pandemic with Weibo (Weibo saw a notable share price increase in social media users), and Twitter was one of the winners of the development of Weibo. As reported by Kantar, social networking use has expanded by thirty percent, while social media for Chinese expansion has increased by 58% (Olum & Bongomin, 2020).

A downside to social networking is that there is a lot of useless knowledge on social media as well as there is misleading, fake, and biassed facts and incorrect information that get posted by individuals but still cannot be addressed by a consumer base on-the-the-the-the-ground reporting of important events, allowing everybody to let their thoughts and ideas out. Covid-19 (Cochliobravia fever) was discovered in India in 2012 and has been controlled since then by the government. The Indian government already has an ongoing plan that seeks to link citizens through social networking. It started new initiatives in March 2020 to keep citizens updated on their government's pandemic actions. Many U.S. government organizations use Twitter accounts to convey knowledge about various topics. Fake content is dangerous on social networking platforms such as Facebook, Twitter, and Pinterest. Fake news, conspiracy theories, and propaganda, as well as bias, have the potential to be distributed via social media across different vectors, such as racism, bigotry, resentment, and so on (Sathish et al., 2020).

Later in China, there was talk that bio-weapons research at the Wuhan Center for Biologic and Bacteriological Engineering was used in genetic engineering released later on the internet. Basing their ideas on these speculations, these Western scientists deal with the possibility of aning vaccine for CO-19 in collaboration with Chinese scientists. Clinical studies showed that misinformation, fabricated evidence, and unsubstantiated medical claims were widespread in the observed information. Several natural and humanistic cures have been proposed for CO19, such as traditional turmeric tea and drinks. On the other hand, virtual turd cures and advertising efforts for alternative antibiotics, such as tweets and photos, are concentrated in countries like Iran. Facebook and WhatsApp took down this data from the World Health Organization within a few hours of it going viral, but it was later found false. However, in contrast, Facebook, Instagram, and Twitter blocked an uploaded video, although YouTube left it accessible (Waheed et al., 2020).

Personal well-being issues are discussed, and personal health-related material is disseminated as widely as ever. There is a general push to use innovative tactics to inform the public regarding current health problems and their continuing resolution, which leads to the conclusion that governments and healthcare workers are both focused on the same A more appropriate way to illustrate this argument is to state that the emergence of social media was a central component in the overall growth of the world's knowledge network. Today's social media strategies use better approaches to getting patients and clients informed about healthcare issues, goods and services, and campaigns all around the globe. As soon as new media came around, they took on the conventional promotional practices, which were historically costly and limited. According to the researcher, the relevance, influence, and audience reaction to on-line ads proved much stronger. Data derived from in- in-depth interviews and content review on Social Networking sites, as well as field research, found that people clearly understand how important information on social media is to healthcare. Most of the respondents frequently choose multimedia media when they want to learn about the latest health news and wellness tips, and they are doing even better because they have more tools available. Thus, several academic studies focused on examining the effect of disease awareness programs, and pharmaceutical firms began to study the impact of these factors. Often, expanding the network to include health providers is another great way to meet the healthcare demands with your product's demands is to prove the effectiveness of these ads. To investigate the levels of disease knowledge that various healthcare workers have as part of the wellness programs they believe necessary to get an idea of doctors' views about the quality of online contact. Even though the overall growth in the number of these online healthcare awareness campaigns, the plurality of healthcare providers felt they were good because they reinforce healthier habits. It was recommended that these marketing programs be backed by non-profit groups rather than aimed solely at a financial profit, but this did not have the desired impact. Commercial organizations also began participating as partners. It would lead to more results if famous people supported the awareness drives and lent their weight to them, too (Fan and Gordon, 2014).

This is due to the current medical advancement and people's worries regarding their longevity because more people are worried about the long-term effects. Many have medical problems that are still growing, making it imperative that they keep up with healthcare provider news to remain abreast or so as such patterns develop. Social Networking is used in all mass media, such as newspaper and billboard ads, as well as programs and advertisements encouraging people to take up a healthier lifestyle. Many brands concentrate on expanding their presence on social media sites, providing the greatest benefit for their customers, and customers are still getting the most value out of these investments. One of the primary reasons for this is because of this and we believe that healthcare advertisement is essential. Because of modern technological advances, such as the internet and social networking, it is now possible to connect with the world in a way we never could before. Often healthcare companies employ digital networking features to distribute healthcare information across different avenues to increase the visibility of their services. So as a second phase, we wanted to look at the advertisements from the University of Missouri Health and Medical Sciences (UHS) and MU HealthCare and banner, respectively, and see how far they will go. The research found that advertisements about the flu's possible effect on public behavior are favorable in most cases. When they saw the letter, they spoke of how it was ingrained in their lives and only agreed to obey the recommendations. An additional randomized-controlled trial (RCT) was conducted to see if following a healthier lifestyle with the appropriate diet and exercise measures affects healthy aging. Additionally, they mentioned adopting a healthier lifestyle and working out to enhance their fitness as a strong benefit for people to seek (Mejova and Kalimeri, 2020).

OBJECTIVES

The study's objective was to identify whether Social Media Visual Advertisements can engage and influence individuals during the pandemic. Further, to identify the important factor influencing an individual in Social Media Visual Advertisements.

METHODOLOGY

The study adopted a Descriptive research design, for which data was collected from 456 samples and scrutinized by 408. The data was collected through an online questionnaire using a simple random sampling technique. The data were collected between May 2019 to January 2020. Table 1 shows the outcomes of the assessment Univariate analysis (Visual Advertisements in Social Media influence you to engage Some of Your time to perceive the content) of Type III Sum of Squares data. The results revealed that there were 0.21 gender, 7.199 age, and 0.024 marital. Table 2 shows the outcomes of the assessment Univariate analysis (Visual Advertisements in Social Media influence decision) of Type III Sum of Squares data. The results revealed that there were 1.087 genders, 1.416 ages, and 0.024 marital. Table 3 shows the outcomes of the assessment Multivariate Analysis (Factors in visual advertisements influencing the most in Awareness Campaign) of Type III Sum of Squares data. The results revealed that there were 0.031 genders, 0.158 ages, and 0.021 marital. The researcher used a purposive sampling approach because the respondents offered significant differences in participating in the research. The students of various ages and colleges studying at different levels of various Advertisements in Social Media samples. The respondents' significant difference data was measured through IBM SPSS Statistics ver. 23 and documented.

ANALYSIS AND INTERPRETATION

Herein Univariate analysis was carried out to identify whether there is a significant difference in opinion among the respondents belonging to different demographic profiles for the Question, "Do Visual Advertisements in Social Media influence you to engage Some of Your time to perceive the content."

The estimated significance value is greater than 0.05. This indicates the null hypothesis is accepted, meaning there is no significant opinion among the respondents despite their gender, age category, and marital status. Further from the mean score, it can be well interpreted that most of them Agree and Strongly agree that Visual Advertisements in Social Media influence them to engage Some of their time perceiving the content.

Herein Univariate analysis was carried out to identify whether there is a significant difference in opinion among the respondents belonging to different demographic profiles for the Question, "Do Visual Advertisements in Social Media influence your decision."

The estimated significance value is greater than 0.05. This indicates the null hypothesis is accepted, meaning there is no significant opinion among the respondents despite their gender, age category, and marital status. Further from the mean score, it can be well interpreted that most agree and Strongly agree that Visual Advertisements in Social Media influence their decision.

Herein Multivariate analysis was carried out to identify whether there is a significant difference in opinion among the respondents belonging to different demographic profiles to identify which among the following factors in visual advertisements influence the most in Awareness Campaign.

The estimated significance value is greater than 0.05. This indicates the null hypothesis is accepted, meaning there is no significant opinion among the respondents despite their gender, age category, and marital status. From the rank analysis performed using the mean score, it can be interpreted that Quotes, Timing of advertisements, Picture presentations, and celebrities are the most influencing factor in visual advertisements.

Table 1. Univariate analysis - visual advertisements in social media influence you to engage some of your time to perceive the content

Tests of Between-Subjects Effects					
Dependent Variable: Do Visual Advertisements in Social Media influence you to engage Some of Your time to perceive the content.					
Source	**Type III Sum of Squares**	**df**	**Mean Square**	**F**	**Sig.**
Gender	.021	1	.021	.063	.802
Age	7.199	3	2.400	7.110	.110
Marital	.024	1	.024	.072	.789

Do Visual Advertisements in Social Media influence you to engage Some of Your time to perceive the content.		
Gender	**Mean**	**Std. Deviation**
Male	4.4384	.52643
Female	4.4293	.66504
Total	4.4338	.59937
Age	**Mean**	**Std. Deviation**
Below 25	4.5366	.50019
26 - 35	4.4595	.50005
36 - 45	4.1167	.94046
Above 45	4.3889	.49441
Total	4.4338	.59937
Marital Status	**Mean**	**Std. Deviation**
Unmarried	4.4366	.60810
Married	4.4308	.59124
Total	4.4338	.59937

Source: (Primary data)

FINDINGS

From the result obtained through analysis, it can be interpreted that most of them Agree and Strongly agree that Visual Advertisements in Social Media influence them to engage some of their time perceiving the content. Further from the mean score, it can be well interpreted that most agree and Strongly agree that Visual Advertisements in Social Media influence their decision. Also, it was found that Quotes, Timing of advertisements, Picture presentations, and celebrities are the most influencing factor in visual advertisements in the awareness Campaign.

CONCLUSION

The whole planet is waiting breathlessly for COVID-19 to depart. Every nation is anxiously waiting for their researchers to develop a treatment for COVID - nobody to date. Medical and paramedical personnel must maintain their honorable, committed, and selfless duty in order to save lives. The custodial workers must keep the sanitation up and the disease at bay with their effortless and unselfish effort. It is

Table 2. Univariate analysis - visual advertisements in social media influence decision

Tests of Between-Subjects Effects					
Dependent Variable: Do Visual Advertisements in Social Media influence your decision?					
Source	Type III Sum of Squares	df	Mean Square	F	Sig.
Gender	1.087	1	1.087	3.242	.073
Age	1.416	3	.472	1.408	.240
Marital	.024	1	.024	.072	.789

Do Visual Advertisements in Social Media influence your decision

Gender	Mean	Std. Deviation
Male	4.4384	.55393
Female	4.5415	.60592
Total	4.4902	.58221
Age	**Mean**	**Std. Deviation**
Below 25	4.5000	.50153
26 - 35	4.5068	.50165
36 - 45	4.3667	.91996
Above 45	4.5833	.50000
Total	4.4902	.58221
Marital Status	**Mean**	**Std. Deviation**
Unmarried	4.4883	.62654
Married	4.4923	.53118
Total	4.4902	.58221

Source: (Primary data)

incumbent on all public organizations to meet the government's demands. These charities and non-profit organizations would strive to assist those in need. The country's law enforcement is within the jurisdiction of the local police department. Everyone has a moral responsibility to provide the information given to the public, whether or not the information given to them by the media agrees with them. We must make others conscious and help them cooperate to prevent fear. The agents tell us what we should and shouldn't do. Better safe than sorry. Don't leave home without permission. That's the best way to slow the progression of COVID - this is the only method to combat it.

Table 3. Multivariate analysis – factors in visual advertisements influencing the most in awareness campaign

Multivariate Tests						
Effect		Value	F	Hypothesis df	Error df	Sig.
Gender	Pillai's Trace	.031	1.526[b]	8.000	385.000	.146
Age	Pillai's Trace	.158	2.683	24.000	1161.000	.070
Marital	Pillai's Trace	.021	1.035[b]	8.000	385.000	.409

Tests of Between-Subjects Effects

Source		Type III Sum of Squares	df	Mean Square	F	Sig.
Gender	Concept	.622	1	.622	.867	.352
	Emotions	.113	1	.113	.348	.556
	Celebrity	1.899	1	1.899	5.088	.025
	Quotes	.244	1	.244	.819	.366
	Timing	7.410E-05	1	7.410E-05	.000	.989
	No. Viewers	1.509	1	1.509	2.225	.137
	No. Followers	.170	1	.170	.222	.638
	Picture Presentation	1.486	1	1.486	4.032	.045
Age	Concept	5.651	3	1.884	2.623	.050
	Emotions	.835	3	.278	.856	.464
	Celebrity	5.873	3	1.958	5.245	.001
	Quotes	2.499	3	.833	2.797	.040
	Timing	8.868	3	2.956	7.103	.000
	No. Viewers	7.176	3	2.392	3.528	.015
	No. Followers	3.192	3	1.064	1.388	.246
	Picture Presentation	11.976	3	3.992	10.833	.000
Marital	Concept	1.220	1	1.220	1.699	.193
	Emotions	.283	1	.283	.870	.352
	Celebrity	.411	1	.411	1.102	.294
	Quotes	.148	1	.148	.497	.481
	Timing	.078	1	.078	.187	.666
	No. Viewers	1.207	1	1.207	1.781	.183
	No. Followers	1.290	1	1.290	1.683	.195
	Picture Presentation	.388	1	.388	1.054	.305

Which Among the Following in visual advertisements influence you the most	Mean	Rank
Concept	3.985294	6
Emotions	3.519608	8
Celebrity	4.404412	4
Quotes	4.504902	1
Timing	4.446078	2
No. Viewers	3.965686	7
No. Followers	4.007353	5
Picture Presentation	4.426471	3

Source: (Primary data)

REFERENCES

Bal, M. (2008). Visual analysis. *SAGE Handb. Cult. Anal.*, *46*, 163–184. doi:10.4135/9781848608443.n9

Brindha, D., Jayaseelan, R., & Kadeswaran, S. (2020). *Social media reigned by information or misinformation about COVID-19: a phenomenological study.* Research Gate.

El-Awaisi, A., O'Carroll, V., Koraysh, S., Koummich, S., & Huber, M. (2020). Perceptions of who is in the healthcare team? A content analysis of social media posts during COVID-19 pandemic. *Journal of Interprofessional Care*, *34*(5), 622–632. doi:10.1080/13561820.2020.1819779 PMID:32962452

Fan, W., & Gordon, M. D. (2014). The power of social media analytics. *Communications of the ACM*, *57*(6), 74–81. doi:10.1145/2602574

Habes, M., Alghizzawi, M., Ali, A., Salihalnaser, A., & Salloum, S. A. (2020). The Relation among Marketing ads, via Digital Media and mitigate (COVID-19) pandemic in Jordan. *Int. J. Adv. Sci. Technol.*, *29*(7), 12326–12348.

Hackley, C., (2014). Introducing Advertising and Promotion. *Advert. Promot. Commun. Brand.*, pp. 1–24, . doi:10.4135/9781446278789.n1

Hawn, C. (2009). Report from the field: Take two aspirin and tweet me in the morning: How twitter, Facebook and other social media are reshaping health care. *Health Affairs (Project Hope)*, *28*(2), 361–368. doi:10.1377/hlthaff.28.2.361 PMID:19275991

Khalifa, H., Khalifa, H., Badran, S.A., Al-absy, M. S. M., & Ahmed, Q. (2020). Social Media and Spreading the News of Covid-19 Pandemic. In the *Arab World*, *11*(5), 680–685.

Lee, J. E., Hur, S., & Watkins, B. (2018). Visual communication of luxury fashion brands on social media: Effects of visual complexity and brand familiarity. *Journal of Brand Management*, *25*(5), 449–462. doi:10.105741262-018-0092-6

Mejova, Y. & Kalimeri, K. (2020). Advertisers Jump on Coronavirus Bandwagon: Politics, News, and Business. *arXiv*.

Olum, R., & Bongomin, F. (2020). Social media platforms for health communication and research in the face of COVID-19 pandemic: A cross sectional survey in Uganda. medRxiv. doi:10.1101/2020.04.30.20086553

Radwan, E., & Radwan, A. (2020). The Spread of the Pandemic of Social Media Panic during the COVID-19 Outbreak. *European Journal of Environment and Public Health*, *4*(2), em0044. doi:10.29333/ejeph/8277

Sathish, R., Manikandan, R., Silvia Priscila, S., Sara, B. V. J., & Mahaveerakannan, R. (2020), A report on the impact of information technology and social media on covid-19. *Proc. 3rd Int. Conf. Intell. Sustain. Syst. ICISS 2020*, (pp. 224–230). IEEE. 10.1109/ICISS49785.2020.9316046

Sutton, J., Renshaw, S. L., & Butts, C. T. (2020). The First 60 Days: American Public Health Agencies' Social Media Strategies in the Emerging COVID-19 Pandemic. *Health Security*, *18*(6), 454–460. doi:10.1089/hs.2020.0105 PMID:33047982

Venigalla, A.S.M., Vagavolu, D., and Chimalakonda, S., (2020). SurviveCovid-19 - A game for improving awareness of social distancing and health measures for Covid-19 pandemic. *arXiv*.

Waheed, U., Wazeer, A., Saba, N., & Qasim, Z. (2020). Effectiveness of WhatsApp for blood donor mobilization campaigns during COVID-19 pandemic. *ISBT Science Series*, *15*(4), 378–380. doi:10.1111/voxs.12572

Chapter 17

Romanian Preschool Teachers' Perceptions About Early Childhood Online Education:
A Qualitative Study on the Inclusiveness of Zoom Kindergartens

Dana Rad
https://orcid.org/0000-0001-6754-3585
Aurel Vlaicu University of Arad, Romania

Raul Lile
Academy of Romanian Scientists, Romania

Alina Costin
Aurel Vlaicu University of Arad, Romania

Gabriela Vancu
Aurel Vlaicu University of Arad, Romania

Henriette Torkos
Aurel Vlaicu University of Arad, Romania

Edgar Demeter
Aurel Vlaicu University of Arad, Romania

Gavril Rad
Aurel Vlaicu University of Arad, Romania

ABSTRACT

COVID-19 replaced face-to-face instruction with online learning. This study examines preschool teachers' online ECE attitudes. 375 preschool teachers took an online course on quality and inclusive early childhood education. 195 out of 375 preschoolers completed this study's online questionnaire about internet learning. The authors coded responses to find pros, cons, and mixed viewpoints. Romanian preschool instructors see the challenge of online learning in Zoom kindergarten, the requirement of online teaching instead of not retaining contact with kids and families, and tightening the connection with parents as advantages of early childhood online education. Romanian preschool teachers have mixed opinions about Zoom kindergarten's pros and cons, including that online classes can be used as integrated online educational sequences but never replace traditional kindergarten.

DOI: 10.4018/978-1-6684-6682-7.ch017

INTRODUCTION

Children nowadays are being born into the digital age. According to Neumann (2015), children aged 2-4 spend roughly 80 minutes each day at home using cell phones and tablets. This is undoubtedly the major reason for instructors in early childhood education to have a greater knowledge and understanding of the use of Information and Communication Technology (ICT) in the classroom (Güneş & Bahçivan, 2018). The findings of the research (Nuri, & Cagiltay, 2017; Blackwell, Lauricella, & Wartella, 2014) also revealed that early childhood teachers' views and attitudes had a favourable influence on ICT use. However, using ICT in early childhood education has become a necessity in order to improve children's learning experiences (Masoumi, 2015; Jalongo, 2021; Chen et al., 2018). The necessity for research on early childhood teachers' perspectives of ICT appears to have piqued the interest of multiple academics, leading to a study by Dong (2018) suggesting that instructors have acknowledged the value of incorporating ICT into their teaching process. A similar study (Nikolopoulou & Gialamas, 2015) found that many early childhood instructors are comfortable incorporating ICT into the educational process. Furthermore (Yurt & Cevher-Kalburan, 2011; Fotakopoulou et al., 2020), early childhood educators believe that the use of ICT is appropriate in early childhood education, particularly in the creation of varied activities to enhance children's cognitive development.

Digital learning for young children has also been contested and condemned. Some researchers (Jiang & Monk, 2015; Radesky et al., 2016) expressed worry about online hazards and dangers, video addiction, social isolation, and physical health problems. Others stated that parents have a mediating role in preventing damage and regulating children's internet activity by establishing and monitoring technology use regulations for their children (Nouwen & Zaman, 2018). These issues, however, have had little effect on online learning's fast expansion over the last decade, which has reached millions of young learners at an unprecedented rate (Silverman, 2020, Zalaznick, 2019). An increasing number of online programs have been developed and offered to help young children with impairments and/or living in distant or impoverished environments (Smith et al., 2016, Zalaznick, 2019).

Furthermore, internet technologies have evolved into social, cultural, and personal artifacts in the multimodal lifeworld' of today's children (Arnott & Yelland, 2020). It should thus be supported to create a multimodal learning ecosystem for today's children, parents, and teachers. While online learning looks to be becoming increasingly common in the future (Franklin et al., 2015; Hansen & Hansen, 2017), there is a lack of research on online learning in the early years. This study will address this gap by polling Romanian preschool instructors who were involved in online instruction during the COVID-19 outbreak.

Because of the Covid-19 epidemic, ICT is now mandatory at all school levels, including early childhood education. Even while the use of ICT has many benefits for supporting the learning process, it will undoubtedly be a problem for levels of education where the majority of the learning process has not utilised ICT substantially, such as in early childhood education in Romania (Anghel, 2020). Before the Covid-19 epidemic, all early childhood education institutes in Romania used a face-to-face learning style. The Covid-19 pandemic, on the other hand, mandates that all early childhood schools integrate online learning. This is undoubtedly concerning for Romanian early childhood educators who are unfamiliar with the usage of ICT in the classroom (Hasbi & Hasanah, 2020).

Numerous research from all across the world has looked at the new educational issues brought on by the COVID-19 epidemic (Pacheco, 2021; Morgado et al., 2020; Pacheco et al., 2021, Flores et al., 2021; Rad et al., 2022; Rad et al., 2022). Given that the pandemic affected different regions of the world at different times and intensities, as well as the fact that local and national educational responses

214

to school closures were not uniform, the novelty of this research lies in the fact that we have thought a contextualised analysis to be valuable.

As a result, the goal of this study was to find out how early childhood instructors in Romania felt about using ICT in the classroom. The findings of this study give an overview of how ICT is used to enhance the teaching and learning process in early childhood education, as well as how online learning is used in early childhood education during the Covid-19 epidemic.

METHODS

Research Design

This study took a qualitative approach, with theme coding utilized to examine the qualitative data received from one open-ended question and statistical summaries of the 195 respondents' basic demographic data. Thematic coding, also known as thematic analysis, is a qualitative data analysis that identifies themes in the text by examining word meanings and sentence structure. It focuses on detecting, evaluating, and interpreting meaning patterns in qualitative data. This method is thought to aid researchers in obtaining in-depth and complete information regarding perspective (Buetow, 2010). The online investigation form was divided into two parts, with the first part focusing on demographic information from respondents and the second part using an open-ended response scale to answer the following research question: "*Please describe in one paragraph what impression the online preschool teaching left on you.*"

Individual online responses, in our opinion, bring more personalization when argumenting personal opinions in preschool teachers, that otherwise, in a focus group or an interview, tend to conform to the majoritarian opinion or give a highly socially desirable response out of the fear of not being judged when presenting a piece of sensitive information, like the impact of early childhood online education on their professional life.

Data Collection and Analysis

Our team has invited 375 early childhood instructors who were enrolled in a nationwide online training program financed by the Romanian Ministry of Education to participate in the current study by filling out an online questionnaire on the program's website https://etic.cf/, from November 2021 to December 2021 (Rad, et., al., 2022). A total of 195 Romanian early childhood instructors agreed to participate in this qualitative study and offered further consent to answer the questions. The online response procedure took approximately 5 minutes, with Google Forms recording the responses. Table 1 shows the description of our respondents regarding their age (a mean of 42 years) and professional experience in years (an average of 20 years of experience).

Data coding and analysis were done cooperatively by the study team. The coding procedure was circular and iterative, including multiple interactions between the two coders to remove inaccurate data interpretation caused by subjective coding. Coders used the same coding instructions throughout the coding procedure, allowing each study team member to examine the data consistently and reliably. The qualitative data consisted primarily of 1–2 short lines from preschool instructors responding to the open-ended inquiry. In most cases, establishing categories from qualitative data was clear. The two coders also met to address any coding issues and established techniques for reaching a coding consensus.

Table 1. Descriptive statistics for preschool teacher participants

	N	Minimum	Maximum	Mean	Std. Deviation
1. Age	195	23	62	42.08	7.634
3. Professional experience (years)	195	2	43	19.57	8.748
Valid N (listwise)	195				

To detect, evaluate, and summarize patterns created from the data, thematic analysis (Terry et al., 2017) was used. In six steps, the qualitative data analysis followed their step-by-step method. (1) Getting to know the data; (2) making primary codes, such as pros, cons and mixed opinions; (3) searching for themes; (4) refining and reviewing themes; (5) defining and labelling themes; and (6) writing qualitative results (Braun, & Clarke, 2021). Preschool instructors' answers were originally categorised into three main categories: supporting online learning, opposing online learning, and having mixed opinions. The original categories were then rearranged and divided into themes based on several categories' justifications, which will be further discussed.

FINDINGS

Preschool Teachers' Beliefs and Attitudes Regarding the Advantages of Zoom Kindergarten

Among the advantages listed by preschool teachers, the most frequent thematic appeared to be the challenge of online learning: *"Teaching online has been a challenge, something new."* and *"It was a challenge and a privilege to learn web tools and digital stories"*. The challenging aspect of learning new strategies to improve the early educational activities proposed by preschool teachers due to Zoom kindergarten is consistent with other qualitative research results (Sanchez-Vera, Solano-Fernandez, & Recio-Caride, 2019). Other preschool teachers stated that: *"It was a unique experience, with many challenges, which took us out of our comfort zone"*, while others viewed early education online teaching as: *"An interesting and challenging way."* and also *"Teaching online has been a challenge for both me and my parents and children."* In the same coding criterion, we have included the creativity aspect of the teaching that was empowered: *"Teaching online to the group of preschoolers seemed to me a new and interesting experience."* and *"Challenging and full of creativity!"*, results consisted with other qualitative studies (Gomes, Almeida, Kaveri, Mannan, Gupta, & Sarkar, 2021).

The second most important advantage of Zoom kindergarten was the necessity of online teaching instead of not keeping contact with kids and families at all: *"Teaching online has helped me keep in touch with the little ones, see them progress, do the activities I propose."*, *"An alternative in case of closing schools"*, *"Far away, but still close!"*, *"The online teaching helped us to adapt to the current conditions to be able to continue the didactic act."*, *"Necessary for the current context"* and *"It seems to me an interesting and beneficial thing in these times."* results were also identified by Forne (2021). In the same category, we have also included the beneficial aspect of online learning in the context of social restrictions and kindergartens temporarily closing: *"It was a more difficult period, but in which I learned and developed my skills and competencies, I worked on the platform, I created materials, and I used various applications. I say it was beneficial."* results supported by another recent qualitative research (Hong, Zhang, & Liu, 2021) and: *"Online teaching is effective for missing children when they are sick."*

The third most important advantage of Zoom kindergarten identified by Romanian preschool teachers was tightening the connection with parents, who have been largely involved with helping their children connect and participate in online activities: *"Parents very involved with their little ones." "I found parents eager to get involved, who had never been involved before.", "Pleasant, effective communication with parents", "Teaching online can work very well if both educators and parents and preschoolers are involved.", "Parents were actively involved in their children's education.", "Because the parents also participated in the activities, everything went well, and the relationship between kindergarten and family developed"*. These results are consistent with another recent qualitative research (Oke, Butler, & O'Neill, 2021). Furthermore, this aspect appears to be controversial in the current research because this involvement of patents was also considered one of the main disadvantages of Zoom kindergarten; the result is also supported by the research literature that will be analyzed in the disadvantages section of the present paper.

The fourth most mentioned advantage was the novelty of this teaching method to children drawn towards interacting with mobile devices and immersed in some of the proposed activities. This emersion in activity aspect also represents a controversial finding because the lack of children's focus on activity was considered one of the main disadvantages. Further, we can conclude that if the online activity is properly designed and approached with interest by preschool teachers and parents, Zoom kindergarten might represent a powerful learning tool even for the youngest participants: *"Online teaching comes with challenges, but I have discovered ways to integrate children and motivate them to participate actively, even online."*, results consistent with other recent findings (Dayal, & Tiko, 2020). Some preschool teachers mentioned: *"The children were fascinated by the diversity of activities and", "The online activities are interactive, interesting, the children are curious and react positively to technology."*

The fifth category included the professional development opportunity offered by learning online educational strategies and tools for Zoom kindergarten: *"I liked it. It would be even easier if the children had the same devices. I have experienced online teaching in large and small groups; the children's interest is maximum in both situations, and the teaching was exciting and included many novelty elements. This makes me want to grow."*, consistent with other research findings (Negrette, Laixely, Cordoba, & Sanders-Smith, 2021) and *"An experience that marked my vision of teaching and professional development. Online teaching will be the new normal."* results were also published in another recent qualitative study (Hu, Chiu, Leung, & Yelland, 2021).

Preschool Teachers' Mixed Beliefs and Attitudes Regarding Zoom Kindergarten

Regarding the mixed perception about both advantages and advantages of Zoom kindergarten, the most important signalized aspect was that online classes could be used in addition to integrated online educational sequences but never to replace traditional kindergarten. Furthermore, the qualitative data revealed that preschool instructors thought traditional learning in educational settings was superior to online learning in terms of providing a learning environment that resulted in increased learning outcomes:" *Online group teaching is a compromise solution that has been used in a crisis. At this age, the efficient use of digital platforms and online applications, I think, would prove to be effective only when used as sequences of activities, given the fact that at this age, children are extremely attracted to whatever digital technology means."*. At the same time, other teachers stated then "The beginning of online group teaching was very difficult, with many problems, both technical and emotional, because it was a novelty for all of us. Still, *over time, I got used to it, gained confidence, and started to document myself, attend classes and do better. However, I believe that online activities are not suitable for preschoolers."* then other teachers responded, *"Develop skills in the use of technology and awareness of the functions that digital tools have. Still, they must be used in addition to physical teaching and not exclusively."* Other teachers considered that: *"Useful, it is not long-term, it cannot be an exclusive education for the little ones, exhausting for the teacher."* and *"Useful, it is not long-term, it cannot be an exclusive education for the little ones, exhausting for the teacher",* and also *"Online teaching was necessary and very important during the pandemic, but I consider that it cannot completely replace face-to-face teaching, socialising"* all of these reasons being depicted in the scientific literature (Dong, & Mertala, 2021). Some teachers also stated, *"Teaching online is a great way to educate parents to teach the content, which we cannot do directly, for kindergarten children is only beneficial for a short period. Digital platforms can be used successfully in the case of online teaching. I think they can be used sparingly in class as well."* and *"It is an activity that cannot replace face-to-face activity; at most sequences of learning activities can be done with the help of technology."*

The second most important aspect of mixed views about the opportunities of Zoom kindergarten was related to parents' dependence on organizing online educational activities: *"The effectiveness of the online activity with preschoolers depends largely on the involvement of parents."* and *"Novelty, but for preschoolers, you depend 100% on your parents to be able to carry out activities.",* then *"In the middle group it was difficult to keep the children's attention for more than 20 minutes for an activity, even if we used various applications, interactive digital games, often the children needed the help of the adult.",* then

Transferring activities online is a compromise solution, which has created a bridge of communication between educators-children-parents, facilitating children's access to education. But because the development of activities through technology means the involvement of parents, their lack of time or interest are factors that have determined a low impact among children.

Other teachers mentioned that:

Apart from the fact that they see each other, with the children from the small group, I haven't been able to carry out online activities for 3 years old kids, because they don't even sit in their parent's arms, they don't answer questions and they don't want to participate. Some parents do not know how to turn off the microphones, and they do not know how to correct their children. With the 5-6s, we managed to do online activities only twice a week and in the afternoon, from 5.30 pm, when the parents arrived home from work. It was a little easier with them, but they only connected 30%. When returning to classes with a physical presence, I did recovery activities with the others.

Other teachers mentioned another aspect of parental time: "After the time spent online, I fully realised that the parents *take kindergarten seriously. It helped us somehow to involve the parents in the life of the preschooler.",* and also *"Online teaching differs in the level of age peculiarities of preschoolers, but also in the willingness of parents to collaborate, to get involved in solving teaching tasks."* results depicted in the literature (Bigras et al., 2021). Some teachers also consider that in rural areas, it is almost impossible to constantly involve parents in Zoom kindergarten: *"In case of force majeure, it is useful to teach online asynchronously rather than synchronously, because automatically parents must be involved in this activity, and the effectiveness of the educational act depends on the availability of parents, which in the village is impossible."*

The third most important thematic in mixed views was the age appropriateness for Zoom kindergarten: "*At the age of 6-7, work on the platform is acceptable, but there should be no online education for younger children.*", then "*With the 6-7s the online teaching is satisfactory, and in the rest it is in vain, in my opinion!*", then "*The age peculiarities of the children as well as the specifics of the activities carried out in the kindergarten are incompatible with the online teaching.*", also "*Online teaching is not suitable for preschoolers. In my opinion, the use of digital platforms is effective only in the context of face-to-face teaching.*" and "*Teaching online seems to me to be effective for medium and last kindergarten class groups, not for the small group (my group this year).*", also "*You can work well with preschoolers in the last kindergarten class, but with those in the small group, it is very difficult to work.*" results consistent with recent research conclusions (Hurwitz, & Schmitt, 2020).

The forth aspect reflected in preschool teachers' responses was the impossibility of replicating an authentic socio-emotional connection: "*technology is important, but it cannot replace socio-emotional interaction, an essential condition in the evolution and development of the preschooler's personality.*", then "*It is challenging, but with low socio-educational efficiency.*", and also "*From my point of view, it is not beneficial to teach online in kindergarten because children need socialisation, interaction.*", while other teachers stated that "*Using digital platforms has allowed us to hone our digital skills, to discover applications that can help us create attractive and interactive teaching aids for preschoolers, but the preschooler is the child who needs socio-emotional interaction to it also develops to form skills and habits.*", results consistent with existing literature (Levine Brown et al., 2022)

The fifth aspect reflected in mixed preschool teachers' opinions about Zoom kindergarten was the less attention span for cognitively predominant oriented activities: "*In preschoolers, the attention span is weak in the online system. I can socialise, listen to stories, easy things, but acquisitions of new knowledge or training of skills and abilities cannot be made*" results consistent with the literature (McClelland el. al., 2013).

The sixth aspect was related to screen time in early childhood: "*If I connected once a week or several hours per day, it was much better than if I connected every day because both my parents and my children were eager to see each other and me. On the other days, I sent themes/activity suggestions to the WhatsApp group. Screen time is important in early ages.*" this is an important aspect depicted in the literature (Duch, Fisher, Ensari, & Harrington, 2013).

The seventh and last mixed aspect considered by Romanian preschool teachers was the appropriateness of existent family technology knowledge and devices. Online learning demands physical resources and professional knowledge from parents: "*Online teaching has both advantages and disadvantages depending on the internet access and the appropriate technological devices/means.*" also ", *It is difficult in the meeting not to be able to control the children's microphones, I liked the interaction, and I felt connected with the preschoolers using online teaching*", aspect creating inequalities between children's access to the Zoom kindergarten, also reflected in the scientific literature (Oliemat, Ihmeideh, & Alkhawaldeh, 2018).

Preschool Teachers' Beliefs and Attitudes Regarding the Disadvantages of Zoom Kindergarten

Regarding the disadvantages of Zoom kindergarten, qualitative descriptions were abundant and twice as many positive and mixed opinions.

Among Romanian preschool teachers, the most important signalized aspect was questioning the appropriateness of online learning and similarly stated, "*Online learning at this age is not appropriate. It is very difficult to master the kids."* and *"Online teaching does not work for preschool education. Children are not cognitively developed enough to assimilate online teaching.",* also *"It is a tiring teaching for both children and teachers.".* Some preschool teachers even stated, *"It is not possible to teach online to preschoolers. It is done online with parents, not with preschoolers".* With this aspect seen above as an advantage of early online education, some teachers stated that: *"Inefficient in the long run, especially due to age peculiarities, useful in the short run."* ambivalence described in the scientifical literature (Hatzigianni & Kalaitzidis, 2018). The lack of appropriateness was also approached: *"Teaching online to the group of preschoolers is ineffective because the parents do not give time for the activities proposed by the educators, by the children. Thus, the educators propose interesting activities using digital platforms and applications, but out of a group of children, an average of about 3 children participate, and the other children stay at home without doing anything useful in their educational journey. So online teaching could NEVER replace face-to-face teaching."* also, *"Teaching online is difficult, requires extra effort, and the lack of direct interaction with children decreases the quality of the educational activity, and diminishes their socio-emotional development."* Some teachers even stated that some parents were totally against Zoom kindergarten: *"We do it because we had to do it, it is not effective, the parents did not agree to the online activity."*

The second most important theme was the lack of physical interaction: *"This activity is not good for children. At their age, they need socialising."* and "Preschool education is based on the development of child-child and child-educator interactions". In a more detailed answer, one preschool teacher stated: *"It is almost impossible to teach online at the preschool level. The children depend on their parents' presence to sit in front of the computers, and they are busier and busier and less available (they only have a little time in the evening). It is efficient to use materials present on certain platforms, but the physical presence of children and educators in the group room is necessary. In a world where parents go to work in the morning to make a living for themselves and their children and recover their children in the afternoon at 16-17, how could online activities be carried out synchronously? No platform in the world replaces the physical presence, the direct interaction."* also, *"Preschoolers need socialisation and physical interactions through the games they initiate. Online learning deprives children of these actions, and they work at home individually, the only play and learning partners are only family members, and most children want to come to kindergarten.".* Also, preschool teachers stated that: *"Teaching online to the preschool group left me with a "bitter taste", the feeling of not fulfilling what I set out to do - or of fulfilling to a very small extent - due to the disturbing factors generated by the family environment and the lack of interaction. Between preschoolers and between preschoolers and the teacher, vital interactions for the development of children at this age." "Hard to manage without parents, lacking the human factor and thus physical contact, which is a price for preschoolers. Interpersonal connection is more difficult and short-lived in preschoolers through platforms."* Such finding is also supported by other qualitative research findings (Aliyyah et al., 2020; Bennette et al., 2021).

The third main disadvantage considered by the preschool teachers was the lack of socio-emotional support and the impersonation and emotionlessness of the Zoom kindergarten approach: *"Socio-emotional development and interaction between everybody suffer".* And *"Inefficient, impersonal, totally inadequate for interaction with preschoolers, during the period when the foundations of socio-emotional education are being laid!"* similar argumentation was also found in existing literature (Lang, Jeon, Sproat, Brothers, & Buettner, 2020). Preschool teachers also stated that: *"In the preschool group, online teaching is not considered effective because the preschooler learns through play and requires a lot of affection and socialisation."* and *"The children suffered socio-emotionally. strangely, you can only have contact with* children visually.", and also "*Emotion is missing*" and "*Online teaching is mechanical, without feelings.*" and "*Children need to socialise and interact physically with other children so that they do not become emotionally traumatised.*"

The forth considered disadvantage was total parental dependence: "*I depended on my parents, and it was more difficult to catch the attention of the little ones. We lacked the movement, the game, the interaction, the collaboration, the socialisation, and the embracing of what binds us humans. We missed meeting in kindergarten*", and even some encountered "*Disinterest on the part of the parents*". In general Romanian preschool teachers acknowledge that Zoom kindergarten was "*A real mess, disinterested parents, bored children*", results consistent with recent research (McFarland-Piazza, & Saunders, 2012; Burns, Jegatheeswaran, & Perlman, 2022). Also, teachers stated that: "*It depends on the involvement of the parents. If we are talking about preschoolers, they need to be present at all stages of the activity to help them.*" and "*Disinterested parents - online activity in vain*" also "*In the case of preschoolers, it is useless considering the most important factor on which the beginning of preschool is based: socialisation. It is impossible without the direct and complete involvement of the parents, from home, requiring continuous parental involvement.*". The parental dependence was also described as: "*It does not reflect the real knowledge of the children and requires maximum involvement from the parents, who, in most cases, are either absent or too involved, solving the work tasks of the little ones.*" Preschool teachers also stated some particular aspects: "*Online teaching is not relevant at the preschool level. At an early age, children need to socialise. Online activities in kindergartens are more carried out with parents and depend on the parents' schedule.*" "*Online teaching is unsuitable for preschool groups. To access the platform, preschoolers need the help of parents who are often very busy.*" results supported by the scientific literature (Lau, Li, & Lee, 2021)."

The fifth disagreement argument was the lack of feed-back in consolidating skills: "*Teaching online does not have the necessary feed-back, it is not possible to fix knowledge optimally, it is not possible to consolidate the necessary skills.*" and also "*I tried to convey the information through the most accessible games, but I did not have real or complete feed-back from all the children.*", argumentation described in the scientific literature (Djonko-Moore, 2022). One teacher stated: "*Missing face-to-face interaction, children's play, no matter how good and useful new web tools are, no matter how digital native children are, they are all missing the real kindergarten, missing ... many ... even if it's technology time, communication and feed-back is missing ...*" and also "*Without the support of parents, most online teaching activities are practically impossible. But even with their help, their efficiency is low.*" The lack of feed-back was also seen as: "*A challenge for both teachers and parents, but the results are not visible as the effort goes.*" and "*Online activity is a demanding job in which not all children are involved and the knowledge transmitted is difficult to assess.*"

The sixth most used argument against Zoom kindergarten was the lack of learning self-regulation skills of the preschoolers: "*After a while, they can't attract preschool children because they lose focus.*" And also: "*I was left with a bitter taste. Preschoolers without parents cannot log on to the platform and participate in activities, especially the small group; these skills should be formed in time; they were not ready for this.*" results consistent with the research (Montroy et al., 2016; McClelland et al., 2011; Williford et al., 2013)

The seventh important thematic referred to rural-urban parental technology knowledge and material resources disparities: "*In the rural area where I work, my online activities were unsatisfactory because the children did not enter due to the lack of gadgets, the helplessness and the ignorance of their parents.*" and also: "*A lot of training from the teacher, a little involvement of the parents from rural areas regard-*

ing the mediation of the online educational activities for the preschool child." Another detailed aspect was also considered: "*Unattractive for children, tiring for parents and teachers, impossible to use for some parents who do not know the technology.*" results consistent with the research (Liao et al., 2016; Whiteside-Mansell et al., 2019; Tieken, 2017)

The eighth thematic and the last one was not being able to reach preschoolers with special educational needs: "*Having a small group this school year, it was almost impossible for me to carry out my activity online, although the number of participating preschoolers was higher than I had hoped. Preschoolers lost their concentration, were distracted by other external things, and found it quite difficult to communicate because those who spoke in kindergarten, being next to one of the parents, often refused communication; other children do not speak at all, others have speech problems and it was quite difficult for me to get along with them,*" also results consistent with the scientific literature (Kuutti et al., 2021).

CONCLUSION

Because of its benefits, such as greater flexibility, wider access, and lower costs, digital and online learning is gaining popularity (Beatson et al., 2022; Luo et al., 2021; Kim, 2018; McKenna et al., 2021). However, the application of online learning during the COVID-19 epidemic was complex and demanding for Romanian preschool instructors, according to this study. In early childhood educational contexts, Romanian instructors held unfavorable opinions and attitudes regarding the values and benefits of online learning and favored conventional learning (Edelhauser & Lupu-Dima, 2021). They have suffered due to the COVID-19 epidemic, making them more resistant to online learning.

Romanian preschool teachers consider as advantages of early childhood online education the challenge of online learning in Zoom kindergarten, the necessity of online teaching instead of not keeping contact with kids and families at all, tightening the connection with parents, the immersive capacity of online digital tools for some highly interactive and vivid activities and none of the less, the professional development opportunity offered by learning online educational strategies and tools for Zoom kindergarten.

Romanian preschool teachers consider main mixed perceptions about both advantages and advantages of Zoom kindergarten, that online classes can be used in addition as integrated online educational sequences but never to replace traditional kindergarten, parents' dependence on organising online educational activities, the age appropriateness for Zoom kindergarten, the impossibility of replicating an authentic socio-emotional connection, the less attention span for cognitive predominant oriented activities, screen time in early childhood, and the appropriateness of existent family technology knowledge and devices.

On the other hand, Romanian preschool teachers considered disadvantages the questioning of the appropriateness of online learning, the lack of physical interaction, the lack of socio-emotional support and the impersonation and emotionlessness of the Zoom kindergarten approach, the total parental dependence, the lack of feed-back in consolidating skills, the lack of learning self-regulation skills of the preschoolers, rural-urban parental technology knowledge and material resources disparities and not being able to reach preschoolers with special educational needs.

Preschool instructors' perceptions about online educational settings in early and preschool educational Romanian institutions varied according to their years of experience according to certain sociodemographic variables. The more in-service experience participants have, the less they agree with Zoom kindergarten and its good impacts on the child's development. Preschool instructors with more in-service experience are more likely to require extra training in integrating online digital resources into daily instruction than those with less experience. Moreover, preschool instructors who completed extra education felt more competent in incorporating digital technologies into their normal instructional job. The findings point to the relevance of developing awareness about the importance of lifelong learning for a high-quality educational practice in which preschool instructors would be more prepared to respond to ever-changing modern-day educational challenges.

This research could represent a starting point for future research envisaging intentional qualitative and inclusive practices in online activities dedicated to preschool children.

Limitations

However, there are certain limitations to this research. To begin, a large-scale quantitative study can give representative and diverse evidence on the issue of interest. It cannot still obtain a comprehensive knowledge of unique scenarios and challenges. To fully understand Romanian preschool teachers' actual viewpoints, concerns, and challenges, interviews or mixed-methods research should be performed. Second, this online study relied solely on self-report data, which might be distorted in a socially acceptable way. More research is needed to double-check these findings.

Thus, the limitations of this current qualitative research reside in the fact that under this methodology, it is difficult to investigate causality unless an experimental design is applied and the fact that this research's results are not statistically representative of the general preschool teacher population. These results are limited to the Romanian preschool population from West Romania's 15 counties. The work can further be used for experimental verification under different cultural settings.

Implications

It may be stated that the requirement for integrating digital technologies into children's routine activities in kindergarten has become essential in current education. Given the lack of research on the effects of Zoom kindergarten on children's development with preschool teachers' online education competency, it would be beneficial to draw attention to this fact in future research that will significantly contribute to an improvement in the quality of Romanian early childhood educational practice. The findings of the study show that preschool teachers do not have many opportunities to attend meaningful pieces of training dedicated to the online designing of ECEC activities, leading to the conclusion that early and preschool educational institutions should focus professional development for preschool teachers on this critical area of effectively integrating technology and online activities into regular kindergarten activities.

Nonetheless, this study is the first to examine Romanian preschool teachers' views and ideas about digital and online learning during the COVID-19 pandemic. The national lockdown has impacted many children's physical attendance at educational venues, making online learning an emerging alternative to keep learning and playing at home (Silverman, 2020). Although online learning was heavily promoted in Romania to replace conventional schooling during the epidemic, the results of this study show that Romanian preschool instructors were neither equipped nor prepared to do so. This means that educational authorities must do more to prepare Romanian preschool instructors for online learning and consider young children's age and learning interests. The conclusions of this study have ramifications for governments and educators worldwide who are pushing online learning to young children and their families as a pandemic option. In emerging scenarios like COVID-19, the promotion and deployment of online learning to replace conventional early childhood education must be carefully examined and effectively organised to assist preschool instructors rather than introducing additional obligations and eventually burnout (Jeon et al., 2021; Višnjić Jevtić, A., & Halavuk, 2021).

REFERENCES

Aliyyah, R. R., Rachmadtullah, R., Samsudin, A., Syaodih, E., Nurtanto, M., & Tambunan, A. R. S. (2020). The perceptions of primary school teachers of online learning during the COVID-19 pandemic period: A case study in Indonesia. *Journal of Ethnic and Cultural Studies*, *7*(2), 90–109.

Anghel, D. (2020). Challenges of Homeschooling in Romania during Pandemic Times. *Revista Românească pentru Educaţie Multidimensională, 12*(2supl1), 1-11.

Arnott, L., & Yelland, N. J. (2020). Multimodal lifeworlds: Pedagogies for play inquiries and explorations. *Journal of Early Childhood Education Research*, *9*(1), 124–146.

Beatson, R., Molloy, C., Fehlberg, Z., Perini, N., Harrop, C., & Goldfeld, S. (2022). Early Childhood Education Participation: A Mixed-Methods Study of Parent and Provider Perceived Barriers and Facilitators. *Journal of Child and Family Studies*, *31*(11), 1–18. doi:10.100710826-022-02274-5 PMID:35282609

Bennette, E., Metzinger, A., Lee, M., Ni, J., Nishith, S., Kim, M., & Schachner, A. (2021). Do you see what I see? Children's understanding of perception and physical interaction over video chat. *Human Behavior and Emerging Technologies*, *3*(4), 484–494. doi:10.1002/hbe2.276

Bigras, N., Lemay, L., Lehrer, J., Charron, A., Duval, S., Robert-Mazaye, C., & Laurin, I. (2021). Early childhood educators' perceptions of their emotional state, relationships with parents, challenges, and opportunities during the early stage of the pandemic. *Early Childhood Education Journal*, *49*(5), 775–787. doi:10.100710643-021-01224-y PMID:34131378

Blackwell, C. K., Lauricella, A. R., & Wartella, E. (2014). Factors influencing digital technology use in early childhood education. *Computers & Education*, *77*, 82–90. doi:10.1016/j.compedu.2014.04.013

Braun, V., & Clarke, V. (2021). Can I use TA? Should I use TA? Should I not use TA? Comparing reflexive thematic analysis and other pattern-based qualitative analytic approaches. *Counselling & Psychotherapy Research*, *21*(1), 37–47. doi:10.1002/capr.12360

Buetow, S. (2010). Thematic analysis and its reconceptualisation as 'saliency analysis'. *Journal of Health Services Research & Policy*, *15*(2), 123–125. doi:10.1258/jhsrp.2009.009081 PMID:19762883

Burns, S., Jegatheeswaran, C., & Perlman, M. (2022). I Felt Like I was Going Crazy: Understanding Mother's and Young Children's Educational Experiences at Home During COVID-19. *Early Childhood Education Journal*, 1–14. doi:10.100710643-022-01306-5 PMID:35153466

Chen, L., Chen, T. L., Lin, C. J., & Liu, H. K. (2018). Preschool teachers' perception of the application of information communication technology (ICT) in Taiwan. *Sustainability*, *11*(1), 114. doi:10.3390u11010114

Dayal, H. C., & Tiko, L. (2020). When are we going to have the real school? A case study of early childhood education and care teachers' experiences surrounding education during the COVID-19 pandemic. *Australasian Journal of Early Childhood*, *45*(4), 336–347. doi:10.1177/1836939120966085

Djonko-Moore, C. M. (2022). Diversity education and early childhood teachers' motivation to remain in teaching: An exploration. *Journal of Early Childhood Teacher Education*, *43*(1), 35–53. doi:10.108 0/10901027.2020.1806151

Dong, C. (2018). 'Young children nowadays are very smart in ICT'–preschool teachers' perceptions of ICT use. *International Journal of Early Years Education*, 1–14. doi:10.1080/09669760.2018.1506318

Dong, C., & Mertala, P. (2021). It is a tool, but not a 'must': Early childhood preservice teachers' perceptions of ICT and its affordances. *Early Years*, *41*(5), 540–555. doi:10.1080/09575146.2019.1627293

Duch, H., Fisher, E. M., Ensari, I., & Harrington, A. (2013). Screen time use in children under 3 years old: A systematic review of correlates. *The International Journal of Behavioral Nutrition and Physical Activity*, *10*(1), 1–10. doi:10.1186/1479-5868-10-102 PMID:23967799

Edelhauser, E., & Lupu-Dima, L. (2021). One year of online education in COVID-19 age, a challenge for the Romanian education system. *International Journal of Environmental Research and Public Health*, *18*(15), 8129. doi:10.3390/ijerph18158129 PMID:34360421

Egan, S. M., Pope, J., Moloney, M., Hoyne, C., & Beatty, C. (2021). Missing early education and care during the pandemic: The socio-emotional impact of the COVID-19 crisis on young children. *Early Childhood Education Journal*, *49*(5), 925–934. doi:10.100710643-021-01193-2 PMID:33935481

Flores, M. A., Barros, A., Simão, A. M. V., Pereira, D., Flores, P., Fernandes, E., Costa, L., & Ferreira, P. C. (2022). Portuguese higher education students' adaptation to online teaching and learning in times of the COVID-19 pandemic: Personal and contextual factors. *Higher Education*, *83*(6), 1389–1408. doi:10.100710734-021-00748-x PMID:34493877

Forne, M. F. (2021). Online Meetings in Early Childhood Education: A Bonding and Educational Experience in Times of COVID-19. *Páginas de Educación*, 52–72.

Fotakopoulou, O., Hatzigianni, M., Dardanou, M., Unstad, T., & O'Connor, J. (2020). A cross-cultural exploration of early childhood educators' beliefs and experiences around the use of touchscreen technologies with children under 3 years of age. *European Early Childhood Education Research Journal*, *28*(2), 272–285. doi:10.1080/1350293X.2020.1735744

Gomes, J., Almeida, S. C., Kaveri, G., Mannan, F., Gupta, P., Hu, A., & Sarkar, M. (2021). Early Childhood Educators as COVID Warriors: Adaptations and Responsiveness to the Pandemic Across Five Countries. *International Journal of Early Childhood*, *53*(3), 345–366. doi:10.100713158-021-00305-8 PMID:34840345

Güneş, E., & Bahçivan, E. (2018). A mixed research-based model for pre-service science teachers' digital literacy: Responses to "which beliefs" and "how and why they interact" questions. *Computers & Education*, *118*, 96–106. doi:10.1016/j.compedu.2017.11.012

Hansen, A. D. O., & Hansen, A. D. O. (2017). Digital technology in early childhood education. *Cadernos Educacao Tecnologia E Sociedade*, *10*(3), 207–218.

Hasbi, M., & Hasanah, L. (2020). Early Childhood Learning from Home: Implementation of Distance Learning in Early Childhood Education during the Covid-19 Pandemic Period in Indonesia. International Journal of Innovation. *Creativity and Change, 14,* 763–778.

Hatzigianni, M., & Kalaitzidis, I. (2018). Early childhood educators' attitudes and beliefs around the use of touchscreen technologies by children under three years of age. *British Journal of Educational Technology, 49*(5), 883–895. doi:10.1111/bjet.12649

Hong, X., Zhang, M., & Liu, Q. (2021). Preschool teachers' technology acceptance During the CO-VID-19: An adapted technology acceptance model. *Frontiers in Psychology, 12,* 2113. doi:10.3389/fpsyg.2021.691492 PMID:34163416

Hu, X., Chiu, M. M., Leung, W. M. V., & Yelland, N. (2021). Technology integration for young children during COVID-19: Towards future online teaching. *British Journal of Educational Technology, 52*(4), 1513–1537. doi:10.1111/bjet.13106 PMID:34219754

Hurwitz, L. B., & Schmitt, K. L. (2020). Can children benefit from early internet exposure? Short-and long-term links between internet use, digital skill, and academic performance. *Computers & Education, 146,* 103750. doi:10.1016/j.compedu.2019.103750

Jalongo, M. R. (2021). The effects of COVID-19 on early childhood education and care: Research and resources for children, families, teachers, and teacher educators. *Early Childhood Education Journal, 49*(5), 763–774. doi:10.100710643-021-01208-y PMID:34054286

Jeon, H. J., Diamond, L., McCartney, C., & Kwon, K. A. (2021). Early Childhood Special Education Teachers' Job Burnout and Psychological Stress. *Early Education and Development,* 1–19. PMID:36353579

Jiang, Y., & Monk, H. (2015). Young Chinese-Australian children's use of technology at home: Parents' and grandparents' views. *Asia-Pacific Journal of Research in Early Childhood Education, 10*(1), 87–106.

Kamal, T., & Illiyan, A. (2021). School teachers' perception and challenges towards online teaching during COVID-19 pandemic in India: An econometric analysis. *Asian Association of Open Universities Journal, 16*(3), 311–325. doi:10.1108/AAOUJ-10-2021-0122

Kim, K. (2018). Early childhood teachers' work and technology in an era of assessment. *European Early Childhood Education Research Journal, 26*(6), 927–939. doi:10.1080/1350293X.2018.1533709

Kuutti, T., Sajaniemi, N., Björn, P. M., Heiskanen, N., & Reunamo, J. (2021). Participation, involvement and peer relationships in children with special educational needs in early childhood education. *European Journal of Special Needs Education,* 1–16.

Lang, S. N., Jeon, L., Sproat, E. B., Brothers, B. E., & Buettner, C. K. (2020). Social emotional learning for teachers (SELF-T): A short-term, online intervention to increase early childhood educators' resilience. *Early Education and Development, 31*(7), 1112–1132. doi:10.1080/10409289.2020.1749820

Lau, E. Y. H., Li, J. B., & Lee, K. (2021). Online learning and parent satisfaction during covid-19: Child competence in independent learning as a moderator. *Early Education and Development, 32*(6), 830–842. doi:10.1080/10409289.2021.1950451

Levine Brown, E., Vesely, C., Mehta, S., & Stark, K. (2022). Preschool Teachers' Emotional Acting and School-Based Interactions. *Early Childhood Education Journal.* doi:10.100710643-022-01326-1 PMID:35233161

Liao, P. A., Chang, H. H., Wang, J. H., & Sun, L. C. (2016). What are the determinants of rural-urban digital inequality among schoolchildren in Taiwan? Insights from Blinder-Oaxaca decomposition. *Computers & Education*, *95*, 123–133. doi:10.1016/j.compedu.2016.01.002

Luo, W., Berson, I. R., Berson, M. J., & Li, H. (2021). Are early childhood teachers ready for digital transformation of instruction in Mainland China? A systematic literature review. *Children and Youth Services Review*, *120*, 105718. doi:10.1016/j.childyouth.2020.105718

Masoumi, D. (2015). Preschool teachers' use of ICTs: Towards a typology of practice. *Contemporary Issues in Early Childhood*, *16*(1), 5–17. doi:10.1177/1463949114566753

McClelland, M. M., Acock, A. C., Piccinin, A., Rhea, S. A., & Stallings, M. C. (2013). Relations between preschool attention span-persistence and age 25 educational outcomes. *Early Childhood Research Quarterly*, *28*(2), 314–324. doi:10.1016/j.ecresq.2012.07.008 PMID:23543916

McClelland, M. M., & Tominey, S. L. (2011). Introduction to the special issue on self-regulation in early childhood. *Early Education and Development*, *22*(3), 355–359. doi:10.1080/10409289.2011.574265

McFarland-Piazza, L., & Saunders, R. (2012). Hands-on parent support in positive guidance: Early childhood professionals as mentors. *Australasian Journal of Early Childhood*, *37*(1), 65–73. doi:10.1177/183693911203700108

McKenna, M., Soto-Boykin, X., Cheng, K., Haynes, E., Osorio, A., & Altshuler, J. (2021). Initial development of a national survey on remote learning in early childhood during COVID-19: Establishing content validity and reporting successes and barriers. *Early Childhood Education Journal*, *49*(5), 815–827. doi:10.100710643-021-01216-y PMID:34092995

Montroy, J. J., Bowles, R. P., Skibbe, L. E., McClelland, M. M., & Morrison, F. J. (2016). The development of self-regulation across early childhood. *Developmental Psychology*, *52*(11), 1744–1762. doi:10.1037/dev0000159 PMID:27709999

Morgado, J. C., Sousa, J., & Pacheco, J. A. (2020). Educational transformations in pandemic times: From social confinement to curriculum isolation. *Praxis Educativa (Santa Rosa)*, *15*, 1–10. doi:10.5212/PraxEduc.v.15.16197.062

Negrette, G. M., Laixely, J., Cordoba, T. E., & Sanders-Smith, S. C. (2021). So we start from zero: Lessons and reflections from online preschool during the COVID-19 pandemic. *Journal of Early Childhood Research*, 1476718X221083410.

Neumann, M. M. (2015). Young children and screen time: Creating a mindful approach to digital technology. *Australian educational computing*, *30*(2), 1–15.

Nikolopoulou, K., & Gialamas, V. (2015). ICT and play in preschool: Early childhood teachers' beliefs and confidence. *International Journal of Early Years Education*, *23*(4), 409–425. doi:10.1080/09669760.2015.1078727

Nouwen, M., & Zaman, B. (2018). Redefining the role of parents in young children's online interactions. A value-sensitive design case study. *International Journal of Child-Computer Interaction*, *18*, 22–26. doi:10.1016/j.ijcci.2018.06.001

Nuri, K. A. R. A., & Cagiltay, K. (2017). In-service preschool teachers' thoughts about technology and technology use in early educational settings. *Contemporary Educational Technology*, *8*(2), 119–141.

Oke, A., Butler, J. E., & O'Neill, C. (2021). Identifying Barriers and Solutions to Increase Parent-Practitioner Communication in Early Childhood Care and Educational Services: The Development of an Online Communication Application. *Early Childhood Education Journal*, *49*(2), 283–293. doi:10.100710643-020-01068-y

Oliemat, E., Ihmeideh, F., & Alkhawaldeh, M. (2018). The use of touch-screen tablets in early childhood: Children's knowledge, skills, and attitudes towards tablet technology. *Children and Youth Services Review*, *88*, 591–597. doi:10.1016/j.childyouth.2018.03.028

Pacheco, J. A. (2021). The "new normal" in education. *Prospects*, *51*(1), 3–14. doi:10.100711125-020-09521-x PMID:33250528

Pacheco, J. A., Morgado, J. C., Sousa, J., & Maia, I. B. (2021). Educação básica e pandemia. Um estudo sobre as perceções dos professores na realidade portuguesa. *Revista Iberoamericana de Educación*, *86*(1), 187–204. doi:10.35362/rie8614346

Rad, D., Egerau, A., Roman, A., Dughi, T., Balas, E., Maier, R., Ignat, S., & Rad, G. (2022). A Preliminary Investigation of the Technology Acceptance Model (TAM) in Early Childhood Education and Care. BRAIN. *Broad Research in Artificial Intelligence and Neuroscience*, *13*(1), 518–533. doi:10.18662/brain/13.1/297

Rad, D., Magulod, G. Jr, Balas, E., Roman, A., Egerau, A., Maier, R., Ignat, S., Dughi, T., Balas, V., Demeter, E., Rad, G., & Chis, R. (2022). A Radial Basis Function Neural Network Approach to Predict Preschool Teachers' Technology Acceptance Behavior. *Frontiers in Psychology*, *13*, 13. doi:10.3389/fpsyg.2022.880753 PMID:35756273

Rad, D., Redeş, A., Roman, A., Ignat, S., Lile, R., Demeter, E., Egerău, A., Dughi, T., Balaş, E., Maier, R., Kiss, C., Torkos, H., & Rad, G. (2022). Pathways to inclusive and equitable quality early childhood education for achieving SDG4 goal—A scoping review. *Frontiers in Psychology*, *13*, 4306. doi:10.3389/fpsyg.2022.955833 PMID:35936241

Radesky, J. S., Eisenberg, S., Kistin, C. J., Gross, J., Block, G., Zuckerman, B., & Silverstein, M. (2016). Overstimulated consumers or next-generation learners? Parent tensions about child mobile technology use. *Annals of Family Medicine*, *14*(6), 503–508. doi:10.1370/afm.1976 PMID:28376436

Sanchez-Vera, M. D. M., Solano-Fernandez, I. M., & Recio-Caride, S. (2019). Digital storytelling using videos in early childhood education. *PIXEL-BIT-REVISTA DE MEDIOS Y EDUCACION*, (54), 165-184.

Silverman, A. (2020). Play, child development, and relationships: A preschool teacher in China shares her virtual teaching experience. *Teaching Young Children*, *13*(4).

Smith, S. J., Burdette, P. J., Cheatham, G. A., & Harvey, S. P. (2016). Parental role and support for online learning of students with disabilities: A paradigm shift. *Journal of Special Education Leadership*, *29*(2), 101–112.

Terry, G., Hayfield, N., Clarke, V., & Braun, V. (2017). Thematic analysis. The SAGE handbook of qualitative research in psychology, 2, 17-37. doi:10.4135/9781526405555.n2

Tieken, M. C. (2017). The spatialisation of racial inequity and educational opportunity: Rethinking the rural/urban divide. *Peabody Journal of Education*, *92*(3), 385–404. doi:10.1080/0161956X.2017.1324662

Višnjić Jevtić, A., & Halavuk, A. (2021). Early childhood teachers and burnout syndrome–perception of Croatian teachers. *Early Years*, *41*(1), 36–47. doi:10.1080/09575146.2018.1482260

Whiteside-Mansell, L., McKelvey, L., Saccente, J., & Selig, J. P. (2019). Adverse childhood experiences of urban and rural preschool children in poverty. *International Journal of Environmental Research and Public Health*, *16*(14), 2623. doi:10.3390/ijerph16142623 PMID:31340510

Williford, A. P., Vick Whittaker, J. E., Vitiello, V. E., & Downer, J. T. (2013). Children's engagement within the preschool classroom and their development of self-regulation. *Early Education and Development*, *24*(2), 162–187. doi:10.1080/10409289.2011.628270 PMID:23441104

Yurt, Ö., & Cevher-Kalburan, N. (2011). Early childhood teachers' thoughts and practices about the use of computers in early childhood education. *Procedia Computer Science*, *3*, 1562–1570. doi:10.1016/j.procs.2011.01.050

Zalaznick, M. (2019). Online service intends to expand pre-K access. EQUITY). *District Administration*, *55*(8), 12.

Chapter 18
Review of the Research on Design Education and Practices

Shweta Vivek Tiwari
Karnavati University, India

ABSTRACT

Since time immemorial, the space where teachers and students assembled for traditional learning was the classroom. But the internet has changed how people think about place, time, and space. The physical dimension no longer confines space; it also includes the virtual domain. Futuristic methods of teaching and learning have emerged based on improved cognitive understanding. As a result, the concept of a classroom has expanded and evolved. Spaces are no longer defined by their physical notions but identified by their intangible usefulness. Today, though technology and the internet have drastically reduced the importance of distance, space is still a crucial determinant for collaborative creative work. Building on the premise that the physical environment influences learning, this research intends to identify spatial characteristics that play a role in facilitating creativity and innovation, especially in the context of design education.

INTRODUCTION

Design

A specification of an object specified by an agent that aims to achieve a goal in a particular environment using a set of primitive components that meet the set of requirements subject to constraints. Here, specifications can be manifested as plans or finished products, and primitives are the elements that make up a design object (Broadbent, 1973).

Design is an interdisciplinary profession that meets several needs. Designers work in multidisciplinary teams, the type and composition of which vary from project to project. This makes it challenging to discuss a range of abilities or even particular knowledge areas. On the educational side, these will vary depending on the location and focus of the program and curriculum (Friedman, 2012).

DOI: 10.4018/978-1-6684-6682-7.ch018

Objectives

- Recognizing the needs (physical, social, and contextual) of a design process in creative education to foster creativity.
- Identifying the role of the space in learning environments (design education institutes and design studios) to facilitate the design process in the context of creative education.

Methodology

- With the help of systematic empirical and theoretical investigation, we determine the pedagogical framework and methods and ascertain a design process's needs (physical, social, and contextual).
- Based on qualitative research, identifying the typologies and qualities of spaces conducive to creativity and facilitating student learning in the context of creative education.

Design Process

'You cannot hold a design in your hand. It is not a thing. It is a process. A system, a way of thinking.' Bob Gill, Graphic Design as a Second Language. Design as a system, a method for structuring the thinking process. Therefore, design is a process-oriented activity. The design process follows a schematic phase structure. Information and decisions made in one phase of the design process form the basis of subsequent steps. It typically goes back and forth between phases so that you can generate and solve ideas to develop creative solutions that meet the specified goals of your assignments. Each design area follows a specific process. The design process is inevitably cyclical. The design process helps ensure that the design meets all activities that serve both economic and design goals. This process creates several possible solutions and uses various techniques and mechanisms to encourage participants to think outside the box when looking for creative or innovative solutions.

Stages of the Design Process

The design process can be identified in the following seven steps:

1. DEFINE: First, one must define the design issues and the target audience. An accurate understanding of the problem and its boundary conditions can lead to the development of more accurate solutions.
2. RESEARCH: The investigation step reviews information such as design problem history, end-user investigations, and opinion-led interviews to identify potential obstacles.
3. IDEATE: Ideate is the phase in which end-user motivations and needs are identified and, perhaps through brainstorming, ideas are generated to meet them.
4. PROTOTYPE: Prototyping is a solution or modification of these ideas, submitted for review by user groups and stakeholders and then presented to customers.
5. SELECTION: Selection sees the proposed answers reviewed toward the design brief objective. Some answers are probably realistic however won't be the fine ones.
6. IMPLEMENT: Implementation includes design development and final delivery to the customer.

7.   LEARN: Learning helps improve designer performance. For this reason, designers need to seek feedback from customers and target groups to determine if the solution meets the purpose of the design brief.

In many cases, the design is linear, but it is often necessary to revisit the previous segment to evolve it as a development (Ambrose & Harris, 2009).

Creativity is an integral part of the design. Without creativity, the design doesn't exist. Therefore, creativity is a part of the design process by default (Thoring et al., 2017).

'Design process can be broadly divided into four stages:
   ◦   Preparation (investigation of the problem in all directions)
   ◦   Incubation (unconscious processing)
   ◦   Illumination (sudden insight and creation of solution)
   ◦   Verification (critical elaboration and validation of the idea)

Building on this, there are two concepts of thinking:
   ◦   Divergent thinking (producing a large quantity & variety of ideas)
   ◦   Convergent thinking (the process of narrowing down to one solution)

They can be further differentiated as:
   ◦   Flexibility (a variety of ideas; diverging in different directions)
   ◦   Fluency (the number of ideas produced)
   ◦   Fixation (the inappropriate repetition of existing solutions)
   ◦   Priming (the activation of a specific mindset)
   ◦   Serendipity (the unexpected finding of valuable ideas, persons, & things)' (Thoring et al., 2021).

The definition of the design process is more relevant in our study, as our interests focus on creativity and the ability of the spatial environment to facilitate the design process.

DESIGN PRACTICES

Design practice studies have revealed that designers who are adept at coping with difficult design issues employ a method known as creative thinking or action (Stolterman, 2008).

'The nature of the designers' problem-solving can be called the designerly way of thinking' - Nigel Cross, Designerly way of Knowing (Cross, 2006).

For decades, a large component of design research has focused on developing theoretical approaches, methodologies, tools, and procedures to support designers' activities. This study has advanced significantly, and the discipline currently contains various approaches, methodologies, and strategies. Some of these ideas are novel, but many have conceptual origins in other fields, such as physics, engineering, social sciences, and humanities, as well as conventional arts and design.

Making something that is not universal is the goal of design practice. It is about making anything with defined goals, scenarios, consumers and users, features and qualities, limited time, and limited resources (Stolterman, 2008).

Coming to the space where these design practices are practiced - workspaces, there has been a huge evolution in its role and functioning. Looking at the historical evolution of workplace design reveals three implications: organizational culture, new technologies, and workplace design. On the one hand, the workspace reflects current management practices. Leading the observatory on the upper floors was similar to enabling the leadership style. On the other hand, workspace design allows for certain work practices, such as the Google Office privacy pods, which allow for personal evaluation and more focused work). After all, technology enables certain forms of work that allow people to work anywhere, with the availability of mobile laptops and wireless networks. When designing a creative space, one must carefully consider management styles, technological developments, and workplace interactions (Thoring, 2019).

Design Education and Design Education Institutes

Any design involves an unusual thought process. Design is more prescriptive than descriptive. Instead of narrating or deciphering the world, the design suggests what the world can be like. Scientists strive to interpret our world, historians tell us what it was in the past, but designers simply tell everyone how it will be in the future. In design-based courses, there is no great theory to learn from. Nevertheless, it is quite practical. While many university courses tend to break things down and study them in separate components or modules, design courses focus on putting things together, mostly with large chunks of unplanned work. It's more about synthesis than analysis. All of this leads to unconventional teaching and learning methods and to very novel-looking places where this happens (Lawson, 2018).

Design Education

Learning to design is not something that can be learned from books. One needs to experience and understand the design for oneself. The type of learning that one undertakes requires not only the acquisition and absorption of knowledge but the development of a complete range of skills and knowledge. In addition, one needs to acquire a variety of practical skills, understand their implications, and be able to apply them in the design process (Lawson, 2018).

Design education calls for diverse teaching, learning, and designing methods and activities, which include concept generation, writing, sketching, digital work, planning, lecturing and listening to presentations, collaborative work, discussions, prototype making, etc. All those activities require unique environments. To understand the requirements of these unique environments, we must study the modes of learning and teaching in design education.

The Bauhaus School in Dessau believed that design instruction should be tri-structured - technical / art / scientific structures - rather than polarized - art / technical structures.

The philosopher who taught a course on "intellectual integration" was one of the prominent representatives of the Vienna Circle in the United States. He was a co-editor of the Unity of Science Encyclopedia, which might be considered the bible of logical positivism. - Charles Morris attempted to express his thoughts about the three fundamental design parts: art, science, and technology. In a nutshell, Morris regarded the design approach as semiosis. He established parallels between the sign's syntactic, semantic, and pragmatic characteristics and the design's aesthetic, scientific, and technical aspects.

In the early 1950s, Tomas Maldonado said at the Hochschule für Gestaltung (HfG) under Ulm, "A new educational philosophy is already in development; its base is scientific operationalism." As a result, the original curriculum's aesthetic features became obsolete, while its scientific substance was improved and highlighted, particularly through contributions from the humanities and social sciences. The new tagline was "Science and technology; a new union." A new theoretical model of the concept that design was applied (human and social) science had overpowered its identity as applied aesthetics. But the underlying dual knowledge structure remains the same; in Dessau and Ulm (Findeli, 2001).

Learning studies show that competence is active, exploratory, and develops in a social context. Learning is enriched when participants think conceptually and critically while involving peers and professionals. This learning study also influences the design of the space where the learning takes place. These learning spaces (classrooms) need to be designed differently than in the 1900s for a teaching method focusing on active learning and constructive knowledge building. For example, does this constructivist approach require flexible seating so that participants can collaborate, discuss, and debate? (Oblinger, 2005).

Design Pedagogy

Teaching design through design practice in universities has been a time-immemorial tradition. The ultimate goal of graduates is to acquire the ability to function as a designer in the professional world. The core goals include programmers that enable graduates to approach and be a member of a community of professionals, with practitioners involved in the process and diverse educational methodologies that may accommodate these approaches. Traditional components of this technique include studios, tutorials, libraries, and reviews. Still, their effective usage necessitates an in-depth comprehension of the designed style of knowing, and its effectiveness supports agile navigation through the design process. Students need time, space, and structure to immerse themselves in design briefs which will occupy them in a reflective process to resolve inconsistencies in dual-processing analytical models (Tovey, 2015).

PRACTICE-BASED TEACHING

Traditionally, art and design education are built on doing, generally through modeling professional conditions via project briefs. There are various aspects of the practice-oriented design theory approach. Students are practitioners from the start, frequently with lengthy project stages requiring various technical abilities, and many activities take place in a studio or workshop setting. Constructive criticism is typically used to give assessment and feedback, supplemented by peer learning. Open-ended solutions, practice variations, and implicit knowledge are accepted without a considerable focus on formal knowledge. It aims to help students become autonomous, self-analyzing, and critical thinkers in an atmosphere emphasizing important skills rather than academic comprehension. Teachers are frequently working artists and designers (Tovey, 2015).

Setting the Scene

Students who aim to become accomplished designers commit to working on design project activities. Gradually, with practice, the students develop the experience to tackle more complex design problems, increasing in intensity and detail. The ultimate goal is usually to achieve some ability to function as a designer in the professional world. Creative knowledge makes use of several sorts of intelligence, particularly visual-spatial reasoning. This is a one-of-a-kind and complicated technique that often solves issues that have not been properly stated and addressed. Parallel thought pathways that leverage continuous and simultaneous cognition are used in design thinking. Such a model is compatible with the solution-oriented approach that serves as the foundation for its creative activity. Reflective practice is a method for reformulating issues and solutions by utilizing implicit knowledge. A variety of teaching methodologies can accommodate these methods. Studios, tutorials, libraries, and constructive critique are classic components, but their effective usage depends on a methodology marked by thoroughly comprehending the designerly style of knowing (Tovey, 2015).

Motivation and the Learning Escape in Design

Designers are well-equipped to cope with competing demands and possibilities, and their techniques of examining challenges and developing ideas are frequently targeted toward discovering and publicizing tensions. This necessitates knowledge of the multifaceted nature of design and design. Today, there are some special challenges and possibilities in developing motivation in design education. Students can be personally motivated by conflict stimuli, failure acceptance, and good self-management conducive to design creativity and creative assessment. Motivation, in essence, promotes successful creative and analytical thinking. The ultimate reward in design is successful innovation connected to bringing a product to market and making it renowned as part of a team. Designers need agile navigation support in the design world. One needs a learning experience that leverages their students' natural motivations to create resiliently, informed, and sustainable abilities (Tovey, 2015).

Design and Transformative Learning

Transformative learning is used to successfully teach design practice. The ability to think creatively, as well as the creative skills and knowledge of implementing and developing ideas, are essential for success as a designer. The process that demands integrating both holistic and linear thinking into a dual-processing model through practical relevance is at its heart. This strategy focuses on establishing mechanisms that assist pupils in overcoming uncertainty thresholds. This is frequently linked to the unpleasant experience of dealing with and resolving design challenges. Activities may be managed efficiently and profitably by putting them into a studio-based culture that draws students via practice and practical learning. The necessity is a learning environment that overcomes the fragmentation that might occur in modular curricular frameworks and, in particular, provides a safe place for problem-oriented learning (Tovey, 2015).

Amplifying Learners Voices Through Global Studio

As a result, design students must learn to convey their tales. Master-apprentice models, widely employed in areas such as skill acquisition, are not ideal for students to relate their tales. Other techniques are required to provide future design graduates with the reflexes needed to comprehend the increasingly complicated environment of the information economy. The Global Studio's mission is to promote a student education approach in which tutors retain distance to foster autonomy. The goal is to expose students to the context of complicated projects, preparing them for professional job life. It varies from supervised design training because teachers are further away from teaching and learning activities. Students construct dialogues and results mostly via peer interaction (Tovey, 2015).

Design Education Institutes

Design-based schools have similarities internationally and even across key disciplines such as industrial design, interior design, and architecture. Design schools originally emerged more or less as a complement to fine arts, especially during the influential Ecole des Beaux-Arts. The most influential European school was the Bauhaus in the early 20th century. Presently, the general view of Bauhaus is a kind of minimalist and intrinsically modernist style. Still, its original concept was much more basic, with ideas for processes and pedagogy included. As a result, our design schools began to identify themselves uniquely, different from art, despite having much in common. Bauhaus was interested in the design of virtually all forms but developed many principles that rejoined manufacturing and crafts with design. It was a new form of manufacturing that included advanced technology for mass production and brought new, highly controlled advantages. The Ulm School developed it further in the mid-20th century and adopted an interdisciplinary approach that included subjects such as sociology, psychology, economics, and even philosophy in its curriculum. It shared the position of understanding and teaching the design process. This has had a major impact on the development of industrial and product design schools (Lawson, 2018).

Curricular and Disciplinary Needs

Universities - higher education institutions are typically composed of various colleges and confer various academic degrees. In addition to institutions, they might also include various departments, orders, research centers, and other organizations. Originally, university courses were categorized in a disciplinary and pedagogical hierarchy. The student's job was to acquire knowledge from the teacher until the degree was obtained. However, the new university model recently introduced in the European Union based on the Bologna project challenges this traditional view. It promotes greater interaction with new technologies, more freedom for individual research and field research initiatives, and with a flexible curriculum. Without constant renewal, through courses at universities and other institutions, or even through the process of self-study, the profession is at risk of becoming obsolete and not considered appropriate by the market. The greater demand for higher education and training is fueled by the large number of people graduating high school. Today's society lives in the information age, where the need for physical work is being replaced by tasks that require technical information with the ability to build one's knowledge. The Internet is a powerful tool. It is accelerating the accumulation and production of knowledge, expanding the capabilities of professionals, and increasing their demand. The development of the Internet has led to thinking about future university revolutions, as face-to-face education can be complemented and even replaced by distance learning (F, n.d.,2020).

Curriculum reforms often encourage the rethinking of spaces. As the program evolves to more aggressive, collaborative, or project-based learning, their spatial needs shift from those based on lecture-based pedagogy. Interdisciplinary activities may require the redesign of spaces that can also combine disciplines. Many learning activities are generic, but many are also closely related to the discipline. For example, the design of learning spaces for physics may differ from that of a history or visual arts space. The need for a laboratory, studio room or project room is often related to the need for specific disciplinary requirements and may be related to accreditation criteria. Ideally, the design of a learning space should be specific for a single discipline, but it is not the case as there are needs to accommodate many programs. In some cases, it may be necessary to integrate different disciplines, such as multidisciplinary programs (Oblinger, 2005).

Infrastructure and Facilities

Faced with increasing IT use, student and staff migration, support system implementation, and legal requirements, today's universities have rethought their infrastructure organization. The patchwork of isolated solutions reduces the university's flexibility and makes it more difficult to collaborate with other institutions. Like many institutions, universities today are challenged by the increasing use of IT. Internet-based communication, digital learning materials, distance lectures, online meetings, support systems, digital certifications, and approvals are just a few of the deliverables and mechanisms institutions need to process today. The 2009 Horizon Report identifies and describes new technologies that can significantly impact education, learning, and research in learning-oriented organizations (Zender & Tavangarian, 2009). The report highlights the key trends that will be introduced over the next 1-5 years:

- Integrated mobile systems- Smart devices that replace multiple other devices
- Cloud computing- Ultra thin client with everywhere remote access to distributed sources and services with well-defined interfaces
- Geo everything- Enrichment of data with geographic information
- Personal web- Individual online representations and content compositions
- Semantic-aware applications- Applications that utilize the meaning of information
- Smart objects- Physical objects that are connected to a rich store of contextual information (Zender & Tavangarian, 2009)

Educational institutions and their design have a significant impact on student learning. Recent research shows that current university students spend less time on campus and more time interacting with peers through technology. The study points out many characteristics of how students interpret the relationship between university learning and teacher expectations and institutions (McLaughlin & Faulkner, 2012). These are:

- Both formal and informal settings were utilized for the learning of these students.
- Timetabled facilities governed the teaching style used, as well as opportunities for collaborative learning - which was evidential.
- These students' active learning is likely to occur outside the classroom, more so in informal spaces.
- These students placed great importance on the technology available everywhere, especially within the university.
- Lastly, these students preferred communal social spaces for learning and sharing technology (McLaughlin & Faulkner, 2012).

The conclusions drawn from their answers show that these university students prefer flexible learning spaces that can accommodate individual and collaborative learning, focusing on social learning and advanced technology. The answers also show the discrepancy between existing lecture rooms and laboratories and the third space these students' desire. These results should impact the design and construction of future education and learning spaces at universities and other institutions. It should be noted that the significance of safety, natural ventilation, lighting, and other physical features is beneficial for effective learning. These students also indicated the need for multipurpose spaces for intensive work and study opportunities. These spaces should encourage students to interact with the global environment via technology. The last 25 years have shown significant changes in learning and education, with functional roles of technology, collaboration spaces, and third room learning putting pressure on universities and staff to meet the demands of the modern academic community. The learning needs of students in higher education and the relationship between learning and institutions are now much emphasized. Freshman responses show that this relationship is crucial (McLaughlin & Faulkner, 2012).

Design Studios

The physical embodiment of the studio in a design-based school cannot be missed. This place is home to learning practical design and discussions on individual design projects, with architecture, interior design, and product design as topics of heated debate. The physical equipment of the design studio has evolved with the advancement in technology, with drafting boards and basic machines now having computers, printers, and internet connectivity (Lawson, 2018). Design courses vary by subject, context, culture, interests, and expertise of the faculty. However, there is an underlying genetic structure and organization. Subjects of technical, historical, social, and even philosophical subjects are required and mainly taught in lecture rooms or seminar rooms. Subjects of skill development are taught in a variety of ways. These include the drawing- manual and digital, especially computer-aided design, and in some cases, surveying and measurement. The most common feature of timetables is sometimes referred to as "studio" or something similar. This is usually the largest single course per week. Essentially, the studio is more than just a place, and it's also a process with recognizable features. Students are assigned problems and then encouraged to work on them in groups or individually. At the beginning of the course, these issues are very specific and can be minor. Subsequently, they become more complex and larger and are selected and defined by both students and tutors (Lawson, 2018).

Without exception, studios include collocations and unstructured schedules. This means that students in the cohort of the year tend to share the same space, if not always. There have been many studies on how much students learn from each other. The course is generally unstructured, and students are encouraged to organize their time themselves though the timetable may contain important events such as project presentations, visits, discussions, critiques, etc. All of these work effectively, but they also come with many risks. Some people find it difficult to focus on their work because the place is so lively and busy. Most importantly, the studio is not a space for formal instruction but a place to learn by doing (Lawson, 2018). Studios are almost always a single place where students can get together and learn from each other. It is based primarily on design issues and uses practical rather than theoretical teaching. Students learn by doing. Students are responsible for planning their time and work, as it has an unstructured timetable. It is very different from the practical courses in the modules of other courses. This encourages students to draw ideas from all modules of their degree program. This process of integrating ideas is one of the most valuable features of a design degree (Lawson, 2018).

DISCUSSION

Student engagement in any teaching method is an essential aspect of examining students' learning process, and the extent of engagement is a significant sign of learning effectiveness. Student engagement is multifaceted, considering factors like attitudes, awareness, and emotion, including straightforward, emotional, and rational behaviors (Hu & Li, 2017). This allowed us to explore the role of the learning environment in promoting student engagement and overall performance. This study attempted to understand the relationship between learning and the spaces within which it happens. There has been a growing interest in learning spaces in the last few years. Several architectural experts in the field of education and design have researched this field and published several studies, with many innovative examples currently being built. Be that as it may, the core issue of what we mean by *space* and spatial matters to learning remains unsolved. *'What kinds of space are we talking about - conceptual, physical, virtual, social, and/or personal? What are the relationships between the nature of these various spaces, and how do they impact learning activities?'* (Boys, 2011).

Training future designers are not limited to curriculum development, student education, and project assignments. The query of space being a facilitator to the student's learning process, enhancing their well-being along with that of teachers, and especially, being a promoter of creativity and innovation, is quite under-researched. At the same time, there is growing interest in a creative learning environment in elementary and kindergartens. However, much research has not been done in designing adult education environments (design schools and universities) (Thoring et al., 2017). A lot of focus has been given to the environments of design educational institutes. However, what is lacking is attention to the environs of a classroom - or better termed - a design studio - in these design educational institutes.

CONCLUSION

The study found that spatial characteristics of the physical learning environment (i.e., design studios and design educational institutes) positively impact and influence creativity. This finding could help to avoid ignoring aspects of design education that affect student engagement, creativity, and the well-being of its occupants (i.e., students) in the physical environment. The physical environment is one of the most neglected areas of design education, despite the fact that it has a significant impact on student engagement, creativity, and the overall wellbeing of its residents, who are the students. In the context of design education, a "design studio" refers to the physical learning environment. The purpose of this study is to determine the spatial aspects of design studios that have a good impact and influence on creative output. Further, this study could support futuristic teaching and learning methods to improve cognitive understanding.

REFERENCES

Ambrose, G., & Harris, P. (2009). *Basics Design 08: Design Thinking*. Bloomsbury Publishing Plc.

Boys, J. (2011). *Towards Creative Learning Spaces: Rethinking the Architecture of Post-compulsory Education*. Routledge.

Broadbent, G. (1973). *Design in Architecture: Architecture and the Human Sciences*. Wiley-Blackwell.

Cross, N. (2006). *Designerly ways of knowing*. Springer.

F, A. (2020). The Role of the University of the Future. Ernst & Young.

Findeli, A. (2001). Rethinking Design Education for the 21st Century: Theoretical, Methodological, and Ethical Discussion. *Design Issues*, *17*(1), 5–17. Advance online publication. doi:10.1162/07479360152103796

Friedman, K. (2012). Models of design: Envisioning a future design education. Academia. https://d1wqtxts1xzle7.cloudfront.net/30525217/Friedman_D_2012_Models_of_Design_-with-cover-page-v2.pdf?Expires=1640843489&Signature=PCG84r9HIFbffpJDTWTsv4QbmGgBANSyfWntNPCUGELaTfeY1giAtusEvUJkXCMykiFqWYI-g7xNNXZsE1srnv0PMUIg00bq9S46lJvGOevenFxGsNEoquEBrzt

Hu, M., & Li, H. (2017). Student Engagement in Online Learning: A Review. *2017 International Symposium on Educational Technology (ISET)*. IEEE. 10.1109/ISET.2017.17

Lawson, B. (2018). *The Design Student's Journey: Understanding how Designers Think*. Routledge. doi:10.4324/9780429448577

McLaughlin, P., & Faulkner, J. D. (2012). Flexible spaces...what students expect from university facilities. *Journal of Facilities Management*, *10*(2), 140–149. doi:10.1108/14725961211218776

Oblinger, D. (2005). Leading the Transition from Classrooms to Learning Spaces. *Educause Review*. https://er.educause.edu/articles/2005/1/leading-the-transition-from-classrooms-to learning-spaces

Stolterman, E. (2008). The Nature of Design Practice and Implications for Interaction Design Research. *International Journal of Design*, *2*(1). http://www.ijdesign.org/index.php/IJDesign/article/view/240/148#anchor0

Thoring, K. (2019). Designing Creative Space: A Systemic View on Workspace Design and Its Impact on The Creative Process. TU Delft, Delft University of Technology.

Thoring, K., Goncalves, M. G., Mueller, R. M., Badke-Schaub, P., & Desmet, P. (2017). Inspiration Space: Towards a theory of creativity-supporting learning environments. *Conference Proceedings of the Design Management Academy*. https://research.tudelft.nl/en/publications/inspiration-space-towards-a-theory-of-creativity-supporting-learn

Thoring, K., Luippold, C., & Mueller, R. M. (2021). Creative Space in Design Education: A Typology of Spatial Functions. *The Design Society*. https://www.designsociety.org/publication/33233/Creative+Space+in+Design+Education%3A+A+Typology+of+Spatial+Functions

Tovey, M. (Ed.). (2015). *Design Pedagogy: Developments in Art and Design Education*. Gower.

Zender, R., & Tavangarian, D. (2009). *"Service-oriented university: Infrastructure for the university of tomorrow,"* in *Intelligent Interactive Assistance and Mobile Multimedia Computing*. Springer Berlin Heidelberg.

Chapter 19
Systematic Literature Review on the Relationship Between Entrepreneurship and Cultural Capital in the Role of Transnationality, Education, and Gender

Sreejith P. M.
Cochin University of Science and Technology, India

Sreejith S.
Cochin University of Science And Technology, India

ABSTRACT

Along with the upcoming opportunities it presents in the market, entrepreneurship is a topic that receives a great deal of attention in academic study. The nature of running a business has been shifting for some time now, which has resulted in many changes to the dynamics of entrepreneurship in more recent times. The revolution that has taken place in the cultural and social components of society has also contributed to the occurrence of this transition. The approach that Bourdieu takes to entrepreneurship deals with the cultural components of the subject matter and delivers a great lot of insightful new information. For the purpose of this study, a comprehensive review was carried out in order to determine the primary topics that correspond to the connection between the two. Transnational entrepreneurship, the role of gender, and the impact of education and skills on the concept of entrepreneurship are the three subjects that have been identified for the study.

DOI: 10.4018/978-1-6684-6682-7.ch019

INTRODUCTION

Entrepreneurship is an emerging prospect in the world today due to its wide range of opportunities associated with it. Entrepreneurship has been defined by Onuoha (2007) as the practice of initiating new organisations in response to opportunities focusing particularly on starting new businesses or revitalising organisations already in a mature state. Schumpeter (1965) also defined entrepreneurs as individuals ready to exploit the opportunities in the market with the help of technical or organisational innovations. Hisrich (1990) stated that an entrepreneur who exhibits creative thinking could take risks and organise social and economic happenings into practical accounts. In many ways, cultural norms inform the very definition of entrepreneurship. These linkages can be traced back to the individuality, power distance, and uncertainty aversion that make up Hofstede's cultural dimensions (Eroglu & Picak, 2011). Values linked with collectivism emphasise the importance of consensus and group work, while individualism emphasises the importance of the individual's achievements and initiatives. Although belonging to different regions and cultural values, the entrepreneurs are tied together with some collectivist values and individual entrepreneurial beliefs based on their culture (McGrath et al., 1992).

The concept of "cultural capital" as we know it now may be traced back to the work of Pierre Bourdieu (Sullivan, 2002). Bourdieu and Passeron (1977) defined cultural capital as attitudes in linguistics, formal knowledge, academic culture and general culture. It consists of standards and attributes regarding informal knowledge related to school or linguistic competence, traditional culture in a humanist approach or a personal or specific style. Bourdieu (1993) stated that cultural capital has theoretically and radically different aspects associated with it. While the former plays the role of an indicator, and the latter is based on the position of class. According to Bourdieu & Wacquant (1992), individuals are socially active and active in the field because they possess some properties necessary for being effective in the field. Bourdieu offered a conceptual framework to conduct research agendas in a methodological approach. The main components of Bourdieu's framework are field, habitus and capital. Here field refers to the space covering social positions, which is related to the capital endowment; habitus states the individual's principles for judgement and practice; and capital refers to the resources that enable that enables the individuals to advance or preserve their relative position in the field (Delmestri & Brumana, 2017). When it comes to regularities in social action and structure and the reality of the actors' purposeful reasoning, Bourdieu's work focuses on resolving the tension between these two perspectives, which he calls "the actor's subjectivism" and "objectivism."

If what Purwanto (2016) says is true, an entrepreneur's cultural capital is crucial to his or her success. Entrepreneurs with high levels of cultural capital have better communication skills and are easier to interact with, both of which are crucial to the success of any business. It is very important for entrepreneurs to have an educational background and to provide training in skill development to better understand the cultural capital aspect. The relationship between entrepreneurship and Bourdieu's approach is increasingly being questioned due to the amalgamation of social practice in entrepreneurship. The social and cultural aspects of entrepreneurship are crucial as a more practice-based approach is gaining momentum in the present times (Sklaveniti & Steyaert, 2019). There are different cases in the context of entrepreneurship that has its relevance to the cultural capital dimensions. With transnational entrepreneurs increasing, they need to be accustomed to the varied cultural differences to match the class position to flourish in their venture while travelling across geographies for their businesses. Moreover, with an increase in the breaking of stereotypical cultural and social taboos, the advancement made in entrepreneurship through them is an interesting area to deal with. Therefore, it can be established that with the novel concepts of entrepreneurship coming into the scenario and development in the cultural capital demonstration of the actors, looking into the relationship between the two prime aspects is of utmost importance. The study conducted in the previous literature would help better understand the changing dynamics of the two areas. This study is thus an attempt to systematically review the relationship between entrepreneurship and Bourdieu's approach in the context of evolving dynamics of both aspects.

RESEARCH METHODOLOGY

Webster and Watson (2002) suggested a pattern for conducting a literature review based on concepts, popularly known as the concept-driven systematic review approach. This particular method is based on reviewing the literature across time from the perspective of the authors conducting these studies. It stands out from other approaches as it involves an individual author's perspective across some concepts in these articles rather than being author driven. Discussion on entrepreneurship's association with Pierre Bourdieu's approach can be systematically reviewed as the literature involved in the topic is vast. This review method would provide a concrete idea about the research on the topic and help in assimilating them in a particular order. Entrepreneurship is a highly looked upon the topic in the present times due to its increasing popularity and wide range of opportunities. Moreover, Bourdieu's approach is related to the social aspects of entrepreneurship which is necessary for every individual to focus upon. Hence, the relationship between entrepreneurship and Bourdieu's approach would provide a detailed understanding.

Sources of Data

In order to conduct a systematic review, it is required to go through research articles from the past corresponding to the area of interest. A search for the research has been initiated in databases including SCOPUS, ScienceDirect and Web of Science to collect the corresponding articles. As the SCOPUS database incorporates the databases of ScienceDirect and Web of Science databases, it can be assumed that SCOPUS as a whole has been used as the primary source for collecting data for conducting the review. The search has been conducted using keywords such as "Entrepreneurship", "Pierre Bourdieu'", "Bourdieu's Approach", etc., to arrive at the research articles sought. From the results generated, relevant papers were selected to conduct the systematic review.

Identifying the Themes

Selecting themes is essential to conducting a systematic review as they provide important insights into the crucial topics discussed in the past literature. A strict process involving analysis of the research papers retrieved from the databases browsed is followed. Screening of the research papers is based on the paper's title for the research framework constructed for the analysis. The framework created for the research helped to recognise major issues related to the social aspects of Bourdieu's Approach to entrepreneurship. These factors identified when browsing through the papers helped in dividing them into themes for the study. The themes thus formulated helped me understand some of the important aspects of entrepreneurship from a social aspect. These themes are reviewed in detail to conclude the entrepreneurship scenario in academic research.

Data Extraction and Synthesis

After identifying themes for the review, the step includes a detailed reading procedure of the papers involving the themes. Extensive reading of the associated papers guides one in learning about the perspective of each researcher on them over time. The papers considered are shortlisted for reading based on the title and abstract. Finally, those papers involving high-quality research on the topic are selected to arrive at the themes to be chosen for the review. Preferred Reporting Items for Systematic Review and Meta-Analysis (PRISMA) and a flow chart representing the entire procedure of selection are created. Further, bibliometric analysis for the SCOPUS database is used to find the topic's contribution to past literature.

RESULTS AND DISCUSSION

The search conducted across the database using the abovementioned keywords gave many results (n=453). After considering the papers based on the criteria laid down for the study and discarding the research papers on the topic beyond 2010 to 2020, a total of 283 papers were finally shortlisted for identifying the relationship between entrepreneurship and Bourdieu's cultural capital approach. Once the papers are selected, and a thorough reading is done through them, three major themes have been identified. The themes chosen are mentioned below.

- Theme 1- Transnational Entrepreneurship
- Theme 2- Gender Disparities
- Theme 3- Role of Education/ Skills

All these three factors are important to the relationship between entrepreneurship and Bourdieu's Approach. The three themes are found to be discussed in the past literature over and over again. This reveals the importance of these aspects in the entire process; thus, conducting this systematic review would help gain further interesting insights into the topic.

Figure 1 is a flow chart representing the systematic review process

The results from the data extraction process conducted is shown in table 1.

In the next section, a list of all the articles selected for conducting the systematic review is given, which contains the authors' names, the type of study (quantitative or qualitative) and the three themes identified from the review. The boxes are marked 'x' for the presence of the corresponding variable in the study considered (table 2).

Transnational Entrepreneurship

The concept of transnational entrepreneurship has been highlighted as the first theme of the systematic review. According to Drori et al. (2009), "Transnational Entrepreneurs" (TA) are social actors who are searching for business opportunities or maintaining business limited within social fields, and who are also enacting ideas, networks, and information that force them to be engaged in various strategies related to actions to promote their entrepreneurial activities. In other words, TA are people who are looking for business opportunities or maintaining business limited within social fields. According to recent research, transnational entrepreneurs are entering a new phase of business strategies that are

Figure 1. PRISMA for the Systematic Review

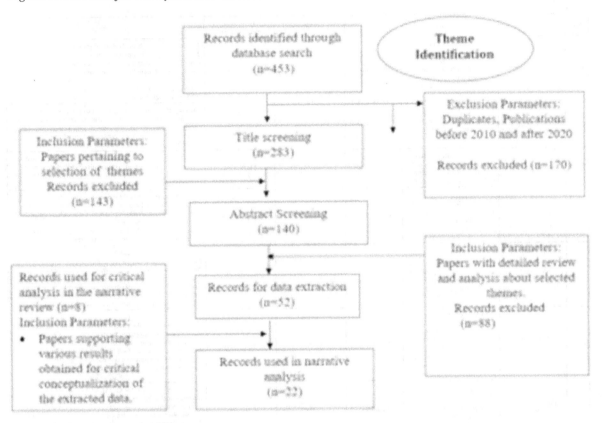

tailored to the environment of the country in which they are based (Dimitratos et al., 2016; Outsios & Kittler, 2017; Walsh & Windsor, 2019). When looking at the Bourdieu's cultural capital that is present in transnational entrepreneurs, it is found that there are challenges in surviving across geographies due to major disparities in the dynamics of the mentorship relationships (Spigel, 2012; Spigel, 2013; Spigel, 2016a; Spigel, 2016b). Entrepreneurs operating on a global scale are obligated to put their technological expertise, professional contacts, and linguistic and cultural fluency to work for the benefit of their businesses (Liu, 2017; Gurau et al., 2020). It is necessary for the growth and development of a company, for transnational entrepreneurs to be able to adjust to the cultural capital setting of the country into which they relocate in order to successfully make relationships and assist in the expansion of the company.

Gender Disparities

One of the rising concerns in entrepreneurship is the minimal number of women. It is established as a dominantly male field, and as the impact of culture is found to be more impact, considering this aspect of the topic is of utmost importance. Karatas-Ozkan and Chell (2013) mentioned the lower number of females in higher education in the science stream leads to their lower number in the field of innovation. Stereotypical beliefs that women-led enterprises would underperform are still prevalent in society (Ahl & Marlow, 2012; Marlow, 2014; Ahl & Nelson, 2015). Yeroz (2019) states three types of habitus for women through Bourdieusian class analysis -women immigrant entrepreneurs, migrant women entre-

Table 1. A literature review on cultural capital and entrepreneurship

No.	Authors	Objective	Research Methodology	Data Collection	Domain of entrepreneurship	Findings
1.	Lutz et al., 2021	To determine the impact of inherited cultural capital on growth expectations, particularly among business owners at the bottom of the pyramid (BoP) in less developed nations.	Qualitative	Secondary	Small Businesses	The entrepreneur's inherited cultural capital, which is anchored in the social background of the entrepreneur, is seen as an essential factor in understanding the success of these business owners. In this case, the bottom of the pyramid scenario is used, especially in less developed countries. Using the data gathered for the study, it was discovered that the entrepreneurs' inherited cultural capital substantially impacted their business objectives.
2.	Jorgensen, 2021	To establish the role of 'change agents' in subverting the company's revenue-focused 'Doxa.'	Qualitative	Secondary	Cultural entrepreneur	The study examined the cultural capital notions proposed by Bourdieu and the alternative forms demonstrated by cultural entrepreneurs. By diverting it into the revenue-focused components of entrepreneurship, the study demonstrated the strong impact caused by change agents available in the process.
3.	Kalu & Dana, 2021	Establish "a deduction on the importance of social and cultural capital for community-wide entrepreneurial outcomes".	Qualitative	Primary	Community entrepreneurship	Communality, trust, social capital, and social network were found to have a substantial impact. Communities can develop innovative ideas as well as consensual partnerships to go forward and for entrepreneurial firms based on the networks they create.
4.	Doanh, 2021	To examine the function of self-efficacy in the entrepreneurship cognitive process among Vietnamese students.	Quantitative	Primary	Entrepreneurship	According to the findings, the subjective norm is seen to considerably impact the intention to start a business out of all the variables evaluated. Examining the moderating influence of self-efficacy, on the other hand, it is discovered that it has a considerable impact on the relationship between the attitude generated toward entrepreneurship and the intention to start a business.
5.	Emre Avci et al., 2020	The purpose of this study was to look at the relationship between teacher self-efficacy and cultural capital levels.	Quantitative & Qualitative	Primary	Entrepreneurship	The study's findings revealed that teachers' self-efficacy levels are adequate, while their cultural capital indicators are moderate. The cultural capital competencies that are engaged are found to have a substantial impact on the teachers' self-efficacy judgments. The instructors' cultural capital competencies have been suggested for enhancement based on features of reading, engagement in cultural activities, and cultural training and education aims.
6.	Markowska & Wiklund, 2020	To develop a process model that explains how changing perceptions of complexity and self-efficacy influence a person's propensity for experimentation (opening out) or modeling (focusing) when learning new skills.	Qualitative	Primary	Entrepreneurship	The findings revealed that entrepreneurship is indeed tied to learning, with the entrepreneurs' process involving timelines, reasons, and other contextual elements. The authors' model demonstrates the impact of self-efficacy and perceived complexity on entrepreneurs' experimentation and modeling process, particularly when they are attempting to have a fresh experience.
7.	Huang & Zhang, 2020	To examine the use of social media as a predictor of students' entrepreneurial ambition was explored, with the role of self-efficacy as a mediating factor.	Quantitative	Primary	Entrepreneurship	The findings revealed that when it comes to assessing entrepreneurial ambitions, self-efficacy mediates the association between entrepreneurial experience and risk inclination. When the demographics of the respondents were taken into account, it was discovered that non-white ethnicities have low self-efficacy in terms of entrepreneurial goals.
8.	Zheng et al., 2020	To investigate the link between proactive personality and social capital using underlying processes (such as internet self-efficacy and online interaction quality), focusing on data collected during the COVID-19 pandemic's peak.	Quantitative	Primary	Entrepreneurship	The study discovered that proactive personalities in the online interaction medium in the education forum during the pandemic could boost social capital intake for both teachers and students. The usage of perceived social support appears to strengthen the mediating influence of the quality of online contact.
9.	Ciuchta & Finch, 2019	To find the relationship between entrepreneurial self-efficacy and entrepreneurial intentions	Quantitative	Primary	Entrepreneurship	The findings implied that social media use has an impact on a student's desire to start a business. The association is also observed to benefit from the mediating role of self-efficacy. The importance of self-efficacy is emphasised throughout the research.
10.	Pillai & Ahamat, 2018	To compare two different entrepreneurial ecosystems in order to identify emergent factors that stimulate and/or stifle the genesis of youth entrepreneurship while identifying similar and divergent entrepreneurial identities and traits among young people from these two sovereign contexts.	Qualitative	Primary	Youth Entrepreneurship	The findings of the study show that when it comes to business expansion, the entrepreneurs' relationships with their family and friends in terms of social-cultural capital are beneficial. Furthermore, for entrepreneurship purposes, relation-based networks are favoured over technology networks and even social media.
11.	Essig, 2017	to examine the conceptual evolution of "arts entrepreneurship" in the United States as opposed to "culture entrepreneurship" in Europe and other parts of the world.	Quantitative	Primary	Cultural entrepreneurship and Arts Entrepreneurship	According to the findings, the notion of cultural entrepreneurship arose as a result of management or leadership studies. It developed as a subset of the above two areas of study in the U.S. higher education system.
12.	Muhammad et al., 2017	To identify obstacles that inhibit rural entrepreneurship in Pakistan, as well as the "cultural, social, economic, and religious traditions and circumstances that discourage entrepreneurship and consequently stifle economic development."	Qualitative	Primary	Rural entrepreneurship	The findings revealed that the low number of entrepreneurs in Pakistan's rural areas is due to the suppressive influence of both social and cultural capital, which is assisted by religious, structural, and other socio-economic forces. According to the authors, both "social and cultural capital require a socio-economic framework in order for entrepreneurship to prosper".

Table 2. List of data extraction review papers for the identified themes

Author	Methodology	Transnational	Gender Disparities	Role of Education/ Skills
Jones (2011)	Qualitative		×	×
Karataş-Özkan & Chell (2015)	Qualitative		×	
Spigel (2012)	Qualitative	×		
Jones (2014)	Qualitative		×	×
Dimitratos et al. (2016)	Qualitative	×		
Liu (2017)	Qualitative	×		
Gurau et al. (2020)	Qualitative	×		×
Brown et al. (2019)	Qualitative	×	×	
Harima et al. (2020)	Qualitative	×		×
Lin & Tao (2012)	Quantitative	×	×	×
Solano (2019)	Qualitative	×		×
Marlow (2014)	Qualitative		×	
Spigel (2013)	Qualitative	×		×
Ahl & Marlow (2012)	Qualitative		×	×
Smaguc (2020)	Qualitative		×	×
Nkongolo-Bakenda & Chrysostome (2020)	Quantitative	×		×
Drori et al. (2010)	Qualitative	×		
Kalin & Oleg (2014)	Qualitative	×		×
De Silva (2015)	Qualitative	×		
Spigel (2016a)	Qualitative	×		×
Spigel (2016b)	Qualitative	×		×
Sklaveniti & Steyaert (2019)	Qualitative		×	×
Walsh & Windsor (2019)	Qualitative	×		×
Huggins & Thompson (2016)	Quantitative	×		×
Nicolopoulou et al. (2016)	Qualitative	×	×	×
Schäfer & Mayer (2019)	Qualitative	×		
Ikeatuwegwu & Dann (2017)	Qualitative			×
Ahl & Nelson (2015)	Qualitative		×	×
Scott et al. (2014)	Qualitative		×	×
Zapała & Zięba	Qualitative		×	×
Yeroz (2019)	Qualitative	×	×	×
Kalfa & Taksa (2013)	Qualitative			×
Gidley et al. (2010)	Qualitative			×
Rowlands (2013	Qualitative			×
Yonni & Manolova (2013)	Quantitative	×	×	×
Schilling & Klamma (2010)	Qualitative			×
Humbert & Drew (2010)	Quantitative		×	
Levie & Hart (2011)	Quantitative		×	×
Tundui (2012)	Quantitative		×	×
Dezalay & Madsen (2012)	Qualitative	×		×
Tegtemeier & Mitra (2015)	Qualitative		×	×
Kakabadse et al. (2015)	Qualitative		×	×
Delmestri & Brumana (2017)	Qualitative	×		×
Soong et al. (2018)	Qualitative	×		×
Outsios & Kittler (2017)	Qualitative		×	×
Santamaria-Alvarez et al. (2018)	Qualitative	×		×
Yu (2018)	Qualitative	×		
Blok et al. (2018)	Qualitative	×		
Anderson & Ronteau (2017)	Qualitative	×		
Jones & Warhuus (2018)	Qualitative		×	×

preneurs and hybrid entrepreneurs. Women are mostly categorised as social entrepreneurs rather than business entrepreneurs because of the societal belief of them being socially committed in the pace of being business-oriented (Levie & Hart, 2011; Tegtemeir & Mitra, 2015). The socio-cultural beliefs surrounding women are too traditional and go way back in time. With the upcoming women entrepreneurs, it is very important to address this issue frequently in order to break the cultural barriers associated with the role of women.

Role of Education/ Skills

As mentioned by researchers, education is a major drawback regarding the difference in the number of male and female entrepreneurs. Having the appropriate level of education or the apt amount of skills (*based on the requirement of the venture*) becomes a crucial part of entrepreneurship. High quality of education is of great importance in terms of globalisation practice as it considers inclusive ideologies (Gidley et al., 2010; Schilling & Klamma, 2010; Tegtemeier & Mitra, 2015). Here it is worth noting that the previous themes correlate to the entrepreneurs' education. The higher education possibilities of women would further lead their way into the field of entrepreneurship, 2hile in the case of transnational entrepreneurs, high-quality education or the skills acquired in their respective countries would help them cope with the transitions better (Lin & Tao, 2012; Yonni & Manolova, 2013; Nicolopoulou et al., 2016; Soong et al., 2017; Yeroz, 2019). A giant step towards achieving Bourdieu's approach to entrepreneurship is thus to avail high-quality education, helping in every aspect of the process and acquiring skills to enhance the scopes better.

CONCLUSION

Future Outlook

The review is an attempt to determine the important factors contributing to the relationship between Bourdieu's Approach and entrepreneurship. Bibliometric analysis has been conducted to further demonstrate the opportunities associated with the research (figure 2).

The bibliometric analysis is conducted in one of the major databases, namely SCOPUS (fig.3). The database identifies and stores research conducted on relevant topics over time. It is seen that for a bibliometric analysis conducted from 2010 to 2020, the number of articles on Bourdieu's cultural capital has been quite consistent. Researchers have put forward an approximate number of articles on the same over some time. However, when research specifically relates to the relationship between Bourdieu's cultural capital and Entrepreneurship, the studies are much lesser. The research area has recently started to gain the attention of scholars and has seen a rise in its number since 2018. This points out the underresearched aspect of the topic, although a high demand for the same seems to exist in the real world. With entrepreneurship gaining its participants, the requirement to look into their social status has increased. The relationship between an entrepreneur and the cultural values of the areas nearby demands an amicable and understandable state. The themes identified in the research highlight some of the most important ones that aptly capture the present situation arising in society based on cultural capital terms about entrepreneurship. The role of gender in entrepreneurship has always been overpowering towards the male section. However, with the increasing empowerment of women worldwide, their stepping into

Figure 2. Bibliometric Analysis in SCOPUS for No. of Articles on Bourdieu's Cultural Capital

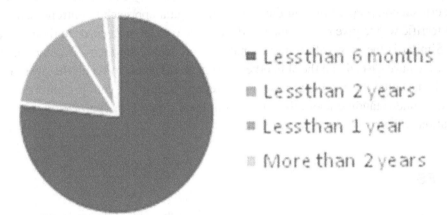

the shoes of an entrepreneur has also seen a rise. The changing norms of genderism in entrepreneurship form an important aspect of tying up the relationship between the two theories. The general culture in a society, an aspect of Bourdieu's cultural capital, acts as a relevant part of the theme.

Similarly, with technological advancement, the entire world has become home to entrepreneurs. Cross-national modes of doing business are constantly increasing, and with that comes the issue of transnational entrepreneurship and its roles in the socio-cultural aspects of society. Entrepreneurs need to respect the culture of the region they attempt to expand their business. This is important in setting up the relationship between Bourdieu's cultural capital approach and entrepreneurship. Education and the acquisition of marketable skills are the common threads that support gender equality and multinational

Figure 3. Bibliometric Analysis in SCOPUS for No. of Articles on Bourdieu's Cultural Capital & Entrepreneurship

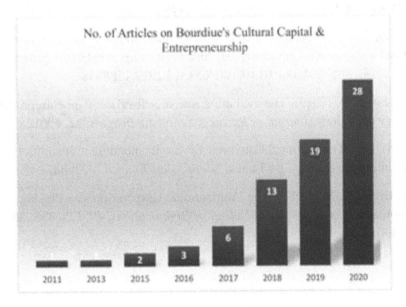

enterprise. It has been demonstrated via this analysis, as stated by Purwanto (2016), that education and skills are crucial components of Bourdieu's cultural capital approach to entrepreneurs. Getting an education is a terrific way to give women more independence, and it often leads to their success as business owners. Similar is the case with transnational entrepreneurs, and their efficiency increases with the education they have earned and the skills they have learnt. Hence, to tie up the overall relationship between Bourdieu's cultural capital approach and entrepreneurship, the entrepreneurs must have a sufficient amount of understanding about the situation at hand through the knowledge they have gained through education and entrepreneurship experience.

REFERENCES

Ahl, H., & Marlow, S. (2012). Exploring the dynamics of gender, feminism, and entrepreneurship: Advancing debate to escape a dead end? *Organisation*, *19*(5), 543–562. doi:10.1177/1350508412448695

Ahl, H., & Nelson, T. (2015). How policy positions women entrepreneurs: A comparative analysis of state discourse in Sweden and the United States. *Journal of Business Venturing*, *30*(2), 273–291. doi:10.1016/j.jbusvent.2014.08.002

Anderson, A., & Ronteau, S. (2017). Towards an entrepreneurial theory of practice; emerging ideas for emerging economies. *Journal of Entrepreneurship in Emerging Economies*, *9*(2), 110–120. doi:10.1108/JEEE-12-2016-0054

Blok, A., Lindstrøm, M. D., Meilvang, M. L., & Pedersen, I. K. (2018). Trans-local professional projects: Re-scaling the linked ecology of expert jurisdictions. *Journal of Professions and Organization*, *5*(2), 106–122. doi:10.1093/jpo/joy003

Bourdieu, P. (1993). *The Field of Cultural Production*. Columbia University Press.

Bourdieu, P., & Passeron, J. P. (1977). *Reproduction in Education, Society and Culture*. Sage.

Bourdieu, P., & Wacquant, L. (1992). *An invitation to reflexive sociology*. University of Chicago Press.

Brown, R., Mawson, S., Lee, N., & Peterson, L. (2019). Start-up factories, transnational entrepreneurs and entrepreneurial ecosystems: Unpacking the lure of start-up accelerator programmes. *European Planning Studies*, *27*(5), 885–904. doi:10.1080/09654313.2019.1588858

Ciuchta, M. P., & Finch, D. (2019). The mediating role of self-efficacy on entrepreneurial intentions: Exploring boundary conditions. *Journal of Business Venturing Insights*, *11*, e00128.

De Silva, R. (2015). How Transnational Entrepreneurs are Responding to Institutional Voids: A Study of Transnational Entrepreneurs from Sri Lanka. *South Asian Journal of Management*, *22*(2), 61–80.

Delmestri, G., & Brumana, M. (2017). The Multinational Corporation as a Playing Field of Power: A Bourdieusian Approach. *Research in the Sociology of Organizations*, *49*, 325–353. doi:10.1108/S0733-558X20160000049011

Dezalay, Y., & Madsen, M. R. (2012). The Force of Law and Lawyers: Pierre Bourdieu and the Reflexive Sociology of Law. *Annual Review of Law and Social Science*, *8*(1), 433–452. doi:10.1146/annurev-lawsocsci-102811-173817

Dimitratos, P., Buck, T., Fletcher, M., & Li, N. (2016). The motivation of international entrepreneurship: The case of Chinese transnational entrepreneurs. *International Business Review*, *25*(5), 1103–1113. doi:10.1016/j.ibusrev.2016.01.012

Doanh, D. C. (2021). The moderating role of self-efficacy on the cognitive process of entrepreneurship: An empirical study in Vietnam. Journal of Entrepreneurship. *Management and Innovation*, *17*(1), 147–174.

Drori, I., Honig, B., & Ginsberg, A. (2010). *Transnational and Immigrant Entrepreneurship in a Globalised World* (B. Honig, I. Drori, & B. Carmichael, Eds.). University of Toronto Press.

Drori, I., Honig, B., & Wright, M. (2009). Transnational Entrepreneurship: An Emergent Field of Study. *Entrepreneurship Theory and Practice*, *33*(5), 1001–1022. doi:10.1111/j.1540-6520.2009.00332.x

Emre Avci, Y., Tösten, R., & Sahin, Ç. Ç. (2020). Examining the Relationship between Cultural Capital and Self-Efficacy: A Mixed Design Study on Teachers. *Athens Journal of Education*, *7*(2), 169–192.

Eroglu, O., & Picak, M. (2011). Entrepreneurship, National Culture and Turkey. *International Journal of Business and Social Science*, *2*(16).

Essig, L. (2017). Same or different? The "cultural entrepreneurship" and "arts entrepreneurship" constructs in European and US higher education. *Cultural Trends*, *26*(2), 125–137.

Garnham, N., & Williams, R. (1980). Pierre Bourdieu and the sociology of culture: An introduction. *Media Culture & Society*, *2*(3), 209–223. doi:10.1177/016344378000200302

Gidley, J., Hampson, G., Wheeler, L., & Bereded-Samuel, E. (2010). From Access to Success: An Integrated Approach to Quality Higher Education Informed by Social Inclusion Theory and Practice. *Higher Education Policy*, *23*(1), 123–147. doi:10.1057/hep.2009.24

Gurău, C., Dana, L.-P., & Katz-Volovelsky, E. (2020). Spanning transnational boundaries in industrial markets: A study of Israeli entrepreneurs in China. *Industrial Marketing Management*, *89*, 389–401. doi:10.1016/j.indmarman.2020.01.008

Harima, A., Harima, J., & Freiling, J. (2020). The injection of resources by transnational entrepreneurs: Towards a model of the early evolution of an entrepreneurial ecosystem. *Entrepreneurship and Regional Development*, 1–28.

Hisrich, R. D. (1990). *Entrepreneurship/intrapreneurship, 45*(2) 209. American Psychological Association.

Huang, Y., & Zhang, J. (2020). Social media use and entrepreneurial intention: The mediating role of self-efficacy. *Social Behavior and Personality*, *48*(11), 1–8.

Huggins, R., & Thompson, P. (2016). Socio-Spatial Culture and Entrepreneurship: Some Theoretical and Empirical Observations. *Economic Geography*, *92*(3), 269–300. doi:10.1080/00130095.2016.1146075

Humbert, L. A., & Drew, E. (2010). Gender, entrepreneurship and motivational factors in an Irish context. *International Journal of Gender and Entrepreneurship*, *2*(2), 173–196. doi:10.1108/17566261011051026

Ikeatuwegwu, C., & Dann, Z. (2017). *Bourdieu's Sociology: A Structured Approach for Entrepreneurship Studies.* ECRM 2017 16th European Conference on Research Methods in Business and Management. Dublin, Ireland.

Jones, S. (2014). Gendered discourses of entrepreneurship in UK higher education: The fictive entrepreneur and the fictive student. *International Small Business Journal, 32*(3), 237–258. doi:10.1177/0266242612453933

Jones, S., & Warhuus, J. P. (2018). This class is not for you: An investigation of gendered subject construction in entrepreneurship course descriptions. *Journal of Small Business and Enterprise Development, 25*(2), 182–200. doi:10.1108/JSBED-07-2017-0220

Jones, S. A. (2011). *The gendering of entrepreneurship in higher education: a Bourdieuian approach.* Leeds Metropolitan University.

Jorgensen, B. (2021). The "cultural entrepreneurship" of independent podcast production in Australia. *Journal of Radio & Audio Media, 28*(1), 144–161.

Kakabadse, N. K., Figueira, C., Nicolopoulou, K., Hong Yang, J., Kakabadse, A. P., & Özbilgin, M. F. (2015). Gender Diversity and Board Performance: Women's Experiences and Perspectives. *Human Resource Management, 54*(2), 265–281. doi:10.1002/hrm.21694

Kalfa, S., & Taksa, L. (2013). Cultural capital in business higher education: Reconsidering the graduate attributes movement and the focus on employability. *Studies in Higher Education, 40*(4), 580–595. doi:10.1080/03075079.2013.842210

Kalin, R., & Oleg, S. (2014). *Transnational Entrepreneurs: Implications of the dual background on opportunity recognition.* LUND University Libraries. https://lup.lub.lu.se/student-papers/record/4461730

Kalu, E. U., & Dana, L. P. (2021). Socio-cultural web and environmentally-driven community entrepreneurship: a portrayal of Abia Ohafia community in South-Eastern Nigeria. *Journal of Enterprising Communities: People and Places in the Global Economy.*

Karataş-Özkan, M., & Chell, E. (2013). Gender Inequalities in Academic Innovation and Enterprise: A Bourdieuian Analysis. *British Journal of Management, 26*(1), 109–125. doi:10.1111/1467-8551.12020

Levie, J., & Hart, M. (2011). Business and social entrepreneurs in the UK: Gender, context and commitment. *International Journal of Gender and Entrepreneurship, 3*(3), 200–217. doi:10.1108/17566261111169304

Lin, X., & Tao, S. (2012). Transnational entrepreneurs: Characteristics, drivers, and success factors. *Journal of International Entrepreneurship, 10*(1), 50–69. doi:10.100710843-011-0082-1

Liu, Y. (2017). Born global firms' growth and collaborative entry mode: The role of transnational entrepreneurs. *International Marketing Review, 34*(1), 46–67. doi:10.1108/IMR-05-2015-0130

Lutz, C., Noseleit, F., & Tundui, H. (2021). Inherited cultural capital and growth aspirations in Tanzanian business at the bottom of the pyramid. *Journal of the International Council for Small Business, 2*(3), 223–249.

Markowska, M., & Wiklund, J. (2020). Entrepreneurial learning under uncertainty: Exploring the role of self-efficacy and perceived complexity. *Entrepreneurship and Regional Development, 32*(7-8), 606–628.

Marlow, S. (2014). Exploring future research agendas in the field of gender and entrepreneurship. *International Journal of Gender and Entrepreneurship, 6*(2), 102–120. doi:10.1108/IJGE-01-2013-0003

McGrath, R. G., MacMillan, I. C., Yang, E. A., & Tsai, W. (1992). Does Culture Endure, or is it Malleable? Issues for Entrepreneurial Economic Development. *Journal of Business Venturing, 7,* 115–135. doi:10.1016/0883-9026(92)90008-F

Muhammad, N., McElwee, G., & Dana, L. P. (2017). Barriers to the development and progress of entrepreneurship in rural Pakistan. *International Journal of Entrepreneurial Behaviour & Research, 23*(2), 279–295.

Nicolopoulou, K., Kakabadse, N. K., Nikolopoulos, K. P., Alcaraz, J. M., & Sakellariou, K. (2016). Cosmopolitanism and transnational elite entrepreneurial practices: Manifesting the cosmopolitan disposition in a cosmopolitan city. *Society and Business Review, 11*(3), 257–275. doi:10.1108/SBR-01-2016-0001

Nkongolo-Bakenda, J.-M., & Chrysostome, E. V. (2020). Exploring the organising and strategic factors of diasporic, transnational entrepreneurs in Canada: An empirical study. *Journal of International Entrepreneurship, 18*(3), 336–372. doi:10.100710843-020-00268-2

Onuoha, G. (2007). Entrepreneurship. *AIST International Journal, 10,* 20–32.

Outsios, G., & Kittler, M. (2017). The mindset of UK environmental entrepreneurs: A habitus perspective. *International Small Business Journal: Researching Entrepreneurship, 36*(3), 285–306. doi:10.1177/0266242617739343

Pillai, T. R., & Ahamat, A. (2018). Social-cultural capital in youth entrepreneurship ecosystem: Southeast Asia. *Journal of Enterprising Communities: People and Places in the Global Economy.*

Purwanto, A. (2016). Cultural capital and business success among entrepreneurs. *Journal of Economics, Business, and Accountancy Ventura, 19*(2), 227–236. doi:10.14414/jebav.v19i2.583

Rowlands, J. (2013). Academic boards: Less intellectual and more academic capital in higher education governance? *Studies in Higher Education, 38*(9), 1274–1289. doi:10.1080/03075079.2011.619655

Santamaria-Alvarez, S. M., Muñoz-Castro, D. C., Sarmiento-González, M. A., & Marín-Zapata, S. I. (2018). Fragmented networks and transnational entrepreneurship: Building strategies to prosper in challenging surroundings. *Journal of International Entrepreneurship, 16*(2), 244–275. doi:10.100710843-017-0215-2

Schäfer, S., & Mayer, H. (2019). Entrepreneurial ecosystems: Founding figures and research frontiers in economic geography. *Zeitschrift für Wirtschaftsgeographie, 63*(2-4), 55–63. doi:10.1515/zfw-2019-0008

Schilling, J., & Klamma, R. (2010). The difficult bridge between university and industry: A case study in computer science teaching. *Assessment & Evaluation in Higher Education, 35*(4), 367–380. doi:10.1080/02602930902795893

Schumpeter, J. A. (1965). Economic Theory and Entrepreneurial History. In H. G. Aitken (Ed.), *Explorations in enterprise*. Harvard University Press.

Scott, J. M., Harrison, R. T., Hussain, J., & Millman, C. (2014). The role of guanxi networks in the performance of women-led firms in China. *International Journal of Gender and Entrepreneurship*.

Sklaveniti, C., & Steyaert, C. (2019). Reflecting with Pierre Bourdieu: Towards a reflexive outlook for practice-based studies of entrepreneurship. *Entrepreneurship and Regional Development*, 1–21. doi:10.1080/08985626.2019.1641976

Smaguc, T. (2020). *Gender Stereotypes In Entrepreneurship Process: Evidence From The Croatian Ict Industry*. 59th International Scientific Conference on Economic and Social Development – Online Conference.

Solano, G. (2019). The mixed embeddedness of transnational migrant entrepreneurs: Moroccans in Amsterdam and Milan. *Journal of Ethnic and Migration Studies*, 1–19.

Soong, H., Stahl, G., & Shan, H. (2017). Transnational mobility through education: A Bourdieusian insight on life as middle transnationals in Australia and Canada. *Globalisation, Societies and Education*, *16*(2), 241–253. doi:10.1080/14767724.2017.1396886

Spigel, B. (2012). *Cultural contexts and entrepreneurial intentions. Entrepreneurship Research Conference*. Texas. United States.

Spigel, B. (2013). Bourdieuian approaches to the geography of entrepreneurial cultures. *Entrepreneurship and Regional Development*, *25*(9-10), 804–818. doi:10.1080/08985626.2013.862974

Spigel, B. (2016a). Bourdieu, culture, and the economic geography of practice: Entrepreneurial mentorship in Ottawa and Waterloo, Canada. *Journal of Economic Geography*, *19*, lbw019. doi:10.1093/jeg/lbw019

Spigel, B. (2016b). Developing and governing entrepreneurial ecosystems: The structure of entrepreneurial support programs in Edinburgh, Scotland. *International Journal of Innovative Research and Development*, *7*(2), 141. doi:10.1504/IJIRD.2016.077889

Sullivan, A. (2002). Bourdieu and Education: How Useful is Boourdieu "s Theory for Researchers? *The Netherlands Journal of Social Sciences*, *38*(2), 144–166.

Tegtmeier, S., & Mitra, J. (2015). Gender perspectives on university education and entrepreneurship: A conceptual overview. *International Journal of Gender and Entrepreneurship*, *7*(3), 254–271. doi:10.1108/IJGE-05-2015-0016

Tundui, H. P. (2012). *Gender and Small Business Growth in Tanzania: The Role of Habitus*. University of Groningen.

Walsh, J., & Winsor, B. (2019). Socio-cultural barriers to developing a regional entrepreneurial ecosystem. *Journal of Enterprising Communities: People and Places in the Global Economy*, *13*(3), 263–282. doi:10.1108/JEC-11-2018-0088

Webster, J., & Watson, R. (2002). Analysing the Past to Prepare for the Future: Writing a Literature Review. *MIS Quarterly, 26*(2), Xiii-Xxiii.

Yeröz, H. (2019). Manifestations of social class and agency in cultural capital development processes: An empirical study of Turkish migrant women entrepreneurs in Sweden. *International Journal of Entrepreneurial Behaviour & Research, 25*(5), 900–918. doi:10.1108/IJEBR-03-2018-0146

Yonni, R.B., & Manolova, T.S. (2013). Institutional context for entrepreneurship in emerging economies: a nine-country comparison of university students' perceptions. *Modern competition, 6* (42), 118-138.

Yu, C. (2018). *Exploring immigrant and transnational entrepreneurship in the Australia and China context.* University of Adelaide, Entrepreneurship, Commercialisation and Innovation Centre.

Zapała, A. & Zięba, K. (2014). Gendered entrepreneurship and its impact on firm innovativeness – a literature review. Przedsiębiorstwo we współczesnej gospodarce – teoria i praktyka [Enterprise in Modern economy- theory and practice], *4,* 5-12.

Zheng, F., Khan, N. A., & Hussain, S. (2020). The COVID 19 pandemic and digital higher education: Exploring the impact of proactive personality on social capital through internet self-efficacy and online interaction quality. *Children and Youth Services Review, 119*, 105694.

Chapter 20
Underprivileged Children and COVID-19:
Visamo Kids Case Studies in Ahmedabad Shelter

Sudeshna Jayant Bhojia
Visamo Kids Foundation, India

ABSTRACT

The pandemic has disrupted lives and is continuing to affect the right to education across the world; a shelter home housing underprivileged kids in the state of Gujarat is no exception. The crisis that hit the world unannounced, and led to hurried closing down of the educational institutions for indefinite periods. After a hiatus, a new mode of imparting education was sought to be adapted –the online mode. And the inequalities in access to education were striking. With online education becoming an only way to maintain continuity, the fragility of the public education system and institutions that were under funded became vivid. The pressure on the parents, educators, and administrators increased manifold. A tiny section of students at a shelter home in Ahmedabad—the Visamo Kids Foundation—endeavoring to access quality education in the finest English medium schools under RTE, were marginalized and deprived of their right to access to quality education.

INTRODUCTION

"I missed my friends a lot. Since childhood, we have been together and suddenly got separated for almost two years. I can live without parents but not without my friends now." A young Jiya who dreams of becoming a physiotherapist describes her feelings sitting in her room at Visamo Kids Foundation. She adds, "We are having a lot of fun as we are together after almost two years." India has been one of the hardest hit nations by the Covid-19 pandemic. The total recorded cases have crossed 43 million in the United States. India also has recorded the highest number of deaths caused due to Covid19, which has now crossed 520,000 (*Coronavirus (COVID-19) Cases*, n.d.). While children have been observed

DOI: 10.4018/978-1-6684-6682-7.ch020

to have lesser health risks, the pandemic seriously impacts their well-being. The harmful effect is expected to be most damaging for children in the poorest countries, neighborhoods, and those in already disadvantaged or vulnerable situations (UNSDP). There are several childcare homes taking care of underprivileged children across the length and breadth of India. This study revolves around the personal experiences shared by the children studying in various top-notch schools of Ahmedabad facilitated by an NGO, Visamo Kids Foundation.

BACKGROUND

During the lockdown in 2020, the schools closed abruptly, and all the children were at the shelter home. Maintaining social distancing as per the norms was becoming a challenge. The non-residential staff found it difficult to reach the workplace owing to the imposition of a curfew. The institution was closed down, and kids were indefinitely sent back to their homes. From mid-April onwards, one of our partnering schools, DPS, Bopal, started their online classes, and soon enough, the other schools started virtual classrooms. We were faced with the challenge of providing access to online education to our students, who are now in remote villages in Gujarat. With the support of local NGOs, family members of the children, community members, Panchayats, and youth groups, somehow, access was ensured, though not for all.

The students of VKF are enrolled across 20+ schools under four boards (ICSE, CBSE, GSEB, and IB). Every school has a different pedagogy with diversity in the online platforms used. Access to a device, access to time for the use of the device for dedicated use for online education, access to a strong internet service, access to privacy, safety, access to an environment that is conducive to studies, access to warm meals and sanitation and many more factors started to impact the education of these kids. Gradually, as and when the situation started improving and depending on the case-to-case assessment of situational factors, feedback provided by teachers at school and of VKF, and recommendations made by the counselor, we started bringing the students back to the shelter home from September 2020 onwards. By January 2021, 14 kids were back at home. The maximum number of students was called back by mid-2021; after Diwali in 2021, 90% were on campus. Finally, in 2022, when the new session was to start, all the students were on campus. During their stay at their homes, the students experienced myriad life situations, and we have captured select stories by documenting 12 case studies. The names have been changed to protect their identities.

Context

Coronavirus disease 2019 (COVID-19) is a contagious disease caused by a virus, the severe acute respiratory syndrome coronavirus 2 (SARS-CoV-2) (*COVID 19,* 2022). The Covid-19 disease has been registered globally since its onset in Wuhan, China, in December 2019. The mass spread of this disease led to what came to be known as the Covid-19 pandemic. The world has changed post-pandemic compared to before the advent of this disease. Nearly half of the world's 3.3 billion global workforce risk losing their livelihoods (*Impact of COVID-19 on people's livelihoods, their health and our food systems,* 2020). The loss of an unprecedented number of human lives and the trauma following those losses has been enormous. This report intends to introduce the readers to the hardships faced, the social and mental impact of the pandemic, and the preference and high spirits of underprivileged children living in childcare homes. The childcare home in focus for this study is Visamo Kids Foundation, Ahmedabad. Visamo Kids Foundation has created a facility that can house 100+ kids with the mission to transform the lives of less privileged yet high-potential kids through formal K-12 education in English (from classes I to XII) in partnership with the finest schools under CBSE, ICSE, and State Board (*Visamo kids' foundation,* 2020).

CASE STUDIES

Case Study 1

Name of the child: Nayan Vasava
Father's name: Mansinghbhai Vasava, Illiterate
Mother's name: Muktiben, Illiterate
Year of joining VKF- 2012 Village- Gangapur, Tapi District
Class- XI- Commerce, DPS, Bopal, Ahmedabad

Focus is My Middle Name

I spotted Nayan for the first time when he was participating in an inter-school Carom competition. Quiet, thin in appearance, and bland, Nayan's presence was not registered by his opponents on the board till his skills made him the tournament winner. I also woke up to his special skills, apart from the facts that he was good at drawing and had the condition of dysgraphia (a learning disability of written expression that affects the ability to write, primarily handwriting, but also coherence). Nayan's father suffered from kidney failure and expired a decade ago. His mother had deserted the kids and eloped with someone. Nayan and his siblings (six sisters and one younger brother) were left with each other. The eldest sister did not marry, and their uncle supported the family.

Nayan's Lockdown Story

During the lockdown, he and his foi (aunt) engaged in several activities to raise money to support the family. They plucked minor forest produce- like tendu patta, mahua, and anwla and sold them. They worked in agricultural fields, and Nayan herded the cattle. One of his sisters suffered from sickle cell anaemia had a paralytic attack during the pandemic, and was treated in a Surat-based hospital. She died last year. The money raised was used partly to support the cost of treatment and partly to buy a secondhand cell phone, with which he attended online classes at his school. He completed Class X in 2022 and has secured 76% marks.

***

Case Study 2

Name of the child: Vali Bhati
Father's name: Dhanabhai Kanabhai, Illiterate
Mother's name: Jenniben, Illiterate
Year of joining VKF- 2013

Residence- Street child- The family lives under a flyover near the IIM (A)
Class- X- Satyamev Jayate International School, Bopal, Ahmedabad

Resilience is My Middle Name

Vali is a child from the streets. The family lives under the flyover opposite the Blind People's Association, Ahmedabad. Her parents work as caretakers in the Hanuman mandir near IIM(A) crossroads. Her father sells coconut, flowers, and garlands. She has five brothers and one sister. All her siblings are either physically handicapped or mentally retarded. Vali has a hearing impairment in her right ear. She is excellent at painting and sports.

Vali's Lockdown Story

During the lockdown, she returned to the streets in Ahmedabad and spent time taking care of her younger siblings. She helped her mother in washing the clothes of her siblings. Her father goes to pluck the flowers (Aakda na Phool- for offering to Lord Hanuman), and she learned to make garlands out of them. She also kept the count while selling the garlands to the temple visitors. Vali is the only child without any deformities. During this stay at home, she learned to cook. She loved making chutney of tomatoes, khichdi, and jowar rotors (thick Indian pieces of bread made of jowar- sorghum) was the first time she bonded closely with her father and siblings. Her parents were amazed to see how Vali could communicate with her siblings- as their verbal expressions are different. Her elder sister is mentally retarded and quarreled with her, but once Vali came to VKF, she missed her and called her. Vali's father had collected bricks strewn here and there and made a makeshift home. During Dashama (a deity popularly worshipped in Gujarat during the Sravan maas) festival, she decorated the place of worship and painted the house's walls. She also continued her online studies while taking care of household work. Visamo collected cell phones in donations and distributed them to those who needed them. Within a few months, we brought back the child to the home, as it was becoming difficult for Vali to focus on his studies – she was in Class IX that year. She was associated with a mentor at Visamo and a volunteer to help her in Math.

***

Case Study 3

Name of the child: Anjali Dantani
Father's name: Pravinbhai, III Pass
Mother's name: Bhavnaben Pravinbhai, Illiterate
Year of joining VKF- 2016
Residence- Streets of Ahmedabad, Navrangpura area
Class- VI, Anand Niketan School, Shilaj, Ahmedabad

Steel is Her Middle Name

Anjali, a six-year-old girl found begging in Ahmedabad streets, was brought to Visamo Kids in 2016. Her father is a house painter, and her mother is a street-based sex worker. There are five sisters. Anjali and her sisters were into begging while one of the elder sisters managed the siblings and the household work. Both parents are alcoholics. Her eldest sister was later married off and forced into sexual relationships with multiple partners. With the support and intervention of a local NGO (Slum Shine), Anjali's parents were convinced to send Anjali to Visamo Kids and continue her studies. She is currently in Class VI, in Anand Niketan School- Shilaj. When Anjali stepped into the institution to appear for the entrance test, she was so afraid of the formal setup that she started crying. So much so that she could not take the paper. The partnering NGO (Slum Shine) requested us to allow the kid to reappear in the test after a few days. The NGO provided roadside nonformal education classes to the children on the streets. This time, the NGO collaborated with a local school, took the kids inside the campus, and started providing classes in a formal setup. After a few days, they brought Anjali back to VKF, and she reappeared for the exam, was cleared with a good score, and was shortlisted for admission. During the final interview, her parents had come in a drunken state and created an uproar on the campus, threatening us with dire consequences if we retained the child. They were somehow managed and sent home. Anjali continued her stay at VKF. Having led six years on the streets, she hated the rules and strict norms of institutional living. She shouted, Howled, wailed, hurled abuses, and hit anyone trying to come near her. It took a few days for her to settle down. And after the summer / Diwali break was so difficult to bring her back to the campus. She pelted stones at our team members and needed to be forcefully lifted and put into the van. At times, there would be a crowd assembled of curious onlookers, trying to oppose our team members from forcibly taking away the child- as Anjali would make such a scene- which generated sympathy from the bystanders.

Anjali's Lockdown Story

This time, when the duration of her stay extended from one month to three when she was unable to join the school, when she was not getting a safe and clean home to stay in, regular hot meals, a warm bed, and a place to bathe and defecate, she asked her father to contact VKF and request to take her back.

***

Case Study 4

Name of the child: Janvi Varsakiya
Father's name: Devubhai SamjibhaiVasava, Illiterate
Mother's name: Dipuben Devubhai, Illiterate
Year of joining VKF- 2012 Village- Gangapur, Tapi District
Class- XI- Commerce, DPS, Bopal, Ahmedabad

I am Tough as a Rock, but I have a Soft Heart Inside

Janvi has two sisters and one brother. She had a habit of stealing things from school, from fellow mates at VKf, and even had stolen money from one of the international volunteers at the institute. Sharp, intelligent, and quiet in her ways, she regularly saw the counselor to get help to overcome her habits. Her mother is the sole earning member is the family. Her father is an alcoholic and stays in police custody for most of the year due to petty crimes. He would come home and impregnate his wife whenever he was out of lockup. Janvi's mother has applied for divorce, and the process is underway.

Janvi's Lockdown Story

When we asked Janvi about life at home during the pandemic, she was so overwhelmed with her emotions that she could not speak up, so she wrote down her experience on a paper and handed it over. "My family struggled a lot during the pandemic. Before the lockdown, my mother used to wake up every day before sunrise to make 'far batata' (a local cuisine- street food) –and later, go to the beaches of Dwarka (a popular pilgrim place in Gujarat) to sell them. During the pandemic, this business came to a standstill. She continued to make the food and sell it in the neighborhood, but her earnings were severely impacted. To supplement the income, she started sweeping the streets and was not ashamed to do so. Under the sun in the afternoons, my heart bled to see her working so hard to feed us. My brother, who was just ten years old, started working in a hotel to bring home money. I started taking private tuition alongside doing all household work to support my family. I have stayed away from home since a very early age. Life at Visamo is protected and very sheltered. These two years of Covid made me experience my family's daily difficulties. I learned how hard my mother works to ensure that I get a good education. My mother had back pain and had to undergo an operation. But she never told me this, fearing that this would affect my stay at Visamo and distract me from my studies. Due to the pandemic, I learned how tough life can be and how privileged I am.

***

Case Study 5

Name of the child: Preshita Parmar
Father's name: Vinod Kumar,
B.A Pass;
Mother's name: late Jyotiben Vinodkumar, VII Pass
Year of joining VKF- 2009
Residence- Pandad, Khambhat, Anand
Completed Class XII- Humanities from Anand Niketan, Satelite.
Currently studying Hotel Management (First year) at IHM – Delhi- Pusa Road.

Conquering Inner Demons: That's how I Meet Life

The mother had committed suicide while she was 11 years old - She was staying at Visamo Kids when the mishap occurred. Her father worked as a caretaker in a hostel run by the Catholic church in Dakor in the Kheda district.

Preshita's Lockdown Story

When the lockdown struck, initially, it was "I never got to spend time with my father. We cooked, cleaned the home, washed clothes, and cleaned the home. I also started online classes as I had access to his phone". But after a few months, as her father had to leave home to rejoin his work at the hostel in Dakor, she was left alone. "The home is very old and due to lack of maintenance- as no one stays here, there are ants all over, the walls are peeling off, and I felt very scared to stay here alone. I felt as if my deceased mother's ghost would appear from nowhere. I learned to do all household chores by myself, which kept my mind off the fear of staying alone. I prayed for Visamo Kids to re-open and call me back. And finally, after nine months of self-quarantine is my home, I got to get back 'home.' Very few friends were called back, but I felt so relieved. I plunged into my preparation for the JEE for hostel and hospitality management and alongside preparing for boards (XII)". Preshita has been admitted to the topmost hotel management institute, IHM, Pusa, after securing 1738 AIR (SC category) in JEE -- IHM. Preshita will reach Delhi on the 18th of August to complete the admission formalities and join the IHM. "During the pandemic, when I was alone in my home, I was petrified and depressed by the loneliness. The fear was, however, not real. It was like a demon in my head. Soon, I learned to cope with that by looking into the eyes of fear. Now I will be staying in the capital city of India all by myself. But I am very confident. I am dealing with my fear of the unknown very constructively. I have started working with an entrepreneur in Ahmedabad as a volunteer. Through my work, I am learning new skills, administration, people handling, data entry, record keeping, computer handling, etc. I am getting comfortable with speaking with strangers and responding to their queries. Pusa- I am getting ready to brave you!"

***

Case Study 6

Name of the child: Rajsi Chavda
Father's name: Arjunbhai Virambhai, Illiterate
Mother's name: Jeeniben Arjunbhai, Illiterate
Year of joining VKF- 2012
Village- Mekhdi, Junagadh District
Class- XI- Commerce, DPS, Bopal, Ahmedabad

My Identity is my Heritage: Rajsi's Lockdown Story

"There is some problem in the child's family," said the counselor from Red Bricks School during a special online meeting we were summoned to attend with the class teacher and counselor. "Rajsi does not put on his video and audio. Once when the audio was on- as he was responding to my question, I heard the adults speaking at high volume- as if a conflict was going on. I kept probing Rajsi to share anything affecting him at home, but he is withdrawing. Please look into the matter urgently" We had another video call with Rajsi and asked him about the same. And what he told us was something we never imagined. Rajsi: "Ma'm, the general tone of speaking is like that only- very high- my parents were not quarreling- they were discussing something important." VKF-"Yes, but why don't you open the video?" Rajsi: "Ma'm, I don't want my classmates to see the poor condition of my house. They see me as a Visamokid. They don't know my real background". VKF: "Are you ashamed of your home and parents' background, Rajsi?" Rajsi: "No, Ma'm. I take pride in being their son. But there is no need to share your background unless needed. Not everyone will appreciate and understand. Also, whenever I opened my phone to connect with online classes, my cousins and other kids in the neighborhood would huddle to see curiously, peek into the class, and demand me to point out my teacher and my classmates. They are simply curious. But if I open the video, it may distract the whole class". Identity building-Children take pride in telling that they are Visamokids. The alumni also take pride in sharing how tough life is for their parents and siblings at home. They know that they are no longer 'underprivileged.' They are far more privileged than those left behind at home in their villages. At a very early age, the kids of VKF shape their identities.

***

Case Study 7

Name of the child: Vikas and Suresh Damore
Father's name: Jamubhai & Alambhai Gulabhai, Illiterate
Mother's name: Lalliben and Motliben - Illiterate,
Joining VKF- 2016
Village- Junapani, Dahod District Class- VII- DPS, Bopal, Ahmedabad

Born Free

The selection process was going on. The panelists of the final interview, with the members of the interview panel, asked for the next candidate to be sent in. And in came a group of five adults and 13 children. Before the panelists could express their amazement and confusion, they sat on the floor. We requested the shortlisted children and parents to sit in the chair and meet the panelists. With great effort and hesitation, a selected few came forward. *Panelists:* So many? We asked for only one child and the parents. *VKF:* This is the family of one child only, Ma'm. The father has two wives, and together, they have 12 kids. Both the wives have come. And they have requested one child from each wife to be provided with admission- else no one will study. (Per policy, we do not give admission to more than one child from one family. Only ten kids are taken each year at home after an admission test, so the services should not be concentrated on a single family). Looking at the condition of the family members, the panelists discussed among themselves, appraised the situation, and made an exception to the rule. The families are

Vikas and Suresh's Lockdown Story

The family is from the tribal belt of the Dahod district in Gujarat. During the lockdown, with the vulnerability increasing due to the shrinking livelihoods in the villages, one night, the animal stock was stolen from this family's shed. This led to a huge fight between the father and other male members of this family with the suspected family, and in the conflict, a member of the suspected family died. Following this, the family had to flee the village and remain underground till the *khap panch* took matters into their hand and decided to a fine (monetary settlement of 5 L to be made by this family to the family of the deceased). The family took loans from private moneylenders and paid the amount within the stipulated time. During this period of hiding, the phones were switched off and sim cards removed/destroyed, so their hideouts were not tracked. The children could not attend online classes. The tutors (part-time hired personnel at the shelter home) could not connect with them to support them in 'After school studies.' Finally, after the settlement, the family returned to their house, and 'schooling' started. We provided online counseling to the children to help them overcome the trauma they faced during uncertainty and fear. And after a few more months, they were brought back to the campus.

***

Case Study 8

Name of the child: Tejasvi Vala
Father's name: Jayeshbhai, B.Com
Mother's name: Anitaben, M.A, B.Ed.
Year of joining VKF- 2014
Residence- Ajak, Junagadh District
Class- IX- Redbricks school, Ahmedabad

With a Storm in My Heart, I Walk On

Tejasvi is a serious and studious child, with her mother working as a gruhmata (housemother) at the VKF. It is difficult for a child to stay in a 'home' where her mother may not be the 'assigned' gruhmata. The boundaries overlap- that professional and personal spaces intersect often. Within a few years, the mother, a survivor of domestic violence who divorced her oppressive partner before joining VKF, re-signed from her job as a gruhmata from the VKf. She was ambitious and had completed her MA while working as a gruhmata. Now, she wanted to do B.Ed and appear for government jobs. She tried her luck but did not get a job of her choice. She was staying with her parents and brother's family in their village, and soon, she felt suffocated, unwanted, and like a burden in the household. She expressed her desire for remarriage, and through his contacts, the father arranged for her remarriage to another person, a divorcee himself, who was looking forward to remarrying. The marriage happened just before the lockdown, and she seemed happy to resettle. The child was happy to know that her mother does not need to stay at her parental home.

Tejasvi's Lockdown Story

During the pandemic, Tejasvi was excited as she met her new father and stayed in a new house with her mother. The new father's house looked affluent. But after a few days, we got a call from Tajasvi's school complaining about her irregularity and reluctance to put on the audio and video. Tejasvi was a hard-working student and used to score well. But in the first online exams held at school, there was a dip in the marks. The school team thought this was not unusual as the contexts have changed overnight, and many kids face difficulty in online education. But when we tried to learn about Tejasvi's new home (through a partnering grassroots NGO in that area), we realized that the new husband was even worse than the previous one. And that Tejasvi is extremely afraid of her new father. After a few months, we brought Tejasvi back to the shelter home. These children were, to date, not allowed access to phones in the 'home,' but after the pandemic, they were allowed to access phones, and we put in place infra-structure so that they have access to the internet. Once, a gruhmata found a cell phone charging on the terrace during her routine check walk. It was found that the phone belonged to Tejasvi. The trained mind of the gruhmata sniffed.

She was troubled, and she enquired about why the device was lying on the terrace and not in the designated charging station. And it was found that Tejasvi wanted to get updated about the day-to-day domestic activities at her new home to remain aware of her mother. And to get this information, she was taking the help of the back door neighbor, a young man several years older than Tejasvi. And in exchanging messages, the man proposed love to the girl, and she got involved with him deeply. Now, she wanted privacy to talk with that man and hence needed to go to the terrace without anyone knowing – under the pretext of washing/ drying clothes and would stay on the chat on the phone. Her marks in school dived low, and the daily reports of her mother's plight made her depressed and all the more dependent on the newfound friend from her village. Once this was uncovered, the child was in counseling and daily conversations with the boarding In Charge at VKF. After the lockdown lifted in 2021, the mother of Tejasvi approached VKF and pleaded to be taken back as a gruhmata. She rejoined VKF as a gruhmata and also as a part-time tutor. She recalls the trauma and pain inflicted at her parental home and from her second marriage. She and her daughter attend the counseling sessions and try to embrace life again.

***

Case Study 9

Name of the child: Riya Nayak
Father's name: Khodabhai Nayak, IX pass;
Mother's name: Mayaben; VI
Year of joining VKF- 2014
Residence- Memnagar, Ahmedabad
Class- VII- St. Kabir, Naranpura, Ahmedabad

The Battles I Fight are Hidden in Me: Riya's Lockdown Story

Riya's mother works as a bus conductor/helper, and her father is a tempo driver. She has a younger brother, and she has seen her mother having fights with her daadi at home. The father is a peace-loving simple man and feels helpless amid the women fighting at home. During the lockdown, she came face to face with a fact that was kept under wraps. She caught her mother red-handed in an intimate sexual act with their neighbor, whom she used to visit frequently, to babysit their kid in the absence of the neighbor's wife. Following this, she raised a ruckus at home, and soon, the daadi threw them out of the house, and they were deported to their maternal uncle's house in a village. This severely affected the emotional state of the mother and, in consequence, had an impact on Riya and her online studies. During one of her interactions, the teacher of VKF came to know about this shift and how the child was deeply impacted. Riya was brought back to VKF when other selected kids were called back. She attended sessions (individual and group therapy) with the counselor at VKF. She has expressed her concern for her younger brother staying with her mother. The counselor informed us that she has built a fantasy world and is nurturing herself in that world. The child is under close monitoring and attends counseling sessions regularly.

***

Case Study 10

Name of the child: Riya Bilwal Father's name: Late Sh.
Ravikant Bilwal, B.Ed
Mother's name: Minaben Bilwal, XII pass Year of joining VKF- 2012
Village- Ratiya, Dahod District Class- VIII- DPS, Bopal, Ahmedabad

Handle Me with Care

Riya's mother is a child widow from the tribal belt of Dahod. Her husband died when Riya was 3 years old. Riya's father had appeared for a physical test the previous day as a part of recruitment in the police and had been put through rigorous physical activity. The next day, he suffered a heart attack and died. The young widow, with a small kid, felt helpless, especially when the jeth (elder brother-in-law) started making indecent approaches. The other members of her law's home wanted her to marry her elder brother-in-law and settle down- as per the norm in the community. She fled from her Sasural and came to her maiden home. No one in the family was ready to accept her back, as sheltering her would be like breaking the community's norms, which they could not put at risk. One of her relatives suggested she go to Ahmedabad and join VKF- one of the children from that village had been admitted to VKF a few years ago. Riya 's mother shifted to Ahmedabad and took up the job as a gruhmata at VKF. Riya was given admission to VKF and enrolled in DPS-Bopal when she reached the appropriate age. Since then, the shelter home has been their home. Meenaben- Riya's mother was a highly efficient and dedicated worker. With an eye for perfection, she came across as a stiff person with a non-negotiable approach. And she was hurt, pained, angered. She channelized her energies into work. But mes, she lost control over her emotions and would. We learned that at home – soon after the death of her husband, Riya used to get beaten up often.

Riya's Lockdown Story

During the lockdown, the mother-daughter duo left VKF, which was closed down, and stayed with a distant relative's home. Meenaben started doing odd jobs to put her time to use. Riya, by now, has developed apathy for her mother; the relationship was not peaceful. There were frequent fights, and Riya, now a teenager, started resisting her mother. By now, we had received requests from children from the streets of Ahmedabad to allow them to come and stay at VKF. But without support staff, we could not decide how to bring back the kids. The kitchen crew members were from Rajasthan, and the trains had not started. Who will run the kitchen? With Meenaben calling us to open up the living quarters, we got the answer. We requested she handle the kitchen temporarily until the kitchen crew resumes duty. She agreed, and we asked the other two girls to return to the campus. The boarding was sorted. But what about academics? With a break in studies, the three girls struggled to keep abreast with the school classes.

We looked for a local teacher who could come to VKF without being held up by the police (as the restrictions on mobility were still on) and teach the kids. We got the answer- an alumnus of VKF- having completed engineering just before the lockdown and still waiting for the job sector to start recruitment. The alumnus was asked to join as a private tutor for the three kids. Things seemed to fall into place. There was life flowing in the lonely corridors of the home. After a month or more, the tutor started complaining about their disrespectful attitude of Riya towards him. We asked Riya the reason behind her behavior, but she did not give any. We assumed that Riya is behaving this way due to the strain in her relationship with her mother and because it is not easy for the kids to attend online classes and stay locked in rooms with limited playmates and playtime. Little did we guess that the reason was something else. A bond was getting built between Riya's mother and her tutor. The tutor would visit them occasionally, even during non-work hours, and spend quality time with Riya's mother. Once, the girls found them in a compromising position. Once this came to our notice, we took stern action against misuse of the property, our trust, and affecting the girls, threatening their mental peace. After much talks with both parties, they made it very clear that they are serious about each other- but can't marry, as the community norms of the mother were highly restrictive. They decided to leave the shelter home and stay as living partners.

There was a lot of discussion on the child and her fate. Where will she stay during the one-month summer break or Diwali break when the shelter home is closed? What about Meena ben's association with VKF as a gruhmata? This is a residential job. What about her association as a parent? What is the status of her live-in partner- is he having a stable job- is he supporting the costs? Is he ready to take up the responsibilities of a teenage kid? Is the kid safe to be with her mother's lover? The questions remain. The child is in our custody. Meenaben has taken up two jobs (one day - babysitting and the other taking care of an old couple in the night). During vacations, Riya stays with her mother- goes with her to work during the day and at night. Our alumnus was facing ostracism from his family in his village when they came to know about this relationship.

***

Case Study 11

Name of the child: Hina Rathod Father's name: Late Sh.
Ravindra Rathod
Mother's name: Niru Rathod, XII pass
Year of joining VKF- 2003
Village- Vasadara, Anand District Amunus of VKF
Currently studying BA-FY at LD Arts college, Ahmedabad
Stays at VKF

My Experiences have Taught Me not to Subject Myself to Self-stigma

Heena is a special child; has studied from PRERNA- DPS Bopal till Class X. She could not complete XI XII from mainstream school and opted for appearing XII in Humanities from the Gujarat board as an external student. Her mother brought her to VKF after her husband died in an accident. Niruben got a job as a gruhmata at VKF. Heena completed XII and started studying in college. Being a dyslexic child, she found it difficult to clear her papers, and her graduation was met with breaks.

Heena's Lockdown Story

She went with her mother to her village post-lockdown, and the stay was extended indefinitely. Later, when VKF started opening up, she returned with her mother to the campus. After a few months, her mother found a suitable match for her and, with the consent of the elders of the family, finalized her again (engagement) with the boy. A month ago, one fine day, Niruben came to meet us teary-eyed and said that the boy's family had called off the proposed marriage with Heena. On asking for the reasons, she said reluctantly that Heena was in a relationship for a brief time with some other boy from her village. This relationship grew when she went to her village with her mother for a few months. The boy started making some undue advances, following which Heena refused to continue the relationship with him and broke off the bond. But now, that boy has come to know about Heena's engagement and has sent some intimate pictures of Heena with him to the other boy, and the family called off the marriage. Heena, an otherwise bright, chirpy, helpful girl with good IT skills, suddenly shrunk with shame. She andh her mother are seeking legal advice to combat cybercrime and are trying to move on. A local complaint in the village police station has been filed. A community meeting was held with the village and family elders. The smile is getting restored.

Case Study 12

Tales of Two Villages: Dharampur's Lockdown Story

Bhagwan Das comes across as a simple man from Tamachhadi, and a remote village tucked off in a Dharampur block of Gujarat. He looks simple but has a strong resolve to ensure his child gets an education. During the lockdown, three students at VKF from Dharampur were stranded in their remote village, 30 km from the district headquarters. There was no connectivity, and the boys had no one to turn to for help. The decision was taken after a meeting with the other parents. Bhagwan Das and his wife borrowed money, dug into their savings, pooled resources with the other families, shifted to Dharampur, took a house on rent, and subscribed to a strong internet supply. The online classes started after a tutorial over a video call. For months, the three kids stayed in that rented house under Bhagwan Das's and his wife's supervision.

Dang's Lockdown Story

Eight kids were in the district of Dang at the southernmost tip of Gujarat. In monsoons, the area is inaccessible due to the submerged bridges and several villages being cut off from the mainstream. During the lockdown, we thought of keeping a few children behind at VKF so that we provide them with remedial classes. Little did we know that what we assumed to be an interim phase was becoming the new normal. By mid-April, we were trying to connect with the district administration to get transport support to send the kids back to their homes. Finally, we got local help, and the kids were sent back home on the 16th of April 2020. Once the kids were safely reunited with their parents, we breathed relief. But soon, we started getting reports from the schools that they were neither attending classes nor available on their numbers. This was expected. Since Dangs comes under the forest division, internet obstructers are installed at several places in the district. The parents of these kids had to come to the district HQs to connect with VKF, as they had connectivity from there. Study material from school (online) was sent to the parents over WhatsApp. They would take printouts and go back. The children would study from their books and take the help of these online resources from school, solve papers/worksheets…and the parent would go back to the HQs to send over to VKF once a week. This continued for some time. Academics was getting affected. Some students walked up a distance to reach a hillock to get access to the net. The use of zoom / other platforms would soon discharge the phone, and the kids hardly got to attend all the classes without a charging point. One parent sent their daughter to another relative's family- where there was connectivity.

***

CONCLUSION

The stories are unending. They are appalling. Yes, we are celebrating the Amrit Mahotsav. But a look at the remote pockets of rural India fills us with despair. Even after 75 years of independence, many children are not having access to education. The divide between the rich and poor, haves and have-nots, is gnarling! Yes, every cloud has a silver lining. In this lockdown, the children at VKF recognized the value of their families. They were filled with gratitude towards their parents and siblings. They acknowledged the privileges they received as part of the Visamo family. Help poured in from different places, 8in the form of volunteering, financial and emotional support, and kind support. Red Bricks school, e.g., had sent eight sets of PC, keyboards, mice, headphones, and subscriptions for the internet for eight of our students studying in Red Bricks to ensure that their online education is not affected. The teachers of VKF and the schools made superhuman efforts to communicate with the families of every child who missed classes. Any misbehavior by a student during online classes was diligently handled and reported to help us nip the problem in the bud. Young college students across the nation formed volunteering groups to provide online tuition to children from underprivileged backgrounds (IDIYA, LOCKDOWN Project—to name a few). It was a joint effort. A story of the collaboration between diverse stakeholders such as parents, the VKF team, donors, volunteers, and students. It was a story of adaptation, resilience, fraternity, and co-creation. It was a lesson worth learning from. It's a personal journey of each – a journey meant to make the passengers fitter- better as a species that refused to become obsolete.

REFERENCES

Coronavirus (COVID-19) Cases. (n.d.). Our World in Data. http://ourworldindata.org

COVID-19 (2022). Wikipedia, The Free Encyclopedia. https://en.wikipedia.org/w/index.php?title=COVID-19&oldid=1127052423

Impact of COVID-19 on people's livelihoods, their health and our food systems (2020) Word Health Organization. https://www.who.int/news/item/13-10-2020-impact-of-covid-19-on-people%27s-livelihoods-their-health-and-our-food-systems

Visamo kids' foundation (2020) Visamokids.org. https://visamokids.org/

APPENDIX

About Visamo Kids Foundation (VKF) (*Visamo kids' foundation,* 2020): The Parentage Home: Visamo Kids Foundation (VKF) was initiated with 18 unprivileged children in Ambawadi, Ahmedabad, as a part of the response program of CALORX Foundation under the leadership of Dr. Manjula Puja Shroff. A shelter camp was set up for relief, rescue, and rehabilitation services to those affected by the earthquake, which shook Gujarat's state in 2001. In 2002, Visamo, meaning Shelter in Gujarati, was registered as Visamo Kids Foundation as a home providing foster care for underprivileged kids of the state. We are a shelter home working towards empowering lives through access to 'Quality Education' for underprivileged children from all over Gujarat in a secured environment of the '*parentage home.*'

Screening for Admission: Every year, in collaboration with grassroots NGOs, VKF conducts screening tests by reaching out to Gujarat's economically and socially disadvantaged communities. The grassroots NGOs are the key stakeholders who act as the bridge between the communities and Visamo, the institution. The screening is done by administering pictorial tests. Qualified psychologists assess the test papers. Those children (10) with the potential to excel academically are shortlisted.

Bridge In Program

Visamo Camp and Home Visit: These shortlisted children attend a ten-day- camp at VKF's shelter at Bopal, Ahmedabad, with the due consent of their parents, wherein a series of mental and physical tests are conducted. The residential staff – '*Gruhmatas*' (house mothers), observe the kids very closely and help them to get settled in the new milieu. Meanwhile, home visits are conducted to verify the background of all the shortlisted candidates. The home visits are done per the format provided by Visamo, by field teams of partnering institutions, as third-party evaluators.

Interview of parents: The camp culminates in an interview process wherein the parents are met by the managing trustee and a panel of selection board members to complete the selection process and admission to Visamo. Admission to VKF is conditional to the admission of the kids to schools.

Grooming and homeschooling: During the four months of their stay at VKF (before admission to the respective schools), the kids are groomed to be school and ready to readied to live in the institution. We partner with local pre-schools for the pre-schooling.

Admission in school: Admission to the Visamokids is made in some of the most prominent schools like DPS, Anand Niketan, Zydus, St. Kabir, Udgam, Zebra, Satyamev Jayate, AIS, etc. The admission gets over by December or early January. A bridge in the program is initiated wherein the kids are groomed for their stay at Visamo and prepared for admission to our partnering schools. Admission to the schools is made per the norms of the Right to Education (RTE) Act.

Academic Excellence: Visamo provides the kids with supplementary teaching classes after returning home from school. The teachers are hired part-time to help the kids cope with their studies at school, understand the concepts, and prepare them for exams/assessments. The teachers prepare Individual Educational Plans (IEPs) for each kid. Specialized care is taken for kids identified with special learning needs. Volunteers are one of the major contributors in helping us provide one-to-one attention to select kids.

Co-Curricular activities at Visamo: To ensure their all-round development, VKF organizes life skill training, counseling, personality grooming, career guidance /counseling sessions and interactions with eminent persons from diverse fields for the children.

Bridge out Programme: The kids start their journey at Visamo from Class I and complete twelve years of school education under diverse boards (CBSE, ICSE, GSEB). Just like the kids get groomed while they come into Visamo, there is a well-structured Bridge out Programme in place that supports the kids to get prepared to move out of Visamo, feeling confident, informed, and empowered about how to deal with their lives after stepping out of the seclusion of Visamo. Mentoring, Aptitude testing, career guidance and counseling, annual career fairs, interaction with field experts, exposure to diverse fields of study and career building, life skill coaching, etc., are the activities undertaken for the senior kids of Class VIII to XII.

Alumni of Visamo: To date, 44 kids have completed Class XII and graduated from Visamo. With the cadre growing in strength, the alumni are making a mark and making us proud.

Few of our alumni have completed their higher studies (Engineering, B.Com/Chartered Accountancy, Hotel Management) and are pursuing jobs. One alumnus, Ashish Badaniya, has shifted base to Bangalore and working with a reputed real estate group therein. One girl, Rinki, has pursued her dreams of becoming a fitness instructor and is popular among her students. Almost all the kids are pursuing part-time jobs to support their incidental costs and contribute to their families. Rohit worked at VKF as a part-time teacher alongside pursuing his Engineering studies. Mohsin and Raju are working as sports coaches at their alma mater, DPS, Bopal. Three of the students married and settled in their own spaces.

Marking a unique gesture of giving back, the alumni have pledged to support a kid at VKF and express their gratefulness to the institution. Jignesh Kalal extended his first stipend money and handed over the monies to his favorite person at Visamo, Ambien Shah, the Administrator. Rinki and Chandni have extended a part of their earnings towards child sponsorship. Vikas, Suresh, Sudhir, and other kids volunteer at Visamo and teach the younger kids in their leisure after college. Rakesh Chauhan helps us set up a thrift shop to raise funds through the garage sale of pre-loved clothes by cleaning, refurbishing, and packing the clothes, in his laundry shop.

The stories multiply. The bond continues. The ripple effect is evident. The camaraderie is felt. Giving back to the community rules the hearts of all.

Friends of Visamo: Visamo networks with multiple stakeholders to implement the program.

- *Parents:* The parents of the children at Visamo have bestowed their faith in the team and us and have supported the cause. They participate in routine events and have given consensus to the activities created for their kids at Visamo.
- *Vendors:* The timely delivery of quality services at reasonable costs helps us maintain service quality and achieve cost savings. The vendors associated with Visamo are a family to us, ready to help under all circumstances.
- *NGOs:* The organizations working at the grassroots, having strong community connections, are the link between Visamo, an institutional program, and the underprivileged/ disadvantaged groups/ communities.
- *Schools:* Our kids are studying across 11 schools in the city. Over the years, the bond between Visamo and the schools has been cemented with trust, commitment toward excellence, and gratitude.

- *Volunteers:* Visamo is blessed to have volunteers stepping in and becoming one with the *parivaar* (family). They bring joy and hope to the young lives nurtured in the parentage home. The silent and steady patrons who invest their most precious resource, *time,* at Visamo. We have local and international interns associating with kids this year to strengthen academic support and extracurricular activities.
- *Donors:* To sustain the current activities and initiate new ones, as per the needs of the time, bringing in new sources of sponsorships/ donations, Visamo has always received support and encouragement from the organization's donors. They are our ambassadors and spokespersons for the cause addressed.
- *Visamo Task Group (The VTG):* A group of experts from diverse fields forms a vibrant platform that meets every month and contributes towards bridging the gaps in the existing activities and strengthening the same. From fundraising to training staff to volunteering, each member of this group remains a source of hope and aspiration for the Visamoites.
- *Kalorex:* Visamo is integral to Kalorex, and team Kalorex is a source of energy for us. Kalorex ignites us, fuels us, steers the direction of our work, shapes us, holds us to account, holds our hand during challenging times, and celebrates the joys with us.

Access to Quality Education

Visamo partners with schools to ensure access to quality education. Kids study at the finest English Medium schools in the city, under CBSE, ICSE, IB, and Gujarat board (State).

We have hired teachers to ensure that the post-school support for the kids is in place. Part-time teachers help the students once they return from school.

Bridge in the program helps the initial grooming of the kids (at the age of 5 years) to undergo and cope with the rigors of formal schooling.

Bridge out program empowers the kids to feel confident to make choices after stepping out of Visamo (after finishing XII, kids step out of Visamo. The services under bridge out are:

- Mentoring
- Career counseling and guidance
- Aptitude testing
- Linking with donors to sponsor the costs of higher education
- One-to-one support for kids is provided through the help of volunteers.
- Kids detected with special abilities are supported to enhance their areas of interest.

Collaborations

Kalorex- parent organization Volunteers

Corporate partners

NGOs – A network of 11 NGOs helped us in rural networking and identification of eligible children to attend the screening tests

Schools- Education partners to VKF

Visamo Alumni are the ambassadors of Visamo. They are the source of strength and lead by example for the kids at Visamo. The support routed to kids for higher studies after they pass out of Visamo after completing XII is not a grant but a loan that has to be re-paid to the Visamo revolving fund, which will sustain other kids' education.

We organize small-scale sales for income generation, such as the sale of paintings/ artwork of kids, the sale of pre-loved clothes, the sale of mats and other articles made out of the paintings of the kids, the sale of fertilizers made in Visamo by decomposing kitchen waste, and so on.

Child sponsorship and donor engagement programs are important for sustaining the activities at Visamo.

Visamo Alumni are the ambassadors of Visamo. They are the source of strength and lead by example for the kids at Visamo. The support routed to kids for higher studies after they pass out of Visamo after completing XII is not a grant but a loan that has to be re-paid to the Visamo revolving fund, which will sustain other kids' education.

We organize small-scale sales for income generation, such as the sale of paintings/artwork of kids, the sale of pre-loved clothes, the sale of mats and other articles made out of the paintings of the kids, the sale of fertilizers made in Visamo by decomposing kitchen waste and so on.

Child sponsorship and donor engagement programs are important for sustaining the activities at Visamo.

CSR engagements are equally important for sustaining the activities.

Partnerships and collaborations with Kalorex, schools, the local community of volunteers, and business houses are key to the operations of the shelter home.

Exit Plan- Visamo is adopted by the business houses to support underprivileged kids across the state.

We do not have plans to upscale or expand. Visamo may be replicated. This is one of its programs. We are poised as a resource center; we will share our experiences and train people or institutions on residential care programs.

Chapter 21
Mobile Journalism and Dissemination:
Use of Smart Phones in Traditional News Reporting

Sandeep Kumar
Karnavati University, India

ABSTRACT

Communication and dissemination of information forever changed after 1990, and media is changing to adapt or survive the emerging trends in use with new media. Smartphones with touch screens and online connectivity are more prevalent than computers in the digital age. Emerging new technologies have changed the journalism and styles of news presentation and dissemination as smartphones changed their audience. Mobile journalism is a journalistic practice in which a reporter uses a smartphone for reporting, recording, editing, and even uploading content on media port or air. The researcher is study-ing how journalists adapt the culture of mobile journalism in their journalistic tasks and the effects of mobile journalism on their work. It also tries to analyze news organizations' responses toward using mobile phones in journalism instead of traditional equipment and studio setups.

INTRODUCTION

1990 was a landmark year as the inventions of the world wide web, the internet, and then social media changed the communication and dissemination of information forever. After 1990, media is changing to adapt or survive the emerging trends in media use with new media. Smartphones with touch screens and online connectivity are more prevalent than computers in the digital age (Marler, 2018). The low rates for internet facilities in smartphones initially changed the readership patterns in newspapers and, magazines, even books. Countries. The American use of public libraries has changed a lot, as a survey done by Pew Research Centre in 2012 and 2015 concluded that it was 53% in 2012 and 44% in 2015 (Horrigan, 2016). The number of people visiting the libraries was decreasing continually; it was 35%

DOI: 10.4018/978-1-6684-6682-7.ch021

in 2016. The reason remained for using library websites and mobile apps (Horrigan, 2016). Emerging new technologies have changed the journalism and styles of news presentation and dissemination as smartphones changed their audience.

News on Radio, Television, and Newspaper is also affected by smartphones. Journalism is studied as print, broadcast, radio, and online or web journalism. New terms such as video journalist (VJ), backpack journalism, and mobile journalism are applied to journalistic practices (Cameron, 2008). Mobile journalism is a journalistic practice in which a reporter uses a smartphone for reporting, recording, editing, and even uploading content on media port or air. Whatever the media, reporting with smartphones is no new concept anymore; the advanced version of smartphones like Apple has made the phone no less than a computer and equal enough to a still and motion camera. When smartphones provide all the facilities of typing, recording, texting, linking, and editing, it is as good as working in a newsroom. The footage and phone recordings of the 9/11 terrorist attacks in the USA and footage of the use of chemical weapons in the Syrian war got the fastest and maximum viewership, establishing the impact of mobile journalism.

2015 was perhaps the worst year for print media before the lockdown shock in 2020, as it showed a 7% fall in readership, which was the greatest decline after the 2010 recession period; in this time, advertising revenue also showed an 8% decline in print media and digital media too (Barthel, 2016) . In 2016, Pew research canter conducted a survey and found that most of the citizens in America use digital media for news, and print media is showing a further downfall in readership. Digital audiences expanded and moved beyond news websites and moved to social media, mobile apps, podcasting, and email newspapers, giving more control to the hands of tech companies like Apple, Facebook, etc. (Barthel, 2016). The data from various research organizations confirmed that the population is turning to digital sources for the news. The momentum is driven by mobile users, with other digital media like Facebook, Instagram, Snapchat, and e-news websites (Barthel, 2016).

Journalists are working on the frontline to deliver news in these tough times; while looking at 2020 and 2021, we will also study the effects of mobile phones as journalists used them during covid pandemic reporting. To see the effectiveness of MOJO in their daily tasks.

Forecast Number of Mobile Users Worldwide 2019-2023 (In Billion)

In 2013 there were 6.8 billion mobile users, 96% of the world's population. Out of these, 2.1 were using the internet on mobile phones, using it for research, news, shopping, music and entertainment viewing, navigation, placing food orders and searching the option for all kinds of services, and for keeping personal socializing and interactions (Mak, Nickerson, and Sim, 2015). The author identified the importance of using mobile phones in affecting customer attitudes toward location-based services and how developing new strategies to include mobile promotion and service information dissemination brought great results in this concerned industry (Mak, Nickerson, and Sim, 2015). Mobile news and cross-media news consumption are showing record rising and simultaneously decreasing the readership of newspapers. Mobile journalism is providing new opportunities for news media, and surely it is regularly transforming (Fardigh, 2014).

Keeping the proximity factor in focus and getting all smaller to bigger news from all areas, the use of the mobile phone in locative news was an obvious step taken by many news organization as the number of smartphone users were increasing, the stats were showing the world is glued to smartphones for news, forced media to find new formats and writing skills suitable to digital media, the need was to invent the right strategies to write content specifically for mobile as a medium (Vaage, 2016). A mobile phone being a personal device and in movement always with the users, forced the news media to focus on location-based news content, here news can be added in the second person to show more closeness, and content can be more utility cantered based on the location and other information of users (Vaage, 2016).

Goggin analyzed the scope of mobile media rigorously on a global level by discussing its technical and cultural practices (Goggin, 2012). The development of audio and video tools in mobile phones changed the political and cultural economics of phones. The music, films, news, information, gaming, and study materials on the phone gave birth to many new markets and business avenues (Goggin, 2012). Kristine Lu, on the Pew Research Centre website, mentioned the growth of mobile devices at a fast pace and how they became a favourite platform to get news in America (Lu, 2017).

Lu stated that eight out of ten American adults watch the news on their mobile phones, and it is increasing rapidly with each passing year; even old age people in the age bracket of the 50s and older are showing the sharpest growth (Lu, 2017) This increase was equally observed in the low-income groups, about eight out of ten adults from low-income households doubled the use of phones for watching the news (Lu, 2017).

The traditional media need to bring lots of updating and changes in organizations to survive the new media journalism, including mobile journalism (Kueng, 2017). Within two decades of the internet and new media, the structure of the new media ecosystem is very clear and poses enough challenges to existing traditional media (Kueng, 2017). Journalism, data, and technology are merging and bringing huge transformations in the media industry. Product is equally important in putting the right content at the right time in the right media; thus, products play a central role in changing the media. Media should not fall behind in implementing and adopting these tools with upcoming changes (Kueng, 2017)

Digital storytelling formats are evolving, and it is disturbing the traditional media trends of writing. Digital storytelling formats are important to mobile consumption and digital business models, the relationship between writer and reader is changing, and it is more interactive than traditional media (Kueng, 2017).

Legacy media organizations use mobile news apps, and radio stations also provide news apps. Still, media organizations are not quick enough to merge these changes and adapt to the mode of mobile journalism; there is still much to improve (Rau, 2018).

Will Marler explored the uses and reasons for the increasing number of smartphone users. He added that smartphones got more users than computers, specifically in poor and minority communities (Marler, 2018). He investigated research investigations for two decades regarding the impact of smartphones on the economic and social status of disadvantaged populations. He used his observations to write this research article depicting the relationship between the use of smartphones with the elevation of the economic and social status of people belonging to economically weaker sections (Marler, 2018). The mobile phone users have increased the total number of world population due to multiple subscribing; it also showed a connecting thread of alleviation or reproduction of socioeconomic inequalities (Marler, 2018). The number of smartphone users also showed a noticeable increase in the productive use of phones like economic updates, health, educational information, and social and entertainment uses. Still, such productive usage was more in higher income groups compared.

Salah Mohammed Salih from Uppsala university under Professor Annika Waem in 2017 on "How smartphones help journalists in their work concerning risky tasks" (Mohammedsalih, 2017) . He applied the phenomenological approach and Survey, Interviews with professionals in journalism; he concluded in his research that the use of smartphones is becoming a norm and is replacing many traditional equipments used in journalism. He also added that mobile journalism is reaching a high level of professionalise with time. Although, it will still take time for bigger news channels, filmmakers, and other media workers to adopt and announce the smartphone as the main equipment in creating media production (Mohammedsalih, 2017).

Stephen Quinn wrote in his book on, "MoJo-Mobile Journalism in the Asian Region" in 2011 to explore and analyze the use of mobiles in journalism work in Asia (Quinn, 2011). In this book, he took an extensive field-based study to see the MOJO in different countries in Asia and analyzed the trends of mobile journalism reporting and its acceptance in media houses, and he also studied the technical advancement of MOJO and techniques of mobile journalism; in the concluding chapter, he writes about the future of mobile journalism. He was sure that using mobile phones in journalism is the norm and common, easy, and preferable for journalists. They are using it in research, sharing, and dissemination of information, taking photos and video recordings, and even editing print, audio, and visual productions. With smart techniques, they were using it for uploading the news too. Future equipment in journalism surely has smartphones; sure rest of all traditional equipment, like heavy cameras and mics, etc., can change. Media should be ready for a changing newsroom (Quinn, 2011).

While conducting the study, the researcher found that Mobile journalism is not really a new trend in Indian media, but people are often using mobile phones for journalistic practices. Covid-19 was declared a pandemic, affecting almost every part of the world. Talking about India, things were imposed immediately to prevent infections, and journalists kept society informed and updated; hence they were working day and night. While doing their job, they were at a higher risk of getting infected with the virus. Mobile Journalism has been a trend in Indian media, and how well they have adapted this concept to continue their work. Is it affecting their work positively or taking it to the downside?

RESEARCH QUESTIONS

- How journalist is adapting the culture of Mobile journalism in their journalistic tasks?
- What are the effects Mobile journalism is having on their work?
- What is news organizations' response to using Mobile in Journalism tasks by journalists?

RESEARCH METHODOLOGY

Content analysis and survey as a research methodology have been adopted for this research. Surveys are a systematic way of asking people to volunteer information about their attitudes, behaviours, opinions, and beliefs (Polland). Survey as a research method plays a very important role in social sciences as the survey method has the advantage of having a great deal of information from a larger population; it can also be created in a way to get personal and social facts, beliefs, attitudes (Mathiyazhagan and Nadan, 2010). Herbert McClosky in 1996 defined the survey as a "planned procedure in which data are collected systemically from a population or from a sample of that population through some form of direct solicitation, like face-to-face interviews, deep interview, telephone interviews, or mail questionnaires," it is also used for collecting primary data based on verbal or written communication with a representative sample of individuals or respondents from the largest population (Mathiyazhagan and Nadan, 2010).

Here convenient sampling has been used as a research methodology. It is also called opportunity sampling. The target population was working journalists in India's print, electronic or digital media. Many journalists were contacted through phone on the phone, and efforts were made to get their confirmation for filling out this questionnaire. The rest of the journalists were approached by taking the information from known working journalists. It was requested the working journalists fill out the questionnaire. Due to covid 19 restrictions and changed circumstances, reporters were found busy and having less field work for safety measures.

Content analysis is a scientific study of communication content; it is the study of content concerning the meanings, context, and intentions contained in messages, it is 75-year-old, and Webster's dictionary includes this word in 1961 (Prasad). Content analysis is the analysis of what is contained in the content or message, and it is a method where the content is the basis from which inferences and conclusions have been drawn (Nachmias)(Prasad). Content analysis conforms to three basic principles of the scientific method: objectivity, systematic, and Generalizability (Prasad). It is most widely used in social sciences and mass communication research. It has been used broadly to understand a wide range of themes such as social change, cultural symbols, changing trends in the theoretical content of different disciplines, verification of authorship, changes in mass media content, nature of news coverage, and many social issues (Prasad).

Content Analysis

MOJO (Mobile Journalist) and VJ (Video Journalist) are two different terms for news reporters regarding the nature of their job. While everybody cannot be a mojo or VJ, each has its parts to be performed, and mobiles can be used for breaking news and some similar and urgent situations where reporting cannot wait for the crew or the broadcasting van. The New York Times, for the first time, published a photo taken with a mobile phone in 2004 from the event of a merger of two giants in telecommunications, AT&T and Cingular. The photograph appeared to be very ordinary, but the point was that it was taken by a phone, and it might be considered as first mojo reporting. A few years later, mojo was being used all around the globe (Quinn, 2011).

Newspapers ruled their monopoly in the news market for a great time, and then the radio came, and things changed. Gradually radio was overtaken by television in the 60s and 70s. As the next cycle evolved with the emergence of the internet and mobile phones, people are now turning their heads to the new trend, be it the provider or the consumer; all of them are using the same platform. Over the last decade, people have increased internet use for news, work, and entertainment purposes. In the name of hardware, one just needs a mobile device with a camera and internet connection. For the software, most media organizations are using their website and some apps so that the reporter can report live on their website, and then it could be broadcasted on television (Quinn, 2011).

Mobile phones have changed the perception of people reading or watching the news. Most people are using mobile phones to satisfy their need for news. Earlier mobile phones were communication devices, and then still camera was introduced, and very soon, these devices were equipped with video cameras. Mobile journalism was not a new big thing in the media industry; people used it according to their needs. There were situations where news channels also used footage or images shared by people, such as bombings in Iraq or Tsunami hitting the lands. In 2005 when London was bombed, BBC received tons of data from people within hours after the announcement. After the evolution of video platforms like YouTube, millions of videos are watched daily and not all content is shot with professional cameras or by professional people. There are some problems while using mobile phones for reporting; sometimes, you may not get the right sound, or maybe the footage is very shaky. Background noises are another problem.

People may ignore the quality of video content on YouTube, but when they turn to mainstream media, they tend to watch in good quality. It is acceptable in different situations where reporting is given more priority over quality or equipment, and people are adapting to mobile journalism (RISJ Admin, 2014).

Mojo is no longer a term; it is widely accepted by people, reporters, and media houses. In Austria, few universities have made it a part of their syllabus to be taught in the first year of the course, so when these students are out in the field, they are technically more advanced and aware of how to take on the thing with time. Mojo is a basic skill and an advanced concept in the newsroom culture. BBS and MTV are using mobile phones for content creation for their shows. Wan Ifra is organizing workshops on mobile journalism in different parts of the world. "Rajasthan," A 360-degree workshop organized in India, where reporters were learning mojo techniques and all types of android smartphones were on display. A fully trained mojo reporter can create amazing content by using mobile devices. The future is bright by looking at the opportunities in mobile reporting (Tjaardstra, 2017).

One of the biggest newspapers in India, Hindustan Times, is out on a new road where they are building a team of fully trained and equipped mobile journalists. Yosuf Omar from Hindustan Times is leading the team as he is the mobile editor of the paper. He was awarded for the news coverage that he did on Snapchat, saying, "Social media for Social good." In an interview with story hunter, he mentioned that everyone is using mobile phones and social media, be it for US election results or maybe some personal problem; this is all mobile journalism stories created by mobile devices giving new meanings to media. (Kovacs, 2017). The duration of these mobile-generated sources is of utmost importance to newsrooms. Fact-checking, quality control, verifying data, and professional authentication is also required before these can be broadcasted. While using Snapchat for journalism, Omar used different filters available in the app to safeguard the interviewee's identity or according to the situation. This also started a new term, "Selfie Journalism". The same strategy was followed in Punjab to connect youth to social issues and drug awareness (Kovacs, 2017).

Many famous movements started with mobile phones, e.g., Arab springs and #Blacklivermatter. These were started with mobile devices. The concept of fake news is getting stronger in this era of selfie journalism. Everyone with a social media account creates a post for their viewers without validating facts. This is when the traditional media stand against this fake news and safeguard society with such news. Newsrooms are changing, and the need for freelancers is only growing. Being a master in one area is not enough nowadays; one must learn all the trades in journalism (Kovacs, 2017).

Research suggests that mobile journalism is a more appropriate way to pursue people for interviews. To test the research, Karhunen interviewed 11 journalists from the United Kingdom, the Netherlands, Germany, Ireland, Australia, Qatar, and Italy. All of them agreed that while doing their regular job with traditional equipment, they got lesser responses, and while using mobile phones for the same purpose, they got a good number of responses. People's turning out more in front of mobile may be psychological. Still, as the journalists mentioned, the task would have been nearly impossible if they were to do it on a traditional camera and with a team. Karhunen tried it by himself; being a journalist and editor for a news website, he pursued people with both methods, and it was for that while using the camera, the team could approach only 200 people in two days, and while using a mobile phone, he was able to approach 400 people in the two days' time. Age and gender might be other factors affecting people's interview decisions. The majority of people who turned out for interviews were at a young age. While mobile journalism was easily approachable, people may have trust issues; some said they trusted the crew and setup of journalists, while some were in favour of mobile phones; on the contrary, some people showed a lack of credibility in the use of mobile phones (Karhunen, 2017).

BBC has a platform for recording, editing, and sharing videos or image files on a mobile device known as Portable News Gathering. Mark Settler from Shoulder pod, a trainer for BBS, said in an interview that MOJO is the biggest revolution in decades. It is cost-effective, fast, Lightweight, and fully digital on a single device. The wide accessibility of smartphone devices makes it a powerful tool. At the same time, citizen journalism comes into a more active phase and has a potential threat to publishers. The media industry is undergoing changes, which may become the new normal (WNIP, 2018).

Mojo or Mobile Journalism is a widely accepted term for a new workflow in the media field where reporters do day-to-day jobs using a mobile device, such as content creation, editing, and sharing of information for news purp. Most media organizations find mobile journalism of more importance, followed by some very valid reasons as it is cheap, always on the go, discreet, and anyone can be a mojo as it requires a skill set which is very common for a smartphone user (seamedu, 2019).

While increasingly organizations are using mobile journalism regularly for most of their associates, Uma Shankar Singh from NDTV has been using mobile for every reporting task for over a decade and finds it very convenient, on time, and hassle-free. He has been using his mobile phone, a selfie stick, and a mic. Be it any political event or a piece of breaking news, Singh can be seen reporting with his smartphone (Granger, 2019).

Technology gets increasingly compact and coming right into our hands Paul Wilson from Exposure video, in an interview with Allied London, said that with lenses, tripods, audio apps, and accessories, mobile phones have increased capability to capture quality content. A smartphone may not provide results equivalent to a professional camera, but results may make some difference if used correctly. Operating a mobile phone is not enough to make movies; you must also have good knowledge about composition and framing, sound and lighting, and how to continue things from one to another. It is when consumers are also shifting to online media, not sticking to television anymore, and making mojo a 24/7 job. Many people are using mobile devices such as iPhones to make movies, and the work is getting acknowledged (London, 2020).

Working in any media field, the need to be on time and on the ground is one of the most important things. Caroline Scott explained how mobile devices are a weapon in Journalism in a podcast for Journalism.co.uk. As Caroline mentioned, Breaking news is something to be reported very first. And you cannot achieve it unless you are not sure what apps you will use for shooting, editing, and sharing. Using many apps for the same content is not a good idea rather than mastering one and achieving a solid workflow. Most people need a little training to get good results compared to high-end technology, especially in crowded areas. Shooting for a blog and shooting for a news channel are two different things (Granger, 2020).

Mobile Journalism is no longer a new term anymore, and it's just how well people adapt to it. MOJO is about permitting storytellers to use whatever technology is available and make the most out of the visual story they can. Mobile Journalism means portability, which started back when the Leica cameras with 35MM film were invented in 1925. Walkie-lookie was another benchmark in video capturing yet being very portable. Not long back iPhone was launched in 2007, and several other mobile devices offered Internet connectivity, a Camera, and Music features. Peter Keresztes from TVR Timisoara, Romania, learned to shoot and edit a story on the phone and share it on social media in just four days; Harriet Hadfield, a reporter at Sky News, used her mobile phone to go live in 90 seconds. Another reporter in Syria used a mobile phone and stayed unnoticed while covering his documentary for Al-Jazeera. Leonor Suarez, Editor at Asturias´ Public Radio and TV, was the first person to film inside the caves of Pozu'l

Fresno, Spain. All these stories share their point of view regarding mobile journalism; it is easy to use, convenient, goes unnoticed, and is cost-effective simultaneously (Mulcahy, 2020).

SURVEY

Online Surveys, using the internet to conduct quantitative research, are in trend now; earlier, it was not a part of conventional research. Web-based surveys are superior to email surveys in many ways, but the email method combined with the offline method is an excellent vehicle. If conducted properly, online surveys have significant advantages over other formats, and they should be used only when appropriate (Evans and Mathur, 2005). Many third-party research firms now provide online survey services, and few specialized survey designs follow the all-important steps required for proper research (Evans and Mathur, 2005). The field of the survey has become more scientific and is further developing. Over the last 25 years, technology has revolutionized survey methods, making them fast, easy, and trying for making error-free (Evans and Mathur, 2005).

Including descriptive and objective questions in the survey gave them a practical experience to further introspect and strengthen their opinions. The respondents were asked to answer 14 questions with the help of nominal, interval, and ordinal measurement scales.

RESULTS, INTERPRETATION AND DISCUSSIONS

The researcher has selected 100 working journalists from different age groups working in the field of Journalism and working with either Print media or Digital media. The sample was selected from different regions, so that researcher could study the effects on a national level. Most respondents are associated with news channels in different parts of the country, holding various positions in journalism. The researcher included different age groups so that the effects of age and experience in handling the technology could also be studied. Out of the hundred journalists, only 48 responded to the research questionnaire. Forty-eight complete responses were used for interpretations and discussion, and simple analysis was applied.

Increased use of Mobile Phones

Figure 1 indicates that almost every journalist is using mobile phone devices for journalistic purposes. Some use it very frequently, and a few people use it less frequently, but no person in the sample was not using mobile phones in Journalism.

Engagement with Mobile Phones

Figure 2 show that most people have been using mobile phones for journalistic purposes for more than two years. As time passes, everyone is being consumed by technology at some level. A few people started using mobile for journalistic purposes in less than six months and less than a year, and it is a positive sign of people using technology for their work.

Figure 1. Increased use of Mobile Phones

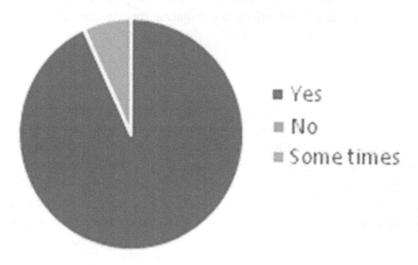

Figure 2. Engagement with Mobile Phone

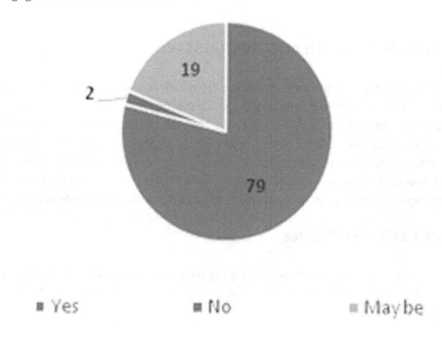

Use of Mobile Devices for Live Reporting

In the previous analysis, it was clear that people have already to mobile technology in Journalism in one way or another, and sooner or later, they are adapting to mobile phones for journalistic purposes; this analysis talks about how many people are using mobile devices for live reporting. 23% of the total population has agreed that they were using mobile phones for a living- reporting very often, and another

Figure 3. Equipment used for Reporting during Corona epidemic

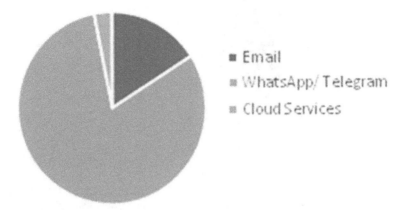

42% of people used it often. 21% were using mobile devices for live reporting rarely, while there were 14% people were not using mobile phones for live reporting at all.

Equipment used for Reporting during Corona Epidemic

Figure 3 clearly shows that most respondents were regularly using mobile devices for their reporting work, as 88% of respondents agreed to use mobile phones during the epidemic. 7% of respondents were using mic as their equipment as they were in front of the camera, and 5% of respondents were operating cameras during the same period. None of the respondents agreed to use the traditional methods (Notebook-Pen) or tablets as these were not convenient as the time is very hard for everyone.

The Medium Used for Sharing Information

Figure 4 represents the responses on what medium was used to share information between colleagues, and more than 80% of the respondents were using messaging apps such as WhatsApp and Telegram. 16% of respondents relied on emails, and only 3% used cloud services for information exchange.

Convenient Use of Smartphones Over Traditional Media Tools

To find out the convenience of use with the smartphone over traditional media tools researcher has used a 7-point Likert scale (Gracyalny, 2017).

Analyzing figure 5 gives a clear impression that the majority of people are in favour of the convenience that is given by mobile phones over traditional media tools in journalistic practices. 37% of respondents strongly agreed on the convenience of smartphones, and another 30% strongly agreed on the same side. On the other hand, very few people very strongly disagreed (3%) and strongly disagreed (9%). The majority of people agree with the new technology.

Figure 4. The medium used for sharing Information

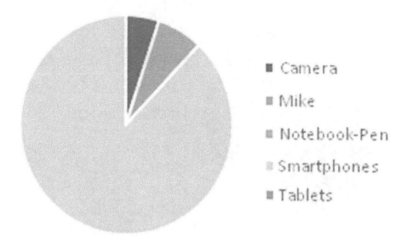

Increased Utility of Smartphones During Covid-19

Statistics in the figure 6 clearly shows the highly increased usage in journalism and sharing of small information in real-time using their smartphone devices which were not that easy before the indulgence of these devices. A few people have a different perspective on the same with a different disagreed response.

Difference Between Uses of Smartphones Versus Traditional Equipment

Figure 7 shows a very positive response, with a great number of respondents agreeing to the fast and portable usage of smartphones as compared to the traditional media tools such as camera, mic, and other accessories required for the shoot.

Figure 5. Convenience of Use Over Traditional Media Tools

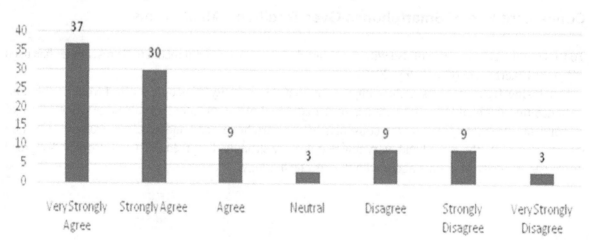

Figure 6. Increased use of Smartphones during Covid-19

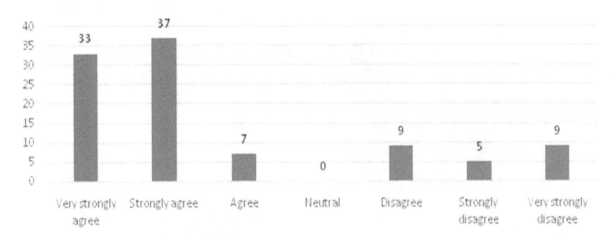

Two respondents have also mentioned that it makes their workflow a little slow, yet five other respondents agreed to moderate time and portability. All respondents were clear with their thought and work schedule, as there was no response for "Can't say."

Figure 7. Increased use of Smartphones during Covid-19

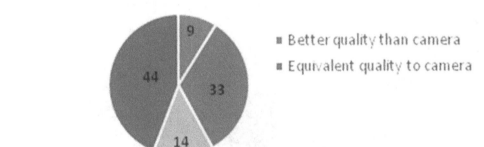

Smartphones Affect the Writing Style in Journalism Practices

Smartphones affect the writing style on one level or another in different practices. 26% of respondents agreed that there are changes in writing style as they are using mobile devices for reporting purposes. Few use it for other things as they minimize any grammatical errors in their writing. Almost half of the respondents said they had witnessed changes in content and structure in their writing style for reporting purposes. 9% of the respondents agreed with the appropriateness of their writing style (figure 8).

Comparison Between Cameras and Phone Cameras in Journalistic Practices

While talking about utility on different levels in journalistic practices, the researcher also compared the smartphone devices based on their camera capabilities, as many companies offer cameras with a straight

Figure 8. Smartphones affecting writing style in Journalism

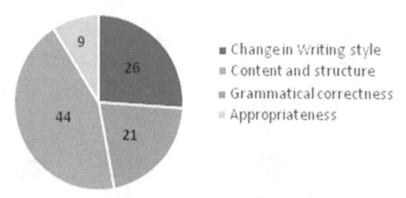

comparison of professional cameras. People yet find professional gear more appropriate for quality. Still, it gives workable quality compared to professional cameras, according to 44% of respondents, and another 33% of respondents agreed that phone cameras offer equivalent quality to professional equipment used for taking photographs (figure 9).

Figure 9. Smartphones vs Traditional media tools

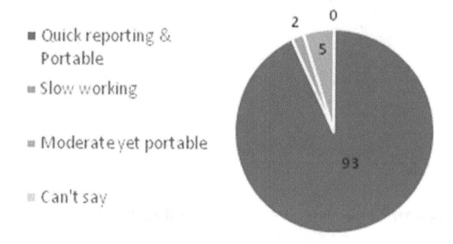

Smartphones Affecting the Speed of Work of Journalists

Ease of portability comes with both pros and cons; on the positive side, smartphones are affecting the speed of work of journalists to a great extent as you can record audio and videos and take photographs and instantly share them over a variety of platforms for the information to be used by the media houses or on social media to be consumed by the people. Almost 80% of the respondents agreed to the same, and another 19% were unsure whether they did (figure 10).

Figure 10. Smartphones affecting speed of work

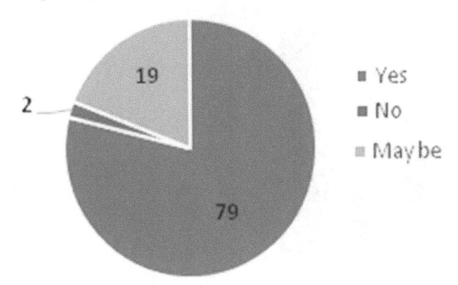

Smartphones Helping Hygiene and Safety From Covid-19

Figure 11 here represents People's acceptance of smartphones as helping media professionals maintain their safety and hygiene during the COVID-19 epidemic 70% of respondents agreed on the same, and 21% were not sure of it. Only 9% of respondents have denied that smartphones are not helping in safety.

Figure 12 here shows how it is helping as it helps in not touching different equipment used by different people; they maintain social distancing. Staying distant is again agreed by 30% of people, and when using one device for all the work, a personal device helps even more, as agreed by 40% of the respondents. Smartphones may not provide safety directly, but they help people maintain safe distance during COVID.

Media Organizations in favor of Using Smartphones

The figure 13 show a clear difference in the media organizations favouring the use of smartphones for journalistic purposes. The 7-pointLikert scale was used to analyze the behaviour. It shows a very strong and strong agreement among the respondents, as most respondents favour using smartphones for different reasons.

Smartphones can Replace Cameras and Mics in the Future

It might take some time to replace professional cameras and mics for reporters as smartphones may provide equivalent quality but cannot beat them. Smartphones at the current stage require more refinement in technology as the figure 14 indicates that almost 60% of people agreed and strongly agreed with smart devices, but many disagreed.

Figures 11. Smartphones helping hygiene and safety from Covid-19

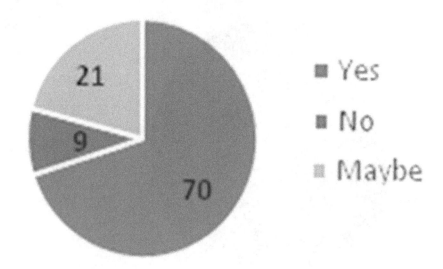

Preferred Equipment for Field Work

More than 50% of respondents have shown smartphones as their preferred equipment for field work, while only 9% are strictly in favour of using professional equipment for their work purposes. 40% of respondents preferred the situation; if the situation permits, they may use professional gear; if not, they will prefer using their smartphones and not miss the information on the spot and report it to their media agency (figure 15).

Figures 12. Smartphones helping hygiene and safety from Covid-19

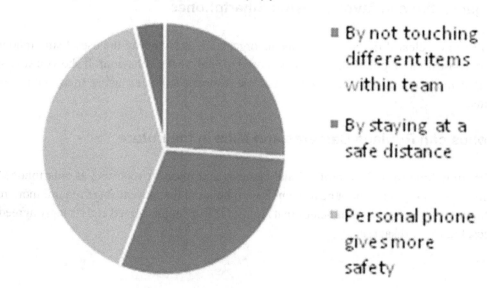

Figure 13. Media organizations over the use of smartphones

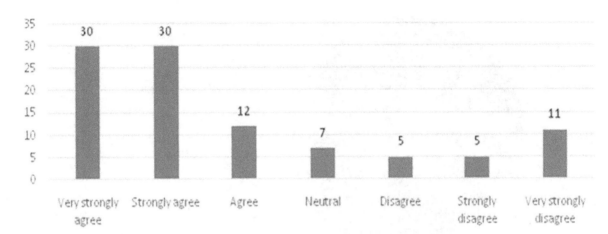

Media Affected by Increased Use of Smartphones

Some respondents mentioned that digital media is affected by the increased use of smartphones, while others mentioned as print media is affected, whereas some mentioned that web or online media is affected, but it is without any doubt very clear that all media types are affected by the smartphone's heavy usage as 77% respondents have agreed for it (figure 16)

Scenario After COVID-19

Talking about the scenario after COVID may not really seem right to discuss at this point, but we can always look for new changes and opportunities, and people seem to be ready for this, as 60% of respondents said that the media would be adaptive to mobile journalism and a great number of respondents said that they are ready if there are any new changes in future, they are ready for it. A few respondents

Figure 14. Smartphones can replace camera and mic

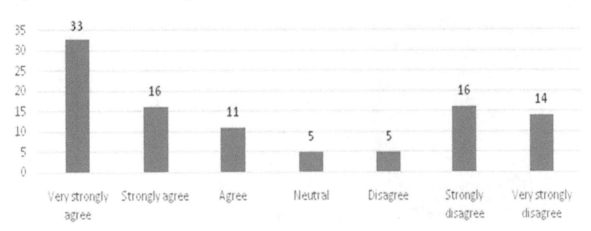

Figure 15. Preferred equipment for field work

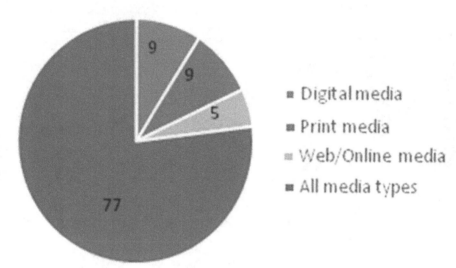

said that media might switch back to traditional methods of reporting and journalism and only 5% were not sure about what will happen in the future (figure 17).

Smartphone Portability Over Traditional Equipment

Smartphones are portable, one can tell by looking at their size, but portability is not all about size but more about doing the thing that previously required a bigger setup and a longer time to complete it. 40% and 28% of respondents Very strongly and strongly agreed in favour of portability over traditional equipment. Almost 20% of respondents on various levels showed disagreement over the portability of these smart devices (figure 18).

Figure 16. Media affected by increased use of smartphones

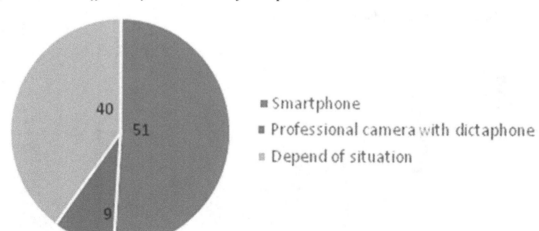

Figure 17. Media scenario after Covid-19

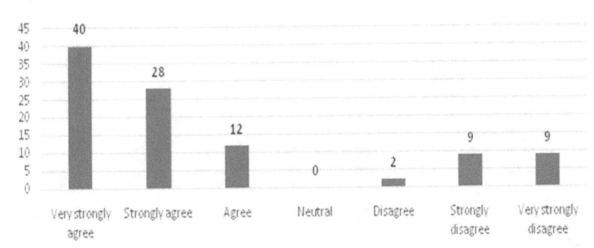

Figure 18. Smartphones portability over traditional equipment

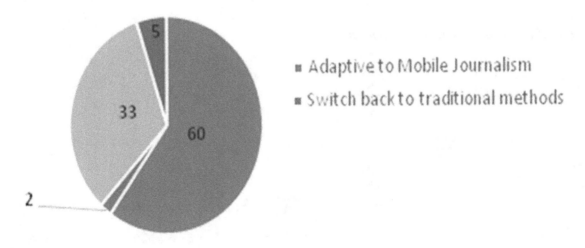

Affordability of Smartphones Compared to Traditional Equipment

Most respondents agreed on the affordability of smartphone devices compared to traditional equipment used in journalistic practices. Professional equipment always comes with a hefty price tag, whereas smartphones are available in different budgets and specifications as the user requires (figure 19).

Smartphones Helping in Discreet Reporting

Discreet reporting is not that often, but it is required for some very sensitive issues that must be reported to the people. And figure 20 represents that smartphones can help in reporting discreetly for many rea-

Figure 19. Affordability of smartphones

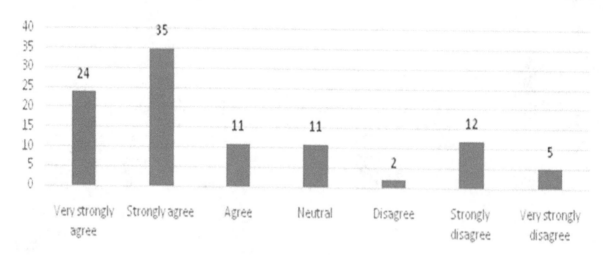

sons and portability and instant sharing are at the top of the list. Few respondents also disagreed that smartphones help in reporting discreetly.

Figure 20. Smartphones in discreet reporting

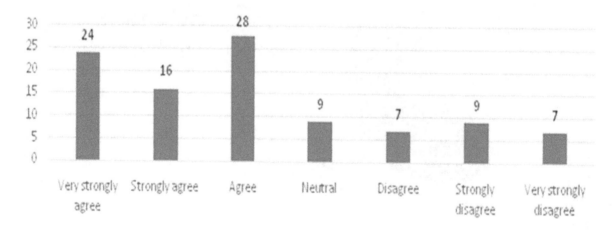

People in front of Smartphones Versus in front of Camera and Mic

People behave differently in various situations, and facing a camera is one of those where people become more conscious and can't talk as freely as they normally do. The smartphone is a solution for such people as 26% of respondents strongly agreed, and 21% strongly agreed. Facing a phone becomes easier than facing a camera. On the other hand, a few respondents very strongly disagreed and strongly disagreed with this as they feel it makes no difference while facing a phone camera or a professional camera (figure 21).

Figure 21. People facing Smartphones vs Camera

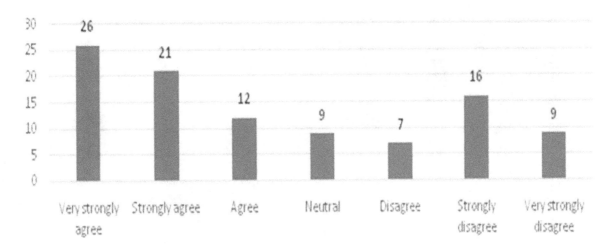

Can Smartphones be Used for Print, Audio, Digital, and Video Mediums

More than 60% of respondents said that smartphones could also be used for print media, audio & video, and digital media as it produces good quality as compared to professional equipment and in near future, there will be developments in the technology which will help in sharing even better-quality files for the same usage. Almost 25% of respondents showed disagreement on different levels of smartphones being used for these purposes (figure 22).

Figure 22. Using Smartphones for Print, Audio, Digital & Video

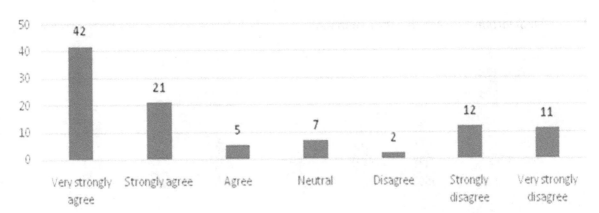

Figure 23. Smartphones giving more control to reporters

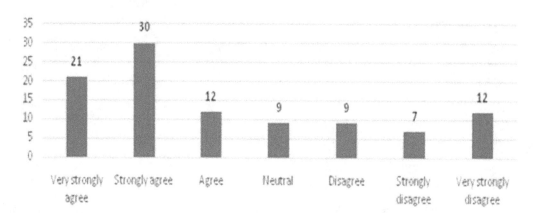

Smartphones Give More Control to Reporters (in Terms of Equipment)

More than 60% of respondent agreed on various levels that smartphones give more control to reporters as it is easy to use, and you do not need a bigger crew to hand the device as compared to a professional camera. Reporters can report more confidently when they are more in control of the situation (figure 23).

Smartphones Changing the Newsroom

More than 50% of respondents agreed that smartphones are changing the newsrooms as reporting has become faster and prompter. There are fewer chances of mistakes for reporters when using digital mediums for writing and reporting from distant locations (figure 24).

Figure 24. Smartphones changing the newsroom

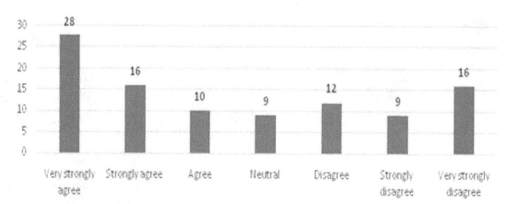

Also, almost 40% of respondents disagreed on various levels that newsrooms are changing. This might have just the effect of tough times, and things may return to normal post-pandemic.

CONCLUSION

Everyone is adapting to the new technology; some are using it to share information with colleagues, while some are doing a major portion of the regular work using smartphones. Smartphones are offering more advanced features to compete with professional equipment. People use them for their regular work very often, which has positively affected their workflow. Phones provide some safety while maintaining a safe distance from other people, from the team, or outwards. Mobile Journalism was a term in the Indian media, but now it has been adopted by the media professionals very well, and they are using it to their best. Mobile phone helps journalists to capture short video, interviews, and photos and to edit the content, and it also helps them forward the content to their agency for final publication. It helps them create their stories more freely and quickly with the least support. The trend is increasing as more people watch and read news on mobile phones. Multi-tasking phones help them in facing the pressure of deadlines. Most of the devices used are smartphones and are laced with all media technologies sufficient for writing, photography, video production, editing, uploading, downloading, etc. Due to this ease of access, more journalists adapt to MOJO in their routine work.

Recommendations

News organizations should incorporate these MOJO techniques and appreciate the speed and fast-paced delivery of the content, whether print or audio-visual. Mobiles have global reach and constantly updating technology. As youth is the largest social media consumer, with increased screen time each year, mobile use is a habit, if not an addiction; it makes it normal for professional use. Media Organisations are favouring mobile journalism. Most of the time, information was indirect, but it was through valid sources. In transferring news from one source to another, there are chances of missing details in between. Nobody anticipated that the pandemic would go on this long or take a fierce take on people's lives. Many industries, like entertainment media, have shifted to online platforms, and other work fields, such as journalists, must think of concrete solutions; temporary solutions will not go in the long run. More concrete solutions require long-term research and studies.

REFERENCES

Admin, R. I. S. J. (2014, March 04). *How mobile phones are changing journalism practice in the 21st Century*. Reuters Institute. reutersinstitute.politics.ox.ac.uk/: https://reutersinstitute.politics.ox.ac.uk/risj-review/how-mobile-phones-are-changing-journalism-practice-21st-century

Barthel, M. (2016). *State of the News Media 2016: Fact Sheet*. Pew Research Center. https://assets.pewresearch.org/wp-content/uploads/sites/13/2016/06/30143308/state-of-the-news-media-report-2016-final.pdf

Cameron, D. (2008). Mobile Journalism: A snapshot of current research and practice. *Research Gate*, 1-6.

Evans, J. R., & Mathur, A. (2005). The value of online surveys. *Internet Research*.

Fardigh, O. W. (2014). Accessing the news in an age of mobile media: Tracing displacing and complementary effects of mobile news on newspapers and online news. *Mobile Media & Communication, 3*(1), 53–74.

Goggin, G. (2012). Google phone rising: The Android and the politics of open source. *Continuum, 26*(5), 741–752. doi:10.1080/10304312.2012.706462

Gracyalny, M. L. (2017). Scales, Likert Statement. *The SAGE encyclopedia of communication research methods,* 1555-1557.

Granger, J. (2019, July 29). A day in the life of a mojo-only TV newsroom. *Journalism.co.uk.* https://www.journalism.co.uk/video/mojo-newsroom/s400/a742390/

Granger, J. (2020, January 13). 10 tips for introducing mobile journalism into local newsrooms. *Journalism.co.uk.* https://www.journalism.co.uk/news/10-tips-for-introducing-mobile-journalism-into-a-local-newsroom/s2/a750186/

Horrigan, J. B. (2016, September 9). *Library usage and engagement.* Pew Research Center. https://www.pewresearch.org/internet/2016/09/09/library-usage-and-engagement/

Karhunen, P. (2017, July 14). *Research: Do Mobile Journalists Get More Interviews?* EJO. https://en.ejo.ch/digital-news/research-do-mobile-journalists-get-more-interviews

Kovacs, S. (2017, January 31). How the Hindustan Times Is Building the World's Largest Mobile Journalism Team. *MediaShift.* http://mediashift.org/2017/01/how-the-hindustan-times-building-worlds-largest-mobile-journalism-team/

Kueng, L. (2017, November 16). *Going digital: A Roadmap for organisational Transformation.* Reuters Institute for the study of Journalism. https://reutersinstitute.politics.ox.ac.uk/our-research/going-digital-roadmap-organisational-transformation

London, A. (2020). Find your MOJO: The rise of mobile film makers and journalists. *Allied London.* https://alliedlondon.com/find-your-mojo-the-rise-of-mobile-filmmakers-and-journalists/

Lu, K. (2017, June 12). *Growth in mobile news use driven by older adults.* Pew Research Center. https://www.pewresearch.org/fact-tank/2017/06/12/growth-in-mobile-news-use-driven-by-older-adults/

Mak, B., Nickerson, R., & Sim, J. (October, 2015). A model of Attitude towards Mobile Location- Based Services. *Journal of Quality Assurance in Hospitality & Tourism, Routledge Taylor & Francis Group,* 414-437.

Marler, W. (2018). Mobile phones and inequality: Findings,trends and future directions. *New Media & Society,* 3498–3520.

Marler, W. (2018). Mobile Phones and inequality: Findings, trends, and future directions. *New Media & Society, 20*(9), 3498–3520.

Mathiyazhagan, T., & Nandan, D. (2010). Survey research method, Media Mimansa. National Institute of Family & Welfare.

Mohammedsalih, S. (2017, August). *Mobile Journalism: Using Smartphones in Journalistic work.* Research Gate. https://www.researchgate.net/publication/342546973_Mobile_Journalism_Using_smartphone_in_journalistic_work

Mulcahy, G. (2020). What is mobile journalism. *Shoulder Pod.* https://www.shoulderpod.com/mobile-journalism#:~:text=A%20Mobile%20Journalist%20or%20MOJO,social%20media%20by%20the%20Mojo

Nachmias, D. (1976). *Content Analysis. Research methods in the social sciences.* Adward Arnold.

Polland, R. J. (n.d.). *Essentials of Survey research and Analysis.* University of North Florida. http://www.unf.edu

Prasad, B. D. (n.d.). Content ANalysis, A method in SOciao Science Research. *Retrieved from CSS.in.*

Quinn, S. (2011). *MoJo - Mobile Journalism in the Asian Region.* Konrad-Adenauer-Stiftung.

Rau, A. E. (2018, June). *Context-related information in mobile news. A study on the adoption of localization technology by Legacy media organizations.* Research Gate. https://www.researchgate.net/publication/323486231

Seamedu. (2019, May 13). Understanding Mobile Journalism & Its Relevance in Today's Times. *Seamedu.* https://www.seamedu.com/blog/understanding-mobile-journalism-its-relevance-in-todays-times/

Tjaardstra, N. (2017, April 30). This is what Mobile Journalism looks like today. *World Assosciation of News Publishers.* https://wan-ifra.org/2017/04/this-is-what-mobile-journalism-looks-like-today/

Vaage, K. (2016). News narratives in locative journalism- rethinking news for the mobile phone. *Journal of Media Practice,* 245–262.

WNIP. (2018). *The rise of mobile journalism: Publishing's new frontier?* WNIP. https://whatsnewinpublishing.com/the-rise-of-mobile-journalism-publishings-new-frontier

Chapter 22
An Empirical Study of Distraction in Work–Life Balance of Teachers During COVID–19 Turmoil Circumstances

Himanshu Barot
Karnavati University, India

Sunil H. Patel
Karnavati University, India

ABSTRACT

COVID-19 was a crucial time to survive and created unprecedented challenges for every industry globally. This unexpected event distracted the work-life balance to where many are physically and mentally tired. Being pushed to quickly adapt to the new work environment and online teaching pedagogy was a challenge for the entire education system. Many studies have been conducted on the impact of COVID-19 in work-life balance of teachers, but the authors observed not a single study has revealed the strength of association between gender, employability, post lecture energy, and domestic responsibilities. This study aimed to measure the strength of this association using chi-square and Cramer's v analysis as well as impact of the pandemic on teaching faculty and subsequent implications of policy. The major outcomes of the study are that personal and professional life was imbalanced with affected mental health, which leads to less productivity.

INTRODUCTION

A healthy work environment is an essential variable to enhance productivity and success. During the COVID-19 pandemic breakout, work and life had badly disrupted routines. While the world stopped moving, work did not, and staff shifted to working from home. During the Covid-19 pandemic, an unanticipated shift from office to remote work was taking a toll on the employees' mental health, even in

DOI: 10.4018/978-1-6684-6682-7.ch022

the comfort of their homes. The work-life balance remains to be an essential element of a good work environment, even if it is remote. Work-life balance and job satisfaction are issues that are difficult to fix and require constant concerns that have to be addressed (Chakrawarti, 2021). The pandemic has revamped how the faculties split their time between personal and professional (coaching, engaging with students, and administration responsibilities). According to a survey in Brazil, 83 percent faculties did not prepare to teach remotely, 67 percent were nervous, 38 percent sensed drained, and fewer than 10 percent were satisfied. This result highlights that most teachers were unprepared for such change, which requires a comprehensive socio-emotional monitoring and psychological support strategy to ensure teacher well-being (Barron et al., 2021). Due to lockdown and remote working, many institutions have cut costs by easing the salary, which disturbs the personal finance metrics. Managing finance and high job insecurity may be additional variables of work-life balance during the pandemic.

The role of the teachers is unique in society. Education is the skills and knowledge-based industry which is the backbone of any nation as a supplier for other industries (Al-Busaidi, 2014). Here students are trained as per current industry requirements in different domains. Throughout the pandemic, the education system encountered several obstacles, making it challenging for teachers to sustain a healthy work-life balance while delivering a high-quality education (Singh, Nakave, & Shah, 2022). The effectiveness and efficiency of the education sector depend on the employees. In modern times, the work-life balance to be developed and maintained by teachers is supremely challenged. Teachers must give additional time each day for effective and creative results, which may face a challenging atmosphere. The consequences of imbalance in work life can negatively impact mental and physical stability in the long run, which could be a prolonged effect on performance, concentration, efficacy, and work-family conflicts (Sunitha & Gopal, 2021).

WORK-LIFE BALANCE THEORIES

Spillover Theory

The spillover model describes the connection between work and family. This theory is that the experiences and satisfaction in one domain results impact the other domain similarly (Edward & Rothbard, 2000). Spillover theory is also categorized as horizontal and vertical. Horizontal spillover impacts one domain's life on the neighboring domain. In contrast, vertical spillover is based on the transmission of emotions or moods between those who are regularly connected, such as family members or organizational colleagues (Sirgy, Efraty, Siegel, & Lee, 2001).

Conflict Theory

Work-life conflict arises when incompatible with meeting the demands of family life due to fulfillment of demands of work life. It is also known as inter-role conflict, and it creates role pressure and stress which influence a person's contribution behavior or strain (Greenhaus & Beutell, 1985). Time–based conflicts are enormous working hours, and scheduling makes it challenging to participate in different roles. Second behavior-based conflict occurs when behavioral issues in family roles or work roles due to unable to adjust expectations of different roles. And third, strain-based conflict occurs when family or work demands spill over, and difficult to fulfill the responsibilities of both roles, which produces psychological symptoms such as anxiety, tension, fatigue, irritability, and depression (Pleck, Stainnes, & Lang, 1980).

Concept of Work-Life Balance

The work-life balance consists of three words work, life, and balance means equilibrium between professional and personal life. The above three words widely include appropriate arrangement amongst work, i.e., profession and aspirations, life, i.e., leisure, health, family, pleasure, and spiritual development, and the balance of both of them in getting satisfaction and good functioning at both the places, i.e., workplace and home which reduces the conflict (Campbell, 2000) (Hill, Hawkins, Ferris, & Weitzman, 2021). Work-life balance brings holistic integration of professional, personal, social, and family life and thereby leads to the satisfaction of the individual.

LITERATURE REVIEW

In India, both government and private sector teaching fraternity are not exposed to work-life balance practices even though it is not designed and implemented by their employers. The study is on the education sector and observed that flexi-time and working from home would not be feasible options for the teaching field. The teaching community needs to design work-life balance policies. The growing diversity of family structures heightened the relevance of balancing work and life. So, the management should focus on flexible working time and incorporate work-life balance strategies in the organization, which can positively impact employees' well-being (Muthulakshmi, 2018). Studies have proved that work-life balance positively impacts family and work satisfaction and psychological distress. Married and working women find it more difficult to manage the balance due to long working time, overtime and traveling from home. In the case of women in the teaching profession have too much burden on their responsibilities and feel more stress, anxiety, and pressurize, so it is very difficult to maintain a work-life balance. In today's busy schedule, well-being and healthcare programs can help to balance and maintain professional and personal life (Memon, Shah, & Shaikh, 2017). Educational institutes play an important role in developing and motivating young minds, and teachers' responsibility lies on the shoulders of teachers. The educational employees working life and environment play a crucial role. Quality of work life encourages employees and makes and maintains the balance between professional, personal and social life with enhancing job satisfaction (Pandey & Jha, 2014). In teaching, job satisfaction is essential for effective and efficient results. The quality of work-life balance depends on designation, nature of the appointment, academic stream, and nature of serving institutions. Accordingly, there is a negative impact on the personal and professional life of teachers due to the heavy work pressure of excessive teaching workload with administrative tasks, research, and many more extensive activities (Punia & Kamboj, 2013).

In India, female workers generally face difficulties and stress through excessive work time and avoiding or limited recognition of their work, which leads to demotivation. This new normal work environment of working from home is a completely unpredictable working scenario. Due to unavoidable situations, conducting classes online remotely was mandatory. It was very hectic and stressful to operate, maintain and balance personal and professional life in the same place parallel (Rawal, 2021). The study reveals that most employees are unsatisfied due to the excess working hours and high-stress levels, which impact their work-life balance. In today's era, the teaching fraternity's role is very dynamic, and there is heavy pressure on them with evolving new teaching-learning environments (Senthilkumar, Chandrakumara-mangalam, & Manivannan, 2012). During COVID-19, the challenging task was the average person was unable to enhance or meet the effective outcomes because of the complex process where they required technology support at every moment. Back-to-back meetings and workload put people under tremendous stress. During work from home, people have found that they are just away from one call or message and expected to work 24X7 and unable to concentrate on other work and devote quality time to family, which causes more stress. Positive work-life balance is essential during such a pandemic, encouraging and motivating employees for growth and productive outcomes (R. Ramakrishnan,2020).

Working from home positively affects the work life of teaching professionals (Sunitha & Gopal, 2021) (Putri & Ali Amran, 2021). So the study expects that working from home positively influences work-life balance. Autonomy in organizing the work schedule makes it possible to impact positively and motivate employees working from home (Rupietta & Beckmann, 2018). Working from home also imbalances employees' work lives if it is not done properly. Organizations must pay more attention to the working hours and duration of work through which the employees can balance and maintain their work-life (Putri & Ali Amran, 2021).

STATEMENT OF THE PROBLEM

Nowadays, employers' expectations are increasing from the employees, putting excessive pressure to get the expected results. In modern scenarios, employees have various competing responsibilities and duties like professional careers, kids, elderly parent care, etc. Work-life balance forms and sustains a supportive and healthy working environment, strengthening employee loyalty and productivity. And between this unprecedented COVID-19 challenge, the already existing issue of work-life balance got worse. For teaching professionals, sudden changes in the work environment from the office to remote working, changes in teaching pedagogy compatible with online mode, and insufficient infrastructure were challenges in balancing and maintaining work and life. Thus, the effectiveness of online teaching during COVID-19 became a challenging factor contributing to mental unrest among teachers (Verma, Panigrahi, & Alok, 2021). Maintaining balance in work-life is not restricted to individual well-being and relationship but is also important for improving performance and productivity in work. Hence, researchers have attempted to study the work-life balance among teachers during COVID-19 challenges.

OBJECTIVES, RESEARCH QUESTIONS, AND HYPOTHESIS

The COVID-19 pandemic has challenged teachers to change the teaching pedagogy in different environments. How many teachers can replicate the offline practices in the new setup and when it is through work from home? When teachers are working from home, they have to maintain a work-life balance in one place. It is a little bit tough, especially for women. The consequences of work-life imbalance may harm teaching productivity and associated activities such as research, participation in FDP/conferences, etc., and mental health. To unfold the answers to these questions, the researchers have carried out the research with the following objectives.

Objective

- ○ To understand the amount of time spent on online classes
- ○ To understand the energy level post lecture
- ○ Whether the domestic responsibilities were clashing with work responsibilities
- ○ Employability status during the pandemic
- ○ Whether the faculties were able to manage the work-life balance

The research questions are answered by testing the following null hypothesis:

H_1: Gender is not associated with time spent online, Post-lecture Energy level, and domestic responsibilities clashing with work responsibilities.

H_2: Employability is independent of post-lecture energy level and domestic responsibilities.

RESEARCH METHODOLOGY

The exploratory research has been used for this study to explore the impact of working from home on work-life balance. The data for the study has been collected through a structured questionnaire. Further, the study has defined the research problem right from its inception of the concept of work-from-home and work-life balance. The data analysis has been done using SPSS and carried out cross tabulation, chi-square, phi, and Cramer's analysis.

Research Sample

The primary participants for this research were the teaching staff of schools, colleges, and coaching institutes. The sample space has been chosen from the teaching staff switched from offline teaching mode to online mode due to Covid-19 lockdowns.

Research Design

For this study, primary data has been obtained through a structured questionnaire, while secondary data has been collected from the platforms and blogs, sharing teachers' experiences in lockdowns. The nature of data is both qualitative and quantitative.

RESEARCH ANALYSIS AND INTERPRETATIONS

Inferences from the Table 1

- 58% and 42% of respondents were male and female, respectively.
- 46% of the teaching staff spent more than 4 hours daily online teaching.

Table 1. Analysis and profile of the respondents

Profile		In %
Gender	Male	42
	Female	58
Type of institution	School	30
	College / University	40
	Coaching Institution	30
Hours spend online	1-3 hours	15
	3-4 hours	39
	More than 4 hours	46
Retained Energy level of the Teaching Staff after the completion of working hours.	Low	36
	Neutral	52
	High (Motivated)	12
Teaching Staffs were able to take part in the carrier advancement activities	Yes	36
	No	64
Frequency of Clashing of responsibilities (Between Domestic and professional responsibilities)	Always	36
	Sometimes	52
	No	12
Managing parenting responsibility along with session preparation	Cakewalk	3
	Easy	6
	Neutral / Manageable	46
	Difficult	42
	Very Difficult	3
During the ongoing pandemic, have you ever felt job insecurity?	Yes	37
	No	63
Was work-life balance maintained?	Yes	21
	No	63
	Maybe	16
Did you feel that mental health was compromised?	Yes	48
	No	27
	Maybe	25
The type of lecture mode is preferred	Online	21
	Offline	79

- More than half of the respondents replied about the neutrality of their nature at the end of completing their job. This can be seen in 2 ways: positive and negative. On a positive note, one is not completely drained of energy. While on the negative side, neutrality means no add-on. This indicates that one is not satisfied with the task done, i.e., how the classes were conducted. It can be because of a lack of student response, absenteeism, no interaction with colleagues, or maybe even pre-occupancy with the housework.

Table 2. Crosstab gender versus hours spend online

			Hours Spend Online			Total
			1-3	3-4	More than 4	
Gender	Male	Count	6	12	24	42
		% within Gender	14.3%	28.6%	57.1%	100.0%
	Female	Count	9	27	22	58
		% within Gender	15.5%	46.6%	37.9%	100.0%
Total		Count	15	39	46	100
		% within Gender	15.0%	39.0%	46.0%	100.0%

- 64% of the faculties said they could not participate in career advancement activities like online FDPs, certification programs, online conferences, and so on. The reasons for this might be many; house duties, health issues, lack of motivation, confusion, etc.; all these reasons majorly point to one single issue: lack of work-life balance.
- 52% of the respondents said that work and home duties sometimes overlap. 36% of respondents said they had overlapping responsibilities in both domains. The major reason behind the clash might be the time overlapping. Mostly, the regular/important housework/duties were to be carried out in the morning, and the same would be the time for online classes.
- 46% said it was the manageable house and work, both responsibilities. 42% said they found it difficult to manage both responsibilities.
- 63% of respondents confessed to having an imbalanced work-life. And if it is counted the 'maybe' is yes, then the number goes up to 79% of respondents having work-life balance issue. The reasons for this could be many such as spending huge time in front of the screen and not getting proper responses from the students, not being able to explain things as could be done in offline classes, and so on.
- 48% of respondents said yes that their mental health was being compromised, and it could be so because of continuously sitting in front of the screen and talking against the blank screen.
- After having a new experience of online classes, when it was asked the respondents, 79% said that they would prefer offline classes, as now they could compare and say which one was better. As with online classes, they found it difficult to manage their work-life balance.

Hypothesis Testing

H_1: Gender is not associated with time spent online, Post-lecture Energy level, and domestic responsibilities clashing with work responsibilities (table 2).

The p-value, .135, is greater than 0.05, and the study fails to reject H1, which means the gender and hours spent online are independent (table 3).

As the p-value is .135, there is a moderate association between gender and hours spent online (table 4).

As the p-value, .408 is greater than 0.05, the study fails to reject H_1, and the gender and the energy level after the classes are found to be independent (tables 5 and 6).

The p-value is .408, which shows a strong association between gender and energy level (table 7).

Table 3. Chi-Square test of gender versus hours spent online

	Value	df	Asymp. Sig. (2-sided)
Pearson Chi-Square	3.999a	2	.135
Likelihood Ratio	4.041	2	.133
N of Valid Cases	100		

Table 4. Symmetric measures

		Value	Approx. Sig.
Nominal by Nominal	Phi	.200	.135
	Cramer's V	.200	.135
N of Valid Cases		100	

Table 5. Crosstab gender versus energy level

			Energy Level			Total
			High	Neutral	Low	
Gender	Male	Count	6	24	12	42
		% within Gender	14.3%	57.1%	28.6%	100.0%
	Female	Count	6	28	24	58
		% within Gender	10.3%	48.3%	41.4%	100.0%
Total		Count	12	52	36	100
		% within Gender	12.0%	52.0%	36.0%	100.0%

Table 6. Chi-Square Test of Gender Versus Energy Level

	Value	df	Asymp.Sig. (2-sided)
Pearson Chi-Square	1.794a	2	.408
Likelihood Ratio	1.815	2	.404
Linear-by-Linear Association	1.602	1	.206
N of Valid Cases	100		

Table 7. Symmetric measures

		Value	Approx. Sig.
Nominal by Nominal	Phi	.134	.408
	Cramer's V	.134	.408
N of Valid Cases		100	

Table 8. Crosstab gender versus house/work responsibilities

| | | | House responsibilities clashing with work responsibilities | | | Total |
			Always	Sometimes	No	
Gender	Male	Count	9	27	6	42
		% within Gender	21.4%	64.3%	14.3%	100.0%
	Female	Count	27	25	6	58
		% within Gender	46.6%	43.1%	10.3%	100.0%
Total		Count	36	52	12	100
		% within Gender	36.0%	52.0%	12.0%	100.0%

Table 9. Chi-Square test gender versus house/work responsibilities

	Value	df	Asymp. Sig. (2-sided)
Pearson Chi-Square	6.688a	2	.035
Likelihood Ratio	6.924	2	.031
Linear-by-Linear Association	4.823	1	.028
N of Valid Cases	100		

As the p-value, .035 is less than 0.05 so reject H_1, and the gender and house responsibilities clashing with work responsibilities depend on each other. Generally, we find ladies having the responsibilities of the house, so the clashing of responsibilities was found to be on the higher side with females (tables 8 and 9).

Table 10. Symmetric measures

		Value	Approx. Sig.
Nominal by Nominal	Phi	.259	.035
	Cramer's V	.259	.035
N of Valid Cases		100	

The p-value is 0.35, which shows a weak association between gender and house/work responsibilities (table 10).

As the p-value, .012, is less than 0.0, reject H1, the gender, and managing child/ parent responsibilities depend on each other. Generally, we find ladies having the dual responsibilities of caring for children and parents. Hence, their responses towards managing both are found to be a bit difficult with females (tables 11 and 12).

The p-value is .012, which shows a weak association between gender and child/ parent responsibilities (table 13).

Table 11. Crosstab gender versus managing child/parent responsibilities

			Level of difficulty in managing child/parent responsibilities and preparing for the online classes					Total
			Cakewalk	Easy	Neutral / Manageable	Difficult	Very Diffi.	
Gender	Male	Count	3	0	23	15	1	42
		% within Gender	7.1%	0.0%	54.8%	35.7%	2.4%	100.0%
	Female	Count	0	6	22	30	0	58
		% within Gender	0.0%	10.3%	37.9%	51.7%	0.0%	100.0%
Total		Count	3	6	45	45	1	100
		% within Gender	3.0%	6.0%	45.0%	45.0%	1.0%	100.0%

H_2: Employability is independent of the post-lecture energy level and domestic responsibilities (table 14).

As the p-value, .072 is greater than 0.05, the study fails to reject H_2 and the employability, i.e., whether he or she is working with the school, coaching institute, or university/ college, the energy level used by them to deliver the lectures are found to independent. So, whether the faculty is from any of these places, they have been putting the same effort into delivering the sessions (tables 15 and 16).

The p-value is 0.072, which shows a weak association between employability and energy level (table 17).

As the p-value, .188, is greater than 0.05, accepting H_2 and the employability, i.e., whether he or she is working with the school, coaching institute, or university/ college, the responsibilities of managing

Table 12. Chi-Square test managing child/parent responsibilities

	Value	df	Asymp Sig. (2-sided)
Pearson Chi-Square	12.790a	4	.012
Likelihood Ratio	16.411	4	.003
Linear-by-Linear Association	1.016	1	.313
N of Valid Cases	100		

Table 13. Symmetric measures

		Value	Approx. Sig.
Nominal by Nominal	Phi	.358	.012
	Cramer's V	.358	.012
N of Valid Cases		100	

Table 14. Crosstab employability versus energy level

			Energy Level			Total
			High	Neutral	Low	
Institution Type	School	Count	0	18	12	30
		% within Employed	0.0%	60.0%	40.0%	100.0%
	Coaching	Count	3	15	12	30
		% within Employed	10.0%	50.0%	40.0%	100.0%
	Uni / College	Count	9	19	12	40
		% within Employed	22.5%	47.5%	30.0%	100.0%
Total		Count	12	52	36	100
		% within Employed	12.0%	52.0%	36.0%	100.0%

child/parents are found to be independent. So, whether the faculty is from any of these places, they have been putting the same efforts into managing child/parent responsibilities (tables 18 and 19).

The p-value is .188, which shows a strong association between employability and managing child/parent responsibilities.

FINDINGS

This research study has been conducted to know about the work-life balance of teachers/faculties in a pandemic situation where the classes were conducted online. The following is the takeaway from this research:

- Most faculties spend more than four hours a day on online classes.

Table 15. Chi-Square test employability versus energy level

	Value	Df	Asymp. Sig. (2-sided)
Pearson Chi-Square	8.590a	4	.072
Likelihood Ratio	11.438	4	.022
Linear-by-Linear Association	4.414	1	.036
N of Valid Cases	100		

Table 16. Symmetric measures

		Value	Approx. Sig.
Nominal by Nominal	Phi	.293	.072
	Cramer's V	.207	.072
N of Valid Cases		100	

Table 17. Crosstab employability versus managing child/parents' responsibilities

| | | | Level of difficulty in managing child/parent responsibilities and preparing for the online classes | | | | | Total |
			Cakewalk	Easy	Neutral / Manageable	Difficult	Very Diffi.	
Employed where	School	Count	0	3	15	12	0	30
		% within Employed	0.0%	10.0%	50.0%	40.0%	0.0%	100.0%
	Coaching	Count	0	0	12	18	0	30
		% within Employed	0.0%	0.0%	40.0%	60.0%	0.0%	100.0%
	Univ / College	Count	3	3	18	15	1	40
		% within Employed	7.5%	7.5%	45.0%	37.5%	2.5%	100.0%
Total		Count	3	6	45	45	1	100
		% within Employed	3.0%	6.0%	45.0%	45.0%	1.0%	100.0%

- There was a mix of responses regarding energy level after the classes; the majority replied neutrally.
- Most of the faculties said they could not participate in career advancement activities like online FDPs, certification programs, online conferences, and so on.
- Clashing of responsibilities was found to be on both the front.
- Most of them replied neutrally regarding having their work impact family life and vice versa.
- Most of them responded that they were getting their family support to carry out their office work.
- More than fifty percent said that their management was not bothered to look for the mental health of their faculties, and faculties had compromised with mental health even though the majority of respondents did not have any kind of insecurity related to their jobs.

Table 18. Chi-Square employability versus managing child/parents' responsibilities

	Value	df	Asymp. Sig. (2-sided)
Pearson Chi-Square	11.250a	8	.188
Likelihood Ratio	14.128	8	.078
Linear-by-Linear Association	.531	1	.466
N of Valid Cases	100		

Table 19. Symmetric measures

		Value	Approx. Sig.
Nominal by Nominal	Phi	.335	.188
	Cramer's V	.237	.188
N of Valid Cases		100	

- Respondents confessed to having an imbalanced work-life, and it was somewhat difficult to manage domestic and work responsibilities during online classes, which impacted productivity.
- Certain hypothesis test was carried out, which says that gender and online hours spent, energy level after the classes, and work-life balance were found to be independent. Whereas house/ work responsibilities and managing domestic responsibilities were found to be dependent on gender as females generally managed both these responsibilities and they find it a bit difficult to manage both things properly.
- The other hypothesis related to employability, i.e., Whether the faculty is from school, coaching institute, or college/university, and their energy level, as well as managing domestic responsibilities along with the work, is found to be independent.

CONCLUSION

This paper aimed to provide an overview of work-life balance for teachers when working from home during the pandemic. As far as work-life balance is concerned, many discussions and research have been carried out by various researchers. But sudden changes in the working environment of teaching professionals during the pandemic were one of the big challenges. Also, learning new techniques to maintain a work-life balance when academicians have to work from home added instability. The study has found that it is very difficult to manage home responsibilities and prepare for online classes from home, which imbalance the mental health and deteriorating productivity of female teachers compare to male teachers. From the overall outcomes of the study, it is concluded that even after resuming the physical office (classroom), management should have a proper work-life balance policy for the employees for the expected results and retaining employees. Due to high disturbance and home responsibility, most teachers cannot participate and attend the conference or FDP for their career enhancement, which reflects a high impact cost for the management.

Practical Implications

The outcomes of this research can be used effectively to evaluate and implement the work-life balance policy in academia and other organization as well. Employee satisfaction does not depend on monetary benefits but most on the working environment and policies of the organization also.

REFERENCES

Al-Busaidi, K. A. (2014). Linking ICT to the Development of Knowledge] Based Economy Pillars. *European Conference on Knowledge Management*, (*vol.* 1, p. 15).

Barron, M., Cobo, C., Munoz-Najar, A., & Ciarrusta, I. S. (2021). *The changing role of teachers and technologies amidst the COVID 19 pandemic: Key findings from a cross-country study*. World Bank Blogs.

Campbell, C. S. (2000). Work/Family border theory: A new theory of work/family balance. *Human Relations*, *53*(6), 747–770. doi:10.1177/0018726700536001

Chakrawarti, N. (2021). Quality Work Life Balance in Education Sector. *International Journal of Education, Modern Management, Applied Science &. Social Science*, 3(2), 9–13.

Edward, J., & Rothbard, N. (2000). Mechanisms Linking Work and Family: Clarifying the Relationship between Work and Family Constructs. *Academy of Management Review*, 25(1), 178–199. doi:10.2307/259269

Greenhaus, J., & Beutell, N. (1985). Sources of Conflict between Work and Family Roles. *Academy of Management Review*, 10(1), 76–88. doi:10.2307/258214

Hill, E. J., Hawkins, A., Ferris, M., & Weitzman, M. (2021). Finding an extra day a week: The positive influence of perceived job flexibility on work and family life Balance. *Family Relations*, 49–58.

Memon, A. R., Shah, A., & Shaikh, F. (2017). Work Life Balance Of Working Women In Education Sector: A Case Study Of. *International Case Studies Journal*, 6(2), 27–46.

Muthulakshmi, C. (2018). A study on work life balance among the teaching professional of arts and science colleges in Tutocorin district. *ICTACT Journal of Management Studies*, 4(1), 657–662. doi:10.21917/ijms.2018.0089

Pandey, A., & Jha, B. (2014). Review and Redefine: Quality of Work Life for Higher. *Global Journal of Management and Business Research. Administrative Management*, 14(11), 35–41.

Pleck, J., Stainnes, G., & Lang, L. (1980). Conflicts between work and family life. *Monthly Labor Review*, 103(3), 29–32.

Punia, V., & Kamboj, M. (2013). Quality of Work-life Balance Among Teachers in Higher Education Institutions. *Learning Community- An International Journal of Educational and Social Development*, 4(3), 197-208. doi:10.5958/j.2231-458X.4.3.010

Putri, A., & Amran, A. (2021). Employees' Work-Life Balance Reviewed From Work From Home Aspect During COVID-19 Pandemic. *International Journal of Management Science and Information Technology*, 1(1), 30–34. doi:10.35870/ijmsit.v1i1.231

Rameshkumar, M., & Chiluka, N. (2012). Work-Life Balance Amongst Teachers. *The IUP Journal of Organizational Behavior*, 11(1), 1-10. https://ssrn.com/abstract=2148284

Rawal, D. M. (2021). Work life balance among female school teachers [k-12] delivering online curriculum in Noida [India] during COVID: Empirical study. *Management in Education*, 20, 1–9. doi:10.1177/0892020621994303

Rupietta, K., & Beckmann, M. (2018). Working from Home. *Schmalenbach Business Review*, 70(1), 25–55. doi:10.100741464-017-0043-x

Senthilkumar, K., Chandrakumaramangalam, & Manivannan. (. (2012). An empirical study on teaching professionals work-life balance in higher learning institutions with special reference to Namakkal District, Tamilnadu. *Bonfring International Journal of Industrial Engineering and Management Science*, 2(3), 38–41. doi:10.9756/BIJIEMS.1389

Singh, J., Nakave, P., & Shah, B. (2022). An empirical study on the impact of Covid-19 on work-life balance of Teaching employees in higher Education sector of Vadodara (India). *International Journal of Creative Research Though*, *10*(2), 779–787.

Sirgy, J., Efraty, D., Siegel, P., & Lee, D.-J. (2001). A New Measure of Quality of Work Life (QWL) Based on Need Satisfaction and Spillover Theories. *Social Indicators Research*, *55*(3), 241–302. doi:10.1023/A:1010986923468

Sunitha, K. S., & Gopal, N. (2021). Work from home improves or impairs the work-life balance – A study conducted among teachers. *Journal of Contemporary Issues in Business and Government*, *27*(4), 22–31. doi:10.47750/cibg.2021.27.04.005

Verma, S., Panigrahi, T., & Alok, D. (2021). COVID 19 and Online Learning in Post Graduate Management Programme: An Empirical Analysis of Students' Perception. *Journal of Applied Business and Economics*, *23*(2), 108–123.

Compilation of References

Abidin, M. J. Z., Mohammadi, M. P., & Lean, O. C. (2011). The Reading Habits of Malaysian Chinese University Students. *In Journal of Studies in Educat*ion, 1(1), E9.

Abri, A. A. (2021). Exploring EFL learners' comm*ents on web-base*d peer feedback: Local and global revisions. English Language Teaching, 14(6), 114–124. doi:10.*5539/elt.v14n6p114*

*Abulrub, A. G., Attridge, A. N., & Willi*ams, M. A. (2011). Virtual reality in engineering education: The future of creative learning. 2011 IEEE Global Engineering *Education Conference (EDUCON), (pp. 751–757). IEEE.* 10.1109/EDUCON.2011.5773223

AbuSa'*aleek, A. O., & Shariq, M. (2021). Innovative practices in ınstructor e-feedback: A ca*se study of e-feedback given in three linguistic courses during the COVID 19 Pandemic. Arab World English Journal (AWEJ) Special Issue on Covid 19 Challenges (1), 183 -198. doi:10.24093/awej/covid.*14*

*Admin, R. I. S. J. (2014, M*arch 04). How mobile phones are changing journalism practice in the 21st Century. Reuters Institute. reutersinstitute.politics.ox.ac.uk/: https://reutersinstitute.politics.ox.ac.uk/risj-review/how-m*obile-phones-are-changing-journalism-practice-21st-c*entury

Ahl, H., & Marlow, S. (2012). Exploring the dynamics of gender, feminism, and entrepreneurship: Advancing debate to escape a dead end? Organisation, 19(5), 543–562. doi:10.1177/1350508412448695

Ahl, H., *& Nelson, T. (2015).* How policy positions women entrepreneurs: A comparative analysis of state discourse in Sweden and the United States. Journal o*f Business Venturing, 30(2), 273–291.* doi:10.1016/j.jbusvent.2014.08.002

Ahmed, A. A., Kumar, T., Iksan, M., Subrahmanyam, S., Kokhichko, A. N., Ali, M. H., Tuama, H. M., & Mousavi, M. S. (2022). Comparing the effectiveness of massive o*pen online course (MOOC) and flipped in*struction on EFL learners' reading comprehension. Education Research *International. doi:10.1155/2022/6543920*

*Aicha, B. A. (2014). The im*pact of Whatsapp mobile social learning of the achievement and attitudes of females students and compared with face to face learning in the classr*oom. European Scientific Journal, 10(22), 116–136.*

Ajmal, M., & Kumar, T. (2020). Using DIALANG in assessing foreign language proficiency: The interface between learning and assessment. Asian ESP Journal, 16(2.2), 335 - 362.

Aktas, B. Ç., & Can, Y. (2019). The effect of Whatsapp usage on the attitudes of students toward English self-efficacy and English courses in foreign language education outside the school. Interna*tional Electronic Journal of Elementary Educat*ion, 11(3), 247–256. doi:10.26822/iejee.2019349249

Al-Busaidi, K. A. (2014). Linking ICT to the Development of Knowledge] B*ased Economy Pillars. Europea*n Conference on Knowledge Management, (vol. 1, p. 15).

Al-Gahtani, S. S. (2016). Empirical investigation of e-learning acceptance and assimila*tion: A structur*al equation model. Appl. Comput. Inform., 12(1), 27–50. doi:10.1016/j.aci.2014.09.001

Aldohon, H. (2021). Writing centre conferences*: Tutors' perc*eptions and practices. Educational Studies, 47(5), 554–573. doi:10.1080/03055698.2020.1717931

Alfalagg, A. R. (2020). Impact of teacher-student writing *conferences on frequency and accuracy of using cohesive devices in EFL st*udents' writing. Asian-Pacific Journal of Second and Foreign Language Education, *5(1), 1–19. doi:10.118640862-020-00104-z*

Alharahsheh, H. H., & Pius, A. (2020). A review of key paradigms: Positivism vs interpretivism. Global Academic Journal of Humanities and Social Sciences, 2(3), 39–43.

Alharbi, M. A. (2020). Exploring the potential *of Google Docs in facilitating innovative teaching and learning* practices in an EFL writing course. Innovation in Language Learning and Teaching, *14(3), 227–242. doi:10.1080/17501229.20 19.1572157*

*Ali, A., Ishtiaq Khan, R. M., Kumar, T., Shahbaz, M., & Alou*rani, A. (2022). An investigation of the educational challenges during COVID-19: A case study of Saudi students' experience. European Journal of Educational Research, 11(1), 353–363. doi:10.12973/eu-jer.11.1.353

Aliyyah, R. R., Rachmad*tullah, R., Samsudin, A., Syaodih, E.*, Nurtanto, M., & Tambunan, A. R. S. (2020). The perceptions of primary school teachers of online learning during the COVID-19 pandemic period: A case study in Indonesia. Journal of Ethnic and Cultural Studies, 7(2), 90–109.

Almeida, R., Bueno, T., & Gimenez, T. (2013). O uso das tecnologias de informação e comunicação para a*prendizagem colab*orativa: percepções de alunos e professores do ensino médio de uma escola pública de Londrina. In Denise Ismênia Bossa Grassano Ortenzi, Kleber, Aparecido da Silva, *Luciana Cabrini* Simões Calvo et al. (Orgs.). Re exões sobre ensino de línguas e formação de professores no Brasil: uma homenagem à professora Thelma Gimenez [The use of information and communication technologies for collaborative learning: perceptions of high school students and teachers at a public school in Londrina. In Denise Ismênia Bossa Grassano Ortenzi, Kleber, Aparecido da Silva, Luciana Cabrini Simões Calvo et al. (Org.). Reactions on language teaching and teacher education in Brazil: a tribute to Professor Thelma Gimenez], (pp. 389–410). Pontes.

Alota*ibi, S. S., & Kumar, T. (2019). Promot*ing teaching and learning performance in mathematics classroom through e-learning. Opción, Año 35. Especial, 2019(19), 2363–2378.

Al Rawashdeh*, A.Z., Mohammed, E.*Y., Al Arab, A.R., Alara, M. and Al-Rawashdeh, B., (2021) "Advantages and disadvantages of using e-learning in university education: Analyzing students' perspectives." Electronic Journal of e-Learning, 19(3), pp.107-117.

Ambrose, G., & Harris, P. (2009). Basics Design 08: Design Thinkin*g. Bloomsbury Publishing* Plc.

Anderson, A., & Ronteau, S. (2017). Towards an entrepreneurial theory of practice; emerging ideas for emerging economies. Journal of Entrepreneurship in Emerging Economies, 9(2), 110–120. doi:10.1108/JEEE-12-2016-0054

Anderson, R. M., Heesterbeek, H., Klinkenberg, D., & Hollingswo*rth, T. D. (2020). How will country-based mitiga-tion me*asures influence the course of the COVID-19 epidemic? Lancet, 395(10228), 931–934. doi:10.1016/S0140-6736(20)30567-5 PMID:32164834

Andújar-Vaca, A., & Cruz-Martínez, M. S. (2017). Mobile instant messaging: WhatsApp and its potential *to develop oral skills. Comunicar. Med*ia Education Research Journal, 25(1), 43–52. doi:10.3916/C50-2017-04

Anghel, D. (2020). Challenges of Homeschooling in Romania during Pandemic Times. Revista Românească pentru Educație Multidimensională, 12(2supl1), 1-11.

Annamdevula, S., & Bellamkonda, R. S. (2016). *Effect of student perceived* service quality on student satisfaction, loyalty, and motivation in Indian u*niversities: The development of HiEduQual.* Journal of Modelling in Management, 11(2), 488–517. doi:10.1108/JM2-01-2014-0010

Ansari, J. A., & Khan, N. A. (2020). Exploring the role of social media in collaborative learning the new domain of learning. Smart L*earning Environments, 7(1),* 9. doi:10.118640561-020-00118-7

Archer-Kuhn, B., Samson, P., Damianakis, T., Barrett, B., Matin, S., & Ahern, C. (2020). Transformative *learning in Field education:* Students bridging the theory/Practice gap. British Journal of Social Work, 51(7), 2419–2438. doi:10.1093/bjsw/*bcaa082*

Arnott, L., & Yelland, N. J. (2020). Multimodal lifeworlds: Pedagogies for play inquiries and explorations. Journal of Ear*ly Childhood Education Research, 9(1), 124–146.*

*Arr*ow, K. M., & Grant, Z. S. (2021). Pandemic Possibilities in Crip Time: Disrupting Social Work Field Education. Intersectionalities: A Global Journal of Social Work Analysis. Research, Polity, and Practice, 9(1), 98–114.

Atmowardoyo, H. (20*18). Research methods in* TEFL studies: Descriptive research, case study, error analysis, and R & D. Journal of Language Teaching and Research, 9(1), 197–204. doi:10.17507/jltr.0901.25

*Aulkemeier, F., Iacob, M. E., & va*n Hillegersberg, J. (2019). Platform-based collaboration in digital ecosystems. Electronic Markets, 29(4), 597–608. doi:10.100712525-019-00341-2

Bacha, M. S., Kumar, T., Bibi, B. S., & Yunus, M. M. (2021). Using English as *a lingua franca in Pakistan: Influences an*d implications in English Language Teaching (ELT). Asian ESP Journal., 17(2), 155–175.

Bachman, L. F., & Palmer, A. S. (1996). Language Testing in Practice. Oxford University Press.

Baisel, A., Vijayakumar, M., & Sujatha, P. (2020). An Experiential Study on the Learners' Perception of E-Learning and Traditional Learning. In Innovations and Technologies for Soft Skill Development and Learning (pp. 46–52). IGI Global. d*oi:10.4018/978-1-7998-3464-9.ch006*

Bakoko, R., & Waluyo, B. (2021). Learning reading through current news events: Newsela.com. Teaching English as a Second Language Electronic Journal (TESL-EJ), 25(3), 1-6.

Bakr, A. F., El Sayad, Z. T., & Thomas, S. M. *S. (2018). Virtu*al *r*eality as a tool for children's participation in kindergarten design process. Alexandria Engineering Journal, 57(4), 3851–3861. doi:10.1016/j.aej.2018.10.003

Bal, M. *(2008). Visual analysis. SAGE Handb. Cul*t. Anal., 46, 163–184. doi:10.4135/9781848608443.n9

Balas-Timar, D., & Lile, R. (2015). The story of Goldilocks told by organizational psychologists. Procedia: Social and Behavio*ral Sciences, 203, 239–243. doi:10.1016/j.sb*spro.2015.08.288

Barbot, M. J., Pugibet, V. (2002). Apprentissages des langues et technologies: usages en émergence. Paris: Clé International. Berdal-Masuy, F., Briet, G. & Pairon, J. (2004). Apprendre seul, à son rythme et *encadré. Études de lingui*stique appliquée [Learning languages and technologies: emerging uses. Paris: Key International. Berdal-Masuy, F., Briet, G. & Pairon, J. (2004). Learn a*lone, at your own pace and supervised. Studies in Applied Linguistics], 134*(2), 173-190.

Barr, A. H. (1936). Cubism and Abstract Art exhibition catalogue cover. Museum of Modern Art (1902-1981), Jr. Cubism and Abstract Art. The Museum of Modern Art.

Barron, M., Cobo, C., Munoz-Najar, A., & Ciarrusta, I. S. (2021). *The changing role of teachers and technologies amidst the COVID 19 pandemic: Key findings from a cross-country study*. World Bank Blogs.

Barrot, J. S. (2020). Integrating technology into ESL/EFL writing through Grammarly. *RELC Journal*, 0033688220966632.

Barteit, S., Guzek, D., Jahn, A., Barnighausen, T., Jorge, M. M., & Neuhann, F. (2020). Evaluation of e-learning for medical education in low- and middle-income countries: A systematic review. *Computers & Education*, 145, 103726. doi:10.1016/j.compedu.2019.103726 PMID:32565611

Barthel, M. (2016). *State of the News Media 2016: Fact Sheet. Pew Research Center*. https://assets.pewresearch.org/wp-content/uploads/sites/13/2016/06/30143308/state-of-the-news-media-report-2016-final.pdf

BasmaIssa, A. A. (2013). The effect of "Whatsapp" electronic dialogue journaling on improving writing vocabulary word choice and voice of EFL undergraduate Saudi students. *Arab World English Journal*, 4(3), 213–223.

Bates, T., & Sangra, A. (2011). Managing technology in higher education: strategies for trans forming teaching and learning. *Wiley/Jossey-Bass. https://www.researchgate.net/publication/ 279513336_Managing_Technology_in_Higher_Education_Strategies_for_Transforming_Teaching_and_Learning*

Bayraktar, A. (2012). Teaching writing through teacher-student writing conferences. *Procedia: Social and Behavioral Sciences*, 51, 709–713. doi:10.1016/j.sbspro.2012.08.229

Bayraktar, A. (2013). Nature of interactions during teacher-student writing conferences, revisiting the potential *effects of self-efficacy beliefs. Eğitim Araştırmaları*-Eurasian Journal of Educational Research, 50, 63–86.

Beatson, R., Molloy, C., Fehlberg, Z., Perini, N., Harrop, C., & Goldfeld, S. (2022). Early Childhood *Education Participation: A Mixed-Methods Study of Pare*nt and Provider Perceived Barriers and Facilitators. Journal of Child and Family Studies, 31(11), 1–18. *doi:10.100710826-022-02274-5 PMID:35282609*

Beck, J., & Flinn, A. (2021). Say it: English pronunciation. Teaching English as a Second Language Electronic Journal (TESL-EJ), 25(2), 1-7.

Becker, B. E., & Luthar, S. S. (2002). Social-Emotional Factors Affecting Achievement Outcomes Among Disadvantaged Students: Closing the *Achievement Gap. Educati*onal Psychologist, 37(4), 197–214. doi:10.1207/S15326985EP3704_1 PMID:23255834

Bell, K. & Anscombe, A.W. (2013). International field experience in social work: Outcomes of a short-term study abroad programme Social Work Education to India., 32(8), pp.1032-10*47. doi:10.1080/02615479.2012.730143*

*Benne*tte, E., Metzinger, A., Lee, M., Ni, J., Nishith, S., Kim, M., & Schachner, A. (2021). Do you see what I see? Chil*dren's understanding of perception and physical interaction over v*ideo chat. Human Behavior and Emerging Technologies, 3(4), 484–494. doi:10.1002/hbe2.276

Bensalem, E. (2018). The impact of WhatsApp on EFL students' vocabulary learning. Arab World English Journal (Vol. 9). AWEJ.

Benyo, A. & Ku*mar, T. (2020). An analysis of* Indian EFL learners' listening comprehension errors. Asian ESP Journal, 16(5.2), 69-85.

Benyo, A., Alkhaza'leh, B. A., & Kumar, T. (2022). Using unfair mea*ns in undergraduate E-learning* programmes in English: An analytical survey. World Journal on Educational Technology: Current Issues., 14(1), 329–341. doi:10.18844/wjet.v14i1.6761

Bertenthal; J. P. G. M. W., *& Curtis, J. B. L. P. C. (2002).* Learning and Understanding. Kartografija i Geoinformacije, 12(20). National Academies Press. doi:10.17226/10129

Bhatt, S. (2016). Social Work Educational Institut*ions in India: An Analysis. Journal of Social Work Education, Rese*arch and Action, 2, 46-67. https://www.researchgate.net/publication/349324328_Social_Work_Educational_Institutions_in_India

Bhatti, R., & Bart, W. *M. (2013). On the effect of lea*rning style on scholastic achievement. Current Issues in Education (Tempe, Ariz.), 16(2).

Bigras, N., Lemay, L., Lehrer, J., Charron, A., Duval, S., Robert-Mazaye, C., & Laurin, I. (2021). Early childhood educators' perceptions of their emotional state, relationships with parents, challenges, and opportunities during the early stage of the pandemic. Early Childhood Education Journal, 49(5), 775–787. doi:10.100710643-021-01224-y PMID:34131*378*

*Blackwell, C. K., L*auricella, A. R., & Wartella, E. (2014). Factors influencing digital *technology use in early childhood education. Computers & Education,* 77, 82–90. doi:10.1016/j.compedu.2014.04.013

Blok, A., Lindstrøm, M. D., Meilvang, M. L., & Pedersen, I. K. (2018). Trans-local professional projects: Re-scaling the linked ecology of expert jurisdictions. Journal of Professions and Organization, 5(2), *106–122. doi:10.1093/jpo/joy003*

*Borgmey*er, A. R., Garand, J. C., & Wilks, S. E. (2021). Examining academic entitlement through the lens of field education. Social Work Education, 41(6), 1336–1350. *doi:10.1080/02615479.2021.1950672*

Bourdieu, P. (1984). Distinction. A Social Critique of the Judgement of Taste (R. Nice, Trans.). Harvard University Press.

Bourdieu, P. (1993). The Field of Cultural Production. Columbia University Press.

Bou*rdieu, P., & Passeron, J. P. (1977). Re*production in Education, Society and Culture. Sage.

Bourdieu, P., & Wacquant, L. (1992). An invitation to reflexive sociology. *University of Chicago Press.*

Bowen, M. M. (2018). Effect of virtual reality on motivation and achievement of middle-school students. Pro-Quest Dissertations and Theses, 125. ht*tps://search.proquest.com/docview/2050*000008?accountid=156 37%0Ahttp://sfx.car.chula.ac.th:3410/sfxlcl41?url_ver=Z39.88 -2004&rft_val_fmt=info:ofi/fmt:kev:mtx:dissertation&genre=di ssert*ations+%26+theses&sid=ProQ:ProQuest+D*isser*t*ations+%26+T heses+Global&at

Boys, J. (2011). Towards Creative Learning Spaces: Rethinking the Architecture of Post-compulsory Education. Routledge.

Brahimi, T., *& Sarirete, A. (2015). Learning* out*s*ide the classroom through MOOCs. Computers in Human Behavior, 51(1), 604–609. doi:10.1016/j.chb.2015.03.013

Braun, V., & Clarke, V. (2021). Can I use TA? Should I use TA? Should I not use TA? Comparing reflexive thematic analysis and other pattern-based qualitative analytic approaches. Counselling & Psychotherapy Research, 21(1), 37–47. doi:10.1002/capr.12360

Briggs, A. (2015), Ten ways to overcome barriers to student engagement *online. On-line Learning Consortium. ht*tps://onlinelearningconsortium.org/news_item/tenways-overc omebarriers-student-engagement-online/

Brindha, D., Jayaseelan, R., & Kadeswaran, S. (2020). Social media reigned by in*formation or misinformation about COVID-19:* a phenomenological study. Research Gate.

Broadbent, G. (1973). Design in Architecture: Architecture and the Human Sciences. Wiley-Blackwell.

Broadbent, J. (2017). *Comparing online and bl*ended learners' self-regulated learning strategies and academic performance. The Internet and Higher Education, 33, 24–32. doi:10.1016/*j.iheduc.2017.01.004*

*Brookhart, S. M. (2017). H*ow to give effective feedback to your students. ASCD.

Brown, D. A. (2018). Instructor-student conferencing as pedagogy: Measuring ISC pedagogy's impact on student writing and self-Efficacy [Doctoral dissertation, Indiana University of Pennsylvania].

Brown, H. D. (20*16). Teaching by Principles. An In*teractive Approach to Language Pedagogy. Prentice Hall.

Brown, R., Mawson, S., Lee, *N., & Peterson, L. (2019). Start-up factories, t*ransnational entrepreneurs and entrepreneurial ecosystems: Unpacking the lure of start-up accelerator programmes. European Planning Studies, 27(5), 885–904. doi: 10.1080/09654313.2019.*1588858*

Bruinsma, M. (2004). Motivation, cognitive processing and achievement in higher education. Learning and Instruction, 14(6), 549–568. doi:10.1016/j.learninstruc.2004.09.001

Buck, G. (2001). Assessing listening. Cambri*dge University Press. doi:10.1017/CBO9780511732959*

Buetow, S. (2010). Thematic analysis and its reconceptualisation as 'saliency analysis'. Journal of Health Services Research & Policy, 15(2), 123–125. doi:10.1258/jhsrp.2009.009081 PMID:19762883

Bureau, E. (n.*d.). Direction of Schools' C*urriculum Development - Balanced Development. Continuous Enhancement.

Burns, S., Jegatheeswaran, C., & Perlman, M. (2022). I Felt Like I was Going Crazy: Understanding Mother's and Young Children*'s Educational Experiences at Home During COVID-19. Early Childhood E*ducation Journal, 1–14. doi:10.100710643-022-01306-5 PMID:35153466

Butt, A. L., Kardong-Edgren, S., & Ellertson, A. (2018). Using Game-Based Virtual Reality with Haptics for Skill Acquisition. Clinical Simulation in Nursing, *16, 25–32. doi:10.1016/j.ecns.2017.*09.010

Cameron, D. (2008). Mobile Journalism: A snapshot of current research and practice. Research Gate, 1-6.

Campbel*l, A., & McNamara, O. (2009). Mapping the field of practitioner research, inquiry and professional learnin*g in educational contexts: a review. In A. Campbell & S. Groundwater-Smith (Eds.), Connecting inquiry and professional learning *in education: international perspec*tives and practical solutions (pp. 10–26). Routledge.

Campbell, C. S. (2000). Work/Family border theory: A new theory of work/family balance. Human Relations, 53(6), 747–770. doi:10.1177/0018726700536001

Cardoso, A. P., Ferreira, M., Abr*antes, J. L., Se*abra, C., & Costa, C. (2011). Personal and Pedagogical Interaction Factors as Determinants of Academic Achievement. Procedia: Social and Behavioral Sciences, 29, 1596–1605. doi:10.1016/*j. sbspr*o.2011.11.402

Carini, R. M., Kuh, G. D., & Klein, S. P. (2006). Student Engagement and Student Learning: Testing the Linkages*. Research in Higher Education, 47(1), 1–32. doi:10.100711162-005-8150-9

Carroll, J. D. (1968). Generaliz*ation of Canonical Correlation Analy*sis to Three of More Sets of Variables. APA.

Cassidy, S. (2004). Learning Styles: An overview of theories, models, and measures. Educational Psychology, 24(4), 419–444. doi:10.*1080/0144341042000228834*

Castro, M., Expósito-Casas, E., López-Martín, E., Lizasoain, L., Navarro-Asencio, E., & Gaviria, J. L. (2015). Parental involvement on student academic achievement: A meta-analysis. Educational Research Review, 14, *33–46. doi:10.1016/j. edurev.2015.01.002*

Chadah, S. (2010). Operationalising right to Education Act: Issues and challenges. The Indian Journal of Public Administration, 56(3), 616–634. doi:10.1177/0019556120100318

Chakrawarti, N. (2021). Quality *Work Life Balance in Education Se*ctor. International Journal of Education, Modern Management, Applied Science &. Social Science, 3(2), 9–13.

Chan, Y. C. (2007). Elementary school of EFL teachers' beliefs and practices of multiple assessments. Reflections on English Language Teaching, *7(1), 53.*

Chang, V. (2016). Review and discussion: E-learning for academia and industry. International Journal of Information Management, 36(3), 476–485. doi:10.1016/j.ijinfomgt.2015.12.007

Chang, Y. (2021). Investigating L2 teacher-student writing conf*erences in a college ESL composi*tion classroom. English Teaching, 76(2), 25–55. doi:10.15858/engtea.76.2.202106.25

Chanier, T., & Vetter, A. *(2006)*. Mu*l*timodalité et expression en langue étrangère dans une plate-forme audio-synchrone [Multimodality and foreign language expression in an audio-synchronous platform]. (Vol. 9). Alsic.

Charliet, B., Deschryver, N., Peraya, *D. (2006). Apprendre en présence e*t *à* distance: une définition des dispositifs hybrides. Distances et savoirs [Learning in the presence and at a distance: a definition of hybrid devices. Distances and knowledge], 4(4), 469-496.

Chatterjee, P., & Nath, A. (2015). Massive open online *courses (MOOCs) in education – a case study in Indian conte*xt *a*nd vision to ubiquitous Learning. Proceedings of the 2014 IEEE International Conference on MOOCs, Innovation and Technology in Education, (pp. 36–41). IEEE.

Chen, L., Chen, T. L., Lin, C. J., & Liu, H. K. (2018). Preschool teachers' perception of the application of information communication techn*ology (ICT) in Taiwan.* Su*s*tainability, 11(1), 114. doi:10.3390u11010114

Cheng, D. (2018). WordSift: Having fun with learning words. Teaching English as a Second Language Electronic Journal (TESL-EJ), 22(2), 1-9.

Chick, R. C., Clifton, G. T., Peace, K. M., Propper, B. W., Hale, D. F., Alseidi, A. A., & Vreeland, T. J. (2020). Using techn*ology to maintain the e*du*c*ation of residents during the COVID-19 pandemic. Journal of Surgical Education, 77(4), 729–732. doi:10.1016/j.jsurg.2020.03.018 PMID:32253133

Cho, B.-H., Ku, J., Jang, D. P., Kim, S., Lee, Y. H., Kim, I. Y., *Lee*, J. H., & Kim, S. I. (2002). The effect of virtual reality cognitive training for attention enhancement. Cyberpsychology & Behavior, 5(2), 129–137. doi:10.1089/109493102753770516 PMID:12025879

Chu, T. H., & Chen, *Y. Y. (2016). With Good, We Become Goo*d: Understanding e-learning adoption by the theory of planned behaviour and group influences. Computers & Education, 92, 37–52. doi:10.1016/j.compedu.2015.09.013

Chuaphalakit, K., Inpin, B., & Coffin, P. (2019). A study of the quality of feedback via t*he Google Classroom-mediate*d-anonymous online peer feedback activity in a Thai EFL writing classroom. International Journal of Progressive Education, 15(5), 103–118. doi:10.29329/ijpe.2019.212.8

Chunjian, Z. (2009). Ap*plication of multimedia in English Teach*ing and learning. Journal of Technology for ELT.

Ciuchta, M. P., & Finch, D. (2019). The mediating role of self-efficacy on entrepreneurial intentions: *Exploring boundary conditi*ons. Journal of Business Venturing Insights, 11, e00128.

Clark, R. C. (2005). Multimedia Learning in e-Courses. In R. Mayer (Ed.), The Cambridge Handbook of Multimedia Lear*ning (pp. 589–616). Cambridge University Pr*ess. doi:10.1017/CBO9780511816819.036

Consalvo, A., & Maloch, B. (2015). Keeping the teacher at arm's length: Student resistance in writing conferences in two high school classrooms. Journal of Classroom Interaction, 120–132.

Coronavirus (COVID-19) Cases . (n.d.). Our World in Data. http://ourworldindata.org

Costa, D., Lopes, J. (2015). A perspectiva docente quanto ao uso do WhatsApp como ferramenta adicional ao ensino de inglês: um experimento em um curso livre de idiomas [The teaching perspective regarding the use of WhatsApp as an additional tool for teaching English: an experiment in a free language course].

COVID-19 (2022). Wikipedia, The Free Encyclopedia. https://en.wikipedia.org/w/index.php?title=COVID-19&oldid=1127052423

Cremona, L., Ravarini, A., & Viscusi, G. (2015). Fitness of business models for digital collaborative platforms in clusters: a case study. Lecture Notes in Business Information Processing. Springer Verlag.

Cross, N. (2006). Designerly ways of knowing. Springer.

Cruz-Benito, J., Sanchez-Prieto, J. C., Theron, R., & Garcia-Penalvo, F. J. (2019). Measuring students' acceptance to AI-driven assessment in eLearning: proposing a first TAM-based research model. International Conference on Human-Computer Interaction, (pp. 15–25). Springer, Cham, 10.1007/978-3-030-21814-0_2

Cummings, J. J., & Bailenson, J. N. (2016). How Immersive Is Enough? A Meta-Analysis of the Effect of Immersive Technology on User Presence. Media Psychology, 19(2), 272–309. doi:10.1080/15213269.2015.1015740

Czerniewicz, L. (2020). What we learnt from "going online" during university shutdowns in South Africa. Phil on EdTech. https://philonedtech.com/what-we-learnt-from-going-online-during-university-shutdowns-in-south-africa/

Damanik, E. S. D. (2020). Student attitude toward the use of Whatsapp in EFL class. Vision (Basel), 15(2).

Davis, F. D. (1989). Perceived usefulness, perceived ease of use, and user acceptance of information technology. Management Information Systems Quarterly, 13(3), 319–340. doi:10.2307/249008

Daweli, T. W. (2018). Engaging Saudi EFL students in online peer review in a Saudi university context. Arab World English Journal, 9(4), 270–280. doi:10.24093/awej/vol9no4.20

Dayal, H. C., & Tiko, L. (2020). When are we going to have the real school? A case study of early childhood education and care teachers' experiences surrounding education during the COVID-19 pandemic. Australasian Journal of Early Childhood, 45(4), 336–347. doi:10.1177/1836939120966085

Delmestri, G., & Brumana, M. (2017). The Multinational Corporation as a Playing Field of Power: A Bourdieusian Approach. Research in the Sociology of Organizations, 49, 325–353. doi:10.1108/S0733-558X20160000049011

de l'Europe, C. (2001). Cadre européen commun de référence en langues [Common European Framework of Reference for Languages]]. Didier.

Demeter, E., Rad, D., & Balas, E. (2021). Schadenfreude and General Anti-Social Behaviours: The Role of Violent Content Preferences and Life Satisfaction. BRAIN. Broad Research in Artificial Intelligence and Neuroscience, 12(2), 98–111. doi:10.18662/brain/12.2/194

Deouël, J., & Granjon, F. (Eds.). (2011). Communiquer à l'ère numérique. Regards croisés sur la sociologie des usages. Presses des Mines. [Communicate in the digital age. Perspectives on the sociology of uses. Paris: Presses des Mines] doi:10.4000/books.pressesmines.387

DePorter, B., & Hernacki, M. (1992). Quantum learning: Unleashing the genius in you. Dell.

Depover, C., De Lièvre, B., Peraya, D., Quintin, J., & Jaillet, A. (2011). Le tutorat en formation à distance *[Distance education tu*toring. Louvain-la-Neuve, Belgium] De Boeck Supérieurdoi:10.3917/dbu.depov.2011.01

De Silva, R. (2015). How Transnational Entrepreneurs are Responding to Institutional Voids: *A Study of Transnational Entrepreneurs from Sri Lanka. S*outh Asian Journal of Management, 22(2), 61–80.

Dezalay, Y., & Madsen, M. R. (2012). The Force of Law and Lawyers: Pierre Bourdieu and the Reflexive Sociology of Law. Annual Review of Law and Social Science, 8(1), 433–452. doi:10.1*146/annurev-lawsocsci-102811-173817*

*Dhawan, S. (2020). Online Learnin*g: A Panacea in the Time of COVID-19 Crisis. Journal of Educational Technology Sy*stems, 004723952093401(1), 5–22. doi:10.1177/0047239520934018*

*Dhodmis*e, T. (2021). Values in Field work for social work: Value ethics for sustainable and ethical future, for the field work in social work. Mahratta, 1(1), 1–3.

Dimitratos, P., Buck, T., Fletcher, M., & Li, N. (2016). The motivation of international entrepreneurship: The case of Chinese transnational entrepreneurs. *International Bu*siness Review, 25(5), 1103–1113. doi:10.1016/j.ibusrev.2016.01.012

Djonko-Moore, C. M. (2022). Diversity education and early childhood teachers' motivation to remain in teaching: An explora*tion. Journal of Early Childho*od Teacher Education, 43(1), 35–53. doi:10.1080/10901027.2020.1806151

Doanh, D. C. (2021). The moderating role of self-efficacy on the cognitive process of entrepreneurship: An empirical study in Vietnam. Journal of Entrepreneurship. Management and Inno*vation, 17(1), 147–174.*

Dockstader, J. (2008). Teachers of the 21st century know the what, why, and how of technology integration. MIT. http://the-t*ech.mit.edu/Chemicool*

*Dogbey, J., Kumi-Yeb*oah, A., & Dogbey, J. (2017). Dialogue pedagogical strategies perceived to enhance online interaction: *The instructor's pe*rspective. International Journal of Online Pedagogy and Course Design, 7(3), 70–85. doi:10.4018/IJOPCD.2017070105

Dong, C. (2018). 'Young children nowadays are very smart in ICT'–preschool teachers' p*erceptions of ICT use. Inter*national Journal of Early Years Ed*ucation, 1–14. doi:10.1080/09669760.2018.1506318

Dong, C., & Mertala, P. (2021). It is a tool, but not a 'must': Early childhood preservice teachers' perceptions of *ICT and its affordanc*es. Early Years, 41(5), 540–555. doi:10.1080/09575146.2019.1627293

Doucet, A., Netolicky, D., Timmers, K., & Tuscano, F. J. (2020, March 2). T*hinking about pedagogy in an unfolding pandemic (Version 2.0*). Independent Report written to inform the work of Education International and UNESCO. https://issuu.com/educationinternational/docs/2020_ research_covid-19_eng

*Downes, S. (2012). Connectivism and Connect*iv*e* Knowledge: essays on meaning and learning networks. Stephen Downes Web. https://www.downes.ca/post/58207

Drolet, J., & Harriman, K. 2020. A conversation on a new Canadian social work field education and research collaboration initiative. Field Educator, 10(1). h*tps://fieldeducator.simmons.edu/ar ticle/a-conversation-on -a-new-canadian-social-work-field-education-and-research-col laboration-initiative/*

*Drori, I., Honig, B., & Ginsberg, A. (2010). Transnational and Immigrant Entrep*reneurship in a Globalised World (B. Honig, I. Drori, & B. Carmichael, Eds.). University of Toronto Press.

Drori, I., Honig, B., & Wright, M. (2009). Transnational Entrepreneurship: An Emergent Field of Study. Entrepreneurship Theory and Practice, 33(5), 1001–1022. doi:10.1111/*j.1540-6520.2009.00332.x*

Duch, H., Fisher, E. M., Ensari, I., & Harrington, A. (2013). Screen time use in children under 3 years old: A systematic review of correlates. *The International Journal* of Behavioral Nutrition and Physical Activity, 10(1), 1–10. doi:10.1186/1479-5868-10-102 PMID:23967799

Dunnagan, C. L., Dannenberg, D. A., Cuales, M. P., Earnest, A. D., Gurnsey, R. M., & Gallardo-Williams, M. T. (2020). Production and Evaluation of a Realistic Immersive Virtual Reality Organic Chemistry Laboratory Experience: Infrared Spectroscopy. Journal of Chemical Education, 97(1), 258–262. doi:10.1021/acs.jchemed.9b00705

Durst, D., Lanh, T. H., & Pitzel, M. (2010). A Comparative Analysis of Social Work in Vietnam and Canada: Rebirth and Renewal. Journal of Comparative Social Work, 5(2), 77–88. doi:10.31265/jcsw.v5i2.63

Dutta, S. (2020, May 20). Telemedicine is the new call *for action at the moment. The Indian* Express.https://indianexpress.com/article/lifestyle/health/in-telemedicine-virtual-healthcare-futu re-scope-india-mindsets-doctors-6421192/

Ebadi, S., & Alizadeh, A. (2021). The effects of online learner-driven feedback on IELTS writing skills via Google Docs. Teaching English with Technology, 21(3), 42–66.

Eckstein, G. (2013). The interaction of theory, philosophy, and practice in ESL writing conferences. *The CATESOL Journal, 24(1), 174–186.*

Edelhauser, E., & Lupu-Dima, L. (2021). One year of online education in COVID-19 age, a challenge for the Romanian education system. International Journal *of Environmental Research and Public Health, 18(15), 8129. doi:10.3390/ ijerph18158129 PMID:34360421*

Edelson, P. J. (1998). The organization of courses via the internet, academic aspects, interaction, evaluation, and accreditation. ERIC. National Autonomous University of Mexico.

Edward, J., & Rothbard, N. (2000). Mechanisms Linking Work and Family: Clarifying the Relationship between Work and Family Constructs. Academy of *Management Review*, 25(1), 178–199. doi:10.2307/259269

Egan, S. M., Pope, J., Moloney, M., Hoyne, C., & Beatty, C. (2021). Missing early education and care during the pandemic: The socio-emotional impact of the COVID-19 crisis on young children. Early Childhood Education Journal, 49(5), 925–934. doi:10.100710643-021-01193-2 PMID:33935481

El-Awaisi, A., O'Carroll, V., Koraysh, S., Koummich, S., & Huber, M. (2020). Perceptions of who is in the healthcare team? A content analysis of social media posts during COVID-19 pandemic. Journal of Interprofessional Care, 34(5), 622–632. doi:10.1080/13561820.2020.1819779 PMID:32962452

El Lissitzky (1928), The Constitution of the Soviets and The Newspaper Transmissions. Soviet Pavilion, Pressa, Cologne, 1928, Pinterest.

El Massah, S. S., & Fadly, D. (2017). Predictors of academic performance for finance students: Women at higher education in the UAE. International Journal of Educational Management, 31(7), 854–864. doi:10.1108/IJEM-12-2015-0171

Emre Avci, Y., Tösten, R., & Sahin, Ç. Ç. (2020). Examining the Relationship between Cultural Capital and Self-Efficacy: A Mixed Design Study on Teachers. Athens Journal of Education, 7(2), 169–192.

Eroglu, O., & Picak, M. (2011). Entrepreneurship, National Culture and Turkey. International Journal of Business and Social Science, 2(16).

Essig, L. (2017). Same or different? The "cultural entrepreneurship" and "arts entrepreneurship" constructs in European and US higher education. Cultural Trends, 26(2), 125–137.

Evans, J. R., & Mathur, A. (2005). The value of online surveys. Internet Research.

Ewert, D. E. (2009). *L2 writing conferences: Investigating teacher talk. Journal of Second Language Writing, 18(4),* *251–269. doi:*10.1016/j.jslw.2009.06.002

Ezeh, C. (2020). A comparison of Storyjumper with Book Creator, and *Storybird for multimodal storytelling. Teaching* *English as a Second Language Electronic Journal (TESL-EJ), 24(1), 1*-9.

F, A. (2020). The Role of the University of the Future. Ernst & Young.

Fan, W., & Gordon, M. D. (201*4). The powe*r of social media analytics. Communications of the ACM, 57(6), 74–81. doi:10.1145/2602574

Fardigh, O. W. (2014). Accessing the news in an age of mobile media: Tracing displacing and complementary effects of mobile *news on newspapers a*nd *o*nline news. Mobile Media & Communication, 3(1), 53–74.

Farrah, M., & Al-Bakry, *G. H. (2020). Online learning for EFL stu*dents in Palestinian universities during corona pandemic: Advantages, challenges and solutions. Indonesian Journal of Learning and Instruction, 3(2), 65–78.

Fehrmann, P. G., Keith, T. Z., & Reimers, T. M. (1987). Home Influence on School Learning: Direct and Indirect Ef-*fects of Parental* Involvement on High School Grades. The Journal of Educational Research, 80(6), 330–337. doi:10.1 080/00220671.1987.10885778

Findeli, A. (2001). Rethinking Design Education for the 21st Century: Theoretical, Methodological, and E*thical Discus-*sion. *Design Issues, 17(1), 5–17.* Advance online publication. doi:10.1162/07479360152103796

Finlay, S. E. (1969). Student Achievement. Lancet, 294(7618), 495. doi:10.1016/S0140-6736(69)90200-1 PMID:4185483

Fisher, P. J. L. *(1996). Who reads when and why. In E. H., Cramer, M. Castle (*Ed.*).* Fostering the love of reading: The effective domain in reading educa*tion. Newark: International Reading Association.*

*F*letcher, T., & Bullo*ck*, S. M. (2015). Reframing pedagogy while teaching about teaching online: A collaborative self-study. Professional Development in Education, 41(4), 690–706. doi:10.*1080/19415257.2014.93835*7

*F*lores, M. A., Barros, A., Simão, A. M. V., Pereira, D., Flores, P., Fernandes, E., Costa, L., & Ferreira, P. C. (2022). Portuguese higher education students' adaptation to online teaching *and learning in times* of the COVI*D*-19 pandemic: Personal and contextual factors. Higher Education, 83(6), 1389–1408. doi:10.100710734-021-00748-x PMID:34493877

Forne, M. F. (202*1). Online Meetings in Early C*hildhood Education: A Bonding and Educational Experience in Times of COVID-19. Páginas de Educación, 52–72.

Fotakopoulou, O., Hatzi*gianni, M., Dardanou, M., Unstad, T., & O'Connor, J.* (2020). A cross-cultural exploration of early childhood educators' beliefs and experiences around the use of touchscreen technologies with children under 3 years of age. European Early Childhood Education *Research Journal, 28(2), 272–285. doi:10.*1080/1350293X.2020.1735744

Fowsar, M. A. M. (2020). Local Democratic Crises in Sri Lanka: A Study based on Kalmunai Municipal Council. Journal of Educational and Social R*esearch, 10(5), 34–43. doi:10.36941/jesr*-2020-0085

Fowsar, M. A. M., Raja, N. K. K., & Rameez, M. A. M. (2022). COVID-19 Pandemic Crisis Management in Sri Lanka. Slipping away from Success. In D. Brisen, *T.T.T. Nguyen, & Q.M. Pha*m (Eds.). Times of Uncertainty: National Policies and International Re*lations under Covid 19 in Southeast –Asia and Beyond (401-422).* Kanishka Publishers.

Fowsar, M. A. M., Rameez, M. A. M., & R*ameez, A. (2020). Muslim Minorit*y in Post-war Sri Lanka: A Case Study of Aluthgama and Digana Violence. *Academic Journal of Interdisciplinary Studie*s, 9(6), 56–68. doi:10.36941/ajis-2020-0111

Fox, M., McHugh, S., Thomas, D., Kiefel-Johnson, F., & Joseph, B. (2021). Bringing together podcasting, social work field education and learning about practice with Aboriginal peoples and communities. *Social* Work Education, 1–17. doi:10.1080/02615479.2021.1972963

Friedman, K. (2012). Models of design: Envisioning a future design education. Academia. https://d1wqtxts1xzle7.cloudfront. net/30525217/Friedman_D_2012_Models_of_Design_-with-cover-page-v2.pdf?Expires=1640843489&Signature=PC-G84r9HIFbffpJDTWTsv4QbmGgBANSyfWntNPCUGELaTfeY1giAtusEvUJkXCMykiFqWYI-g7xNNXZsE1srnv0PMUIg-00bq9S46lJvGOevenFxGsNEoquEBrzt

Fuchs, C. (2020b). Communication and capitalism: A critical theory. *University of Westminster* Press., doi:10.16997/book45

Gao, T., & Liu, J. (2021). Application of improved random forest algorithm and fuzzy mathematics in *physical fitness of athle*tes. Journal of Intelligent & Fuzzy Systems, 40(2), 2041–2053. doi:10.3233/JIFS-189206

Gao, X., Samuel, M., & Asmawi, A. (2016). Online features of Qzone w*eblog for critical peer feedback to facilitate business English writing. Journal of Educational* Technology Systems, 45(2), 285–301. doi*:10.1177/0047239516659865*

*Garib, A. (2021). Learn languag*es with music: Lyrics Training app review. Teaching English as a Second Language Electronic Journal (TESL-EJ), 24(4), 1-11.

Garnham, N., & Wi*lliams, R. (1980). Pierre Bourdie*u a*n*d the sociology of culture: An introduction. Media Culture & Society, *2(3), 209–223. doi:10.1177/016344378000200302*

Ghada, A. (2016). Effect of *WhatsApp on critique writing proficiency and perceptions toward learning. Cogent Educa*tion, 1-26.

Ghahderijani, B. H., Namaziandost, E., Tavakoli, M., Kumar, T., & Magizov, R. (2021). The comparative effect of group dynamic assessment (GDA) and computerized dynamic assessment (CDA) on Iranian upper-intermediate EFL learners' speaking complexity, accuracy, and flu*ency (CAF). Language Testi*ng in Asia, 11(1), 25. doi:10.118640468-021-00144-3

Gidley, J., Hampson, G., Wheeler, L., & Bereded-Samuel, E. (2010). From Access to Success: *An Integrated Approach* to Q*uality Higher Education Informed by Social Inclusion Theory and Practic*e. *Higher Education* Policy, 23(1), 123–147. doi:10.1057/hep.2009.24

Gilliland, B. (2014). Academic *language socialization in high school writing conferences. Canadi*an Modern Language Review, 70(3), 303–330. doi:10.3138/cmlr.1753

Global Newswire. (2022). Global Online Education Market (2022 to 2027). https://www.globenewswire.com/fr/news-release/2022/02/03/2378224/28124/en/Global-Online-Education-Market-2022-to-2027-by-User-type-Provider-Technology-and-Region.html

Godw*in-Jones, R.* (2017). Smartphones and language learning. Language Learning & Technology, 21(2), 3–17. 10125/44607

Goggin, G. (2012). Google phone rising: The Android and the politics of open source. Continuum, 26(5), *741–752. do i:10.1080/10304312.2012.706462*

Golonka, E. M., Bowles, A. R., Frank, V. M., Richardson, D. L., & Freynik, S. (2014). Technologies for foreign language learning: A review of technology types and their effectivene*ss. Computer As*sisted Language Learning, 27(1), 70–105. doi:10.1080/09588221.2012.700315

Gomes, J., Almeida, S. C., Kaveri, G., Mannan, F., Gupta, P., Hu, A., & Sarkar, M. (2021). Early Childhood Educators as COVID Warriors: Ad*aptations and Responsiveness to the Pand*emic Across Five Countries. International Journal of Early Childhood, 53(3), 345–366. doi:10.100713158-021-00305-8 PMID:34840345

Gracyalny, M. L. (2017). Scales, Likert Statement. *The SAGE encyclo*pedia of communication research methods, 1555-1557.

Granger, J. (2019, July 29). A day in the life of a mojo-only TV newsroom. Journalism.co.uk. https://www.journalism.co.uk/video/mojo-newsroom/s400/a742390/

Granger, J. (2020, January *13*). *10 tips for intro*ducing mobile journalism into local newsrooms. Journalism.co.uk. https://www.journalism.co.uk/news/10-tips-for-introducing-mobile-journalism-into-a-local-newsroom/s2/a750186/

Grasha, A. F., & Yangarber-Hicks, N. (2000). Integrating *Teaching Styles and Learni*ng Styles with Instructional Technology. College Teaching, 48(1), 2–10. doi:10.1080/87567550009596080

Grassin, J.-F. (2016). Échan*ges en ligne sur un réseau social dans le cad*re d'une formation en Français Langue Étrangère: pratiques discursives et modes de participation [Online exchanges o*n a social network as part of a French as a Foreign Language course: discursive practice*s and modes of participation]. In Liénard, F. & Zlitni, S. (éd.), Médias numériques et communi*cation électronique, Actes de colloque, Bruges, 295-*303.

Greenhaus, J., & Beutell, N. (1985). Sources of Conflict between Work and Family Roles. Academy of Management Review, 10(1), 76–88. doi:10.2307/258214

Gr*oundwater-Smith,* S., & Mockler, N. (2005, July 4-6). Practitioner research in education: Beyond celebra*tion. Paper presented to the Australian Association for Research in Education Focus* Conference, James Cook University, Cairns, Australia.

Grégoire, R. (2016). Cours en ligne ouverts et massifs: état des lieux et adoption au Canada français. Guide et bilan de l'impact des cours en ligne *ouverts et massifs (CLOM) au Canada fra*ncophone [Open and massive online courses: inventory and adoption in French Canada. Guide and assessment of the impact of open and massive *online courses (OLOC)* in French-speaking Canada]. REFAD.

Guiamalon, T. (2021). Teachers Issues and Concerns on The Use of Modular Learning Modality. IJASOS-International E-journal of Advances in Social Sciences, 7(20), 457–469. doi:10.18769/ijasos.970927

Guiamalon, T. S., & Hariraya, P. G. (*2021). The K-12 Senior High School Programl: The Case Of Laboratory High School, Cotabato City State Po*lytechnic College, South Central Mindanao, Philippines. IJASOS-International E-jo*urnal of Advances in Social Sciences, 7(19), 391–399. doi:10.18769/ija*sos.820171

Gunawan, W., Kalensun, E. P., Fajar, A. N., & Sfenrianto. (2018). E-Learning through social media in the virtual learning environment []. IOP Publishing.]. IOP Conference Series. Materials Science and *Engineering, 420(1), 012110.* d*oi:*10.1088/1757-899X/420/1/012110

Gurău, C., Dana, L.-P., & Katz-Volovelsky, E. (2020). Spanning transnational boundaries in industrial markets: A study of Israeli entrepreneurs in China. Industrial Marketing Management, 89, 389–401. doi*:10.1016/j.indmarman.2020.*01.008

Guthrie, J. T. (2000). Contexts for engagement and motivation in reading. Handbook of reading Research, (vol 3), 1-15.

Güneş, E., & Bahçivan, E. (2018). A mixed research-based model for pre-service science teachers' digital literacy: Responses to *"which beliefs" and "how and why they interac*t*" q*uestions. Computers & Education, 118, 96–106. doi:10.1016/j.compedu.2017.11.012

Habermas, J. (1987). Théorie de l'agir communicationnel [[Communication action theory]]. Fayard.

Habes, M., Alghiz*zawi, M., Ali, A., Sali*halnaser, A., & Salloum, S. A. (2020). The Relation among Marketing ads, via Digital Media and mitigate (COVID-19) pandemic in Jordan. Int. J. Adv. Sci. Technol., 29(7), 12326–1234*8.*

Hackley, C., (2014). *Introducing* Advertising and Promotion. Advert. Promot. Commun. Brand., pp. 1–24, . doi:10.4135/9781446278789.n1

Haelewyck, S. (2014). *L'acquisitio*n du français à l'usage d'applications mobiles: un état de question. (Mémoire de Master). Université de Gent. [The acquisition of French for the use of mobile applications: a state of question. [Master memory, University of *Gent]*

Hall, B. (2017). *Follo*wing the Lat*est Trends to Shape Customiz*ed E-Learning Experiences. Brandon Hall [online]. https://www.brandonhall.com/blogs/tag/*e-learning/*

Halliday, M. (1993). *Towards a language-based theory of learning. Linguistics and Education, 5(2), 93–116. doi:10.1016/0898*-5898(93)90026-7

Hansen, A. D. O., & Hansen, A. D. O. (2017). Digital technology in early childhood education. Cadernos Educacao Tecnologia E Soc*iedade,* 10(3), 207–218.

Harima, A., Harima, J., & Freiling, J. (2020). The injection of resources by transnational entrepreneurs: Towards a model of the early evolution o*f an entrepreneurial ecosystem. Entrepreneurship and Regional Development, 1–28.*

Harmer, J. (2007). *The Practice of English Language Tea*ching. Pearson Education Limited.

Harw*ell, D. (2020). Mass schoo*l closures in the wake of the coronavirus are driving a new wave of student surveillance. Washington Post. https://www.washingtonpost.com/ technology/ 2020/04/01/online-proctoring-college-exams-coronavirus/

H*asbi, M., & Hasanah, L. (2020). Early Childhood Learni*ng from Home: Implementation of Distance Learning in Early Childhood Education during the Covid-19 Pandemic Period in Indonesia. International Journal of Innovation. Creativity and Change, 14, 763–778.

Hatipoğlu, Ç. (2015). English language testing and evaluation (ELTE) training in Turkey: Expectations and needs of pre-service English language teachers. ELT Research Jour*nal, 4(2), 111*–128.

Hattie, J., & Timperley, H. (2007). The power of feedback. Review of Educational Research, 77(1), 81–112. doi:10.3102/003465430298487

Hatzigianni, M., & Kalaitzidis, I. (2018). Early childhood educators' attitude*s and beliefs around the use of touch-scr*een technologies by children under three years of age. British Journal of Educational Technology, 49(5), 883–895. doi:10.1111/bjet.12649

Haw*n, C. (2009). Report from* the field: Take two aspirin and tweet me in the morning: How twitter, F*acebook and other social media are reshaping* health care. Health Affairs (Project Hope), 28(2), 361–368. doi:10.1377/hlthaff.28.2.361 PMID:19275991

Hayes, J., & Allinson, C. W. (1996). The Implications of Learning Styles for Training and Development: A Discu*ssion of the Matching Hypothesis. B*ritish Journal of Management, 7(1), 63–73. doi:10.1111/j.1467-8551.1996.tb00106.x

Heggart, K. R., & Yoo, J. (2018). Getting the most fr*om Google Classroom: A Pedagogical Framewo*rk *f*or Tertiary Educators. The Australian Journal of Teacher Education, 43(3), 140–153. doi:10.14221/ajte.2018v43n3.9

Herrington, J., Reeves, T. C., & Oliver, R. (2010). A guide to authentic e-learning. Routledge. *https://researchrepository.murdoch.edu.au/id/eprint/1903/1/*a _guide_to_authentic_learning.pdf

Hess, E. (2019). Book Creator. Teaching English as *a Second Language Electronic Journal (TESL-EJ), 23(1), 1-9.*

Hetesi, S. (2021). A comparative review of Kahoot and Socrative. Teaching English as a Second Language Electronic Journal (TESL-EJ), 24(4), 1-11.

Hill, E. J., Hawkins, A., Ferris, M., & Weitzman, M. (2021). *Finding an extra day a week: The positive in*fluence of perceived job flexibility on work and family life Balance. Family Relatio*ns, 49–58.*

Hisrich, R. D. (1990). Entrepreneurship/intrapreneurship, 45(2) 209. American Psychological Association.

Hitchcock, L. I., King, D. M., Johnson, K., Cohen, H., & Mcpherson, T. L. (2019). Learning outcomes for adolescent SBIRT simulation training i*n social work and nursing education. Jo*urnal of Social Work Practice in the Addictions, 19(1-2), 47–56. doi:10.1080/1533256X.2019.1591781

Holland, A., & Museum, S. (1952). The f*irst museum audio guides. Stedelijk Museum.*

Hong, X., Zhang, M., & Liu, Q. (2021). Preschool teachers' technology acceptance During the COVID-19: An adapted technology acceptance model. Frontiers in Psychology, 12, 2113. doi:10.3389/fpsyg.202*1.691492* P*M*ID:34163416

Hoque, M., Yusoff, A. M., Toure, A. K., & Mohamed, Y. (2019). Teaching Hadith Subjects through E-Learning Methods: Prospects and Challenges. International *Journal of Academic Research in* Progressive Education and Development, 8(2), 507–514. doi:10.6007/IJARPED/v8-i2/6164

Horrigan, J. B. (2016, September 9). Library usage and engagement. Pew Research Center. https://www.pewresearch.org/internet/2016/09/09/library-usag e-and-engagement/

Hossain, M. A., Jahid, M. I., Hossain, K. M., Walton, L. M., Uddin, Z., Haque, M. O., Kabir, M. F., Arafat, S. M., Sakel, M., Faruqui, R., & Hossain, Z. (2020*). Knowledge, attitudes, and fear of COVID-19 during the ra*pid rise period in Bangladesh. PLoS One, 15(9), e0239646. doi:10.1371/journal.pone.0239646 PMID:32970769

Hoven, D. (1999*). A Model for reading and viewing comprehension in multimedi*a environments. Language Learning & Technology, 3(1), 88–103.

Howland, J. L., Jonassen, D. H., & Marra, R. M. (2011). Meaningful learning with techn ology (4th ed.). Pearson Education.

Hu, K., Deng, Y., & Liu, X. (2022). WordSift: Reading easier by understan*ding key words. RE*LC Journal, 00336882221087464. doi:10.1177/00336882221087464

Hu, L. T., & Bentler, P. M. (1999). Cutoff criteria for fit indexes in covariance structure analysis: Conv*entional criteri*a *v*ersus new alternatives. Structural Equation Modeling, 6(1), 1–55. doi:10.1080/10705519909540118

Hu, M., & Li, H. (2017). Student Engagement in Online Learning: A Review. 2017 International Sympos*ium on Edu-cational Technology (ISET). IEEE. 10.1109/ISET.2017.17*

Hu, X., Chiu, M. M., Leung, W. M. V., & Yelland, N. (2021). Technology integration for young children during CO-VID-19: Towards future online teaching. British Journal of Educationa*l Technology, 52(4), 1513–1537. doi:*10.1111/ bjet.13106 PMID:34219754

Huang, C. S., Yang, S. J., Chiang, T. H., & Su, A. Y. (2016). Effects of situated mobile learning approach on learning motivation and performance of EFL students. Journal of Educational Technology & Society, 19(1), 263–276.

Huang, Y., & Zhang, J. (2020). Social media use *and entrepreneurial intentio*n: *T*he mediating role of self-efficacy. Social Behavior and Personality, 48(11), 1–8.

Huggins, R., & Thompson, P. (2016). Socio-Spatial Culture and Entrepreneurship: Some Theore*tical and Empirical Observations.* Ec*o*nomic Geography, 92(3), 269–300. doi:10.1080/00130095.2016.1146075

Humbert, L. A., & Drew, E. (2010). Gender, entrepreneurship and motivational factors in an Irish context. International Journal of Gender and Entrepreneurship, 2(2), 173–196. doi:10.1108/17566261011051026

Hurwitz, L. B., & Schmitt, K. L. (2020). Can children benefit from early internet exposure? Short-and long-term links between internet use, digital skill, and academic performance. Computers & Education, 146, 103750. doi:10.1016/j.compedu.2019.103750

Hussein, Z. (2017). *Leading to Intention:* The Role of Attitude in relation to an Acceptance Model in E-Learning. Procedia Computer Science, 105, 159–164. doi:10.1016/j.procs.2017.01.196

Huver, *E., & Springer, C. (2011).* L'évaluation en langues [Language assessment]. Didier.

Hyland, K. (2002). Authority and invisibility: Authorial identity in academic writing. Journal of Pragmatics, 34(8), 1091–1112. doi:10.1016/S0378-2166(02)00035-8

IBM. (2019). IBM e-learning content. IBM. https://www.ibm.com/training/W961341C20522X82,

Ikeatuwegwu, C., & Dann, Z. (2017). Bourdieu's Sociology: A Structured Approach for Entrepreneurship Studies. ECRM 2017 16th European Conference on Research Methods in Business and Management. Dublin, Ireland.

Impact of COVID-19 on people's livelihoods, their health and our food sy*stems (2020) Word Health Organization.* https://www.who.int/news/item/13-10-2020-impact-of-covid-19-on-people%27s-livelihoods-their-health-and-our-food-systems

Insights, G. M. (2022). E-Learning Market Size. Competitive Market Share & Forecast, 2022 – 2028. *GM Insights. https://www.gminsights.com/industry-analysis/elearning-marke*t-size#:~:text=E%2DLearning%20Market%20size%20s*urpassed,to%2* 0economical%20internet%20connectivity%20p*lans

İşman, A. (2012). Technology and technique: An educational perspective. The Turkish Online Journal of Educational Technology, 11(2), 207–213.

Jab*er, O. A. (2016). An* examination of variables influencing the acceptance and usage of e-learning sy*stems in Jordani*an higher education institutions. [PhD dissertation, London School Commerce, *Cardiff Metropolitan Univ., Cardi*ff, U.K].

Jaggars, S. S., & Xu, D. (2016). How do online course design features influence student performance? Computers & Education, 95, 270–284. doi:10.10*16/j.compedu.2016.01.014*

*Jalongo, M. R. (2021). The effects of COVID-*19 on early childhood education and care: Research and resources for children, families, teachers, and teacher educators. Early Childhood Education Journa*l, 49(5), 763–774. doi:10.1*00710643-021-01208-y PMID:34054286

Jandrić, P. (2020). Deschooling. In M. Peters (Ed.), Encyclopedia of teacher education. Springer. doi:10.1007/978-981-13-1179-6_115-1

Jarrett, C. (2018). "A*nother nail in the coffin for* learning styles" – students did not benefit from studying according to their supposed learning style. The British Psychological Society. https://digest.bps.org.uk/2018/04/03/a*nother-nail-in-the-cof fin-for-learning-styles-*students-did-not-benefit-from-studyi ng-according-to-their-supposed-learning-style/

Jayakumar, P., & Ajit, I. (2016). Android app: An instrument in clearing Lacuna of English gramma*r through teaching 500 sentence str*uctures with reference to the verb eat. Man in India, 96(4), 1187–1195.

Jayakumar, P., & Ajit, I. (2017). The Pedagogical Implications on the Root and Route of English Basic Ve*rbs: An Ex-ten*sive Study through Android Application. Social Sciences, 12(12), 2244–2248.

Jayakumar, P., Suman Rajest, S., & Aravi*nd, B. R. (*2022). An Empirical Study on the Effectiveness of Online Teaching and Learning Outcomes with Regard to LSRW Skills in COVID-19 Pandemic. In Technologies, Artificial Intelligence and the Future of Learning Post-COVID-19 (pp. 483–499). Springer. doi:10.1007/978-3-030-93921-2_27

Jena, P. K. (2020). Challenges and Opportunities created by Covid -19 for ODL: A case study of IGNOU. Interna*tional Journal for Innovative Researc*h in Multidisciplinary, 6(5):217-222.7.https://10.31235/ doi:osf.io/jy2td

Jena, R. (2020). Measuring the impact of business management student's attitude towards entrepreneurship education on entrepreneurial intention: A case study. Computers in Human Behavior, 107, 106275. doi:10.1016/j.chb.2020.106275

Jeon, H. J., Diamond, L., McCartney, C., & Kwon, K. A. (2021). Early Childhood Special Education Teachers' Job Burnout and Psychological Stress. Early Education and Development, 1–19. PMI*D:36353579*

*Ji, S. (2017). Exploring L2 wri*ting conferences: Discourse and effects [Doctoral dissertation, Purdue University].

Jiang, L., & Yu, S. (2021). Understanding changes in EFL teachers' feedback practice during COVID-19: *Implications for teacher feedback literacy at* a time of crisis. The Asia-Pacific Education Researcher, 30(6), 509–518. doi:10.100740299-021-00583-9

Jiang, Y., & Monk, H. (2015). Young Chinese-Australian children's use of technology at home: Parents' and grandparents' views. Asia-Pacific J*ournal of Research in* Early Childhood Education, 10(1), 87–106.

Jogan, S. N. (2019). Higher Education in India: Avision of 2030. International Journal of Research, 6(7), 365–370. https://files.eric.ed.gov/fulltext/ED596145.pdf

Jones, S. (2014). Gendered discourses of entrepreneurship in UK higher education: The fictive entrepreneur and the fictive student. International Small Business Journal, 32(3), 237–258. doi:10.1177/0266242612453933

Jones, S., & Warhuus, J. P. (2018). This class is not for you:An investigation of gendered subject construction in entre-preneurship course descriptions. Journal of Small Business and Enterprise Development, 25(2), 182–*200. doi:10.1108/ JSBED-07-2017-0220*

Jones, S. A. (2011). The gendering of entrepreneurship in higher education: a Bourdieuian approach. Leeds Metropolitan University.

Joore, P., Brezet, H., & Care, S., Sykes, A. O., Giesen*, D., Meertens, V., Vis-visschers, R., Be*ukenhorst, D., Moghimipour, I., & Seminar, E. (2016). Online library : Digital copies. BMJ Open. doi:10.1177/1468794107071*408*

*Jorgensen, B. (2021). The "cultural entrepreneurship" of independ*ent podcast production in Australia. Journal of Radio & Audio Media, 28(1), 144–161.

Kabilan, M. K., Ahmad, N.*, & Abidin, M. J. Z. (*2010). Facebook: An online environment for learning of English in institutions of higher education? The Internet and Higher Education, 13(4), 179–187. doi:10.1016/j.iheduc.2010.07.003

Kaieski, N., Grings, J. A., & Fetter, S. A. (2015). Um E*studo Sobre as Possibilida*des Pedagógicas de Utilização do WhatsApp. Renote - Novas Tecnologias na Educação [A Study on the Pedagogical Possibilities of Usin*g WhatsApp. Renote - New Techno*logies in Education], 13(2), 1–10.

Kakabadse, N. K., Figueira, C., Nicolopoulou, K., Hong Yang, J., Kakabadse, A. P., & Özbilgin, M. F. (2015). Gender Diversity and Board Performance: Women's Experiences and Perspectives. Human Resource Management, 54(2), 265–281. doi:10.1002/hrm.21694

Kalfa, S., & Taksa, L. (2013). Cultural capital in bu*siness higher education: Recon*sidering the graduate attributes movement and the focus on employability. Studies in Higher Education, 40(4), 580–595. *doi:10.*1080/03075079.2013.842210

Kaliisa, R., & Picard, M. (2017). A systematic review on mobile learning *in higher education: The African perspective. The Turki*sh Online Journal of Educational Technology, 16(1), 1–18.

Kalin, R., & Oleg, S. (2014). *Transnational En*trepreneurs: Implications of the dual background on opportunity recognition. LUND University Libraries. https://lup.lub.lu.se/student-papers/record/4461730

Kalu, *E. U., & Dana, L.* P. (2021). Socio-cultural web and environmentally-driven community entrepreneurship: a portrayal of Abia Ohafia community in South-Eastern Nigeria. Journal of Enterprising Communities: People and Places in the Global Economy.

Kamal, T.*, & Illiyan, A. (2*021). School teachers' perception and challenges towards online teaching during COVID-19 pandemic in India: An econometric analysis. Asian Association of Open Universities Journal, 16(3), 311–325. doi:10.1108/AAOUJ-10-2021-0122

Kamińska, D., Sapiński, T., Wiak, S., Tikk, T., Haamer, R. E., Avots, E., Helmi, A., Ozcinar, C., & Anbarjafari, G. (2019). Virtual reality and its applications in education: Survey. Information (Switzerland), 10(10), 1–20. doi:10.3390/info10100318

Kapasia, N., Paul, P., Roy, A., Saha, J., Zaveri, A., Mallick, R., Barman, B., Da*s, P., & Chouhan, P. (2020).* Im*p*act of lockdown on learning status of undergraduate a*nd postgraduate students during COVID-19 pandemic in West Bengal, India. Children and Youth Services Review, 116, 105194. doi:10.1016/j.childyouth.2020.105194 PMID:32834270*

Karataş-Özkan, M., & Chell, E. (2013). Gender Inequalities in Academic Innovation and Enterprise: A Bourdieuian Analysis. British Journal of Management, 26(1), 109–125. doi:10.1111/1467-8551.12020

Karhunen, P. (2017, July 14). Research: Do Mobi*le Journalists Get More Interviews?* EJO. *https://en.ejo.ch/*digital-news/research-do-mobile-journalists-get-more-interviews

Karim, A., Hasan, A., & Shahriza, N. (2007). Reading Habits and Attitude in the Digital Age: Analysis of Gender and Academic Program Differences in Malaysia. *The Electronic Library. http://umpir.ump.edu.my/5/1/Reading*_habits_and_attitude _at_digital_age_-_amelia_2.pdf

Katz, E. (1961). The social itinerary of technical change: Two studies on the diffusion of innovation. Human Organization, 20(2), 70–82.

Kemmis, S. (2006). Participatory action research an*d the public sphere. Educational Action Research, 14(4), 459–476.* doi:10.1080/09650790600975593

Kgosietsile, N. (2018). Social Work Education and Human Rights A Comparative Study of Learning and Teaching of Human Rights in University of Gothenburg, Sweden and M*akerere University, Uganda [Master's thesis, University of Got*henburg]. https://gupea.ub.gu.se/bitstream/handle/ 2077/57127/gupea_2077_57127_1.pdf;jsessionid=8C59CF3D2 4AF9DBBC53DA6D2FBF027FA?sequence=1

Khalifa, H., Khalifa, H., Badran, S.A., Al-absy, M. S. M., & A*hmed, Q. (2020). Social Media a*nd Spreading the News of Covid-19 Pandemic. In the Arab World, 11(5), 680–685.

Khan, A. (2019). Testing in English Language Teaching and its Significance in EFL Contexts: A Theoretical Perspective. *Global Regional Review (GRR), 4.*

Khan, M. J., Chelliah, S., & Ahmed, S. (2017). Factors influencing destination image and visit intention among young women travellers: Role of travel motivation, perceived risks, and travel constraints. Asia Pacific Journal of Tourism Research, 22(11), 1139–1155. doi:10.1080/10941665.2017.1374985

Khan, R. M. I., Kumar, T., Benyo, A., Jahara, S. F., & Haidar, M. M. F. (2022). The reliability analysis of speaking test in computer-assisted language learning (CALL) environment. Education Research International. doi:10.1155/2022/8984330

Kiesler, F. (1924), International Exhibition of New Theater Technique. Vienna, 1924, Avant-garde on Display: Frederick Kiesler's Exhibition of New Theatre Technique.

Kim, J.-H. K., Thang, N. D. T., Kim, T.-S. K., Voinea, A., Shin, J., Park, S. B., Jang, S. H., Mazuryk, T., Gervautz, M., & Smith, K. (2013). Virtual Reality History, Applications, Technology and Future. Digital Outcasts, 63(ISlE), 92–98.

Kim, K. (2018). Early childhood teachers' work and technology in an era of assessment. European Early Childhood Education Research Journal, 26(6), 927–939. doi:10.1080/1350293X.2018.1533709

Kinni, R. (2020). Integration of theory and practice in social work education. Analysis of Finnish social work students' field reports. Social Work Education, 40(7), 901–914. doi:10.1080/02615479.2020.1754385

Kirby, J. R., Moore, P. J., & Schofield, N. J. (1988). Verbal and visual learning styles. Contemporary Educational Psychology, 13(2), 169–184. doi:10.1016/0361-476X(88)90017-3

Klavas, R. D. J. S. B. A. (2002). California Journal of Science Education. Journal of Science Education, II(2), 75–98.

Klem, A. M., & Connell, J. P. (2004). Relationships Matter: Linking Teacher Support to Student Engagement and Achievement. The Journal of School Health, 74(7), 262–273. doi:10.1111/j.1746-1561.2004.tb08283.x PMID:15493703

Kochem, T. (2019). Mondly for kids. Teaching English as a Second Language Electronic Journal (TESL-EJ), 23(1), 1-7.

Kohnke, L., & Moorhouse, B. L. (2021). Using Kahoot! to gamify learning in the language classroom. RELC Journal, 1–7.

Kohnke, L., & Moorhouse, B. L. (2022). Facilitating synchronous online language learning through Zoom. RELC Journal, 53(1), 296–301. doi:10.1177/0033688220937235

Kolb, A. Y., & Kolb, D. A. (2005). Learning Styles and Learning Spaces: Enhancing Experiential Learning in Higher Education. Academy of Management Learning & Education, 4(2), 193–212. https://www.jstor.org/stable/40214287. doi:10.5465/amle.2005.17268566

Kolb, A. Y., & Kolb, D. A. (2012). In N. M. Seel (Ed.), Experiential Learning Theory BT - Encyclopedia of the Sciences of Learning (pp. 1215–1219). Springer US. doi:10.1007/978-1-4419-1428-6_227

Koltovskaia, S. (2019). Storybird. Teaching English as a Second Language Electronic Journal (TESL-EJ), 23(1), 1-9.

Kovacs, S. (2017, January 31). How the Hindustan Times Is Building the World's Largest Mobile Journalism Team. MediaShift. http://mediashift.org/2017/01/how-the-hindustan-times-building-worlds-largest-mobile-journalism-team/

Koşar, G. (2021). The progress a pre-service English language teacher made in her feedback giving practices in distance teaching practicum. Journal of English Teaching, 7(3), 366–381. doi:10.33541/jet.v7i3.3145

Kress, G. (2009). Multimodality: A Social Semiotic Approach to Contemporary Communication. Routledge. doi:10.4324/9780203970034

Kress, G., & Van Leeuwen, T. (2001). Multimodal discourse: The modes and media of contemporary communication. Edward Arnold.

Kudto, N. M., Lumapenet, H. T., & Guiamalon, T. S. (2022). Students' Learning Experiences in The New Normal Education. Central Asian Journal of Theoretical & Applied Sciences, 3(5), 221–233.

Kueng, L. (2017, November 16). *Going digital: A Roadmap for organisational T*ransformation. Reuters Institute for the study of Journalism. https://reutersinstitute.*politics.ox.ac.uk/our-resear*ch/going-digital-roadmap-organisational-transformation

Kukulska-Hulme, A. (2009). Will mobile learning change language learning? ReCALL, 21(2), 157–165. doi:10.1017/S0958344009000202

Kukulska-Hulme, A. (2012). Mobile-Assisted Language Learning. In C. A. Chapelle (dir.), The Encyclopedia of Applied Linguistics. Blackwell Publishing. doi:10.1002/*9781405198431.*wbeal0768

Kukulska-Hulme, A., & Shield, L. (2008). An overview of mobile assisted language learning: From content del*ivery to supported collaboration and* interaction. ReCALL, 20(3), 271–289. doi:10.1017/S0958344008000335

Kumar, A. & Ambrish. (2015). Higher Education: Growth, Challenges and Opportunities. International Journal of Arts, Humanities *and Management Studies, 1(2). https://* www.academia.edu/11996755/Higher_Education_Growth_Challenges_And_Opportunities

Kumar, D. N. S. (2020, April 29). Impact of COVID-19 on h*igher education. High-er Educatio*n Digest. https://www.highereducationdigest.com/impact-of-covid-19-on-higher-education/

Kumar, D. N. S. (29 April 2020). Impact of COVID-19 *on Higher Educa*tion. Higher Education Digest. https://www.highereducationdigest.com/impact -of-covid-19-on -highereducation/

Kumar, T. (2020). Assessing lang*uage need an*d proficiency of English graduates of Prince Sattam Bin Abdulaziz University for designing pre-placement training and workshops. Asian ESP Journal., 16(4), 153–168.

Kumar, T. (2021a). 'Desire to learn, *learn to shine': Idolizing* motivation in enhancing speaking skill among L2 learners. Cypriot Journal of Educational Science., 16(1), 411–422. doi*:10.18844/cjes.v16i1.5542*

*Kumar, T. (2021b). Social Networki*ng Sites and Grammar Learning: The Views of Learners and Practitioners. International Journal of Early Childhood Special Education (INT-*JECSE), 13(2), 215-223. doi:10.9756/INT-JECSE/V13I2.21*1057

Kurt, S. (2022). Speakometer: English pronunciation coach. Teaching English as a Second Language Electronic Journal (TESL-EJ), 26(1), 1-6.

Kurtus, R. (*2002, January 27). Gaining* knowledge by reading. The Courier Mail, p. 22.

Kuutti, T., Sajaniemi, N., Björn, *P. M., Heiskanen, N., &* Reunamo, J. (2021). Participation, involvement and peer relationships in children with special educational needs in ear*ly childhood educatio*n. European Journal of Special Needs Education, 1–16.

Lang, S. N., *Jeon, L., Sproat, E. B.,* Brothers, B. E., & Buettner, C. K. (2020). Social emotional learning for teachers (SELF-T*): A short-term, online intervention to increase early childhood educato*rs' resilience. Early Education and Development, 31(7), 1112–1132. doi:10.1080/10409289.2020.1749820

Lau, E. Y. H., Li, J. B., & Lee, K. (2021). Online learning and parent satisfa*ction during covid-19: Child competence in independent learning as a moderator. Early Education and Development, 32(6), 830–842. doi:10.1080/10409289.2021.1950451

Laukenmann, M., Bleicher, M., Fuß, S., Gläser-Zikuda, M., Mayring, P., & von Rhöneck, C. (*2003*). *An in*vestigation of the influence of emotional factors on learning in physics instruction. International Journal of Science Education, 25(4), 489–507. doi:10.1080/09500690210163233

Lawson, B. (2018). The Design Student's Journey: Understanding how Designers Think. Routledge. doi:10.4324/9780429448577

Leandro, D., & Weissheimer, J. (2016). Facebook e aprendizagem híbrida de inglês na universidade. In Júlio Araújo & Vilson Le a (Orgs.). Redes sociais e ensino de línguas: O que temos de aprender? [Facebook and *hybrid English learning at* university. In Júlio Araújo & Vilson Le a (Orgs.). Social networks and language teaching: What do *we have to learn?*]. *Parábola Edit*orial.

Lebrun, M., Lacelle, N., Boutin, J.F. (2012). La littératie *médiatique multimodale De nouvelles approches en lecture-écriture à l'école et hors de l'école. Presses de l'université du Québec.* [Multimodal Media Literacy New approaches to reading-writing in and out of school. Press of the University of Quebec.]

Lee, J. E., Hur, S., & Watkins, B. (2018). Visual communication of luxury fashion brands on social media: Effects of visual complexity and brand familiarity. Journal of Brand Management, 25(5), 449–462. doi:10.105741262-018-0092-6

LeLoup, J. W. (1997). But I *only have e-*mail—What can I do? Learning Languages, 2, 10–15.

Lenders, O. (2008). Electronic glossing–is it worth the effort? Computer Assisted Language Learning, 21(5), 457–481. doi:10.108*0/09588220802447933*

Lerner, D. (1958). The passing of traditional society: Modernizing the Middle East. APA.

Lessig, L. (2001). The Future of Ideas–The fate of the commons in a connected world. Random H House.

Levie, J., & H*art, M. (2011). Business and social entrepreneurs in the UK: Gender, context a*nd commitment. International Journal of Gender and Entrepreneurship, 3(3), 200–217. doi:10.1108/17566261111169304

Levine Brown, E., Vesely, C., Mehta, S., & Stark, K. (2022). Preschool Teachers' Emotional Acting and School-Based *I*nteractions. Early Childhood Education Journal. doi:10.100710643-022-01326-1 PMID:35233161

Lewis, G. D. (2018). Museum- Definition, history, types & operation. Britannica. https://www.britannica.com/topic/mus*eum-cultural-institution*

Li, Q., Li, Z., & Han, J. (2021). A hybrid learning pedagogy f*or surmounting the challenges of the COVID-19 pandemic* in the performing arts education. Education and Information Technologies, 26(6), 7635–7655. doi:10.100710639-021-10612-1 PMID:34220284

Li, X. (2022, January). The Effectiveness of Mobile-assisted Language Learni*ng (MALL) Applications on the Spoken* Engl*ish Assessments in China's Universities. In 2021 International Conference on Social Development and Media Communication (SDMC 2021) (pp. 751-756).* Atlantis Press. 10.2991/assehr.k.220105.137

Li, Z., Li, Q., Han, J., & Zhang, Z. (2022). Perspectives of hybrid performing arts education in the post-pandemic era: An empirical study in Hong K*ong. Sustainability, 14(15), 9194. doi:1*0.3390u14159194

Liao, P. A., Chang, H. H., Wang, J. H., & Sun, L. C. *(2016). What are the determinants of rural-urban digital inequality amon*g schoolchildren in Taiwan? Insights from Blinder-Oaxaca decomposition. Computers & Education, 95, 123–133. doi:10.1016/j.compedu.2016.01.002

Lin, X., & Tao, S. (2012). Transnational ent*repreneurs: Characteristics, drivers, and success facto*rs. Journal of International Entrepreneurship, 10(1), 50–69. doi:10.100710843-011-0082-1

Linjawi, A. I., & Alfadda, L. S. (2018). Students' perception, attitudes, and readiness toward online learning in dental education in Saudi *Arabia:* A cohort study. Advances in Medical Education and Practice, 9(1), 855–863. doi:10.2147/AMEP.S175395 PMID:30538597

Liu, S., & Kunnan, *A. J. (2016). Investigating th*e *A*pplication of Automated Writing Evaluation to Chinese Undergraduate English Majors: A Case Study of "WriteToLearn". calico journal, 33(1), 71-*91.*

Liu, Y. (2017). Born global firms' growth and collaborative entry mode: The role of transnational entrepreneurs. International Marketing Review, 34(1), 46–67. doi:10.1108/IMR-05-2015-0130

Liu, Z. (2005). Reading behavior in the digital environment: Changes in reading behavior over the past ten years. The Journal of Documentation, 61(6*), 700–712. doi:10.1108/00220410510632040*

Loh, T. H. & Fishbane, L. (2022, March 8). COVID-19 makes the benefits of telework obvious. Brookings. https://www.brookings.edu/blog/the-avenue/2020/03/17/covid-1 9-makes-the-bene*fits-of-telework-obvious/*

Lo*kh*andwala, S., & Gautam, P. (2020). Indirect impact of COVID-19 on environment: A brief study in Indian context. Environmental Research, 188, 109807. doi:.2020.109807 do*i:10.1016/j.envres*

London, A. (2020). Find your MOJO: The rise of mobile film makers and journal*ists. Allied London. https://alliedlondon.com/find-your-mojo-the-rise-of-mobile-f ilmmakers-a*nd-journalists/

Longuet, F. (2016). Former des enseignants par le biais d'environnements d'apprentissage numérique multimodaux [Train teachers through multimodal digital learning environments]. In Revue de Recherches en LMM (r2lmm.ca), vol. 3.

Lu, K. *(2017, June 12). Growth in mobile news use driven by older adults. Pew Re*search Center. https://www.pewresearch.org/fact-tank/2017/06/12/growth-in-m obile-news-use-driven-by-older-adults/

Lumapenet, H. (2017). Determinants of Bangsamoro Teacher's Identity. In *Lumapenet, HT, & Sagadan, SA* Determinants of Bangsamoro Teacher's Identity. 7th CEBU International Conference on Civil, Agricultural, Biological and Environmental Sciences (CABES-17) Sept (pp. 21-22).

Lumapenet, H., Usop, M. (2022). School Readiness towards the Delivery of Learning in the New Normal. Int*ernational Journal of Early Childho*o*d S*pecial Education (INT-JECSE),Vol 14, Issue 03 2022, 2629-2637.

Luo, W., Berson, I. R., Berson, M. J., & Li, H. (2021). Are early childhood teachers ready for digital transformation of *instruction in Mainland China? A* systematic literature review. Children and Youth Services Review, 120, 10*5718. doi:10.1016/j.childyouth.2020.105718*

Lutz, C., Noseleit, F., & Tundui, H. (2021). Inherited cultural capital and growth aspirations in Tanzanian business at the bottom of the pyramid. Journal of the International Council for Small Business, 2(3), 223–249.

Lv, X., Ren, W., & Xie, Y. (2021). T*he effects of online f*eedback on ESL/EFL writing: A meta-analysis. The Asia-Pacific Education Researcher, 30(6), 643–653. doi:10.100740299-021-00594-6

Lévy, P. (1997). L'intelligence collective: pour une anthropolo*gie du cyberspace* [[*Co*llective intelligence: for an anthropology of cyberspace.]]. Ed. La Découverte.

Ma, *M., Wang, C., & Teng, M. F.* (2021). Using learning-oriented online assessment to foster students' fe*edback literacy in L2 writing during COVID-19 pandemic: A case of misalignment between micro-and macro-contexts. The Asia-Pacific Education Researcher, 30(6), 597–609.* doi:10.100740299-021-00600-x

Ma, Q. (2020). Examining the role of inter-group peer online feedback on wiki writing in an EAP context. Computer Assisted Language Learning, 33(3), 197–216. doi:10.1080/09588221.2018.1556703

Mahajan, M., and Singh, M.K.S. (2017). Importance and benefits of learning outcomes. OSR Journal *of Humanities* and Social Science (IOSR-JHSS), 22(3), 65–67.

Mahajne, I., & Meler, T. (2021). Retraining in social work for Arab academic women: Motivation and integration into the Field. Affilia, 37(2), 300–319. doi:10.1177/08861099211057504

Mahapatra, S. K. (2021). Online formative assessment and feedback practices of ESL teachers in India, Bangladesh and Nepal: A multiple case study. The Asia-Pacific Educa*tion Researcher, 30(6), 519–530. doi:10.100740299-021-00603-8*

Mahmodi, M. (2017). The Analysis of the Factors Affecting the Acceptance of E-Learning in Higher Education. Interdisciplinary Journal Virtual Learn. Med. Sci., 8(1), e11158.

Mahmood, R., Shah, A. H., & Kumar, T. (2020). En*glish language learn*ing and its socio-cultural effects: A comparative study of private and government schools of Islamabad. Asian EFL Journal, 27(3.3), 150-164.

Mak, B., Ni*ckerson, R., & Sim, J. (O*ctober, 2015). A model of Attitude towards Mobile Location- Based Services. Journal of Quality Assurance in Hospitality & Tourism, Routledg*e Taylor & Francis Group, 414-437.*

Ma*liborska, V., & You, Y. (2016). Writing conferences in a second language writing classroom: Instructor and student perspecti*ves. TESOL Journal, 7(4), 874–897. doi:10.1002/tesj.249

Mangenot, F., & Soubrié, T. (2014). Le web social au service de tâches d'écriture [The social web at the service *of writing tasks]. Recherch*es.

Markowska, M., & Wiklund, J. (2020). Entrepreneurial learning under uncertainty: Exploring the role of *self-efficacy and perceived complexity. Entrepreneurship and Regional* Development, 32(7-8), 606–628.

Marler, W. (2018). Mobile Phones and inequality: Findings, trends, and future *directions.* New Media & Society, 20(9), 3498–3520.

Marler, W. (2018). Mobile phones and inequality: Findings, trends and f*uture directi*ons. New Media & Society, 3498–3520.

Marlow, S. (2014). Exploring future research agendas in the field of gender and entrepreneurship. International Journal of Gender and *Entrepreneurship, 6(2), 102–120. doi:10.11*08/IJGE-01-2013-0003

Marquillo Larruy, M. (2012). «Littératie et multimodalité ici & là-bas... [Literacy and multimodality here & there]». Rech*erches en didactique des langues et des cultures: Les Cahiers de l'Acedle,* n° 9 (2): 47- 84.

Martin, G. (2012). Les amis de vos amis sont-ils vos amis ? Idées économiques et *sociales [Are your friends' friends your friends? Economic and social* ideas], 169(3), 1-1. Doi:10.3917/idee.169.0001

Masoumi, D. (2015). Preschool teachers' use of ICTs: Towards a typology of practice. Contemporary Issue*s in Early Childhood, 16(1), 5–*17. doi:10.1177/1463949114566753

Mathiyazhagan, S. (2021). Field practice, emerging technologies, and human rights: The emergence of tech social worker*s. Journal* of Human Rights and Social Work, 7(4), 441–448. doi:10.100741134-021-00190-0 PMID:34518805

Mathiyazhagan, T., & Nandan, D. *(2010). Survey research method, Media Mimansa. National Institute of F*amily & Welfare.

McClelland, M. M., & Tominey, S. L. (2011). Introduction to *the special issue on self-regulation in early childhood. Early Educati*on and Development, 22(3), 355–359. doi:10.1080/10409289.2011.574265

McClelland, M. M., Acock, A. C., Piccinin, A., Rhea, S. A., & Stallings, M. C. (2013). Relations between preschool attention span-persistence and age 25 educational outcomes. *Early Childhood Research Quarterly, 28*(2), 314–324. doi:10.1016/j.ecresq.2012.07.008 PMID:23543916

McFarland-Piazza, L., & Saunders, R. (2012). Hands-on parent support in positive guidance: Early childhood professionals as mentors. Australasian Journal of Early Childhood, 37(1), 65–73. doi:10.1177/183693911203700108

McGrath, R. G., MacMillan, I. C., Yang, E. A., & Tsai, W. (1992). Does Culture Endure, or is it Malleable? Issues for Entrepreneurial Economic Development. Journal of Business Venturing, 7, 115–135. doi:10.1016/0883-9026(92)90008-F

McKenna, M., Soto-Boykin, X., Cheng, K., Haynes, E., Osorio, A., & Altshuler, J. (2021). Initial development of a national survey on remote learning in early childhood during COVID-19: Establishing content validity and reporting successes and barriers. Early Childhood Education Journal, 49(5), 815–827. doi:10.100710643-021-01216-y PMID:34092995

McLaughlin, P., & Faulkner, J. D. (2012). Flexible spaces...what students expect from university facilities. Journal of Facilities Management, 10(2), 140–149. doi:10.1108/14725961211218776

Meece, J. L., Anderman, E. M., & Anderman, L. H. (2006). Classroom Goal Structure, Student Motivation, and Academic Achievement. Annual Review of Psychology, 57(1), 487–503. doi:10.1146/annurev.psych.56.091103.070258 PMID:16318604

Mehdizadeh, M. (2020). National Public Radio. RELC Journal, 51(3), 461-465.

Mei, B., Huang, S., & Zhao, Q. (2021). Using clips in the language classroom. RELC Journal, 1–4.

Mei, B., Qi, W., Huang, X., & Huang, S. (2022). Speeko: An artificial intelligence-assisted personal public speaking coach. RELC Journal, 1–5. doi:10.1177/00336882221107955

Mejova, Y. & Kalimeri, K. (2020). Advertisers Jump on Coronavirus Bandwagon: Politics, News, and Business. arXiv.

Memon, A. R., Shah, A., & Shaikh, F. (2017). Work Life Balance Of Working Women In Education Sector: A Case Study Of. International Case Studies Journal, 6(2), 27–46.

Metropolitan Museum of Art. (1810), The Public Viewing David's 'Coronation' at the Louvre Louis Léopold Boilly. Metropolitan Museum of Art.

Miller, M. (2019). Youglish. Teaching English as a Second Language Electronic Journal (TESL-EJ), 23(2), 1-10.

Min, P. (2013). The use of multimedia technology in English language teaching: A global perspective. Crossing the border. International Journal of Interdisciplinary Studies, 1(1), 29–38.

Mirzaee, M., & Yaqubi, B. (2016). A conversation analysis of the function of silence in writing conferences. Iranian Journal of Language Teaching Research, 4(2), 69–86.

Misra, Y. (2002). Empowering People - Grassroots Organizations and Rural Development. UOC.

Mochizuki, N. (2017). Contingent needs analysis for task implementation: An activity systems analysis of group writing conferences. TESOL Quarterly, 51(3), 607–631. doi:10.1002/tesq.391

Mody, B. (1991). Designing messages for development communication: An audience participation based approach. Sage Publications.

Mohammedsalih, S. (2017, August). Mobile Journalism: Using Smartphones in Journalistic work. Research Gate. https://www.researchgate.net/publication/342546973_Mobile_Journalism_Using_smartphone_in_journalistic_work

Mohanty, M., & Parhi, P. (2011). F*olk and traditional media: A powerful tool for rural developmen*t. Journal of Communication, 2(1), 41–47. doi:10.1080/0976691X.2011.11884781

Monrad, M., & Mølholt, A. (2017). Problem-based learning in social work educa*tion: Stude*nts' experiences in Denmark. Journal of Teaching in Social Work, 37(1), 71–86. doi:10.1080/08841233.2016.1271382

Montroy, J. J., Bowles, R. P., Skibbe, L. E., McClelland, M. M., & Morrison, F. J. (2016). The development of sel*f-regulation across early childhood. Devel*opmental Psychology, 52(11), 1744–1762. doi:10.1037/dev0000159 PMID:27709999

Moore, D., & Coste, D. (2006). Plurilinguismes et école [[Plurilingualism and scho*ol]]. Didier.*

Moorhouse, B. L., & Kohnke, L. (2022). Creating the conditions for vocabulary learning with Wordwall. RELC Journal, 1–6. doi:10.1177/00336882221092796

Morgado, J. C., Sousa, J., & Pacheco, J. A. (2020). Educational trans*formations in pandemic times: From soci*al confinement to curriculum isolation. Praxis Educativa (Santa Rosa), 15, 1–10. doi:10.5212/PraxEduc.v.15.16197.062

Morrison, G. R., Ross, S. J., Morrison, J. R., & Kalman, H. K. (2019). Designing Effective Instruction. John Wiley *& Sons.*

Mou, J., Shin, D. H., & Cohen, J. (2017). Understanding trust and perceived usefulness in the consumer acceptance of an e-service: A l*ongitudinal investigation. Beha*viour & Information Technology, 36(2), 125–139. doi:10.1080/01449 29X.2016.1203024

Mudliar, P., & Rangaswamy, N. (2015). Offline Strangers, Online Friends: Bri*dging Classroom Gender Segre*gation With Whatsapp. In Conference on Human Factors in Computing Systems - Proceedings (Vol. 2015-April, p. 3799– 3808). 10.1145/2702123.2702533

Muhammad, N., McElwee, G., & Dana, L. P. (2017). Barriers to th*e development and progress of entrepreneurship in rural Pakistan. International Journal* of Entrepreneurial Behaviour & Research, 23(2), 279–295.

M u l c a h y ,   G .   (2 0 2 0) .   W h a t   i s   m o b i l e   j o u r n a l i s m .   S h o u l -
d e r   P o d .   h t t p s : / / w w w . s h o u l d e r p o d . c o m / m o b i l e - j o u r n a l i s m # : ~ : t e x t = A % 2 0 M o
bile%20Journalist%20or%20MOJO,soc*ial%20media%20*by%20the%20Mo
jo

Murre, J. M. J., & Dros, J. (2015). Replication and analysis of Ebbinghaus' forgetting curve. PLoS One, 10(7), 1–*23. doi:*10.1371/journal.pone.0120644 PMID:26148023

Muthulakshmi, C. (2018). A study on work life balance among the teaching professional of arts and science colleges in Tutocorin district. ICTACT Journal of Management Studies, 4*(1), 657–662. doi:10.21917/*ijms.2018.0089

Muzaza, S., & Tembo, G. (2020). Testing and Evaluation Towards Teaching and Testing. Journal Educational Verkenning, *1(1), 21–24.* doi:10.48173/jev.v1i1.26

Mäkipää, T., Hahl, K., & Luodonpää-Manni, M. (2021). teachers' perceptions of assessment and feedback practices in Finland's foreign language classes during the covid-19 pandemic. CEPS Journal, 11(Special Issue), 219–240.

Nachmias, D. (1976). Content Analysis. Research methods in the social sciences. Adward Arnold.

*Narula, U. (2006). Dynamics Of Mass Communicati*on. Theory And Practice. Atlantic Publishers & Dist.

Nedungadi, P. P., Menon, R., & Raman, R. (2018). Towards an inclusive digital literacy framework for digital India. Education + Training, 60(6), 516–528. doi:10.1108/ET-03-2018-0061

Negrette, G. M., Laixely, J., Cordoba, T. E., & Sanders-Smith, S. C. (2021). So we start from zero: Lessons and reflections from online preschool during the COVID-19 pandemic. Journal of Early Childhood Research, 1476718X221083410.

Neumann, M. M. (2015). Young children and screen time: Creating a mindful approach to digital technology. Australian educational computing, 30(2), 1–15.

Newswire, P. R. (2022). E-Learning Market Size in the UK to grow by USD 11.57 billion by 2026. Technavio. https://www.prnewswire.com/news-releases/e-learning-market-size-in-the-uk-to-grow-by-usd-11-57-billion-by-2026--packaged-content-segment-to-be-significant-for-revenue-generation--technavio-301563094.html

Nguyen, T. (2015). The effectiveness of online learning: Beyond no significant difference and future horizons. Journal of Online Learning and Teaching, 11(2), 309–319.

Nicklas, R. (2017). Memrise. Teaching English as a Second Language Electronic Journal (TESL-EJ), 21(1), 1-12.

Nicolopoulou, K., Kakabadse, N. K., Nikolopoulos, K. P., Alcaraz, J. M., & Sakellariou, K. (2016). Cosmopolitanism and transnational elite entrepreneurial practices: Manifesting the cosmopolitan disposition in a cosmopolitan city. Society and Business Review, 11(3), 257–275. doi:10.1108/SBR-01-2016-0001

Nielsen, J. (2021 November 7). 6 Environmental Benefits of Online Learning That Will Blow Your Mind. Sustainable Business Toolkit. https://www.sustainablebusinesstoolkit.com/social-and-eco-benefits-of-online-learning/

Nikolopoulou, K., & Gialamas, V. (2015). ICT and play in preschool: Early childhood teachers' beliefs and confidence. International Journal of Early Years Education, 23(4), 409–425. doi:10.1080/09669760.2015.1078727

Nissen, E. (2011). Variations autour de la tâche dans l'enseignement / apprentissage des langues aujourd'hui [Variations around the task in language teaching/learning today]. Alsic, 14(Vol. 14). Advance online publication. doi:10.4000/alsic.2344

Nkongolo-Bakenda, J.-M., & Chrysostome, E. V. (2020). Exploring the organising and strategic factors of diasporic, transnational entrepreneurs in Canada: An empirical study. Journal of International Entrepreneurship, 18(3), 336–372. doi:10.100710843-020-00268-2

Nobre, A. (2018a). Multimedia Technologies and Online Task-Based Foreign Language Teaching-Learning. Tuning Journal for Higher Education, 5(2), 75–97. doi:10.18543/tjhe-5(2)-2018pp75-97

Nobre, A. (2020). The Pedagogy That Makes the Students Act Collaboratively and Open Educational Practices in Personalization and Collaboration in Adaptive E-Learning. IGI_Global. Doi:10.4018/978-1-7998-1492-4.ch002

Nobre, A. (2021). Educational Practices Resulting From Digital Intelligence in Handbook of Research on Teaching With Virtual Environments and AI. IGI_Global. Doi:10.4018/978-1-7998-7638-0.ch003

Nobre, A., & Martin-Fernandes, I. (2018b). «Pratiques pédagogiques de mobile-learninget FLE: une étude de cas [Pedagogical practices of mobile-learning and FLE: a case study]». Thélème. Revista Complutense de Estudios Franceses, Vol. 33. Núm., 2, 195–211.

Nouwen, M., & Zaman, B. (2018). Redefining the role of parents in young children's online interactions. A value-sensitive design case study. International Journal of Child-Computer Interaction, 18, 22–26. doi:10.1016/j.ijcci.2018.06.001

Nuri, K. A. R. A., & Cagiltay, K. (2017). In-service preschool teachers' thoughts about technology and technology use in early educational settings. Contemporary Educational Technology, 8(2), 119–141.

Nushi, M., & Momeni, A. (2021). English listening and speaking: A review. Teaching English as a Second Language Electronic Journal (TESL-EJ), 25(3), 1-8.

Oblinger, D. (2005). Leading the Transition from Classrooms to Learning *Spaces*. *Educause Review*. *https://er.educause*.edu/articles/2005/1/leading-the-transition-from-classrooms-to learning-spaces

Oke, A., Butler, J. E., & O'Neill, C. (2021). Identifying Barriers and Solutions to Increase Parent-Practitioner Communication in E*arly Childhood Care and Educa*tional Services: The Development of an Online Communication Application. Early Childhood Education Journal, 49(2), 283–293. doi:10.100710643-020-01068-y

Oli*emat, E., Ihmeideh, F., & Alkhaw*aldeh, M. (2018). The use of touch-screen tablets in early childhood: Children's knowledge, skills, and attitudes towards tablet technology. Children and Youth Services Review, 88*, 591–597. doi:10.1016/j. child*youth.2018.03.028

Olmos, E., Cavalcanti, J. F., Soler, J.-L., Contero, M., & Alcañiz, M. (2018). In S. Yu, M. Ally, & *A. Tsinakos (Ed*s.), Mobile Virtual Reality: A Promising Technology to Change the Way We Learn and Teach BT - *Mobile and* Ubiquitous Learning: An International Handbook (pp. 95–106). Springer Singapore. doi:10.1007/978-981-10-6144-8_6

Olum, R., & Bongom*in, F. (2020)*. Social media platforms for health communication and research in the face of COVID-19 pandemic: A cross sectional survey in Uganda. medRxiv. do*i:10*.1101/2020.04.30.20086553

Onuoha, G. (2007). Entrepreneurship. AIST International Journal, 10, 20–32.

Outsios, G., & Kit*tler, M. (2017). The mindset of UK* environmental entrepreneurs: A habitus perspective. International Small Business Journal: Researching Entrepreneurship, 36(3), 285–306. doi:10.1177/0266242617739343

Pacheco, J. A. (202*1). The "new normal" in education. Prospects, 51(1), 3–14. doi:10.100*711125-020-09521-x PMID:33250528

Pacheco, J. A., Morgado, J. C., Sousa, J., & Maia, I. B. (2021). Educação básica e pande*mia. Um estudo sobre as perceções dos profess*ores na realidade portuguesa. Revi*sta Iberoamericana de Educación, 86(1), 187–204. doi:10.35362/rie8614346*

Pan, H., Xia, F., Kumar, T., Li, X., & Shamsy, A. (2022). Massive open online course versus flipped instruction: Impacts on foreign *language speaki*ng anxiety, foreign language learning motivation, and lea*rning attitude. Frontiers in Psychology, 13, 833616. doi:10.3389/fpsyg.2022.833616 PMID:35197908*

Pandey, A., & Jha, B. (2014). Review and Redefin*e: Quality of Work Life for Higher. Global Journal of Man*agement and Business Research. Administrative Management, 14(11), 35–41.

Pandey G. P. (1999). Traditional media and development. Communicator, July-Sept. 1999.

Papanastasiou, C. (2002). Effects of Background and School Facto*rs on the Mathematics A*chievement. Educational Research and Evaluation, 8(1), 55–70. doi:10.1076/edre.8.1.55.6916

Parga, J., & Doyle, K. (2020). Field Instructor Training: Implications of Low *Completion Rates. Field Educator, 10*(2). https://fieldeducator.simmons.edu/article/field-instructor-training-impli*cations-of-low-completio*n-rates/

Parong, J., & Mayer, R. E. (2018). Learning science in immersive virtual reality. Journal of Educational Psychology, 110(6), 785–797. *doi:10.1037/*edu0000241

Parong, J., Pollard, K. A., Files, B. T., Oiknine, A. H., Sinatra, A. M., Moss, J. D., Passaro, A., & Khooshabeh, P. (2020). The mediating role of presence differs across types of spatial learning in immersive technologies. Computers in Human Behavior, 107, 106290. doi:10.1016/j.chb.2020.106290

Parveen, J. J., & Rajesh, V. (2011). Multimedia in English Language Teaching: An empirical analysis. Journal of Technology for ELT, 1(4), 112–116.

Pashler, H., McDaniel, M., Rohrer, D., & Bjork, R. (2008a). Learning Styles. Psychological Science in the Public Interest, 9(3), 105–119. doi:10.1111/j.1539-6053.2009.01038.x PMID:26162104

Pask, G.PASK. (1976). Styles And Strategies Of Learning. The British Journal of Educational Psychology, 46(2), 128–148. doi:10.1111/j.2044-8279.1976.tb02305.x

Patel, C. (2013). Use of multimedia technology in teaching and learning communication skill: An analysis. International Journal of Advancements in Research & Technology, 2(7), 116–123.

Pearson, W. S. (2021). A review of the Kaizena app for feedback on second language writing. RELC Journal, 1–5. doi:10.1177/00336882211045776

Peraya, D., Bonfils, P. (2014). Détournements d'usages et nouvelles pratiques numériques: l'expérience des étudiants d'Ingémédia à l'Université de Toulon [Diversion of uses and new digital practices: the experience of Ingémédia students at the University of Toulon]. Revue des sciences et techniques de l'information et de la communication pour l'éducation et la formation, 21. Doi:10.3406/stice.2014.1098

Petra, M. M., Tripepi, S., & Guardiola, L. (2020). How many hours is enough? The effects of changes in field practicum hours on student preparedness for social work. Field Educator, 10(1). https://fieldeducator.simmons.edu/article/how-many-hours-is-enough-the-effects-of-changes-in-field-practicum-hours-on-student-preparedness-for-social-work/

Phipps, L., Sutherland, A., Seale, J., Ball, S., Dilloway, M., Evans, S., Lakey, M., Peacock, S., Skelton, J., & Wiles, K. (2002). Access All Areas: disability, technology and learning. In Access All Areas: disability. https://eprints.soton.ac.uk/6181

Phoophuangpairoj, R., & Pipattarasakul, P. (2022). Preliminary indicators of EFL essay writing for teachers' feedback using automatic text analysis. International Journal of Educational Methodology, 8(1), 55–68. doi:10.12973/ijem.8.1.55

Phusawisot, P. (2018). The use of Rogerian reflections in responding to doctoral student's research paper in one-on-one writing conferences. LEARN Journal: Language Education and Acquisition Research Network, 11(1), 110–124.

Pillai, T. R., & Ahamat, A. (2018). Social-cultural capital in youth entrepreneurship ecosystem: Southeast Asia. Journal of Enterprising Communities: People and Places in the Global Economy.

Plana, M. G., Hopkins, J. E., Gimeno, A., & Appel, C. (2013). Improving Learners Reading Skills Through Instant Short Messages: A Sample Study Using WhatsApp. In IV World CALL Conference (p. 10–13).

Pleck, J., Stainnes, G., & Lang, L. (1980). Conflicts between work and family life. Monthly Labor Review, 103(3), 29–32.

Polland, R. J. (n.d.). Essentials of Survey research and Analysis. University of North Florida. http://www.unf.edu

Poole, R. E. (2011). Concordance-based glosses for facilitating semantization and enhancing productive knowledge of academic vocabulary [Doctoral dissertation, University of Alabama Libraries, USA].

Prasad, B. D. (n.d.). Content ANalysis, A method in SOciao Science Research. Retrieved from CSS.in.

Prasnig, B. (2007). The Power of Learning Styles :Memacu Anak Melejitkan Prestasi dengan Gaya Belajarnya. Kaifa.

*Priajana, N. (2013). Student teachers' reading habits and pre*ferences.In [JEFL]. Journal on English as a Foreign Language, 3(2), 71. doi:10.23971/jefl.v3i2.65

Punia, V., & Kamboj, M. (2013). Quality of Work-life Balance Among Teachers in Higher Education Institutions. Learning Community- An International Journal of Educational and Social Development, 4(3), 197-208. doi:10.5958/j.2231-458X.4.3.010

Punjab University. (2020). Guidelines. Punjab University. https://*www.edexlive.com/news/2020/mar/25/p*anjab-uni ve rsity-issues-guidelines-for-online-teaching-through-google-classroom-10873.html

Purwanto, A. (2016). Cultural capital and business success among entrepreneurs. Journal of Economics, Business, and Accountancy Ventura, 19(2), 227–236. doi:10.14414/jebav.v19i2.583

Putri, A., & *Amr*an, A. (2021). Employees' Work-Life Balance Reviewed From Work From Home Aspect During CO-*VID-19 Pandemic. International Journal of Management Science and Infor*mation Technology, 1(1), 30–34. doi:10.35870/ijmsit.v1i1.231

Pérez-Sabater, C., & Montero-*Fleta, B. (2015).* ESP vocabulary and social networking: The case of Twitter. Ibérica. Revista de la Asociación Europea de Lenguas para Fines Específicos, (29), 129–154.

Quinn, S. (2011). MoJo - Mobile Journalism in the Asian Region. Kon*rad-Adenauer-Stiftung.*

*Rad, D., Balas, E., Ignat, S., Rad, G., & Dixon, D. (2020). A Predictive Model of Youth Bystanders' Helping Attitudes. Rev*ista romaneasca pentru educatie multidimensionala-Journal for Multidimensional Education, 12(1Sup2), 136-150.

Rad, D., Dughi, T., Demeter, E. (2019). The Dynamics of the Relationship between Humor and Benevolence as Values. Revista romaneasca pentru educatie multidimensionala-Journal for Multidimensional Educ*ation, 11(3), 201-212.*

*Ra*d, *D*., Egerau, A., Roman, A., Dughi, T., Balas, E., Maier, R., Ignat, S., & Rad, G. (2022). A Preliminary Investigation *of the Technology Acceptance Model (TAM) in Early Childhood Educa*tion and Care. BRAIN. Broad Research in Artificial Intelligence and Neuroscience, 13(1), 518–533. doi:10.*18662/brain/13.1/297*

Rad, D., Magulod, G. Jr, Balas, E., Roman, A., Egerau, A., Maier, R., Ignat, S., Dughi, T., B*alas, V., Demeter, E., Rad, G., & Chis, R. (2022).* A *Radial Basis Function Ne*ural Network Approach to Predict Preschool Teachers' Technology Acceptance Behavior. Frontiers in Psychology, 13, 13. *doi:10.3389/fpsyg.2022.880753 PMID:35756273*

Rad, D., Redeş, A., Roman, A., Ignat, S., Lile, R., Demeter, E., Egerău, A., Dughi, T., Balaş, E., Maier, R., Kiss, C., Torkos, H.*, & Rad, G. (2022).* Pathways to inclusive and equitable quality early childhood education for achieving SDG4 goal—A scoping review. Frontiers in Psychology, 13, 4306. doi:10.3389/fpsyg.2022.955833 PMID:35936241

R*adesky, J. S., Eisenberg, S., Kis*tin, C. J., Gross, J., Block, G., Zuckerman, B., & Silverstein, M. (2016). Overstimulated consumers or next-generation learners? Parent tensions about child mobile technology use. Annals of Family Medicine, 14(6), 503–508. doi:10.1370/afm.1976 PMID:28376436

Radwan, *E., & Radwan, A. (2020). The Spr*ead of the Pandemic of Social Media Panic during the COVID-19 Outbreak. European Journal of Environment and Public Hea*lth, 4(2), em0044. doi:10.29333/ejeph/8277*

Ra*h*imi, E., van den Berg, J., & Veen, W. (2015). Facilitating student-driven constructing of learning environments using Web 2.*0 personal learning environments. Computers & Ed*ucation, 81, 235–246. doi:10.1016/j.compedu.2014.10.012

Ramazani, J. (1994). Student writing by e-mail: Connecting classmates, texts, instructors. *University* of Virginia. https://www.virginia.edu/~trc/tcemail.htm

Rambe, P., & Bere, A. (2013). Using Mobile Instant Messaging to Leverage Learner Participation and Transform, Pedagogy at a South African University of Technology. British Journal of Educational Technology, 44(4), 544–561. doi:10.1111/bjet.12057

*Rameez, A. (2018). Political Participation of Women in Local Governance: Case Study of Selected Local Gov*ernment Bodies in Eastern Sri Lanka. Journal of Asian and African Studies, 53(7), 1043–1061. doi:10.1177/0021909618762559

Rameez, A. (2019). English Language Proficiency and Employability of Universi*ty Students: A* Sociological Study at Faculty of Arts and Culture, South Eastern University of Sri Lanka. International Journal of English Linguistics, 09(4), 199–209. doi:10.5539/ijel.v9n2p199

Rameez, A., & Fowsar, M. A. M. (2018). An Empirical Survey on Factors Affecting Citizens' Trust in Public Institutions in the Eastern Province of Sri Lanka. Journal of Politics a*nd Law, 11(2), 88–100. doi:1*0.5539/jpl.v11n2p88

Rameez, A., Fowsar, M. A. M., & Lumna, N. (2020). Impact of Covid-19 on Higher Education Sectors in Sri Lanka: A Study based on South Eastern University of Sri Lank*a. Journal of Educational and Social Research, 1*0(6), 341–349. doi:10.36941/jesr-2020-0132

Rameshkumar, M., & Chiluka, N. (2012). Work-Life Balance Amongst Teachers. The IUP Journal of Organizational Behavior, 11(1), 1-10. https://*ssrn.com/abstract=2148284*

*Rao, C. (2006). An analysis of creati*ve *w*riting skills in English among college students and development of creative mobilization technology. Indian Educational Abstract*s, 6(2). Best, J. W. (1986). Research in Education, 1986.*

Rau, A. E. (2018, June). Context-related information in mobile news. A study on the adoption of localization technology by Legacy media organizations. Research Gate. https://www.rese*archgate.net/publication/*323486231

Rawal, D. M. (2021). Work life balance among female school teachers [k-12] delivering *online curriculum in* N*oid*a [India] during COVID: Empirical st*udy. Management in Education, 20, 1–9. doi:*10.1177/0892020621994303

Reed, B. (2010, 23.09). A brief history of smartphones. Blog Post.

Reynolds, M. (1997). Learning Sty*les: A Critique. Mana*gement Learning, 28(2), *115–133. doi:10.1177/1350507697282002*

*Richman-Adbou, K. (2018). How Museums Evolve*d Over Time From Private Collec*tions to Modern Institutions. Cabi*nets of Curios*i*ties.

Rie*ner, C., & Willingham, D. (2010). The My*th of Learning Styles. Change: The Magazine of Higher Learning, 42(5), 32–35. doi:10.1080/00091383.2010.503139

Rivkin, S. G., Hanushek, E. A., & Kai*n, J. F. (2005). Teachers, Schools, and Academic Achievement. Econometrica, 73(2), 417–*458. doi:10.1111/j.1468-0262.2005.00584.x

Rodrigues, H., Almeida, F., F*igueiredo,* V., & Lopes, S. L. (2019). Tracking e-learning through published papers: A systematic review. Computers & Education, 136, 87–98. doi:10.1016/j.compedu.2019.03.007

Rogers, E. M. (1962). Diffusion of innovations. Free Press.

Roman, A., R*ad, D., Egerau, A., Dixon, D., Dughi, T., Kelemen, G., Bala*s, E., & Rad, G. (2020). Physical Self-Schema Acceptance and Perceived Severity of Online Aggressiveness in Cyberbullying Incidents. Journal of Interdisciplinary Stud*ies in Education, 9(1), 100–116. doi:10.32674/jise.v9i1.1961*

Rourke, L. & Lysynchik, L. (2000). The Influence of Learning Style on A*chievement in Hypertext [microform]. ERIC C*learinghouse. https://eric.ed.gov/?id=ED446102

Rowlands, J. (2013). Academic boards: Less intellectual and more academic capital in higher education governance? Studies in Higher Education, 38(9), 1274–1289. doi:10.1080/03075079.2011.619655

Roy, A. (2020). The pandemic is a portal: An online teach-in. Arundhati Roy.

Rupietta, K., & Beckmann, M. (2018). Working from Home. Schmalenbach Business Review, 70(1), 25–55. doi:10.100741464-017-0043-x

Sabatier, C., Moore, D., & Dagenais, D. (2013). Espaces urbains, compétences littératiées multimodales, identités citoyennes en immersion française *au Canada [Urban spaces, multimodal literacy skil*ls, civic identities in French immersion in Canada]. Glottopol, 21, 138–161.

Saidin, N. F., Halim, N. D. A., & Yahaya, N. (2015). A review of research on augmented reality in education: Advantages and *applications. Interna*tional Education Studies, 8(13), 1–8. doi:10.5539/ies.v8n13p1

Saiful, W., Sulistyo, G. H., & Mukminatien, N. (2019). Confronting effect of online teacher and peer feedback on the students' writing performance. Pro*blems of Education in the 21st Century, 77(5)*, 650-666.

Sakar, A., & Ercetin, G. (2004). Effectiveness of hypermedia annotations for foreign language reading. Journal of Computer Assisted Learning, 21(1), 28–38. doi:10.1111/*j.1365-2729.2005.00108.x*

Salsberg, E., Quigley, L., Mehfoud, N., Acquaviva, K. D., Wyche, K., & Silwa, S. (2017). Profile of the Social Work Workforce. Health Sciences Research Commons. https://hsrc.himmelfarb.gwu. edu/sphhs_policy_workforce_ fac pubs/16

Sanchez-Ver*a, M. D. M., Solano-Fernandez, I. M., & Reci*o-Ca*ri*de, S. (2019). Digital storytelling using videos in early childhood education. PIXEL-BIT-REVISTA DE MEDIOS Y EDUCACION, (54), 165-184.

Sandström, G. (2007). Higher education for social work in Sw*eden. Australian Social Wor*k, 60(1), 56–67. doi:10.1080/03124070601166711

Santamaria-Alvarez, S. M., Muñoz-Castro, D. C., Sarmiento-González, M. A., & Marín-Zapata, S. I. (2018). Fragmented networks and transnational entrepreneurship: B*uilding strategies to prosper in challengi*ng surroundings. Journal of International Entrepreneurship, 16(2), 244–275. doi:10.100710843-017-0215-2

Sarica, G. N., & *Cavus, N. (2009). New trends in 21st century E*nglish learning. Procedia: Social and Behavioral Sciences, 1(1), 439–445. doi:10.1016/j.sbspro.2009.01.079

Sarkar, S. (2020). GC goes ahead with final year exam plan, students and teachers highlight digital divide, anxieties. The Hindu.

Sathi*sh, R., Manikandan, R.,* Silvia Priscila, S., Sara, B. V. *J., & Mahaveerakannan, R. (2020), A report on the impact of information technology and social media on covid-19. Proc. 3rd* Int. Conf. Intell. Sustain. Syst. ICISS 2020, (pp. 224–230). IEEE. 10.1109/ICISS49785.2020.9316046

Scales, A. M., & Rhee, O. (2001). Adult reading habits and patterns. Reading Psychology, 22(3), 175–203. doi:10.1080/027027101753170610

*Schcol*nik, M., Kol, S., & Oren, A. (2007, June). Are handhelds suitable *for reading academic texts? I*n EdMedia+ Innovate Learning (pp. 888-895). Association for the *Advancement of Comp*uting in Education (AACE).

Scheerens, J. (2016). Educational effectiveness and ineffectiveness. A Critical Review of the Knowledge Base, 389. Springer.

Schibeci, R. A. (1989). Influences on Student Attitudes and Achievement in Science. Science *Education, 73(1), 13–24. doi:10.1002ce.3730730103*

Schilling, J., & Klamma, R. (2010). The difficult bridge between university and industry: A case study in computer science teaching. Asse*ssment & Evalua*tion in Higher Education, 35(4), 367–380. doi:10.1080/02602930902795893

Schrader, C., & Bastiaens, T. J. (2012). The influence of virtual presence: Effects on experienced cognitive load *and learning outcomes* in *e*ducational computer games. Computers in Human Behavior, 28(2), 648–*658. doi:10.1016/j.* chb.2011.11.011

Schramm, W. (1964). Mass Media and National Development: The role of information in the developing countries. Stanford University press.

Schroeder, C. C. (1993). New Students—New Learning Styles. Change: T*he Magazine of Higher Learning, 25(5), 21–26. doi*:10.1080/00091383.1993.9939900

Schumpeter, J. A. (1965). Economic Theory and Ent*repreneurial History. In H. G. Aitken (Ed.), Explorations in enter-prise.* Harvard University Press.

Schäfer, S., & Mayer, H. (2019). Entrepreneurial ecosystems: Founding figures and research frontiers in economic geography. Zeitschrift für W*irtschaftsgeographie, 63(2-4),* 55–63. doi:10.1515/zfw-2019-0008

Scott, J. M., Harrison, R. T., Hussain, J., & Millman, C. (2014). The role of *guanxi network*s in the performance of women-led firms in China. Internat*ional Journal of Gender and E*ntrepreneurship.

Seamedu. (2019, May 13). Understanding Mobile Journalism & Its Relevance in To-day's Times. Seamedu. https://www.seamedu.com/blog/understanding-mobile-journalism -its-relevance-in-todays-times/

Sedrakyan, G., Malmberg, J., Verbert, K., Jarvela, S., & Kirschner, P. A. (2020). L*inking le*arning behaviour analytics and learning science concepts: Designing a learning analytics dashboard for feedback to support learning regulation. Computers *in Human Behavior, 107, 105512. d*oi:10.1016/j.chb.2018.05.004

Selwyn, N. (2020). After COVID-19: The longer-term impacts of the corona virus crisis on educa-tion. Melbourne Monash University. https://educationfutures.m*onash.edu/all%2D%2D-pre* s*ent/after* -covid-19

Senthilkumar, K., Chandrakumaramangalam, & Manivannan. (. (2012). An empirical study on teaching profes*sionals work-life balance in higher* learning institutions with special reference to Namakkal District, Tamilnadu. Bonfring In-ternational Journal of Industrial Engineering and Management Science, 2(3), 38–41. *doi:10.9756/BIJIEMS.1389*

Serdyukov, P. (2017). Innovation in education: What works, what doesn't, and what to do about it? Journal of Research in Innovative Teaching & Learning, 10(1), 4–33. doi:10.1108/JRIT-10-2016-0007

Servotte, J. C., Goosse, M., Campbell, S. H., Dardenne, N., Pilote, *B., Simoneau, I. L., Guillaume, M., Braga*rd, I., & Ghuysen, A. (2020). Virtual Reality Experience: Immersion, Sense of Presence, and Cybersickness. Clinical Simulation in Nursing, 38, 35–43. doi:10.1016/j.e*cns.2019.0*9.006

Setién, A., Nobre, A., Chenoll, A. (2017). El proceso de enseñanza-aprendizaje en contextos ubicuos y universitarios. Tres estudios de casos Virtualidad, Educación y Cienc*ia [The teaching-learning process in ubiquitous and un*iversity contexts. Three case studies Virtuality, Education and Science], 14 (8), pp. 123-135.

Shaffer, W. R. (2017), Exhib*ition Design and The E*volution of Museum-goer Experience. Master's Green, Cooper Hewitt, PA]. https://repository.si.edu/bitstream/handle/10088/35449/Shaffer%20Thesis.pdf?sequence=1&isAllowed=y

*Shang, H. F. (2017). An exploration o*f asynchronous and synchronous feedback modes in EFL writing. Journal of Computing in Higher Education, 29(3), 496–513. doi:10.100712528-017-9154-0

Shang, H. F. (2022). Exploring online peer feedback and automated corrective feedback on EFL writing per*formance. Interac*tive Learning Environments, 30(1), 4–16. doi:10.1080/10494820.2019.1629601

Siemens, G. (2004). Connectivism: A learning theory for the digital age. http://www.ingedewaard.net/*papers/connectivism/2005_siemens_ ALearning*TheoryForThe DigitalAge.pd

Siemens, G. (2020). A Google scholar search of prominent voices quickly reveals those who have earned the right to provide guidance [tweet]. Twitter.

Silverman, A. (2020). Play, child d*evelopment, and relationshi*ps*:* A preschool teacher in China shares her virtual teaching experien*ce. Teaching Young Children, 13(4).*

*Singer-Nourie, B. D. P. M. R. and S. (2001). Quantu*m Teaching. Kaifa.

Singh, J., Nakave, P., & Shah, B. (2022). An empirical study on the i*mpact of Covid-19 on work-life balance o*f Teaching employees in higher Education sector of Vadodara (India). International Journal of Creative Research Though, 10(2), 779–787.

Sirgy, *J., Efraty, D., Siegel, P.*, & Lee, D.-J. (2001). A New Measure of Quality of Work Life (QWL) Based on Need Satisfaction and Spillover Theories. Social Indicators Research, 55(3), 241–302. doi:10.102*3/A:1010986923468*

*Sklaveniti, C., & Steyaert, C. (*2019). Reflecting with Pierre Bourdieu: Towards a reflexive outlook for practice-based studies *of entr*epreneurship. Entrepreneurship and Regional Development, 1–21. doi:10.1080/08985626.2019.1641976

Smaguc, T. (2020). Gender Stereotypes In Entrepreneurship Process: Evidence From The Croatian Ict Industry. 59th International Scientific Conference on Economic and Social Development – Online Conference.

Smith, S. J., Burdette, P. *J., Cheatham, G. A., & Harve*y, S. P. (2016). Parental role and support for online learning of students with disabilities: A paradigm shift. Journal of Special Education Lead*ership, 29(2), 101–112.*

*So*lano, G. (2019). The mixed embeddedness of transnational migrant entrepreneurs: Moroccans in Amsterdam and Milan. Journal of Ethnic and Migration Studies, 1–19.

Solomon, Z., Ajayi, N., Raghavjee, R., & Ndayizigamiye, P. (2019). In S. Kabanda, H. Suleman, & S. Gruner (Eds.), Lecturers' Perc*eptions of Virtual Reality as a Teaching and Learning Platform BT - ICT Educati*on (pp. 299–312). Springer International Publishing.

SoniV. D. (2020)" Global Impact of E-learning during COVID 19. https://ssrn.com/abstr*act=3630073 doi:10.2139/ ssrn.3630073*

*Soong, H., Stah*l, *G.*, & Shan, H. (2017). Transnational mobility through education: A Bourdieusian insight on life as middle transnationals in Australia and Canada. Globalisation, Societies and Education, 16(2), 241–253. doi:10.1080/1 4767724.2017.1396886

Sooryanarayan, D. G., & Gupta, D. (2015). *Impact of lear*ner motivation on MOOC preferences: transfer vs made MOOCs. International Conference on Advances in Computing, Communications, and Informatics, (pp. 929–934). IEEE. 10.1109/ICACCI.2015.7275730

Souza, C. (2015). Aprendizagem sem distância: tecnologia digital móvel no ensino de língua inglesa. In Texto Livre. Linguagem e Tecnologia. [Lear*ning* without distance: mobile digital technology in English language teaching. In Free Text: Language and Technology] doi:10.17851/1983-3652.8.1.39-50

Sowell, J. (2020). Let's be direct: Making the student-teacher writing conference work for multilingual writers. MEX-TESOL Journal, 44(4), 1–8.

Spigel, B. (2012). Cultural contexts and entrepr*eneurial intentions. Entrepreneurship Rese*arch Conference. Texas. United States.

Spigel, B. (2013). Bourdieuian approaches to the geography of entrepreneurial cultures. Entrepreneurship and Regional D*evelopment, 25(9-10), 804–818. do*i:*10.*1080/08985626.2013.862974

Spigel, B. (2016a). Bourdieu, culture, and the economic geography of practice: Entrepreneurial mentorship in Ottawa and Waterloo, Canada. Journal of Economic Geography, 19, lbw019. doi:10.1093/jeg/lbw019

Spigel, B. (2016b). Developing and governing entrepreneurial ecosystems: The structure of entrepreneurial support programs in *Edinbu*rgh, Scotland. International Journal of Innovativ*e Research and D*evelopment, 7(2), 141. doi:10.1504/IJIRD.2016.077889

Spinath, B. (2012). Academic Achievement. In Encyclopedia of Human Behavior (pp. 1–8). Elsevier. doi:10.1016/B978-0-12-375000-6.00001-*X*

*Srinivas, M. N. (Ed.). (1993). India's Village*s. M*edia Promoters & Publishers.

St. Amour, M. (2020). Privacy and the online pivot. Inside Higher Ed, 25.

Stemler, L. K. (1997). Educational characteristics of multim*edia: A literature review. Jo*urnal of Educational Multimedia and Hypermedia, 6, 339–360.

Stolterman, E. (2008). The Nature of Design Practice and Implications for Interaction Design Research. International Journal of Desi*gn, 2(1). http://www.ijdesign.org/index.*php/IJDesign/article/view/240/148#anchor0

Storey, M. A., Phil*lips, B., Maczewski, M., & Wang, M. (2002). Evaluating the usability of Web-based learn*ing tools. Journal of Educational Technology & Society, 5(3), 91–100.

Strauss, S., & Xiang, X. (2006). The writing conference as a locus of emergent agency. Written Communication, 23(4), 355–396. doi:10.1177/0741088306292286

Strong, P. (1990). Epidemic psychology: A model. Sociology of Health & Illness, 12(3), 249–259. doi:10.1111/1467-9566.ep11347150

Sullivan, A. (2002). *Bourdieu and Education: How Useful is Boourdieu "s Theory for Researchers? The Netherlands Jour*nal of Social Sciences, 38(2), 144–166.

Sunitha, K. S., & Gopal, N. (2021). Work from home improves or impairs the work-life balance – A study conducted among teachers. Journal of Contemporary Issues in Business and Government, 27(4), 22–31. doi:10.47750/cibg.2021.27.04.005

Sutton, J., Renshaw, S. L., & Butts, C. T. (2020). The First 60 *Days: American Public Health Agencie*s' S*ocial Media Strategies in the Emerging COVID-19 Pandemic. Health Security, 18(6), 454–460. doi:10.1089/hs.2020.0105 PMID:33047982

Tan, A. (2012). Study intonation: *A mobile-assisted pronunciation training application. Teaching English as a Second* Language Electronic Journal (TESL-EJ), 25(3), 1-8.

Taras, H. (2005). Physical Activity and Student Performance at School. The Journal of School Health, *75(6), 214–218.* doi:10.1111/j.1746-1561.2005.00026.x PMID:16014127

Tardy, M. (1966). Le professeur et les images [The teacher and the pictures]. PUF.

Tarhini, K., Hone, K., Liu, X., & Tarhini, T. (2017). Examining the moderating effect of individual-level cultural values on users' acceptance of E-learning *in developing co*untries: A structural equation mo*delling of an extended technology acceptance mode*l. *Interactive Learning Environments,* 25(3), 306–328. doi:10.1080/10494820.2015.1122635

Taylor, L. (2021). Discursive stance as a pedagogical tool: N*egotiating literate identities in writing* conferences. Journal of Early Childhood Literacy, 21(2), 208–229. doi:10.1177/1468798419838596

Taylor, M. C. (2001). The Moment of Complexity: Emerging Network Culture. University of Chicago *Press.*

*Tegtmeier, S., & Mitr*a, J. (2015). Gender perspectives on university education and entrepreneurship: A conceptual overview. International Journal of Gender and Entrepreneurship, 7(3), 254–271. doi:10.1108/IJGE-05-2015-0016

*Teras, H., & Kartoglu, U. (2017). A ground*ed theory of professional learning in an authentic online professional development progra*m. The International Review of* Research in Open and Distributed Learning, 18(7). doi:10.19173/irrodl. v18i7.2923

Teras, M., *Suoranta, J., T*eras, H., & Curcher, M. (2020). Post-Covid-19 Education and Education Technology 'Solutionism': a Seller's Market. Postdigital Science and Education. Google Scholar.

Terry, G., Hayfield, N., Clarke, V., & Braun, *V. (2017). Thematic analysis.* Th*e* SAGE handbook of qualitative research in psychology, 2, 17-37. doi:10.4135/9781526405555.n2

Thomas, S. (2007). "Transliteracy: Crossing divides". Web. October 2015.

*Thoring, K. (2019). D*esigning Creative Space: A Systemic View on Workspace Design and Its Impact on The Creative Pro*cess. TU Delft, Delft Universi*ty of Technology.

Thoring, K., Goncalves, M. G., Mueller, R. M., Badke-Schaub, P., & Desmet, P. (2017). Inspiration Space: Towards a theory of cre*ativity-supporting learning environments.* Con*f*erence Proceedings of the Design Management Academy. https://research.tudelft.nl/en/publications/inspiration-spac e-towards-a-theory-of-creativi*ty-supporting-learn*

Thoring, K., Luippold, C., & Mueller, R. M. (2021). Creative Space in Design Education: A Typology of Spatial Functions. The Design Society. https://www.designsociety.org/publication/33233/Creative+Spa ce+in+Design+Education%3A+A+Typology+of+Spatia*l+Functions*

Tieken, M. C. (2017). The spatialisation of racial inequity and educational opportunity: Rethinking the rural/urban divide. Peabody Journal of Educa*tion, 92(3), 385–404. doi:10.1080/0161956X.2017.1324662*

Tjaardstra, N. (2017, April 30). This is what Mobile Journalism looks like today. World As-sos*ciation of News Publishers. h*ttps://wan-ifra.org/2017/04/this-is-what-mobile-journalism-looks-like-today/

Todey, E. *(2019). MReader. Teaching E*nglish as a Second Language Electronic Journal (TESL-EJ), 22(4), 1-9.

Tomlinson, B. (2005). Testing to learn: A personal view of language testing. ELT Journal, Oxford University Press, 59(1), 44. doi:10.1093/elt/cci005

Tovey, M. (Ed.). (2015). Design Pedagogy: Developments in Art and Design Edu*cation. Gower.*

Tundui, H. P. (2012). Gender and Small Business Growth in Tanzania: The Role of Habitus. University of Groningen.

UNESCO. (2020). COVID-19 educational disruption and response. UNESCO. h*ttps://en.unesco. org/covid19/educa-*ti*on*response

UNESCO. 2012. TIC UNESCO: Un référentiel de compétences pour les enseignants [UNESCO ICT: A competency framework for teachers]. Paris. https://unesdoc.unesco.*org/images/0021/002169/216910f.pdf*

Unni Krishnan, J.P. & Ors. Vs State of Andhra Pradesh & Ors. 1993 AIR 217, 1993 SCR (1) 594, 1993 SCC (1) 645, JT 1993 (1) 474, 1993 SCALE (1)290.

Vaage, K. (2016). News narratives in locative journalism- rethinking news for the mobile phone. Journal of Media Practice, 245–262.

Vadia, M. N., & Ciptaningrum, D. S. (2020, August). Improving students' writing skill using online feedback. I*n 1st International Conference on Language, Literature, and Arts Educ*ation (ICLLAE 2019) (pp. 178-182). Atlantis Press. 10.2991/assehr.k.200804.034

Vainshtein, I. V., Shershneva, V. A., Esin, R. V., & Noskov, M. V. (2019). Individualization of Education in Terms of E-learning: Experience and Prospects. Journal of Siberian Federal University. Humanities & Social Sciences, 12(9), 1753–1770. doi:10.17516/1997-1370-0481

Van De Bogart, W., & Wichadee, S. (2015). Exploring students' intention to use LINE for academic *purposes based on technology acceptance model. Internat*ional Review of Research in Open and Distributed Learning, 16(3), 65–85. doi:10.19173/irrodl.v16i3.1894

Vandenhoek, T. (2013). Screen reading habits among university students. International Journal of Education and Development using I*CT, 9(2). https://*www.learntechlib.org/p/130282/

Varma, M., & Verma, A. (2017). Rural development and channels of grass root communication with reference to health information. Journal of Content, Community & Communicatio*n, 6(12), 101–110.*

Vasquez, M. J. T., & Duran, R. P. (1985). Hispanics' Education and Background: Predictors of College Achievement. The Journal *of Higher Education, 56(2), 233. doi:10.2307/1981674*

Venigalla, A.S.M., Vagavolu, D., and Chimalakonda, S., (2020). SurviveCovid-19 - A game for improving aw*areness of social distancing and healt*h measures for Covid-19 pandemic. arXiv.

Verma, S., Panigra*hi, T., & Alok, D. (2021). COVID 19 and Online Learning i*n Post Graduate Management Progra*mme: An Empirical Analysis of Students' Perception. Journal of* Applied Business and Economics, 23(2), 108–12*3.*

Vidanagama, D. U. (2016). Acceptance of E-learning among undergraduates of computing degrees in Sri Lanka. Int. J. *Mod. Educ. Comput. Sci., 8(4), 25–32. doi:10.5815/ijmecs.2016.*04.04

Visamo kids' foundation (2020) Visamokids.org. https://visamokids.org/

Višnjić Jevtić, A., & Halavuk, A. (2021). Early childhood teachers and burnout syndrome–perception *of Croatian teach-*ers. Early Years, 41(1), 36–47. doi:10.1080/09575146.2018.1482260

Vyver, A. G., Williams, B., & Marais, M. A. (2015). Using social media as a managerial platform for *an educational developme*nt project: Cofimvaba. International Journal of Information and Education Technology (IJIET), 5(12), 910–913. doi:10.7763/IJIET.2015.V5.636

Waheed, M., Kaur, K., & Qazi, A. (2016). *Students' perspective on kno*wledge quality in eLearning knowledge quality in eLearning. Internet Research, 26(1), 120–145. doi:10.1108/IntR-08-2014-0199

Waheed, U., Wazeer, A., Saba, N., & Qasim, Z. (2020). Effectiveness of WhatsApp for blood d*onor mobilization campaigns during COVID-19 pandemic. ISBT Science Se*ries, 15(4), 378–380. doi:10.1111/voxs.12572

Waller, R. E., Lemoine, P. A., Mense, E. G., & Richardson, M. D. (2019). H*igher education in search of competitive advantage: Globalizati*on, technology and e-learning. International Journal of Advanced Research and Publications, 3(8), 184–190.

Walsh, J., & Winsor, B. (2019). Socio-cultural barriers to develo*ping a regional entrepreneurial ecosystem. Jo*urnal of Enterprising Communities: People and Places in the Global Economy, 13(3), 263–282. doi:10.1108/JEC-11-2018-0088

Warschauer, M., & Kern, R. (2000). Network-ba*sed language teaching: Concepts and practice. Cambridge University Press. doi:10.1017/CBO9781139524735

Webster, J., & Watson, R. (2002). Analysing the Past to Prepare for the Future: Writing a Literature Rev*iew. MIS Quarterly, 26(2), Xiii-Xxiii.

Wenger, E. (2005). La théorie des communautés de pratique. Apprentissage, sens et identité [The theory of communities of practi*ce. Learning, meaning and identity]. Les Pre*sses de l'université Laval.

Whiteside-Mansell, L., McKelvey, L., Saccente, J., & Selig, J. P. (2019). Adverse childhood e*xperiences of urban and rural pre*school children in poverty. International Jo*urnal of Environmental* Research and Public Health, 16(14), 2623. doi:10.3390/ijerph16142623 PMID:31340510

Widyaningsih, T. L. (2018). An analysis of online corrective feedback implementation in writing *class. BRIGHT: A Jo*urnal of English Language Teaching. Linguistics and Literature, 2(1), 63–78.

Wieman, C. E. (2019). Expertise in university teaching & the implications for teaching effectiveness, evaluation & *training. Daedal*us, 148(4), 47–78. doi:10.1162/daed_a_01760

Wihastyanang, W. D., Kusumaningrum, S. R., Latief, M. A., & Cahyono, B. Y. (2020). Impacts of providing online teacher and peer feedback on students' writing perform*ance. Turkish Online Journal of Distance Education, 21(2),* 178–189. doi:10.17718/tojde.728157

Wilder, S. (2014). Effects of parental involvement on academic achievement: A meta-synthes*is. Educational Review, 66(3), 377–397. doi:10.1080/00131911.2013.780009*

*Willi*amson, E. C. (2020). Guest editorial: Advancing field education as a key area of *focus in the 2022 EPAS. Field Educator, 10(1). https://*fieldeducator.simmons.edu/article/guest-editorial-adv a n c i n g - f i e l d - e d u c a t i o n - a s - a - k e y - a r e a - o f - f o c u s - i n - t h e - 2 0 2 2 - epas/

Williford, A. P., Vick Whittaker, J. E., Vitie*llo, V. E., & Dow*ner, J. T. (2013). Children's engageme*nt within the preschool classroom and their development of self-regulatio*n. Early Education and Development, 24(2), 162–187. doi:10.1080/1 0409289.2011.628270 PMID:23441104

Winans, M. D. (2021). Grammarly's tone detector: Helping students write pragmatically appropriate texts. RELC Jo*urnal, 52(2), 348–352. doi:10.1177/00336882211010506*

*Winne, P. H., & Nesbi*t, J. C. (2010). The Psychology of Academic Achievement. Annual Review of Psychology, 61(1), 653–678. doi:10.1146/annurev.psych.093008.100348 *PMID:19575616*

WNIP. (2018). The rise of mobile journalism: Publishing's new frontier? WNIP. https://whatsnewinpublishing.com/the-rise-of-mobile-journalism-publishings-new-frontier

Woiceshyn, J., & Daellenbach, U. (2018). Evaluating inductive vs deductive research in management studies: Implications for authors, editors, and reviewers. Qualitative Research in Organizations and Management: An International Journal, 13(2), pp.183-195. doi:10.1108/QROM-06-2017-1538

World Economic Forum. (2020). The COVID-19 pandemic has changed education forever. We Forum. https://www.weforum.org/agenda/2020/04/coronavirus-education-global-covid19-online-digital-learning/

Wright, J. (2020). Researchers, teachers, and learners seeing new possibilities with Voyant tools. Teaching English as a Second Language Electronic Journal (TESL-EJ), 24(2), 1-10.

Wu, W. S. (2005). Web-based English learning and teaching in Taiwan: Possibilities and challenges. Paper presented at The First Hsiang-shan Area Intercollegiate International Conference on English teaching. Crane Publishing.

Xiao-Dong, L., & Hong-Hui, C. (2020). Research on VR-supported flipped classroom based on blended learning— A case study in "learning english through news.". International Journal of Information and Education Technology (IJIET), 10(2), 104–109. doi:10.18178/ijiet.2020.10.2.1347

Xu, J. (2021). Chinese university students' L2 writing feedback orientation and self-regulated learning writing strategies in online teaching during COVID-19. The Asia-Pacific Education Researcher, 30(6), 563–574. doi:10.100740299-021-00586-6

Xu, Q., Chen, S., Wang, J., & Suhadolc, S. (2021). Characteristics and effectiveness of teacher feedback on online business English oral presentations. The Asia-Pacific Education Researcher, 30(6), 631–641. doi:10.100740299-021-00595-5

Yadav, J. S. (1979). Communication strategy and the challenge of rural development. Communicator, 14(2), 6.

Yamada, M., Kitamura, S., Shimada, N., Utashiro, T., Shigeta, K., Yamaguchi, E., & Nakahara, J. (2011). Development and evaluation of English listening study materials for business people who use mobile devices: A case study. CALICO Journal, 29(1), 44–67. doi:10.11139/cj.29.1.44-66

Yang, A. (2007). Cultivating a reading habit: Silent reading at school. Asian EFL Journal, 9(2), 115–129.

Yang, L. (2022). Focus and interaction in writing conferences for EFL writers. SAGE Open, 12(1), 1–13. doi:10.1177/21582440211058200

Yang, M., Mak, P., & Yuan, R. (2021). Feedback experience of online learning during the COVID-19 pandemic: Voices from pre-service English language teachers. The Asia-Pacific Education Researcher, 30(6), 611–620. doi:10.100740299-021-00618-1

Yang, Y. F., & Meng, W. T. (2013). The effects of online feedback training on students' text revision. Language Learning & Technology, 17(2), 220–238.

Yeh, C. C. (2017). Shared time, shared problems? Exploring the dynamics of paired writing conferences. Pedagogies, 12(3), 256–274. doi:10.1080/1554480X.2017.1356232

Yeh, E. (2018). Voxy. Teaching English as a Second Language Electronic Journal (TESL-EJ), 22(3), 1-10.

Yeröz, H. (2019). Manifestations of social class *and agency in cultural capital deve*lopment processes: An empirical study of Turkish migrant women entrepreneurs in Sweden. International Journal of Entrepreneurial Behaviour & Research, *25(5), 900–918. doi:10.1108/IJEBR*-03-2018-0146

Yin, R. K. (2009). Case *study research: Design and methods (4th ed.). SAGE Publications, Inc.*

Yoke, S. K., Rajendran, C. B., Sain, N., Kamaludin, P. N. H., Nawi, S. M., & Yusof, S. (2013). the use of online *corrective* feedback in academic writing by L1 Malay learners. English Language Teaching, 6(12), 175–180.

Yonni, R.B., & Manolova, T.S. (2013). Institutional context for entrepreneurship in emerging economies: a nine-country comparison *of university students' perceptions. Modern competition, 6 (42)*, 118-138.

Yu, C. (2018). Exploring immigrant and transnational entrepreneurship in the Australia and China context. University of Adelaide, Entrepreneurship, Commercialisation and Innovation Centre.

*Yuk, A. C. K., & Yunu*s, *M.* M. (2021). Using peer-modo feedback at the pre-writing stage to im*prove year 4 pupils' writing performan*ce. Journal of Education and e-Learning Research, 8(1), 116-124.

Yurt, Ö., & Cevher-Kalburan, N. (2011). Early childhood teachers' thoughts and practices about the use of computers in early childhood education. P*rocedia Computer Science, 3,* 1562–1570. doi:10.1016/j.procs.2011.01.050

Yılmaz, R., & Kılıç-Çakmak, E. (2012). Educational interface agents as social models to influence learner achievement, attitude and reten*tion of Learning. Comp*uters & Education, 59(2), 828–83*8. doi:10.1016/j.compedu.2012.03.020*

*Zalaznick, M. (2019). Online service intends to exp*and pre-K access. EQUITY). District Administration, 55(8), 12.

Zapała, A. & Zięba, K. (2014). Gendered entrepreneurship and its impact on firm innovativeness – a literature review. Przedsiębiorstwo we współczesnej gospod*arce – teoria i praktyka [Enterprise in Modern* economy- theory and practice], 4, 5-12.

Zender, R., & Tavangarian, D. (2009). "Service-oriented university: Infrastructure for the university of tomorrow," in Intelligent Interactive Assistance and Mobile Multimedia Computing. Springer Berlin Heide*l*berg.

Zhang, D. (2022). Engaging, impressing an*d captivating language learners by interactive presentations – a review of Mentimeter. Teaching English as a Second Language Electronic Journal (TESL-EJ)*, 26(1), 1-8.

Zhao, J., Xu, X., Jiang, H., & Ding, Y. (2020). The effectiveness of virtual reality-based technology on anatomy teaching: A meta-analysis *of randomized controlled studies. BMC Medical Education, 20(1), 127.* Advance online publication. doi:10.118612909-020-1994-z PMID:32334594

Zhao, X. (2022). Leveraging artificial intelligence (AI) technology for English writing: Introducing Wordtune as *a digital writing assi*stant for EFL writers. RELC Journal, 1–5. doi:10.1177/00336882221094089

Zheng, F., Khan, N. A., & Hussain, S. (2020). The COVID 19 pandemic and digital higher education: Exploring the impact of proactive personality on social capital through *internet se*lf-efficacy and online interaction quality. Children and Youth Services Review, 119, 105694.

About the Contributors

S. Suman Rajest is currently working as a professor at Bharath Institute of Higher Education and Research, Chennai, Tamil Nadu, India. He is an Editor in Chief of the International Journal of Human Computing Studies and The International Journal of Social Sciences World, He is the Chief Executive Editor of the International Journal of Advanced Engineering Research and Science, International Journal of Advanced Engineering, Management and Science, The International Journal of Health and Medicines, The International Journal of Management Economy and Accounting Fields and The International Journal of Technology Information and Computer and also he is an Editorial Board Member in International Journal of Management in Education, Scopus, Inderscience, EAI Endorsed Transactions on e-Learning, and Bulletin of the Karaganda university Pedagogy series. He is also a Book Series Editor in IGI Global Publisher, Springer, etc. All of his writing, including his research, involves elements of creative nonfiction in the Human Computing learning system. He is also interested in creative writing and digital media, Learning, AI, student health learning, etc. He has published 111 papers in peer-reviewed international journals. He has authored and co-authored several scientific book publications in journals and conferences and is a frequent reviewer of international journals and international conferences and also, he is also a reviewer in Inderscience, EAI Journals, IGI Global, Science Publications, etc..

Salvatore Moccia is a former professor of Strategic Management at the International University UNIR – La Rioja, Spain, and holds visiting positions in Germany, Switzerland, and Thailand. He is also Editor-in-Chief of ISSIP (), The International Society of Service Innovation Professionals, a professional association co-founded by IBM, Cisco, HP and several Universities with a mission to promote Service Innovation for our interconnected world. He is also the founder of Tech Valley Management, a Tech company that owns several digital magazines, including , and www.sharedmobility.news and organizes Tech Conferences all around the world. He has vast experience as manager in the higher education sector, and as business consultant. He is also serving as Board Member and Secretary General of the foundation "A Bridge to the Holy Land", founded and presided by HRH Monika zü Lowenstein. In addition to that, he also serves as "Innovation Expert" for the Katerva's. He is also guest editor of Scopus and ABDC indexed journals.

Karthikeyan Chinnusamy is a senior principal with more than 25 years of experience in IT, Product Dev, R&D and Education fields. Fellow IETE, Fellow IE, Sr Member IEEE, Sr Member ACM, Project management Institute (PMI), Reviewer, Editorial Board Member of R&D Journals. Board Member & Program Director SF DAMA. SME in Data Governance, GDPR, HIPAA Compliance, Data Management, Data Architecture, Master Data, Data Quality, AI/ML, Analytics and reporting in Payment processing,

Customer, Finance, CRM and License domains. Mentor in SFDC Mig, Data.com, ERP, Architecture, R&D, Embedded systems, VLSI,Adv Information processing. I am also reviewer for IEEE Silicon Valley Sr Member Elevation and Speaker, Volunteer for SFBay ACM. Reviewer of Journals in Springer Nature. Link:

Bhopendra Singh is an associate professor in Engineering & Architecture Department, Amity University Dubai, UAE, from October 2011 to date. He is a competent & versatile professional with 25 years of experience in Strategic Planning, Academic Operations, Teaching & Mentoring. He is currently serving as a Head of Industry Relations-Engineering and senior faculty at Amity University in Dubai. He is an individual with a proactive attitude, thinking out of the box and generating new design solutions and ideas. His research parts are actively involved in accreditation like IET, WASAC, DQA Award, and HCERF Visits. Signed several MOU with industries like Cisco, Emircom, Tele logic, Siemens, Dewa R&D. Coordinating with other reputed institutions like IIT Indore for research and student's internship. Organizing industry visit industry Guest lectures for engineering students. Organizing training for engineering students. Arranging internship for engineering students since July 2018. Coordinator of Board of Studies (2011 to 2014). Member of IQAC (2012-2014). Developed and installed lab for engineering programs (2011-2012). Member of sports committee from (2011-2015). He teaches as per academic curriculum to students, recognizing and nurturing each student's creative potential. Teach students using a systematic instructional methodology comprising lecture plans (following the credit allotted to each subject), discussion groups, seminars, case studies, field assignments, and independent and/or group projects. Recently, he has been the technique program committee, the technique reviews, and the track chair for international conferences published by Springer-ASIC/LNAI Series. He is serving as the editor in chief of the editorial board of international journals, and he authored/edited different books by Springer, Wiley, CRC Press, and filed many Patents. Finally, he is a member of ISTE, IET, IEEE, etc..

R. Regin is currently working as an assistant professor in the Department of Computer Science and Engineering at the SRM Institute of Science and Technology, Chennai, Tamil Nadu, India. He has a specialization in the branch of information and communication. He holds experience of 10+ years in teaching faculty and research. He has also published papers in 55 reputed international journals, 40 international conferences, and 15 national conferences. He is a member of professional bodies like IE and IETE. He is also a Book Series Editor for IGI Global Publisher, Springer, etc. He is the Editor-in-Chief of the International Journal of Technology Information and Computers, Growing Scholar USA, and a member of the Journal Ilmiah Teunuleh's Editorial Advisory Board. He does research work in the fields of VANET, WSN, MANET, Cloud Computing, Network Security, and Information Security. He is a reviewer for many reputed journals like Springer, Inderscience, etc.

***

Aravind B. R. is pursuing his PhD in English Language Teaching at the School of Social Sciences and Languages at VIT Chennai, India. He obtained his UG and PG degrees from Loyola College, Chennai and St. Joseph's College of Arts and Science, Cuddalore respectively. After completing his studies, he taught the English language in his own city, where he was the Head of the Department of English for two years. In 2016, he turned to be a full-time researcher in English Language Teaching. His research interest includes vocabulary teaching and learning, web tools for language learning, literary theory and literary criticism. He has published six Scopus Indexed papers, four Non-Scopus papers, one Book Chapter and a Book on his research areas.

Alina Costin is an associate professor PhD at Aurel Vlaicu University of Arad

Edgar Demeter is an assistant professor PhD at Aurel Vlaicu University of Arad.

Lakshmi Priya GG received her Ph.D.from the National Institute of Technology (NIT), Trichy, India. She has over 17 years of teaching and research experience. Presently, she is working as Associate Professor (Senior) at the Department of Multimedia, VIT School of Design (V-SIGN) at Vellore Institute of Technology (VIT), Vellore, India. She has published papers in more than 50 international journals, conference proceedings, and book chapters. Among these, one of her research works got published in IEEE Transactions on Image Processing. Her research focuses on Multimedia Indexing and Retrieval, Medical Image Processing, Human Action Recognition, Image caption and annotations, Educational usage of VR & AR Technologies. She has received a seed money grant and a research award from VIT, Vellore.

Raul Lile is a PhD candidate.

Raja M. is a recipient of the Gold Medal for securing first rank in the university during his Master's degree. He is presently an internal part-time research scholar and assistant profesor at the Department of Multimedia, VIT School of Design (V-SIGN) at Vellore Institute of Technology (VIT), Vellore, India. With over 17 years of combined experience in India and abroad, he has held various positions in the industry and academia. His research includes the empowerment of rural schools using VR & AR technologies, Extended Reality's impact on education, and Educational Technologies. He also has published books and quality research papers in Scopus-indexed and SCI journals to his credit.

Ana Nobre lived and studied in Paris. She currently teaches at Universidade Aberta where she has taught since 1998, having previously been a professor at the Sorbonne University, Paris. She completed a PhD in Didactologie des langues et des Cultures from the University Sorbonne Paris III. She is dedicated to the teaching of foreign languages in eLearning, to digital resources for learning in online environments and recently to the didactic eLearning and gamification in education. She was coordinator of the project "Teaching / learning languages online" and researcher of @ssess project of the Distance Education Laboratory and eLearning (FCT, 2010-2013) where she investigated the problem of digital alternative assessment of orality.

Sunil Patel has completed his doctoral study in the field of Management in Organised Retail Pharmacy. He has 18+ years of total experience. He has 5 yrs of corporate experience with Dr. Reddy's and Intas Pharma Pvt. Ltd. in sales and Training department respectively. 13+ years of academic experience, during this tenure he has participated in various national and international workshops, seminar and conferences. He has published and presented more than 18 research papers in National and International journals and conferences and has won best paper presentation award in one of the International conferences. He has been invited by various reputed institute as visiting and Expert faculty. He has conducted workshops on Research Methodology, Production & Operations research, and use of software package in data analysis, qm3 for windows and also delivered expert lectures in various seminars organized at reputed Management institutions. His area of interest includes Marketing Management, Advertising, Sales & Distribution Management, Logistics & Supply Chain Management and Consumer Behavior.

|Sambit Pradhan is a cross disciplinary design educator with focus on communication design. Pradan has been a design practitioner and educator since 2010 with diverse professional interests in fields like visual communication, theatre, films, spatial design, writing,p[and poetry. However, nothing has been as fulfilling as teaching and that's where my true passion lies. I believe that the design thinking tenets of empathy, tolerance, universality, inclusivity, functional aesthetics, responsible innovation, and humane sensitivity must go on to be second nature for us all irrespective of age, gender, origins or means.

Dana Rad, PhD. is an associate professor in the faculty of educational sciences, psychology and social sciences at Aurel Vlaicu University of Arad, Romania. She is Head of Center of Research Development and Innovation in Psychology. She holds a double specialization in Psychology (PhD in Applied Cognitive Psychology) and Automation (MD in Automation and Intelligent Systems).

Gavril Rad is a PhD candidate, and an assistant professor at Aurel Vlaicu University of Arad

Sreejith S. is working as an assistant professor of Management at the School of Legal Studies, Cochin University of Science and Technology from 4th September 2014 He is also a research guide of the Faculty of Social Science at CUSAT. Before joining CUSAT, he also served as a member of faculty in Bhavan's Royal Institute of Management, Albertian Institute of Management, and Farook Institute of Management. He started his career as an officer in the finance department at Bharati Airtel. His Ph.D. in Management was earned from Bharathiar University and the topic for the same was "An Empirical Study on Telecentre Sustainability with Special Reference to Akshaya Project, Kerala". He is an MBA graduate from Kerala University through TKM Institute of Management, Kollam. He did his B.Com from MG University Kottayam through M.A. College Kothamangalam. Sreejith is also a FLAIR certified faculty as well as acted as coordinator and resource person for various workshops and FDPs. His areas of interest are in Management Studies, Empirical Research Methodologies, and Community Informatics. He has published books as well as research papers and presented research papers at National and International conferences. He is also serving as an expert member for various academic boards and selection committees of a few institutions in Kerala.

Henriette Torkos once got kicked out for yelling at a talker. Currently, Torkos is studying at the Aurel Vlaicu University of Arad University of Arad.

Gabriela Vancu is a lecturer PhD at Aurel Vlaicu University of Arad.

Venkates Waran is currently working as a professor in the Department of Management Studies, PSNA College of Engineering & Technology, Dindigul affiliated to Anna University, Chennai where he teaches courses in Advertising, marketing and Research Methods. He has served in various faculty positions from Assistant Professor to Professor in leading Arts & Colleges such as Cherran Arts and Science College, Kangeyam and Sree Saraswathi Thyagaraja College, Pollachi. He received MSc in Physics, an M.B.A., from Bharathiar University and MPhil from Alagappa University Karaikudi. He received his Ph.D in Business Administration from Madurai Kamaraj University, Madurai. He is having twenty two years of teaching and nine years of research & consultancy experience. His research activities include on Branding, Advertising and Digital marketing He conducted more than 90 Entrepreneurship Awareness Camps and trained around 8000 Engineering, Arts and Science College students and motivated them towards entrepreneurship. He also conducted 10 Faculty Development programmes, 10 EDP/WEDP programmes and 7 TEDP programmes. He trained more the 200 women entrepreneurs in Dindigul District.

Ahmet Erdost Yastibaş has been working as an English language instructor for more than 10 years. He has a Ph.D. degree in English language teaching. His research interests include foreign language assessment and evaluation, technology-enhanced foreign language teaching, and foreign language education for sustainable purposes.

Index

A

Anxiety 66, 182, 300
Applications 3, 6, 9, 11, 25, 59, 90-91, 99, 102-103, 105-
    107, 111, 115, 117, 178, 203-204, 216-220, 237
Attitude Towards Use 16-18
Audio Feedback 29, 31, 33
Awareness and Training of Teacher 175

B

Behavioral Intention to Use 12, 16, 18
Best practices 178, 191
Bourdieu 179, 184, 241-245, 248-252, 254

C

case studies 101, 256-258, 311
Circumstances 131, 181, 271, 278, 298
Communication Channels 12, 149, 151, 153-154,
    156, 158-159
Computer-based testing 1, 4-6, 9-10
COVID-19 52, 61, 64, 68-69, 71-73, 78-79, 81-82, 89,
    93, 95, 102-103, 114-115, 117, 120-121, 126, 159-
    160, 177, 184-186, 197-198, 201, 204-205, 208,
    211-215, 222-227, 256-257, 269, 277, 284-285,
    287-289, 291, 298, 301-302, 311-312
critical thinking 95, 111, 134, 137, 192
Cultural Capital 241-246, 248-253, 255
Curriculum Innovation 139-140, 143
Curriculum Integration 139, 144-145

D

Design Education 230-231, 233-236, 239-240
developing reading habits 127
Digital Environments 85, 90, 92, 97
Digital Humanities 85, 89, 91, 97
Digital Literacies 85, 87

Digital Tools

Digital Tools 1, 10, 90, 97, 117, 218, 222
Distraction 142, 298

E

early childhood education 213-215, 223-229
Easy Test Maker 1, 4-10
e-book 127
Education 1, 3, 10-15, 19-22, 27, 38-41, 43, 45-46, 53-
    54, 64-67, 71, 73, 76-82, 85-87, 89-90, 92, 95-104,
    106-107, 109, 111, 114-126, 129-130, 137-142,
    144-149, 160, 174-176, 178-199, 213-220, 222-
    231, 233-241, 244-245, 248-258, 260-261, 264,
    268-273, 298-300, 311-312
EFL 3, 11, 23-25, 27-35, 37-40, 53, 64-66, 80-82,
    125, 131, 138
eLearning 12, 20, 22
E-learning 10, 12-17, 19-22, 40, 57, 64-65, 100, 102-
    103, 107-108, 111-114, 117-126, 178, 185
E-learning with VR 102-103
ELTL (English Language Teaching and Learning)
    54, 64
English language teaching 1, 11, 23-24, 27, 37, 39-40,
    54-55, 58-59, 64-66, 101
Entrepreneurship 198, 241, 243-246, 248-255
ESP (English for specific purpose) 54
Evaluation 1-5, 9-12, 20, 27-28, 32, 44, 57, 65, 67, 115,
    139, 142-144, 147, 166, 189, 233, 253
Exhibition Design 162-163, 166-168, 173-174

F

Face-to-face conference 83
Fear 46, 119, 175, 177, 197, 209, 215, 262, 264
Feedback 22-25, 27-29, 31-40, 64, 68-82, 94, 107, 111,
    113, 115, 144, 232, 234, 257
field learning 187-192
Foreign Languages 85, 90, 97
Formal 93, 140, 149, 151, 153-155, 177, 188, 234,

237-238, 242, 258, 260, 272

G

Gender 100, 124, 128-130, 137, 140, 143, 207, 241, 244-245, 248-254, 279, 298, 302, 304-307, 310
General Public 162, 164, 166
Giving Feedback Online 23, 69, 71
Global Advantages in Education 117
Grammatical Errors 25, 41, 46, 48, 285

I

importance of reading 127, 136
Informal 87, 93, 149-151, 154-155, 157-159, 188, 237, 242

L

Language Didactics 85, 88
Language Teaching 1, 11, 23-25, 27, 37, 39-41, 54-55, 58-59, 64-66, 68-69, 81, 85, 88, 90-92, 97-101, 125
Learning 2-4, 9-22, 24-25, 27, 37-41, 44-45, 52-67, 69-71, 82, 85-107, 111-119, 121-126, 130, 135-136, 139-149, 162, 176-179, 181-182, 184-193, 195-198, 200, 213-227, 229-240, 244, 253, 258, 262, 269-270, 279, 310-312
Learning Interest 139, 145
Learning of Communication 149
Learning Social Media 200
Learning Styles 139-143, 145-148

M

Madurai 12, 16
Mobile journalism 274-281, 289, 295-297
MOJO 274-275, 277-280, 295-297
Multimodality 86-88, 98-100
Museums 162-166, 169-174

N

New Journalism 274

O

Online education 12, 14-15, 19, 45, 103-104, 125, 175, 179, 182-184, 213, 215, 219-220, 222-223, 225, 256-257, 264, 269
Online feedback 23-25, 27, 31-34, 38-40, 71-74, 78-79

Online writing conference 72, 74, 76-77, 83
Orthography 41, 47

P

Perceived Ease of Use 12, 15, 18, 20
Perceived Usefulness 12, 16-18, 20-21
Pertaining 230
Practises 177, 230
preschool teachers 213, 215-217, 219-228

Q

qualitative research 126, 195, 213, 216-217, 220, 223, 229, 231

R

reading habits 127-131, 134-138
Research 1, 4-6, 11-14, 16, 19-20, 22, 25, 33-34, 38, 40-45, 48, 53, 55-56, 59, 63-69, 71-73, 79, 81-82, 88, 91, 100, 104, 106-110, 114-116, 119, 125-130, 134, 136-137, 146-148, 159-161, 167, 173, 176-177, 179-180, 182, 184-186, 190, 194-198, 201, 204-207, 211, 213-217, 219-232, 236-237, 239-240, 242-244, 248, 250, 252-255, 274-279, 281, 295-297, 300-302, 308, 310-312
Rural development 149-151, 158-161

S

shelter home 256-257, 263-264, 266-267, 270, 273
Social Issues 150, 153-159, 176, 193, 278-279
Social work agencies and India 187
Social work education 187-198

T

Talk and Comment 23, 25, 27-37
Teaching-Learning 85, 91, 93, 100-101, 103, 107-108, 111, 120-121, 301
technology assisted reading 127
Technology of Communication 162
Testing 1-6, 9-11, 65, 135, 137, 146, 271-272, 302, 304
Transnational 241-242, 244-245, 248-255
Turmoil 298

U

Underprivileged children 256-257, 270

V

Virtual Reality 102-104, 107-108, 111-112, 114-116
Virtual Reality in E-learning 102
Visamo Kids Foundation 256-257, 270
Visual Advertisements 200-202, 206-210
vocabulary 2-3, 23-25, 39, 41-43, 46, 48, 56-63, 65-67, 95
VR 102-109, 111-114
VR and e-learning 102

W

Work-life balance 298-302, 304, 308, 310-312

Writing 2, 11, 23-25, 27-35, 37-48, 51-53, 55-56, 58-63, 65, 67-70, 72-84, 87-88, 90, 92-94, 96-97, 100, 128-129, 141, 216, 233, 254, 275-276, 285-286, 294-295

Writing conference 69-70, 72, 74, 76-77, 82-84
Writing Conferences 68-84

Z

Zoom 38, 68, 71-72, 75, 77-80, 176, 182, 213, 216-223, 268

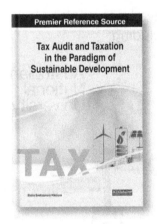

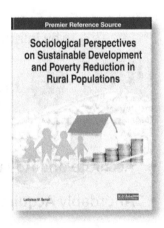

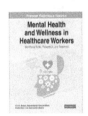

9 781668 466827